X8
A17

215/965

$6-98

IN THE VERY THICKEST
OF THE FIGHT

D1300358

IN THE VERY THICKEST OF THE FIGHT

*The Civil War Service of the
78th Illinois Volunteer Infantry Regiment*

STEVE RAYMOND

Guilford, Connecticut

To Those Who Served

~

To buy books in quantity for corporate use
or incentives, call **(800) 962–0973**
or e-mail **premiums@GlobePequot.com**.

Copyright © 2012 by Steve Raymond

ALL RIGHTS RESERVED. No part of this book may be reproduced or transmitted in any form by any means, electronic or mechanical, including photocopying and recording, or by any information storage and retrieval system, except as may be expressly permitted in writing from the publisher. Requests for permission should be addressed to Globe Pequot Press, Attn: Rights and Permissions Department, P.O. Box 480, Guilford, CT 06437.

Layout artist: Sue Murray
Project manager: Ellen Urban

Maps by Melissa Baker, © Morris Book Publishing, LLC

Library of Congress Cataloging-in-Publication Data is available on file.

ISBN 978-0-7627-8283-3

Printed in the United States of America

10 9 8 7 6 5 4 3 2 1

Contents

INTRODUCTION

MORE THAN TWENTY YEARS HAVE PASSED SINCE I FOUND THE LETTER. HIDDEN IN A collection of old papers, it was obviously much older than the others, a fact confirmed by its date, August 10, 1863. It had been written by Capt. Maris R. Vernon, commander of Company K of the 78th Illinois Volunteer Infantry Regiment, requesting a furlough for Sgt. Jonathan Butler, one of his men.

Butler, the letter said, had "for the last month been unfit for duty, sick in the regimental hospital . . . Sergt. Butler has had little or no sickness prior to this since entering the service. He has always been with the regiment on the march, and without regard to weather has ever discharged his duties in a prompt and soldierly like manner. A furlough would not only benefit him in health and spirits, but would also afford him an opportunity to arrange his business matters at home in a more satisfactory manner for absences. Sergt. Butler has never before asked for a furlough."

As Civil War letters go, this one was not unusual; there were probably thousands like it. Nevertheless, it challenged my curiosity. Who was Jonathan Butler, this soldier who had always been with the regiment and discharged his duties faithfully? What illness confined him to the hospital? What business did he have at home? Was his furlough granted?

And who was Captain Vernon? The letter made it clear he was an educated man who wrote well. It was also clear he cared enough for his men to write such a letter. What was his story?

For that matter, what was the story of the 78th Illinois Volunteer Infantry? In years of studying the Civil War, I had encountered few references to this regiment. Had it spent the war in obscurity? Or merely suffered from lack of a historian to record its exploits?

I decided to try to answer these questions.

At first I searched casually, finding scraps of information here and there and filing them away in a folder. Membership in the Puget Sound Civil War Roundtable brought contact with other members who provided some information, but for a long while my folder remained thin. The Internet, which had been little more than an idea when I started my quest, provided a gradually increasing source of further information and contact with others interested in the 78th Illinois, mostly descendants of men who served in its ranks. From them and other sources I learned of a few published diaries or memoirs and was able to find copies. Through diligent detective work, I tracked down other diaries or letter collections in libraries around the country and obtained copies with the generous help of archivists at these institutions.

Bit by bit, my collection of information on the 78th grew until it occupied not just a single folder but many, and I realized what had begun as a casual search had become an obsession. I also realized I was on the track of a remarkable story, for the 78th Illinois had a very unusual history. It got off on the wrong foot in nearly every way possible, serving under a lackadaisical colonel who was often absent, feuded with his officers and superiors, ended up in arrest, and finally retreated to his tent and did nothing. The regiment was issued ancient rifles, including many that didn't work, and those that did work were almost as dangerous to their users as they were to the enemy. The regiment's companies were posted separately as guards at railroad bridges, which prevented the regiment from drilling and learning to maneuver as a unit. The companies also were beyond mutual supporting distance, so the Confederate raider John Hunt Morgan was easily able to capture two of them. Reduced in numbers, devoid of leadership, distrusted by senior officers, the 78th became a regiment that was always left behind when others went to the front. For the first year of its existence, it fired few shots in anger.

But after the regiment's reluctant colonel was finally forced to resign, his second in command, Lt. Col. Carter Van Vleck of Macomb, Illinois, took over. Van Vleck, a forceful, no-nonsense officer, had been in command only a short time when every available regiment, even the 78th, was called to take part in the campaign to capture Chattanooga. The 78th, part of Maj. Gen. Gordon Granger's Reserve Corps, was summoned urgently to assist Maj. Gen. George Thomas in his desperate defense of the Union left during the second day of the Battle of Chickamauga. And there, in its first real test of combat, the regiment charged up Horseshoe Ridge, drove a veteran Confederate force from its crest, then held against furious counterattacks, helping Thomas earn his sobriquet, "the Rock of Chickamauga." The 78th lost nearly one hundred men that day and ended up under temporary command of a lieutenant, but never again would anyone ever question its bravery or spirit.

The 78th later joined the pursuit of Confederates retreating from Missionary Ridge, then made the brutal winter trek to relieve Union forces besieged at Knoxville. As part of the XIV Corps in the Army of the Cumberland, it joined Sherman's campaign against Atlanta and fought at Buzzard's Roost, Resaca, Rome, and Dallas. It behaved heroically in the assault at Kennesaw Mountain, fought in battles around Atlanta, and achieved perhaps its greatest moment when its determined soldiers braved showers of canister to capture a rebel battery and a Confederate general at Jonesboro.

The 78th then joined Sherman's March to the Sea and was in the thick of the action at the final great bloodletting at Bentonville, North Carolina. After the

Confederate surrender, the regiment marched to Washington, D.C., and stepped proudly through the city as part of the Grand Review—a tough, veteran regiment that had overcome great adversity to forge a record that inspired other soldiers to call it "the Old, Reliable 78th."

Uncovering this remarkable story was a deeply satisfying experience, though some questions remain unanswered. I was able to learn what ailed Jonathan Butler and what became of his requested furlough, but found little else about him. If he wrote letters home during the war, apparently they did not survive, so he is seen here only as others saw him. As for Maris Vernon, he was later promoted to lieutenant colonel and his terse reports appear in the *Official Records of the War of the Rebellion*. A few of his letters also survive. But the man himself remains mostly a mystery.

Fortunately, however, the words and deeds of many other soldiers of the 78th Illinois Volunteer Infantry have been preserved, and their individual stories are as fascinating as the story of their regiment. Their letters and other sources also provide previously unreported details of the fighting at Chickamauga, Kennesaw Mountain, Jonesboro, and other actions and incidents—details new to history.

This history, as so many others, relies in part on the *Official Records of the War of the Rebellion*. The *Records* are invaluable to historians, often providing the best account— sometimes the only account—of battles, skirmishes, or other incidents. But they are far from perfect. Most were written well after the events they describe, when memories were no longer fresh, and nearly all were written in the formal manner demanded by military protocol, which inhibited free expression and opportunities to relate personal experiences. For these we must look to the letters and diaries of the officers and men who fought the battles, endured the drudgery of camp life and the weary exhaustion of the march. Their unfettered accounts and the disclosures of their most private thoughts tell us what the Civil War was really like.

In this volume, I have relied principally on four extensive collections of letters, four diaries, one brief published memoir, and excerpts from many other letters written by members of the 78th Illinois Volunteer Infantry Regiment. Some have never before been accessible to historians.

Most important are the letters of Carter Van Vleck, who joined the 78th as its lieutenant colonel and later became its colonel. For nearly 150 years, his letters to his wife Patty and daughter Nellie have been in the private custody of descendants, and it was only through their generosity that the letters were made available for quotation in this history. They also were made available to my colleague, Teresa Lehr, recently retired from the State University of New York-Brockport, for an edited version of the letters titled *Emerging Leader: The Civil War Letters of Carter Van Vleck to His Wife Patty, 1862–1864*, which should be a valuable complement to this volume.

Van Vleck, a lawyer by profession, was a born leader with more than ordinary common sense. Deeply in love with his wife and daughter, strong in his religious convictions, and devoted to the Union, he set an example for everyone he met. As second in command of the 78th Illinois, he was in the difficult position of being caught between its do-nothing colonel and the growing discontent of the regiment's other officers, yet his integrity assured the respect of both. When he finally ascended to command, his tough-minded approach to discipline quickly turned the 78th into a first-rate fighting outfit. His letters provide the best surviving account of the regiment's transition from one always left behind to one that never failed in its duty. He was also an eloquent, articulate writer, and some of his letters are literary gems.

Second in importance only to the Van Vleck letters are those of Maj. William L. Broaddus, the third-ranking officer of the 78th. The Broaddus collection has long been part of the David M. Rubenstein Rare Book and Manuscript Library at Duke University in North Carolina, but seems to have been previously overlooked by historians.

Broaddus was not an educated man, but he was intelligent, decent, and a devoted patriot. He was also deeply conflicted between his loyalty to the regiment and his love for his family. In letters to his wife, Martha, Broaddus spoke often of obtaining a furlough or resigning from the service so he could return to his family. But whenever his wife pressed him on the matter, he replied that a furlough probably wasn't in the cards just then, or he needed to stay with the regiment until its work was finished. Since his son, Thomas, also was a soldier in the 78th, part of his reluctance to leave the regiment may have been from concern for his son.

The Broaddus letters provide a different perspective on divisions within the regiment and activities during its first year of service. His lack of formal education is evident in his use of phonetic spelling, sometimes with unintentionally hilarious results, but he always managed to make his meaning clear. The phonetic and other misspellings have been left intact to preserve the original flavor of the letters, as they have for other letters or diaries whose writers spelled phonetically. Errors in capitalization and punctuation have been corrected to spare readers a few headaches.

The letters of Thomas Goldsborough Odell, collected, edited, and published by his great-grandson, the late Donald Odell Virdin, contain the most detailed descriptions of camp life in the 78th Illinois. Odell and his younger brother, Risdon, were privates in Company G, and Odell wrote often to his wife, Beliscent, and their children. He was a literate correspondent with an apt turn of phrase, though he mostly used dashes for punctuation, a common practice among Civil War correspondents. Odell was wounded at Chickamauga and the letters he wrote during his subsequent lengthy stay in hospitals shed light on what it was like to be confined in such places.

The letters of James K. Magie are the most skillfully written of any 78th correspondent. That was to be expected, since Magie was a newspaper editor in civilian life. A few excerpts from his letters have been published previously, but most appear here for the first time, courtesy of the Gilder Lehrman Institute of American History.

Magie had gone into debt to purchase an interest in the *Macomb Journal* before the war and also needed money to pay for an operation needed by his son, so financial matters were ever on his mind and many of his letters are devoted largely to that topic. He thought all his problems were solved when he became brigade postmaster and saw a chance to make a profit selling stamps and newspapers to soldiers in the 78th and other regiments. He wrote excitedly to his wife about how much money he could make, suggesting his postmaster's position also might allow him to avoid combat. Sometimes he also seemed to delight in deliberately provoking his wife, as when he sent home an old uniform and told her to "watch out for the greybacks" (lice).

Things didn't work out as Magie hoped. He didn't get rich, and when the 78th finally went into combat he was there in line with the rest of them. Eventually he was promoted to first sergeant of Company C, which increased his pay a few dollars a month. His letters contain many interesting and sometimes hair-raising anecdotes, but they do not always paint a flattering portrait of the man who wrote them.

The diary of John Batchelor is the most important of those kept by men of the 78th because it is the only one yet found that covers the entire period of the regiment's service. Batchelor, a twenty-three-year-old carpenter originally from Warwickshire, England, was a private in Company I. Most of his diary entries are terse—e.g., "Some of the men are drunk"—but Batchelor was never shy about expressing his opinions, and in some ways he is the most likeable of the 78th's correspondents and diarists. The diary, now in the Abraham Lincoln Presidential Library at Springfield, Illinois, has been cited often by other historians.

Charles Vilasco Chandler was nineteen years old and had just completed his first year at Lake Forest Academy near Chicago when he enlisted as a private in Company I of the 78th. Bright and articulate, he was soon appointed regimental sergeant major and was later promoted to lieutenant. His diary, now held by the Putnam County Public Library in Greencastle, Indiana, was started in June 1861, and its first year chronicles the relatively carefree life of a college student who enjoyed socializing with young ladies and playing a game that would later be known as baseball. But there is a mysterious gap in the diary between July 16 and September 13, 1862, when, for reasons not explained, Chandler suddenly joined the army. The remainder of the diary chronicles his service with the 78th, including his studies to become an officer, the mistakes he made, and his junior officer's view of the regiment's internal problems. The diary ends shortly after the Battle of Chickamauga, where Chandler was wounded in the opening moments of action. His wounds eventually forced him to leave the service.

The diary of James M. McNeill contains some of the most flowery writing to be found among the surviving documents of the 78th Illinois. McNeill, a twenty-six-year-old sawyer from Dallas City, Illinois, was a sergeant in Company H. His diary, which covers the first seven months of the regiment's service, was published in *Call Them Men, Then*, a small book compiled and edited by William and Marvel Allen of River Falls, Wisconsin, distributed mostly to family members and libraries (William Allen was the adoptive great-grandson of Capt. John K. Allen, Company H commander). The diary is valuable for descriptions of the regiment's early history and also provides a detailed account of a skirmish at New Haven, Kentucky. The diary ended abruptly on March 16, 1863, and McNeill was discharged from the service in June of that year for reasons not recorded.

The journal of Pvt. James Edgar Withrow of Company I is the briefest of any 78th diary that has surfaced to date. Withrow began keeping the diary shortly after the battle of Chickamauga in September 1863, perhaps realizing he was a participant in historic events. If so, his resolve did not last very long; the final entry was January 4, 1864.

Withrow got off to a bad start in the regiment. He was homesick and hated the army. "He don't like to drill nor to do anything else & has made every body dislike him, so that it is really a very hard place for him," Van Vleck wrote. As a consequence, whenever Company I had to provide men for detached duty, Withrow's name was always near the top of the list, and he spent much of his time away from the regiment. During the period he kept his diary, he served in an artillery battery and on a cattle-butchering detail, so his perspective was more that of an outsider than a member of the 78th. Nevertheless, his diary has useful information, particularly his description of the condition of the 78th when it returned from the harsh winter march to relieve the Union garrison at Knoxville. The diary is now part of the Illinois History and Lincoln Collections at the University of Illinois at Urbana-Champaign.

The only published memoir by a member of the 78th was a little book by Edward Mott Robbins with the weighty title *Civil War Experiences: Chickamauga, Mission Ridge, Buzzard Roost, Resaca, Rome, New Hope Church, Kenesaw Mountain, Peach Tree Creek, Atlanta, Jonesboro, Averysboro, Bentonville*. Robbins, who enlisted in Company H as a private, wrote the memoir in 1919, more than fifty years after the events he described, relying mostly on his memory and the published *Report of the Adjutant General of Illinois*. Both were fallible sources. Robbins's recollection of names and dates was unreliable, so he often used dates supplied by the Adjutant General, also unreliable in many instances. In fact, Robbins was so heavily influenced by the Adjutant General's

Report that he even borrowed some of its language. But there was nothing wrong with Robbins's memory of some of the events he witnessed, and his brief memoir contains some of the best anecdotes of the 78th Illinois.

Other sources include small collections of letters from Dr. William H. Githens and Pvt. Benjamin F. Gill; a single long letter from regimental chaplain Robert Taylor; excerpts from the letters of William E. Summers and the reminiscences of his sister, Lucia Summers; excerpts from letters of Pvts. Isaac Landon and Cornelius Pierce; and a couple of anonymous letters sent by members of the 78th to local newspapers. Githens, a surgeon, wrote feelingly about the wounded men he treated and the dead he saw being carried to their final resting places; unfortunately, most of his letters apparently were auctioned to private collectors and have been lost to historians. Gill, a blacksmith in civilian life, helped keep the regiment's horses and mules well shod. Taylor describes his efforts to attend to the spiritual needs of the unit. Lucia Summers shared her reminiscences and excerpts from letters written by her brother, original first sergeant and later first lieutenant of Company K, in a pair of lengthy newspaper articles. Excerpts from letters and reminiscences of Landon, a private in Company K, and Pierce, a private in Company F, also appeared in newspapers.

The attrition of war took a severe toll on the diarists and correspondents of the 78th, and Batchelor's diary and some reports in the *Official Records* provide the only direct record of events after the Battle of Jonesboro, including the March to the Sea in November and December 1864, and the Carolinas campaign that followed. These records, however, have been augmented by published histories of two regiments that served in the same brigade as the 78th and shared many of its adventures. They are *History of the Thirty-Fourth Regiment of Illinois Volunteer Infantry*, by Sgt. Edwin W. Payne, and *Every-Day Soldier Life, or a History of the Hundred and Thirteenth Reg't, Ohio Volunteer Infantry*, by F. M. McAdams. The diary and letters of Maj. James A. Connolly, published in book form as *Three Years in the Army of the Cumberland*, also was a valuable source.

So these are the voices that speak to us across the years. There may be others yet unheard, their words waiting in tattered, water-stained diaries or yellowed packets of letters hidden away in attics across the land. Perhaps in the future some will surface and fall into the hands of historians who will add to the saga of the 78th Illinois Volunteer Infantry Regiment.

But for the present, these pages include all that is known. It is a story that has been waiting more than 150 years to be told. It is my great privilege now to tell it.

—Steve Raymond

"The Blind Leading the Blind"

AUGUST 2—SEPTEMBER 20, 1862

THEY MET FOR THE FIRST TIME AT THE OLD STONE CHURCH IN DALLAS CITY ON Saturday, August 2, 1862. Few of the men present were strangers to one another; many had grown up together, and some were related. All had answered President Lincoln's latest call for troops to help put down the rebellion.

The purpose of the meeting was to elect officers for a new company of infantry. It would be the third company raised in Dallas City, a remarkable record for an Illinois community of barely a thousand souls. Every man present took an oath to abide by the results of the election. Then the name of John Knox Allen, a thirty-seven-year-old Dallas City merchant and one of the company organizers, was placed in nomination for captain. He was elected by acclamation. George T. Beers, twenty-nine, a civil engineer from neighboring Pontoosuc, was elected first lieutenant, and Samuel Simmons, a forty-two-year-old farmer from Henderson County, was chosen second lieutenant.

"The meeting then adjourned to Gabhart's Beer Saloon" where the new officers "exhibited their thanks by a copious treat, of the company, to what Lager they could drink," James K. McNeill wrote in his diary. McNeill, twenty-six, would become a sergeant in the new company.

Recruiting continued after the meeting until the company had nearly reached its goal of a hundred members and it was time to head for Quincy, where new regiments were assembling and being mustered into federal service. Sunday August 10th was fixed as the date for departure and the community turned out the day before to say farewell to its sons. The young ladies of Dallas City presented the company with a silk flag, accompanied by a "very pretty and befitting address" by Miss Lucie Hinkley.[1]

Early the next morning, the men of Captain Allen's company boarded the 135-foot steam packet *Jennie Whipple* for the journey down the Mississippi to Quincy. With the great river's current behind the *Jennie Whipple*, the trip downstream would be short, and as the steamer edged away from the Dallas City quay the men arranged themselves around her deck and sat back to doze or watch the scenery. Some lit pipes.

They expected a peaceful journey, but they had scarcely grown accustomed to the sounds of the river and the rhythmic thump of the boat's engine when they heard another sound rising above the others—the shouts of an angry mob. The *Jennie Whipple* was approaching the town of Alexandria, on the Missouri side of the river, where a crowd had assembled on the shore, shaking fists, waving black flags, and chanting "Hurrah for Jeff Davis!" The same unsettling scene was repeated at Canton, the next town downstream along the Missouri shore. "It made us very indignant to think so near home we should be insulted in such a manner," wrote Edward Mott Robbins, a twenty-year-old member of the company. "I have never had a very favorable opinion of those two towns since."[2]

Missouri was a bitterly divided state and the attitudes of some of its people were decidedly different from those of their Union-leaning neighbors across the river in Illinois. It was almost as if the Mississippi was a philosophical as well as a physical barrier between the two states, and the jeering Confederate sympathizers on the Missouri shore reminded Robbins and his comrades of the reason for their journey: They were on their way to fight.

The *Jennie Whipple* reached Quincy about three o'clock that Sunday afternoon, and there Captain Allen and his men met a more friendly reception. Another new company, still in process of organization and led by a Major Holten, greeted the Dallas City contingent and escorted them to the town square.

Quincy, the county seat of Adams County, Illinois, was the largest city in the area. Its citizens were proud their city's population had topped 14,000 in the 1860 census, though just barely (the final tally was 14,005).[3] Quincy in 1862 was a busy, noisy, smoky, smelly place, a thriving transportation hub served by three railroads and almost daily visits from cargo-laden steamboats passing up and down the Mississippi. The city's streets, muddy or dusty by turns, were deeply rutted with wagon tracks and crowded with freight wagons, carriages, solitary riders, and pedestrians who stepped carefully through dried mud and horse manure, brushing away flies that seemed to hover everywhere.

Quincy also was a city greatly changed by the Civil War. Nearly the entire population had shifted to a war footing. A local foundry converted production from farm implements to cannon and a local tannery started turning out leather boxes to hold the percussion caps soldiers would need to fire their rifles. Women residents organized the "Needle Pickets" and "Good Samaritans," who met four times a week and began soliciting flannel, lint, and other material that could be used to make bandages or other "articles of comfort" for soldiers.[4]

Women in neighboring Melrose Township established a similar group, the "Melrose Aids," who met twice a week to knit and sew items for soldiers. Lucia Summers, a member, later recalled that the "Melrose Aids" also made havelocks, caps "made of heavy white linen, having a cape to it about 10 or 12 inches deep, to protect the necks of the soldiers from the hot rays of the sun." Soldiers who received the fruits of their labors sometimes wrote letters of acknowledgement. "Some were very thankful for the havelocks, others put them to different uses from what was intended—'Made pretty good dishrags,'" one said.[5]

Several hospitals were built in Quincy to accommodate the anticipated flow of sick or wounded men from the camps and battlefields. Newsboys on street corners shouted war headlines from the city's four newspapers, while bookstores advertised the latest texts on military tactics for aspiring officers. Attorneys proclaimed themselves advocates in settling "war claims," including bounty payments and pensions.

When the war began, Quincy had only two militia companies, the "Rifles" and "Guards." The latter company was commanded by Capt. James Dada Morgan, who had broken his leg while packing ice during the previous winter and was still on crutches. But when the company departed for service on April 21, 1861, less than ten days after the Confederates fired on Fort Sumter, Morgan hobbled along.[6] He would become a general before the war was over.

Responding to the call for volunteers to quell the rebellion, men from Quincy and surrounding farm communities stepped forward in sufficient numbers to fill eight additional companies. Two of these joined the "Rifles" and "Guards" and became part of the 10th Illinois Volunteer Infantry Regiment. Five others joined the 16th Illinois, which formed at Quincy and camped in the Adams County fairgrounds south of the city. A single company mustered into the 27th Illinois.[7]

In November 1861, the city received word of its first battlefield fatality. William Shipley, a twenty-four-year-old first lieutenant and the adopted son of Senator Orville H. Browning, was killed at Belmont, Missouri. His body was sent home and a funeral service was held at the home of Senator and Mrs. Browning on the corner of Seventh and Hampshire Streets.[8]

Such funerals would become sadly routine by the following spring. By then, however, it was beginning to look as if the war would be over soon and the Union would be victorious. New Orleans, the South's largest city, had been captured, Union forces had driven all the way into northern Mississippi, and Maj. Gen. George Brinton McClellan's huge Army of the Potomac was poised on the doorstep of Richmond, apparently on the verge of capturing the Confederate capital. The federal government, anticipating an early end to the war, began shutting down recruiting offices and reassigning recruiters.

Then everything changed. The Confederate Army of Northern Virginia under its new commander, Robert E. Lee, launched a series of savage assaults that would become known as the Seven Days Battles, driving McClellan's army away from Richmond. The defeats changed the whole complexion of the war, and suddenly it was clear the conflict would continue and the Union would need many more men in its armies. In July 1862, President Lincoln issued a call for three hundred thousand more troops, with quotas based proportionally on the population of each loyal state.

Quincy's quota was 225, thanks to its having surpassed the fourteen thousand population mark in the 1860 census. The quota for all of Adams County was 675.[9] Recruiting efforts resumed quickly along with subscription rallies where citizens were asked to pledge sums of money for a fund to pay enlistment bonuses.

So "war fever" was running high in Quincy when the Dallas City men arrived, and the city was already filling with other new companies in various stages of organization. But when Captain Allen's men reached the town square, they learned a camp for new regiments had yet to be established, and no preparations had been made to receive them. They would have to find lodging on their own.

Some headed for the Adams House hotel on Hampshire Street, which advertised "no pains will be spared to make those comfortable that favor us with their patronage." That promise may have won over a few men, but more likely they were attracted by another business on the same premises, the partnership of Whitbread & Wetzell, purveyors of "Lill & Diversey's Chicago Champagne and Stock Ales" with "barrels and half barrels received daily." Other members of the company, perhaps less thirsty, found quarters at some of Quincy's other hotels.

The new company's arrival did not go unnoticed in the city. "A first class company of recruits came in on Sunday afternoon from Dallas City," the *Daily Whig* reported August 11. "They did not arrive as early as expected, but come in now with full ranks, numbering over 100 men. This morning they paraded on the Square, and elicited a good deal of admiring attention."

On the same day, the *Daily Whig* reported a local company recruited by Capt. M. G. Tousely and Lt. H. P. Roberts "is now full and 'running over.' It numbers 102 sworn men." Major Holten was reported to have eighty-two men signed up for his company, and Major Hugo Hollan, "whose headquarters are over Fred's Saloon North of the Court House," had about fifty recruits. "Captain Vernon, we understand, has only about fifty men sworn in, but with the other companies out of the way and the war fever still so high, he will undoubtedly fill up in a few days."

Maris R. Vernon, twenty-seven, was one of several local attorneys who had recently advertised his services on behalf of those who had war claims. Now he was trying to raise a company so he could join the war himself, advertising for recruits to report to his law office at 105 Hampshire Street. His efforts received a ringing endorsement from the *Daily Whig:* "Mr. Vernon is well qualified for the position, being a thorough master of company drill, and admirably fitted by his excellent character to have the control of young men amid the temptations of war . . . He will hold meetings throughout the county, and will be aided by influential speakers. Let all help to make Captain Vernon's company a success."

A day later, August 12th, another new company "of fine looking men" arrived in Quincy, this one from Carthage, Hancock County. It was commanded by Capt. Robert M. Black, a twenty-five-year-old Carthage resident who listed his occupation as "student." "Captain Black is a man of energy," the *Quincy Daily Herald* reported, "for he had been in the city but three or four hours before he picked up six or seven additions to his company and had them sworn."

The same edition of the *Daily Herald* was filled with notices of "war meetings" scheduled that week. "Ellington on the War Path!" was the headline over one advertisement. "The people of Ellington Township will meet en masse at the grove just east of Center School House on Thursday, Aug. 14th, at 10 A.M. to take action upon the subject of bounty for volunteers; to instruct our Town Supervisors to vote for such bounty; to encourage enlistments, and other important matters. Come on! Turn out! Bring on your wives, your children and your sweet-hearts, and let us have a good old-fashioned Basket Pic-Nic, and a general good time."

Another notice told of a recruiting meeting to be held at Chatten Spring in Fall Creek Township August 13th. Yet another, signed by "Many Citizens," summoned "all able bodied and patriotic citizens of this town and neighborhood" to a meeting "at early candle lighting in 'Union Church' at Big Neck Prairie, in Adams County, Illinois, on Tuesday evening. Good speakers will be there."[10]

Jonathan Butler, twenty-four, a blacksmith who had moved to Big Neck from his native Pennsylvania, may have been among those who listened to the "good speakers" at the Union Church. Despite having been married scarcely seven months earlier—or maybe because of it—Butler volunteered to enlist in Maris Vernon's company.[11]

Similar enlistment meetings and rallies were going on in and around the city of Macomb, in McDonough County northeast of Quincy. John Batchelor, a twenty-three-year-old carpenter, was among those who enlisted. Like most people then living in southwestern Illinois, which had not been settled long enough to have many native-born residents, he was from somewhere else—in his case, all the way from Warwickshire, England. Batchelor's name was added to the roll of a new company commanded by Capt. Granville Reynolds, a thirty-seven-year-old farmer from Industry, McDonough County.

The recruits would need officers to lead them, and on August 16th the *Whig & Republican* announced that Quincy attorney William H. Benneson would be one of them. Benneson had been appointed colonel "of one of the regiments now mustering here," the paper said. "Its number is not yet assigned, but [it] will probably be the 78th. Mr. Benneson is generally esteemed a very safe, able and considerate man, and we have no doubt he will do full justice to this appointment."[12]

Born in Newark, Delaware, Benneson had graduated with honors from Delaware College in 1840, then taught school for three years in Virginia while studying law. He moved to Quincy in 1843 and opened a law office in partnership with Stephen A. Douglas, the future US senator who was Lincoln's opponent in the famous Lincoln-Douglas debates and a presidential candidate in 1860. The partnership dissolved when Douglas entered politics, but the two men remained friends.

In 1849, Benneson left his law practice to seek his fortune mining gold in California. Apparently unsuccessful, he returned to Quincy three years later to resume the practice of law. Now, at age forty-three, with a newly signed colonel's commission from Illinois governor Richard Yates in his pocket, Benneson was ready to try his hand as commander of an infantry regiment, a task for which his prior experience had done little to prepare him. There is no record of his physical appearance; his service record contains no description and apparently no photographs have survived.

The following week the *Whig & Republican* reported that "Capt. Vernon turned out yesterday with most of his men and made a fine parade. He has an excellent company. In general his men are of good size and strong look, and we predict they will make their mark on the enemy." The paper also reported the results of elections in Vernon's company: Not surprisingly, Vernon was elected captain. Jeremiah Parsons of Melrose was chosen first lieutenant and William B. Akins of Keene Township, second lieutenant. All the votes were unanimous.[13]

It was standard procedure at that stage of the Civil War for companies to elect their officers. Usually the drive to recruit the company was headed by a leading local citizen, and his election as captain was virtually a foregone conclusion. The choices for first and second lieutenant often were contested, however, and the results were made unanimous only after a clear winner had emerged. Sometimes runners-up in the voting became sergeants, as was evidently the case in Vernon's company. William E. Summers of Quincy, brother of Lucia Summers of the "Melrose Aids," was chosen first sergeant, while Jonathan Butler, the blacksmith from Big Neck, became one of the other sergeants.

Captain Reynolds's company, including John Batchelor, left Macomb for Quincy on Tuesday, August 26. Batchelor noted in his diary that his son, William, was six months old that day.[14]

By that time an encampment for the new regiments had been established on open ground on the north side of Quincy, extending from Sunset Hill on Locust Street eastward to about Tenth Street and southward for several blocks. It needed to be large, because it would have to accommodate a large number of men. A typical Union infantry regiment had ten rifle companies, nominally with one hundred men each (although few companies were able to sustain that number), plus a headquarters company. The latter included three field officers (those with ranks above captain), a colonel, lieutenant colonel and major; an adjutant, usually a lieutenant, who handled much of the regiment's paperwork; a surgeon, assistant surgeons, and hospital stewards; a quartermaster, responsible for rations, forage, and equipage; a chaplain; and a noncommissioned staff. If the regiment had a band, its members also were assigned to the headquarters company; if not, then the company usually included a "principal musician" (bugler or drummer). At full strength, a regiment would have somewhere between one thousand and eleven hundred men. Four new regiments—the 50th Illinois, commanded by Col. M. M. Bane; the 78th, under Col. Benneson; the 84th, led by Col. Louis H. Waters; and the 119th, commanded by Col. Thomas J. Kinney—would be established at Quincy. That meant the new camp would have to accommodate more than four thousand men.

At first the camp had no barracks, so tents were provided—mostly tall, conical Sibley tents that could shelter as many as twenty men each, provided they slept side-by-side with their feet toward the center of the tent and their heads toward the outside, like spokes on a wheel. As soon as the tents were ready for issue, the company from Dallas City left its hotel rooms and moved to the new camp on the edge of town. Five Sibley tents were issued to the company and Captain Allen appointed a sergeant to supervise the men in each tent. The men also were formed into separate "messes," each responsible for preparing its own food.[15]

"We knew absolutely nothing about camp life," Edward Mott Robbins wrote. The Sibley tents were just one of many new things that posed challenges. They "were round with [a] pole in the center to hold them up, and guy ropes to hold them from blowing over . . . It was some time before we got used to those guy ropes, for we were constantly getting too near and falling over them. What was said on those occasions would hardly bear repeating.

"Each man drew a tin plate, tin cup, knife, fork and spoon. The company drew five camp kettles, all of different sizes, to be used in cooking different kinds of food. The greatest trouble we had for a time was how much rice to put in the kettle. The first time cooking . . . we had everything around camp filled with rice. It kept swelling beyond what we had any conception of."[16]

While the Dallas City men adjusted to camp life, more new companies were arriving in Quincy. "A fine company from Liberty came in yesterday afternoon, and were escorted about town by the companies of Captains Holton and Hollan," the *Whig & Republican* reported August 30th. "Captain Holton made quite a handsome little reception speech to them in the Square, for which he was deservedly honored with three cheers. The men are substantial looking soldiers." They were commanded by Capt. George Pollock of Beverly, Adams County.

Two other Adams County companies arrived the next day, one from Camp Point, under command of Capt. Jacob F. Joseph, and the other from Coatsburg, commanded by Capt. Henry E. Hawkins. All these companies were assigned to Colonel Benneson's 78th Regiment along with Captain Reynolds's company from Macomb, Captain Allen's from Dallas City, Captain Vernon's from Quincy, and four others.

The regiment was completing its organization. Carter Van Vleck, a Macomb attorney, was commissioned lieutenant colonel. Van Vleck, thirty-two, was a former Democrat who had switched allegiance to the Republican Party and endorsed Lincoln in the 1860 election. Besides Lincoln, he also may have been the only man in southern Illinois to hold a US patent at the time. Lincoln obtained a patent in 1849 for his design of a device to lift riverboats over shoals. Van Vleck received a patent in 1857 for the invention of "Never-Fail Roofing" material made of gutta percha, a latex-like substance from tropical trees.

Van Vleck's photograph, published in a family genealogy, shows a rather sad-eyed man with dark hair, a short dark beard, high forehead, and resolute expression. Van Vleck had reason to be sad-eyed; he and his wife, Patty, had three children die in infancy, the most recent less than a year before Van Vleck was commissioned. The close-knit couple was sustained by their religious faith and love for their only surviving child, a four-year-old daughter named Nellie.

William L. Broaddus, a thirty-nine-year-old mechanic, also from Macomb, was commissioned major. Broaddus stood five feet, nine inches tall and had dark hair and gray eyes. He started the war as a lieutenant in the 16th Illinois Volunteer Infantry, was promoted to captain, then resigned to accept appointment as major of the 78th. His son, Thomas, eighteen, had enlisted as a private in the new 84th Illinois, but transferred to the 78th when his father joined that regiment; his nephew, Robert Laughlin, also was a member of the 78th.

George Greene, a twenty-year-old clerk from Quincy, was appointed regimental adjutant, and the Rev. Robert F. Taylor, thirty-one, of Quincy, became chaplain. Dr. Thomas M. Jordan, a thirty-two-year-old physician from Macomb, was appointed surgeon. Other appointments would be made from the ranks after the new companies were formally mustered into the service.

That happened September 1st. A few men were rejected by the mustering officer for reasons not recorded, while a few others had drifted away before the regiment could be mustered, including five from Captain Allen's company (one went to Chicago, where higher bounties were paid, and enlisted in another regiment there).[17] The rest were mustered into federal service; for the next three years, they would belong to the government.

Next day there was a drawing to assign each company the alphabetical letter by which it would be known. The letters A through I and K were written on pieces of paper and placed in a hat (the letter J was not used because when handwritten it was too easily confused with the letter I). Chaplain Taylor was appointed to draw letters from the hat and was blindfolded for the occasion.[18]

The chaplain drew letter A for a company of eighty-five troops mostly from St. Clair, Schuyler, McDonough, and Hancock Counties, commanded by Capt. Robert S. Blackburn. The company receiving letter B had ninety men, mostly from Adams County. It was commanded by Capt. John C. Anderson, at age forty-eight one of the two oldest men in the regiment.

The letter C went to a company of eighty-five recruits all from Blandinsville, McDonough County. Its commander was Capt. Charles R. Hume, a lawyer who at age forty-eight was tied with Captain Anderson as the oldest man in the regiment. Among his men was thirty-five-year-old James K. Magie, who had purchased a half interest in the *Macomb Journal* on March 23, 1862, and served as editor until his enlistment, leaving the paper under management of a man named Nichols, who owned the other half interest.

Company D, commanded by Capt. Robert M. Black, was mostly from Hancock County and a few settlements in Adams County. The company's ninety men included the regiment's youngest, Charles N. Bennett, who was only fourteen.[19] Capt. George Pollock's band of "substantial looking soldiers," noticed earlier by the *Quincy Whig Republican*, became Company E. Its ninety-four men were almost all from Adams County. Capt. Henry E. Hawkins' company, seventy-nine men also mainly from Adams County, drew the letter F.

Company G, commanded by Capt. Jacob F. Joseph, was another company of Adams County men. It mustered ninety-five men. Capt. John K. Allen's contingent, including Edward Mott Robbins, became Company H. Most of its ninety-two men came from Dallas City, Pontoosuc or Durham, Hancock County, along with several from Henderson County. Company I—John Batchelor's company, commanded by Capt. Granville Reynolds—was mostly from cities and towns in McDonough County. Its roster numbered eighty-eight.

Company K—Jonathan Butler's company, commanded by Capt. Maris Vernon— had men from nearly every village and township in Adams County. Among its eighty-eight men was twenty-four-year-old Perry Lesure from Liberty, only son of aging parents who wanted him at home. When they learned he had enlisted, they began a campaign to have him discharged; it would continue for two years.

So these were the men who would go to war under the banner of the 78th Illinois Volunteer Infantry Regiment. Their average age was just over twenty-five years, and including six members of the Headquarters Company, 716 gave their occupation as farmers—about eighty percent of the regiment. There were also thirty-six carpenters, twenty-one blacksmiths, twelve teachers, eight shoemakers, six wagon makers, six merchants, five masons, five laborers, four teamsters, four students, four plasterers, four clerks, three lawyers, three saddlers, and a host of other trades, including such esoteric occupations as "plow stocker," "moulder," "tinner," broom maker, and leather inspector.

But their peacetime occupations no longer mattered, for they all had the same occupation now: They were soldiers.

What induced these men to enlist? Why had they pledged their lives to the service of their country for three years or the duration of the war? The war had already been in progress seventeen months when they enlisted; why hadn't they answered the first call for troops when the war began?

One answer is that more than a hundred of them would have been too young; they had reached military age in the months since the war's beginning. But that does not answer for the rest. During the great wave of patriotism that swept the North after Fort Sumter, when thousands flocked to volunteer, these men had not. Those who did enlist at the outset of the war expected a grand adventure with a swift result, but that was not what happened. Instead, the war had become a grim, deadly struggle, and the enormous casualties at Shiloh and the Seven Days battles shocked the nation. Anyone who volunteered now was surely putting his life at risk. So why did these men step forward in the late summer of 1862 when they had not done so in the spring of 1861?

There are probably as many answers to that question as there were men in the 78th Illinois, but patriotism was certainly one factor. The surviving diaries and letters of men who served in the 78th bear ample evidence of that. Some expressed their thoughts eloquently while others were barely literate, but each in his own way voiced a deep commitment to the nation's experiment in democracy and a fear that the rebellion could mean the end of it. The idea of the Union was sacred to them, holding great promise for the future, and they were willing to fight for it not only for themselves but also for their children. The very fact that the war had become a bitter, protracted struggle may have given them greater incentive to enlist, for everyone could now see the war was going to last a long time and the Union would need many more men in its armies if it was going to prevail. So they stepped forward.

Did slavery have anything to do with it? The letters and diaries of men in the 78th reveal that some were morally opposed to slavery and others at least had serious reservations about it, but the idea that the war was a struggle against slavery was still emerging in the late summer of 1862, so it was probably not among the factors that induced these men to enlist. However, when Lincoln announced his draft of the Emancipation Proclamation shortly after the 78th was mustered into service, it may have helped many men feel they had made the right decision when they volunteered.

Peer pressure was certainly a factor motivating some men to enlist. Since Civil War companies were typically raised in small communities where everyone knew everyone else, or in some cases was related to nearly everyone else, everybody knew who had volunteered in the first call for troops and who had not. Those who did volunteer became local heroes. In the year that followed, those who stayed behind sometimes found themselves targets of subtle hints that maybe they also should have volunteered. Sometimes the hints weren't so subtle.

To have one's lifetime friends, neighbors, and relatives suggesting repeatedly that it was one's moral duty to volunteer was a powerful inducement to enlist. Young men also worried that if they didn't volunteer, young women were unlikely to view them favorably as marriage prospects. So some men enlisted at least partly from fear of what others would think of them if they did not.

Enlistment was made easier by the knowledge that one would be serving with relatives, neighbors, or lifelong friends. Most company commanders also were local community leaders, well known and respected by their men, and their companies often included fathers and sons and sets of brothers or cousins. So the prospect that the uncertainties of military service would be shared with familiar faces also was surely a stimulus to enlistment, though how much is impossible to measure.

Economics were another important factor. The previous year's harvest in southwest Illinois had been sub-par and the next one promised to be little better, so farmers' incomes were uncertain at best. The first year of war also had resulted in double-digit inflation, taking a big bite out of the already meager purchasing power of farm families. With so many men in the army, there was also a shortage of farm labor, and labor costs had risen to the point where some crops cost more to harvest than they were worth. For all these reasons, the promise of thirteen dollars a month as a private in the army was appealing to many young men, and the prospect of an enlistment bonus was an added attraction. The bonuses came from funds pledged in local subscription drives and the amounts varied, tending to be higher in larger communities where more people contributed. The enlistment bounty in Quincy, for example, was forty dollars—more than three months' pay for a private soldier—while in smaller Macomb it was twenty-five dollars.

It seems incredible in the twenty-first century to think that anyone would risk his life for thirteen dollars a month, but the dollar was worth a great deal more in 1862 than it is today—at least 113 times more, if one compares a private's pay in 1862 with a newly enlisted private's pay in today's army. By that measure, a private's pay of thirteen dollars a month in 1862 would be worth $1,467.60 in today's dollars. Using the same comparison, an enlistment bonus of twenty-five dollars in 1862 would be equivalent to $2,825 in today's dollars, and a bonus of forty dollars would be worth $4,520. These figures are conservative, and the actual value of an 1862 dollar in modern terms might be even higher. In any case, to an Illinois farmer trying to figure out how he was going to feed his family through the winter of 1862–63, the prospect of earning thirteen dollars a month plus an enlistment bonus was a powerful stimulus to enlist.

Of course, those who did enlist also expected to be paid on a regular basis. In that, they would be sorely disappointed.

Even before they were formally mustered into the service on September 1, 1862, the new soldiers of the 78th Regiment were beginning to learn the mysteries and miseries of military drill. Most men in the regiment were accustomed to the discipline of hard work, but nothing had prepared them for the experience of marching shoulder-to-shoulder in lockstep and responding instantly to a bewildering variety of shouted commands, each with different meaning. Yet they would need to learn these things until they became second nature if they were to be able to respond instantly on the battlefield.

Major Broaddus, by virtue of his earlier service in the 16th Illinois, was well versed in drill, but few if any of the regiment's other officers had any experience; they were starting from scratch. They not only had to learn the commands and what they meant; they also had to learn how to give orders.

It did not go well at first. Men stumbled over one another, formations collided, and embarrassed officers shouted frantically, trying to untangle things and restore order. "It was like the blind leading the blind," recalled Isaac W. Landon, a private in Company K. "Instructor and instructed were both alike ignorant; yet, somehow, we made tolerable progress."

To onlookers, progress was probably difficult to discern and they might have wondered how such stumbling troops could ever hope to win a war. The same thought also later occurred to Landon: "When we remember that our entire army was made up of men as ignorant of the science of war as ourselves, are we not baffled to know from whence our victory came?"[20]

It didn't seem to bother Major Broaddus that everyone looked to him for guidance. "I stand drilling first rate, or rather stand the labor of drilling the officers," he wrote to his wife, Martha, who was home caring for the couple's younger son and daughter. Colonel Benneson "is very busy with other matters."[21]

One of those matters was a meeting with a man named Dills, who was trying to win the colonel's blessing to become sutler of the 78th Regiment. Sutlers were civilian merchants who were given a more or less exclusive franchise to sell goods to a regiment. They accompanied the regiment on the march with a wagonload of merchandise—pies, cakes, other confections, canned goods, articles of clothing, writing materials, and other items not readily available in the field—and, in the absence of competition, sold them at high prices. It seemed an easy way to get rich, because soldiers were a captive market, always hungry and always in need of the delicacies and necessities sutlers had to offer. But being a sutler was not without hazards, because soldiers also were nearly always short of cash and resented being overcharged, and there were stories of regiments that turned on their sutlers and cleaned out their wagons. When a sutler was greatly outnumbered by a mob of angry armed men, there was little he could do about it, and some sutlers were left with nothing.

If Mr. Dills had heard such tales, they apparently didn't bother him. Determined to win Colonel Benneson's favor, he presented the colonel with a splendid horse worth several hundred dollars. The gesture had the desired effect; Dills was promised the sutler's appointment. Later, however, Dills had second thoughts and eventually decided not to accept the appointment, and the sutler's franchise eventually went to someone else. But Colonel Benneson kept the horse anyway.[22]

In addition to their efforts to master the convolutions of military drill, the new soldiers of the 78th also had to struggle with new uniforms. Privates were issued dark-blue woolen frock coats, trousers of lighter blue, wool forage caps with leather visors, and a belt set that included a cartridge box, percussion-cap box, bayonet, and scabbard. But they didn't get everything at once, and many of the things they got didn't fit.

If a soldier knew how to handle a needle and thread, he might be able to fix things himself. He might even be able to make a little money on the side. Thomas Goldsborough Odell of Company G wrote his wife and children that he made ten cents tailoring a pair of pantaloons for another soldier. He also said a lady came into camp and made about four dollars a day fixing uniforms, charging twenty-five cents to alter the waist of a pair of pantaloons or one dollar to make them over.[23] Those prices would put a significant dent in a private's monthly pay, but for sake of appearances or comfort, or both, some men were willing to pay.

Odell wrote the folks at home—his wife, Beliscent, and four children—about a picnic September 3rd arranged by residents of Honey Creek Township. "It was a nice thing to see a whole Co(mpany) surround the good things, which were spread out on the ground," he wrote. "Lieut. Herndon returned thanks."

On the night of September 3 there was excitement in camp. "Orders were received to have four days rations prepared, and to be ready to march at any moment," James M.

McNeill wrote in his diary. "But soon the order to prepare rations was countermanded, and the fires prepared to cook, which were burning brilliantly, making a beautiful scene for the new soldiers, who had never before seen camp fires burning, [were ordered] to be put out. The excitement, which was greate, which we presume is always the case with fresh troops on getting an order to march, soon died down to the usual quiet, which at no time while we stayed here was very extensive."

Next day it was McNeill's turn to be impressed by a picnic. "Quite a stir in camp on account of a huge PicNic being on hand, given by the liberals of Macomb," he wrote. "A large crowd in attendance estimated at two thousand. The ardue [ardor] of whom, especially the young misses in their white drapes and the young lads with their shining collars, etc., was somewhat dampened in the evening by the fall of a very heavy rain, which beside damping the ladies and gents, had an admirable tendency toward testing the capacity of our tents, which held good their reputation as to turning the rain from above, but wonderfully deficient in keeping it out from beneath, the rain having run under and almost floated some of us off."

On September 8th the regiment drew its first pay. Privates in some companies apparently got their full monthly pay of thirteen dollars, but that was not the case in Odell's company. Next day he wrote home that he had been paid ten dollars and expected to receive the remaining three dollars "and perhaps the balance [probably referring to his enlistment bonus] today or tomorrow." That didn't happen, but Odell and his mates were consoled by knowledge that another picnic was scheduled that day and his company was invited to attend. He also noted that daily prayer meetings were being held in each company.[24]

Next day Lieutenant Colonel Van Vleck wrote home to his wife, Patty, and daughter, Nellie, that the regiment was still a long way from being prepared for active service. "We have no tents except for the privates & no knap sacks, haversacks, guns or canteens & [the] government will surely not send us away so, & it will take some time to get a supply."[25]

The regiment also was still making appointments to fill vacancies in the Headquarters Company. Dr. Elihu S. McIntire, thirty-one, of Company H, a Dallas City physician in civilian life and one of the original organizers of the company, was appointed first assistant surgeon. Abner V. Humphrey, a Quincy resident who listed his occupation as clerk, became regimental quartermaster. Pvt. Charles Vilasco Chandler, a nineteen-year-old Macomb resident who had just completed his first year of college at Lake Forest Academy near Chicago, was appointed sergeant major. Seth W. Grammar, a forty-three-year-old farmer from Beverly, Adams County, was named commissary sergeant. The 78th would have no regimental band, but Reuben L. Maynard, thirty-five, a farmer from Industry, McDonough County, was appointed principal musician.

One of the other regiments in camp, the 50th Illinois, did have a band, and it played every evening during dress parade. The 78th had its first dress parade September 13th. "We make a show worth seeing," Odell wrote, "all ranged in two ranks some 50 rods in length, the buttons glistening in the evening sun." He described how Colonel Benneson stood in front of the regiment and saluted and the men in ranks answered the salute. The colonel then put them through several other evolutions and everything went well as long as they were standing in ranks and did not have to march.

Dress parade "was a fine sight," Lucia Summers agreed, "the soldiers in line, the white tents and the inspiring 'Signal March.' A great many people were there to see the parade—people from the county, and many citizens always attended."[26]

But life in camp wasn't all just drill, picnics, prayer meetings, and dress parades. Many young men in the 78th had spent their lives on isolated farms and had never been exposed to common childhood illnesses such as mumps and measles or other diseases. Now that they were crowded in camps with thousands of other men under less than ideal sanitary conditions, it did not take very long for them to start getting sick. Every morning a few more turned out for sick call, complaining of everything from blisters or aches and pains to sore throats, coughs, diarrhea, fevers, measles, or something more serious. The prescribed treatment often was nothing more than a day or two off from drill, perhaps coupled with a dose of "blue pills" (a concoction of chalk and mercury), but the more seriously ill were sent to hospitals. For some, that would be their last stop.

Odell's younger brother, Risdon Odell, eighteen, who also had enlisted in Company G, was among those afflicted, as was Odell himself. His service record shows he suffered from chills, fever, and diarrhea, but apparently it was not serious enough to keep him from duty—or from going to town to spend his first pay on items for his family and some paper and ink for himself.

Most of the regiment's time in camp was spent in drill, but some members of the 78th were able to pick up a little extra money by helping build barracks. However, those structures—each one hundred feet long and twenty feet wide—would not be completed in time for the 78th to occupy them.

On September 17 rifles were issued to the regiment. They were not what the men expected. They were old and in poor condition, and they were huge and heavy—.69-caliber rifled muskets. The reaction was one of universal disgust.

"We got some old guns," John Batchelor wrote in his diary. "We called them Mexican, of very large bore. We then named them, after our Colonel, and called them our Bennisons." Pvt. Cornelius Pierce of Company F was issued a rifle with a firing mechanism that didn't work and a ramrod stuck so solidly in the barrel it could not be removed, but an inspector examined the weapon and declared it ready for use.

Isaac Landon didn't like the rifles either. "They were a dangerous weapon, about as destructive at one end as at the other," he wrote.

The men of the 78th were volunteers and had not yet absorbed the lessons of army discipline, so they did exactly as they would have done in civilian life: They drew up petitions calling on Benneson to reject the weapons. The petitions, however, were never presented to the colonel, probably because the guns were packed up in crates shortly after they were issued and the men of the 78th thought they had seen the last of them. They would not be so lucky.[27]

The consternation over the rifles was forgotten when movement orders were received September 18th. "We got imperative orders this morning to go immediately to Louisville, Ky.," Van Vleck wrote his wife, "but the Col. [Benneson] has telegraphed back that we cannot move until we get guns, our bounty money & canteens. I don't know what the result will be but expect we will be compelled to go."

He was right. The regiment was told to "go with what we have got." Orders were issued for the men to cook four days rations and be prepared to move the following day.[28]

Not everyone received the news enthusiastically. Pvt. Henry William Richter, thirty-five, of Company H, evidently decided that wherever the regiment was going, he did not want to go along. He failed to answer roll call September 19 and was listed as a deserter.

"We Have Bin Seeing Pretty Hard Times"

SEPTEMBER 20–OCTOBER 28, 1862

IF THE MEN OF THE 78TH REGIMENT HAD ANY THOUGHTS OF RIDING TO WAR IN comfort or style, those hopes were quickly dashed when they arrived at the Quincy & Toledo Railroad station on the morning of September 20th. The train that was waiting had no coaches. It did not even have any boxcars. Instead, it consisted of a long string of open cars that had last been used for hauling coal. Two-by-twelve-inch wooden planks had been nailed across the tops of the cars to serve as seats, but the cars themselves had not been cleaned, and some still had coal dust several inches deep in their bottoms.[1]

But there was no help for it, so the men climbed awkwardly into the cars and made themselves as comfortable as possible on the hard wooden benches. By one count, 934 men boarded the train—several seriously ill men had been left in Quincy hospitals—along with their Sibley tents, other equipment, and several horses. About 3:00 p.m. the train started with a spasmodic jolt and began moving slowly out of town. If there was any sort of formal send-off, none of the 78th's diarists or correspondents saw fit to make note of it.

Quincy was left behind and the train headed out across the prairies. Without cover, the men were exposed to smoke and cinders from the locomotive, plus coal dust stirred up by their feet and caught by the wind. Added to the unfamiliar swaying motion of the cars, the smoke and dust made some men feel nauseated. It did not help that most also had received smallpox vaccinations shortly before boarding the train and some were beginning to suffer bad reactions to the vaccine. Soon many were sick.[2]

But the train continued on its way, rocking and belching across a mostly empty land, stopping at isolated stations to take on wood and water and give the cramped men a chance to crawl out of the open cars, stretch their muscles, and answer calls of nature. Then they scrambled back and the train resumed its journey.

Dusk came, then darkness, and the men could see little but the glow from the locomotive's headlamp and the steady stream of sparks issuing from its huge funnel.

Now and then they caught glimpses of dim lanterns or candles in the windows of distant cabins, or clusters of flickering lights as the train lumbered through remote villages or small towns.

Through the vast empty darkness, the train continued on its way. Sleep was nearly impossible, even for men who were not sick, but many tried anyway, curling up on the hard wooden benches or seeking a more comfortable position in the dusty grime at the bottom of a car. After a long, mostly sleepless night for all aboard, the train passed through Decatur, Illinois, around daylight September 21st, and about 1:00 p.m. it crossed the Wabash River at Attica and turned toward Lafayette, Indiana. There it made a longer stop to add an extra car to accommodate some of the men who were sick.[3] The large engine that had been pulling the cars also was exchanged for two smaller ones, one to pull and the other to push. After that the train moved "in much faster time than we had gone before," James M. McNeill wrote in his diary.

Just before dark the train pulled into Indianapolis, "a nice city, displaying much taste and wealth," McNeill wrote. "We remained here from some cause untill 10 or 11 o'clock, and after changing locomotives, pushed on toward Louisville." Batchelor noted that "we are cheered loudly all along the line."[4]

Again the men tried to sleep. Since by this time they were exhausted, some actually succeeded. Odell told his wife he wanted to see the country but nothing was visible in the dark, so he tried to sleep and managed to snooze all the way from Indianapolis until the train reached its destination of Jeffersonville, Indiana, across the river from Louisville. "We arrived here about daylight this morning, rather sleepy and stooped it is true, but after feasting ourselves on some hot coffee, etc., we feel much better," Odell wrote.

Odell was surely in the minority, however. Batchelor complained that "our eyes [were] almost filled with cinders from the engine and dust in the coal carrs." Major Broaddus later told his wife that "I had to sit up all the way and leaned forward on the next seat with my hand under my head. My hand went to sleap and the two small fingers of my left hand is still in that condition. They are some better and I think will get all right again. They doo not hurt me but I have not mutch use of them."[5]

Despite the urgency with which it had been summoned, when the 78th reached Jeffersonville it found there was no immediate need for the regiment to cross the Ohio River to Louisville. Instead, it was ordered to camp on the riverbank near Jeffersonville, where it found several other regiments already camped and awaiting orders. The men spent the night and most of the following day at the riverside camp, drawing their first rations of hardtack and sowbelly. "But we were not hungry," Isaac Landon remembered. "We had traveled several hundred miles in open cars, our eyes and ears and lungs were full of dust and cinders, and just before leaving Quincy nearly all had been vaccinated, by whose orders I don't know, and that infernal virus was now doing its painful work."[7]

Late in the evening of September 23rd, the regiment finally received orders to cross the river. They started about 10:00 p.m., "crossed the river on the ferry, and marched through the city 'till we reached the outskirts, and halted," McNeill wrote. There "we wrap[p]ed ourselves up in our blankets and for the first time, made mother earth our pillow and the starry heavens our covering, where we sweetly slept 'till day (it not being long till that time when we layed down)."

They remained until afternoon of the 24th when the regiment relocated its camp on better ground "neare a high plank fence which enclosed the depot buildings," McNeill wrote.[6] The soldiers picked up all the loose planks they could find and leaned them against the fence to provide makeshift shelters. Their tents, except one for field officers and another for headquarters, had been left in Jeffersonville on orders from Maj. Gen. William "Bull" Nelson, commanding at Louisville. This was done ostensibly so that Nelson's forces "would be able to travel as fast as the rebels," Van Vleck wrote his wife.

News that Lincoln had announced his intent to issue the Emancipation Proclamation reached the regiment, and Van Vleck responded enthusiastically. "Lincoln has hit the nail on the head with the Emancipation Proclamation," he wrote. "God grant us strength to put [it] in to force & blot out the bloody stain from our national escutcheon. I think God will bless us now since we have struck at the root of the evil."[7]

Two matters of importance transpired during the day. One was the mustering of thirty-nine recruits. Most or all were men who had missed the September 1st muster of the regiment; now they would also belong to the government for three years or the duration of the war.

The second matter was less cause for celebration. It was the reappearance of the crates into which the obsolete .69-caliber rifles had been packed in Quincy, with the same dreaded rifles inside. They were reissued to the regiment, much to the men's disgust, and the soldiers began trying to learn the manual-of-arms with the big, awkward weapons.

At three o'clock the following morning, the men were roused from their plank shelters and formed into line of battle by order of Maj. Gen. Charles C. Gilbert. No sooner had they formed in line than they were dismissed and allowed to return to their makeshift quarters. Then General Gilbert appeared in person and demanded to know who commanded the regiment. Escorted to Colonel Benneson's quarters, the general greeted the colonel by asking why his regiment was not still in line of battle.

McNeill recorded what happened next: "The Col. cryed out 'Fall in boys.' Says Gilbert, 'Is your reg. made up of boys?' 'No sir' replied Benneson, 'it is made up of men.'

'Call them men then,' replied Gilbert. So we were called into line again, and had the pleasure of standing there 'till daylight, much to the good of the Union cause, and we presume to the satisfaction of Gen. Gilbert.'"

That was the 78th's introduction to General Gilbert. They would get to know him much better in the months to come, much to their regret.

Later that morning the 78th joined two other regiments and marched down Broadway in Louisville, then marched back, and continued marching until nightfall "when we turned out on a common, eat [ate] our suppers from our haversacks, rolled ourselves up in our blankets, and slept in line till morning," McNeill wrote. The city was crowded with troops, including the army of Maj. Gen. Don Carlos Buell, which had just arrived after a forced march. It had come to defend Louisville from the converging columns of Confederate generals Braxton Bragg and Kirby Smith. Buell's men "look very tired; the men have nothing in the world except shoes, pants, & shirts, & a canteen," Van Vleck wrote his wife.

The morning of the 26th came early for the regiment. It was again called into line at 3:00 a.m. and remained standing for three hours. Then it marched three miles through what Van Vleck called "the thickest cloud of dust ever you heard of" to a new campsite.[8] That same day William Mahil, one of five recruits mustered into Company D two days earlier, was reported as a deserter, establishing a record for the shortest period of service with the regiment.

The 78th had been fortunate to experience dry weather ever since it left Quincy, but its luck ran out September 27th. It began raining that morning and the men, still without tents, got thoroughly soaked. They also had no food. There wasn't much they could do about the rain, but they were determined to get something to eat, and the solution presented itself in the form of a nearby sweet potato patch, where the men soon busied themselves harvesting potatoes. Unbeknownst to them, someone far up the chain of command had issued orders forbidding such foraging, and when a provost marshal's patrol happened by and saw what was happening, they quickly rounded up every soldier who could not run fast enough to escape. The wet, hungry, bedraggled prisoners were marched before Lieutenant Colonel Van Vleck, who was found seated in a fence corner "looking much like a drowned rat" himself. A large pile of sweet potatoes lay at the colonel's feet.

"The Col. laughed, as any other man would, when the prisoners were brought up," McNeill jotted in his diary, "and one of the boys observed that 'he thought the Col. too had been in the potatoe patch from the indications around his feet.' As soon as the potatoes at the Col's. Feet were discovered, the boys thought their [their] cause not a bad one, for it showed most clearly that he too was fond of sweet potatoes on a rainy day, and nothing else to eat. He ordered the boys released, after taking their names, to await the return of the Col. The Col. returned but we heard nothing more respecting the sweet potatoe convicts."[9] That sort of incident went a long way toward endearing an officer to his men.

By next morning the weather had cleared and the sun was out. Men from each company were detailed to go to the Louisville stockyards and draw mule teams for the regiment, one team for each company and three for the headquarters company, plus two ambulances to haul medical supplies and sick or wounded men. Edward Mott Robbins recalled what happened at the stockyards: "I don't think there was one mule in ten in those yards that ever had a halter on, and to see those men catch those mules, harness and hitch six of those unbroken mules to one wagon and start out of those yards was a sight long to be remembered. Most of the time was spent by those men in untangling those teams, all piled up and tangled to the extent of having to unhitch and unharness in order to get straightened out. But it was astonishing how soon those teams were brought into subjection."[10]

Major Broaddus found time that day to write a letter home. "We have bin seeing pretty hard times ever since we started from Quincy," he wrote. "We have bin laying out with out our tents most of the time and it has bin raining. We have to form line of battle every morning at three o'clock and stand at arms till day light rain or shine . . . if we were rid of all West Point officers I think we would squelch out this rebellion in three months. But while they conduct it the Lord knows when it will bee through. They are killing more men by mistreatment and long marches than the rebels doo."[11]

Times were especially hard for Broaddus, who suffered an unusual handicap: He had but a single tooth remaining in his lower jaw, most of the teeth in his upper jaw also had been extracted, and he had no dentures to replace them. This made it almost impossible for him to chew his food. As long as he could get soup, stew, soft bread, vegetables, or fruits, he could manage, but with the regiment in the field such things often were not available. Salt pork or bacon might be cut into small pieces and swallowed whole, though that was tough on digestion, but eating hardtack or anything else that defied being cut up was out of the question. For Maj. William L. Broaddus, war sometimes was truly hell.[12]

Broaddus might have been thinking about getting something soft to eat the next morning when he entered the elegant Galt House Hotel at Second and Main Streets in downtown Louisville. If so, he quickly forgot it when he discovered he had walked in on the immediate aftermath of one of the most bizarre incidents of the Civil War: A Union general with the unlikely name of Jefferson C. Davis had just shot and mortally wounded Gen. William "Bull" Nelson.

The two men had been friends before the war. Nelson, whose nickname was due partly to his physical stature—he was about six feet, four inches tall and weighed more than three hundred pounds—and partly to his aggressive nature, had been a naval officer until summoned by President Lincoln to help raise troops in his native Kentucky. Transferred to the army, he carried out his mission so successfully he was promoted to brigadier general, led a division at Shiloh, then fought well enough at Corinth to be promoted to major general. When the Confederate columns of Bragg and Smith moved north to threaten Louisville, Nelson was placed in command of the city's defenses.

Davis, a small, pale man with hooded eyes and a hangdog look, weighed less than half as much as Nelson, but his diminutive appearance concealed a fiery temper—one historian has called him "volcanic"—with a profane vocabulary to match. At age eighteen he had enlisted as a private in the militia and served with distinction in the Mexican War. Selected for appointment to West Point, he was denied entry due to a bureaucratic error, but continued to serve in the army and won a battlefield commission. He was part of the garrison at Fort Sumter when the Confederates fired the first shots of the Civil War and was promoted rapidly thereafter, winning laurels as a division commander at the Battle of Pea Ridge. He was on sick leave when the Confederates mounted their threat to Louisville, but left his bed and reported to Maj. Gen. Horatio Wright in Cincinnati. Wright promptly sent him to Louisville to assist in the city's defense. There his old friend Nelson gave Davis the job of organizing the local militia, home guard, and new untrained regiments, such as the 78th Illinois, into an effective fighting force.

Still not fully recovered from his illness and perhaps convinced of the futility of his task, Davis failed to embrace it with the vigor Nelson demanded, and after a stormy confrontation Nelson ordered Davis out of the city. Davis was not the sort to take such an order lying down, but he complied—perhaps further evidence he wasn't feeling up to his usually combative self—and returned to Cincinnati.

Meanwhile, the arrival of Buell's army ended the Confederate threat to Louisville, and Wright, evidently believing Davis could still be of use, sent him back. And there, on the morning of September 29, Davis and Nelson met face-to-face at the Galt House.

Broaddus told his wife what happened next: "I was at the Gualt House in a few minutes after the occurrence. I heard a good many persons and officers speak of the matter and they all justify Davis . . . Nelson had slap[p]ed Davis in the faise [face] and cussed him as a coward and Davis turned to a friend and borrowed a revolver and shot him down. He lived about twenty minutes. He was one of the most cruel men that ever lived and it is well enough that he is out of the way."

Davis was taken into custody by civil authorities and turned over to the military for trial. General Buell recommended an immediate court martial, but by then his army had left Louisville and was moving to intercept Bragg, so Buell had no general officers available to serve on a court-martial board. For the time being, Davis remained in legal limbo, confined to his room at the Galt House.[13]

The dramatic incident quickly became the talk of all the soldiers in Louisville. Among the men of the 78th, it almost overshadowed the good news that the regiment's tents had finally been returned, giving them at least a modicum of shelter.

About this time the regiment also got some bad news. Pvt. Henry Gunn, nineteen, of Company K, who had been left in the hospital at Quincy, had succumbed to his illness. He was buried in his hometown of Fall Creek, Adams County. Gunn was the regiment's first fatality, but many other men were suffering from disease. Van Vleck wrote home that the regiment had 106 men in the hospital on October 1st.[14]

The regiment also had suffered its first casualty from the ancient rifles. "A man in Capt. Hume's Co. accidently shot himself," Broaddus wrote. "The ball pas[s]ed through the hand near the wrist [and] made an offul [awful] hole and has ruined his hand for life, and their [there] is some danger of losing his life."

The victim, Pvt. Joseph Tipton of Company C, was shot through the left hand, apparently while loading his weapon. His injury inspired a near mutiny over the dangerous rifles. "A great many of the regiment, thinking them [the rifles] too destructive, went and stacked them at regimental headquarters, swearing they might stay there," Private Landon remembered. "And they did stay there about an hour, and then the owners all quietly went and got them again and the meeting ended." McNeill also mentioned the incident in his diary: "Excitement ran high in camp today, which ended in the stacking of [the rifles] at the Col's. tent, by one or two entire companies and parts of others. The bravery displayed soon cooled off however, and the boys took them up again." Soldiers identified as having participated in the protest were assigned three months' extra duty. [15]

Next day—Friday, October 3rd—four companies of the 78th were detailed for provost marshal duty in downtown Louisville, with directions to arrest any soldiers without passes or those who had consumed too much "tangleleg" (whiskey). That evening they were assigned to guard a "superb mansion" on Hancock Street, which turned out to be a whorehouse according to McNeill. That wasn't exactly what the men of the 78th thought they had signed up to do.[16]

⸻

The regiment was drummed awake at the now-familiar hour of 3:00 a.m. October 6th and was on the march by 9:00 a.m., headed south, with each man carrying his musket, knapsack, haversack, two days of provisions, and forty rounds of .69-caliber ammunition. Their tents, equipment, and commissary stores were packed in wagons pulled by the mule teams they had drawn eight days earlier.

The 78th marched thirteen miles that day, the longest march it had yet made. There would come a time when the regiment would consider a thirteen-mile trek light work, but that was far in the future; meanwhile, if there had been any doubt the 78th was still too raw for combat, it was removed by its miserable performance on this march. It was especially tough for those who were ill or recovering from illness. Cornelius Pierce was among the latter. Along with many others, he had been thoroughly soaked when the regiment was caught in the rain without its tents and "took very sick with a cold settled in my breast and for four days I was unable to sit up. I would have been sent to the hospital, but it was crowded." Nevertheless, he gamely managed to make the thirteen-mile march, but had to put his gun and knapsack on a wagon and walk behind it. "Several [men] gave out before we got through," he said in a letter home.

Pierce also was unhappy about the quality of the food the soldiers had to eat. "We have plenty to eat but the way it is cooked is enough to make anybody sick," he said. "I am dead set against coffee, and have not drunk two cups of it in the last 12 days. Pies and cakes have been brought into the camp but we are afraid to buy now as some of the soldiers here have been poisoned by eating them."[17]

The march took them past cornfields long since stripped of corn and orchards long since stripped of fruit. They stopped to drink from springs and trekked through stands of beech, poplar, white oak, and cedar. Odell thought it a pleasant country, but Van Vleck sharply disagreed, describing it as "the poorest country I ever saw." He also noted that "the men were entirely not used to marching & carrying their heavy knapsacks & nearly half of the reg't. gave out."[18]

The regiment was on the march again by 7:00 a.m. on Tuesday, October 7th, covering another nine miles until it arrived at the village of Shepherdsville on the Salt River. Shepherdsville was a stop on the Louisville & Nashville Railroad, a 185-mile link between its namesake cities. After the Union forces took Forts Henry and Donelson early in 1862 and moved farther south into Tennessee, the railroad became a vital federal supply route. From Louisville, it ran almost due south to Shepherdsville. Four miles beyond that it reached Bardstown Junction, where a spur line ran southeast to Bardstown. The main line then veered southwest and continued ten miles to Lebanon Junction, where another spur ran southeast through Boston and New Haven to the town of Lebanon. The main line continued another thirteen and a half miles from Lebanon Junction past Muldraugh Hill to Elizabethtown, then south into Tennessee.

The railroad's route cut across the sprawling watershed of the Salt River, including the Beech Fork, Rolling Fork, and other tributaries, requiring construction of numerous bridges and trestles. These structures were tempting targets for Confederate cavalry. The bridge over the Salt River at Shepherdsville had twice been burned by Confederate raiders, most recently just two days earlier, and the 78th was ordered to remain in the town—largely abandoned by its inhabitants, most of whom were secessionists—to guard a new bridge under construction. Even while it was being built, the fire that had consumed the old bridge continued burning in an outcropping of sulfurous rock, despite efforts of a crew of railroad workers to put it out. "The more they work and the more water they put on, the more it burns and fumes," Van Vleck wrote.[19]

The 78th camped in a field about five hundred feet from the bridge. Another Illinois regiment, the 91st, was camped nearby. That night brought excitement to both units. "The pickets had been thrown out and about 10 in the evening, after everything had become quiet, a magnificent scare got up by the firing of several guns in the direction of the pickets, who shortly after ran in and reported that they had been fired on, the balls passing over their heads," McNeill wrote in his diary. "The drums in both regiments beat the long roll. After the scare was all over, and we found no enemy to be neare it was truly amusing to think how the boys rolled out. Prior to this it generally took the boys about half an hour to get up, and into line, but this time two minutes had not elapsed before every man was out with gun in hand, looking bewilderingly around to see where the enemy was."

Everyone had a good laugh when they learned the source of the firing. Two hungry privates, Clinton Morgan and Marion Bond of the 78th's Company C, had gone foraging and encountered "a squad of pigs" and opened fire. The two were placed under arrest by an officer and scheduled for trial by court martial. There was no word on the fate of the pigs.[20]

Next day, October 8th, a great battle was fought at Perryville, Kentucky, about thirty-five miles east of Shepherdsville, although the soldiers of the 78th had no way of knowing it. Buell's army had maneuvered to block General Braxton Bragg's thrust into northern Kentucky and the two forces collided in a day-long slugfest in which neither gained decisive advantage. Short of men and supplies, the Confederates withdrew during the night, leaving Buell in possession of the field even though his army had suffered more casualties than the rebels.

Everything was peaceful in Shepherdsville that day. The 78th was ordered to send one company to Elizabethtown, about twenty-seven miles away, to guard a baggage train, but the rest of the regiment remained in camp. Major Broaddus spent part of the afternoon writing to tell his wife he had bought a horse from "a ritch Union widow," that the weather was dry and pleasant, and the regiment had a good place to camp. Then he added: "Our Col. is not very popular in the reg't. but him and I get along first rate. He consults me on allmost every matter of intrist [interest] connected with the reg't."

Colonel Benneson's unpopularity was due to a growing list of gripes by the soldiers of the 78th. Their biggest complaint was that they still had not been paid their enlistment bounties, but there were plenty of others—the long, miserable ride from Quincy to Louisville in open cars, the old rifles hated by the men, the 3:00 a.m. reveilles for no apparent reason, and the decision to leave the regiment's tents at Jeffersonville (they probably had no idea the tents had been left behind in obedience to an order). The men believed a more assertive commander could have solved or prevented such problems.

The men also noticed that Benneson had been frequently absent from the regiment, leading to speculation he was spending most of his time lobbying for a brigadier's commission. But those who had personal contact with him—mostly officers, like Broaddus—usually reported the colonel treated them cordially.

The new railroad bridge over the Salt River was completed September 11th "and the cars are running out some 15 miles farther on the road toward Nashville," Broaddus wrote his wife. He added: "I baught [bought] some peaches yesterday and [illegible word] had some cooked for dinner to day and you would have laughed to have seen Col. Van Vleck sit by and pick out worms as they was cooking, but they ate first rate after they were dun [done]." Cooked peaches, worms and all, were among the few things soft enough for the nearly toothless Broaddus to eat.[21]

About eleven o'clock Monday, October 14th, the regiment left Shepherdsville on the march south along the railroad, leaving Lieutenant Colonel Van Vleck sick with "bilious fever" along with about 90 other men suffering "ague in some form or another." The regiment camped that night at a little place called Belmont and resumed the march next morning, reaching a campsite on the Beech Fork about 4:00 p.m. The 91st Illinois also made the march and Colonel Benneson, as senior officer, took command of both regiments, although Broaddus thought the 91st "the biggest set of thieves I ever saw." That night men from both regiments raided a "Secesh" farmer named Gardner and made off with some chickens, turkeys, and pigs. "Here I caught a turkey that run in between 2 hay stacks and into my arms," Batchelor wrote in his diary.[22]

The 78th broke camp again the morning of October 17th and marched until about 2:00 p.m. "when we stop(p)ed in a beautiful meadow belonging to an old Secesh by the name of Beeler, on the bank of Rolling Fork, opposite too [to] and a little below the town of New Haven," McNeill wrote in his diary. "This was the best camping place we had seen since we left Quincy." Broaddus thought New Haven "a very pretty little town of some four or five hundred inhabitance [inhabitants] . . . We arrived safe had no trouble on the road. I doo not think that there are very many rebels in armes [arms] in this section of the state."[23]

Saturday the 18th was a day of rest for the regiment, but the next morning the men were ordered to be ready to march at noon, "at which time we were packed up, and our knapsacks on the wagon," McNeill wrote. "We crossed the river, having to cross on the rocks as best we could, there being no bridge which is usual in this country, and passed thru town [New Haven] . . . It has a population of about 300."

The regiment started marching on the road to Lebanon but had gone only about four miles when "we met a courier from Gen. Buel[l], ordering us to return to New Haven as quick as we could," Broaddus wrote later to his wife. The courier brought news "that the Rebel John Morgan was marching on that plaice [New Haven] with two thousand cavalry and one peice of cannon." The advance guard of the regiment was ordered to load rifles and Colonel Benneson told company commanders to check their men's cartridge boxes to make certain they were full. "We went back to New Haven faster than we went out, where we arrived about five o'clock," McNeill recorded. "We remained standing in the street till neare dark, when we marched above town a short distance, crossed the river on a bridge and halted, as we thought, to spend the night." But there was hardly time to post pickets before new orders were received, and the regiment started out again, this time in a westerly direction through a wooded area "under the guidance . . . of an old Negro."

The path took them to a bridge over the Rolling Fork, and after posting guards at the bridge and pickets around camp, the regiment finally bivouacked for the night. "Next morning found us guarding a fine bridge which had so far escaped the fate of its neighbors, by the vigilance of the citizens who had so far guarded it," McNeill wrote. The regiment began digging entrenchments around the bridge, except for Companies A and C, which were stationed at another bridge, this one over the Beech Fork, about four or five miles distant.

Then word was received that Morgan's force was in the hamlet of Boston, only about two miles from the Beech Fork camp, apparently intending to move against the bridge over that stream. Colonel Benneson ordered Major Broaddus to take four companies to reinforce the two at Beech Fork. "We went down on the [railroad] cars as quick as we could," Broaddus wrote. "Soon after we got their a lady came in to camp [and] said she lived in Bosten and the rebels had just left the plaice, and she had walked two miles to let us know of their movements. I sent wourd to Col. B that I did not think they ment to attack us but if they did we would give them the best fight we could." Captain Hume of Company C, who had been in command of the two companies at Beech Fork, had already started work on fortifications, and the other companies joined in. "The work was built of logs, layed horizontally and forming a square some 45 by 35 feet, located neare the river, and so as to afford protection to the bridge," McNeill wrote.

Orders meanwhile reached Benneson to leave only a skeleton force at the Rolling Fork Bridge and take the rest of his command to the bridge at Beech Fork, which was a vital link on the railroad spur to Lebanon, where the Union had a large cache of military stores. Benneson left a single company of the 91st Illinois at Rolling Fork and headed for Beech Fork with eight companies of the 91st and the balance of the 78th. They reached Beech Fork that night.

Morgan's men were camped less than four miles away, but there was no contact. "I don't think that Morgan would have at[t]acked us atall, for if he had intended to have dun so, he would have dun it bifore the other reg't. got here," Broaddus wrote. "Their [There] is quite a larg[e] forse [force] of cavalry in persuit of him but I am affraid they will not get him."[24]

Broaddus was right. Morgan escaped, but he would be back.

The 78th and the eight companies of the 91st spent the next two days expanding fortifications around the bridge at Beech Fork. They were joined by Van Vleck, recovered from his illness. Most of the other sick men who had been left at Shepherdsville were expected to rejoin the 78th the following day.

While the 78th marched back and forth and ended up digging trenches at Beech Fork, Gen. Jefferson C. Davis was being freed from house arrest in Louisville and restored to duty. General Wright had ordered his release on grounds that no charges had been filed against him during the period required by military law. Davis had not been court-martialed because there were no general officers to hear his case, and nothing more was done. In retrospect, it appears neither Wright nor Buell pressed the matter very vigorously—possibly because they were in sympathy with what Davis had done. Davis would later be indicted in a civil court, but the case never came to trial. He had literally gotten away with murder.[25]

That was something for the men of the 78th to remember, because their path and Davis's would cross in the future.

～

On the morning of October 23rd, the 91st Illinois left Beech Fork and headed west with a new assignment to defend bridges in the vicinity of Elizabethtown, while the 78th was ordered to split up and protect bridges along the Lebanon Branch of the Louisville & Nashville Railroad—two across the Rolling Fork, including the one at New Haven, one across the Beech Fork near Boston, one at Pottinger's Creek, and one at Wilson's Creek.

The news was not well received. "I have just learned that our reg't is to bee scattered all along this Rail Road," Broaddus wrote his wife. "Just what I was affraid of." The move would make it much more difficult for Broaddus and the other field officers to fulfill their duties. It also meant the still largely undrilled companies of the 78th would be unable to drill together and learn how to maneuver effectively as a regiment in battle. Not only that, but even the least sophisticated soldier in the regiment realized the isolated companies, beyond supporting distance of one another, would be easy targets for capture or annihilation by a larger force, such as Morgan's cavalry.

The bad news was accompanied by a sudden change in the weather. "It is quite could [cold] and chilley this morning," Broaddus told his wife. "We have had but little cold we[a]ther here as yet, but it looks very mutch like snowing just now and nothing but thin tents to stay in, but their [there] is plenty of good wood and there is no danger of freasing. The boys have got good over coats and blankets." There was also some good news—"a prospect of the boys getting their bounty soon. The money is at Louisville and Col. Benneson has bin up to day to see about it." Broaddus's weather forecast was on target; that night it began to snow and two or three inches had fallen by next morning.

In accordance with the new orders, Company F was to return to the fortifications at the Rolling Fork bridge; Company B was stationed at Boston; Company E would defend the bridge over Wilson's Creek; Company G would guard the bridge over Pottinger's Creek; Companies H, I, and K would return to New Haven; and Companies A, C, D, and the Headquarters Company would remain at the Beech Fork bridge.[26]

Chaplain Taylor gave a short sermon on the snowy morning of October 26th, after which the companies assigned to return to New Haven or other points started on their way. "It looked much like winter this morning when we started," McNeill told his diary, "the ground covered with snow, and the trees which were yet green with summer's verdure bending with the frosty emblem of winter." The three companies arrived at New Haven about 3:00 p.m.

Next morning they had a visit from Brig. Gen. Charles C. Gilbert, the same officer who had ordered the 78th into line of battle at 3:00 a.m. back in Louisville. He delivered news that he was now in command of the division to which the 78th had been assigned. Gilbert had started the war as a captain and had been promoted to brigadier general, although his appointment had not been confirmed by the Senate. When Maj. Gen. Horatio G. Wright in Cincinnati decided more senior officers were needed in Kentucky, he made Gilbert a "provisional" major general—something he had no authority to do. Nobody argued with him, however, and Gilbert donned his second star and went on to serve as a corps commander under Buell at the Battle of Perryville. There, through no initiative of his own, Gilbert was presented an opportunity which, had he seized it, might have resulted in a more decisive victory for the Union. But he failed to act, and as a result he had been relegated to secondary command and was once again wearing the single star of a brigadier.

His command consisted of the 10th Division of the Army of the Ohio, including a brigade at Munfordville [south of Elizabethtown], another brigade guarding the military stores at Lebanon, and several detached units guarding the Louisville & Nashville Railroad, including the 78th, 91st, and 107th Illinois regiments and a single company of the 2nd Kentucky Cavalry. Benneson, by virtue of having the earliest date on his commission, was the senior colonel.

Gilbert ordered the companies at New Haven to begin building a stockade fort. The stockade was "to be built of timbers set on end, and about seven feet above ground," McNeill recorded, "so arranged as to set our tents, four in number on each corner, the corners being made circular, the size of the tents, 16 feet in diameter, the whole forming a square 45 feet."[27]

The news that Gilbert was in command did not please those in the 78th's Headquarters Company back at the Beech Fork bridge. "I don't like him at all," Van Vleck wrote. But the lieutenant colonel did like his new tentmate, Major Broaddus, who had given up his own tent for use by other officers. "He is a first-rate man," Van Vleck wrote his wife.

He also told his wife that "we have one woman in the regiment who does our washing, tolerably well, but don't iron much though we don't have much to iron." The snow had melted away within a day, he said, but "all day yesterday that severe cold wind continued & I suffered most intolerably & got down sick again. But I feel a great deal better to day & I hope I shall have no more trouble." The weather "seems to agree with the majority of the men, but some of them wilt like a plucked flower in the sun," he said.

3

"The Maddest Set of Men in the World"

October 29–December 29, 1862

The train from Louisville that rumbled into New Haven on Wednesday, October 29th, dropped off an army paymaster with the 78th's long-awaited enlistment bounties. "We [Company H] were paid $27, the bounty money promised to be paid in advance and two dollars premium," McNeill reported. "Never did money come more acceptable than did this to our boys. Having been promised the bounty money when mustered in, they had brought but little with them, and that they had long before spent."

Soldiers with wives or families rushed to make arrangements to send money home. Batchelor sent home twenty dollars. Those without families paid off loans or gambling debts or offered loans to soldiers who still needed money. Others spent part of their bounty during off-duty hours at the tavern in the New Haven Hotel. They were able to work up a healthy thirst by cutting logs for the stockade General Gilbert had ordered them to build.

The soldiers at Beech Fork also received bounty payments. "I am very glad of it for I have no doubt their families had began to nead it very mutch and they feel mutch better them selves," Broaddus told his wife.

But he also had bad news: "I have just this moment learned that one of our boys has just died," he said. "He had brain fever. He belonged to Capt. Black's Co[mpany]." The soldier, George Kimmel, eighteen, of Chili, Hancock County, was not the only casualty in the 78th that day. Pvt. Benjamin F. Ross, twenty-three, of Company G, of Camp Point, Adams County, died of disease in a Quincy hospital.[1]

Meanwhile, work continued on the stockades at New Haven, Beech Fork, and the 78th's other outposts. The construction method was to set trimmed logs on end side-by-side in palisade fashion, resulting in a log rampart about seven feet high. General Gilbert had altered his original specification that each stockade should be forty-five feet square; he subsequently ordered that one side of each stockade should be pushed out in the center to form a triangle, so the finished structure would have five sides.

Gun ports were cut in the logs and small huts or houses were built at each of the five rounded corners, large enough for Sibley tents to be erected on top.[2]

The regiment suffered another loss November 2nd when Pvt. John A. Burke, twenty-seven, of Company B, a resident of Marcelline, Adams County, died at Boston, Kentucky.

Van Vleck and Broaddus returned from a trip to Louisville two days later. "The more I see of Kentucky and i[t]s people the more I would hate to live here," Broaddus wrote. "I think it is avery [a very] good state to bee born in if one leaves it early. I am very thankful to my parents for taking me out of the state while I was young."[3]

Colonel Benneson was elsewhere, as he seemed to be with increasing frequency, so Van Vleck was in temporary command of the regiment. He was pleased with orders received the day before to move the regiment's headquarters to New Haven, where he expected to spend the winter. He and Broaddus talked of renting a house together and perhaps bringing their wives and Van Vleck's daughter, Nellie, to visit.

Then the daily train pulled into camp and a staff officer found Van Vleck and told him General Gilbert was on the train and wished to see him. "I accordingly went & made my obeisance, & he opened his mouth & said 'You will not heed the orders sent you, for the removal of your headquarters to New Haven, but on the contrary you will move your headquarters across the bridge into that stockade & will hereafter be designated as Garrison No. 10 of the 10th Division until further orders; and you will also keep these several companies here with you.' Then, bowing graciously, he stepped aboard the cars (and) off he went."

In addition to his duties as temporary commander, Van Vleck also was president of a court-martial board "for the trial of delinquent soldiers." One such was Pvt. Clinton Morgan of Company C. He was "guilty of all manner of depredations until we could live with him no longer & we tried him & sentenced him to forfeit one month's pay, to have one-half of his head smooth shaved, and to be drummed out of camp to the tune of Rogues March before all the troops, & the sentence was executed to the letter, & I think I never saw a man who seemed to appreciate his punishment more than he, & I hope it will have a good effect on the other troops." Morgan's transgressions included drunkenness and threatening to kill Capt. Charles R. Hume, Company C's commander. He would be the only man ever drummed out of the 78th Regiment.

After the sentence was carried out, Van Vleck, Broaddus, the rest of the Headquarters Company, and Companies I and K packed up and started marching toward New Haven. General Gilbert's orders of the day before had been modified yet again, and they were headed to the little town on the Rolling Fork after all. When they arrived at New Haven about 1:00 p.m., they found "a very neat little village . . . with some very fine buildings which would be an ornament to any town," Van Vleck wrote.

"There are more Union people here than at Beech Fork, where there really were none but Negroes."[4]

Their arrival did not please the garrison at New Haven. The stockade was finished and "the boys were having what the soldier terms a 'bully time,'" McNeill reported. "No standing guard, having full range of a fine and productive scope of country, which produced luxuries without end, fat chickens and turkeys not excepted, full and undisputed access to the town just across the stream, which had many fair-eyed beauties whos[e] charms were fast claiming the mastery over our boys, big hopes of the good time coming, when in the winter we would have nice parties . . . when much to our regret Headquarters made its appearance and blasted all our hopes . . . The guard was put out and the old ro[u]tine of camp duties devolved upon us."

The regiment had completed six stockades by November 5th, each guarding a crucial bridge. The soldiers at New Haven christened their stockade "Fort Allen" after Captain Allen, commander of Company H. Work then started on a smaller stockade-like structure to accommodate regimental headquarters. The new structure was just west of the main stockade and inside a row of freshly dug rifle pits. Spurred on by a cold rain, the soldiers also began building huts in anticipation of spending the winter in New Haven.

But apparently there would be no visits from wives or children. "We are ordered not to go more than 100 yds. from camp, & not to allow any officers' wives, or soldiers' wives or any laundress or other female, in, or in the vicinity of the camp," Van Vleck wrote. One result was that "our washer-woman" was sent home after having been with the regiment ever since it left Quincy. "She made a big cry, & so did her husband."

The wife of Dr. Thomas Jordan, regimental surgeon, had been staying nearby and he was ordered to send her home. He protested that as a surgeon "his presence was not so necessary as that of other officers, & as he was not so likely to be taken prisoner, away from camp, as others," Van Vleck wrote. So he was given permission to keep his wife a short time, "provided, he would 'keep her a good ways out.'" Ever hopeful of arranging a visit from his wife, the lieutenant colonel added: "I wouldn't wonder if some of the rest of us got similar permission before a great while."[5]

Broaddus meanwhile was recovering from extraction of the last tooth in his lower jaw. He told his wife he would have a set of dentures "put in if I get an opportunity of doing so."

The soldiers awoke November 7th to find snow falling. It later changed to rain, then back to snow. "It was a very disagreeable day," McNeill declared. It was certainly disagreeable to Pvt. Brigham D. Brown of Company K, of Melrose, Adams County. Brown, nineteen, died of disease that day at New Haven.

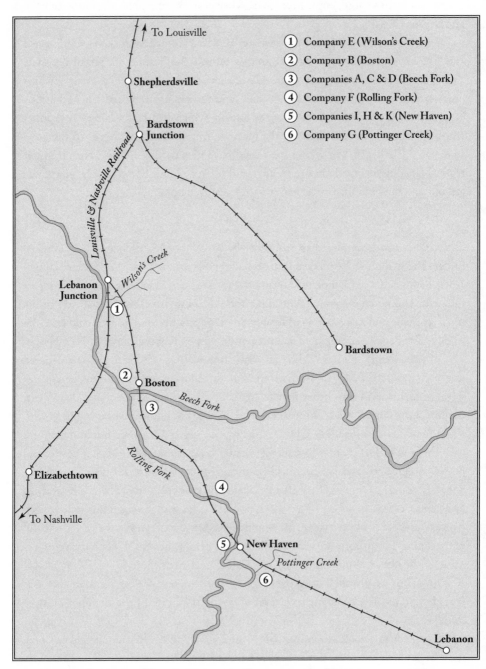

To Louisville

Shepherdsville

Bardstown
Junction

Louisville & Nashville Railroad

Wilson's Creek

Lebanon
Junction

① Company E (Wilson's Creek)
② Company B (Boston)
③ Companies A, C & D (Beech Fork)
④ Company F (Rolling Fork)
⑤ Companies I, H & K (New Haven)
⑥ Company G (Pottinger Creek)

①

② ○ Boston
③

Beech Fork

Bardstown

Rolling Fork

Elizabethtown

④

To Nashville

⑤ ○ New Haven
Pottinger Creek
⑥

Lebanon

78TH ILLINOIS DISPOSITION OF COMPANIES - NOVEMBER 5, 1862

Word also was received that one of "Morgan's brigands" had been seen in New Haven, so 1st Lt. George Beers took twelve men and—mindful but not heedful of Gilbert's order to stay within one hundred yards of camp—led them into town. Leaving six men behind, he led the others about a mile up the Bardstown road, stopping to ask residents if they had seen the man being sought. Soon they heard a horseman coming at full gallop. Concealing themselves behind a fence, they stopped the rider when he appeared and "recognized him as being the man they were after, and a notorious brigand of Morgan's Gang," McNeill wrote. "His name was Johnson and [he] was well known by the citizens of N. Haven, having resided in town a few years before. He was conducted into camp and put under a strong guard to await orders from General Gilbert.

"When we arrived in town, Lieut. Beers took us all over to the New Haven Hotel and cut all our throats, not in anger with glist[e]ning steel, but [with] good old b[o]urbon that made us feel that the cares of war were few and light, especially on that memorable night."[6]

Johnson, the prisoner, had been "lurking around as a spy," according to Van Vleck. "He confesses all & begs very hard for his life."

The lieutenant colonel also responded to a question from his wife: "You ask me what are my daily duties. I hardly know how to answer you for we are now divided into six parcels guarding six different bridges, & of course any thing like the usual routine of drill &c. is out of the question, & as a consequence there is very little to do pertaining to the reg't. for the field officers. We are called up by the reveille at six in the morning, but it is not required of the field officers to rise then, unless they desire, yet it is usual for us to get up at that time & after breakfast I spend my forenoons either in reading military books or in writing, unless it is so cold that I am unable to do either; & so with the afternoons until about 2 o'cl'k., when we have reg't'l or battalion drill, until 4 o'cl'k. At 4 ½ o'cl'k. we have dress parade, and at half past 5 supper, & nothing from that time until bed time.

"You will see that we really have but very little to do . . . To sum up all our duties, in a military point of view, they am[ount]t to this, that we keep a good watch over the bridges."

That's what they were supposed to be doing, anyway. But a letter home from Pvt. Cornelius Pierce of Company F, stationed at the Rolling Fork bridge about a mile and a half from New Haven—the "fine bridge which had so far escaped the fate of its neighbors by the vigilance of the citizens who had so far guarded it"—told a somewhat different story. "There are some hard cases in this company," Pierce wrote. "You can see 25 or 30 sitting around playing cards and cursing and quarreling has become so common that not a day passes that several fights take place among them, and most of them have gambled away their bounty money. The boys borrowed a fiddle from a Negro and they now have music and dancing every night. The Negroes bring pies and bread into camp every day and sometimes cooked turkeys and chickens. Two Union families bring us whatever we want to eat, besides. . . .

"I must tell you how we sleep these cold nights. We lie down on the straw with all our clothes on, except our shoes and caps, with our knapsacks for pillows. We spread a blanket and then put on our two overcoats and then the other blanket and crawl under. We keep our guns and cartridge boxes at our heads. I put on two pairs of socks at night and take off one pair in the morning.⁷"

The cold nights moderated somewhat after the first week of November. "The weather is delightful, & sufficiently warm to be comfortable without my overcoat, which I have left off to day for the first time in two weeks I think," Van Vleck wrote Sunday, November 9th. He told his wife about sparsely attended church services conducted by Reverend Taylor that morning, which prompted him to ponder the chaplain's future: "I . . . fear that he is not likely to meet with the success as an army chaplain . . . that he earnestly labors for. He is thoroughly devoted to his labor & I have the utmost confidence in his piety, but he seems to lack that knowledge of human nature, and of the common affairs of life, which are indispensable to the highest degree of usefulness in the army, or indeed any where else; but still he is doing good & will improve, I think. I pray daily for his success & for grace to cooperate successfully with him in his labors.

"I feel my own weakness here. My lack of courage to do my whole duty to Jesus & my fellow soldiers.

"This [is] an embarrassing field of labor where the Col. [Benneson] does not encourage the efforts made, or has himself no respect for religion. The Major [Broaddus] is a sincere Christian, but like me lacks the courage to do his whole duty, but we both try to preach the gospel, by holy lives, & proper examples in all our intercourse with others. We tent together & of course worship together & I find it much more pleasent than being alone, generally. He is a good man. The more I see of him the better I like him. I am indeed thankful that we could be together in the army. The Col. improves in his bearing & the men like him much better than they did. He has left off much of the austerity of manners that made him so unpopular at first."

Van Vleck's assessment of Benneson's popularity was ironic, because at just about the same time, another soldier in the 78th was sending an anonymous letter to the *Quincy Daily Herald* complaining about the colonel. The letter, whose author signed himself "Seventy-Eighth," criticized Benneson for the miserable train trip to Louisville, for lobbying shamelessly for promotion, and for giving "insulting" answers to orderly sergeants. It also complained the regiment never had been given an opportunity to drill together and was being held back while other regiments were sent to the front. The writer concluded by saying the whole regiment was dissatisfied with the colonel. Whether Benneson ever saw the article is unknown, but others in the regiment did, and at least one would later come to the colonel's defense.[8]

Major Broaddus got a welcome surprise November 10th when word came that his wife, Martha, was at Lebanon Junction. Dr. Elihu McIntire, the regiment's first assistant surgeon, sent an ambulance to bring her the rest of the way to New Haven. While she was en route, Benneson, Van Vleck, and Broaddus found a place where she could stay about a quarter of a mile from camp, General Gilbert's orders to the contrary notwithstanding. "This visit was an entire surprise to the Major & of course he feels very fine," Van Vleck told his wife.[9]

Nobody said anything about the matter to General Gilbert, who called at New Haven that day and ordered the garrison to form line of battle whenever a train pulled into town. The same order was conveyed to the other outposts of the 78th.

November 12th the regiment lost another man when disease claimed Pvt. Albert C. Bennett of Company I, a Macomb resident. Van Vleck attributed his death to "bilious fever," although he added that Bennett had been "exceedingly homesick and dispirited which probably was the mediate cause of his death . . . The doctors say it is a very common cause of death. They pine away like a sick bird & loose their appetites & finally die, apparently of emaciation."

Sunday, November 16th was unseasonably warm and Chaplain Taylor preached another sermon. Van Vleck, who listened, complimented the chaplain, but added that "he is pretty well worn out, having (as he thinks) to visit all the companies every week & it takes him all the time & is very hard on him."[10]

That night there was a hard rain "which tryed the efficiency of our tents, in their new position, to shead [shed] the rain," McNeill wrote. The rain continued "almost constantly" the following day, "sometimes very hard." It bothered Batchelor, too: "Raining all the time am wet through and through," he wrote.

It also rained at Pottinger Creek, where Company G had named its stockade "Fort Joseph" in honor of Captain Jacob F. Joseph, company commander. The rain was a bother to the men who had to turn out and form line each time a train passed their post. The daily train from Louisville came through on its way to Lebanon at 10:30 a.m. and returned at 2:00 p.m. It was usually loaded with provisions, soldiers going to or coming from a hospital, and sometimes with sick prisoners.

Odell wrote his family that his company was trying to reduce conflicts within its ranks. The men had voted to end quarreling, cursing, and lying, with a penalty of forty-eight hours of picket duty for anyone who violated the rule. Card playing had been halted by an earlier vote. "As to whiskey drinking, I cannot say the co[mpany] is entirely clear of it; but very little of the article finds its way into camp." The company also was having occasional prayer meetings, and the chaplain had given testaments to most men and promised to provide hymn books at twenty-five cents each.

Odell also wrote a long letter to his daughter, Mary, describing the fort, the huts where the soldiers lived, and how they made coffee: A fire was built in a ditch lined with rock and water was put on to boil while a "darkey" named George put coffee in a sheet-iron pan and pounded it with a gun butt until it was fine enough to go into the pot, where it was boiled five or ten minutes. Food also was cooked over the fire in the ditch and the men ate standing up at a plank table. Odell told Mary that George was about twenty-two but "hardly knew his letters when he came here." The men in Odell's company had gotten him a book and were trying to teach him to read and write.[11]

It was still raining the next day, November 20th, when a court martial heard the case of Major Broaddus's son, Pvt. Thomas Broaddus of Company I, who was accused of allowing a man through the guard line without a pass, in violation of orders. Van Vleck was president of the court while Captain Vernon of Company K acted as judge advocate. The charge was not sustained, doubtless to the relief of Major Broaddus and his wife.

Next day the rebel Johnson, who had been taken prisoner November 7th, was sent to Louisville, "much to the relief of the boys as a detail of nine men had to be made every day to guard him," McNeill wrote. "Provisions for him had to be furnished out of the rations of the men—the quartermaster would not furnish them."

"Am sick," John Batchelor wrote in his diary November 22. But he attended church services the following day and also managed to weigh himself, finding he carried 154 pounds on his five-foot, eight-inch frame. "Strong as a horse!" he added.[12]

Van Vleck, meanwhile, wrote Patty in another attempt to explain his duties: "It is the lieut. col.'s place to take charge of & command all expeditions of less than a reg't. & more than four companies & to command all posts garrisoned by that no. of troops. 2nd, when with headquarters, to command the camp whenever the col. is temporarily or permanently absent, to see that order & disciplin[e] are enforced at all times, & to drill the reg't. as an instructor when the col. is not so disposed to do (which he seldom is). 3rd, when in battle he takes charge of the right wing of the reg't. (or battalion as it is called when formed in line of battle) & communicates the commands of the col. & sees that they are executed, & keeps the battalion in line, i.e., keeps them from breaking ranks or running off, if he can—(& if he don't run himself). In short he acts for the col. whenever he cannot act or is not disposed to act."

The "Benneson rifles" claimed another victim November 24th. "Joseph Bartlett [Pvt. Joseph Bartlett of Pilot Grove, Hancock County] while on picket, let his gun go off by accident, the ball passing through his right hand, the forefinger of which had to be amputated," McNeill wrote. "We regret much the accident, as Jo was a favorite with all."[13]

Martha Broaddus left for home the same day. She was suffering an apparently serious respiratory infection, and between that and her son's court martial, her stay had not been very pleasant. In addition, the farmer at whose home she stayed presented her a bill for room and board that she thought was too high.

Meanwhile, the soldiers at New Haven received new orders from General Gilbert to enlarge the stockade so it could accommodate all three companies stationed there. "All hands are at work as fast as they can," Major Broaddus wrote. He added: "The boys are talking about the dinner that is to bee sent them from Macomb at Chris[t]mas, but I think that pies and sutch things would not be worth mutch by the time they get here. A lot of good butter and a few green ap[p]les would bee good, or canned fruit." That was a menu that might appeal to a man with very few teeth.

Van Vleck wrote his wife November 25th that he was leaving New Haven to assume command of the companies at the Beech Fork bridge. He was not looking forward to the assignment.[14]

On the 27th the men began cutting and hauling logs to build cabins for winter quarters. Broaddus wrote his wife that since Van Vleck had departed for Beech Fork, he had a new tentmate: Elisha Morse, a thirty-one-year-old Macomb farmer who had enlisted as a private but had shown such talent for writing that he ended up handling most of the regiment's writing chores. Although subject to frequent bouts of illness, he was a favorite of Van Vleck, who had him pegged as officer material.[15]

It was about this time in November—the date on his letter is not clear—that Pvt. Benjamin F. Gill of Company I sat down to write his wife. Gill, a blacksmith from Macomb, was responsible for keeping the 78th's horses and mules shod, which excused him from most other duties. He was another phonetic speller, perhaps even more so than Broaddus.

"Dear Wife," he wrote, "Well I have just got don[e] sup[p]er. I eat a [w]hole pie one buiskit [biscuit] [and] lbs. of stued [stewed] beef, one pint of coffee made rite sweat [right sweet] and I am as full as a tick and I am in a good humor. I never get out of humor only w[h]en I am hungry . . .

"I wish I was ther[e] to night. I would torement you and sing you a song and tell you about war and spit on your carpet and all kinds of fun. I would have but it can[n]ot be ther[e] for I will have fun any how—a writing. You don't know how good it makes me feal [feel] to get a letter from you. It makes me feal good to think that I have got a wife at home with three children and plenty to eat and send me letters and boots and butter and to think that she is getting fat . . .

"I wish you would send me one dollar in your next letter if you [can] spare it. I will pay it back as soon as the officers payes me for a shoeing their horse. The officers is all strap[p]ed too. I can make out but I like to have a little on hands in case of neede and so on. I don't spend much every thing is so high hear . . . I don't buy any thing only what I am oblige[d] to have. . . .

"Ther[e] has been two or three boys wounded in our redgiment. They shot them selves."[16]

Cornelius Pierce also wrote home about the men who accidentally shot themselves: "Two weeks ago one of our company shot his thumb off accidentally and two more got shot through the right forefinger . . . which makes about ten that have got shot since we came into Kentucky." The "Benneson rifles" seemed prone to discharge while being loaded, which nearly always resulted in a hand wound

Pierce himself had been excused from guard duty for three weeks. He had never completely recovered from the cold he caught after getting soaked in the rain at Louisville, and while cutting logs in the cold air at Rolling Fork bridge he suffered a relapse, with the cold settling in his lungs. But he wasn't complaining. "We have easy times since our stockade has been completed," he wrote. "Before it took 12 to stand picket, but now it only takes four in the daytime and six at night. We can live as comfortable as we please. Our mess has not got a stove yet, but the other three messes have theirs. We build a fire in the center of the tent and the smoke passes up and out of the top. We have plenty to eat as usual. We have enough hard crackers to do us a month. The neighbors are nearly all Union around here and they bring us plenty of bread and pies and gingerbread and roasted chickens, but we have to pay dear for them."

Meanwhile, after three days at Beech Fork, Van Vleck decided he liked it there after all. One reason was the presence of a sutler's wagon, from which he obtained oysters, sardines, and some "very fine canned peaches." He also found that since the Headquarters Company had moved to New Haven, things had gotten a bit lax at Beech Fork and the garrison there—Companies A, C, and D—had become "the poorest disciplined and the poorest drilled in the reg't., but they are going to be the best if I am permitted to remain here a month or two. I drill them five hours a day, which is pretty hard work for me as I have never done any thing [like] it before. I got very tired towards the last this forenoon & must go at it again at 2 o'cl'k. this afternoon & drill until 4 p.m. Then comes dress parade, then supper, then study until nine, then bed until 6 a.m., then breakfast, guard mounting at 8. a.m., then drill until 12, then dinner, then write until 2 p.m., & then drill again.

"One thing is certain: I am learning something, I can now go through nearly all the maneuvers, evolutions & performances known to military tactics, & shall not be ashamed if I have good luck, to drill my part of the reg't. in the spring, with any like no. [number] of men in the service."[17]

Two days later he wrote again: "We are getting very comfortably fixed here. My first order was for the men to build themselves & me good houses to live in, & they will in a few days be completed & then we will be at home comparatively . . . Certainly I will have a better chance for study than amidst all this noise. And it takes an immense am[oun]t of study to learn well the art of killing people, without getting killed yourself.

"It is a fearful yet a very pleasant study. I like it much better than I expected to & much better than any thing else I ever studied or practiced. How I should like the sad realities of war, or how I should demean myself in an actual fight, of course I have as little idea as anyone else that knows me. I might disgrace myself & family forever or might win honors worthy to be won. Circumstances as well as courage & skill would have much to do in the matter."

Over the next few days the regiment put finishing touches on their winter huts. They were just in time, for on Friday, December 5th, it began snowing again. The snow ended by nightfall but the temperature plunged sharply and by Sunday morning the ice on the Rolling Fork at New Haven was "sufficiently thick to make good scating [skating]," McNeill wrote.[18]

At Beech Fork, Van Vleck was snug in his new quarters. "I got moved into my new room night before last & feel decidedly at home," he told his wife and daughter. "My quarters are built of logs set on end in the ground like the other parts of the stockade, and form a shield to the main entrance to the fort. It has a good roof & floor & two windows, and a good stove, all 'borrowed' until spring of our Union neighbors.

"I have also built a first rate bed in one corner, wide enough for two, have one good square table, & one round center table, a toilet stand, wood box, clothes, basket, wash stand, water table for the water bucket, one splint bottomed chair with a back to it, one camp stool, five three-legged stools, a cupboard, a broom, two windo[w] curtains, one spare bed (my old cot; but no bed clothes with it) and a great multitude of small articles of necessity, such as all sorts of brushes, stationery, and a House Keeper." The latter was 1st Lt. John B. Worrell of Company B, a "splendid man" in Van Vleck's words. "He rooms with me, & in consideration thereof keeps the room in order, cuts & brings in all the wood, builds the fires, makes the beds, & makes 'herself' generally useful. I can't imagine how I could fix myself more pleasantly if I had the whole army at my disposal."

Of course, since this was the army, it was inevitable that once everyone was comfortably settled in winter quarters they would be ordered to relocate. And that's just what happened: On Monday, December 8th, orders were received for most of the companies in the regiment to move.

The complicated orders were as follows:

Company B was to leave Boston and return to Shepherdsville to guard the railroad bridge there.

Companies I and K, with Major Broaddus in command, were ordered to move from New Haven to guard a bridge on the main line of the Louisville & Nashville railroad about ten miles south of Shepherdsville.

Company C, which had been at Beech Fork, was divided in half, with half ordered to guard a bridge on the L&N main line three miles south of Shepherdsville and the other half to defend another bridge farther south.

Company D, which had been at Beech Fork, also was divided. Half the company, under Captain Black, was sent to Wilson's Creek bridge about five miles away, trading places with Company E, which was ordered to Beech Fork, where Company A remained, with Van Vleck in command of both companies. The other half of Company D, under Lieutenant Worrell, was ordered to guard the bridge at Boston, about two miles from Beech Fork.

Company H remained at New Haven, where Benneson commanded.

Companies F and G remained where they were, the former at the other Rolling Fork bridge, the latter at Pottinger's Creek.[19]

With Lieutenant Worrell's departure, Van Vleck lost his "housekeeper." His was not the only loss; Odell wrote his daughter that George—Company G's black cook—had disappeared. "The last we heard of him he was with Co[mpany] F," Odell said. "We bought him a book and learned him to spell. We paid him for his work. He said we were the best people he ever saw. In the south they don't teach the poor black folks how to read and write. George said he wanted to learn how so that he could write his mother a letter. . . ."

The orders to leave their just-finished winter quarters made the soldiers of the 78th "the maddest set of men in the world," Van Vleck wrote. "They had all got nicely fixed for winter and they are all turned out into the cold . . . And I believe the Col. is the maddest man of the lot that his command has dwindled down to a single company, & that a company fully officered. He threatens to resign but (I) guess he'll not."

The scattering of the companies also meant there would still be no opportunity for them to drill as a regiment, a matter of continued concern to Van Vleck. But at least the weather was pleasant so the companies were able to move to their new stations without interference from the elements.[20]

Broaddus took the move in stride. "We are very comfortably situated here," he wrote from his new post on the L&N Railroad. He was still troubled by his lack of teeth, however. "I have not got my teeth fixed and can't until I get my pay," he said. "I called to see a dentist when I was in Louisville. He said he would charge me thirty dollars for an under set." Of course neither Broaddus nor anyone else in the regiment had any way of knowing when the paymaster might make his next visit.

Van Vleck was troubled by a recent order from General Boyle in Louisville. Boyle had ordered "all officers under his command to allow no slave to enter their lines, & to put out all slaves now in their lines or hereafter coming within them. I admitted one the other day, & have got him here yet. His master was killed in the rebel army. I want to see whether Mr. Lincoln or Mr. Boyle rules this army. You need not be surprised to hear that I am in jail at Louisville any time, for that is the way of all commanders that dare to let a nigger in." [21]

The reasons for Boyle's order are unclear, but Van Vleck was not quite accurate in suggesting the general was violating Lincoln's policy. The president had announced his intention to issue the Emancipation Proclamation, but he had not yet done so, and even when he did—on January 1, 1863—it would apply only to those states in open rebellion against the federal government. That did not include Kentucky, which meant that within its borders slavery and fugitive slave laws would technically remain legal.

On December 17th, the *Quincy Whig & Republican* published a letter written in response to the earlier one signed by "Seventy-Eighth" that was so critical of Colonel Benneson. The letter was from a member of Company B who was evidently well acquainted with the soldier who signed himself "Seventy-Eighth." It was clear no love was lost between them.

It was equally clear the writer was not anxious to see fighting. "I have to say in reply that 'Seventy-Eighth' misrepresented the Colonel in some respects," his letter said, "for is there a regiment in the field that is better situated than the 78th—is there a regiment which has an easier time than this same regiment? Well, who deserves credit for the position that this regiment now holds? Nobody else but Col. Benneson.

"'Seventy-Eighth' flies into quite a passion about the arms that are not of the very best pattern, but there are regiments in the service that would gladly exchange with the 78th. 'Seventy-Eighth' also thinks it very hard that this regiment could not have passenger cars from Quincy to Jeffersonville when he knew that the Colonel used his authority to get good cars and 'Seventy-Eighth' knows as well as I do that the superintendent of the railroad could not furnish the government with any other.

"'Seventy-Eighth' takes it very hard at heart about the Colonel seeking promotion. I suppose he thinks that nobody should be promoted because he was not promoted to the orderlyship of Co. B. . . .

"There is not a colonel in the service that takes more interest in the welfare of his command than Col. Benneson. He is always ready to accommodate any of the 78th. It makes no difference to him whether the applicant be a private or an officer. 'Seventy-Eighth' says that the whole regiment is dissatisfied with the Colonel. I think that he is very much mistaken, for since the regiment has got their bounty, I have not heard a single man murmur against the Colonel. I cannot say that much for 'Seventy-Eighth,' for I have heard a man in his company say that he could not discharge the duties of his office, which is third sergeant of Co. B."

Finally, the writer noted that "Seventy-Eighth" "thinks that this regiment ought to be in active service. He thinks it very hard that some regiments that have entered the service since the Seventy-eighth have been sent South and the Seventy-eighth has to be strewn along the railroad, but he is only talking for effect, as he knows that we are having an easier time than any other regiment in the service of the United States."

The letter was signed "A Private of Company B."

It would be a while before copies of that issue of the *Whig & Republican* reached the regiment because mail deliveries had been temporarily interrupted, possibly due to the wholesale rearrangement of commands. Since no letters were received for a week or more, the soldiers had none to answer—but that still didn't stop them from writing.

Van Vleck wrote his wife and daughter he had taken a new boarding place at the home of a widow named Cox about a half mile from camp, despite General Gilbert's orders that no one was to go more than one hundred yards beyond camp. "It seems quite like civilization to get again where there are women and children," he wrote, "and to have something cooked to eat. We still get no vegetables from the fact that there are none in the country. There was a very severe drought here last season so that vegetables would have been scarce at best. And then the presence of the army has taken every 'green thing.'" He also said he had grown hoarse shouting drill commands and "I bathe my chest every morning in cold water, and find that it strengthens my lungs very much." [22]

Broaddus also wrote his wife to say he "had a call from Gen. Gilbert. He was very pleasant. He invited me up to see him. He has his head quarters at the Junction [probably Bardstown Junction]. We are buisey [busy] at work on our stoc[k]ade. The weather has bin quite could [cold] for a few days but the sun shines very brightly and is very pleasant to day. Col. B(enneson) gets along better than he did when you were here. Col. Van [Vleck] gets along first rate. He is very mutch beloved by the men and officers and is going to make a splended officer I think. . . .

"We doo not have as good a cook as Jake was. He in making pies puts the short[e] ning in the long way and they are so tough that it takes better teeth than I have got to eat them...."[23]

Van Vleck wrote again December 21st to report he had a new roommate at the widow Cox's place, the regiment's new assistant surgeon, Dr. Samuel Moss, "a first-rate surgeon and an excellent gentleman."[24]

<hr>

The far-flung companies of the 78th celebrated Christmas Day as best they could, except possibly for Companies B and C. They were on the move again, having been ordered to join the 71st Indiana Volunteer Infantry in helping guard two long, high, vulnerable trestles over the Sulphur Fork and Broad Run at Muldraugh Hill.

Company F, still at Rolling Fork bridge, enjoyed the holiday generosity of a "good Union man" named Patterson, "who made us a present of a fat hog and some turkeys and chickens for a Christmas dinner, so we had a good time of it," Cornelius Pierce wrote his family. "Only there was a little too much whiskey smuggled into camp." Packages they were expecting from home had not arrived, however, and "the captain sent a man to Louisville to see about them, but he has not yet returned."

Company G, still at Pottinger's Creek, also enjoyed a Christmas feast. Pvt. Lemuel B. Roseberry described the festivities in a letter to the *Quincy Whig & Republican*, including an endorsement of Colonel Benneson: "Gentlemen: You will please insert in your loyal and patriotic paper the heartfelt thanks of the officers and members of Co. G, 78th Ill., to the loyal and patriotic ladies and gentlemen (especially the ladies) of Camp Point and vicinity, for the splendid Christmas dinner sent to us by them ... The members one and all expressed the highest satisfaction.

"All that was lacking materially to complete our happiness was the presence of our Colonel. We would have been glad to have had him with us to share the sumptuous repast set before us. Circumstances being such that he could not possibly be with us on the occasion, was something that we regretted very much, as he has the entire confidence and esteem of the whole company.

"Some persons in the regiment seem to be down on the Colonel in regard to the arms issued to the regiment. There have been absurd articles published against him. I do not think that Col. Benneson merits such abuse from any member of the 78th. Col. Benneson, in the first place, tried to arm his regiment as well as any that had preceded him in the army, but in this he failed; but I do not believe it was through any neglect of his. Even after we had arrived in this state (Kentucky), he tried, and is still trying, to procure better and more efficient arms. The kind that we have is called the Altered Musket—altered from a flint to a percussion lock and rifled. Col. Benneson's

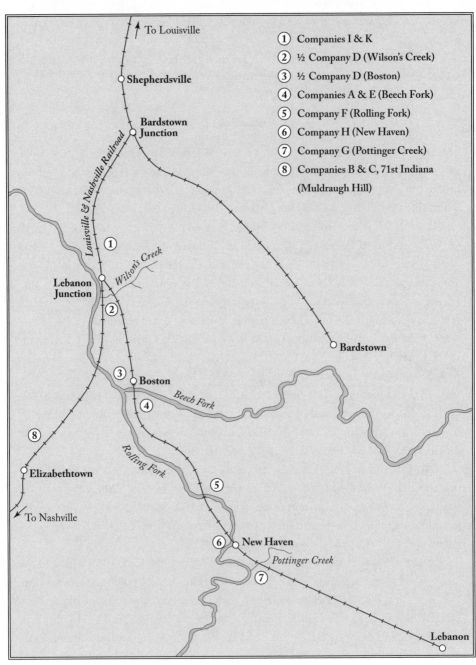

To Louisville

Shepherdsville

Bardstown Junction

① Companies I & K
② ½ Company D (Wilson's Creek)
③ ½ Company D (Boston)
④ Companies A & E (Beech Fork)
⑤ Company F (Rolling Fork)
⑥ Company H (New Haven)
⑦ Company G (Pottinger Creek)
⑧ Companies B & C, 71st Indiana
    (Muldraugh Hill)

Louisville & Nashville Railroad

①

Wilson's Creek

Lebanon Junction

②

Bardstown

③ Boston

④ *Beech Fork*

⑧

Rolling Fork

Elizabethtown

To Nashville

⑤

⑥ New Haven

Pottinger Creek

⑦

Lebanon

78TH ILLINOIS DISPOSITION OF COMPANIES - DECEMBER 26, 1862

headquarters are at present at New Haven, 45 miles southwest of Louisville, on the Lebanon Branch of the Louisville & Nashville Railroad, where he can be found at all hours, day or night, attending to the duties of his office."[25]

At Beech Fork, Van Vleck anticipated a Christmas feast with the widow Cox and her family. "I expect a Big Dinner at my boarding house," he wrote Patty and Nellie. "Turkey, and all the K[entuck]y chicken fixens. I expect a good many kinds of meat, for at no meal, (not even supper) since I have been there, have they had less than four different kinds on the table. So I conclude for a Christmas Dinner they will have at least a dozen kinds. This evening I intend to give the officers here an oyster supper. That's all I can think of to do, except write to you, which is my first treat."

When all the feasts had been consumed, it remained for Vilasco Chandler to write a final word in his diary: "Christmas of '62 has come and gone," he said. "It has awaken[ed] nothing but pleasing emotions, [but] the reality has not been there. In Kentucky with the dull pale apathy of a winter rain. The bright keen sparkle of a sun making bright the glistening snow is not here. What a change in a year."[26]

The Christmas celebration brought more than feasts and packages from home. Rumors were rampant that the rebel raider John Hunt Morgan was on his way north again with a large force of cavalry, bent on destroying the Louisville & Nashville Railroad.

The rumors were true. Morgan had been promoted to brigadier general December 11th. Three days later he married Martha "Mattie" Ready in a ceremony conducted by Confederate General Leonidas Polk, an Episcopal bishop who, when the occasion demanded, could still don clerical vestments over his uniform. A week after the ceremony, Morgan saddled up and led his men northward to carry out Gen. Braxton Bragg's orders to disrupt the Union Army supply line by destroying the bridges on the Louisville & Nashville.

His reputation preceded him. "Today camp is alive with rumors of Morgan's approach in immense numbers," Chandler wrote the day after Christmas. Company G received orders from Colonel Benneson to move to New Haven, but General Gilbert countermanded the orders and the company ended up at Lebanon Junction where "great preparations were making . . . in anticipation of an attack by some of Morgan's forces, such as making a barricade of government wagons, digging rifle pits, etc.," Odell wrote.[27]

Benneson was undoubtedly feeling somewhat lonely at New Haven, with only a single company to defend the stockade. His mood surely was not improved by news of the death from disease that day of Pvt. Stillman Augustus French, nineteen, a member of Company K, who had been left in the hospital at New Haven when his company moved to its new post.

On the morning of the 27th, cannon fire was heard from the direction of Elizabethtown. The cannon belonged to Morgan's forces, shelling positions occupied by eight companies of the 91st Illinois. The fight was one-sided because only the Confederates had artillery, and the 91st surrendered after less than an hour. Morgan paroled about 650 soldiers and put his own men to work tearing up the L&N tracks and setting fire to three bridges.

Next morning Morgan had his men in motion along the L&N toward the high trestles at Sulphur Fork and Broad Run, only about five miles from Elizabethtown. Union soldiers had built earthworks with artillery platforms to guard the trestles, which were about a mile apart, but no guns had been installed. Companies B and C of the 78th had been posted at the Broad Run trestle the night before, but when the rebels appeared at Sulphur Fork trestle, Lt. Col. Courtland Matson of the 71st Indiana, who was in command, called the two companies to join the rest of his troops at Sulphur Fork.[28]

Morgan had all the advantages. His cavalry force not only greatly outnumbered the federals but also enjoyed a high degree of mobility, while the federal troops were tied to a fixed position. Even more important, Morgan had artillery while the Union troops had none. Raw troops, such as those in Companies B and C of the 78th, were usually terrified by their first exposure to artillery fire, especially when they had no means of returning it, and it's likely the troops of Captains Anderson and Hume were no exception. The 71st Indiana was a slightly more experienced outfit, though most of the regiment had surrendered in its first battle at Richmond, Kentucky, on August 30, 1862—not a record to inspire confidence. Its captured soldiers had been paroled and sent to Indianapolis. After they were exchanged, the regiment was reorganized and sent back to Kentucky.[29]

Morgan employed his usual tactics. "I sent in flags of truce, demanding a surrender, which was declined," he wrote later. "I then opened fire, and after some shelling and skirmishing for about an hour the stockades surrendered. The stockades, trestles, and a quantity of army stores were destroyed." About seven hundred prisoners, including Companies B and C of the 78th, were taken and paroled.[30] There were no casualties on either side, but destruction of the two trestles would shut down the railroad until February.

The sounds of cannonading at Muldraugh Hill could be heard by most of the other men in the 78th, including Batchelor and Chandler in their camp along the railroad south of Shepherdsville. "Our anticipation[s] have been harrowing," Chandler wrote. "The booming of artillery towards Elizabeth[town] have been continual between 1 and 4 p.m. They have surrendered. Our time next."

On the 29th Chandler reported "the stream of paroled prisoners has been continuous . . . Co[mpanie]s B & C have passed. Surrendered, nobody hurt. Shameful."[31]

Next stop for the two paroled companies would be at Louisville, but ultimately
they would be sent to Benton Barracks in St. Louis to await exchange. They would have
to wait ten months. Meanwhile, the 78th Illinois would be reduced to eight companies.

After leaving Muldraugh Hill, Morgan moved northeast and camped for the
night on the Rolling Fork. Federal cavalry found him there the next morning as his
troops were crossing the river. Morgan deployed skirmishers to hold off the federals
until his men finished crossing, then kept going northeast. They paused long enough
to tear up the Bardstown spur railroad and burn the stockade and bridge at Boston,
where Lieutenant Worrell and his small garrison—half of Company D of the 78th—
had been hurriedly withdrawn to avoid capture. Morgan's main force continued in
the direction of Bardstown, but three companies of the 9th Kentucky Cavalry were
dispatched with orders to destroy the railroad bridge at New Haven, where Colonel
Benneson and Company H were waiting.

4

"Our Colonel Is Under Arrest"

DECEMBER 29, 1862–FEBRUARY 7, 1863

THE SOUND OF DISTANT CANNON FIRE ADDED URGENCY TO THE EFFORTS OF COMPANY H as its men cleared the stockade for action and deepened the rifle pits around its perimeter. Pvt. James K. Magie, former editor of the *Macomb Journal,* was among them. He had been on detached duty from Company C serving as an orderly to Colonel Benneson; otherwise he would have been captured along with the rest of his company at Sulphur Fork.

"Just at sundown, a man came galloping into camp with the news that the rebels were marching on us and were only about a mile off," Magie wrote later to his wife, Mary. "I was eating supper when the rebels on horseback made their appearance on a side hill about three quarters of a mile distant. We knew then we had to fight . . . By 7 o'clock we heard that the rebels were on all sides of us, and had their pickets stationed in the town."

Dr. Thomas Jordan, the regimental surgeon, was worried about his horse, which was being kept in a stable next to the stockade. "He values him much," Magie wrote, "and he said he would rather shoot him than to let the rebels have him." The stable also housed horses belonging to Colonel Benneson, Lieutenant Colonel Van Vleck, Chaplain Taylor, and Lieutenant Greene, the regimental adjutant. "If they were not killed by the cannon balls it was thought the rebels would capture them and take them if they should overpower us."

There was talk of getting the horses away and hiding them somewhere, but no one seemed anxious to undertake the hazard of spiriting them through Confederate lines. "I then volunteered to lead the way and get them out," Magie wrote. He removed his uniform, donned civilian clothing, then "boldly pushed forward, passed our picket lines, and went over into town and made my way to the house of Dr. Elliott, a good Union man, and talked with him about the best direction to take to get out into the timber or brush. I got what information I could, and then made my way back. I was only gone about an hour. The Colonel and other officers were surprised to see me come back, as while I was gone a contraband (runaway slave) came to our lines and told our boys just where a number of the secesh were and that we were entirely surrounded. I told them that I was willing to make the attempt, and would get their horses out if they (the rebels) killed me for it."

Magie recruited Pvts. Karr McKlintock of Company I and Herman Houk of Company H to go with him and take the horses. He went first and, after making sure the way was clear, signaled the others to follow. Then, "about half a mile or perhaps a mile from our camp I came upon the rebel pickets. They fired a pistol shot at me." The shot missed and Magie dashed back "to the boys" and led them off in a different direction. Eventually they came to "the base of a mountain, which was a mile to the top." The three men, with the horses, made their way to the top and settled down to spend the night.[1]

———

Next morning the men of Company H awoke to a light, misty rain and a heavy overcast that promised more. About 7:00 a.m. they saw three riders coming down the Bardstown Pike with a flag of truce.

Captain Allen and Lieutenant Beers went out to meet the riders "at the farther extremity of the railroad bridge," McNeill wrote. As they did, people began to appear on the surrounding hillsides—civilian spectators come to watch what they thought would be either a surrender or a battle.

One of the riders was Capt. Henry P. Housley of the 2nd Confederate Kentucky Cavalry. A New Haven native, he had been given the honor of presenting a demand for the surrender of Fort Allen. He handed a note to the fort's namesake declaring the stockade was surrounded by cavalry and artillery and promising private property would be respected if the garrison surrendered. It was signed by Brig. Gen. John Hunt Morgan. Captain Allen conveyed the demand to Colonel Benneson, who replied "that he respectfully declined." Captain Housley and his escorts then withdrew and all was quiet, except for the steady drip of rain and distant sounds of conversation among civilian spectators.

Meanwhile, Benneson deployed his meager force of eighty men. He sent Lieutenant Beers with twenty men to occupy the rifle pits on the northwest side of the stockade, placed sentinels at points where they could survey the surrounding countryside, and distributed the rest of Company H inside the stockade.

It was about 9:00 a.m. when the Confederates finally appeared in force on a wooded ridge northwest of the stockade. Again they had the advantage of a larger force, greater mobility, and at least one piece of artillery. The latter, a twelve-pounder mountain howitzer, was rolled into place about a thousand yards from the stockade. Three mounted companies of the 9th Confederate Kentucky Cavalry formed in line of battle behind it.

Then the howitzer boomed and 1st Sgt. Thomas Scott shouted a warning to the men inside the stockade. "Every fellow found his hiding place," McNeill wrote. "The shell came buzzing and struck about 50 yards short of us (but) the ball bounded over us and struck on the farther bank of the creek." The howitzer spoke again, but this time the missile was a shell instead of a solid shot. It exploded in mid-air just outside the stockade "sending fragments in every direction, some of which fell harmless among the men."

More rounds were fired, but no damage resulted. The gun crew limbered up, moved the weapon to a position behind a rail fence somewhat closer to the stockade, and resumed firing. The men of Company H had no way of knowing the gun crew was inexperienced—cavalrymen detailed as gunners—and had failed to adjust the angle of the gun's elevation to account for the move closer to the stockade. Their shots passed over the stockade and began falling in the Rolling Fork or in New Haven on the other side of the stream. Each time a shell passed overhead, a pet rooster inside the stockade crowed and flapped its wings, much to the amusement of the soldiers.

A single company of Confederate cavalry had accompanied the howitzer to its new position. "The boys who were aching to let fly at them now received the order to fire," McNeill wrote. In their excitement, the men forgot the firing ports in the stockade walls; instead, they jumped onto the platforms at the stockade corners, tore down their Sibley tents, and leveled their .69-caliber muskets over the parapets. Concerned about the effective range of the old weapons, Colonel Benneson told them to aim high. The opening volley passed far over the heads of the Confederates, so the men hastily reloaded and fired again, this time aiming lower. The Confederate troopers dismounted and led their horses to concealment behind the home of a local resident named Howell, then took positions behind a pair of rail fences and returned fire.

Captain Allen ordered his men to "'pour it into them' and right willingly did they obey," McNeill recorded. "The firing was rappid and insescent [incessant] for about half an hour." While the bullets flew back and forth, the howitzer crew changed positions again, coming another hundred yards closer to the stockade, but again the shells passed overhead.

While this was going on, part of the remaining Confederate cavalry dismounted and deployed west of the stockade in a cornfield extending north across the railroad tracks. On the far side of the tracks, another small Confederate force began making its way down a wagon road leading to a ford next to the railroad bridge. Simultaneously, the dismounted troopers in the cornfield began advancing toward the stockade.

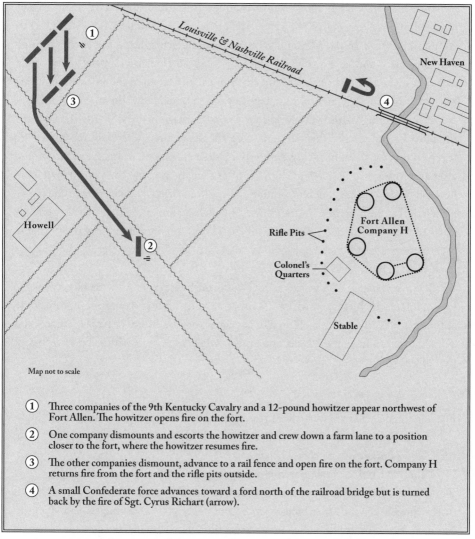

1. Three companies of the 9th Kentucky Cavalry and a 12-pound howitzer appear northwest of Fort Allen. The howitzer opens fire on the fort.

2. One company dismounts and escorts the howitzer and crew down a farm lane to a position closer to the fort, where the howitzer resumes fire.

3. The other companies dismount, advance to a rail fence and open fire on the fort. Company H returns fire from the fort and the rifle pits outside.

4. A small Confederate force advances toward a ford north of the railroad bridge but is turned back by the fire of Sgt. Cyrus Richart (arrow).

SKIRMISH AT NEW HAVEN - MORNING DECEMBER 29, 1862

Benneson sent 2nd Lt. Samuel Simmons with several men to deal with the threat from across the tracks, but they found the Confederates already in retreat when they arrived. The rebels had been turned back by the fire of Sgt. Cyrus Richart, who had been stationed as a sentinel on a bridge abutment.

"At this juncture we commenced a rapid fire upon the enemy with all our disposable force," Benneson wrote later in his after-action report. "The damaging effects of our fire were immediately apparent. The cannoneers abandoned their cannon, and only returned to remove it out of our range. The forces in the cornfield receded from their advanced position. In a few minutes the rout became general, and the enemy, moving at a rapid pace and in a disorderly mass, disappeared from view in the timber from which he had emerged prior to the attack." Some men ran out of the stockade and tried to pursue the Confederates on foot, but they were no match for the mounted men.

So ended the "battle" of New Haven. It was Benneson's finest hour. "The Col. was the most highly pleased man we have seen for many a day," McNeill recorded—"so much so that he thought Co. H deserved a visible expression of his gratification, and after everything had quieted down in the afternoon, he had the company drawn up in line and made a practical demonstration of his gratification by delivering to the boys a pithey [pithy] little speach, in the course of which he remarked that he was 'perfectly satisfied with the courage and bravery of Co. H' and then finished up by presenting to them a couple of well-filled bottles of good old whiskey. The boys received both with a good hearty cheer for Col. Wm. H. Benneson."

Benneson had reason to feel good; the skirmish clearly had been a victory for the Union force, which escaped without a single casualty and no damage to the stockade, although the Confederate shelling did damage several buildings in New Haven. As far as can be determined, the Confederates also suffered no loss, with the possible exception of a single wounded man.[2]

Having failed at New Haven, the three companies of Confederate cavalry went looking for other targets. Their next choice was the bridge defended by Company F over the Rolling Fork north of New Haven.

"About 11 o'clock yesterday the rebs came on to within half a mile of Company F and halted and sent in three men and demanded of Captain Hawkins the surrender of his company," Cornelius Pierce wrote. "His reply was about the same as Colonel Benneson's, and in less time than it takes to write, every man had his gun and cartridge box and was ready for them. The rebels, after a short consultation, wheeled their horses and put back the way they came, but made their appearance again on the other side of the river and again we made ready for them, but they kept out of reach of our guns and passed on."

That evening a slave approached Company G's pickets at the Pottinger Creek bridge to report that about a hundred rebel soldiers were at his master's place a mile away. He said they planned to spend the night and then try to force Company G to surrender in the morning. Captain Joseph sent out three scouts who returned with word they had encountered enemy pickets less than a half mile from the stockade. "We went to sleep in full expectation of trying our guns in the morning," Odell wrote. But when morning came, there was no sign of the rebels. Further investigation "satisfied us that they had left the neighborhood."[3]

That was the end of Morgan's so-called "Christmas Raid." In his official report of the expedition, Morgan did not even mention the skirmish at New Haven.

After the rebels had gone, the soldiers of Company H wandered over the field and were amazed at what they saw. "We found some of our shots had passed over the hill back of where the enemy were posted and lodged in the trees," McNeill wrote. "Some of the balls, even at that incredible distance, lodged in the bodies of the trees and penetrated some inch and a half and two inches. The fence rails around where the [Confederate] sharp shooters were secreted, were literally riddled with balls—some of the balls having passed entirely through large oak rails. Howell's house, some 800 yards distant, had balls penetrate through both walls. Some of our shots went beyond an Irish shantee [shanty] up the railroad over a mile distant. . . .

"The battle had the happy effect of satisfying the boys perfectly with their Benneson rifles—and now they say they would not exchange them for any gun in the service—and the Col. told the boys he had no objection to having them called 'Benneson rifles'—that he believed they were an honor to him and he gloried in the name."[4]

⌐ ⌐

While Company H and the Confederates had been firing ineffectually at one another, Privates Magie, McKlintock, and Houk were still guarding the officers' horses on the nearby mountain. They were visited by two local "Union men" who complained that their brother, a rebel sympathizer, had acted as a guide for Morgan's men. Magie, whose borrowed clothes made him look as if he might have been a Confederate partisan, came up with a plan to capture the rebel sympathizer, whose name was Floyd Price. Magie went to Price's house, pretending to be one of Morgan's men who had become separated from the main force, and asked Price to guide him back to Morgan.

Price fell for the story and told Magie he had indeed been with Morgan's men the night before. He promised Magie he would show him the way to rejoin Morgan's force if Magie would just wait until he milked his cow. When Price began milking the animal, Magie came up on one side of him and one of the other privates came up on the other. Both pointed pistols at Price's head and told him he was their prisoner. Magie, McKlintock, and Houk then returned triumphantly to camp with the five horses and their prisoner.[5]

⌐ ⌐

After all the excitement of December 30th, New Year's Eve was an anticlimax. Odell was on guard duty the last two hours of 1862. It was a bright, moonlit night and "all was calm; not a sound to be heard except the measured footsteps of the sentinel, as he passes to and fro on the beat, and now and then the lowing of ox, or the barking of a dog," he wrote. It was equally quiet at the 78th's other outposts.[6]

January 7th was Magie's birthday. "Yesterday I entered upon my 37th year," he wrote his wife. "Oh, how time flies! I can scarcely realize that I am growing so old. It seems about yesterday that I was a saucy, frollicking boy, and now I am verging upon forty years of age."

It wasn't a happy birthday. He had received a copy of the January 2nd edition of the *Macomb Journal*, the newspaper he had left under management of its other owner, Nichols. "What a sick thing it has become," he said. "Not a local item was printed in it."[7]

On January 10th Broaddus told his wife that Capt. Granville Reynolds of Company I, who had just returned from furlough, had loaned him ten dollars because there was still no prospect the regiment would soon be paid. "If I could borrow thirty dollars I would get my teeth fixed but I guess I will have to wait untill I get my pay," he wrote.

He also had some harsh words for General Gilbert, who had issued an order directing that a noncommisioned officer and four men should start from the stockade every morning at daylight and follow the railroad to the Rolling Fork bridge. If they found damage to the tracks, the patrol was to stand next to the railroad with rifles inverted until the train came along. The inverted rifles would be a signal to warn the train crew of damage ahead. But the order didn't say what the men were supposed to do if the train never came, and in that respect, Broaddus said, it was like many other nonsensical orders issued by General Gilbert.

It rained hard the night of January 13th and continued the next day. "The rain has fallen in torants [torrents] [and] the river is rising very fast," Broaddus wrote. "I am going to New Haven in the morning as a witness in a court marshal [martial]. The Col. wants me to stay two or three days but I don't think I will stay long for I guess the mud must bee about a foot deep up their [there], and if it keeps on raining all night as fast as it has to day they will bee drowned out up their."

By the next day the rain had changed to snow. Broaddus started for New Haven but did not get far. "It has bin snowing all day," he wrote. "The snow has fallen to the depth of 25 inches. The river is rising very fast and there is some fears of it washing the bridge away at this point."[8]

~~~

Sometime earlier a farmer near New Haven—Edward Mott Robbins remembered his name as Sphink—had invited several men from Company H to a dance. "Of course we were crazy to go," Robbins wrote, "but how were we to get outside the lines? We decided to ask the officers for a pass, but this failed. Our officers claimed this was a plan made up to get a lot of us out there and take us prisoners . . . and we decided it was all off. But as the time came near for the event . . . a few of us Yanks' heels began to tickle for a dance and a desire to have a chance at the roast turkey that was promised for the occasion. So we made up our minds we would take our chances on getting by the pickets."

Then the snow came, and it was "the heaviest, the natives said, that had ever been known in Kentucky. It covered the earth to a depth of a little more than two feet. The night for the party arrived, and not Johnnies [rebels], snow, pickets, nor anything else would have stopped that gang.

"During the day we located the guards on picket duty, quite a ways from the main road, and planned to go as close to them as possible without attracting their attention, then to drop on our hands and knees and crawl through the snow to a safe distance on the outside, which we did, and arrived safely at Mr. Sphink's. We had taken the precaution to take our side arms with us, for we had seen service enough to be always on the alert and trust nobody or allow them to get the drop on us.

"When we went into the house almost the first persons we met were men wearing the gray uniform, and the host introduced them to us as Confederate soldiers home on furlough. At first we were just a bit disconcerted until our host assured us that all was on the square, that we need not fear any trouble, as they were home boys and had heard of our coming and for us to pitch in and have as good a time as we could, and we sure did have a fine time, a royal supper, and not a word was spoken to mar the peace and comfort of anyone. When we left for camp we shook hands with the Confeds the same as any one else and bid them goodbye.

"It was some time before the officers found out about our going out, in fact not until we had left Kentucky, consequently we were not disciplined for having the good time, and leaving the camp without permission."⁹

The snow had forced an end to drilling in the camp at Pottinger Creek. Patrols on the railroad also were halted. "We are consequently living very snugly—having nothing to do but eat, sleep and stand guard once a week," Odell wrote.

Slowly the temperature moderated and by January 16th it was warm enough that rain began to alternate with snow. The rising temperature also caused snow on the ground to melt, and the rivers rose rapidly until finally nature accomplished what Morgan had failed to do at New Haven: the swift, raging river carried away the western half of the railroad bridge and threatened to flood the stockade.¹⁰

"The snow is still very deep but is set[t]ling some and the prospect is that we are going to [have] a thaugh [thaw]," Broaddus wrote that day. "I have had a bad cold for too [two] or three days. I have the head ake [headache] to day. I think I will go up to Louisville to morrow to get my teeth fixed. I sold my revolver for twenty dollars and borrowed ten, and think that I can get them fixed for that. I have to go up to New Haven to morrow morning and then if the Col. will let me, I will go on the evening train to Louisville."

Evidently the colonel didn't let him, for it was another three days before Broaddus finally traveled to Louisville to see a dentist.

Meanwhile, back in Quincy, Colonel Benneson was getting a boost from one of the local newspapers. Under the heading "The 78th Regiment All Right," the *Quincy Whig & Republican* printed the following January 17th:

"We learn from John A. White, Esq., who has just returned from a visit to the 78th Regiment, that the troubles existing in this Regiment are all settled, and that a perfect good feeling now exists between them and their officers. The complaints which were frequently made about Col. Benneson were all without foundation, and were made by a few disaffected persons without any cause whatever as far as he was concerned, as he was unable to remedy the difficulties complained of. From our acquaintance with Col. Benneson we were led to suppose that he possessed all the requisite qualifications to make a careful, humane and popular officer, and have declined to publish any of the many articles received reflecting upon him as an officer, being satisfied that all would yet end well, and we are pleased to learn that such is the case."[11]

In Kentucky it was still raining. "Rained all day," Batchelor wrote on the 20th. "Oh the slush." He wasn't the only one complaining. "You would laugh to see our kitchen floor now," Odell wrote. "The mud is about two inches deep."

Broaddus was spending his second day at the United States Hotel in Louisville. "I came up here yesterday to get my teethe fixed," he wrote his wife. "I had the impression of my mouth taken to day. Will have to waite until Friday morning before they will bee dun [done]. They cost Me $20.00. My health is quite good again."[12]

Nobody in the 78th yet knew it, but orders affecting the regiment were being sent out that day. The orders, from Maj. Gen. Horatio G. Wright, commanding the Department of the Ohio, were addressed to Maj. Gen. Gordon Granger and included a long list of infantry, cavalry, and artillery units that "are to be sent to the Department of the Cumberland, to operate with the forces in that department." The 78th was among the units on the list. "The above force is to be under your command, and will be assembled, with the least possible delay, at Louisville, and proceed thence by steamers to Nashville, via the Cumberland River," the orders said. They also included a list of general officers who were being assigned to Granger, including Brig. Gen. Charles C. Gilbert.

Gordon Granger was a forty-year-old graduate of West Point who had seen duty in the Mexican War and on the frontier. He started the Civil War as a cavalry captain but rose rapidly after service at Wilson's Creek, Island No. 10, and Corinth. In an army with some officers who had perfected profanity nearly to an art form, Granger could more than hold his own. In one historian's opinion, he suffered "lack of warmth" and "was not only unpopular with the men but had difficulty with his superiors." Another said his "reputation as a martinet with a decidedly sadistic streak was well deserved."[13]

The orders reached the 78th by telegraph about 9:00 p.m. on the 20th. "It may be three or four days before we get rations cooked and everything ready to start," Magie wrote home from New Haven next day. "The river is coming up again and is within one foot of being as high as it was before. If it rises four feet higher than it is now it will drive us out of our quarters, but we are soon to go anyhow unless our orders are countermanded. I really wish they would be, for I would rather stay here until spring. I have made a number of acquaintances about the town and throughout the country here and I begin to feel attached to the place.

"I spent last Monday evening at a private house in town [word illegible] and had the pleasure of playing Squirt with a very pretty young lady. You must not get jealous about it, although I begin to think I have some right to go about among the girls as you have almost quit writing to me.

"We have a contraband in camp who makes us a great deal of fun. He is the greatest dancer I ever saw. He joins in our debates and makes a right darn good speech. He is employed by the Colonel, and [word illegible] makes fires [word illegible] and &c. He means to stay with us until the war is over and then to go to Illinois with us. He is a slave and ran away from Spencer County about 50 miles distant."

Colonel Benneson left January 22nd to report to Louisville. Broaddus was still there, waiting for his new teeth. "It is quite lon[e]som[e] hear in the city with lots of persons around and knowing no one," he told his wife. He also had seen the article in the *Quincy Whig & Republican* and took issue with it: "Col. Benneson has not resigned. There is not mutch better feeling to ward him than their [there] was before," he wrote.[14]

⌐⌐⌐

As Broaddus was writing those lines, Chaplain Robert F. Taylor was writing to the *Whig & Republican*. His letter, however, was different from any that had so far appeared in the Quincy newspapers; it concerned the spiritual health of the regiment. It was headed "Religion in the 78th:"

> *Mr. EDITOR: A few words in regard to the state of religion and morals in this regiment will be more than acceptable to many of your readers who*

have husbands, sons, and brothers here, in whose moral well-being they are deeply interested.

I may begin by saying that in this regiment of course, as in every other, and every where else, "sin abounds." The prevailing forms of immorality with us are profanity, obscenity and Sabbath desecration. In two or three companies, whose commanding officers are dissipated, intemperate practices prevail to an alarming extent. Jayhawking [stealing] was practiced in a limited degree, [but] has been pretty effectually frowned out.

Our religious services in seven of the ten companies have been well attended. In the other three companies there are a few who show a proper regard for sacred things.

Some of our men who professed piety at home have made shipwreck here, but a majority of professors of religion are struggling nobly and successfully against temptation and their Christian energies and affections are being invigorated by the exercise. The principles and behavior of some of our officers are quite unfriendly to the growth of piety among the men. Were our regimental and company officers all as deeply interested in the spiritual welfare of the men, as some are and ought to be, ours would be one of the most moral and best regulated regiments in the field I think.

We have been detailed as bridge guards on the Louisville & Nashville Railroad, and previous to the capture of Co's B and C, in the late Morgan raid, we occupied ten different posts. Thus divided and scattered it has only been possible for me to make the "grand rounds" about once in three weeks or a little oftener, and in some of the companies there are no religious exercises excepting when I visit them.

Just at this moment a courier has arrived with the intelligence that we are to take the field, and with an order that we be ready to move on short notice. Ours will hereafter be the camp, the march, and the bloody conflict; but thank God we will be together, and as in Union there is strength, I hope the change may be for the better both with regard to the service we render to the country, and the obedience we owe to God.

We have felt—and more especially since we have been so subdivided, the want of some outward bond of union among Christian men in the regiment, and some organized system [of] opposition to prevailing vices. We have accordingly formed an association at each of the stockades, known as "The Christian Association of the 78th Reg't. Ill. Vols." Our basis of Union is the following pledge, which is the preamble to our Constitution:

"For the purpose of preserving our Christian integrity, and promoting each other's usefulness and growth in grace, we, the undersigned members of the 78th Reg. Ill. Vol., do hereby band ourselves together, promising scrupulously to refrain from all unnecessary use of intoxicating liquors, from the use of profane and indecent language, from Sabbath desecration, from falsehood and licentiousness, and promising

further that we will attend punctually, whenever it is practicable, on the preaching of the Word of God, and such other means of grace as may be within our reach; and promising further, that we will pray one for another, that we will faithfully caution and admonish one another, and that we will kindly and thankfully receive cautions and admonitions one from another in regard to any breach of, or departure from the terms of this agreement."

These associations are all formed on the one basis, with the view of consolidating when we are brought together. They each meet once in two weeks, and some of them every week, to receive members, transact business, and to discuss some practical question in Christian morals, interspersing these with other exercises of a devotional character. These meetings are generally interesting and profitable to all who attend them; and the influence of the association on the morals of the regiment is already quite obvious. Having to make arrangements for removal, I [must] close this abruptly, requesting the prayers of the Christian public on our behalf.

R. F. TAYLOR, Chaplain[15]

Company H was still at the stockade at New Haven on January 23rd, awaiting transportation, when a company of the 63rd Indiana Regiment showed up to replace them. "They had to pitch their tents and await our departure," McNeill wrote. Company G left the stockade at Pottinger Creek that day and marched to New Haven to wait for the train. Things were getting crowded in the little Kentucky town, but word was received that a train would arrive in the morning and Companies G and H should be ready to board.

Next morning found Company H "all packed up and our plunder all out only awaiting the train to take us to Louisville," McNeill related. The bridge over the Rolling Fork had been repaired and "the train came at its usual time, but only to sadly disappoint us." Colonel Benneson was on board and told his men that transportation for the two companies could not be furnished until the next day. "So here we were, tents taken down and packed, cooking utensils, provisions etc. all nicely fixed up, enough to ag[g]ravate the patience of a Christian much less soldiers," McNeill wrote. "We fixed up the best we could and awaited impatiently." At least it wasn't raining, although the weather was threatening.

By then Broaddus had returned to his camp on the railroad south of Shepherdsville. "We are under marching orders," he wrote, and "the boys are very ancious [anxious] to go farther South. Any thing to get out of this state for we are heartley [heartily] sick of guarding rail roads."

But the most important thing Broaddus had to tell his wife was that "I got my teeth put in but they are of no use. I can't doo any thing with them. I will see if the dentist can't doo something for them when I go up to the city to morrow. If he can't I don't know what I will do for I can't eat tough meat nor eat hard bread at all."[16]

Sunday, January 25th, was Vilasco Chandler's birthday. "I am 20 years old and so much begin to look grave and sober like a man," he wrote while waiting for the train at New Haven. For a time it appeared no train was going to come, but then, as "we began to think that we were going to have an other trial of our patience," the train finally came into sight about noon, McNeill wrote. "Soon we were all aboard, and as the long line of cars moved off we feelingly bid adieu to the old stockade where we had spent three months of our soldier life so pleasantly.

"We had to stop along the road and take on the different companies at their several stockades, and when we arrived at the Lebanon Junction dark had set in; and here we had to wait till the locomotive and two or three cars ran up . . . to Rolling Fork brid[g]e to take on Cos. I and K. It was long after dark before we arrived at Louisville, and the rain was pouring down in torrents. We spent the night on the cars as best we could, which was bad enough. Some were lucky enough to find some passenger cars at the depot, that were being repaired and the doors of which the key had failed to be turned upon; the cussined [cushioned] seats of which afforded a tolerably comfortable sleeping place."

Magie spent the night in an empty freight car. Chandler found uncomfortable repose on a set of harnesses. It was still raining hard the next morning, but about 10:30 a.m. the regiment marched up Broadway and made camp in an old orchard. "The ground [was] muddy, and here we were without hay or straw or a stick of wood," Chandler wrote. "And yet [General] Gilbert knew we would be here for he had ordered it. We could get nothing to burn, as no fence was near except a graveyard which was religiously preserved."

If there was any consolation for the wet, miserable men of the 78th, it was the warm welcome they received marching through Louisville. They were "greeted at almost every dwelling, by handkerchiefs, and the stars and stripes, streaming from the windows of the upper stories, held by the hands of the fair sex of all ages and sizes," Odell wrote.[17]

Pvt. Leonard Wood, 22, who was ill, had been left behind by Company K at its post south of Shepherdsville, and he died there January 27th. Wood, from Melrose, Adams County, was a cousin of Pvt. Stillman Augustus French, also of Company K, who had died December 26th.

Other soldiers were getting sick in the wet, cold, windy weather, but a load of wood was delivered to the regiment late on the 27th so the men were at last able to build fires. It was just in time, because that night the rain changed to snow. "It was an awful rainy, nasty, muddy time," Magie wrote.

January 28th "was spent in grumbling about the weather, Gen'l. Gilbert, etc., till along in the afternoon we were pleased to again meet our Lieut. Col. [Van Vleck] who had just returned from a visit home bringing two letters for me," Chandler wrote. The regiment also received orders to proceed to Portland, on the Ohio River just west of Louisville, to board the steamer *John H. Groesbeck.*

But the day's most important event was that "we stacked our old guns this morning, prepa[ra]tory to getting new ones, which were then awaiting us at Portland," McNeill wrote. "The boys were delighted with the prospect of exchanging their old guns for Springfield rifles." The .58-caliber Springfields were the workhorse weapons of the Union army.

The regiment was up early for breakfast on the morning of the 29th "and immediately all was bustle and confusion consequent to moving camp," Chandler recorded. "We took up our line of march at 8 ½ [a.m.] and arrived at Portland at 10, a distant [distance] of six miles. We there went on the boat assigned for us, and after working all day, got all things aboard about 8 o'clock p.m." Batchelor's diary entry for the day was characteristically succinct: "Moved to boat."[18]

The *Groesbeck* was a brand-new vessel, a 359-ton sidewheeler yet to make her first trip, but when the 78th attempted to board they found the 6th Kentucky Cavalry already on the boat. The 78th boarded anyway, driving the cavalrymen off to find transportation elsewhere.

The *Groesbeck* may have been new, but once the men of the 78th were on board they found the close quarters anything but pleasant, except for the officers, who were assigned staterooms. Enlisted men who couldn't find room in a cabin had to remain on deck where it was cold, unless they were lucky enough to find a spot close to a boiler or warm smokestack. Eight other steamers were moored at Portland, taking on troops, horses, and artillery, but as yet, none of the rank-and-file soldiers knew their destination.

Four more steamers arrived at Portland the next day and others were rumored to be at Louisville. "Gen. Granger is reported to be going with us and ten days rations (are) to be taken which means something probably," Chandler jotted in his diary. But there was good news: "The paymaster arrived and paid four companies. The remainder will be paid tomorrow."

Colonel Benneson meanwhile had gotten himself in hot water. Van Vleck had details: "Gen'l. Boyle ordered Col. Benneson to turn all *slaves* out of the reg't. & he refused to hunt for any and said he knew of none on board, but acknowledged that he had some *Negroes* aboard & he was ordered by Boyle's inspector to trot 'em out that he might ascertain whether they were *slaves* or not, & the Col. refused, & the insp[ec]tor left, & soon came an order placing the Colonel under arrest, & putting me in command of the reg't. I expect they will renew the demand on me and then I shall go under arrest & next will be the Major's turn.

"I am sorry that any such difficulty should have arisen but I am certain than none of the 78th will prove Negro hunters nor slave catchers for any body, let the consequences be what they may."

It was James K. Magie who had the full story because he was part of it. He had been ordered by Benneson to stash the contraband aboard the *Groesbeck* and keep him out of sight. "Our Colonel is under arrest for refusing to search the boat for runaway niggers," Magie told his wife. "The contraband was put in my charge and I have got him yet. The nigger thinks there is nobody like Massa Magie. The Colonel says he means to take him home with him after the war is over, but the nigger says he will go with me. The Louisville nigger catchers would have got him if I hadn't secreted him."[19]

At 10:00 p.m. on the 30th, orders came for the regiment to disembark from the *Groesbeck* and prepare to board another steamer, the *Bostonia No. 2*. The soldiers worked through the night to unload the boat and by next morning everything was "in a perfect jumble again, out on the levy, all in a heap, waiting for the *Bostonia No. 2* to get ready to receive us," Van Vleck wrote. General Gilbert then issued yet another order: The regiment was to re-board the *Groesbeck*.

Somehow during all this unloading and re-loading, the contraband was kept hidden. And wherever the regiment was going, it would now be under the command of Lt. Col. Carter Van Vleck.[20]

"I dislike exceedingly to take command of the reg't. now that we are going into the field," Van Vleck wrote his wife. "I feel my incompetentcy so greatly & the responsibility, especially of handling an undrilled reg't. is very great. God grant me strength & wisdom & courage to do my whole duty to Him, to my men, and to my country."[21]

<hr>

Speculation about the regiment's destination was rampant. Most believed they were headed for Vicksburg or Nashville, but they were still ignorant of the answer when the *John H. Groesbeck* cast off about seven o'clock Sunday morning, February 1st, and moved out into the broad Ohio River in company with several other steamers. Not everybody from the 78th was on board. "Their [there] was some 30 or 40 of our reg't left behind at Louisville," Broaddus wrote. "We started sooner than was expected, and some of them were out in town and got left, and perhaps some have gone home . . . The Col. is along with us but is still under arrest and some think they will brake [break] him of his office. He talked very saucey to Gen. Gilbert's aide."

Pvt. John McKee of Company K, eighteen, of St. Albans Township, Hancock County, was among those who did not make it aboard the boat. He died in the hospital at Louisville the day before.

The flotilla of transports headed downstream. "I enjoyed the ride very much," Chandler wrote in his diary. "The Ohio was grand. The banks were steep, nearly precipitous, formed mostly of lime stone. The river is high and still rising. [General] Gilbert comes along on the *St. Patrick.*"

McNeill enjoyed it less. "We already knew that our stay on the boat was destined to be very disagreeable," he wrote, "for after getting on the horses, mules, wagon(s) and baggage the chance for comfort was very much sircumscribed [circumscribed]. The men were packed in the cabin and on the decks so thick that he who got an undisturbed foot holt, was extremely fortunate; and added to this, the weather during all our stay on the boat, was extremely disagreeable, alternating from rain to cold. Part of the men had to sleep on the hurricane deck, and in fact every place they could find room to pile down, the attendant consequence of all which was a fearful decimation, by sickness, of our reg[iment]."

Their contrasting impressions of the trip were repeated the next day. Chandler: "We continued our way very pleasantly, this being a fine day. We arrived Shawnee Town about 7 ½ [7:30] and the sight of Illinois shore did us all good. As we continued our journey, the banks grew less precipitous. I was surprised to see so much timber land in Illinois. After the Wabash entered the Ohio, the latter became broader. It was very high, and many houses looked like they would soon be submerged. We arrived at Smithland at the mouth of the Cumberland about three in the afternoon. We stopped here to coal and await the arrival of the remaining fleet."

McNeill: "Made Smithland, at the mouth of the Cumberland, where we found awaiting our arrival six gun boats to convey us up the river." The Cumberland flowed north out of the Tennessee heartland, and the 78th's destination was now obvious; they were headed for Nashville. "We remained here till next morning, and at early dawn commenced the ascent of the deminutive [diminutive] Cumberland. The night we layed [laid] at the mouth of the river was intens[e]ly cold and was accompanied by a snow storm and next morning the ground was covered with snow three inches deep.

"The trip up was almost void of interest; the monotony, occasioned by nothing being seen but the wooded hills along the river, would sometimes be broken by some picture of nature, such as a towering cliff of sollid [solid] rock, still in nature's originality, and still untouched by mortal hands, and from the reigning solitude all along, except once in a greate while where the scene was broken by some lone habitation, and more rarely still, a dirty little vil[l]age striving for a place amid the seeming desolation, one would think that ages still would roll around and leave the scene unchanged."

Chandler again: "After we had coaled, we started up the Cumberland, which is an insignificant stream compared with the Ohio. It is quite narrow, with a swift current, consequently we did not make good headway. It is cold today, having snowed last night. Owing to some defect in the boiler we did not make as good time as the remaining boats, which passed us during the afternoon. Towards evening we saw a large flock of turkeys on shore at which the boys shot. We arrived at Dover along in the night, having passed Fort Donelson during the dark. I wish much to see it but can not. There was a fight here [Dover] today. The rebs were driven off."[22]

There had indeed been a fight that day at the little town of Dover. The 83rd Illinois, with somewhere between six hundred and eight hundred men, had driven off two brigades of cavalry under Confederate Maj. Gen. Joseph Wheeler, and evidence of the battle was visible even before the *Groesbeck* reached the town. "As we came up . . . we saw indications of an enemy ahead; such as burning bales of hay, floating down the river," McNeill recounted, "and this morning our apprehensions of an enemy ahead were verified by learning that a battle had been fought."

The men of the 78th were naturally curious to see the results of a battle where men on both sides had actually been killed or wounded, so "notwithstanding the stringent orders to prevent the men from leaving the boat, we found ourself, about ten in the morning, crossing the river in a skiff, to view the scenes, and horrors of a battlefield," McNeill wrote. "We passed up through the vil[l]age, which is situated on a hill and extends down the slope toward the river. The vil[l]age bore vivid marks of the blighting influences of war and of the more particular and immediate ravages of battle strife often repeated. We saw no signs of inhabitants except the soldiers who were occupying the deserted dwellings for various purposes.

"The houses were nearly all, more or less, racked by the iron and leaden hail that had, now, on two occasions like hurricane passed through them. The first object of battle horror that met our gase [gaze] was a fellow lying upon his back with his bowls [bowels] torn out by a canister shot from the seige gun, upon which we judged he was making a charge up the hill, on the crest of which the gun was posted. The next we came to was an object truly appalling; he lay but a few feet from the mouth of the 32-pounder, upon which he had rashly charged and ordered its surrender; the only answer he received was a full charge of grape which literally tore him in pieces; his horse lay by him in the same horribelly [horribly] mutilated form.

"We next ap[p]roached where a crowd had gathered around some object in the street and found it to be the body of a Rebel col[onel] . . . His clothing was almost entirely cut off him by curious trophy seakers [seekers]. The dead of our own forces awakened a different feeling than that which we looked upon the enemy, whom we thought had met a just reward. Our dead were collected in a room (12 in number) where they had the proper attention due a Christian and loyal soldier. Capt. E.P. Reed of the 83rd was killed, and decently placed in a metallic coffin, which he had purchased for a member of his company a short time before."[23]

Major Broaddus also "went over the river the day after we got here and saw some of the de[a]d rebels," he wrote to his wife. "I saw 14 in one pile. It was a pret[t]y hard-looking sight. Among them was one very youthful looking person, and it was thought by some that it was a woman and I am inclined to think it was a woman in men's clothes. Their [there] was 11, out of all that I saw, that was shot in the eye. They faught [fought] well."

Magie wrote his wife that he also toured the battlefield. "They had picked up the rebel dead and were burying them. I saw one pile of the butternuts in which I counted 23 dead bodies. I looked in a few of the houses and saw a number of the rebel wounded. Col. McNary of an Alabama regiment was one of the killed. I cut off a piece of his hair which I enclose to you, and which you may burn or throw away as you choose." One can only imagine Mary Magie's reaction when she received a lock of hair from the scalp of a dead rebel officer.

"The advance portion of our fleet arrived about an hour after the battle was over," Magie's letter continued. "The gun boats shelled the woods surrounding the town, immediately after their arrival. Whether there were any rebels remaining at that time I did not learn . . . There are now about 50 large steamboats, heavily loaded, lying here, and what they are waiting for I am not able to say."

Nobody knew whether Wheeler's defeated force was still in the neighborhood, so to defend against a possible attack, companies of the 78th took turns standing picket duty on the hurricane deck of the *Groesbeck*.

Chandler took up his pen again on February 5th. "Another day has passed and still this fleet remains stationary, giving the rebels good opportunity to fortify and attack us any where," he wrote. "It snowed all morning, which has made it disagreeable. The victory still increases. Eighty more dead rebels have been found. The cold night has done what our bullets could not do. What a horrible death!

"Nothing has been done to hasten our departure. We will soon be out of rations. This will be a cold night. If we remain here much longer many will be sick. This is a horrible place to place men. We could have marched to Nashville easily in comparison to this method of going."[24]

━━◆━━

It was foggy the next morning—too foggy for safe navigation on the river—but the fog gradually lifted and the *Groesbeck* and her consorts finally got under way. "All the fleet had now come up and soon we were puffing up the river, a grand, magnificent sight,"

McNeill chronicled. "None of those that have witnessed such a scene can imagine the grandeur of a large fleet of transports moving together, with banners streaming from each jackstaff, the decks lined with uniformed soldiers, bands discoursing pleasing airs, and the curling clouds of steam and the volumes of black smoke looming up all combined [to] form a grand sublime picture."

Van Vleck was less interested in the sight of the fleet than the scenery along the river. "The Cumberland river is a very beautiful stream," he wrote Patty. "It is high now so that the largest boats have crossed the shoals without difficulty, & nearly the whole length from the mouth to Nashville the farms come down to the water's edge. The banks do not overflow like the Ill[inois] & Miss[issippi] Rivers, neither are there so many bluffs along the river but excellent farming lands characterize the banks of the whole river, but like all other parts of the south that I have visited, the husbandry is very poor & the improvements are shocking bad. The white folks seem very scarce, & Negroes plenty.

"Our fleet consists of 56 transports & seven gunboats & about 30,000 men which will af[f]ord Gen'l. Rosecrans [who had replaced Buell] quite a reinforcement but in men we will lack the power of endurance because nearly all have been taken out of forts & comfortable winter quarters like our own, & will be in a poor plight to stand long & tedious marches. Many will be the poor fellows that will fall out by the way. We left all that were sick in the hospital at Louisville, some 40 or 50 of them, & there are now fully as many more that will have to be left at Nashville.

"The boat has been very much crowded & we did not look to the matter of ventillation as we ought until we all began to be sick & then we opened up. Until then it had not occurred to any what the matter was, but we all got better soon after the discovery . . . I don't mean to say that all the sickness has been occasioned by the want of ventillation, for exposure has had much to do with it. It has been very cold, and day before yesterday snowed all day, & many of the men could not be comfortably cared for under shelter, & nearly everybody aboard has a cold."

The *Groesbeck* arrived at Nashville about 5:00 p.m. on Saturday, February 7th. "This is the tenth day since we came aboard," Chandler wrote, and "the best day since we came aboard. The sun was bright and pleasant. The waves caused by the fleet long and silvery. The banks high, rocky and lofty covered with pines, etc., giving a grand and somber appearance." The boat dropped anchor opposite the city and the men aboard settled down as best they could to spend the night, hoping it would be their last aboard the cramped vessel.[25]

5

"The Rebels Are Still Crowding Us Pretty Closely"

FEBRUARY 8–MARCH 31, 1863

AT DAYLIGHT THE MORNING OF FEBRUARY 8TH, THE MEN ABOARD THE *JOHN H. Groesbeck* discovered there was no room in Nashville for them to land. They would have to stay on the boat until space finally became available.

The men of Company H got a temporary reprieve from shipboard life, but the occasion was solemn. They filed off the *Groesbeck* Monday morning, February 9th, to attend the burials of Pvts. Martin Ellis and John Pate, both thirty-four, who had died the day before—the former of "congestive chills" and the latter of "Erycipalis" (erysipelas, now recognized as a form of streptococcus infection). Both were sons of Dallas City who would not be going home again.

After the burials, the company returned to the *Groesbeck* and pitched in to help unload. They continued working after dark by the flickering light of torches until all the regiment's wagons and equipment had been unloaded. Even then no orders came for the men to disembark, so the weary soldiers trudged back aboard the steamer to spend yet another night.[1]

It was raining the next morning when the regiment finally got word to leave the *Groesbeck*. "We commenced our march from the levee about ten this morning, through the mud which was only about half knee-deep and mixed up to a very nice sloppy consistency which characterized the road all the way out," McNeill wrote. "We took the Franklin Pike and proceeded due south four miles, where we filed off to the right and camped on nice rolling ground in the woods, which would have made a pleasant camping place had the weather been otherwise than extremely inclement." The rain continued all night, but "we made our muddy *couches* a little more comfortable, by a supply of long reeds which we layed [laid] under us."

The men were not impressed by the city they saw on their way to the Franklin Pike. "Nashville is a mean dirty city with narrow dirty streets and there are many

69

women of ill repute about," Chandler wrote, although he failed to explain how he knew the women's repute. McNeill thought the city "did not equal in appearance what we in our imagination conceived of the wealth, beauty and grandeur of this once celebrated metropolis of Tennessee. However, we presume that *war* has had the effect of tarnishing this once boasted city. The streets are narrow and in some places irregular."

Van Vleck also was "greatly disappointed" in Nashville, but thought the state's capitol was "one of the finest buildings in the world. It excells all other state buildings & is set up on a high hill so that you can see its foundations from any part of the country round about." The countryside beyond the city impressed him, though, as "one of the most beautiful in the world." The war had left its cruel mark, however. "There is not a fence anywhere to be seen, and many of the magnificent residences have been abandoned, & all the shade trees cut down & the houses either left in charge of the Negroes or taken possession of by soldiers."

More than fifty men, including Chaplain Taylor, were left in hospitals at Nashville and many others were "complaining of colds & other camp disagreeables," Van Vleck wrote. "The Col. & Maj. are both quite unwell with colds. So it is with a great many of the officers & men." Dr. Thomas Jordan, the regimental surgeon, also was left behind, hobbled by a badly sprained ankle.[2]

After the 78th set up its muddy camp along the Franklin Pike, Major Broaddus returned to Nashville to visit his son, Thomas, who was among the sick. "The people about the city are mostly Secesh and they are getting punished good for their disloyalty by paying about four prices for everything they have to live on," he wrote to Martha. "Butter is selling at 50 cts. per lb. Syrup is wourth $2 to $2.50 per gallon, a[p]ples from 75 cts to $1 per dozen, and every thing else in proportion. My health is as good as usual except a very bad cold but am able for duty." He was still without a set of working teeth, however.

The regiment was "up and on the march" at 3:00 a.m. on Thursday, February 12th, McNeill recorded. "We learned we were ordered to Franklin, a town 16 miles distant which we reached at 3 in the afternoon. There were five other regiments besides our own and we were in the van. Soon after we started it began to rain and rained hard untill afternoon. We had, however, a splendid road and the only inconvenience from the rain was getting wet."

Earlier that day a division under command of Brig. Gen. Jefferson C. Davis, the slayer of "Bull" Nelson, had vacated Franklin and rebel cavalry had promptly moved in, so the troops marching toward Franklin were told to prepare for battle. The 125th Ohio was sent forward and drove the Confederates away, aided by a few shells from the 2nd Illinois Battery. "Onward we went untill we reached the suberbs [suburbs] of the town and then our regiment filed off into a pasture and stacked arms," McNeill wrote.

Later the 78th was directed to a field next to the Harpeth River, where it made camp. Two companies were detailed to stand picket. "We pityed [pitied] the boys who had to go on picket this evening, without having eaten anything since morning, except of the scant supply in their haversacks, but thought we were lucky not to be in their place," McNeill declared.[3]

"Franklin is said to be the most beautiful town in the south," Van Vleck told his wife. "I have not yet been in the town but expect to one of these days, as Gen'l. Gilbert gave me to understand this morning, that we would remain here for 'some time,' & you know how long that is. I think we will remain here until Gen'l. Granger gets his army corps organized & that will take a week or two. I hope it will take time enough to give us an opportunity to learn something of the drill, for most of the reg't. are very ignorant.

"We are temporarily brigaded with the 124th and the 113th Ohio, commanded by the ranking col. of the 124th, whose name is [Oliver Hazard] Payne," he wrote. "Col. Benneson would command if he was not under arrest. His case gets along very slowly. The charges were handed in to the general court martial, at Nashville, & he will be notified to appear for trial whenever the case is reached. I begin to think that Gilbert will not succeed in breaking him but he will try his very prettiest, & will spare no pains nor trouble nor exertion to accomplish that end, for he has taken a great dislike to him & intends to gratify his malice in that way."

The 78th Illinois would remain at Franklin until nearly the end of June. Much of that time was spent drilling—as acting commander, Van Vleck was determined to make up for all the opportunities the regiment had missed—or working on fortifications, including a work called Fort Granger on a bluff next to the Harpeth River.[4] There was also continual picket duty, frequent foraging expeditions, and other work details.

The days were long. General Gilbert reinstituted his order for the regiment to turn out in line of battle before sunrise, though he modified it slightly; instead of rousing the men at 3:00 a.m., as he had done back in Louisville, he now required them to fall in line at 5:30 a.m. There they stood, in rain or shine, for an hour. Breakfast followed, then guard mounting at 8:00 a.m. Unless it was at work on fortifications, the regiment would hold skirmish drill from 10:00 to 11:30, dinner at noon, battalion drill from 2:00 to 4:00 p.m., and dress parade at 5:00 p.m., followed by the evening meal. Men not assigned to picket or guard duty would then have the remainder of the evening free until lights out, but the officers kept busy studying or reciting the lessons they needed to learn to perform their duties.

For the most part, it was a monotonous existence, punctuated occasionally by brief moments of excitement caused by rebel forays. But as the days of winter lengthened into spring and the men of the 78th watched other regiments march through Franklin on their way to the front, they began wondering if their turn would ever come—or if their regiment had for some reason been found wanting by senior officers and was to be relegated permanently to the drudgery of daily drill and shoveling dirt in the seemingly endless construction of Fort Granger.

Some also began wondering whatever had become of their colonel.

At first the regiment slept on the ground without straw and without fires in their tents. The weather continued cold and wet and soon the 78th had 146 new cases of illness in addition to those still in the hospital at Nashville. Colonel Benneson was among the ill, suffering from dysentery or "bilious fever" as it was commonly called. Van Vleck sent him back to Nashville in an ambulance. "I hear nothing more of his trial," the lieutenant colonel wrote. "I wish it might be over with & he returned to his reg't."

The regiment also had been without mail since leaving Louisville and the regimental postmaster, Pvt. George Painter of Company I, was held to blame. "There has been so much dissatisfaction about Mr. Painter as postmaster that he was removed this morning [February 17th], and I was appointed in his place," James K. Magie wrote his wife. "In less than an hour I was promoted to the office of brigade postmaster." That made him responsible for mail delivery to the 113th and 124th Ohio regiments as well as the 78th. "This gives me the privilege of going out or coming in just as I please," he wrote. "I am also furnished a horse and I have the privilege of selling papers, envelopes, letter paper, &c, by which I can make from 30 to 50 dollars per month." He was also exempt from the new order requiring the regiment to turn out under arms at 5:30 every morning, so while the other men got up, Magie was able to sleep until breakfast.[5]

The new order soon led to a confrontation between Van Vleck and General Gilbert. The general "ordered Capt. Joseph to sleep in the guard house because he was five minutes too late in the morning in getting his company out on parade," Van Vleck told Patty. "We are required to go out on parade, armed and equipped, *ready* for the march, every morning at 5 ½ o'cl'k. at the sound of the bugle at Gilbert's head quarters, a mile away, & are not allowed to make any noise, not to beat the drum nor anything else, but must awake by the sound of the bugle. Tuesday morning [February 17th] it rained hard all the morning, & nobody awoke until quite late, & we then hurried out as fast as possible, but Capt. Joseph and Lieut. Brown, of Co's. G & A respectively, were about five minutes behind the rest when Gilbert's Inspt [inspector]. Gen'l. came up & ordered the two delinquent companies on extra duty & ordered their commanders under arrest & to report to Gilbert's H'd. Qtrs. immediately."

There they "were treated with greatest indignity" and made to stand outside in the rain. Gilbert finally ordered them to remain under arrest for twenty-four hours and spend the night in the brigade guard house. "Captain Joseph very properly declined going," Van Vleck wrote, "& the next morning I was waited on by the Inspector Gen'l. to know why Capt. Joseph didn't sleep in the guard tent, & I told him I supposed he prefer[r]ed to sleep in his own tent. He replied that he was ordered to sleep in the guard tent & I told him that no body had any authority to issue such an order & that no such orders would be respected by the officers of this reg't. & he replied 'that he should go in to the guard tent that night, if it took the whole command to put him there.' I told him if he was put there by an overpowering force there would be a 'rumpus' & he rode off in great rage & I was soon ordered before the general.

"I went & found him much excited. He wanted to know if I intended to *resist* his orders. I told him *not* & he wanted to know if this reg't. would obey orders. I told him we would if they were *legal* but that he nor any body else had a right to send one of my captains to the guard house and that no such orders would be obeyed except at the point of the bayonet, that such an order was an indignity alike to every officer in the reg't. & would be resented as such. He *knew* I was in earnest & he began to cool off, & finally to back down, & said he would modify the order & send it to me in writing.

"Towards night it came, requiring Captain Joseph 'to report at bedtime to Col. Payne [the brigade commander] & to *sleep with the officer of the guard if Colonel Payne should so direct.*' Capt. Joseph accordingly went to Col. Payne & was informed by him that Gen. Gilbert had directed that he might go back to his *own* quarters & sleep, & not be required to sleep even with the *officer of the guard.* Did you ever hear of a more complete backdown?

"I have used my whole sheet telling you about this little fracus [fracas], but I have done it to show you some of our numerous trials, & to let you see that we don't propose to be tread in the dirt without some good reason for it. I confess I felt a little vicious & was ready to suffer consequences, let them be never so terrible, but I was determined, come what would, *never* to submit to such an outrage."

Almost as an afterthought, Van Vleck added that the regiment now had "*300* sick out of the 8 companies left us. I am about the only officer that is quite well."[6]

Magie, meanwhile, had wasted no time consolidating his new position as postmaster. He went to Nashville the day after his appointment, found the regiment's accumulated mail, and brought it back to Franklin. "The mail came today and an immense one," Chandler wrote. The mail delivery was a big boost to morale, which helped men stomach the news later that day that the regiment was being divided into two shifts to alternate an hour at a time digging fortifications.

A day later, February 19th, one of the regiment's many sick, Pvt. Samuel R. Driver, 22, of Company A, succumbed to his illness.

Magie brought another mail on the 20th, and the consensus was that he was doing a fine job as postmaster. He had established a routine and told his wife about it in a letter written at Nashville: "I come up here to Nashville each alternate day [to fetch mail] and go back to Franklin early next morning," he said. "I have a good little pony that Co. D captured from the rebels at Boston, Ky. I have exclusive use of the horse . . . I have a good chance of making some money. I buy about a hundred papers each day at 5 cts. and sell for 10 cts. If I don't have to move soon I shall make a good thing out of my postmastership."

Magie's diligence soon won him promotion to division postmaster, along with the privilege of riding the train between Franklin and Nashville. "I leave Franklin on the cars every afternoon at 4 o'clock and leave Nashville every morning at 7 o'clock," he wrote Mary. "I have to pay a dollar per night in Nashville for supper, breakfast and lodging. The government however allows me 75 cts per day for rations and 40 cts extra per day for [word illegible]. I have however the monopoly of selling newspapers. I pay 4 ½ cts a piece and sell for 10 cts. I think I will be able hereafter to sell about 200 per day which will net me $11 per day profits.

"I think this is too good a thing to last long . . . but if I can keep the position of division postmaster a month I know I can make a clear one hundred dollars if not more. I also sell postage stamps for a dime and do errands for the different regiments in Nashville, such as buying their rubber blankets and many other articles, on which I make the usual profit. I have got now about $40 by me, and if I prosper for a month to come as I hope to I will send you about the middle of March $50." Money was important to Magie. He was still in debt from his purchase of the *Macomb Journal*, and he needed money to pay for an operation needed by his son, Eddy, who had a foot problem.

"I had some interesting adventures on my last trip on horseback to Nashville," Magie wrote. "There are many splendid residences all the way from here to Nashville, but there are very few white persons visible, and little niggers however in abundance. But to my adventures: I was just nearing the top of a hill when I suddenly discovered about half a dozen butternuts, all sitting down by the roadside. It was too late for me to turn back if they should have evil designs upon me so I rode up to them with all the confidence and authority of a general commanding. I asked them what they were doing there. You must know that I felt a little streaked, for I couldn't imagine why they were there, apparently hidden unless they had evil designs upon me. They told me they had been sent out from Nashville to put up telegraph poles. They were native laborers in homespun clothes, and looked just like the rebels that we captured. It was some relief to me and I passed on."

Then he told his wife about another "adventure"—but first warned her not to read his letter out loud to anyone. "I was galloping along in a secluded portion of the road when I discovered something that looked like calico in a niche formed by what they call a crook fence. I soon perceived clearly the object of my gaze. There was a man and a woman in a horizontal position—the man uppermost.

"I got within about four rods before they discovered me. The pair jumped instanter, and a more foolish looking couple I never saw. The man began to ask questions about his regiment—said that he and his *wife* had got left behind, and they had set down to rest."[7]

<hr>

Another soldier from the 78th, Private Lindorft Butts, twenty-one, of Company F, died of illness at Nashville February 22nd. Two days later, Pvt. John Reed, twenty-two, of Company K, died at Franklin.

"Col. Benneson has not had his tryal [trial] yet," Broaddus wrote on February 25th. "I doo not know whether they will doo any thing with him or not. We are very mutch in hopes that we will get rid of Gilbert."

Magie also wrote home on the 25th, telling his wife what it was like to ride the train from Franklin to Nashville to pick up the mail. "The locomotive and train is [run] altogether by soldiers," he wrote. "We burn [fence] rails for fuel. Every train carrys one company for guard. When we get short of wood we stop near a good fence and a dozen or twenty boys soon have a large pile of rails cut up into convenient lengths.

"It is awful to see the devastation of this war. The soldiers will pull off the weather boards [of houses] for fuel when they are satisfied the owner is a rebel. There is plenty of timber or green wood hereabouts, but the soldiers would rather have *dry* wood, and it makes no difference whether it is some nicely painted ornamental piece around a rich man's door yard, or fence rails around a pig pen—it is all the same."[8]

On February 27th, Van Vleck updated his wife on the regiment's situation: "I hear nothing as yet from Col. Benneson's case," he wrote. "They can keep him under arrest only two days longer without a trial. He will then be entitled to go back to his reg't. & take command, which I hope he will do."

The regiment suffered another loss next day when Pvt. William T. Walker, thirty-nine, of Company A, died at Nashville.

<hr>

Sunday, March 1st, was beautiful and springlike, but it was not a day of rest because the men were called again to work on fortifications, which they did until noon. They expected to resume work after the noon meal, "but a scare got up in camp that we were going to have a fight and we did not work anymore," McNeill wrote in his journal. The "scare" occurred when rebel skirmishers drove in federal pickets, but it was over quickly and did not amount to anything. Such incidents were becoming an almost daily occurrence.

Magie, meanwhile, was beginning to worry about his position as postmaster even as the dollar signs in his eyes were growing larger. "I am fearful all the time that some untoward event will happen to break in upon my present arrangements," he wrote his wife. "If I can hold my position, and have the monopoly of the express and newspaper business for 100 days, I can send you home $1,000, which will buy us a snug little house.

"You need not tell the soldiers' families how much I am making, for I don't let them [the soldiers] know that I am making so much, for it might create jealousies, or the like. The feeling so far is high in my favor. They get their mail regularly, rain or shine."

Odell also wrote home that day, noting that because of all the sickness in the regiment, the 78th was barely able to muster 350 men fit for duty. Odell had been ill himself, but thought he would "soon be as hearty as ever."[9]

Batchelor was part of a foraging expedition on March 2nd. "Got 39 loads corn, six loads hay," he wrote. Back in camp there were apprehensions of another attack. "The pickets reported skirmishing in front," McNeill wrote, "and that our cavalry had taken several rebels prisoners, which latter was confirmed by several being brought into camp. In consequence of the anticipated attack, we did nothing all day."

Magie was in Nashville that day, picking up mail as usual. "I am still running the mail between here and Franklin, and I average about eight dollars per day profit," he wrote Mary. "As long as I am doing so well I shall content myself with being absent from you, knowing that I am gaining something to add to our future comfort.

"The rebels are still crowding us pretty closely at Franklin. We have some skirmishing every day, and we are making some few captures. I have had frequent opportunities of conversing with some of these rebels. A portion of them are heartily sick of the rebellion, while others talk pretty saucy. If a battle comes off, I don't think I will be able to take a part, as in my present business I have no business with a gun."[10]

Batchelor went foraging again March 4th, but this time it was a big operation with a train of eighty wagons accompanied by five regiments of infantry, a cavalry force, and an artillery battery. "We had a pretty sharp scrim[m]age with the Rebels," Batchelor wrote. "Lasted all the afternoon. Supposed about 12 or 15 Rebels killed. Drove Rebels 2 ½ miles. Our loss slight."

Back in camp, Broaddus told his wife in a gossipy letter that his nephew, Private Bob Laughlin of Company I, was "sick with the mumps but presume he will bee abel [able] to cook again in a few days [Laughlin had been cooking for the colonel]." He sent the letter with 1st Lt. Matthew Henry of Company E, who had resigned and was starting for home.[11]

Van Vleck also gave Lieutenant Henry a letter to take home. "We had reinforcements to the extent of two brigades yesterday," he wrote Patty, "so that we now have here, 13 reg'ts. of Inft. [infantry], 3 or 4 reg'ts. [of] cavalry & 3 batteries, & have built quite forminable [formidable] fortifications on both sides the river & the rebels must not come with less than 25 or 30 thousand men, expecting to accomplish anything." He also admitted having felt unwell for several days, "but am better again now."

Back in Louisville, where he had been left in a hospital, Pvt. Azariah Frazelle of Company E, aged thirty-two or thirty-three, died of disease March 4th.[12]

The eighty-wagon foraging expedition, under command of Col. John Coburn of the 33rd Indiana Volunteer Infantry Regiment, moved out again the next day toward a place called Thompson's Station, about eight miles south of Franklin. There Coburn blundered into Confederate Maj. Gen. Earl Van Dorn's cavalry and a brisk fight broke out. Dismounted cavalry under rebel Brig. Gen. "Red" Jackson made a frontal attack on Coburn while a division of mounted cavalry under Brig. Gen. Nathan Bedford Forrest moved around his flank and got into his rear. Nearly surrounded, low on ammunition, and "convinced that a massacre would ensue," Coburn surrendered. More than a thousand men from the 33rd and 85th Indiana, the 19th Michigan, and the 22nd Wisconsin became prisoners. The 124th Ohio, which had been held in reserve to protect the foraging train, was not involved in the action and escaped capture.[13]

The men of the 78th could hear the sounds of battle but again did not participate. "We were left idle spectators of the roar of the tumult, with the 113th Ohio untill noon of today, and then, but unfortunately when too late, were ordered out," McNeill wrote. "We went out about a mile and a half, on the Columbia Pike and formed in line of battle. The 124th Ohio, which had been out, but did not take part in the battle, soon returned and joined us . . . We awaited for the approach of the enemy . . . but fortunately nothing appeared but the broken, thin[n]ed ranks of our defeated columns; victims to miss management [mismanagement] and consequent defeat.

"After all of our strug[g]ling forces had gone by, and we had concluded that the enemy were satisfied with what they had accomplished, and were not intending to follow up, [we] started back to camp leaving the [1st Illinois] Battery unprotected, where it remained until night, when, Gilbert ordered it in, remarking 'he had forgotten it.' Had the enemy come on, they would have had no trouble in capturing the whole battery; thus would have added another favor to the many already given them.

"A heavey detail was made from our regiment, at night, to fell timber on two points east of camp. We worked hard all night thinking it would add to our security, and when morning came we had made clear the two hills, of the jiant [giant] monarchs of the forest. We were thus on the allert for an attack was expected next day."[14]

Trainloads of reinforcements began arriving in Franklin before the night was over and continued coming in all the next day under a torrential rainfall. The expected attack did not materialize, giving the troops time to start assessing blame for the defeat. Major Broaddus thought he knew who was to blame: "Dear Wife," he wrote, "we got badly whip[p]ed [yesterday]. Most of four reg'ts was taken pris[o]ner after giveing them [the rebels] a very hard fight and the loss must have bin very heavey, as they faught hand to hand for some time . . . If we had bin sent out to their relief we could have extricated them with out any difficulty. Some of the officers say that they sent three messengers to [General] Gilbert for reinforsements but he sais [says] he did not get the dispatch. But he did know that their [there] was heavey fighting going on, for we could hear muskatrey [musketry] very plainly.

"Gen. Granger and Gen. Beard [Baird] are here and I am in hopes as Gen. Gilbert has not bin confirmed he will slink out of sight . . . I must close as my sheat is about full."[15] Absalom Baird, a native of Washington, Pennsylvania, was a West Point graduate who had served in the Peninsula Campaign before being appointed a brigadier general of volunteers in the Army of the Ohio.

It remained quiet the next day, but on Sunday, March 8th, the 78th received orders to be ready to march early next morning "as a forward movement was ordered and we expected to have the satisfaction of accompanying the expedition this time," McNeill wrote. Odell wrote home that the regiment was "expecting to go out a rebel hunting tomorrow." It looked as if the 78th was finally going to get a chance to see some real action, and the anticipation expressed by McNeill and Odell was doubtless shared by most of the regiment. Van Vleck, however, was an exception. "I am sorry that Col. Benneson is not here to take charge of the reg't.," he confided to his wife. "I dread the responsibility of taking so many men into a fight, but know of no way, but to rely in the strength of Him who is Ruler of us all, & to go boldly forward & do my duty as best I can."

He was also unhappy with the weather. "It rains all the time," he said. "Last night and the night before, it rained as hard as I ever knew it to, so that most of the tents were but little use, not turning the water, & the mud is very deep every where. Is it any wonder the men are sick?"

A lot of men were sick, all right, but the order for the regiment to move had a sudden beneficial effect on their health. "When the boys thought their [there] was a prospect of getting in to a fight they got well fast and more reported for duty than common," Broaddus observed.[16]

Yet it was all for naught, for when the movement south began on Monday morning, the 78th again was ordered to stay behind. "The troops were moving early this morning and we were again allowed the privilege of being spectators, merely, and have the duty of guarding the camp assigned us," McNeill recorded. That was not their only duty; they were also expected to continue working on fortifications.[17]

That night it began raining again and continued through the next day and into the following night, "which made us appreciate our good luck in being left behind in camp," McNeill wrote, "but we pityed [pitied] the poor fellows who had gone out front without tents to protect them from the descending torrents. No fighting in front yet." In fact, the rebel force had fallen back and the Union advance met little or no resistance.

On the 12th news came that Van Dorn's Confederate troops had retreated across the Duck River and the force that had been sent after them was returning to Franklin. General Gilbert came with them. "I saw General Gilbert kick a soldier to day," Batchelor wrote in his diary. "I wish the soldier had shot him. I *doo*."

On the morning of the 14th, the men of the 78th were ordered "to have our boots blacked, clothing, etc., in good order for division inspection at 2 o'clock," McNeill wrote. "So at the appointed time we came out all gay and shining to try the test of a critical inspection. We crossed the river and went out a mile on the pike and were drawn up in an old field.

"Soon Gen. Granger made his appearance, brilliantly equip[p]ed and followed by a cavalcade, consisting of his staff, body guard etc. After he rode along our lines we were marched in *grand review* before him. The sun shone out . . . and we suffered much from heat and thirst. Aside from the fatigue, heat, etc., it was an occasion well worthy [of] attention to see a large army drawn up in line, or marching by column of company with flags and banners displayed, music discoursing pleasing airs at the head of each regiment, and long lines of cavalry and batteries of artillery, to any one but a soldier, who sees such almost daily, is a grand thing."

Van Vleck didn't think so. "Yesterday we had a grand review of all the troops here, before Maj. Gen'l. Gordon Granger," he wrote Patty. "There were some 10,000 or 12,000 troops reviewed & of course made a very fine appearance & that is all there was of it. A great show of fine clothes. A humbug that ought to be abolished, for surely this is not the time for display of tinsel & broadcloth.

"Still it has a moral effect in discovering to us the horrors of war, if we reflect that all that fine body of men are but food for the cannon & the musket, & remember that they may at any hour be confronted by even a greater body of men pitted against them in deadly strife & thousands of the brave fellows made to bite the dust & left to be burried with their mangled limbs by careless and unfeeling strangers, no dear ones near to lament their loss, nor to administer consolation in the dying hour. And thousands of others who must languish for weeks and months in the loathsome hospitals with mangled or disseevered limbs, with no friends to minister to their wants & sufferings, who will care for them above the thousands of others, who are groaning and dying around them.

"Such is war. . . ."

Changing subjects, Van Vleck reported that Colonel Benneson "is still [feeling] quite poorly. His time of arrest has expired & Gilbert has never filed any charges against him. He expects to return to the reg't. this week & to assume command, though he talks strongly of resigning on Gilbert's account, but guess he will become reconciled after a while."[18]

For most of the regiment, Sunday the 15th was "truly a day of rest; not even so much as company inspection," McNeill wrote happily. "The sun too was shining out [a] lot and joined to the rest [it] was a very lazy day." Batchelor went to church in Franklin.

The day wasn't peaceful for Van Vleck, however. "I had another little encounter with Gen'l. Gilbert," he wrote his wife. "Saturday night I rec'd a written order from Gen'l. Gilbert to march all my commissioned officers to his quarters for sword drill 'every day.' Next day was Sunday and I did not expect to drill, but the officers of all the other reg'ts. went up and drilled without the 78th. Shortly afterwards I was ordered to report myself to Gen'l. Gilbert, which I did. He wanted to know if I & my officers were at the drill. I told him they were not. He wished to know why they were not. I told him it was Sunday.

"He wanted to know if I had rec'd. his order. I told him I had. He asked if that didn't say that I must drill 'every day.' I told him it did. 'Well,' says he, 'isn't Sunday a day?' I replied, 'It's no day for drill, Gen'l.'

"'But,' said he, 'the order makes no exceptions & should have been obeyed.' I replied that many of my officers were religious men & did not propose to drill on the Sabbath. He replied that they might have to do worse. I told him they would do worse when they were compelled to. He answered that time was short & every minute ought to be improved. I told him that we were ready to do our whole duty at all times & to do all *necessary* work on the Sabbath, but I did not believe that it was necessary to drill on the Sabbath when there were six days in the week for that business.

"He hesitated and stammered & turned several colors & finally replied, 'Colonel, I believe you have my idea, better than I have myself. *I didn't think about it being Sunday.*' Then calling to his adjutant he said, 'Mr. Speed, you send around to the different reg'ts. a modification of that drill order, *excepting Sundays.*' Said I, 'Have you any further business with me, Gen'l.?' 'Nothing further,' & I returned to my tent wondering how such pusillanimous specimens of humanity ever attain to the command of a division of an army of Americans. Surely but *few* need doubt their capacity to command a thousand men, so long as such generals are counted capable of commanding ten thousand.

"Thus the second time I have had the *proud* satisfaction of standing before my commanding general, & making him back square down from his positions of wrong and tyranny, and have then seen him try to sneak away from the positions he had taken like a whipped spaniel.

"Col. Benneson is still away & has had no trial. I expect him here in a few days, as he is released from arrest but still has the charges hanging over him."[19]

The 78th and other regiments resumed work on the fortifications at Franklin on March 16th. "Since Gen Granger has taken command, the work is being done more vigorously," McNeill wrote, "and a part of the work Gilbert had done he has abandoned, and the work begins now, to assume the appearance of a fortification. When completed it will be a very strong position; being situated on the crest of a hill . . . From any portion of the works a range for miles can be had for artil[l]ery."[20]

The March 16th entry was the last in McNeill's journal. He offered no explanation for the abrupt ending. His service record shows he remained with the 78th another three months before being discharged June 16, 1863, for unspecified reasons.

Next day the regiment received the unhappy news of the death of another man who been left in the hospital at Nashville. The victim was Pvt. John Davis, twenty-two, of Company A, whose home was Birmingham, Schuyler County.

Batchelor "went forraging" on the 19th and 20th, but his diary does not mention a skirmish that took place on the 19th. Broaddus had the details: "We had a little skirmish between the cavalry out in front yesterday and one capt[ain] and man of our forse [force] were killed and three or four wounded," he wrote. "We captured three pris[o]ners and drove the rebels off. I doo not know whether we killed any of them or not. Their pickets are about ten miles off. We are fortifying this place as fast as posable [possible] and making very strong earth works."

He also told Martha that their son, Thomas, had recovered from his illness and returned from Nashville "looking pret[t]y well." After a week of fine weather, it was threatening to rain, but "the reg't. has drawn gum blankets for the men so we will bee in a mutch better fix for the rain."

Magie, meanwhile, had hit a snag in his continuing quest to get rich. "I don't know as I shall have an opportunity to make much more money," he wrote his wife. "A government mail agent has now been appointed and he brings out all the mail for this place. I suppose I can continue to keep up a little speculation by which I can make one or two dollars a day, and perhaps more. The boys are now making preparations to express home their overcoats, extra blankets, &c., and they will employ me to see to it, by which I expect to make a few dollars."[21]

The regiment lost another man March 20th. Pvt. George W. Swan, twenty-two, of Company K, a resident of Keene Township, Adams County, died at Nashville.

Since there was no sword drill for officers on Sunday, March 22nd, they had time to write letters. Broaddus wrote to his son, Reuben: "We had agood old fashion[ed] surmon [sermon] (Methodist) to day, and it made me think of home. The preacher belonged to an Ohio reg't. and he was a first rate preacher. Our chapl[a]in is a very good man, but he has very poor health and does not preach very often, but we like him very mutch. . . .

"Our cavalrey have a skirmish al most every day with the rebels. Some times we drive them and then again they drive us. I suppose turn about is fare [fair] play. We are incamped on a hill, and the country around is some what broken and the camps are stre[t]ched as fare [far] as the eye can reach, and at night it looks very pret[t]y. Looks like a large city illumminated when the camp fires are li[gh]ted."

Van Vleck wrote to his wife and daughter. "A general court-martial has been ordered to begin its sessions here tomorrow for the trial of several person[s], including Col. Benneson," he said. "Gen'l. Baird is the president of the board & I am sorry to say that I am also a member of the board, but hope to be excused from sitting in judgment in the case of my colonel. The duties of the court will doubtless occupy several weeks of my time, which I very much dislike."

He reported that the chaplain's health had improved, "but I begin to fear he will not stand it much longer, he cannot get rid of his cough, which I fear is taking the form of consumption. He also fears it. He is a good man, need not fear to die, & if it is God's will he may well rejoice when he is summoned home."

Enlisted men had time to write letters, too. Magie told his wife that his prospects seemed to be withering: "I believe I wrote you that my newspaper speculations have been sadly interfered with. I have things now arranged so that I make about three dollars a day, but I am set back by an overstock some days so that I lose a dollar or two."

Odell described his surroundings to his family: "I look around me—I see the green grass, I see the peeling brook, the pure living water gushing forth from the earth," he wrote. "I look where the farmer sowed his wheat last fall, and where from those noble trees he gathered so much delicious fruit—and . . . it is checkered over with soldier tents, mules, wagons, artillery—the fence is gone—the orchard is cut down—and in some cases, the houses have been torn to the ground . . . When I lift my eyes I see soldiers, teams, darkies, moving in every direction. This is indeed a fine country, and was it not for the curse of African slavery, and the war which has grown out of it, I would love to have you down here. . . ."[22]

Colonel Benneson returned to Franklin March 23rd, apparently restored to good health. He had been released from arrest because he was not tried within the required length of time, though the charges against him were still pending. As senior colonel present, he took command of the brigade. Van Vleck was on court-martial duty, so Major Broaddus took temporary command of the regiment. The major reported delivery of several thirty-two-pound rifled cannon, with more expected. "Then we [will] have three batries [batteries] of field peices and if the enemy should come we can give them a warm reseption," he told his wife.

Magie was responding rather defensively to something his wife, Mary, had told him in a letter. "You say Mrs. Clark [apparently an acquaintance] says if there is any fighting I am obliged to take a gun. I am obliged to obey orders, but it is not the rule to put men on detached service, as I am, in the ranks. If there is any fighting to be done I may take a gun and do my share, but it will be at my own option. I will never play the sneak or coward, or run unnecessarily in danger. If a battle comes off there is nothing to hinder me from going out of all danger if I want to as I have passes to go outside the lines when I please. I am subject to no roll call, am perfectly independent—my duties are simply to see that the regiments get their mails promptly and in good time, and that the mails go out as promptly."[23]

On March 25th, Dr. Elihu McIntire, the Dallas City physician who was first assistant surgeon of the regiment, submitted his resignation for reasons of unspecified disability. With Dr. Jordan, the chief surgeon, still hobbled by a sprained ankle, that left Dr. Samuel Moss as the only able-bodied surgeon left to administer to the needs of the 78th.

Of more immediate importance, however, was the fact that a rebel cavalry force had circled behind the Union position at Franklin, cut the telegraph line to Nashville, burned a railroad bridge, and captured a wagon train and a number of prisoners, mostly remnants of the unfortunate brigade that had earlier suffered defeat at Thompson's Station. Federal cavalry tracked the rebels, recaptured the wagon train, and took some Confederate prisoners in turn. The 78th and other regiments were ordered into battle line during the night, but all remained quiet in Franklin.

It was an especially bad week for Company A of the 78th, which lost three men. Pvt. Hiram Scott, aged forty-three or forty-four, died in a hospital at Nashville on March 27th. Next day Pvt. John E. Reed, twenty-one, also died at Nashville and Pvt. Shepard Graham, also twenty-one, died at Franklin. Scott and Graham were both from Birmingham, Schuyler County; Reed was a resident of Brooklyn, St. Clair County.

Van Vleck had spent the week listening to apparently endless court-martial testimony. "We have been ever since Monday noon trying one case and are not yet through with the witnesses for the prosecution, & there are 46 witnesses for the defense," he wrote Patty on March 28th. "There are 30 cases to look after besides this, so that I have got a permanent berth so long as we remain here." The charges against Colonel

Benneson "have been filed for his trial in this court; but as many of us are of inferior rank to him, he will not be compelled to stand trail before us & I doubt whether he will choose to be tried.

"I know Gen'l. Gilbert is afraid of the court, because we are made [up] of Western men, & [he] is flattering the Col. with a good many promises to persuade him from being tried by this court. But at the same time, he has told others that he hated the very sight of the Col. [and] didn't think the Col. ought to be tried by this court because some of its members were of inferior rank to him . . . The Col. is very easily flattered & I presume will be induced to waite for a trial until Gen'l. Gilbert gets a court called to suit him & then the poor Col. will wake up to a sense of his situation."

That night brought a torrential rainstorm. "I was sleeping with a man named McClellan [there were four McClellans on the 78th's roster]," Magie wrote his wife. "We had that day moved our camp about a quarter mile and on a sloping ground. Mac and I had cut two logs about 8 feet long, and on these logs we placed boards across and then laid our blankets on the boards or slats and this made a comfortable bed. During this heavy rain a large stream of water ran right between our logs and went dashing on through the tent.

"I was awake enough to know it was a powerful rain, but I didn't know that the water was five or six inches deep in the tent. I had hung up my coat and vest, but my pants lay at the foot of the bed. In the morning I found my pants had floated and [were] almost buried in the mud. In the seat there was about 15 pounds of gravel. I have borrowed another pair and have put the pants out to wash this morning and have put on my white shirt probably for the last time, as it has now got pretty thin."

He added the latest camp gossip: "Lieut. McCandless in Co. I has sent in his resignation and there begins to be much speculation respecting his successor." As for Colonel Benneson, he "is very kind to me. I am better suited with my present position that I would be with a lieutenancy."

Presumably having gotten all the gravel out of his pants, Magie wrote again a day later to say the weather had greatly improved. "This morning was a clear, gusty morning. The sun shines out beautifully and the birds sing merrily and it is growing warmer every moment. We will send our box, containing overcoats, etc., home this week."[24]

Two more men were stricken from the roster of the 78th on the last two days of March. Sgt. Charles A. Smith, twenty-two, of Company K, a Quincy resident, died at Nashville on the 30th. Pvt. Stephen Avery of Company A was discharged as disabled on the 31st.

"The Government Has Commenced Giving Us a Few Pickles"

April 1–May 31, 1863

COLONEL BENNESON WAS JUBILANT. HE HAD SENT A TELEGRAM TO THE WAR Department in Washington, D.C., asking whether Gilbert ever had been confirmed by the US Senate as a brigadier general. The answer had come late in the evening of March 31st: "Chas C. Gilbert was *not* confirmed as Brigadier General," the telegram said. "His rank is a Captain in the 1st Reg't. of US Infantry." It was signed, "E. M. Stanton, Sec. of War."

Benneson couldn't wait to share the news. But it was April Fools' Day—a tradition dating long before the Civil War—so he probably had to show the telegram to convince others it wasn't a joke. However he did it, the word spread like wildfire, and soon every officer in camp had heard about the telegram, almost certainly including General Gilbert himself.

The news triggered celebrations. "There was a general Jubilee, a wide expression of joy, & had there been anything ardent to be had [to drink], I think there would have been a high old time in camp," Van Vleck wrote Patty. "'*The Captain*' has not yet rec'd. official information of the fact, but no doubt he will in a few days, & will then take his departure from his *much loved & very loving* flock."

The celebrations were premature. The telegram changed nothing. Gilbert still had not been formally divested of his rank or command. He still wore a star on each shoulder and for the time being at least he was still Benneson's superior officer. Relations between the two had already deteriorated badly; now they were certain to become even worse.

The rancor between the two began escalating the day after Benneson returned to Franklin and took command of the brigade. When rebels cut the telegraph line to Nashville, Gilbert had ordered out all the regiments in the brigade, except the 78th, which again was left behind, and had issued the orders directly to the regimental commanders, without going through Benneson. This, as Van Vleck later noted, was a gross insult, but Benneson, "very much to the mortification of us all, pocketed the insult without complaint."

A few days later "the Col. woke up and very much to his surprise he found that he was the only man (able to travel) left in camp, the whole command, including his brigade, had been sent out during the night on an expedition without his having the least intimation of it, under command of Col. Payne (a young man 23 years of age)," Van Vleck wrote.

"Of course this was more than any human could stand. Accordingly as soon as we got in, he [Benneson] called on me to show me a letter written by him directed to General Granger, in which he set forth his *last* grievance & the fact that Gilbert is only a capt., & positively refused to obey another order from him . . . [But] Gilbert soon tested him by sending the ordinary order for daily details for duty, & the Col. refused to obey. The only course for Gilbert, if he is what he *pretends* to be, was to arrest the Col. for disobedience of orders. But instead of doing this, he got *Granger* to issue the order for the details—a plain confession that *he* had no right to issue orders or that the Col. was under no obligations to obey *his* orders."

Next day Gilbert issued an order relieving Col. Benneson from brigade command "on account of *feeble health*," and placing Colonel Payne—Benneson's junior—in command. "Imagine our mortification and disgust when the Col. [Benneson] expressed himself satisfied to obey the last order of Gilbert," Van Vleck wrote—"& yet refused to take command of the reg't.

"He is thus left without anything in the world to do, but to eat, sleep, & draw his pay, *& he is satisfied* . . . Such a complete & disgraceful back down I never have seen, it surprises & disgusts every body. It is a plain confession of cowardice and imbecility. It shows a desire to be relieved of any command or responsibility. He [Benneson] is satisfied to compell others not only to do *his* duties, while *he* draws the pay, but to share his disgrace & the thousand discomfitures that a vindictive general can heap upon a hated & disgusted & vanquished inferior and his subordinates, while the power of redress is in his hands & all the rest of us are powerless.

"To all intents & purposes it is a voluntary arrest. You can immagine, knowing me as well as you do, how such an unmanly & disgraceful surrender of a conflict in which I was interested would effect [affect] me, & you can immagine how it would effect [affect] the Maj. [Broaddus], who is the very soul of honor & manhood. I told the Col. in so many words that I would rather be a 'Yellow Dog,' & belong to Gilbert than to occupy his position. And so I would. I shall never hereafter be satisfied to go in to a fight under him, after such a display of the most dastardly cowardice. But I have no fear of being called on to do so. He will never be *well* enough to command the reg't. *in time of a fight.*"[1]

All this occurred before Benneson sent his telegram to the War Department and elicited the response that was sure to infuriate Gilbert even further. While Benneson probably didn't realize it, he also had doomed any aspirations he might still have had for promotion. Such an overt display of disloyalty to a superior officer—even one who might have it coming—would surely not go unnoticed by other senior officers, especially West Pointers. Benneson had made himself a marked man.

If there was such a thing as an April Fool, he was it.

⸻

While these events transpired, Van Vleck remained on court-martial duty and Broaddus commanded the regiment. He kept the men busy with drill, rifle practice, and preparations for inspection. His son, Thomas, was acting as Colonel Benneson's orderly, a job he liked because, in his father's words, "it is mutch easier than standing guard." It was easy because Benneson had hardly anything for him to do.[2]

Broaddus had the regiment practicing "shooting at a mark every day," Odell wrote his family. "There is to be a silver medal given to the best marksman in each Co. Monday." Odell's Company G, however, lost two of its officers April 2nd when Capt. Jacob F. Joseph and 2nd Lt. Pleasant M. Herndon resigned, the latter for reasons of ill health. Joseph's place would be taken by 1st Lt. Thomas L. Howden, who would be promoted captain before the month was out. Tobias E. Butler of Camp Point, Adams County, who had enlisted as a private, would be promoted to first lieutenant to replace Howden.

Dr. Jordan, the regimental surgeon, also had resigned "on account of his lameness." The doctor was still on crutches from a severe ankle sprain he had suffered stumbling over a cobblestone at New Haven.

On April 3rd Broaddus climbed to the top of Roper's Knob, the dominant topographical feature near Franklin and site of an army signal station. "It is several hundred feet from its base to its top," he wrote Martha. "I had a field glass and I had a fine view of the surrounding country. I believe I have told you that this is [the] pret[t]iest country I ever saw. The vallies [valleys] are from one to two miles in width surrounded by high hills. Some would call them mountains and then there is a second range not so high and on them are some very fine residences. But the rav[a]ges of ware [war] will leave its marke on this country for years to come."

The major also had distressing news: "Gen. Gilbert has gone to day to see Gen. Rosecrans to see if he [Rosecrans] can't doo something for him and we are very mutch affraid that he will try and get the President to appoint him agane [again] and that would give him power to act as Brig. Gen until the next Congress. All the field officers of this brigade are going to sind [send] a petition by tellagraff [telegraph] to the President not to appoint him over us."[3]

Word also came that sickness had claimed the life of another member of the 78th. Pvt. Robert Gardiner of Company E, aged nineteen or twenty, had died at Louisville, where he had been left in a hospital.

Van Vleck got a break when General Granger dissolved the court martial that had occupied his attention for so long. The general "thought it was not a paying institution in as much as we were two weeks in session & only got through with one case," the lieutenant colonel wrote his wife.

Dissolution of the court-martial board left Colonel Benneson's case still up in the air, but "there are a great many cases of company officers for trial, & a court martial of captains will soon be called to attend to them," Van Vleck said. "Among others is Lieut. Harvey McCandless [he appears on the 78th's roster as 2nd Lt. James H. McCandless]. You know he was at home about the same time I was. He went without authority, & since he has been back, he has been exceedingly anxious to resign notwithstanding he was warned of the danger.

"His resignation was sent up to Gen'l. Rosecrans stating the facts of his absence in as mild terms as possible, but it was no go. It was returned with a peremptory order that he be court martialed. The penalty for the offense is fixed by law & is dismissal from the service, & as a full confession of the matter is contained in his application to resign, his fate cannot be uncertain nor long postponed."

Two days later, on Sunday, April 5th, Pvt. Benjamin Gill penned another letter to his wife, speculating on the fate of a daguerreotype image he had sent her but she had not received. "I expect that lik[e]ness of ours got lost when the cars runn off of the track and throwed all of the mail in the warter [water] between Abington and Macomb and I think we lost the lik[e]ness and two letter[s] ther[e]," he wrote. "I think we give three dol[l]ars for our pictures. It was [a] fancy one. If it is lost I will be sorry and I want you to write and tell me w[h]ether you get it or not. . . .

"I got a letter from Aunt Hanah [Hannah?] yesterd[ay] and was sorry to lurn [learn] that she bur[i]ed one of her daughters. She have lots of tr[o]uble. I feel sorry for her but we all haft [have] to die some time. You should be surprised to see how used to sickness and death the soldiers will get. I thought [it] was awful to see a dead man or see one shot but know [now] I don't mind it no more than I would if it was a horse or mule. I have seen so many de[a]d men since I have bin in the army and some shot and wounded and crippled every how. I expect it seems hard to you. . . ."[4]

Broaddus told his wife about "quite a lit[t]le skirmish" that occurred near Franklin, "but every thing was very quiet while we were on [picket]. Our head quarters were at the house of a very we[a]lthy old man by the name of Carter. He had three very pret[t]y girls and they profes[s]ed to bee in favor of the Union. We eat dinner and supper with them. The old man has three hundred acres of land well improved laying [ad]joining the town of Franklin, and at one time he was offered three hundred dollars per acre for all he had and now he could not sell it a[t] any price. He had sixteen Negroes leave at one time, but has about fifty yet.

"The Pay Master is here and has paid off some of the reg'ts and I presume we will get our pay in afew days. The weather is very pleasant . . . I will try and get to go to Nashville as soon as we get our pay so that I can send it home and get some things that I nead."[5]

Magie wrote his wife on the 7th to tell her that "a man died in the same tent I slept in last night. He was from Adams Co[unty]. I sleep in the hospital tent." The unfortunate victim was Pvt. George W. Hedrick, thirty-two, of Company E, whose home was McGee, Adams County.[6]

On Friday, April 10th, the Confederates attacked. "About 2 o'clock the rebels made a dash upon the town of Franklin, drove in our pickets, and came dashing on as though they meant to take the whole of us," Magie wrote the next day. "The ball opened in fine style. The troops nearest the point of attack were soon in line of battle and charged upon the enemy, slaying them without mercy. The firing was kept up all the afternoon, sometimes at one point and sometimes at another. The 78th was formed in line of battle and held as a reserve . . . Not one in the 78th was hurt, or is missing."

Never one to miss an opportunity to make a few dollars, Magie told how "at the same time the cannon was thundering, and the rifles cracking, I went out and sold about a dozen papers to the reserve, and they set down to read them, while within a quarter of a mile of them the deadly conflict was going on.

"About sundown the 78th was ordered out, and they started for the scene of action, but the firing by this time had ceased. I got my blanket and went along. We only went about a quarter of a mile when they stacked arms, and after remaining there about an hour were ordered back to cook rations for two days. This morning about half of the regiment is ordered out on picket but at this time (8 o'clock) there are no indications of renewing the fight. . . ."

Referring to a boxful of clothing he had sent earlier, Magie said: "I trust that you will have received it by the time this reaches you. Look out for *greybacks* [lice]. They may be on some of the blankets."[7]

The 78th again was the only regiment General Gilbert did not order out when the Confederates attacked. Instead, Gilbert waited until evening, after the fighting was over, to summon the 78th. Magie and the other enlisted members of the regiment did not seem to attach any significance to this, but Van Vleck interpreted it as another deliberate insult to the regiment, or at least another slap at Colonel Benneson.[8]

Magie wrote his wife April 13th to report four or five members of Company C who escaped capture at Muldraugh Hill in December had rejoined the regiment.

Where they had been since then was not explained. One of them, Pvt. Charles H. Magie of Blandinsville, McDonough County, was Magie's relative, though Magie's letters never explained their relationship. Since most of Company C was still in St. Louis awaiting exchange, Charles Magie joined Company D, the same company James had joined. He was assigned duty as a hospital cook and "appears to like it better than to go in the ranks," Magie wrote his wife. "You know I board with the hospital mess, that is the doctors, nurses, &c. and so Charley and I, we may say, live together.

"We have had no more battles since the one of Friday last. The enemy however is close upon our front in large numbers, and are unusually lively of late. We are on the alert ready for them if they attack us." He again expressed hope he might have enough money saved by the war's end to buy out Nichols's interest in the *Macomb Journal*.

"The reg't. has gon[e] over the river on picket to day and as I did not feel quite well enough I am pretty much alone," Broaddus wrote on the 15th. "I have not been able for dutey for the last ten days but I am a good deal better and think I will bee able for dutey in afew days. I have had something like bil[i]ous fever and [have been] troubled some with diarrhe[a]. The fever is broke and the diarrhea[a] is nearly stop[p]ed.

"We have agood deal of sickness in our reg't. We have about two hundred and fifty men for dutey in our reg't. and then we have about one hundred on detached survice which would make three hundred and fifty. We started from Quincy with over nine hundred. So you see we have run down pretty fast.

"You will ask what has become of them. Well about forty have died, about the same number discharged, about twenty five deserters (the most of them will come back.) there is two co[mpanies] at St. Louis and the balance are sick at dif[f]erent hospitals, some in Louisville, some in Nashville and some at this place."[9]

In one of his longer diary entries, Batchelor wrote on April 16th that the "Rebels sent in a flag of truce [asking] for our surrender. But General Granger now commanding sent word back if they wanted the place come and take it."[10]

Broaddus meanwhile was growing bored with army life: "Every thing mooves along in camp after the same old montonus [monotonous] way," he wrote his wife on the 17th. "Work and drill and then drill and work . . . I have got about well and go on duty as field officer of the day.

"We got our pay yesterday. I drew two hundred and thirty four dollars after deducting out the tax. In a few days their will bee two months more pay due me, but [I] doo not know when we will bee paid. I will send two hundred and fifty dollars home soon. Will have about fifty left.

"You ask me how my teeth does. They doo not work well. If I had an upper set they might doo some good but then I am affraid they won't. I mean to try and come home after awhile and then I will try and have a full set put in. . . ."

Saturday the 18th was very warm. The 78th received orders that day to turn in their well-worn Sibley tents. In their place "we were issued what we called dog tents," Edward M. Robbins wrote later. "Each man drew a piece of canvas cloth 4x6 feet, buttons on one end, so that two men could button their respective pieces together and sleep together."

Odell added his own description of the new tents: "Each tent contains about eight y[ar]ds of white cotton drilling—it will be much more healthy for two or three men to sleep in a tent at this season of the year, than for eighteen or twenty to be crowded into one and then when we want to move, the teams will have nothing to haul except provisions, cooking utensils, etc., ammunition, etc."

Broaddus didn't think much of the new tents. "They will not be of much account in wet weather," he wrote.[11]

Van Vleck had sent home a photograph of himself and Patty apparently told him she liked it, for he wrote her on the 18th and said "I am glad I have a sad look if that is what first interested you, and if you admire I shall not be sorry that others dislike it, for you know that your wishes and admirations are my desired laws." He also remarked in passing, without explanation, that Benneson had been restored to command of the brigade.

Broaddus made another trip to the summit of Roper's Knob. "It was a very clear day, and with a field glass I could see a signal post nine miles off," he wrote Martha. "I could see their tent very plainly. The surrounding country is the most b[eau]utiful I ever saw. The more I see of this country the better I like it. And I am in hopes that Uncle Sam will confiscate all the rebels' property and then I will try and buy a farm and move down here. . . ."

Magie also was busy with pen and paper that Sunday, April 19th. He began the letter by chastising his wife for writing letters with a pencil instead of a pen. Then, after his usual remarks about financial matters, he added: "A fine large house was burned yesterday in Franklin because it obstructed the view from our fort. It was owned by a secesh captain.

"I was over in Franklin yesterday at the hospital. I saw some of the wounded rebels that we took a week or two ago. I talked with one young man who had his arm shot off close to his shoulder. He was from Mississippi. I saw others of our own men who I suppose are dead this morning for I thought there were some sick who could not live many hours. . . ."[12]

Things were quiet the next several days, with neither side making any aggressive movements. The weather was pleasant and the soldiers at Franklin remained busy drilling and working on fortifications. On April 22nd, Batchelor reported sick with "bilious fever" and by the next day it was serious enough to land him in the hospital.

He wasn't alone. "Mr. [Elisha] Morse has been quite sick for several days, in fact ever since I wrote you last," Van Vleck told Patty. "He is some better to day. The Col.& Maj. are not any better since I last wrote. And I am not entirely well. For the Colonel being in command of the brigade & having taken the adj[utant] with him, and the Maj. & Morse being sick, it leaves what there is to be done for the Sergt. Major [Vilasco Chandler] & me. But fortunately we are not doing a great deal now, except to work on the fortifications & standing at arms in the morning which we have to do every morning from 4:00 o'cl'k until near sun up, which last I think does more to keep the men sick than everything else. I hope still, someday to see an end of Gilbert's reign & then we can sleep till morning . . . .

"Our officers are still mostly sick. We only have one captain and only seven lieut's able for duty. Several of the officers are very sick. When we get acclimated we will get along better.[13]

Magie wrote his wife April 23rd to report that he had made about six dollars the day before. "I have got almost fifty dollars now on hand . . . As matters appear now I shall probably make another $100 by the first of June, and if we are kept here all summer and I keep on I should certainly have enough by next fall to have all debts paid, and a surplus sufficient to buy out Nichols. I hope we may continue to prosper.

"And there is Eddy [his son] we need [illegible symbol] $100 for him. I wish this war might end this summer, we would then take Eddy to New York and have his feet attended to."

The gossip in camp that day, as reported by Broaddus, was that "there is a man in the 125th Ohio Reg't. . . . that is to be shot next Tuesday at this place for desertion. It looks pret[t]y hard to have men shot but I presume it becomes nessary [necessary]."[14]

Magie had more details in a letter written two days later: "There is to be a man shot next Tuesday in the 125th Ohio Reg't, which is camped a few rods from us. He has been found guilty on three charges, viz—desertion, stealing and using threatening language. I don't know whether I shall witness the execution or not.

"I was over in Franklin yesterday. Six more rebel families were ordered outside the lines, and went yesterday. There was a quite imposing funeral procession yesterday—a lieutenant in the 4th Regular US Cavalry. He was wounded at the battle two weeks ago Friday. There was a splendid brass band out on the occasion. I went with the procession to the cemetery, and after the burial spent an hour or two looking at the tomb stones."

In a letter to Patty the following day, Van Vleck described the fortifications under construction at Franklin: "We are building eight different works," he wrote. "The principal one is nearly completed & is a very extensive affair & very strong & commands all the rest. The others are small & only intended to protect a few guns & about one reg't. of inf[antr]y. One is on top of a very high knoll, 300 ft. high, which is perfectly inaccessible to an assaulting party & is out of range from any position where the enemies' guns can be placed, & yet it commands all the country for miles round about [this was an apparent reference to Roper's Knob]. It is to be armed with guns of the heaviest calibre that can be got up there & will protect all the other works. In fact each of the forts protects all the others so that this will be one of the most impregnable places in the world when completed & armed, which will not be long hence, as the whole force are at work with all their might."[15]

April 27th brought an end to the quiet period. Major Broaddus described what happened in a letter written a day later: "Our cavalry went out on the Colombia [Columbia] Pike about six miles and surprised and captured one hundred and eighteen officers and privates of a Texiss [Texas] reg't. Their [there] was nine commissioned officers.

"Later in the day our cavalry pickets was driven off on the Louisburg Pike by three reg'ts of the enemy. They advansed to within about one mile of us and we made preparations for giving them a warm reseption and fully expected they would try and gob[b]le up some of us to pay for those we had captured in the morning but they did not come...."

That Tuesday also was the day the soldier from the 125th Ohio was scheduled to be shot, but "I have not heard any thing about it," Broaddus reported. It turned out President Lincoln had commuted the death sentence and ordered the soldier sent to prison.

But the grim reaper would not be denied. Pvt. Tracey Pelsor of Company A of the 78th had died in a hospital at Quincy a day earlier. A resident of Brooklyn, St. Clair County, he was seventeen or eighteen years old.

Odell wrote home on the 28th to list "some of the prices of eatables here." Pies and corn dodgers cost twenty-five cents each. Milk was fifty cents a gallon. Apples went for five to ten cents each. Dried peaches could be had for thirty cents a pound and dried apples for forty cents. Potatoes were twelve and a half cents a pound and a barrel of green apples cost twenty-five to twenty-eight dollars. "The government has commenced giving us a few pickles, potatoes and baker's bread once in awhile," Odell concluded. "We need such food now in order to prevent scurvy with which we are threatened."[16]

Benjamin Gill had a bad habit of not dating his letters, but sometime in late April he wrote the following to his wife: "You thought it strange at me sending my Bible home. It was to[o] he[a]vy to carry. I have got a little one the preacher gave me and I thank you for your rebuck [rebuke]. I will tray [try] and profit by it. I still try and live a C[h]ristain [life]. I find it is good to wait upon the Lord. I hope you will pray for me.

"I don't know any nues [news] to tell you only the calv[a]ry brought in 300 prisoners . . . The rebles say they are glad to be taken fore they will go north and get plenty to eat. They look well, only ragged and dirty. They was Texas Rangers the best troops the South has got."[17]

The last days of April expired quietly in camp. Magie informed his wife of his latest profit-making scheme: He had bought a watch for $16 and hoped to sell it for $20. But he was concerned about the illness of some of his comrades, particularly Pvt. Solomon Huff of Company H, who "was very sick with pneumonia. I thought two or three days ago that he would die, but he is better now and there is some hope of his recovery. I wrote to his father a day or two ago in reference to his case."

Batchelor and Cornelius Pierce also were among the sick, the former still in the hospital. Pierce had never fully recovered from the respiratory ailment he had contracted in the rain at Louisville, then aggravated working in the cold winter air of Kentucky. Now, he wrote his family, he was scarcely able to sit up. "I have got that old complaint again, that misery and pain in my breast and side, ever since I have been lying on the ground here in camp. I know very well that no mustard which the doctor gives me, or any other kind of draught, will cure that lump in my breast."[18]

Even though he was in the hospital, Batchelor still knew what was going on outside. "Our brigade was called up at 12 o'clock at night—to go after some rebels," he wrote in his diary May 1st. "There is quite a fuss between Gilbert's staff officers and officers of the 78th as Gilbert ordered out the brigade but slighted the 78th as they won't obey him as he is only a captain of regulars."

Broaddus was on picket duty and did not go with the regiment, but in a letter to his wife he reported what he heard about the affair: "Our reg't. was sent out to the front last night with the ballence [balance] of our division some eight miles. They went to try to surprise a rebel camp but did not sucsede [succeed] very well. They took twelve pris[o]ners and killed about as maney and did not loose a man.

"I think Col. Benneson will get him self in a scrape. He refused to obey Gilbert's orders to day, and I think Granger will put him under arrest. They are trying to get a hold on him and I think they will sucsede. Benneson has but little discression [discretion]. He may work his own boat."

Two days later Broaddus wrote again to say "we got one large Parrot gun out from Nashville day before yesterday and have [it] in position in the main fort. We have three thirty-too [two] pounders in that fort and if we had two more large guns for the fort on Roper's [K]nob I think we would be ready for the rebels. We have three bat[te]ries of light artil[le]ry that we can use to very good advantage in the forts.

"Well I told you something about Col. Benneson's trouble with Gilbert—I have come to the conclusion that he [Benneson] has lost all of his manhood if he had any."

His recital of conflicts between Gilbert and Benneson was amazingly similar to the account Van Vleck had sent earlier to his wife, almost as if Broaddus had copied parts of Van Vleck's letter. They were now condemning Benneson with a single voice.[19]

Odell returned to camp from picket duty about 10:00 a.m. that Sunday. He attended church services, then went with another man to climb Roper's Knob. "On this hill is stationed a part of what is called the Signal Corps," he wrote his family. "But as you don't know what is meant by this I will try to tell you. There is one post on the hill here and another 9 miles in direction of Murfreesboro, on another hill. The communications are made by means of flags, which may be seen by means of a telescope, at night torches are used. These flags and torches are waved or moved so that the signals understand each other."[20]

The next two days brought unfortunate news to the regiment. On Monday, May 4th, Pvt. Henry H. Barrow, twenty-one or twenty-two, a member of Company K from Melrose, Adams County, died in the hospital at Nashville. On Tuesday, a freak accident wounded one of the regiment's best young officers, 1st Lt. John B. Worrell of Company D. "Lieut. Woorl [Worrell] of Co. D drop[p]ed his revolver out of his pocket and it went off and shot him in the right arm just above the elbow," Broaddus wrote his wife. "The ball struck the bone did not brake [break] it but it is thought that parte of the ball is in the bone and I am very mutch afraid his arm will have to come off."

Worrell would not lose his arm, but in addition to being wounded he soon fell ill with fever and diarrhea. He would eventually recover and return to service.

The day after Worrell was wounded, Gilbert's command—six regiments, including the 78th—crossed the Harpeth River, marched about a mile south of Franklin, and set up a new camp in a driving rainstorm. "Ever since [we] have been hard at work cutting down the timber which is the only object I can see in the move," Van Vleck wrote his wife, "& that is no reason for the move, for we could have sent over men every day to do the work with less trouble. . . .

"There are no other changes to note that I think of. Col. Benneson still refuses to take command of the reg't. and Gilbert will not let him command the brigade so that he still has nothing to do and feels perfectly satisfied."

On May 8th or 9th—records differ—Gilbert's command moved back to its old camps in Franklin and resumed work on the fortifications. "As I predicted in my last, we moved back to our old camp on the north side of the river yesterday," Van Vleck wrote Patty May 10th. "What the object of the move [south of Franklin] was I am unable to determine but guess it was to see how quick we could tear up the camps and make the men miserable during that severe cold rain. It was one of the worst times to move that could possibly have been selected. But we are back all safe and sound again."[21]

On Saturday, May 9th, Private Solomon Huff of Company H—the soldier Magie had been worried about—died of his illness at Franklin.

Broaddus had submitted a request for leave and it was approved, but for only seven days, "and of course that would not doo me any good," he told Martha—it would not allow time for him to travel home and return, or to get his teeth fixed, which was what he was hoping to do. "I will have to wait for awhile and perhaps it will bee a more faverable time. This you know is not a very faverable time to make an ap[p]lication and if I had know[n] that Hook[er] was agoing to git whip[p]ed I would have waited a while [this was a reference to Union General Joseph Hooker's defeat at the Battle of Chancellorsville, Virginia]."

Broaddus wrote home again May 12 with "nuse [news] that Van Dorn is dead. I presume it is true. He was found in bed with another man's wife and her husband shot him and killed him." The news was true; the Confederate cavalry general was shot dead May 7th by an angry husband.

Van Vleck, meanwhile, was growing heartily tired of camp life. In a letter to his wife, written May 13th, he offered a lengthy description: "If you would really like to know just how comfortable a thing a tent life is in hot weather imagine yourself here some hot sultry day. Take a sheet and fasten one edge to the ground, say four or five feet from the south side of the house, and fasten the other edge up against the house four or five feet from the ground. But to get the full benefit of camp life you should for about two or three weeks before the experiment deposit all the slops and offal from the table nearby so as to secure the attendance of more flies than were ever before congregated in the same space.

"When you have the arrangement complete, crawl under your shelter with all your winter clothes on and try to sleep; and if you are not *sleepy* take up Hardie's [Hardee's] Tactics and try to study and you soon will be, but if you find it difficult to *gratify* your disposition to sleep remember there is no place you can go to except to some other pleasant place just like the one you are in, or one still more so, and that there is nothing you can do until *dinner time* and that is a long way off.

"After you are sufficiently *refreshed* from your rest, though you may not have slept very soundly, you will find quite a relief to crawl out and walk around in the sun awhile wishing at every step that you had some summer clothes and lived farther north, and looking every few minutes at your watch to see whether it is not most noon. After looking a good many times, you hear dinner called at some of the tents and are glad to think that the sun is near the meridian when you can spend a few minutes at something beside tactics and bliss. And you grasp your watch quite nervously to be assured of the time and are somewhat surprised to find that it is only half past 10 o'cl'k."

After dinnertime finally did come and go "you are heartily glad of it for such another fight with flies you never had before and it will ever remain a question of doubt whether you or they scored the greater share of army rations for that meal. It will not be so bad at supper time. It will be cooler and the flies will have gone to rest, but that is a long way off and a deal of energy it will require to kill time and flies till then. Brighter and more intensely shines the sun, hotter and hotter grows the day! More numerous still the flies! How tantalizing to be reminded just now of ice creams and lemonades and of the cool shade of our garden bowers and broad trees at home, where flies, though bad, are not the worst of all the ills with which we're cursed.

"You are faint and exhausted with the heat and worried out of patience with the flies. You can not longer endure the scorching rays of the sun. You will be excused from walking further, and be permitted to return to your tent to rest and refresh yourself with a short nap. You undertake it, and are surprised to find the place as warm again as when you left it. The sun having passed the meridian is pouring out his rays in a direct flow upon the tent which carefully gathers and retains it all. It is wholly untenable even for the flies and you crawl to the shady side and put in the afternoon in a highly exaggerated imitation of your forenoon's work, longing for the time to come when the fortifycations will be done and drill again begun, that you may have *something* to do.

"I often have heard it said that solitary confinement is one of the most severe of all punishments and I now make no doubt of it, unless the victim happens to be one of those peculiar specimens of humanity naturally adapted to that kind of existence."[22]

Batchelor, finally out of the hospital, recorded a landmark in construction of the fortifications on May 14th: "Cover the [ammunition] magazine with dirt and sod."

That day Broaddus visited with Pvt. George Painter of Company I and found him "stupefied" over news of the death of a family member. "Death is a very common thing here in the army," the major wrote his wife. "We hear the low muffled role [roll] of the drum and see the slow measured steps of a s[q]uad of soldiers following some poor fellow to his last resting place almost every day. But we think but little about it, for it is a thing we expect. But when we [learn] that some loved one has died and we [are] fare [far] away and will never get to see their loved forms any more in this wourld we are startled and wonder if it can bee so. . . ."

He had more cheerful news the following day: "Our chapl[a]in has got back. Looks a gradeal [great deal] better. The weather is very pleasant."[23]

Vilasco Chandler, after neglecting his diary a long while, chose that day [May 15th] to return to it: "Have been reading in 'Recreations of a Country Parson' which has induced me once more to do my duty to my diary," he wrote. "I will endeavor to give some thing that happens in my daily course of duty . . . Have been very irritable all day. Rec'd letters from home. Ed bought some lager beer out."

As good as his word, Chandler made another entry on May 16th, recording "a bright beautiful day. After guard mounting I studied for some time [he was studying to become an officer] and also read in 'Country Parsons.' Gen. Gilbert came around and called out all the shirks and they go on picket for three days. Serves them right. This business of shirking one's duty is extremely contemptible. It is a shame to Union soldiers.

"Went down to the brook and had a fine bath. It is very pleasant to cast off the dirt of a week's accumulation, would that we could as well and easily cast off the multitude of little sins of a week's accumulation."

Next day was Sunday and Chaplain Taylor preached his first sermon since returning from leave. "Quite interesting," was Chandler's assessment.

Ever the faithful correspondent, Broaddus told his wife that "the health of the reg't. is improving though one man has just died and another one will not live untill night. The one that has died was stab[b]ed by another man in our reg't. The one that has died belonged to Company A and the one that did the stab[b]ing belonged to Co. E. They were under the influence of liquor. The one that is not expected to live belongs to Co. F. He has bin troubled with 'heart disease' for some time."[24]

The victim, Samuel Deiser, twenty-three, a native of Londonderry, Ireland, actually belonged to Company E. A resident of Beverly, Adams County, he was a teamster. So was the man who stabbed him with a pocket knife, though Broaddus did not mention his name.

Pvt. George Eyman, thirty-eight or thirty-nine, of Company F, the man with "heart disease," fulfilled Broaddus's prediction and passed away before the day was out. He was a resident of Columbus, Adams County. A third member of the 78th, Private John D. Hartwell, of Company K, also died that day at Franklin. It was a bad day for the regiment.

Van Vleck also had news for his wife that day: Colonel Benneson had applied for leave but his application was refused. "All the Generals, even Rosecrans, advised him to resign . . . but he has no notion of taking their advice but is going to apply to the Secretary of War for leave. Mr. Morse's and the Major's applications [for leave] were also rejected. It is not a very easy thing to get a leave now."

The lieutenant colonel also reported he had ordered two of his lieutenants to appear before an army board of examination, established to determine whether volunteer officers were fit for their posts. Neither lieutenant passed, "so that there will be some vacancies for good material to fill before a week from this time . . . There will be more of them in a few days, for I am determined not to run a machine involving the responsibility of a Col.'s position with engineers that know nothing of their business and do not care to learn." One of the lieutenants who failed the examination was Harvey McCandless [James H. McCandless] of Company I; Van Vleck did not identify the other. McCandless resigned before the end of the month. Van Vleck hoped he would be able to promote Elisha Morse, still a private, to fill one of the vacancies.

Colonel Benneson, perhaps stricken by his failure to get leave, had fallen ill again and entered the hospital in Franklin. Chandler and two other men went to visit the hospital May 18th and found him "looking better than when he left . . . The hospital is very neat, with its long rows of white cots."[25]

The regiment received word that day that Dr. William Githens had been appointed second assistant surgeon to fill the vacancy left by the resignation of Dr. McIntire. Less welcome was the news that Pvt. William J. Beard of Company F had died in a hospital at Nashville.

Next few days were occupied with drill—sometimes starting as early as 4:00 a.m.—and work on the fortifications. The weather was growing warmer and the flies Van Vleck complained about were becoming even worse. Continuing dry weather also added to another annoyance, steadily increasing dust.

Dr. Githens arrived on the 23rd and was quickly mustered into the service. Chandler noted the occasion: "Our new Doctor came. He may be a good one, but he will belie his looks."

Patty Van Vleck had written her husband to ask how he thought his men viewed him as acting commander of the regiment. "Of course a man is a very poor judge of his own popularity, but I am perfectly satisfied with their continued manifestations of approval," he wrote her on May 24th. "Neither officers nor men are at all backward in expressing themselves as not only willing but anxious that I should retain command. It would be very foolish for me to say this to anybody but you, or even to you had you not called for it. Suffice it to say, that I have never been able to discover the least dissatisfaction among either officers or soldiers, either in word, deed, or looks, for anything I have done thus far, but on the contrary, have often rec'd unmistakable expressions of their confidence, esteem & approval. I could ask for nothing more, & only thank God for his goodness, & pray that He will continue to bless me, & that he may grant me wisdom & courage to fill, profitably to Him, to my country, to my men and to myself the responsible position to which He has called [me], so unexpectedly to myself. For I confess I had never dreamed or even aspired to the position until I saw it plainly set before me."

Switching subjects, he reported that Benneson was still in the hospital "and his name is never mentioned. No body seems to realize that he has any connection with this part of the army. I understand his health is much improved, but [he] is talking some of resigning, but I have no idea he will do that soon [even] if Gilbert, Granger, & Rosecrans *did* advise it . . . He has engendered a bitter animosity against himself & the reg't. on the part of all our commanding generals, & he slips out the way, avoiding all the consequences . . . But it will all come out right I think in the end . . . He will ultimately be compelled to resign by the outside & inside pressure. Of course all this talk is for you only, it would appear very improper to anybody else.

"All the feeling I have in the matter, is probably the improper one, of hating to see a man draw a large salary for doing nothing at all. For the Col. has really *never* done anything. He has yet to drill the reg't. for the first time & never has done any other duty except to exercise command on our march from Louisville to New Haven . . . But I have said much more than I intended to & have a notion now to destroy my letter. It looks so foolish for a subordinate to complain of doing his superior's duty. I should hate very much for any body but you to see this."[26]

Chandler complained on the 25th that he was not feeling very well "in consequence of what I have been eating." Major Broaddus was the field officer of the day and Chandler and Elisha Morse "went with him around the pickets. We found Col. Banning [of the 121st Ohio] some what excited as the cavalry pickets had just been driven in. We rode out and purchased some butter and strawberries and came in with a hard headache. We had no dress parade, but there was division drill. Was remarkedly dusty."

The regiment suffered another loss that day when Pvt. Ezra Tatman, nineteen, of Company F died in the hospital at Franklin.

Chandler still didn't feel well the next day. "I was out in the sun too much yesterday," he wrote in his diary. The diarrher [diarrhea] has started on me a little and I must be very carefull of what I eat. Mr. Morse had a hard chill in the afternoon. I wrote for the Quartermaster nearly all day, for which he pays me $1. A warm day."

A day later his condition had not improved. "Am not feeling any better," he wrote. "Have stopped eating anything. I have company as Mr. Morse had another hard chill. He is quite sick. I have not been sick, but enough unwell to feel listless and without energy."

That day Company G was on duty at the fort on Roper's Knob, Odell wrote his family. "We came in Monday morning [May 25th] and since that time have been busily engaged making preparations for examination [inspection] by Capt. Stacy, chief of Gen. Gilbert's staff. It is all over now—the examination came off this forenoon, and Co. G was pronounced equal to the best in the reg't. and but very little behind the best in this command. So you see we got praised for our labor."[27]

By the 28th Chandler reported himself feeling "some better, so is Mr. Morse." The 78th was on fatigue duty that day, while Van Vleck and Capt. Granville Reynolds of Company I were assigned to court-martial duty, the former as president of the court.

"A very dusty day till eve when a few drops fell to tantalize us," Chandler recorded. "Had dress parade, I took an opium pill, and am going to bed in the chaplain's tent in a few minutes."

Broaddus, as usual, was writing to his wife. "I think if I had my teeth in that my health would improve," he said. "Thos. looks better than I ever saw him.

"Col. Benneson has bin ordered before a commity [committee] of examination [examination board] but he sais [says] he will not attend. But they will keep after him untill they brake him. Serg[t]. Howland [Sgt. Nathaniel Howland of Company K, a Quincy native] is still in Nashville has not bin discharged looks very bad and it is doubtful whether he ever gets well." The ailing sergeant would be discharged two days later for reasons of disability.

That night Wheeler's Confederate cavalry attacked and drove the Union soldiers at Franklin within the walls of their forts, then circled behind them to damage the railroad and cut the telegraph line to Nashville. The 78th was ordered out with sixty rounds of ammunition per man, but in the end the regiment stayed put.

The excitement of Wheeler's raid was exceeded in the regiment by news that Van Vleck and Reynolds had both been placed under arrest by General Gilbert. Broaddus communicated the details in a hastily written letter on the 31st: "As I am in com[mand] of the reg't. I have but little time to write. Old Gilbert has put the Lt. Col. under arrest and I suppose he will keep him under arrest for the next forty days, but I have no idey [idea] that he will ever bring him to tryal. The offence was refusing to let the pr[o]vost guard take Sergt. Hamilton to the guard house when the sergt. had not bin guilty of any offence. I think the Col. did just right but the old hound [Gilbert] will devil us as mutch and as long as he can, and it would not surprise me if he picks a quarrel with me and puts me under arrest at any time.

"I had a talk with him the other night and talked very plain to him. He is one of the most vindictive over bearing old vill[a]ins in the wourld and if he does not get what Gen. Nelson got I miss my guess, for I have heard more than one hundred men sweare that they would kill him if they ever got a chance. Their would bee no sympathy for him if he was to go up the spout one of these days.

"The reg't. is getting along very well. The sick are doing well and if we could get out from under Gilbert I think we would bee pret[t]y well satisfied. Every officer has petitioned Gen. Granger to take us out from under his command [and] put us under Gen. Beard's [Baird's] but I doo not know what will be the result. But we can't make things any worse.

"Col. Benneson has gone to Nashville and I think he does not intend to come back to the reg't. any more. He won't if he can help it. All he cares for is the pay. I don't believe he cares one cent for the welfare of the reg't."[28]

The arrests came after Van Vleck was called to a disturbance in the quarters of Company I of the 78th, where he found one of Gilbert's provost guards "surrounded by a large crowd of excited soldiers." The guard had seen a light in one of Company I's tents after the 8:00 p.m. "lights out" order Gilbert had issued previously. The guard stuck his head into the tent, which was occupied by four soldiers including Sgt. Perminion Hamilton, and ordered them "in a burly and authoritative tone," to extinguish the light.

Not knowing the guard, Hamilton asked him—politely, he later said—to identify himself. The guard swore and told him again to put out the light. Things went downhill from there, and after several heated exchanges the guard declared Hamilton under arrest. By then the ruckus had brought other men out of their tents, some with loaded weapons. Captain Reynolds was called and tried to calm the angry guard, who was still shouting profanities. Then Van Vleck was summoned.

When the lieutenant colonel arrived and ascertained what was going on, he called for Sergeant Hamilton, only to find he had gone to bed. Van Vleck got him up and took him to his own tent to spend the night, and the crowd dispersed. Reynolds went to the provost marshal to complain of the guard's conduct, but instead of punishing the guard the marshal ordered Reynolds to send Sergeant Hamilton to the guard house for the night. Reynolds reported to Van Vleck, who refused to let the sergeant go on grounds that "he had committed no offense, and while I have life and strength, my men shall not be dragged to the guard house to suit the caprice of anybody's dog." Later, in a letter to his wife, Van Vleck described Hamilton as "one of the most faithful, gentlemanly & Christian soldiers of my acquaintance."

As a consequence of all this, Van Vleck and Reynolds were placed under arrest for *"mutiny in exciting a large crowd of soldiers to the resistance of the provost guard, whereby Sergeant Hamilton was forcibly released from the lawful custody of the guard."*

"The charge is of course perfectly groundless & we ... should be glad to have a trial immediately but will not be gratified," Van Vleck wrote. "He [Gilbert] has the power to keep us under arrest for 'forty days & nights' & then release us without trial, & we have no redress & I doubt not, that is his intention. Indeed he intimated as much to Maj. Broaddus when he told him that 'he presumed nothing would ever be done with the charges.'

"After the arrest every officer in the regiment excepting Capt. Reynolds & myself who were prohibited by our arrest signed a petition to be relieved from Gilbert's command & they say if the petition is not granted they will all resign in a body. I have long expected to be under arrest for something, but supposed he would seize upon some more plausible excuse than he now has.

"He knows & don't hesitate to say, that we all hate him & he intends to punish us at every opportunity. Under the circumstances the question very naturally arises, how long is it my duty to stay under the command of such a man? To resign only to rid *myself* of the nuisance, I never will, for I cannot find it in my heart, to leave my gallant men, to suffer under his contemptable treatment & myself slip out, unless by my going I can improve *their* condition.

"I know his hate is all occasioned by his difficulty with Col. Benneson, & whenever I am of the opinion that he has transfer[r]ed his vindictiveness from the Col. to me, I shall get out [of] the way, that the reg't. may not be made to suffer on my acct.

"Col. Benneson has played out entirely. As I told you in my last, he was ordered to appear before the Board of Examiners, & he refused to appear, & the next morning got on to the cars & went to Nashville with the convale[s]cent sick, & left word that he should probably not come back to the reg't. soon, as he intended to go to Louisville with the first load of sick ones, & get into the hospital there & send for his wife, unless he could get into the hospital at Quincy, & as soon as he is well enough, he expects to get detailed on detached service, to be provost marshall of some town or the like. He may make it work nicely, but from what I hear I shall not be surprised if he is brought back in close confinement, & if he is, it will go hard with him for he not only went away without the proper authority, but he took a soldier off with him as a waiter, both of which are great military offenses.

"I think he acted very foolish, & if he is found out as I think he certainly must be, he will be dishonerably dismissed [from] the service.

"I never saw a man for whom I formed so great a contempt in so short a time. He expressed his true sentiments when he told us that, *he* had got out from under Gilbert, & we could get out the best way we could. He cares no more for the reg't. nor for what may become of it, than as though he lived in the moon."[29]

The arrest of Van Vleck and Reynolds led to dissolution of the court-martial board to which they had been appointed, for it left the board without a quorum. That didn't bother Van Vleck, who hated court-martial duty.

So May ended with Colonel Benneson apparently having abandoned his regiment, with Lieutenant Colonel Van Vleck and one of his company commanders under arrest, and with the 78th's other officers petitioning for a change in commanding generals.

This was not the war they had expected to fight.

7

"The Most Melancholy and
Painful Sight I Ever Saw"

ON THE COOL MORNING OF JUNE 1ST, THE 78TH ILLINOIS VOLUNTEER INFANTRY
Regiment marked the beginning of its tenth month of service with what Vilasco
Chandler thought was a "great drill." His comrades might not have agreed, but since
Chandler had begun studying to become an officer the evolutions of drill had become
increasingly interesting to him.

Lieutenant McCandless, who had tendered his resignation, started home that
day, as did 1st Lt. Clinton B. Cannon of Company F, who also had failed his examination. They were joined by the wounded and ailing Lieutenant Worrell, going home
on furlough.

Next day Major Broaddus went to see General Granger to ask for Van Vleck's
release from arrest "and I would bee glad if he could have it dun [done] and he said he
would and did right a way." Granger must have been in a good mood; either that, or he
had become as disgusted with Gilbert as everyone else. In any event, he ordered Van
Vleck and Reynolds both released immediately.[1]

Van Vleck wasted no time doing what he had wanted to do for some time: He
sent Chandler to report to Reynolds as replacement for Harvey McCandless as second
lieutenant of Company I and ordered Elisha Morse to report to Capt. Henry Hawkins
as replacement for 1st Lieutenant Cannon in Company F, then started the paperwork
to make the promotions official.

The 78th was visited by a paymaster that day and the soldiers were paid through
April 1st, leaving the government only a month in arrears. The men had scarcely finished collecting their pay when the cavalry pickets were driven in by rebels. The 78th
was called into line and ordered "to march up to the main fort," except for Companies
A and I, which were stationed on Roper's Knob.

The regiment cooled its heels inside the fort until about 8:00 p.m. while great movement was going on outside. The rest of Gilbert's division and all of Gen. Absalom Baird's broke camp, fell into line, and marched out on the road to Triune. Once again the 78th was left behind, alone except for remnants of Coburn's Brigade that escaped capture at Thompson's Station. Col. John P. Baird of the 85th Indiana was in command of those troops. As senior officer present, he also was in temporary command at Franklin.

The 78th lost another man that day with the death in a Nashville hospital of Pvt. George W. Askew of Company E, a resident of Richfield, Adams County.

— • —

The regiment was "ordered up to Roper's Knob to hold it" on the morning of June 3rd, Chandler reported in his diary. The 78th tramped up the hill after the noon meal and "camped around the knob and by dark had our tents fixed up nicely."

Van Vleck sent his wife a description of Roper's Knob and its fortifications. "The hill is quite round," he wrote, "& the defenses are built to encircle it." They included "a stockade built very strong," a "stone and earthwork fort, strong enough to resist any artillery," and "rifle trenches that encircle the brink of a precipice some 50 or 60 feet high that extends around the whole [k]nob, which makes it look like one hill set upon another, or like a monstrous wart.

"At the bottom of this precipice is a table of a moderate slope outward some 50 or 60 feet wide, covered with a beautiful blue grass sod; on this table we are encamped & have the most beautiful prospect, all around that can be imagined . . . We are up above the fog, the dust & the many bad smells incident to a large camp, & feel very happy.

"We are in a very precarious situation. There are no troops nearer than Nashville. Although our works are very strong, yet there are not enough of us to man them well. We could attend to this one, but the others are not so well protected. Just outside our camp is a very strong abatis that I forgot to mention in the description of our camp. All we have to fear is starvation. We will however keep water & provisions enough for 30 days constantly on hand, so that we can stand a pretty fair siege."[2]

If the regiment was happy in its new camp, Colonel Baird was not. He sent off a telegram complaining about the order to station the 78th on Roper's Knob. "This order changes my whole disposition of the forces, and I don't feel satisfied at all," he wrote. "I will command my own brigade, but will not obey this order. If I have not done my duty, say so. My brigade consists of the uncaptured force of the 85th and 33rd Indiana, 19th Michigan, and 22nd Wisconsin, amounting to about 400. There are 242 convalescents, and this force is in the main fort. The 78th Illinois numbers about 400, and only 332 for duty. Granger knew before he left here how I had disposed the forces, and approved it."[3]

The Confederates had noted the movement of two divisions away from Franklin and wasted little time mounting an attack on the remaining force. About 2:00 p.m. on the 4th "our pickets were driven in, and in an hour the firing was very brisk," Chandler wrote. "The big guns of the fort opened and the rebels skedaddled. At length they formed and made a charge on our cavalry, who beat a hasty retreat." Union artillery then took over and held the rebels at bay. "We were all ordered out and had a fine view of the contest from the top of Roper's," Chandler continued. "We shelled the town a little. Our cavalry came up in the rear and quite a fight ensued. How it resulted is not known. The rebels have possession of Franklin tonight. Our company on picket duty." Colonel Baird telegraphed for reinforcements and four regiments of infantry, four of cavalry, and a company of artillery arrived at Franklin during the night.

June 5th dawned gray and drizzly. About 9:00 a.m. the pickets began firing and the Union artillery opened. Cavalry from both sides skirmished most of the day, but the rebels eventually fell back. "The rebs gutted the town," Chandler reported. "Railroad communication cut off."[4]

While this was transpiring, Granger responded to Colonel Baird's protest over the posting of the 78th on Roper's Knob by sending his chief engineer, 1st Lt. H. C. Wharton, back to Franklin to "superintend the reorganization of the garrison at that place. He will see that the 78th Illinois Volunteer Infantry is posted in and around the large fort, and that 150 men from the remainder of the command be stationed on Roper's Knob."

So, after a sermon by Chaplain Taylor—whose persistent cough was returning—the 78th left Roper's Knob the afternoon of June 7th and returned to the main fort. "It began to rain about the time we got there," said Chandler. "Had green peas and strawberries for dinner. A mean stinking camp where we are." The remnants of the 33rd Indiana took the 78th's place on Roper's Knob.[5]

Chandler took his first turn commanding a picket detail the following day. It was "a fine day for standing picket," he wrote. "All quiet during the day. We had all the milk we wanted. In evening fell back to the edge of town . . . A few rebels in sight at sundown."

—◦—

That evening Van Vleck and Colonel Baird were having a quiet conversation, never dreaming they were about to become involved in one of the most disturbing incidents of the Civil War. It began when "two very fine-appearing officers rode up," Van Vleck wrote. "They were both rigged out with fine white worsted havelock, & both had very beautiful horses, and fine rigs generally, but especially the older one. His horse was one of the finest I ever have had the pleasure of seeing, & he had a magnificent sword & sword belt & had two silver drinking cups strung on his belt. . . .

"The older one (a man about 30, the younger being not more than 22, or 23) introduced himself to Col. Baird as Col. Antrin [Auton] from Washington City, detailed as special inspector gen'l. of the Dept. of Ohio & the Cumberland, and introduced the young man as Major Dunlop, his assistant also from Washington. He said they had just come from Murfreesboro, that they lost their way & came by the way of Eaglesville (nine miles south of our lines) & were pursued by the rebels, & lost their coats & all their money & that their private servant was captured, & [they] wanted a pass to Nashville & then [they] took Col. Baird [to] one side and wanted to borrow $50. He not having it asked me to let him have it to loan to them.

"I declined. I told him their story was to me a very strange & improbable one. I did not think they were what they pretended to be, for [the] government would certainly not send two field officers from Washington here, to inspect troops, when we already had so many inspectors. And I could not understand how they could lose all their money and their coats & servant & yet escape themselves unharmed, nor how they should leave Murfreesboro without an escort, & even if all that was true, if they were what they represented, they could when they got to Nashville draw their draft for any amt. of money they might need. I thought they were spies."

Colonel Baird "differed with me somewhat, but still was made to doubt, & demanded to see all their papers, & they showed him the order from our Sec't. of War, a pass from Rosecrans & also a letter from Rosecrans & a pass from Gen'l. Morgan. So he borrowed the money from some other person & let them have it."

The two officers then rode out of camp, "but they were no sooner gone than he [Colonel Baird] was more & more troubled & ask[ed] Col. Watkins, of the 6th Ky. Caval[ry], who had by this time come up, what he thought of them & he thought they were doubtful & Baird told him to follow them & see where they went, which he did & soon overtook them." Colonel Watkins "insisted on sending an escort with them, as it was now about dark, but they declined an escort, & he then insisted upon their staying all night, & they at last agreed to go to the tavern and stay, but he told them that was not the way for soldiers to do, & as he had good quarters, they must stay with him & were finally induced to alight & go with him to his tent."

Once the officers were in the tent, Colonel Watkins posted a guard around it, arrested the two and took them back to Colonel Baird, who interrogated them and became "quite mad." Baird telegraphed Rosecrans, who answered "that no such men had left there or were known to him" and confirmed "that they were doubtless spies, & must be tried immediately & if found guilty hung before morning."

After Rosecrans's dispatch was received late in the evening, the two officers were searched, over "Colonel Auton's" protest, though it was pointed out to him that if he and his assistant were loyal to the Union, they should have nothing to fear. But when

"Major Dunlop's" sword was removed from its scabbard, the words "Lt. W. G. Peter, C.S.A." were found engraved on the blade. Further search revealed the two were carrying papers that identified them as Confederate spies.

"They confessed their guilt and acknowledged that they were rebel officers, the first a colonel of cavalry & the other a lieut. & his adjutant," Van Vleck wrote. "They [had] served together in the same reg't. in the regular [US] Army & his real name is [William] Orton Williams. At the time the war began he was a lt. col. on Gen'l. [Winfield] Scott's staff & resigned & was, on account of it, for a time imprisoned on Governor's Island . . . He is a first cousin to Gen'l. [Robert E.] Lee, the commander in chief of the rebel army & was engaged to marry his daughter. In the rebel service he is known as Col. Thompson or Col. Orton, I can[t] tell which." The younger officer was twenty-year-old Lt. Walter Gibson Peter, of Montgomery County, Maryland.

"We have a darkie in our reg't. that left him [Williams] only a month ago, that has been his servant ever since the Col. has been in the rebel service. The Col. recognized him & called to him & shook hands with him & talk[ed] with him for some time. The darkie says he is a regular spy, spent half his time that way, but that he is col. of a fine reg't., & the young man is his adj't. The Col. however insisted that he was now inspector general of Bragg's army.

"The parties were both arraigned, & I was called up about 10 o'cl'k. to sit on court martial for their trial, but in waiting for instruction from Rosecrans we did not get to work until 3 o'cl'k. The trial however took but a short time as they confessed their guilt, or rather all the facts that constituted the *deepest* guilt, & as Rosecrans had ordered imperatively, in three different dispatches, that they be hung before morning, there was little for us to do but to sign the finding of guilty against them. But although they acknowledged the justness of their sentence & that they knew the risk they were running when they started out, yet they were very anxious to be shot & not hung, & got permission to telegraph for that priviledge to Rosecrans, & we waited until 9 o'cl'k. a.m. for an answer but no answer came.

"They were then taken out in the presence of all the troops & both hung to the same tree. It was the most melancholy & painful sight I ever saw. They walked up to [the] gallows with a firm step & were both noble-looking fellows. They did not exhibit the least emotion until they had the ropes adjusted & the handkerchiefs tied over their heads. They then embraced each other. The young man sobbed & nearly gave way to his pent-up feelings, but the Col. promptly checked it, by saying 'Let us die like Men.' And they did. I never saw nor read of so fine an exhibition of self-sacrificing devotion to a cause, nor so heroic and philosophical a resignation to such a terrible fate.

"I could not help admiring them as men & sympathized deeply with them. Oh, how many such bitter fruits are being continually gathered in this bloody harvest of Death!"[6]

The two rebels asked Chaplain Taylor to pray for them and requested the sacrament, which he administered. They also wrote letters to their families and gave them and their personal belongings to Taylor.

The execution made a deep impression on everyone who saw it. That probably would have been true in any event, but especially in this case because the unidentified man responsible for preparing the nooses didn't know his job and it took the prisoners an excruciatingly long time to die. Broaddus described the scene to his wife. The rebel officers "walked some two or three hundred yards to the gallo[w]s [and] got on the cart," he wrote. "I neve[r] see[n] any one meet death with more c[o]urage than they did. The[y] examined the ropes, and spoke about the matter of hanging as if it was a matter of no great importance . . . The men who had charge of their execution did not doo up the job very well. The ropes did not slip good and their hands were not tied behind them. The oldest one [Williams] caught the rope and said 'Tighter.'

"The feelings of the young[er] man [Lieutenant Peter] came very near over coming him after they had put the rope over his neck and had blind folded him, he shuck [shook] all over and said 'O Collin!' [Colonel]. The Col. said 'We will die like men' and they imbraced each other and were very soon in the etearnal world.

"There was a feeling of sadness on all the troops here . . . and yet all felt as if they aught [ought] to bee hung. I think if ever any one deserved hanging, they did. The Col. [Williams] said he did not ask for mursey [mercy] for him self for he knew what would bee his fate if he was detected and had run the risk and did not expect mursey but he would like for us to spare the young man if we could, for he said he had followed him in this matter, and would not have come if it had not bin for him, but we could not find one guilty and let the other go. I guess it will be aleson [a lesson] to others."

Sensing opportunity as always, the indefatigable James K. Magie found a way to insert himself into the proceedings and ended up sketching the execution and writing a vivid account for *Harper's Weekly*. "The gallows was constructed by a wild cherry-tree not far from the depot, and in a very public place," he wrote. "A little after nine o'clock a.m. the whole garrison was marshaled around the place of execution in solemn sadness. Two poplar coffins were lying a few feet away. Two minutes past nine the guards conducted the prisoners to the scaffold—they walked firm and steady, as if unmindful of the fearful precipice which they were approaching. The guards did them the honor of marching with arms reversed.

"Arrived at the place of execution they stepped upon the platform of the cart and took their respective places. The Provost Marshal, Captain Alexander, then tied a linen handkerchief over the face of each and adjusted the ropes. They then asked the privilege of bidding last farewell, which being granted, they tenderly embraced each other. This over, the cart moved from under them, and they hung in the air. What a fearful penalty!

"They swung off at 9:30—in two minutes the Lieutenant ceased to struggle. The Colonel caught hold of the rope with both hands and raised himself up at 3 minutes, and ceased to struggle at 5 minutes. At 6 minutes Dr. Forester, surgeon 6th Kentucky Cavalry, and Dr. Moss, 78th Illinois Infantry, and myself, who had been detailed to examine the bodies, approached them, and found the pulse of both full and strong. At 7 minutes the Colonel shrugged his shoulders. The pulse of each continued to beat 17 minutes, and at 20 minutes all signs of life had ceased. The bodies were cut down at 30 minutes and encoffined in full dress.

"The Colonel was buried with a gold locket and chain on his neck. The locket contained the portrait and a braid of hair from his intended wife—her portrait was also in his vest pocket—these were buried with him. Both men were buried in the same grave—companions in life, misfortune, and crime, companions in infamy, and now companions in the grave."[7]

Magie was undoubtedly paid for the article and sketch published in *Harper's Weekly*—he did nothing for free—but his surviving letters (the collection is incomplete) make no mention of the amount he received.

———

The hangings were the major topic of conversation in the regiment for the next few days, but camp routine had returned to normal by the following day, at least outwardly. It rained most of the day and Chandler complained there were "flies in abundance." Van Vleck was busy fielding complaints about his promotion of Chandler to second lieutenant of Company I. Most of the men in the company had petitioned to elect an officer of their own choice, "but I of course could not do that for I think [Chandler] will make one of the very best & most popular officers in the reg't.," Van Vleck told his wife. He also admitted his appointment of Elisha Morse as first lieutenant of Company F had been "much against the wishes of the company & officers . . . yet they are beginning to like him very much . . . The capt's. name is Henry E. Hawkins . . . He told me last night that his tent was like another place since Mr. Morse came there. Everything was now so quiet & all study, & everything nice. He said he would not give him up for any thing & was obliged to me for appointing him."

Word came from Nashville that Colonel Benneson had at last managed to get a twenty-day leave of absence and had gone home. "I do wonder what next," Van Vleck wrote. "It may be when he gets back he will be more satisfied to take hold & do his duty or at least a part of it, but I have but little hope of him."

That evening there was "a poor dress parade, several mistakes," Chandler recorded in his diary. He did not say whether the mistakes were his.[8]

The regiment was up at 3:00 a.m. the next day for drill in the rain. Chandler said he "read an account of the 'Execution at Franklin,'" probably the one Magie had written. "Studied in afternoon and was out to battalion drill from three to five. Recited lesson and went to bed early . . . Capt[s] Black and Blackburn were both *drunk*. Our Capt. [Reynolds] says he will resign if this is not stopped."[9]

The regiment was awakened at 2:30 a.m. on the morning of the 12th, "much to the dislike of all," in Chandler's words. Van Vleck established the daily picket lines around the post, and later that morning the troops of the 85th Indiana, who had been captured at Thompson's Station in March, returned to Franklin, having been exchanged for rebel prisoners. "We received them with all honors," Chandler wrote.

The regiment drilled in the afternoon, "a bad one," Chandler said. "I did not go to lesson but to the river, and had a good wash."

Next day, Saturday, June 13, the regiment received a dispatch from General Granger warning of an expected attack. "Our scout came in and said that a large body of the enemy were about five miles off on the Columbia Pike marching this way," Broaddus wrote. The men went to bed that night "with accoutrements on, and [were told to] have our canteens," Chandler reported. There was no attack, but during the night "the Tellagraph [telegraph] was cut and the rail road bridge was burned between her[e] and Nashville," Broaddus said. "So you see," he wrote his wife, "we are agane [again] cut off from communication with Nashville, and I doo not know when the train will bee through agane, but hope it won't bee long."

The 14th was "a warm dusty day, very unpleasant and disagreeable," in Chandler's words. "Did not have inspection as most of the boys were on picket. Went to church . . . Excitement some what high. Ordered [again] to sleep with accoutrements on . . . Rebs reported all around." That day also brought word of the death of Pvt. Gordon Scott of Company E, who had been in the hospital at Nashville.

The warm, dusty weather continued for several days. So did rumors of an impending attack, but Broaddus discounted them. "We doo not feeal [feel] any uneaseyness for we doo not think the Rebels intend to attack us at this place for they have not the forse [force] to spare to garrison it if they were to take it and they know that they would have to sacrifise a good maney lives to take the place," he wrote. "We have about twenty five hundred men at this place, and are well fortified, and think that we can whip five times our number. . . ."

Nevertheless, "we have made up our minds to burn the town of Franklin if we are attacked her[e] agane. We did through [throw] a few shells in to the town when we were attacked the other day, and knocked some pre[t]ty big holes in some of the buildings. One shot wounded a black woman in the arme. The Doctor thought that the arme would have to come off. The Rebels planted their batry [battery] in the town, and we were compelled to fire in that direction, and they have fare [fair] warning now if they doo it again the town will have to go up, and it is a very pret[t]y place.

"The Negro population is increasing very rappidly here at this time. One women [woman] had three little darkies at one litter the other night over in town. Before this rebel[l]ion she would have bin very valuable but Negroes are not worth mutch down here [now].

"We have one or two cases of smal[l] pox in our camp. They belong to the 7th Ky. Cavalry but they are kept off to them selves . . . The train has just got in. The [rail]road is all right agane. . . ."

The 78th had about five hundred men on its muster roll June 15th, not including Companies B and C, which were still in St. Louis awaiting exchange. About two dozen men were on detached duty with an artillery battery with Granger's force in Triune, others were serving as teamsters, and many were sick in hospitals.[10]

June 16th brought joyous news to the regiment. "Gilbert is at last extinguished," Van Vleck wrote. "Colonel Baird rec'd. a dispatch yesterday, saying '*Captain* Gilbert, late Brig. Genl., has just left for Murfreesboro to join his company. Bully.'

"If he [Gilbert] could have been present here last evening he would have had more hate for the 78th than ever. I formed the reg't. into a square and read the dispatch to the men. Such yelling you cannot immagine. It roused the whole country. Col. Baird, whose head quarters are now more than a mile away, was soon over here on his horse to know what on earth was the matter. When he understood it he shook hands with me & rejoiced as much as the rest of us.

"I have never seen a man or officer but what entertains the same opinion of the scamp that we do . . . So the contempt is universal . . . We all feel happy & wonder what will now become of us. Surely no worse fate can befall us than to have remained under Gilbert."

Van Vleck and his men were not the only ones celebrating. "I am out of Gilbert's command thank heaven," wrote Col. Emerson Opdycke of the 125th Ohio. "He [Gilbert] is rather an enigmatical individual, and has not a single friend in his command, outside of his staff. His Q.M. [quartermaster] and Commissary are public plunderers, whether he is implicated with them or not is an open question. I do not think him competent, or *very loyal;* he cannot maneuver his division half as well as some colonels in it, and he is only a capt. in regular service. The Senate did not confirm him, but he has been allowed to keep his place until now; his whole command has been taken from him. I cannot help but feel a little sympathy for him, but his fate is *just,* we have too many such officers. . . ."[11]

That day was the "warmest day of the season," according to Chandler. Odell commented on it too. "The weather is getting quite warm here," he wrote his family, "so much so that we get in the shade during the heat of the day as much as possible. The nights are pleasant. To one who has been in Illinois it would seem that all the house flies in creation had concentrated their forces near Franklin where they make it their daily business [to] annoy the 'dwellers in the tents.' They are so plenty in my tent as I ever saw them in a kitchen. . . .

"A black woman gave me a good plate full of green peas and beans and beets yesterday. I thanked her—says she, 'Oh! Massa, you is welcome to all dat I gib you. I wish I had mo to gib you!' Today I gave 15 cts. for 7 onions."[12]

1st Lt. Jeremiah Parsons of Company K resigned June 17th. 2nd Lt. William B. Akins was promoted first lieutenant to take his place.

Broaddus wrote his wife on the 18th to report that "we had quite a spree in camp yesterday. Two cavalry men fel[l] out about cards. One drew his revolver and shot at the other but mist [missed] him and killed the brother of the man he shot at. The other then drew his revolver and shot the one that shot at him, killing him on the spot & the other one died in afew minutes. They were both hauled off to [the] grave this morning in the same wagon."[13]

Van Vleck was pleased next day with news that "we have been transferred to Brig. Gen'l. A[bsalom] Baird's command. He is very much of a gentleman. I am quite well acquainted with him. I served for two weeks on a court martial with him. I like him very much. He is very popular with all his men & officers. He is a West Pointer, for many years a teacher there."

———

Van Vleck and the other men in the 78th did not yet realize it, but the regiment at last had found a home. It was now part of the Second Brigade of Baird's Division along with the 98th, 113th, and 121st Ohio Volunteer Infantry Regiments. These four regiments would serve together through the remainder of the war.

The 98th Ohio had been recruited in Belmont, Carroll, Harrison, Jefferson, and Tuscarawas Counties and mustered into service at Steubenville, Ohio, August 22, 1862. Though still fearfully green, the regiment was pressed into service at the Battle of Perryville, where it suffered 229 casualties. After that its movements had been similar to those of the 78th.

The 113th included men from Champaign, Franklin, Licking, Logan, Madison, and Montgomery Counties and was mustered into service December 12, 1862. It was sent to Louisville December 27th and a week later to Muldraugh Hill to replace the 71st Indiana and Companies B and C of the 78th after their surrender to Morgan's raiders. After that its movements had been similar to those of the 78th.

The 121st Ohio, organized at Camp Delaware, Ohio, in September 1862, resembled the 78th in a number of ways. Its men—from Delaware, Knox, Logan, Marion, and Morrow Counties—were mostly farmers. The 121st also had been issued old muskets, although theirs were of European manufacture and were in even worse shape than the rifles issued to the 78th. The regiment's first service was guard duty in Cincinnati. Without having an opportunity to drill, and still armed with the almost unserviceable European muskets, the regiment also saw limited duty at Perryville, where it suffered forty-two casualties. Its colonel, William P. Reed, was senior among the officers of the four regiments in the Second Brigade of Baird's Division, and thus took command of the brigade.[14]

Van Vleck wrote his wife that the 78th was "improving very fast in every respect, in health & strength, & drill & discipline. It makes no difference what I want done, I only have to say the word & it is done with alacrity." He also indulged in a little vanity, perhaps forgivably. "I confess I felt a little flattered last night," he wrote Patty. "I allowed the Major [Broaddus] to hold the dress parade, & I took a position off to one side where I had a fine view of their performance, & it was so fine I couldn't help but speak in high terms of it to the officers, & one of them, Capt. [Henry E.] Hawkins, spoke up & said 'Yes the men have improved *very* much,' & then as we started off together he said, 'The reg't. to a man love you, Col., they perfectly worship you, the men all think as much of you as though you was their own father. They think so much of you they can't keep from talking about it & speak of it every day.'

"I mention this for *your* special benefit, & for the reason that it is only one of a good many similar testimonials that I have rec'd. within the last few days, & for the further reason that I presume every man's wife, like himself, is glad to know whether his labors are acceptable as a military commander or not, & when he receives such bountiful testimonials, is he not justified in telling his wife?

"I have feared so much that I should fail, in the command of a reg't., that I should not willingly have accepted the place. You know that from the first I desired only a 2nd position but when I remember how poorly Col. B[enneson] manages things & how poor a faculty he has for getting along with the men & officers, I can't blame them for wishing he may never come back, but I think he will. I rec'd. a letter from him yesterday saying he was much better & would be back as soon as his leave expired."[15]

On the 20th the regiment "got up at our unreasonable time," Chandler reported. Drill was "as usual" and after that it was "dusty and nothing to do. Studied [Hardee's]

Tactics, and loafed after drill." Broaddus noted "their [there] was firing among the pickets this morning and we had one man killed. We captured two or the [three] Butternut...."

Next day was Sunday and Broaddus complained there was no preaching. "Our Chapl[a]in [Taylor] is very sick and I doubt whether he ever preaches agane [again]," the major wrote. "He has not bin well for some time and yesterday evening he was taken with hemerage [hemorrhage] of the lungs and is still bleeding [bleeding] quite freely and unless the doctor gets it [stopped] I fear he will not stand it long. He expects to resign soon any how. I think the warm weather is not good for him.

"We have another yo[u]ng man in the hospital that I think will not live long. He is by the name of James Carrol[l], fife major and a brother in law to Capt. Reynolds. He has diaria [diarrhea] and is very low. The rest of the sick are doing very well. There is but six or eight in the hospital at this place.

"One yo[u]ng man had bin sick for a long time, and was sent to Nashville and got his discharg[e] a short time ago and started home and died on his way home in the cars some where between Indiannaplis [Indianapolis] and Shicago [Chicago]. His father is in the reg't. and will not live long if he does not get a discharge."[16]

The regiment received orders that day to prepare to march to Triune the next morning, but Van Vleck got the orders modified to give the 78th another day of preparation. He also wrote a long letter to Patty covering a number of subjects: "We have a Negro boy named Archy, that takes care of the horses of the field officers, & formerly of the chaplain's but he sold his [horse] a week or so ago to Asst. Surgeon [William H.] Githens ... Mr. Taylor is very bad with bleeding at the lungs, was taken last night. He is a little better now, & [we] think he will get over it. He has made up his mind to resign & will send up his papers tomorrow. I think he had better, for the hot weather will soon use him up. It is rather hard on all of us.

"I only weigh 143½, less than ever before since I was 14 years old, yet I can't see but what I am well. I have to be careful with my diet as I always did but I feel more like work & have less of that trouble[d] feeling that I never could describe than ever before, but I am always scared to look in the glass, for my cheeks are as hollow as Uncle Eleazer's. I can't understand it, for I have a good appetite & digest all I eat. But I think it is the weather, the nights & the fore part of the day are very cool, & the middle of the day very hot, & then the drill I guess has something to do with it, & also the continued excitement of first one kind & then another. I hope & pray that my health may be spared...."

The regiment was excused from picket duty on the 22nd so it could spend the day getting ready to break camp. Those too sick to join the march to Triune were sent to hospitals in Nashville. Broaddus worried about what the 78th would find when it got to Triune; he had heard there were twenty-five thousand troops in the town and feared it would be impossible to find anything to eat—especially for a man with no lower teeth.[17]

The 78th had been in Franklin nearly four and a half months, but if there was any sorrow in parting it was not reflected in any surviving diaries or letters. The regiment started at 6:00 a.m. on the 23rd and had "a very pleasant march" of thirteen miles to Triune. "The roads [were] fine and the boys stand the march well," Broaddus wrote. They arrived "just in time to see the rear guard of the entire army that was here, moving out south," Van Vleck wrote his wife. "I found Gen'l. Granger waiting to give me orders, which were for me to follow him, tomorrow morning, to Salem, south east from here & near Murfreesboro. The whole line is moving southward . . . We are in the rear of the whole line, but of course we can not tell how long we will remain so."

Granger also inquired "whether we had Col. Benneson's things along. I told him I had, & he peremptorily ordered me to leave them here & not to haul them another rod. He said Col B. had gone to *hell* & would never see this reg't. again. I don't of course *know* what he meant. But I am inclined to believe that if there was any significance at all to the remark, the Col. has been, or will, soon be dismissed the service by order of Rosecrans, for some of his numerous errors.

"We expect to start early tomorrow morning."[18]

That evening, however, the regiment received new orders: its destination was no longer Salem; instead, it was to escort a large wagon train to Murfreesboro. And when the men turned out the next morning, the weather was no longer pleasant for marching. It had started raining, and by noon, when the march finally got under way, the roads were already muddy. Much worse was to come.

"Such a march is not yet of record," Van Vleck wrote his wife from Murfreesboro three days later. "You can have no conception of it even if I should attempt a description.

"We had 300 teams in our train, all heavyly loaded, & there were in those teams 1,800 mules, & those mules had 7,200 legs, all prone to kick out the traces, and every time one succeeded in getting out, the whole train had to stop until the driver could put it back. But this was not the most serious difficulty.

"We got started at 12 o'cl'k. Wednesday & it was raining, a cold driving drenching rain & wet[t]ing the ground more & more at every step, and every one of the 7,200 mule legs was punching away as nervously as possible, stir[r]ing up the mud. So that by the time the infantry, which was in the rear, got along, it was well stirred to the bottom, & if the mules lacked anything in mixing the water & dirt thoroughly the deficiency was supplied by the two regiments of cavalry which were in advance of all the wagons.

"Little, however, would we have cared for rain and mud if we could have been permitted to move along without other hinderances, but the road aside from the mud surpasses anything I have ever seen or heard of. Hills of great length & of the most rocky, corrugated surface that can be imagined. No team could go more than a few feet at a time. A little reflection will give you some thing of an idea how long we must be in getting over such a place with our train, which was between four & five miles long. But we were at last over the first long hill and down into the bottom, a marshy cedar bottom. You know what kind of roads a rainy day would find here. So bad were they, that no attempt was made to use them, but we went through the sloughs, through plowed fields where a patch of ground could be found which was not too mushy to be plowed.

"We soon began to see the effects of the low ground. Heaps of corn, boxes of bread, & barrels of pork were scattered in piles at every place where it was possible for the road to be worse than the general average. Here we would find also, wagons disabled, one with the coupling broken, another with the tounge [tongue] ruined, & others with axletrees & wheels broken. Wagons sunk in the mud to the axles, and others with the mules in all over and the drivers completely exhausted from whipping & swearing & sitting down beholding the objects of their care, appearing the very personifications of despair.

"But the drivers were not alone, there must be a whip for every mule, and men at every wheel with rails & jacks to give a helping hand in time of need. And then a push with all the [force] that could be brought to bear upon the wagon helped many pounds toward getting out of the worst places. And in winding through the swamp among the trees, many a time the wagons would be brought up square against a hugh [huge] cedar, that had not the least notion of getting out of the way, & the wagons must be run back by the muscle of soldiers, or [by] 'the ax laid at the root of the tree,' which would equally claim the services of the ever willing boys. Thus we journeyed, rather we thus labored from twelve until eight, when it was too dark to proceed further, when we turned in to a rolling field & the weary patriots lay down in the water & mud and slept in the drenching rain till morning."

The regiment made only three and a half miles that first day. Van Vleck went on to describe two more days of slogging through mud before they finally reached Murfreesboro. "Considering the roads & all the other circumstances," he concluded, "I think this one of the most remarkable marches of the war. The men were indeed tired & sore, and all their feet badly galled & blistered. Wet boots or shoes are very poor things to march in, & they were all soon laid aside after haulting. Soldiers you know carry but one pair of pants, & those they wear, & it was quite necessary that they should be washed in our reg't. before they were dried or the men could never ground arms in them again. It was curious to see the men all barefooted & standing around in the rain

& *in their drawers,* washing their pants. Some however did not go to the pains to take them off but would step into some convenient mud puddle & wash off the thickest of the mud with them on.

"Such is Soldiering down in Dixie."

The march had left the lieutenant colonel's sword "so rusted as to be entirely ruined." His saddle bags also "were soaked through . . . spoiling sundry boxes [of] pills & other medicines. I am glad I have so little use for them. I feel as well as ever I did this morning. You will know how well I am when I tell you that I can chew tobacco all day & not feel badly from its effects."

Batchelor's description of the march was almost as brief as Van Vleck's was lengthy. His diary entry for June 24th was "Raining." For June 25th he wrote: "Raining. Can hardly get wagons through the mud and slush." June 26th: "Raining in torrents but we keep going to ar[r]ive at Murfreesborrary at noon." He was impressed by the sights of the Stones River battlefield near Murfreesboro: "We pass many graves [of] men killed in late battle and many dead horses. One rail pen was arround 7 of the 89[th] Illinois boys another some of the 34th Illinois."[19]

<hr>

The regiment finally had a chance to rest on the 27th, remaining in camp all day. It continued raining, but that didn't stop Batchelor from taking a bath in Stones River, trying to wash away the mud. Chandler was feeling sick, perhaps from exposure on the march, and took some medicine. He still felt well enough to make out part of the muster roll and noted in his diary that the 78th had orders to march at 5:00 a.m. the next day.

They got up at 3:00 a.m. "and fussed around till 5 a.m. when we started," Chandler recorded. "Marched through Murfreesboro, and of all the meanest, dirtiest places, this is the climax. We marched out on the Shelbyville Pike nine miles when we went into camp. I with difficulty made the trip. The medicine I took last night made me weak."

That afternoon they witnessed the passage of a column of rebel prisoners, brought in after Rosecrans's advancing army had fought its way into the town of Shelbyville. Odell counted 495 captives, some wounded, plus two cannon. "We are now upon ground occupied by the enemy a few days ago," he wrote. "For some four or five miles this side of Murfreesboro not a [fence] rail was to be seen—but here, there are some small crops in cultivation, principally wheat & cotton. Every farm has an orchard, peaches are plenty here, blackberries are getting ripe."[20]

Broaddus, meanwhile, was worried about his son, Thomas, who had been sent back to Nashville with others who were sick. "I have not heard what hospital Thos. went too," he wrote Martha, "but he told me he would write as soon as he got to Nashville, but he is very car[e]les[s] about writing, and he may not doo it.

"Capt [Henry] Hawkins accident[al]ly shot him self in the hand yesterday. It will bee quite soar [sore] but not dangerous . . . ."

More prisoners were brought in on the 29th and a company of the 78th was dispatched to escort them back to Murfreesboro. Broaddus spoke to one of the prisoners, an artillery captain, and wrote to tell his wife that the captain said the rebels "will soon have to give up, that the Southern Confed[e]racy is about plaid [played] out. They were a good deal discurajed [discouraged] and I think did not feal [feel] very bad about being taken pris[o]ners."

About 3:00 p.m. orders were received for the balance of the regiment to march to Shelbyville. "In ten minutes we were ready, and the rain poured," Chandler reported. "It rains very easy here. We marched 12 miles and camped in a meadow four miles from Shelby. I go to bed soon on the ground and am tired enough to sleep."

The march took the regiment through some "very good country," Broaddus said. "Wheat and corn look fine and it must bee pret[t]y hard for the rebels to have to leave this section just as the harvest is ripe, for they have bin living very hard, mostly on corn bread and bacon . . .

"We have got with our brigade at last and Cols Warner, Banning and Pierce [of the three Ohio regiments] have all called on us and are very friendly and I think we will like them. They appear to bee very mutch of gentle men."[21]

On the last day of June the regiment marched within a mile of Shelbyville. "This is a Union neighborhood," Chandler noted. "Saw an old lady with a Union flag. Several young ladies came out from Shelbyville and sang several Union songs.

"Granger's order about pilfering was read—and the penalty is severe, but may be needed. Saw an Atlanta paper.

"We will move to Shelbyville tomorrow morning."[22]

8

"I Expect We Will Have a Big Mess"

July 1–August 19, 1863

The 78th Illinois marched into Shelbyville, Tennessee, on the afternoon of Wednesday, July 1, 1863, crossed the Duck River, and made camp in a grove about a mile beyond the river. "The river stinks with dead men and horses," Batchelor wrote. He was right; many rebels and their mounts had drowned trying to escape the federal cavalry charge that had captured the town June 27th. "About sixty bodies have been taken out," Chandler reported. "The river is very high indeed and remarkably swift."[1]

Home in Illinois, Mary Magie wrote a letter to her husband that day. Perhaps irked by some of his complaints, she let him know things were not always pleasant on the home front, either. "You must excuse a very short letter from me today as I am tired," she wrote. "We are getting our cherries picked and I have been very busy all day. This morning I did not get up untill near six o'clock then I made a fire and ironed my collored [collared] clothes, got breakfast, washed dishes, went out and hoed the cucumbers, tomatoes, and corn, then went to work at the cherries. I helped Mrs. Clark today and she will help me tomorrow. . . .

"Yesterday morning I got up at half past four o'clock, and got to my washing at five o'clock, and got it out before nine, cleaned my room and porch, then went out and scrub[b]ed the privy, and just as I got done my boil broke, and discharged a quantity of matter."

She told Magie she had gone to the local bookstore where the proprietor told her about that week's issue of *Harper's Weekly*, which contained Magie's sketch and story about the execution of the rebel spies. The bookseller already had sold his last copy, but Mary was able to borrow it from the man who bought it. She offered no critique of either the sketch or the article. However, she did report she had twice gone to the office of the *Macomb Journal* to see Nichols, the man left in charge, in hopes of getting some money from him, "but he was not to be found . . . Now I must tell you that Dr.

Sandford called this afternoon. He has taken the measure of Eddie's feet, and is going to send to N.Y. [New York] for the shoes. I am going to see Nichols and see if I cannot get him to give me some money to pay for shoes."[2]

It was very warm in Shelbyville on July 2nd and some men in the regiment went swimming in the Duck River, despite the decomposing humans and horses. Next day brought rain, and the 78th received its first mail since leaving Franklin. Broaddus wrote his wife that day to tell her that "all the cavalry left here yesterday and one of our brigades leave[s] to day. Our brigade and apart of another is all the troops that are left here.

"I wrote you [earlier] about some Rebels getting drouned [drowned] at this place," he said. "Their [there] has bin quite a number of bodies taken out since we came here. I was down at the river yesterday and they took one out while I was thir [there]. He was a hard looking sight had bin in the water four days.

"Shelby Ville is larger than Macomb and has bin a very pret[t]y place, and a place of a good deal of business, but there is a good maney old houses in the place. The day we marched in the women and children waived their handkerchiefs and flags from quite a number of houses. I think this the most loyal place we have found in the South."

Pvt. Thomas J. Vail, twenty-three, of Company I, one of the sick who had been sent to the hospital in Nashville, died that day. He was a resident of Industry, McDonough County.

❦

July 4th "passed off very quietly, no firecrackers, no gingerbread, no ice cream, no soda-water," Van Vleck wrote his wife. The lieutenant colonel was a bit under the weather, though, suffering from a cold, and his mood was not improved when he received a letter from Colonel Benneson announcing he would return to the regiment July 12th.

The regiment was not happy either. It had orders to leave its pleasant camp in the wooded grove and move to the public square in Shelbyville. "It rained all morning and at intervals in the afternoon," Chandler wrote. "We moved camp to a most miserable place. All the troops moved into town. Most of them are quartered in houses . . . The worst camp we have ever had. . . ."[3]

Sporadic rain continued the next two days. "I am ashamed to say I did nothing today but read in a novel, *The Woman in White,*" Chandler confessed to his diary on the 5th. "I have no excuse for doing this except a desire to do something, and having nothing to do." Next day, however, he and his newly minted fellow officer, Elisha Morse, started for Nashville to buy clothing and officers' shoulder straps.

Batchelor wrote only one word in his diary that day: "Sick." Broaddus was concerned about sickness, too, but not his own. His wife had complained of a lingering cough, and the major wrote to say that if she did not soon get better he would resign and return home. He also told her he still had not heard from their son, Thomas, since he was sent to the hospital in Nashville.[4]

Odell attended a Union meeting in town that day and listened to several speeches. "The one which most interested me was a speech from an old gray-bearded farmer of this vicinity, who had to lie low while the Rebs were here—but who has been a Union man of the right stripe all the time," Odell wrote his family. "Says he, 'I told 'em, I had but four niggers, but rather than be precipitated into a war by rebellion, I would rather lose them all—but this would not do. We were involved in a war and I lost my niggers too.' He called on his Rebel friends to throw down their arms and secede from Jeff. Davis." Another speaker told how he had hidden in a hollow log in order to avoid Confederate conscription. "A very large Union flag has been raised which for months has been concealed in a straw bed on which the Rebel officers slept," Odell wrote. "The house had been searched and researched but still, the good old flag was preserved."

Van Vleck had Colonel Benneson on his mind, as usual. Lieutenant Worrell had just returned from Quincy, where Benneson was spending his leave, with news the colonel had "talked strongly of resigning," Van Vleck wrote Patty. "Granger is as much down on him as Gilbert was & if he comes back, I fear he will have us all in hot water in short time. [His] greatest trouble is that he outranks all the other colonels & is entitled to the command of the brigade, & none of the reg'ts. or generals want him in that position, believing him to be deficient in health & every other respect, so that he cannot stay long should he come."

If Benneson did return to the regiment, he probably wouldn't like what he found. "I believe I have told you that Gen'l. Granger ordered me to leave all the Col.'s things at Triune," Van Vleck wrote, "but I sent them to Nashville except a box of eatables, which we have taken care of for him ever since last spring long before we went to Nashville & those including some wines & liquors, [which] we felt justified in using up rather than storing them where he never could get them. And his horse we brought along, and a night or two ago the cavalry stole that. So that when he does come & finds his things left behind, his goodies eat up & his liquors drank up, and his pet mare stolen, I expect there will be a storm that will blow us all away; but let it come, who cares; we have got three years to take it in.

"Rosecrans is still marching victoriously on, & we are as usual left to shut the gates behind him. I had rather be here than anywhere else I have ever been but I should like to go along with the army once, to see how it would seem."[5]

"Sick, but do duty," was Batchelor's diary entry July 7th. Broaddus wrote to his younger son, Reuben: "Your Ma sais you want to come down here very mutch. It would bee very nice to make a visit and see all the boys, to see the large arma [army] and especial[l]y the cavalry, and to see the forts and large guns and all these things. But it is not so pleasant to bee compel[l]ed to stay here, as some of our poor fellows have to when they are sick. I went through the grave yard at Franklin a few days before we left their [there], and I counted the graves of our men that had bin buried after we went thier and their was one hundred and fourteen that had died from sickness and wounds and had bin kil[l]ed. I think thier was but ten or twelve kil[le]d and then we sent a great maney of our sick to Nashville and quite a number of them died.

"I have seen stout healthy looking men take sick and die in a few days. It is tear-able [terrible] to be through the hospitals and see the suf[f]ering but [I go] because I thought it my duty. The sick soldiers like to have their comrad[e]s visit them, and especial[l]y their officers, for they think that the officers care som[e]thing for them. And I have bin surprised at some officers for not going to see their sick boys.

"Well Reuben I doo not think you would like the arma [army] if you were to get in it. Nothing but duty would keepe me in it. . . ."[6]

⌒

By July 8th Batchelor apparently was feeling better. "Go forraging get corn eatables mules and horses," he wrote. Chandler recorded that it cost ten dollars for his officer's shoulder straps. He also said he had seen nearly all the regiment's sick men in the hospitals at Nashville, including Dr. Moss, the assistant surgeon, who accompanied Chandler and Lieutenant Morse on their return to the 78th.

They made the trip July 10th, leaving Nashville at 7:30 a.m. and arriving in Wartrace at 11. "We walked from there to Shelbyville, and enjoyed the day," Chandler wrote. "The road was lined with blackberries and I had all I could wish . . . I have enjoyed this five-day vacation. The first I have had since Aug. 20th 1863 [this was an error; he meant 1862]. I have not been off duty a day in all that time."

When they reached Shelbyville they found the regiment had moved again, this time to "a vacant lot in a very pret[t]y part of the town," as Broaddus put it. The major also told his wife he had received a pair of boots she had sent him. They "were very good but I could not get them on until I got them stretched . . . The shoe maker where I got them fixed sais [says] they would have sold for seventy dollars before we came here.

"By the way rebels them selves doo not have mutch confidence in their money . . . A little boy talking to Capt. Allen the other day said the rebel soldiers had plenty of money, had arms full. He said it was so plenty that their piggs made beds of it all winter last winter. So you see that their money is so plenty that it is almost worthless."[7]

Sgt. Jonathan Butler of Company K was admitted to the regimental hospital at Shelbyville that day, July 10th. Records show he was listed as "sick" without defining the nature of his illness. But the major event of the day was news of the Union victory at Gettysburg and the Confederate surrender at Vicksburg. "I wonder if it can all be true," Van Vleck wrote. "If so, what is to prevent a peace before Christmas? Oh what a time of rejoicing when we all get home!"[8]

July 11th brought word of the death in Nashville of Pvt. Charles Viars of Company F, who was from Columbus, Adams County. It also brought Benneson's return to the regiment. "Col. Benneson has got back," Broaddus wrote next day. "He is not dismis[s]ed. I doo not know what will bee dun [done] with him. Gen. Granger and Beard [Baird] both want to get rid of him and if he is put in command of the brigade their [there] will be trouble for all the field officers will oppose it."

The major had other news for his wife: Their son, Thomas, had returned from the hospital in Nashville, "but he does not look as stout as he did before he got sick." Also, the regimental surgeon, Dr. Moss, "is quite sick and we feal [feel] that there is some doubt whether he gets well and we will be very sorry for he is a first rate doctor and a perfect gentleman. If we should loose him I presume Doc Githens will take his place but he is not thought to be so good a doctor as Moss. . . ."

"Their [there] was a man shot at this place a short time before we came here by order of [Confederate General] Brag[g] for desertion. He had bin conscripted or pres[s]ed in to the arma, and just before he was shot he said all he regret[t]ed was that he could not die under the old flag."[9]

July 13th brought "an unpleasant rain," in Chandler's words. He also reported that Harmon Veatch of Company I had been appointed regimental sergeant major, replacing Chandler.

In a postscript to his letter of the day before, Major Broaddus cautioned his wife not to send any money to Thomas "for he does not nead [need] it. I let him have some and he used all he got last pay day. The Col. [Benneson] does not have an orderly all the time and I think there is not mutch chance to get Thos. in their [there]. Standing guard is not so hard as it was in the winter. I will get him an easy place if I can."

Batchelor was feeling poorly again July 14th. "Am very bilious," he wrote. "Have head acke [ache] so mutch but do duty." Chandler recorded his company "had morning drill again till it commenced raining. Spent all morning in making a bunk. Had it about done when we received orders to 'strike tents.' Moved a mile beyond town near the river and pitched our tents, not knowing when we move again."[10]

The new camp was about a half mile south of town in a grove near the Duck River. "The river makes a bend here, nearly in the shape of a horseshoe," Odell wrote. The place had been used previously by the rebels as a campground, but Odell thought it "a much healthier place than town."

The good news about recent federal victories was followed July 16th by reports of draft riots in New York. That day Major Broaddus also reported having more trouble with what remained of his teeth. "I have bin troubled with tooth ake [ache] and I have lost one [tooth] in the last weak [week] and I wish they were all out," he wrote Martha. "The sun has not shown it self a day at a tim[e] for the last month."[11]

Van Vleck, meanwhile, wrote his wife that "Col. Benneson still declines to take command of the reg't. on the plea that he has reported to Gen'l. Baird & must await his orders. I went yesterday to see the Gen'l. & he told me that the Col. didn't seem to care whether he was on duty or not & he thought he would let him slide along for the present. I told him he had been sliding along for the last six months, & I thought it was time he was doing at least some of the work. The Gen'l. replied that he should be *ordered* immediately to duty. But the order has not yet arrived.

"The Col. [Benneson] told the Maj[or] & me, that he was as well as ever & had his usual weight, but he didn't feel quite so strong as he used to, and he didn't intend to go on duty until he was *perfectly* strong if it took a year longer. He said he would take command every sixty days *for a few days at a time,* so as to keep out of the hands of the authorities, for he had understood, that a man off duty for more than 60 days could be mustered out the service.

"Is not that a very laudible [laudable] ambition? The Gen'l. told me that he [Benneson] would be ordered before a Board of Examiners again. I wonder what plea will excuse him this time. *He was too sick before.*"

—

Next few days passed quietly in camp. The rain eased up and the weather cleared each day after morning fog. Odell reported the dry weather allowed his company to resume drilling for the first time since it had left Franklin. The regiment held dress parade on the 18th and there were church services and an inspection the next day, Sunday. Chandler raved over some turtle soup made by Capt. Henry Hawkins of Company F, who shared it with him.

Van Vleck attended the church service, then wrote to Patty. "The Col. still stays in his tent caring for nobody, & nobody caring for him. He still waits for some body to order him to duty & I begin to believe that Granger intends to let him remain just as he is; as long as he is contented to keep out the way . . . & [Benneson] is perfectly satisfied to remain till the end of [the] war with nothing to do but to eat & draw his pay."[12]

Broaddus caught the regiment's relaxed mood in a letter to his wife the next day. "We are having rather a lasey [lazy] time of it of late. We ust [used] to have to stand at armes every morning at three o'clock with out regard to weather and I assure you it was not very pleasant to have to git up at that [hour] of the night and stand in the cold rain untill day light, but we doo not have to git up until five o'clock now and the Col. and I have to bee waked up ev[e]ry morning to breakfast.

"Rather easy soldiering this. But I would prefer more action duties for this thing of laying about loose looks to me as if we was not putting down the rebel[l]ion very fast. . . .

"Gen. Beard [Baird] has gon[e] home on a sick leave and I doo not think he is mutch worse off than I am. But he is a gen[eral], that [is] the diferance."

Broaddus wasn't the only one writing letters that day. Pvt. Cornelius Pierce of Company F was among those who had been left in a hospital at Nashville, where the respiratory ailment that had troubled him since the first rainy day in Louisville was gradually wearing him down. But on July 20th he wrote his family to tell them he had received a very important visitor: "General Rosecrans and staff were here last week. I had the honor of conversing with the general. He thought it would do me good to get to the front and pick blackberries. I think the general not only a good but a great man. He talked freely with the boys and everybody seemed pleased with him." Pierce added, however, that he thought the general cursed too freely.[13]

The regiment had three hours of battalion drill July 21st, learning a couple of new maneuvers. As usual, rumors abounded; the latest was that General Granger's Reserve Corps, including the 78th, was about to be transferred to the Army of the Potomac.

Brig. Gen. Walter Chiles Whitaker, who had received his brigadier's star the month before, visited the regiment July 22nd. Whitaker, who had served in the Mexican War and had been colonel of the 6th Kentucky Infantry (Union), was taking Baird's place while the latter was on leave. He was known as a hard drinker, but made a good impression on Van Vleck, who said "he seems to be a man of considerable ability & a thoroughly interested soldier." Chandler thought "he appears like a pleasant man. He saluted the guard very politely."

Whitaker told the officers he wanted to review the brigade on Sunday, and that disappointed Van Vleck. "I don't like the idea of his having review on Sunday," he wrote, "but know of no way to help myself since it is authorized by military law & custom, which no doubt ought to be changed."

Van Vleck also told his wife he had again been detailed as president of a court martial, "although I protested strongly against it. I don't like the idea of doing all that kind of work, when there are a plenty of others just as competent as I that have never done any of that labor. We have a quarter master of the 98th Ohio Vols. to try for selling provisions belonging to the men, which is a very common sin among that class of officials. There is great corruption among quarter masters at best; there are so many opportunities for them to steal that they find it hard work to resist the temptations."

Broaddus, meanwhile, told his wife that "most of the deserters from our reg't. have got back. Some of them had gon[e] to [word illegible] but concluded after thinking over the matter that they had better return. They blame the Cop[p]erheads for persuading them to leave. I think they as well as the Cop[p]erheads will have a beautiful record to leave to their children. I think the Cop[p]erheads are responsable for the ryot [riot] in New York."[14]

Although they had purchased their shoulder straps and were acting as officers, Chandler and Elisha Morse were wondering when they would receive their commissions. The paperwork had been sent to General Rosecrans more than a month earlier, but the commissions still had not arrived. It was a matter of importance to them, for without their commissions in hand they could not be formally mustered as officers and receive officers' pay.

For the next three days, the weather was warm and the regiment drilled three times a day. "No work except guard duty and drill," Odell wrote. "Plenty to eat—citizens furnish plenty of vegetables at reasonable prices . . . We are expecting to be paid off every day—as the Pay Master is here—and the Pay Rolls have been made out and signed . . . J.T. Pickler [Pvt. Joseph Pickler of Company G] and I bought us some eggs and potatoes today and had a fine mess. . . ."

On July 26th General Whitaker reviewed the brigade. It was "an excessively warm day . . . but fortunately, the sun was obscured by clouds the most of the time until we got through the review, which passed off very smoothly," Van Vleck wrote. "My reg't. was highly complimented by the general, the brigade commander & many spectators, not only for their neat appearance but for the excellent manner of their marching. Every gun was as bright as steel can be polished, not the least speck of dirt or rust could be found upon any part of the poorest gun. It is a very pretty sight to see a review of several reg'ts."

Next day's mail finally brought Chandler and Morse their long-awaited commissions. The following day the 78th was detailed to guard a forage train and left Shelbyville shortly after noon, "rather dreading the trip, as we did not know but we would have to walk, and it was very hot," Odell wrote. "We were agreeably disappointed when Major Broadus ordered six men to get into each wagon. There were about 60 wagons in the train."

The wagon train crossed the Duck River and headed south on the Louisburg Pike for eight miles until it reached "a very rich Reb's farm" where soldiers hitched four mules to a reaper and loaded the wagons with oats and hay. "As we came back the Major had the assurance to go into the stable and lead out the old man's fine black horse which he had kept concealed for fear 'Uncle Sam' would get him . . . We had the pleasure of riding back. It was dark when we got here."[15]

Having been stricken with "bilious fever" on the 28th, Van Vleck checked into the regimental hospital on the 30th. There, he said, "I could be better taken care of than it is possible to be in a tent. I have the best of a bed & the very best of care, as well as though I was at home. The surgeons give their personal attention as though I was [their] own brother. The hospital is a large college building & I have a fine airy room. I have no doubt but by the grace of God I shall be able for duty in a day or two."

Chandler visited the lieutenant colonel and was not encouraged. "I fear that he [Van Vleck] and the Major will leave suddenly sometime and leave us here in the cold under O.B.," he confided to his diary ["O.B." was his abbreviation for "Old Benneson"].[16]

Hot, dusty weather continued as July passed into August, and the men of the 78th bathed and swam in the Duck River at every opportunity. On August 1st, Chandler reported that Company D had a competition for prizes. The nature of the competition was not recorded, but 1st Sgt. James Abbott emerged the winner.

Next day was Sunday. The paymaster visited and paid the men for the months of May and June, again leaving the government a month in arrears. Although they had their commissions in hand, Chandler and Morse still had not been mustered as officers so they were not paid for the time they had served as lieutenants, but Major Broaddus gave both men a loan—thirty dollars for Chandler and sixty-five dollars for Morse, who promised to write his wife and tell her to pay that sum to Martha Broaddus back in Macomb.

"Col. Benneson sais he will take command of the reg't. in the morning," Broaddus wrote. "I think it is about time he was dooing something. Col. Van. is sum [some] better . . . As Col. Benneson will take command of the reg't. in afew days Col. Van. does not feel at liberty to make any offer of the chapl[a]incy of the reg't. to any one."[17]

Another of the sick who had been left behind in Nashville succumbed to his illness August 3rd. This time the victim was Pvt. Samuel M. Ewing of Company A, who was from Camden, Schuyler County. Cornelius Pierce also remained in the hospital there, and his condition was worsening. "I am too sick now to write," he said in a brief note to his wife. He also told her not to try to visit him because she would not be allowed through the lines. Sometime after this brief letter was written—the date is not certain—Pierce was given a discharge for disability, and though his condition was grave, he was placed on a train that would take him home to Quincy.

Van Vleck, though, was feeling better. He had been without fever several days, but told Patty he was "quite weak & my head troubles me some, so that I can not sit up yet, more than a few minutes at a time. The unceasing care & kindness of the officers of the reg't. have been exceedingly gratifying, for I have thus been able more perfectly than ever before to learn their genuine feelings towards me . . . It has more than paid me for my sickness. They have all been to see me. Many every day, some still oftener, although the camp is two miles out.

"Gen'l. Rosecrans has been here to day [August 3rd] & reviewed the troops. He *specially* complimented the 78th for their appearance & movements. He said he did not know who had drilled them, but who ever it was understood his business well. This set our officers & men all pretty high & the Ohio reg'ts. didn't like it I understand." The regiment had come a long way since its first fumbling attempts to drill on the fields outside Quincy.

"Benneson is very kind to me, comes to see me every day, & urges me to ask for leave of absence," Van Vleck continued. "But I tell him that the next leave belongs to the Major & I shall not take it from him, & that when I go home again I want to go to stay. He expresses much solicitude lest I resign."[18]

Odell provided a detailed account of the review by General Rosecrans. "The brigade formed and marched across the river into a large pasture on the Columbia Pike, under command of Brig. Gen. Whittaker. We formed in a line of battle fronting to the north, 78th on the right, next Miller's Chicago Battery. The left and center was made up of the 113th, 98th and 121st Ohio Reg'ts. As soon as this was done, the Gen. made his appearance—in company with Gen. Whittaker and staff and taking position, some 30 or 40 rods in front of the center, we were ordered to open ranks (that is, the rear rank moves back four paces, the commissioned officers four paces to the front, as on dress parade). All things being ready, the Gen. and his suite rode along the line, beginning on the right.

"Although he passed briskly along, he had something to say to most of the officers and men—he wore a pleasant smile on his face—talked in a clear and decisive tone—calculated to animate and encourage . . . He said the 78th was the healthiest and best drilled reg't. in the brigade. He told the officers to take great care to keep the men healthy."

Chandler also described Rosecrans: "He is a strong advocate of lager and goes in for singing. About 5.10, broad shoulders, very compactly built, large head projecting backward, light whiskers, full face, eagle nose, very prominent."[19]

There was no battalion drill next day because Benneson still had not taken command of the regiment, Van Vleck was still recovering from his illness, and Major Broaddus also had fallen ill. The weather continued very hot and humid, but on the afternoon of August 5th a rain shower cooled the atmosphere and left a pleasant evening.

Broaddus, for one, was glad to see the change. "The last few days [of hot weather] has bin pret[t]y hard on the men," he wrote Martha. "Col. Van does not git along as fast as he aught too. He is clear of fever but [word illegible] quite weak but the doctor sais he will be around in afew days. I hope he will for I doo not feel very well and I am in command of the reg't. and am not really able to doo the woork. My back has bin troubling me agoodeal [word illegible]. The hot weather I think perhaps has bin the cause of it. I would make an application for a leave of absance but I doo not know whether I would git it or not and it cost so mutch [to travel home] and I would bee about half of the time on the road and if I don't git better soon, I will resign and come home. . . .

"If it did not cost so mutch and thier [there] was any place for you to stay I would have you come . . . but we are one mile from town, and have to git a pass to go up when we want to go, and I would not be permit[t]ed to stay out of camp at night, and in day time I have to command the reg't. So you see I could not be with you any po[r]tion of my time, and you must not let your disier [desire] over come your judgement in this matter."

Van Vleck at least was out of bed. "I have sit up nearly half the time today in the rocking chair which Mr. Morse borrowed for me, of a good Union lady," he told his wife. "It is very agre[e] able to be able to be up, for I had become very tired lying in bed so long."[20]

President Lincoln declared Thursday, August 6th a day of national prayer and thanksgiving for the recent Union victories, so church services were held both in the morning and afternoon at Shelbyville, with passes given to all the men so they could attend. Drill was suspended, which was just as well because another hard rain fell in the afternoon. A train headed for Shelbyville ran off the tracks and killed three soldiers and the accident delayed delivery of the mail to the 78th and other regiments.[21]

Drill resumed the next day, but with Van Vleck and Broaddus both sick, Capt. Granville Reynolds took temporary command of the regiment. That left Chandler in temporary command of Company I. "Made a few mistakes, as all beginners are liable to," he wrote.[22]

August 8th was Van Vleck's tenth day in the hospital. "I have never known what homesickness is, until I came here," he wrote Patty. "To have nothing to do but to think of home. I don't wonder the poor boys in hospital get homesick & desert. I shall never pass sentence of death on a man for deserting from hospital." He did report, however, that his appetite was beginning to return, which he regarded as a hopeful sign.

Chandler spent the day on picket duty on the Murfreesboro Pike. "Was kept busy all day reading passes," he wrote. Broaddus visited Van Vleck in the hospital and each tried unsuccessfully to convince the other to apply for a leave of absence and spend some time at home.[23]

Even though he still felt poorly, Broaddus resumed command of the regiment the next day because General Whitaker had scheduled another grand review, even though the day was frightfully hot. "Our Gen. is great on reviews," the major wrote Martha. "I think they are almost to[o] often this hot weather. Especially when we don't feel very well.

"You ask how the boys are pleased with Lt. Chandler. Very well as fare [far] as I know. He is agoing to make a first rate officer and he is a first rate fellow. Very few boys of his age that are his euquel [equal]. He is not puffed up at all but a very modest un assuming boy and if he lives and this ware [war] should continue he will make his marke. Lt. Morse is very popular withe his men and he deserves to bee for he is a good officer and a good fellow."

—— ~

Monday, August 10th marked a year to the day since the men of Captain Allen's Company H left Dallas City to begin their service in the war, but there is no mention in any surviving letters or diaries indicating that anyone in the company remembered the anniversary. The regiment kept up its usual camp routine, drilling in the morning and afternoon despite continued hot weather.

Van Vleck remained in the hospital, but "I am living quite high," he told Patty. "I have oysters three times a day & stewed ripe apples or peaches, & London porter or good ale. I have been blessed with presents from the officers of the reg't. in the way of wine, porter, oysters, whiskey, brandy & ripe fruit. They are very grateful to my feelings as tributes of respect, & I ought not to forget the privates, for there is not a day passes but many of them come to see me & the most of them are sure to bring a ripe apple or peach.

"We have done nothing as yet about getting another chaplain. I had expected to call a meeting of the officer[s] before I was sick, but one thing and another hindered until I was taken down."

It had been a month since Sergeant Butler of Company K entered the hospital. Whatever was ailing him, he was no better, so his company commander, Capt. Maris R. Vernon, wrote a letter requesting a furlough for him. "Sergt. Butler has had little or no sickness prior to this since entering the service," Vernon wrote. "He has always been with the regiment on the march, and without regard to weather has ever discharged his duties in a prompt and soldierly like manner. A furlough would not only benefit him in health and spirits, but would also afford him an opportunity to arrange his business matters at home in a more satisfactory manner for absences. Sergt. Butler has never before asked for a furlough." The request was sent up the chain of command.

Broaddus wrote his wife again on the 11th to tell her that two of the brigade's Ohio regiments were leaving that day. "I hear they go to Waretrase [Wartrace]," he wrote. "That leaves but two reg'ts of infy [infantry] here and one reg't. of cavalry . . . As the arma [army] is on the moove I would not be surprised to git marching orders at any time."

The major also noted that Colonel Benneson had been back for a month but still had not taken command of the regiment. The colonel "poaks [pokes] around and sais nothing to any one and no one sais any thing to him. We have all quit messing [eating] with him. He has one Negro to cook for him and one to take care of his horses and no one to mess with him. There is agreat deal of dissatisfaction with his course in the reg't. I have bin thinking that the officers would petition him to resign but I don't know as they will. . . ."

Odell wrote his family that day to report the army was beginning to organize Negro regiments. "There is a call for more commissioned officers and privates to take charge of them," he said. "The 78th will furnish some. How would you like for me to join one?"[24]

Several days earlier, Cornelius Pierce had arrived home in Quincy, having miraculously survived the rail journey from Nashville. Back in the hands of his family, he was placed in the same comfortable featherbed he had slept in before his departure to the service—a bed he had often dreamed of while trying to sleep on cold or wet ground in Kentucky and Tennessee. And there, on Tuesday, August 11th, surrounded by his family, he quietly passed away. He was thirty years old.

Back in Shelbyville, the 78th again moved camp August 12th, this time to a location nearer town. Van Vleck felt well enough to visit the camp, although he was still too weak to resume duty. He told Patty that that Colonel Benneson "remains in his tent doing nothing" but "comes every day to see me & talks exceedingly nice to me, but I can see through his thin mask, for I know that he is as jealous of me as he would be of a successful suitor to his own wife; but I can get along with him without any outbreak or expressed ill feeling. I only hope that somebody may order him to some kind of duty, or [otherwise get him] out of the way, before a great while for I am very tired of seeing him lie around doing nothing."[25]

As Van Vleck and Broaddus intimated in their letters, the regiment's other officers had grown increasingly resentful over Benneson's peculiar behavior and refusal to take responsibility. Their resentment finally boiled over that night. Unknown to Benneson and unattended by Van Vleck, who remained in the hospital, the officers met and resolved to sign a petition calling on the colonel to resign. The petition "will ra[i]se a brease [breeze] I think but let it come as well now as any time," Broaddus wrote. "He [Benneson] knows nothing of [it] yet but will know it soon. I think every officer in the reg't. will sign the petition."

The officers' meeting preceded a "grand ball in the city last night," the major added. "Quite a number of the officers of the 78th was their [there]. I had an invitation but did not go. I hear agood deal of brag[g]ing on the beauty that was in attendance but I must confess I have seen but very few pret[t]y women since I have bin in Tennessee . . . ."

The ball was sponsored by General Whitaker. Van Vleck attended, traveling by ambulance. "There were about 50 ladies present & I had a good chance to see characteristics of the Southern people in the way of dress," the lieutenant colonel told his wife. "The dresses of the most of them were relics of the days of peace and plenty. Indeed, I think there was not a dress there that was not bought before this rebellion began, & to my mind, it was a serious commentary on the folly of the rebellion.

"Our young officers went in on their nerves and did some tall dancing, but they all agreed that the girls were a good deal below the average of Northern girls, both in beauty & intelligence. I suppose they danced until the morning was near at hand, but I became quite tired and returned shortly after nine, only remaining there about an hour. . . ."[26]

Next day the officers of the 78th notified Colonel Benneson of their petition. Benneson immediately went to see Van Vleck in the hospital.

"The storm I predicted in my last [letter] has broken," Van Vleck wrote Patty. "The company officers unanimously signed a petition requesting the Col. to resign & go home, & then sent a representative to him & advised him of the fact, & gave him the choice to resign honorably without having the petition sent to him, or to receive the petition; and if he would not then resign they would publish the petition, and prefer charges against him that should dismiss him from the service.

"The Col. seemed very much surprised & agitated and took time to consider the matter. I don't know what he will conclude to do. He says that he is hunted on all sides. Gen'l. Granger is just as bitter against him as Gilbert was, and he has not one friend to whom he can go for consolation or advice. All above him, all below him and those of his own rank alike, care nothing for him. And all alike express the same opinion, that he was never made for a military commander. Still he has such an ardent love for money, that nothing will induce him to resign, except the belief, that it is the only thing that will save him from being dismissed [from] the service.

"It is quite embarrassing to me to have matters stand as they do. I well wish that he might either go home or go to work, to save this unpleasant mode of trying to get rid of what the regiment regard[s] as an encumberance. But I really suppose that he will do neither until he is compelled to. He is now busy I am told talking with some of the more pliable officers who signed the petition, to know why they signed it, and to induce them if possible to recant.

"One of the captains that he thus talked with was inconsiderate enough to tell him that the reg't. was afraid if they didn't get rid of the Col. that the Lt. Col. would resign; and that they much prefer[r]ed to loose the Col. to the Lt. Col. and that they liked the Lt. Col. much better for a commander than they did the Col. This kind of talk of course could do nothing but harm as it raised the Col.'s suspicions that I was at the bottom of a conspiracy to dethrone him, and served to inflame his jealousy against me which already burned brightly enough.

"So much were these feelings raised in the Col. that he could not resist coming to see me this morning, to tell me, that he supposed I thought that he accused me of this conspiracy against him. Oh no, I told him, that I had never thought of such a thing. That I was entirely innocent, and had not the least doubt but he so regarded me. He said that was true, that he had always entertained for me, the very highest regard, & wanted to assure me that he had not the *least* suspicions against me. I told him that I had entire confidence in his assurance, since I knew that I had never given him any grounds for suspicions. He reassured me of his high regards & suggested that we had always got along together with the utmost harmony. I readily assented to this & knew no reason for interrupting the harmony existing. He then bid me good day & started back for camp with much less consolation than he expected to find.

"Thus matters rest."

Matters did not rest long, however. "There were several of the officers in to see me, last night," Van Vleck wrote again next day. "They inform me that the Col. has visited all the company officers, except those from McDonough Co[unty], & privately labored with them to induce them to reconsider their action & withdraw their names from the petition. He used every argument & pled with them promising to do better than he had done, and asking that they would withhold their action & try him for three weeks longer, & warning them against this McDonough County influence, which was control[l]ing the whole regiment; but the result of a whole day's labor did not erase a single name from the petition. [Company I, commanded by Capt. Granville Reynolds, was largely from McDonough County.]

"The officers all stood remarkably firm & told him, many of them, some wholesome truths that served to refresh his memory of things that he had forgotten. He asked each the question whether he doubted his capacity to drill the reg't. The reply was, 'I don't know, sir, *I have never seen you try.*' Rather a knockdown argument to a col. who had been with his reg't. for twelve months. He gathered very dry consolation wherever he went & was very much cast down & was feeling exceedingly bad, for he told the adj't [adjutant] that he couldn't resign, that [such] a matter [was] out of the question, *for his wife had rented their house for three years & gone to boarding.*

"That settles the question, so far as he is concerned, but it don't quite satisfy the officers who have got their 'dander up,' & will send in the petition this morning, and will send up charges tomorrow morning that they think will produce the same general result as a resignation, & the petition will be published. So that the beginning of the end, is not yet."

The rank and file of the regiment was largely unaware of the ferment among the officers; they were mostly preoccupied by the usual daily camp routine. A squad from Company G, including Odell, was assigned to guard a forage train on Saturday, August 15th. The foragers "brought in about 25 loads of hay," Odell wrote. "We took it off a rebel captain's farm, who was killed in the last fight we had at Franklin. The farm is a very large one—good orchard, good spring and very fine house. A few 'darkeys' hold possession, while Uncle Sam's boys gather the crops." It was a hot day—about ninety degrees in Odell's estimation—and he told his family he was bathing in the Duck River about three times a week, before breakfast.[27]

Word came next day of a change at the division level, with Gen. James Steedman replacing Baird as division commander. Steedman had been a newspaper editor in civilian life, served in the Ohio State Senate, and became chief of police in the city of Toledo. He had seen action at Perryville and Stones River and enjoyed the nickname "Old Steady." Not everyone agreed with that assessment, however. John Grant Mitchell, who would later command the Second Brigade, including the 78th, conceded that Steedman was a fighter, but otherwise "no more worthless man ever commanded men . . . He had no idea of the needs of his men, no thought of their food or clothing or comforts, 'no more than (of) a hog.' His devotion to cards and whiskey and women filled the measure of delight except when under fire and then he was a lion."[28]

"I know too little of the new man to express an opinion of the change," Van Vleck wrote. "As to our own affairs there is but little change. Last night the Col. was handed the petition to resign, & I know that there are a long string of charges that would sink any ordinary man to eternal infamy, ready prepared, to send up to morrow, in case he still refuses to resign, as we suppose he will.

"He is in a terrible state of mind. There is a fearful struggle going on in his mind between avarice and personal comfort . . . But thus far he has declined to determine what to do, and says that he must have several days to decide. But the officers told him when they handed him the petition that he must decide by tomorrow morning.

"My health continues on the ascendant, & I expect to go to the reg't. and report for duty in the morning."

Broaddus also was keeping his wife informed of the latest developments in the regimental soap opera, but he had more mundane matters on his mind as well—mainly food. "We are getting plenty to eat now," he wrote. "Peaches and ap[p]les are Ripe and pret[t]y plenty. I have tasted of water mellons but twice this season. They are very scarse [scarce]."[29]

Broaddus wrote Martha again on the 18th to report that "Col. Van. is back with the reg't. and is in command. He begins to feel pret[t]y well agane. Col. Benneson is still laying around dooing nothing. The petition that I spoke of was handed to him afew days ago. He will not resign, I think, and to day Capt. Vernon [of Company K] preferred charges against him. So you see that the officers are determined to git rid of him if posable [possible] and I expect we will have a big mess and should not wonder if some of us was put under arrest soon. But let it come, for if he stays we doo not want to."

Van Vleck had a memorable first day back in command. "Yesterday the Col. called me into his tent & wished me to advise him," he wrote Patty August 19th. "I told him that my position was such as to make it a very delicate matter for me to advise him. But he said, that should make no difference as he had never regarded me as ambitious, & if I was I had a right to be & no one could blame me for it. He wanted to talk to me as a Christian & a Mason, as he had ever regarded me as both & he now hoped he was both as he had made a profession of religion when at home recently.

"After the settlement of preliminaries, he said he had no personal feeling against any but the Major, & I assured him that the Major had no *personal* ill will against him. Whereupon he went for the Major & brought him in & they buried the hatchet so far as personal feelings are concerned.

"He then wanted our honest convictions of what was his duty, under existing circumstances. We told him that he could never propitiate the officers of the reg't. and the longer he remained here, the wider would be the breach for the officers had determined to carry the matter to the last extremity & would prefer some very serious charges, if he declined to resign. To cut the matter short, he finally agreed to resign as soon as Doctor Moss gets back, if he would give him the necessary certificate of disability.

"One thing more I must mention. He said that he should not have felt so badly about this movement if the officers had stated their true reasons in the petition for desiring him to resign. That he had talked with all the officers excepting a *very few* (from McDonough I suppose) and that the principal reason assigned by them all for wanting him out the way, was that the Lt. Col. had drilled the reg't. & brought it up to its present high standard of discipline & drill & that he is entitled to the honors & profits of its commander. He said he knew this was true & if this had been stated in the petition as the reason for wanting him to resign, he could have resigned cheerfully.

It struck me that this was a very peculiar exhibition of taste. It is the last reason in the world I should want assigned against me in a petition to resign if I were in his place.

"I am glad there is so good a prospect of an early settlement of the trouble, as it is greatly impairing the efficiency of the reg't. while it hangs over us."

As if that weren't enough for one day, Van Vleck reported he had been "foolish enough" to "eat a small piece of musk mellon, and it gave me the cholera morbus of which I suffered greatly all night last night. But I am well again this morning, & have learned a lesson that will not soon be forgotten. I think I am about as near empty this morning, as a person ever was."[30]

August 19th also was the last day of life for James K. Magie's relative, Pvt. Charles C. Magie, twenty-six, of Company C. He died that day in the hospital at Nashville.

9

"In the Very Thickest of the Fight"

AUGUST 19–SEPTEMBER 20, 1863

THE 78TH REGIMENT STRUCK ITS TENTS AGAIN AUGUST 19TH AND MOVED INTO downtown Shelbyville, occupying the town square and a pair of hotels. Its sojourn there was brief. General Steedman "came last night & orders us to move this morning to the north side of town," Van Vleck wrote. "So we go."

Their new campsite was again near the Duck River about a mile from town. Except for an artillery battery and a cavalry detachment, the 78th was the only infantry regiment remaining at Shelbyville. Once again it had been left behind.

To nearly everyone's surprise, Colonel Benneson announced August 21st that he was taking command of the regiment. Van Vleck wrote his wife that he asked the colonel "whether he still intended to abide by his promise to the Maj. & me, to resign when Doct[or] Moss get[s] back, & he said he did, provided the Doctor would give him the necessary certificate of disability. But if that be his intention I can't understand why he should be so very anxious to get command when he can't remain at most, but a couple of weeks, if he resigns as he agreed . . . But it may be possible that he will keep good faith with us."[1]

There was no chaplain to provide services for the regiment on Sunday, August 23rd. Major Broaddus, for one, could have used some spiritual comfort. He had received a letter from Martha informing him that his teenaged son, Reuben, had been injured in an accident. "It is a very bad hurt and I am affraid it will disfigure him very mutch," he wrote. "I hope to git a letter from you in the next mail giving me the particulars about it and in mean time I hope for the best."

Broaddus did have good news about his other son, Thomas: "Capt. Reynolds offered six prizes to the six best drilled men in his co[mpany] and Thos. was one of the six that got a prize," he wrote.

But there was bad news, too. "We lost a very fine yo[u]ng man out of the reg't. yesterday. He was by the name of Curl [John B. Curl, aged twenty or twenty-one, a member of Company I]. His farther [father] got here a few hours before he died. He was in his right mind untill afew hours before his death. He died of typhoid fever and was not thought to be dangerous."

Broaddus again acknowledged his wife's repeated wish that he resign, but added: "Our arma [army] is on [word illegible] moovement at this time and I doo not like to resign just at this time but I will send in my resignation in the course of the next month if nothing happens to prevent [it]." The major also reported Benneson had taken command of the regiment and "is trying to bee very ple[a]sant."[2]

Two days later, Van Vleck told Patty that after being in command of the regiment several days, Colonel Benneson was "the most changed of any man I ever saw. He works all the time, attends personally to dress parades and drill (something he never did before) and during the day, is in the saddle all the time. He rides up town and back in much haste a great many times a day and rides off in all directions from camp and back every few minutes, into his tent, and off again—the very personification of industry and energy! What on earth he rides around so much for, nobody can guess, but I presume it is for the exercise, and at the same time to put on an air of business.

"We are all satisfied that he does not intend to resign. But Dr. Moss is expected back today. He will, if the Dr. comes, be given an opportunity to tender his resignation, and, should he decline the charges will go forward."

❧

Vilasco Chandler was finally mustered into the service as a second lieutenant August 27th by somebody named "Lt. J.B. Hay—who does not understand his business," Chandler wrote. Elisha Morse was not so lucky. He had gone to a mustering officer only to be told the officer had run out of the necessary forms. He tried again only to be informed there was a War Department order against mustering any new officers into a company that already had two officers and fewer than eighty-three men, which was the case in Morse's Company F (Chandler's company had ninety-one men, so the rule did not apply to him). Unless a waiver could be obtained, Morse would continue to receive a private's pay even while serving as a first lieutenant.[3]

Except for the unusual sight of its colonel busily riding to and fro, the regiment kept to its normal routine over the next few days, although a spell of unusually cool weather forced warmer dress and a return to campfires, especially in the evening. "It is quite chilly in our tents and we have to go out and sit by the fire to keep warm and then smoke nearly puts our eyes out," Broaddus wrote on the 30th.

Doctor Moss returned and met with Colonel Benneson, but the colonel "has not sent in his resegnation yet but sais he will to day," Broaddus wrote. "He is in pret[t]y hot water. He has put five officers under arrest for signing the petition. Sais he will not put me under arrest. I told him I did not ask any favers [favors]. He sais he wants to be friendly with me. We had along [a long] talk yesterday evening."

Broaddus also wrote a stern letter to his injured son, Reuben. "I learned through a letter I got from your Ma that you had met with a very bad accident and had got badly hurt," he said. "I was very sorry to hear it, for I am affraid that it gave you a gradeal [great deal] of pain, and I am very mutch afraid that it will disfigure you for life, and that would be bad. And I can say that I am truly sorry that it hap[p]ened.

"But Reuben, you doo not know with what sorrow and shame I learned that you got hurt while in disobediance of your Ma. Now Reuben I would not have thought that you would have dun [done] so. I told you that I wanted you to obay [obey] your Ma and I thought you would have dun it, especially when she is left almost alone and no one to comfort her but you and Emma. But in sted [instead] of trying to make her burdens lighter you are making them heav[i]er. You know that your Ma has very poor health and you aught [ought] to stay with her and doo all for her that you can.

"Your Ma sais I had better come home and look after your int[e]rest. Is it posable [possible] Reuben that I have to lay down my arms and quit fighting for my country in the hour of her peril and come home to try and persuaid [persuade] you to bee a good boy and obay your Mother[?] So mutch as I love my country yet I feel that I have a duty at home to perform in taking care of my family and Reuben if it was to come home to protect your rights or int[e]rest from others [w]rongs I could doo it chearfuly [cheerfully]. But it is to persuaid you not to doo [w]rong if it becomes ne[ce]ssary for me to come home.

"Now Reuben I doo hope you will try and bee abetter boy. Stay with your Ma at night and doo not run off down in town or go to the creek but stay at home and learn your books and try and make a man of your selfe. . . ."[4]

Van Vleck had some later news about Benneson. "The Col.'s matters have at last come to a head," he wrote Patty. "I have been acting as *mediator* between him and the other officers. And after getting him to agree to resign quite a number of times, I at last succeeded in getting his name signed to the necessary application, & placed in my hands with the agreement that I am to go to Nashville with the resignation and withdraw the charges & get his resignation endorsed as favorably as possible, by [General] Granger, so that there shall be no doubt of its acceptance. So that there is reason to hope that our family troubles are about ended for a time, at least."

Benneson "is most thoroughly tired of trying to stay with the reg't. against its will, & has wisely concluded, to use the language of his resignation that, 'I can better subserve the interests of my country at home than with said reg't.' And the reg't. all [agree] with him & wish him success in his enterprise of serving the country at home.

"It has been a very disagreeable position for me. He *would* insist that I was his best friend & the only man that he could trust, & so did all his plannings, lamentings and negotiatings with me. He has manifested a very great liking for me, as well as unlimited confidence in my religious character & integrity, & has bestowed very fulsom[e] praise not only to me but to others in and out of the reg't.

"He told Col. Reid that I was one of the best men in the world & had a good deal more brains than he had & was a good deal better lawyer than he was &c &c. I am surprised that I could get along through such a fearful struggle as we have had without incurring his displeasure, for I really expected that he would lay the cause of all his troubles at my feet and attribute them to ambitious designs, but he has not only repudiated & denied all such feelings time and again, but has manifested the very kindest regard & the highest respect for me, from the first to the last.

"Poor man! I think he is more to be pitied than blamed or despised."

That morning the unlucky and often unhealthy Lieutenant Morse left for Stevenson, Alabama, in charge of a squad detailed to guard a herd of cattle. "I hope he may come back well but fear the tramp may be too much for him," Van Vleck wrote.

Since it was Sunday, Odell went to church in Shelbyville. "The house was crowded with men, women, and children," he wrote his family. "There were some soldiers—the rest were all black folks. The preacher was black. I expect you would like to see the black people have meeting—they appear to be very good folk. What a pity they were ever brought into slavery and kept in ignorance—only a few of them can read. The preacher can read—I don't know how he learned; for Negroes have not been allowed to go to school in this state—but that time is past."[5]

On the morning of the last day of August, Van Vleck started for Nashville with Colonel Benneson's resignation papers in hand, hoping to get them approved quickly. "All bid him God speed," Chandler wrote in his diary.

The colonel's resignation was on Broaddus's mind, too, as he wrote a letter home. His wife, Martha, had asked him if he and Van Vleck signed the petition asking Benneson to resign. "I did but he [Van Vleck] did not," the major wrote. " . . . I knew he [Benneson] could not charge me with personal motives for our reg't is below the minimum [in manpower] and if [the colonel] gets out we can't elect a col[onel] and as we can't promote the Lt. Col. you see it would not help me any in that direction. But it was for the good of the reg't. and I think we will get rid of him [Benneson] and that is all we want."

Although his admonitory letter to Reuben had not yet reached home, Broaddus was pleased to hear from his wife that his son had already adopted an attitude of contrition. "I was very glad to hear of Reuben's determination to be abetter boy," he wrote. "I hope he will car[r]y out his determination. Nothing would give me more pleasure, and nothing hurst [hurts] me so mutch as to here [hear] of the bad conduct of my children."

The first day of September was another day of camp routine. It was also the first birthday of the regiment, a year since it had been mustered at Quincy. The regiment had come a long way in that time, but if anyone paused to reflect on its progress after a year in existence, they did not mention it in their letters or diaries.

Broaddus, however, was busy writing again on Tuesday the 2nd. "You say in your letter that you are affraid that I doo not tell you how sick I am," he wrote Martha. "I would not dec[e]ive you. I have tryed to tell you all about how I was as near as I could. I have bin able to [do] duty the most of the time altho[ugh] I have not felt well for the last month, but think that I feel some better than I did one month ago, and when cool weather com[e]s on I think I will get better. . . ."[6]

The 78th lost another man Thursday, September 3rd, when Pvt. Bernard F. Roe, eighteen, of Company G, died of disease in Shelbyville. He was from Camp Point, Adams County.

Van Vleck returned from Nashville the next day bringing the acceptance of Benneson's resignation, which he delivered to the colonel "at 5 o'cl'k. last eve., when he ceased to be Col. of the 78th Reg. Ill. Vol. and became a citizen," the lieutenant colonel wrote his wife.

Benneson, however, had one last surprise in store. "All our troubles have been kept entirely from the soldiers," Van Vleck continued, "so that very few of them knew that he [Benneson] had been petitioned to resign, or that charges had been prefer[r]ed against him. It was kept from them not only at his request, but from views of policy. Imagine, then, the surprise of the officers, last night, when they learned that he had employed private soldiers to go all through the companies and get signatures to a paper expressing great regret at his resignation, he telling them that he had been forced to resign by the officers, but forgetting to tell them why.

"The officers feel highly incensed at this underhanded attempt to get up an antagonism between themselves & their men. I will this morning explain to the men the whole story, & the Col. will be lucky if he is not drummed out of camp. He expects to start for home tomorrow, when I hope to be able to date the end of our troubles from him.

"I now have the satisfaction of knowing that I am commander of this regiment & owe no allegiance to so small a man as the Col. has shown himself to be."

Benneson was not drummed out of camp. He simply vanished. "O.B. [Old Benneson] suddenly disappearing this morning, having sold out," Chandler wrote on the 5th. "He went without bid[d]ing any body good bye. Bully for him."

But the colonel didn't make it out of camp without a last conversation with Major Broaddus. "I had very plain tok [talk] with Benneson this morning," the major wrote. "He has bin talking to the men and telling them that we forsed [forced] him [to] resign, and for his sake we have kept it from them [and] never let them know any thing about the charges. I told him this morning I me[a]nt to expose him now, me[a]nt to have the charges published. He is the most contemptable puppy I ever saw. He has no spunk nor man hood about him . . . ."[7]

On Sunday morning, September 6th, Van Vleck scribbled a brief note to Patty: "I have just this minute rec'd. orders to move immediately to Cowan, a little place just this side of the mountains as you go to Ala[bama]. The order was for us to start at 5 o'cl'k. this morning but I did not get the order until 8 so that it makes us in a great hurry. I am well. Mr. Morse returned night before last & started yesterday to Murfreesboro to get mustered, as he has at last rec'd. permission to be, so he is all right. The Col. left for home day before yesterday with the 'Good rid[d]ance' of all."

Broaddus found time to write a longer letter and take one more parting shot at the colonel. "Col. Benneson has left," he told Martha. "He tryed to doo all the dev[i]lement he could before he left. Told the Boys that they could go in to the Vetren [Veteran] Corps and advised them to doo so and got agood maney in the notion of it and told them a great maney lies . . . He went in agreat hurry with out telling any of us good by[e]."[8]

Broaddus's comments closed the book on Benneson, but in fairness it must be noted that the colonel's side of the dispute is missing. If he ever recorded the reasons for his behavior, his explanation has not survived. In the absence of such an account, his actions must speak for themselves.

— ◡ —

The 78th broke camp before noon September 6th, said goodbye to Shelbyville, and started south. They were finally on the move—and this time, they would not be left behind.

The regiment reached Tullahoma about 11:00 a.m. the next day, where it was reunited with the other regiments of the Second Brigade of Steedman's Division. There the 78th received orders to draw five days' rations and march with the rest of the brigade to Bridgeport, Alabama.

Chandler thought Tullahoma "a disolate [desolate] place. Was much surprised at the want of fortifications." The 78th was soon back on the road with its sister regiments and the brigade camped for the night at Decherd, "a miserable place without water" in Chandler's view.

The march resumed at 5:00 a.m. on the 8th with the 113th Ohio in the lead. "We reached Cowan at 9 [a.m.], where we struck the mountains, where the scenery was grand and the roads *awful,"* Chandler wrote. "We passed through Tantallen [Tantalon] at 3 o'clock where we came upon some of the 16th [Illinois]. Saw some of the boys. Camped 6 miles from Anderson [Tennessee]. We had fresh meat and roast corn as the teams were not up. A picturesque valley was our camp."

At 11:30 a.m. next day the regiment crossed into Alabama. "The boys struggled terribly," Chandler recorded. "The roads terribly dusty." That evening they camped about two miles from Stevenson. "Our teams were all up. Had supper. Took a wash. Will have a pleasant sleep."[9]

Van Vleck summed up the regiment's progress in a brief note to Patty: "We have made four day's forced marches, over the mountains & through the poorest country, & the deepest dust and hottest sun, that I ever saw. The dust for the most of the way has been about 4 inches deep. The roads have been used an immense deal for army use, & as an old drover told me, 'They have had no rain this side of Cowan, since the War.'

"I understand we are going to the extreme front. Our entire corps, except the 3rd Brigade of our division & a few other reg'ts. are all coming. Rosecrans expects to do something & we expect to help him . . . My health is first rate & improving all the time. This is true also of all the men; sore feet is the only complaint. We have made from 15 to 22 miles a day. And have done as good marching as can be done by any troops, considering the awful dust & heat."[10]

They were on the road again at daybreak September 10th with the 78th taking the advance. "Passed through Stevenson at 8 [a.m.]," Chandler recorded. "Saw Gen'l Steadman [Steedman] and a colored reg't. Terribly dusty. Very little straggling. Awful dry.

"Arrived at Bridgeport at 3 p.m. Took a swim in the Tennessee. A fine stream, and good water. There has been a splendid bridge here, [but?] was burned off." Batchelor noted that a pioneer regiment was busy building pontoons to bridge the river. Odell wrote his family that he had stood the march, but his younger brother, Risdon, "came with us to the Cumberland mountains and gave out—he was sent ahead on the cars—with some others."[11]

Van Vleck arrived in Bridgeport "very tired and dirty," he wrote his wife. "I have been in the saddle from daylight till dark ever since Sunday [September 6th] & feel pretty sore & tired, but not too much so to write you a word, to tell you that I am well, & have got along without any thing unpleasant transpiring save the heat & dust which have been worse to day than before. You can have no idea how dusty it is; at least six inches covered the roads all the way to day.

"This place is a wilderness [with] only two or three houses. There was a splendid bridge before the Rebels burned it. The country all the way from Shelbyville is the most miserable I ever saw. There is only two or three decent houses on the whole road & not more than that many farms of any value. The people also are the hardest specimens of humanity I have ever met with."[12]

Chandler thought the 78th's camp at Bridgeport, about a mile from the Tennessee River, was "the dirtiest meanest worst camp we ever had." Broaddus, however, said he expected the regiment would "move down close to the river for that is about all the water we will get and that is very warm." The thought of having "to drink warm water and dip it up below where a thousand men are swimming and nearly as maney mules and horses are drinking is pret[t]y rough," he added, "but we have to shut our eyes and go it blind and not stop to think about it."

He also had news that "Chattano[o]ga is in our pos[s]ession" and the 78th was bound there. The news was correct. Rosecrans's deft maneuvering had turned the flank of Confederate Gen. Braxton Bragg's army and made Chattanooga untenable for the rebels. Bragg had ordered it abandoned three days earlier, allowing federal troops to take possession.[13]

Bragg was still determined to oppose the federal advance, however, and thought he saw an opportunity on September 11th. Rosecrans's army had struggled through the gaps of Lookout Mountain on the east side of the Tennessee River and one Union division was isolated in a pocket known as McLemore's Cove, beyond easy supporting distance of other federal troops. The Confederates had at least a temporary advantage in numbers and Bragg ordered an attack he thought would crush the federals. But overcautious subordinates failed to carry out his orders. After repeated prodding, they finally moved forward and found the federals had discovered their danger and pulled back. The opportunity had been lost.

Bragg was furious, but powerful help was on the way, though he didn't know it yet. On September 5th Confederate president Jefferson Davis had approved the transfer westward of two veteran hard-fighting divisions from Gen. James Longstreet's Corps of Robert E. Lee's Army of Northern Virginia. The divisions of John Bell Hood and Lafayette McLaws, accompanied by an artillery battalion, were en route over the rickety Confederate railroad system to join Bragg's army. Longstreet had vowed to defeat Rosecrans or die trying.

On Saturday, September 12th, Rosecrans sent word to Gen. Gordon Granger in Bridgeport to proceed to Chattanooga with three brigades of his Reserve Corps. The orders trickled down the chain of command and reached the 78th about 3:00 p.m. The regiment was ordered to leave nonessential baggage and move in light marching order. Two hours later it crossed the Tennessee River on a pontoon bridge and made camp east of the river.

Since the regiment was down to two field officers after Benneson's departure, the officers held an election that evening. To no one's surprise, Van Vleck was elected colonel and Broaddus lieutenant colonel, both unanimously. George Greene, the regimental adjutant, was elected major. The election had no official meaning—it was only an expression of the officers' sentiments—but it would soon have unexpected consequences.

The regiment was on the road by 6:00 a.m. Sunday morning, leaving behind its wool blankets and knapsacks, and marched through more heavy dust. "Passed some grand bluffs bordering on the river," Chandler wrote. After dinner and a sermon, the regiment resumed the march and made about fifteen miles before going into camp. The men were roused again at eleven o'clock that night and were back on the road by midnight. They marched all night, passing within view of Chattanooga about noon the next day, then turned south to Rossville, Georgia, named for the Cherokee leader John Ross. There they made camp.

"Passed some picturesque places," Chandler wrote. "The view from the mountain [Lookout Mountain] is grand. The dust was intolerable. We marched 42 miles in 48 hours—a hard march. The 78th was the best regiment in the brigade as to marching."[14]

The troops had gotten well ahead of their supply train, and when they arrived in Rossville they were not only tired but hungry and without rations. General Granger had issued strict orders against foraging, but given the circumstances most officers looked the other way while their hungry soldiers went searching for food.

There are varying accounts of what happened next, but all agree that Granger got upset when he saw soldiers with their arms full of the fruits of their foraging efforts. The soldiers were from the 115th Illinois, sometimes called the "Second Methodist Regiment," or the 125th Illinois, depending on the source, and Granger placed them under arrest. He ordered them strung up by their thumbs, according to one source; another said he ordered them to march around camp carrying rails on their shoulders. When he saw other men carrying food seized from nearby farms and fields, the irritable general grew furious and sent cavalry patrols to round up every forager they could find.

Soon Granger had men from every regiment in the division hanging by their thumbs or tied to fences in preparation for a whipping. Word spread rapidly through the camps and before long a growing mob of angry soldiers surrounded Granger's headquarters, demanding release of the men. Again there are conflicting accounts of what transpired next. One version is that Granger ordered an artillery battery to fire blank rounds to disperse the soldiers, and if that failed, to fire on them with canister, but the gunners refused and abandoned their cannon. Another version says the artillerymen responded to the general's order by leveling their guns at his headquarters and threatening to fire.

However it happened, it was obvious the situation had gotten out of hand and threatened to explode into full-fledged mutiny. Fortunately, General Steedman and Col. Dan McCook stepped in to calm things down. Perhaps sensing he held a losing hand, Granger took advantage of the opportunity to turn his captives over to Steedman, with orders to punish them. Steedman wisely released the men with only a reprimand, thus ending what could have been a disastrous confrontation.[15]

The men of the 78th evidently were only marginally involved in the affair, for no surviving account makes mention of it—though Chandler remarked the next day that it was "a great day for foraging—has been carried to a great excess and through a desire to destroy"—but the episode certainly made them more aware of the mercurial personality of their corps commander.

—◦—

"We have a very beautiful camping place, which was but recently used by the rebels," Van Vleck wrote his wife. He also told her the Second Brigade had a new commander, Col. John Grant Mitchell of the 113th Ohio, "who has recently been promoted from Lt. Col. and as Lt. Col. was outranked by me. Since his promotion I stand next in rank to him.

"He is a young man of very fine ability & talent, has been in the service ever since the war began, & is only 24 years old. I like him very much, as does every body else that knows him.

"I have stood the trip remarkably well, feeling better than when I started," he added. "This is true of the entire reg't., not a man gave out except with blistered feet, and we have made one of the hardest marches of the war, & I have been very much surprised to see how well the men have stood it. They straggled less than any other reg't. on the road. Every time we stacked arms to rest, every man was present, except those that had given out [because] of blistered feet, & were permitted to ride. Many of the men marched & kept up all the way, whose feet were raw nearly all over from blisters."[16]

Broaddus had a somewhat different account. "We had to pass over the spear of Lookout Mountain," he wrote Martha. "The road is not only bad but dangerous. One team fell over the side of the mountain killing the driver and six mules. They fell about three hundred feet and another team fell and killed the driver and two mules.

"The weather is very warm and the roads very dusty and the march was very hard on the men but they stud [stood] it without a mummer [murmur] and a parte [part] of the time on half rations." On the subject of rations, he also had this to say: "I have a pret[t]ly hard time in getting something that I can eat. Hard tack, coffee and sow belley and that not very plenty—but if I o[n]ly had teeth to masticate my food I could get along."

He assured his wife that Thomas was in good health and stood the march well. "I let him ride one of my horses apart of the time. My health is not very good but I am able for duty the most of the time. When things gets quiet in this department if I doo not get any better I will resign if nothing happens [to] me before. I feel very grat[e]ful to the officers of this reg't. for the expression of their wish to have me elected Lt. Col."[17]

Next morning, September 17th, Broaddus wrote again. "I am pret[t]y mutch alone to day," he said. "Our brigade has go[ne] out on a reconnais[s]ance and I have caught a very bad cold and my head and back acked [ached] so I did not feel well enough to go and the Doctor told me if I did not keep quiet I would take a spell of bil[i]ous fever and told me I must not go. They did not expect to go but about six miles and only took one day's rations with them so I presume they will bee back to night."

The reconnaissance, toward the town of Ringgold, had been ordered by General Granger to see what was in his front. It was under command of General Steedman, who took six regiments and a battery and started at 3:00 a.m. His force brushed some rebel pickets out of the way, crossed West Chickamauga and Pea Vine Creeks, passed through the village of Graysville, crossed East Chickamauga Creek, and eventually came within view of Ringgold. Steedman posted a section [two guns] of artillery on a hill west of the town and put his regiments in line, with the 78th Illinois on the left. The artillery lobbed a few shells toward the town and an enemy battery replied, with no apparent damage to either side. Dust clouds beyond the town convinced Steedman that heavy enemy forces were moving up, so he ordered his force to retire, "having accomplished the object," as Chandler put it.

Steedman's force withdrew the way it had come, without realizing the Confederates were following, and made camp west of Pea Vine Creek. There, to the federals' surprise, "the enemy opened upon us with artillery" about midnight, Edward Mott Robbins remembered. There was confusion but "no damage except the briars we incorporated in our feet while getting into our clothes and into line of battle. Unfortunately we had camped where there were some rail fences which we burned to cook our suppers, and the fence rows were full of blackberry briars." Steedman's report of the incident says only six rebel shells fell into the federal camp, but Odell was startled by one that landed only fifty feet away.[18]

Back at Rossville, waiting for the regiment to return, Broaddus had time to write another letter to Martha. "I wrote you that I was sick," he said. "I am feeling some better this morning and think that I am not going to have a spell of fever. My back is still troubling me a good deal.

"The reg't. has not got back yet but we are looking for them every minnit [minute].

"The we[a]ther turned quite cool last night and is clowdy [cloudy] to day and I am in hopes it will rain, for the roads are very dusty . . . There is nothing to be had to eat in this section of the country. We can't buy furit [fruit] of any kind nor get milk nor buttar [butter] for love nor money. We are living very hard. Nothing but sow belly and crackers and not enough of them, but when we git the rail road open times will bee better.

"It is now noon. The reg't has just returned. The[y] went out as fare [far] as Ring[g]old, sixteen miles, the object a reconnais[s]ance. They had some lit[t]le skirmishing. No one of our men hurt . . . .

"I believe I have writ[t]en about all the nuse [news] of int[e]rest. I will write agane in afew days. Good by[e] with my love to you and children & kin and friends from your affectionate husband."

It was a five-hour march from the regiment's campsite near Pea Vine Creek to Rossville and the men were tired and hungry when they arrived. They got something to eat—although Batchelor complained that rations were "very short"—and managed to rest until suppertime. They were just sitting down for another meal of short rations when orders came to move again.[19]

———

After days of probes and maneuvers, the armies of Rosecrans and Bragg were now stacked in northeast-to-southwest lines facing one another across the valley of West Chickamauga Creek, although each army remained somewhat in ignorance of the dispositions and intentions of the other. Bragg had started a movement to turn Rosecrans's left flank, pushing forward Bushrod Johnson's Division of Maj. Gen. Simon Bolivar Buckner's Corps to seize Reed's Bridge over the creek. Johnson's men collided with a small federal cavalry brigade under command of Col. Robert H. G. Minty. Minty resisted skillfully, but his force was no match for Johnson's Division and he was forced to withdraw across Reed's Bridge, which he called "a narrow, frail structure, which was planked with loose boards and fence-rails." He took up a position along a ridge west of the bridge, but the rebels followed and soon forced him from that position as well.[20]

Minty appealed for help, and about 4:00 p.m. General Granger dispatched Col. Dan McCook's brigade to his assistance. Simultaneously, Granger ordered General Whitaker to take his brigade to the Red House Bridge downstream. That left Granger with only Mitchell's Brigade, including the 78th Illinois and the 98th, 113th, and 121st Ohio, plus two attached regiments. So when Granger received a message from Rosecrans's chief of staff ordering him to cover Minty's withdrawal, he had no other force to send, and Mitchell's men got their marching orders about 6:00 p.m.

It was nearly three o'clock the next morning before Mitchell's brigade caught up with McCook, who had halted near the junction of the Reed's Bridge and Jay's Mill Roads after hearing noises in the darkness ahead. By that time Minty's force had retired southward, and when McCook sent scouts forward they returned with a number of Confederate prisoners. McCook concluded that a rebel brigade had crossed Reed's Bridge and was somewhere in his front. He thought that if he could destroy the bridge, the enemy force would be trapped on the west side of the creek and he would be able to attack and destroy it after daylight.

When Mitchell arrived, McCook asked him to rest his men briefly, then allow them to have breakfast so they could be ready for action. Meanwhile, he sent the 69th Ohio under Lt. Col. Joseph Brigham to destroy the bridge. The Ohioans captured rebel pickets guarding the bridge and charged across, driving away other surprised Confederates on the eastern side. Then they set the bridge on fire.

When daylight came, McCook tried to organize an attack. Before he could do so, a Confederate cavalry brigade arrived on the scene and ran into a party of federals filling canteens at a spring near Jay's Mill. Firing broke out and spread quickly along the lines. "The engagement was fast becoming general when a peremptory order recalled us to Rossville," Mitchell wrote later in his report of the action. The "peremptory order," delivered by mounted courier, was from Rosecrans to Granger, ordering the withdrawal of McCook and Mitchell "if not already too late."[21]

The 78th and its sister regiments trudged back the way they had come, arriving in camp at Rossville about noon. "Heavy firing off three or four miles," Batchelor wrote. "Wounded men and prisoners are coming in frequently." The first day of the Battle of Chickamauga was under way, but Granger's Reserve Corps, stationed on the far left flank of Rosecrans's army, would not play a role.

The men of the 78th were hungry and they "obtained rations, as much as the haversacks could hold," Chandler wrote. They relaxed for a time, but then orders came to support General Whitaker, whose brigade was guarding the road to Ringgold about four and a half miles southeast of Rossville. Despite still feeling ill and suffering a lame back, Major Broaddus rejoined the regiment for the march, and with the sounds of distant battle still audible, the brigade started about 5:00 p.m. When it reached Whitaker's position, the 78th was halted on a small stream on the right flank of Mitchell's brigade and went into line supporting Company M of the 1st Illinois Battery. Companies D and K of the 78th were posted in front as skirmishers.[22]

It was a cold night and the men settled down next to their campfires and tried to get some sleep. They were rudely awakened about 10:00 p.m. by the sound of a cannon firing. The shell exploded near the picket line and within moments every man was on his feet, the entire division was called into line of battle and orders were given to extinguish all fires. Two more shells were fired but did no damage and the night eventually again became quiet, but the men were told to remain in line and sleep on their arms. Without fires, most of them shivered through the night.[23]

September 20th daylight revealed a thick, smoky haze that obscured the brigade's surroundings. Batchelor remembered it was a year to the day since the regiment had left
Quincy for its uncomfortable train ride to the war, and made note of it in his diary. He
was unaware the regiment was about to begin another journey that would turn out to
be far less pleasant.

The cold, weary soldiers of the 78th got stiffly to their feet, fell into line, and began
marching toward McAfee Church on the Ringgold Road, near its intersection with the
La Fayette Road. The latter ran southward in the direction from which the sounds of
battle had been heard the previous day. Despite a day of desperate fighting, the armies
of Rosecrans and Bragg still faced one another with the issue undecided, and the men
of both armies were rising from an uneasy night to prepare for another day of combat.

At McAfee Church the 78th was posted in line with the 96th Illinois of Whitaker's Brigade across the Ringgold Road. Steedman's whole division was there, as was
General Granger. About 9:00 a.m. sounds of firing were heard from the south, signaling a renewal of the contest between the main armies. It grew steadily louder as the
morning wore on, but isolated as they were on the extreme left of the Union army,
nobody at McAfee Church knew what was happening.

Momentous events were taking place not far away. About 11:00 a.m., Rosecrans
received an erroneous report that the movement of Brig. Gen. John M. Brannan's
division to support General George H. Thomas's XIV Corps on the army's left flank
had opened a gap in the Union line, so he sent orders to Brig. Gen. Thomas J. Wood
to shift his division immediately to fill the gap. Wood complied, but his movement
actually did open a gap where none had existed previously. Just then Gen. James
Longstreet, commanding the Confederate left wing, attacked with three divisions.
They flooded through the gap and rolled up the right flank of Rosecrans's army. With
his position crumbling before his eyes, Rosecrans and his staff were forced to join the
retreat, and soon most of the whole right wing of Rosecrans's army was streaming
off the field.

Most, but not all. Some retreating federals fell back on Thomas's position, which
had been under siege by the right wing of Bragg's army for much of the day. Thomas
gathered them on a promontory called Snodgrass Hill, about four miles south of
Granger's position at McAfee Church.

Granger's soldiers could hear the sounds of battle gradually shifting, indicating
Rosecrans's army was being forced back. Then they saw clouds of smoke and dust rising near Thomas's position. Granger's only orders had been to be prepared to support
Thomas, so the irascible Reserve Corps commander now had to decide whether to stay
put or march to Thomas's assistance.

Maj. J. S. Fullerton, Granger's chief of staff, wrote later that he and the general climbed to the top of a haystack and sat there watching and listening for ten minutes, trying to figure out what was happening to Thomas. Finally Granger jumped to his feet, swore, and said "I am going to Thomas, orders or no orders!"[24]

Gen. James Steedman, the division commander, told what happened next. "At half past 11 o'clock, General Granger becoming satisfied, from the heavy and receding sounds of artillery, that the enemy was pressing the left of our line severely, ordered me to move to the battlefield as rapidly as possible with two brigades of my command, General Whitaker's and Colonel Mitchell's. I moved at once." Steedman's third brigade, McCook's, was left behind to continue guarding the Ringgold Road.

Whitaker's brigade took the lead, followed by Mitchell's, both in column of fours. They moved at quick step, which made the soldiers glad they had thought to fill their canteens from a spring near the church. They headed a short distance back toward Rossville, then turned south on the La Fayette Road, marching through thick dust toward the rising sounds of battle.[25]

Soon they began to encounter stragglers and wounded men fleeing northward from the fighting around Thomas's position. About a mile and a half north of Cloud Springs Church on the La Fayette Road, their column was sighted by Confederate pickets from Brig. Gen. H. B. Davidson's brigade, part of Gen. Nathan Bedford Forrest's cavalry. Forrest had earlier advanced across the La Fayette Road, capturing a Union field hospital at Cloud Springs Church. Alerted to Granger's approach, he ordered his troops back to the east side of the road, then rounded up elements of four artillery batteries and placed them in position to shell Granger's column when it came within range.

Granger's men reached the church and found it still occupied by Union soldiers—some wounded, others dead. They took possession of the field hospital, then resumed their rapid march southward. As they did, the rebel batteries opened fire at a distance of about six hundred yards. Of the six regiments in Whitaker's brigade and four in Mitchell's, only the 98th and 121st Ohio of Mitchell's brigade had been under heavy artillery fire previously (at Perryville). The sudden shelling was an unpleasant baptism for their untried comrades, and at every muzzle flash men threw themselves down in the dusty roadway until the shell passed over.

An Illinois battery tried to return fire and Steedman began to deploy the division in line of battle, but Granger countermanded the order and resumed the march. In fits and starts the column moved south, under fire the whole way, with Davidson's cavalrymen adding small arms fire to the artillery. "The temper of the men was well tried and proved to be of the right material," Van Vleck wrote later.[26]

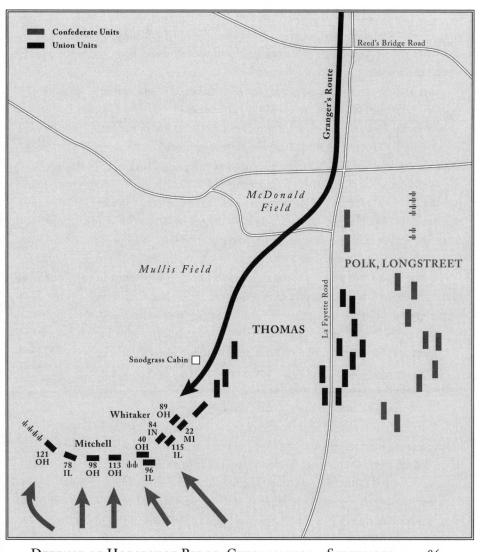

Legend:
- Confederate Units
- Union Units

Reed's Bridge Road

Granger's Route

McDonald Field

Mullis Field

POLK, LONGSTREET

La Fayette Road

THOMAS

Snodgrass Cabin

89
OH

Whitaker
84
IN
22
MI
40
OH
115
IL
Mitchell
121
OH
78
IL
98
OH
113
OH
96
IL

DEFENSE OF HORSESHOE RIDGE, CHICKAMAUGA - SEPTEMBER 20, 1863

Casualties were few, but Granger and Steedman finally decided to move off the road and cut across a large field belonging to a farmer named John McDonald. The soldiers moved into the field at the double-quick, and here they encountered the grim flotsam from a fight that had taken place that morning when Brig. Gen. John Beatty's Union brigade had been broken by an overwhelming rebel attack, leaving the field strewn with wounded men, mutilated corpses, discarded rifles, haversacks, canteens, and other debris. Dry brush still smoldered and flames licked along the fence rails. It was a hellish scene.

But Steedman's men kept going, out of McDonald's field and into an adjoining field on the Mullis farm, where sounds of battle were even louder. Granger had sent a courier to tell Thomas he was on his way, but the courier had not arrived. Now Thomas and his staff, clustered around the Snodgrass cabin, could see clouds of dust rising from the Mullis field, signaling the approach of troops, but they did not know whose troops they were. Thomas's shrinking perimeter was already under heavy Confederate pressure; if the dust clouds meant more Confederates were approaching, it was clear the game was up. He dispatched a mounted officer to determine which troops they were. The officer made the trip under fire and returned safely to report the troops were Granger's, much to Thomas's relief.

Granger and Steedman caught sight of the Snodgrass cabin through a haze of battle smoke and headed in that direction, with their troops following. As the 78th trotted past a rail fence near the north end of Snodgrass Hill, Edward Mott Robbins, who had been detailed to act as a hospital steward, was lagging behind on horseback. He heard a voice call out, "Hello, Yank, have you any water?" He stopped and saw a Confederate soldier lying on the ground just beyond the fence.

"What's the matter with you, Johnny?" he asked.

"I am wounded, and waiting to die," was the response.

"I went to him, raked the leaves away from him (the whole battlefield was ablaze), emptied part of the water from my canteen into his, and Dr. Githens gave him a dose of morphine to relieve his suffering, and [we] left him to die," Robbins recalled.

Robbins and Githens next stopped to help a wounded Michigan soldier. By then Granger's column had passed out of sight, and the two men did not know where to go. They started east and "we could hear voices just ahead of us, but the smoke from fire-arms, cannon and burning leaves was so dense we could not see far. But the wounded soldier I had just befriended called and said, 'Hold on, Yank, don't go that way. Johnnies are thicker than hell just beyond those bushes.' I asked him if he heard troops pass before I came and he said they did but they turned south down the west side of the ridge." Robbins and Githens went that way and eventually caught up with the 78th. "I have mentioned this circumstance to show the feeling among soldiers when one is put out of action," Robbins wrote later in his memoir. "I favored the Confederate and he in turn saved me from walking into the Confederate lines, which I would have done."[27]

The arrival of Granger with Steedman's division at Snodgrass Hill "was one of the most dramatic moments of the battle," one historian has said. It was probably between 1:00 and 1:30 p.m. when Granger rode up to Thomas while Whitaker's and Mitchell's troops tried to catch a little rest after their long, rapid march. Thomas ordered Steedman's division placed on the left next to the brigade of Col. Charles G. Harker, but before the movement could be made there was a sudden roar of musketry off to the right. A courier arrived moments later with word that the rebels were attacking and about to turn the right flank of Thomas's line. Thomas told Granger to order Steedman to move at once to counter the threat.

Whitaker's and Mitchell's troops were again ordered to their feet and started toward the right at the double-quick. The Union line occupied three hills to the south and southwest of the Snodgrass house. Beyond the third hill was a long, narrow, curving ridge known as Horseshoe Ridge, a sort of rugged, rocky natural earthwork, heavily wooded in places. Except for a single Ohio regiment, the ridge was unoccupied by Union troops. Thomas wanted Steedman's division to fill the empty space.

Whitaker's brigade, still in the lead, got there first, faced left and started up the reverse slope of the ridge. Mitchell's brigade passed behind Whitaker, moving farther to the right toward the end of the ridge. As the 78th prepared to go into combat, Robbins turned over his horse and Dr. Githens's with "all of our effects, except the medicine case and surgeon's case of instruments, to the care of a Negro boy we called Jack, and instructed him to keep in the rear so as to avoid getting lost or being captured by the Rebels."

The regiment "passed into a dense piece of timber, where our brigade was formed in two lines," Van Vleck wrote. The 113th and 98th Ohio were posted in front, with the 121st Ohio and 78th Illinois in the rear. But in the difficult, wooded terrain, the lines "very soon became separated," Van Vleck said later; the rear line veered to the right, in effect extending the length of the Union line. When the brigade finally faced left and started up the slope, the 113th Ohio was on the left, the 98th Ohio to its right, the 78th Illinois next, and the 121st Ohio at the end of the line. Van Vleck had detailed Company F of the 78th to guard a field hospital and Companies B and C were still in St. Louis awaiting exchange, so the regiment went into action with only seven companies—a total of 334 men and nineteen officers.

The regiment was halfway up the slope when "the enemy appeared in force on the crest, and opened a murderous fire," Mitchell reported. The rebels belonged to Zachariah Deas's brigade of Alabama troops. At the sight of them, Mitchell gave the order to charge.[28]

Major Broaddus, his illness and lame back forgotten in the excitement, took his post on the left, shouted for the men to follow him, and spurred his horse to the top of the ridge. Holding the reins in one hand, he raised his revolver in the other, but before he could pull the trigger a rebel bullet sliced through his coat collar and ripped through his throat, severing his jugular. Broaddus toppled from his horse and died within moments. The rebel fire also cut down Pvt. Frank Lane of Company I, a twenty-four-year-old farmer from Macomb, with a fatal wound.

Others fell as the regiment rushed up the slope and engaged the Confederates in a brief, bloody, close-quarter fight. When Colonel Mitchell reached the top of the rise, he was knocked momentarily from his horse and General Steedman took his place. Steedman "walked along the line enco[u]raging the men and taking the colors and walking forward with them," Batchelor wrote later in his diary. "When he came to Thomas Edmon[d]son, our color s[e]argent [and] asked him for the flag he refused to give it to him, saying 'I can carry it anywhere.' 'Then step out two paces,' he [Steedman] said, then [shouted], 'Men, rally on your colors!' and they did." Edmondson later fell wounded.[29]

The ferocity of the 78th's assault drove the Confederates from the top of the ridge and the regiment "occupied the crest ourselves, capturing several prisoners," Van Vleck wrote later. Deas's exhausted veterans, who had already suffered heavily in earlier fighting, withdrew down the other side of the ridge.

The fight consumed only about twenty minutes and was followed by a lull when only light skirmishing took place. That gave the men of the 78th a little time to rest, care for their wounded, and perhaps feel good about what they had accomplished in their first real test of battle. But every man knew the afternoon's work was far from finished. Van Vleck took advantage of the opportunity to have Broaddus's lifeless body removed and carried to the rear, and make sure the regiment was prepared for whatever might come next.

⌒

There is a powerful human instinct to try to impose order on chaotic events where no order actually exists. Thus the reports of Van Vleck, Mitchell, Steedman, and others written after the battle, and the accounts of participants scribbled in diaries and letters, all attempt to describe a sequence of events. Not surprisingly, none of those descriptions agree. What occurred over the next few hours happened so swiftly and with such furious and shocking intensity it was beyond the capacity of any human mind to absorb. Some accounts mention three separate rebel assaults on Mitchell's brigade, others four, still others as many as eight.

Van Vleck's report says only that "time and again did the enemy charge upon our lines in superior force, getting as near as 20 or 30 yards, but he was as often hurled back into the ravine from which he vainly struggled to ascend . . . We maintained the admirable position we had gained from about 1 o'clock until after 4, under one of the most terrible fires on record; it was emphatically a hand-to-hand musketry fight." He was seriously in error about the time—it was probably closer to 2:00 p.m. before the 78th gained its position—but he was unquestionably right about the rest of it.

Mitchell's report said only that the enemy attacked "several times . . . but in each instance he was met, and gallantly repulsed."

Steedman said "the enemy attacked us furiously, and after severe fighting for about half an hour we repulsed him, but in a few moments he renewed the attack with increased force, and was again repulsed. Determined to get possession of the ridge, he immediately attacked us again, and for about one hour fought desperately."

Ammunition ran low, so those still able to fight rifled the cartridge boxes of those who could not—the wounded and the dead—searching desperately for a few more rounds. Sometimes they were briefly forced to defend the ridgetop with bayonets, rifle butts, rocks, or even fists. The crest was so narrow in places there was scarcely space for men to fight toe-to-toe, but somehow they did.

Each Confederate lunge brought more casualties to the regiment. Captain Allen, commanding Company H, was shot through the left hand. Newly minted 2nd Lt. Vilasco Chandler of Company I took a bullet through the leg. Capt. Granville Reynolds bound up Chandler's wound and 2nd Lt. Harmon Veatch helped the young officer to the rear.

Sixteen enlisted men, at least one from each company, went down with fatal wounds. Sgt. Harlow Selby of Company G was knocked silly by a bullet that struck him a glancing blow on the head. He would later return to duty, "though his health was never as good as theretofore."

At some point during the immense racket of musketry and screaming men, 1st Lt. Tobias Butler of Company G was shot through the groin and bladder, a wound thought to be mortal. Capt. George Pollock of Company E also was wounded. Another company commander, Capt. Thomas G. Howden of Company G, fell with a serious wound, but when a surgeon approached he refused treatment until the surgeon first looked after another casualty, Pvt. David Vincent of Company I, who was lying nearby even more seriously wounded. The surgeon reached Vincent in time to staunch the flow of blood and save his life. Howden survived as well.[30]

The repeated Confederate assaults finally wore down the 78th and its sister regiments. "Our brigade was in the very thickest of the fight," Van Vleck wrote later. "After maintaining this fearful contest for more than three hours an overwhelming force was thrown against our left wing, which left us no alternative but to retire or be overpowered and captured. Such a shower of grape, canister, and musket-balls as was at this time poured over the regiment can hardly be imagined. We put forth every energy in our power to drive back, or at least hold in check, the massive columns that moved steadily against us, but in vain. Our only salvation was in retreat. The order was reluctantly given and still more reluctantly obeyed."

Odell remembered the Confederates "soon came back with far greater numbers than before—but we kept them back and finally charged them and drove them with heavy loss on both sides." Odell's friend, Pvt. Chamberlain Reed, "was shot dead at my left elbow." Then the Confederates "flanked us and commenced a cross fire on us which forced us to fall back to our old position—but they were so much concealed that we could [not] see them. Consequently, we took shelter as best we could, some behind trees and logs, and others upon the ground.

"I could not get any other shelter and I lay down—at this time shot and shell came in a perfect storm. I was struck [in the foot] when I went to the rear."[31]

As the regiment began to pull back from the crest of the ridge, Van Vleck's horse was shot from under him, leaving him on foot. Seeing his plight, Lt. George Greene, the adjutant, offered his horse. Van Vleck was mounting the horse when a bullet struck his left arm below the elbow. The bullet traveled down his arm under the skin and parallel to the bone, exiting near his wrist. "No important bone was injured," he wrote later. He still managed to mount the horse and lead the regiment across "a large ravine where I formed a new line in perfect order." The enemy followed down the ridge and across the ravine, where the 78th "poured into them a most destructive fire."

With Major Broaddus down and Van Vleck wounded, there was no other field officer left to take command of the regiment, so Van Vleck remained on the field as long as he could, perhaps an hour. But as he grew weaker from pain and loss of blood, he realized he might be on the verge of losing consciousness. Remembering the officers' election a few days earlier in which George Greene had been chosen major, Van Vleck huddled quickly with his remaining company commanders and told them he was preparing to turn command over to Greene. The captains agreed to follow the adjutant's orders, and the twenty-one-year-old lieutenant took command of the regiment.

Van Vleck then found a surgeon, "who dressed the arm & stopped the blood." He also found a discarded saddle and bridle and "a horse voluntarily came to me & so did one of my lieut[enant]s., who helped me onto the horse, & I traveled to Rossville in the dark with Lieut. Vilasco Chandler . . . who had found a cavalry man who let him use his horse."

Odell also was trying to get off the field. He had been struck by a bullet that passed through his left foot, breaking several bones, and was able to walk only a few steps without help. Pvt. Joseph Miller of Company G offered assistance. "It was then near sundown," Odell remembered. "We hobbled on till dark through shot and shell—and by this time our men, who were falling back, came up. The Adjutant, who by then had command of the reg[iment], permitted Risdon [Odell's brother] and the Major's son [Thomas Broaddus] to help me along. Finally I got permission to ride on a battery wagon and rode to camp some four miles. There we got water, the first we had had since morning."

The brigade had held its position for nearly five hours "against the assaults of greatly superior numbers," Mitchell wrote, "and at sundown, after the last cartridge was fired, [we] fell back to the ridge first in our rear."

This time the Confederates did not follow, and Mitchell's brigade finally received the order to retreat.[32]

The Battle of Chickamauga was over.[33]

"Our Lights Are All Over Missionary Ridge"

SEPTEMBER 20–NOVEMBER 25, 1863

INTO THE SMOKY TWILIGHT THEY MARCHED, LED BY LIEUTENANT GREENE, A GRIMY file of bone-weary men, their faces black with powder and their uniforms stained with dirt and blood. Exhaustion erased all thoughts except the need to put one foot in front of the other. For hours they stumbled through the darkness, dimly aware of others also marching toward Rossville, where they hoped to find safety.

Most of the 78th's wounded had been carried from the ridge, but some were left among the bodies of the slain. Those who had been rescued were loaded into over-crowded ambulances and wagons, or placed on horseback, or stumbled painfully on foot with assistance from their comrades. Their cries of pain mingled with the muffled tramp of feet in heavy dust.

Van Vleck and the wounded Lieutenant Chandler made their way on horseback "until we were both completely exhausted." Somewhere along the way they ran into Dr. Samuel Moss, who assisted them. The trio found a log cabin whose occupant gave them coffee and allowed them to rest before they resumed the trip.

It was late when the regiment stumbled into its old camp at Rossville and the men finally had a chance to get something to eat and drink and try to catch a little sleep. But not every man slept. Robbins was up throughout the night ministering to his wounded comrades. He also had a very sore foot. During the battle he had stepped on Dr. Githens's foot and the doctor's spur "tore my shoe in such a manner as to permit small gravel to work between the sole of my shoe and my foot." In all the excitement, he hadn't felt the pain.[1]

Lieutenant Greene, the 78th's acting commander, also had no rest. He was busy trying to figure out how much of a regiment he had left. The 78th had come off Horse-shoe Ridge in good order, but inevitably there was some straggling on the way back to Rossville and men became lost in the darkness. It would take time for them to find their way back to the regiment. Meanwhile, less than 250 men responded to the first roll call.

Casualties had been especially high among the officers. Of nineteen officers who had gone into battle with the regiment, Broaddus had been killed and eight others wounded, including Van Vleck. Each company had suffered at least one man killed and some as many as thirteen wounded or missing. Company E received the worst of it, with six killed, ten wounded, and three missing.

Besides Broaddus, the dead included Martin Fugate, Solomon Toland, and William H. Davis of Company A; John Carroll of Company D; Israel Hendricks, Josiah Starnes, John Hastings, Valentine Fulmer, George W. Campbell, and William Bliven of Company E; Valentine Dilley and Ralph Chamberlain Reed of Company G; Charles Henry Deibert of Company H; Frank Lane of Company I; and Francis M. Moore and Joseph M. Phipps of Company K.[2]

～～

The weary, battle-shocked men of the 78th were roused from their blankets on the morning of September 21st and ordered to march up Missionary Ridge to help guard the approach to Chattanooga. "We threw up breastworks and put out skirmishers and let them remain as a picket," Lieutenant Greene wrote later. At midnight the picket line received orders to pull back to Chattanooga, but not everyone got the word. A staff officer, whose identity was not recorded, was supposed to inform all the men on picket, but the message never got to four officers and fifty-one men of Companies F and I. They stayed where they were, unaware the rest of the picket line was withdrawing in the darkness.

The regiment's wounded men also were being moved, and Dr. Githens was ordered to take charge of an ambulance train bound for Bridgeport, Alabama. Githens was still without his horse and personal effects, which he and Robbins had turned over to the "Negro boy we called Jack" before the battle. They had told Jack to stay in the rear and safeguard their baggage and horses, but had not seen him since. Without a horse or even a blanket, Githens was about to start on foot when Jack suddenly appeared with the horses and all of Githens's and Robbins's baggage.

Wounded officers also were being evacuated. "Came in ambulance train to Chattanooga," Chandler scribbled in his diary. "Have a good hosp[ital] but no attendance. Had my wound dressed for the first time. Col Van, Cap't[s]. Pollock, Howden, and Allen in the same room." Though it was less than twenty-four hours since he had been wounded, Van Vleck spent part of the day writing his official report of the action. He wrote with his right hand, which had not been injured.[3]

When daylight came September 22nd, the fifty-five men on the Missionary Ridge picket line were still there. In the early morning light, they discovered everyone else had gone. They also discovered they were surrounded by Confederates. All were taken prisoner, including Capt. Henry E. Hawkins, newly mustered 1st Lt. Elisha Morse, 2nd Lt. Leander Irvin, and thirty-one men of Company F, plus 1st Lt. Hardin Hovey and twenty men of Company I. This time there would be no prisoner exchange, and nearly half the captives would die in Confederate prison camps, most in the living hell of Andersonville.[4]

Among the 78th's soldiers who did not see action at Chickamauga was Sgt. Jonathan Butler of Company K. His request for a furlough had been granted, and while the regiment fought at Chickamauga, Butler was home in Adams County trying to recover his health and look after his business affairs. But he was not excused from all military duties. On September 22nd—the same day fifty-four of Butler's comrades were being captured on Missionary Ridge—the following notice appeared in the *Quincy Daily Whig*:

"Serg't Jonathan Butler, of the 78th Illinois (late Col. Benneson's reg't) will hold a meeting at Payson on Friday eve., Oct 2, to recruit for the 78th reg't. Lieutenant Jeremiah Parsons, of Melrose, will speak in aid of the enterprise.—The same bounties as heretofore will be paid. A full attendance is solicited." [Parsons, formerly first lieutenant of Company K, had resigned in June.]

Three days after Chickamauga, Rosecrans gave orders for his battered army to pull back and shorten its line. He also abandoned Lookout Mountain. The Confederates quickly moved forward and occupied the latter, giving them control of the wagon road and railroad around its base, cutting two major federal supply routes to Chattanooga.

Help was on its way to Rosecrans. Secretary of War Stanton had dispatched Maj. Gen. Joseph Hooker with the XI and XII Corps of the Union Army of the Potomac, about fifteen thousand men, to board trains for Chattanooga. But it would take a long time for them to get there.

Chattanooga's geography is complex. The Tennessee River skirts the north side of the city, then abruptly turns south and makes a giant U-shaped bend around the appendage of Moccasin Point, then bends north again around Raccoon Mountain. The federals held Chattanooga and Moccasin Point. The Confederates occupied the west bank of the river opposite Moccasin Point, the massive bulk of Lookout Mountain south of Chattanooga, and the heights of Missionary Ridge east of the town, which bristled with cannon. The federals were virtually surrounded on three sides.

During the afternoon of September 23rd, with cannons booming in the distance, what remained of the 78th and its sister regiments in Mitchell's Brigade crossed the river from Chattanooga and made camp on Stringer's Ridge near the base of Moccasin Point. The rest of Steedman's division also crossed, with the first brigade going into camp farther south on Moccasin Point, opposite Lookout Mountain, while McCook's brigade camped at Friar's Ford, about six miles north of the city.

Chandler spent the day on his way back to Bridgeport: "Another horrible day in the ambulance," he wrote. "A mountain road and nothing to eat. Many have been sent on foot, who are slightly wounded, others in army wagons. This the most terrible of all. Rosey [Rosecrans] made a great mistake."[5]

The men of the 78th heard more cannonading on the 24th. Lieutenant Greene spent much of the day trying to reorganize what remained of the regiment. With so many men in Companies F and I having been captured on Missionary Ridge, he decided to consolidate the remainder into a single company.

Chandler's ambulance arrived in Bridgeport about 2:00 p.m. that day. "Had my wound dressed for the second time since it was received," he wrote. Van Vleck and Captains Allen and Howden also arrived in Bridgeport.

Odell, meanwhile, was at a field hospital near Chattanooga. He told his family that Longstreet's men "put a ball through my left foot about two inches forward of the ankle bone. I don't think that any of the bones are injured much, at any rate I can move all of my toes. I think I will be able to get around on crutches in a few days, but it will be some time till I am able to join the reg[iment].

"I have not seen Risdon since Monday morning—he was well then—though he had his canteen shot off him and his blanket riddled with bullets, he was not harmed."[6]

September 24th also was the day Pvt. James Edgar Withrow decided to start keeping a diary. Withrow had enlisted in Company I at age nineteen, but found he didn't like the army and soon became unpopular with his comrades. "He don't like to drill nor to do anything else," Van Vleck once wrote of him, "& [he] has made every body dislike him so that it really is a very hard place for him." Part of the difficulty was that Withrow was severely homesick, but others in his company were unwilling to cut him any slack over that; they would rather have been at home, too. As a consequence, whenever Company I was called to furnish a man for a detail, Withrow was among the first chosen. That actually worked to his advantage September 22nd, when he was on detached duty with the 1st Illinois Artillery; otherwise, he would probably have been among the men of Company I captured on Missionary Ridge.

The Battle of Chickamauga may have made him realize he was a participant in great events and inspired him to begin keeping a journal. Whatever the reason, he began his diary as "simply a general outline of life in camp." His artillery unit was camped on the Chattanooga side of the river. "Very little fighting has taken place today," he wrote. "Rebs are said to be in pos[s]ession of Lookout Mountain . . . Went out & saw the enemy at a distance and our whole line of fortifications for & all."[7]

The Confederates were easy to see. Their batteries hovered over the city from Missionary Ridge and Lookout Mountain, threatening Rosecrans's beleaguered army, which was now on half rations. The only road open to Bridgeport was a sixty-mile route over Walden's Ridge, a torturous trip for both men and animals. The forage required to sustain horses and mules over the route was more than they could carry in wagons, leaving virtually no capacity for other supplies. The wagon trains also were fair game for marauding Confederate cavalry. The men stranded in and around Chattanooga were left to subsist mostly on hardtack and parched corn.

Withrow was awakened about eleven o'clock that night "by quite a little fight out at the fortification. The rebs were said to have come up just after night fall 2-deep [and] at the time of shelling lay in close proximity to our intrenchments. All is quiet this morn' [September 25th]. Down go many fine houses this morn' in order to make way for works . . . Crossed the river several times today on pontoons. Quite a breezy day this . . . At times today the sun was exceedingly warm."[8]

That afternoon the wounded officers in Bridgeport embarked on the next stage of their journey. "Had my wound dressed and felt better," Chandler wrote. "Went to the cars and had to lie down in a hog car. I was with Capt[s]. Allen and Howden. The col [Van Vleck] is very bad today . . . Went to Stevenson [Alabama], where we remain till tomorrow morning. What suffering the army has endured in a week."

From Stevenson the officers went on to Nashville, where they arrived at 2:00 p.m. the next day. Chandler was amazed to find his father waiting at the officers' hospital. "He was much affected at seeing me," Chandler wrote. "Oh, how much I was relieved at seeing him!" But the hospital was "so full that it was impossible to get beds. Slept on floor."[9]

Back in Chattanooga, Withrow recorded a very cold night. "Like to froze," he wrote. "An occasional cannon can be heard today but nothing constant . . . We miss those captured men of the 78th very much."

Sunday the 27th, a week after the battle, some of the more lightly wounded soldiers of the 78th, who also had been evacuated to Nashville, called on their wounded officers in the hospital. Chandler, who said he was feeling "pretty well today," also was visited again by his father. "Father is too kind," he wrote. "His eyes seem full of tears."

<hr />

Van Vleck was cheered by the visitors, but he had other things on his mind. He now faced the task most dreaded by any commanding officer: writing to the widow of a man killed in battle—in this case, Martha Broaddus.

"Dear Lady," he began. "It becomes the most painful duty of my life to write you the particulars, as I have heretofore telegraphed the fact, of your husband's death. We went into the engagement about 1 o'clock on Sunday afternoon after marching for several miles under a continuous fire of bullets and shells. We found the enemy occupying the crest of a high ridge in strong force & the 78th Ills. & 121st Ohio made a charge upon them and drove them, gaining the crest ourselves, which we held until about 4 o'clock. During nearly the whole time there was the most terrific firing of artillery and musketry poured upon us.

"The Major, true to his brave and noble instincts, was foremost in the charge. We had barely gained the crest and halted the line when the Major, sitting on his horse a little to the left of the line, and in the act of raising his pistol to fire, rec'd a musket shot through the neck, severing the jug[u]lar vein. He fell instantly from his horse and died in a few minutes, not being able to speak after he was shot. I ordered some men detailed and his body taken from the field to the ambulance train & thence by [word illegible] 7 miles distant.

"About four o'cl[oc]k I was quite severely wounded in the left arm, which compelled me to leave the field [much of the remainder of the paragraph is illegible] . . . The consequence was that all the dead and many of the wounded were left on the field. The Major's body was carried back to where the ambulances should have been, and the place marked so that his body can be recovered as soon as we can regain the ground where he was left, which will not be many days hence. I left orders for the recovery of his body at any cost, and at the first opportunity. I have just confidence that it will be recovered.

"I have with me the Major's sword and pocket book [most of the remainder of this paragraph and the one following are illegible].

"May God bless you in your terrible affliction . . . Your husband died a true soldier of the Cross as well as the Stars and Stripes, a Christian & a Patriot, the pride of his reg't. and an object of affection to all who knew him.

"Most affectionately, your friend,
Carter Van Vleck."

—⁓—

While the lieutenant colonel performed his painful task, Withrow awoke to a "fine Sabbath morning" in Chattanooga. But he complained of "great destitution of feed for our horses & half rations of ev[e]rything but bread for man. Only a very few corn stalks, no corn for our *animals*. The rebs' camp fires were many & plain last night at a distance of 3 or 4 mi[les]."[10]

Nearly every building in Chattanooga had been converted into a hospital after the battle of the 20th. On that "fine Sabbath morning," Pvt. John T. Miller of Company A, who had been wounded in the battle, died in one of them.

It was a rare Civil War soldier who escaped infection from wounds, and Chandler was no exception. "I have some fever and feel quite miserable," he wrote on the 28th. "I have had several calls today from my soldier friends. . . ."

For Withrow in Chattanooga, the day was cold but "warm about the middle. Another fight took place last night on the front. We now draw only half rations of anything. Still I am doing well." The 1st Illinois Artillery moved its camp and ended up in a canebrake near the Tennessee River.

Chandler had a restless night "and consequently felt very miserable" next morning, "and doubtless looked so. Had several calls today. The ladies are quite numerous. My fever is very high today."

That was the last entry in his diary.

Van Vleck also had not escaped infection. He wrote Patty on the 29th that when he arrived in Nashville "my arm was swol[l]en & inflamed to rather an alarming extent. The surgeon got me on to a bed & fixed me so that I could have a stream of cold water poured over the arm, which has been kept up incessantly ever since." The treatment had reduced the swelling by half, he wrote, and "suppuration has been going on very freely ever since I got here. I have had no chills and but little fever . . . No bone is broken & none materially injured in my arm. The surgeon thinks I will in time, regain the entire use of [it]. The ball entered at the point of the elbow, and pass[ed] out about half way to the wrist.

"There have been between six & seven thousand wounded brought here. Very many are sent home. The worst wounded were left at Chattanooga. Sergt. [Perminion] Hamilton has fever and I fear is not going to get along very well. His wound is not severe, & appears to be doing well, but typhoid is feared. I hope it may be averted.

"A serious accident happened here this morning. A large no. of prisoners were kept in a large hotel building . . . The prisoners were going down the stairs to breakfast, when the stairway leading to the fourth floor, gave way, carrying all the others with it to the bottom, killing and wounding about 100 persons, Confederate prisoners."[11]

Withrow complained about his campsite that morning: "The atmosphere near as this to the river is very cold & damp at night," he wrote. In the 78th's camp on Stringer's Ridge, John Batchelor went foraging, at which he had become an expert. "I got 2 Chickens," he crowed. He went again the next day and "got a shoat and sweet potatoes."

The last day of September was dark and cloudy. Withrow discovered rebels occupied the riverbank opposite his camp, which afforded an opportunity for what he called a miracle. "Often have I heard of conversing across the river with the enemy & did not believe it, but the whole squad here were just engaged in a long conversation [with the rebels] which was indeed quite novel & interesting," he wrote. "They agreed to allow our men to get water without opening fire on them & made several other contracts.

"For the first time in a long while it has commenced to sprinkle," he added. By nightfall the sprinkles had developed into heavy rain and by the morning of October 1st the dust of many weeks had turned to mud. "And a real fall morning it is too," Withrow wrote. "Cool & raining . . . Whiskey was also drawn today by those that wished it. I cared not for it . . . A mud[d]y day. It is with extreem difficulty we banish the water from our dog tents."

The storm passed over that night and October 2nd dawned clear and dry. Withrow "had another converse with 3 mounted rebels across the Tenn[essee] this morning. Queer times these." That evening he visited what remained of Company I in the camp of the 78th. Thomas Broaddus, the major's son, was there—he had not been with the pickets captured on Missionary Ridge—but Batchelor and many others were not; they had gone with a wagon train to Stevenson, Alabama, to collect rations.[12]

Also missing was Pvt. George H. David. He died that day of wounds suffered at Chickamauga.

Van Vleck wrote a letter home October 2nd, with difficulty. "It is hard work to write well lying on my back with no left hand to hold the paper still, but I guess you can make out the most of it," he told his wife. "The inflam[m]ation is out of my arm so that the Dr. discontinued the cold water this morning & thinks there is no doubt but I will recover the full use of my arm by proper care . . . Vilasco [Chandler] has had some fever, but that has subsided. So that he is now doing fine."

The lieutenant colonel said he hoped to recuperate at home, though "it is very hard to be taken away from the reg't. just now, the Major being gone, but I suppose it is for the best & I will chafe under my lot as little as possible . . . But as there is no great loss without some small [gain] . . . I hope that my visit with you will counterbalance all other evils."

October 3rd was cool and windy at Chattanooga, but the night was clear and soldiers camped around the city could see Confederate signal lights on Lookout Mountain and Missionary Ridge, along with a galaxy of rebel campfires blazing on the heights. Next day was Sunday and Withrow visited the hospitals in Chattanooga "& found many friends . . . There is a 20-acre hospital, covered with tents, besides our ambulances filled with wounded officers & men . . . Their occupants however are getting along very well."

It remained cool next morning. "Still the sun banishes the frost early and makes the weather quite agreeable," Withrow wrote. About 11 o'clock that morning he began hearing "very heavy cannonading . . . a steady, constant artillery duel has been the day's programme with long range guns."

Van Vleck meanwhile had arranged a leave of absence and drawn two months pay "so that I am ready to start for home as soon as the doctor will let me off," he wrote his wife. The doctor, however, refused until a "secondary suppuration" of his arm took place, which could be "one day or it may take five . . . You may be assured that it is hard for me to lie here and think of you knowing that nothing but the tardy progress of my wound keeps me from you."[13]

Batchelor returned to the 78th's camp October 6th. "On our way back to Chattanooga we get a hog," he wrote. "I shot him in the creek then went in after him. Then we got 3 chickens, 1 duck and 1 turkey." Then, almost as an afterthought, he added: "The Rebels got into the head of our wagon train and shot the mules and burned 107 wagons." The wagon train was under command of 1st Lt. John Mercer of the 78th's Company E.

Withrow complained that he "almost froze again last night. The enemy saw fit to shell the city or that direction at several different times." He also complained about snakes near his campsite. "Wednesday morn' and a rainy one it is," he wrote next morning. "The moisture came seeping down about midnight . . . The rebs saw fit to throw one shot over our heads this morn'."[14] Pvt. Benager Davis of Company A, wounded at Chickamauga, died of his wounds in one of the Chattanooga hospitals that day.

At the officers' hospital in Nashville, Van Vleck was writing Patty again. "I thought we would start for home tomorrow morning, but after sitting up for half an hour this forenoon I am satisfied that I cannot stand the trip yet. My arm pained me so much that I could only sit up for half an hour when I had intended to remain up all day. How could I stand an all day's ride in the cars? The doctor says this will not be so when suppuration has begun, which seems tardy but [I] hope that I shall be able to start by Friday or Saturday at furtherest. I am getting quite impatient but it does no good."[15]

A day or two after writing this letter, Van Vleck started for home in company with Vilasco Chandler and Chandler's father.

~

October 8th was "a cool, bright, cheerful morning," according to Withrow. "Had a fine tramp down on the river this morning . . . Another large supply train arrived this morn' from Stevenson [Alabama] . . . Cannonading all around today." Another of the 78th's wounded, Pvt. James R. Wisehart of Company G, died in a Chattanooga hospital that day.

On Friday the 9th, Batchelor was with another detail ordered to Stevenson for rations. They took "the River Road [and] the girrallas [rebel guerillas] shoot across the river. Sometimes kill a man, sometimes a mule."[16]

Pvt. Peter L. Felt of Company K died of wounds in Chattanooga that day. Notified that his son was severely wounded, his father had started for Chattanooga in hope of seeing him. He got as far as Nashville where he was told he could not pass farther. Private Felt died without seeing his father.

The army at Chattanooga received a major shakeup that day. President Lincoln had earlier signed an order consolidating three corps—the XX, XXI, and Granger's Reserve Corps—into two, the IV and XIV, and the order was now being implemented. Steedman's division of the Reserve Corps was transferred to the XIV Corps with a new commander, Bvt. Maj. Gen. Jefferson C. Davis, the pale, perennially unhealthy and fiercely temperamental officer who had escaped prosecution for killing "Bull" Nelson. The first brigade of the new division was assigned to Brig. Gen. James Dada Morgan, the officer who had left Quincy as a captain on crutches in the opening days of the war. The second brigade, including the 78th and its three sister Ohio regiments, which had been under Colonel Mitchell's command, was assigned to Brig. Gen. John Beatty, a banker and Republican politician in civilian life (Beatty's old brigade had been decimated at Chickamauga). The third brigade remained under Col. Dan McCook, Jr., who had commanded it in Steedman's division. The XIV Corps badge was an acorn, red for the first division, white for the second, and blue for the third. Davis's division was the second, so the men of the 78th were authorized to wear a white acorn on their forage caps, though few ever did so.[17]

⌒

Early in its existence, the 78th Regiment adopted a practice of forming committees to compose tributes honoring men who died of disease, but the practice was largely abandoned when deaths became numerous. The death in battle of Major Broaddus was a different matter, however, and the regiment's officers—those not wounded or captured—revived the custom to honor him. Capt. M. R. Vernon of Company K, Capt. Granville Reynolds of Company I, and Assistant Surgeon Samuel Moss were appointed to draft a resolution, which was adopted unanimously. It read in part:

"*Resolved,* That in the death of Major Wm. L. Broaddus, the country has lost a valuable citizen and a devoted patriot, the army an efficient officer and a brave soldier who sealed his devotion to his country with his life's blood.

"*Resolved,* That in Maj. Wm. L. Broaddus both officers and men found a sympathizing friend and an upright man; as a commander, he was loved by his officers and all under him; a strict disciplinarian, enforcing obedience of orders, and at the same time commanding the respect and good will of his whole command; in camp he was a lively companion and cheerful friend to all—to the soldier and the soldier's friend. Those of the 78th Illinois who survived the memorable battle of Chickamauga will ever hold in grateful remembrance the name of Major William L. Broaddus, whom they loved while living and mourn now dead.

"*Resolved,* That while we deplore the necessity that calls for such a sacrifice of human life, we rejoice to know that the deceased freely gave the offering, believing that to die in the defense of our country was the highest and most sacred duty devolving upon a citizen.

"*Resolved,* That to the bereaved wife and mourning family we tender our warmest sympathy in their great affliction, and share with them the grief that has fallen heavily upon them."[18]

While the 78th's officers were adopting their resolution October 10th, Withrow, in the camp of the 1st Illinois Light Artillery, was recording a warmer day than "any day for some time. Rebels very plenty just across the river. The boys had quite a conversation with them today. They are supposed to be fixing to make hostile demonstrations, hence a heavier guard. Our rations are so short these days that for a few meals occasionally we have to go without." It wasn't just food that was lacking. "Owing to a general reorganization of the artillery we are to be without guns for a few weeks &c."

Assistant Surgeon William H. Githens had Copperheads (Confederate sympathizers) on his mind when he wrote his wife on Monday, October 12th. "I wish some of our Copperheads could see or know something of what's endured for the sake of the country," he wrote. "I think they would stop throwing obstacles in the way of an honorable peace—but as things are, war must go on—still more butchery, thousands more of the brave fellows must give their bones to bleach on these hills—not to speak of the mangled bodies maimed for life and destined to pass years of suffering and privation.

"To give you some idea of the extent of the last battle—we sent thousands through to Bridgeport of the slightest wounded, or that could be hauled, and yet nearly every building of any size in Chattanooga is a hospital—besides acres of tents here in this field hospital—and from all these, day after day, go burying parties—four men jog along very leisurely with a stretcher on their shoulders and on that is a man wrapped in a blanket—which is to be his winding sheet and coffin—(for there is no lumber to make coffins). Presently they come laughing and chatting back—forgetting that it may be their turn next—but we soldiers and all become very indifferent to death. If they come very fast the diggers put two in one hole—yesterday I saw them digging a larger hole than usual and they said it was for three—two of our men and one Rebel—they did not belong to our division or it would have been stopped pretty soon. . . ."[19]

Batchelor noted on the 15th that it had been raining almost steadily for three days. The wet weather had affected Withrow, who complained of rheumatism. That day Sgt. Perminion Hamilton of Company I died in Chickamauga. His wound at Chickamauga—he was shot through the hand—had not appeared serious, but Van

Vleck thought he might be suffering from typhoid fever. Whatever the cause, his service record would bear the notation that he died of wounds.

The rain stopped on October 16th, although the day was cloudy. "Our whiskey rations however were too much for some of the boys this morning, causing great excitement &c.," Withrow recorded. The 78th lost another sergeant that day when William Glenn of Company E died in Chattanooga of wounds suffered at Chickamauga.

Although nobody in Chattanooga yet knew it, the 16th also was the day Maj. Gen. Ulysses S. Grant was ordered to assume command of a new Military Division of the Mississippi, which included the Department of the Cumberland and all the troops at Chattanooga.

Next day Pvt. Joseph Matthews, another soldier from the 78th who had been wounded at Chickamauga, died at Chattanooga. He was a member of Company E. After another day of rain, Monday the 19th came with "a beautiful morning for a wonder clear, & bright," Withrow wrote. "Had a ride down toward the field hospital where I had an Ambrotype taken."

It wasn't a beautiful morning for Rosecrans. Grant had telegraphed orders relieving him and appointing Thomas in his place, with an injunction to hold Chattanooga at all hazards. "We will hold the town till we starve," Thomas replied. It was a defiant message, but Grant might not have known that starvation of the troops at Chattanooga was more than just a mere possibility.[20]

Withrow's section of the 1st Illinois Light Artillery received Rodman rifles on the foggy morning of the 20th. That evening the unit moved its camp into Chattanooga. "Quite a business place it evidently has been, some stylish residences &c.," Withrow wrote. He also noted that General Rosecrans, having been relieved, left the town that day. He added: "No hard bread for 12 hours & scant prospects ahead!"

Next morning he again took account of the meager rations: "Our next five days rations are: 2/3ds hard bread ¼ sow belly ¼ beef ¼ coffee ¼ tea 1/ Sugar, no pepper soap or candles. Pretty rough times these. With short rations of ev[e]rything else I'm certain of full rations of rheumatism while lying on such wet ground. As usual it's another rain storm. How disagreeable to move in the rain 'but its all for the Union.' Night this time finds us over by fort Negley on the extreem front . . . Thousands of the enemies' tents are very plainly to be seen only 2½ miles distant, on a side hill. Places are fixed here for the men in extreem cases to crawl underground or into shell proof caves. Rain! Rain!! Rain!!!"

The rain stopped that night, but it was cold and Withrow complained the next morning that his "rheumatic pains are so great as to seriously impede my traveling. Our caissons are a half mile in the rear, it not being best to have them so far from water & feed with the horses . . . Two of our siege guns were opened on the enemy for a few shots. No reply."

Pvt. James Kinkade of Company K died that day in Chattanooga of wounds suffered at Chickamauga. Company I also lost a man with the death of Pvt. John W. Soward, although his demise apparently was from disease.

It rained again on the 23rd, but it was a landmark day for the army. "General Grant come to Chattanooga to day," Batchelor wrote. "The [wagon] train could hardly get up the mountain [the weather was] so cold and sloppy and disagreeable."[21]

Next day Withrow received orders to report back to the 78th. "Night finds me over the river in Co. I. Quite a different set of circumstances now surround me."

October 25th was Sunday, but there were no religious services in the 78th. General Davis had the whole division building cabins for what they expected would be winter quarters, and most of the men were engaged in the work.

Pvt. John L. Miller of Company B died of his Chickamauga wounds on the 26th.

The men of the 78th were awakened several hours before daylight on the 27th by the sounds of skirmishing across the river. Federal troops had floated down the river from Chattanooga in pontoon boats past rebel pickets at the base of Lookout Mountain, then around the tip of Moccasin Point, finally landing at Brown's Ferry on the west bank of the river. After a brief fight they secured a beachhead. The move signaled that things would happen quickly now that General Grant was in command.

Construction of winter quarters was halted next day "in order to prepare for an inspection of camp, arms &c &c," Withrow wrote. "Cleaning old guns is a business I never did fancy . . . Cannonading was kept up constantly all day by the rebels on Lookout Mountain."

The regiment was "ordered out of camp at day break" on the morning of the 29th "& passed under the batteries of Lookout, when we reached the XII A[rmy] C[orps] under Gen. Joe Hooker," Withrow reported. Hooker's men had finally arrived and their presence, along with the seizure of Brown's Ferry, gave the federals command of Lookout Valley and reopened the critical supply line to Kelly's Ferry on the Tennessee River west of Raccoon Mountain. Withrow saw General Grant and his staff that day and reported the rebels "kept up an incessant roar of artillery at us all day." Pvt. George W. Dowell of Company C died of disease in Nashville that day.[22]

The first day of November was marked by a large mail delivery, with nearly every man in the regiment receiving at least two letters. Distant firing was heard from the direction of Lookout Mountain, but otherwise it was quiet.

Batchelor "went out foraging" November 2nd. "I got 3 more pigs and we got loads of corn." Meanwhile the enemy continued shelling "from the mountain to the city," Withrow reported.

Fog blanketed Chattanooga the following morning. The Union soldiers didn't know it, but another kind of fog was prevailing in the Confederate camp. Responding to an ill-advised suggestion from Confederate president Jefferson Davis, Gen. Braxton Bragg was about to make a disastrous error. Never able to get along with subordinate officers, Bragg had become alienated from Gen. James Longstreet. On November 3rd he ordered Longstreet to take his two divisions and head for east Tennessee, where he might be able to do some harm to the federal garrison at Knoxville, where Maj. Gen. Ambrose Burnside commanded.

Bragg still held a dominating position around Chattanooga, but lacked strength to capture the city. He hoped reinforcements would make up for the loss of Longstreet's men, but he already had lost control of Lookout Valley and he knew additional Union forces under Maj. Gen. William T. Sherman were on their way to Chattanooga. By sending Longstreet away, Bragg was not only virtually giving up hope of seizing Chattanooga, but risking his ability to hold his positions on Lookout Mountain and Missionary Ridge.[23]

In the camp of the 78th Illinois, Capt. Granville Reynolds of Company I received a letter from 1st Lt. Elisha Morse, among those captured on Missionary Ridge on the morning of September 22nd. Morse said he was being held at Libby Prison in Richmond, Virginia.

November 4th was a fine day but it rained again on the 5th. "Bad time for stiff knees &c.," Withrow commented. "Some of the boys having been sent to the rear for slight wounds on the 20th arrived this afternoon."

Sgt. William E. Summers of Company K wrote home November 6th, sending the letter with a soldier who had been discharged. "We have not been paid off for four months and I cannot get stamps," he explained. Most of the 78th spent that cool, bright day working on a corduroy road to Kelly's Ferry. They had sounds of distant shelling for accompaniment.

Batchelor and others from Company I had wagon train guard duty November 8th and went to Bridgeport where they saw "our companys C and B men." At long last the two companies that surrendered at Muldraugh's Hill had been exchanged and were on their way back to the 78th. They had spent nearly ten months at Benton Barracks in St. Louis, where the men were bored with little to do. Since they were not far from their homes, many had deserted or gone absent without permission. As a result, the two companies had compiled an unenviable record of several dozen courts martial, more than the regiment's eight other companies combined during the entire course of the war. But that was behind them now, and they were warmly welcomed back to the 78th, where their numbers would help replace the losses of Chickamauga.[24]

Batchelor camped "by a nice field of tame[?] grass" on the 9th. With his uncanny ability to find livestock in areas thought to have been picked clean by the armies, he reported "we got 3 more pigs and a young heiffer [heifer]."

It was blustery back on Moccasin Point, where Withrow reported the wind came "near upsetting all our tents . . . Bought a little hard bread today & made some fine hominy. One square meal any way."

After a cold night, with temperatures around freezing, the 78th "drew the first full rations of bread & meat today for a long time & half rations of sugar & coffee," Withrow wrote next day. The supply line from Kelly's Ferry was beginning to deliver.

On Wednesday, November 11th, Brig. Gen. John Beatty arrived to take command of the brigade from Col. John G. Mitchell, who returned to his regiment, the 113th Ohio. "There has been much suffering among the men," Beatty wrote. "They have for weeks been reduced to quarter rations, and at times so eager for food that the commissary store-rooms would be thronged, and the few crumbs which fell from broken boxes of hard-bread carefully gathered up and eaten. Men have followed the forage wagons and picked up the grains of corn which fell from them, and in some instances they have picked up the grains of corn from the mud where mules have been fed. The suffering among the animals has been intense. Hundreds of mules and horses have died of starvation. Now, however, that we have possession of the river, the men are fully supplied, but the poor horses and mules are still suffering. A day or two more will, I trust, enable us to provide well for them also."[25]

November 12th was so nice that Withrow was inspired to write "there was never finer weather since the creation of man." It was cool enough, however, that "a little fire [was] quite pleasant." The news in camp was that Lt. George Greene, who had been acting as regimental commander since Chickamauga, had gotten his promotion. He was now Maj. George Greene.

Odell, still in the hospital near Chattanooga, also had news. His wounded foot had become infected. "I will have to have it amputated, I know," he wrote his family on the 12th. "This is bad news to you but the good Lord will give me strength to survive. My health is as good as ever as far as I know—don't be alarmed about me."[26]

The fine weather that captivated Withrow didn't last long. It was windy the next day, and the wind stirred up so much smoke from campfires that the soldiers could scarcely see Lookout Mountain. They drew new underclothes that afternoon, and continued work on the huts they expected to occupy for winter quarters. Even stronger wind came on the 14th, this time accompanied by rain. Withrow complained his knee was bothering him again.

On the 15th the men of the 78th signed their payrolls in anticipation of being paid for the first time in four months. That day their brigade also welcomed a new addition, the 34th Illinois Volunteer Infantry, commanded by Lt. Col. Oscar Van Tassell. The 34th was a veteran outfit, having seen action at Shiloh and Stones River.

The 34th was glad to join its new brigade. "We were so fortunate as to have left for our use a well constructed camp of log and pole cabins, recently vacated by other troops, which, after being repaired and put in good condition, were the best quarters ever occupied by the regiment during its whole term of service," wrote Sgt. Edwin W. Payne, the regiment's historian. "The camp was located on the west slope of the ridge called Moccasin Point. The top of the ridge was only a few rods from our quarters, from which could be seen the whole of that part of Lookout Mountain occupied by the enemy, and nearly all of Missionary Ridge . . . When the campfires of both armies were lit at night, the spectacle was grand beyond description."[27]

The 78th sent teams into Chattanooga on the 16th to obtain rations for the next week. It was a cool, windy day with "still an occasional thunder" from Lookout Mountain, Withrow wrote. At the field hospital near town, Odell was writing his family to say his infected foot had gotten a reprieve. "I told you that the doctors talked of amputating my foot . . . but they have concluded to wait awhile and perhaps try cutting it open . . . I have come to the conclusion that if I can get it patched up so that I can get home that I will do it and if it becomes necessary to amputate it then I will have it done.

"I hope you will not be uneasy about me. I have no pain to bear. We are furnished with plenty of good food to eat, good bunks and plenty of bed clothing. We are in tents, but we have a good fireplace and my bed is close to it."[28]

Sounds of distant skirmishing could be heard on the 17th and 18th, but the 78th and its sister regiments were not involved. General Beatty inspected the 78th for the first time on the 19th. "No compliments or comments," Withrow reported. That evening the regiment was sent out on picket duty.

It was taking much longer than Grant expected for Sherman's force to make the trip from Bridgeport to Chattanooga, mainly because Sherman's enormous wagon train delayed his movements. Grant was anxious because of news that Longstreet had driven Burnside into his fortifications at Knoxville and Grant could do nothing to help unless he broke out of Chattanooga. He believed he needed Sherman's force to do that. Grant had planned an assault on the Confederate positions Saturday, November 21st, but by Friday evening only one of Sherman's brigades had reached Brown's Ferry, so the attack had to be postponed.

Grant's plan was for Sherman to assault the Confederate right flank on Missionary Ridge. Davis's division, including Beatty's brigade, was ordered to concentrate at the Caldwell Farm across the Tennessee River from South Chickamauga Creek, where Davis would be able to support Sherman once his force arrived. Davis established headquarters on the Caldwell Farm and met with his brigade commanders to explain the plan.

It was obvious to the men of the 78th that big things were afoot. "Very heavy reinforcements coming in all the time," Withrow wrote on the 20th. "Marching orders for tomorrow morning early." It rained heavily that day, and the bad weather caused still further delay in Sherman's approach. Grant had to postpone the attack another day.

But the 78th finally received four months' pay that day—fifty-two dollars in Withrow's case.[29]

⌁

Near dusk on November 22nd, a solitary figure made his way into the camp of the 78th Illinois. After an absence of nine weeks, Lieutenant Colonel Van Vleck had returned to the regiment, having walked the last ten miles from Kelly's Ferry. "My feet were quite sore but otherwise I have had no trouble of any kind," he wrote Patty. His arm also was "as good as new," he said, though that was a severe exaggeration. His wound had healed, but his left arm was still almost useless and he needed help with such simple tasks as donning his coat or mounting his horse.

"I had a glorious reception by the reg't.," he wrote. "It made yesterday the most glorious day of my life. All the officers & most of the privates came & shook hands with me, within three minutes after I got back, & they nearly shook my arm off."

Withrow was there for the welcome and reported "the Col. looks fine." But then Withrow got word of a new assignment: "Seven out of our regiment, among which was I, were detailed to guard a cattle pen. It looks like it will be rather a good thing, more plenty to eat." He didn't mention it, but the detail also would likely keep him out of the battle everybody knew was coming.[30]

Withrow's detail took him across the river to Chattanooga on the 23rd. "Had a fine time over in the city this afternoon," he wrote. "A battle in plain view has been raging all afternoon." He was witnessing Grant's opening move, the advance of the Army of the Cumberland to Orchard Knob, a hill near the base of Missionary Ridge. Thousands of federal troops overran two Confederate regiments while the rest of the rebel army watched from Missionary Ridge as their artillery blazed away in a vain effort to stop the Union advance.

Sherman's men were finally in position, and that night they boarded pontoon boats concealed on the north side of the Tennessee River, floated downstream, and landed near the mouth of South Chickamauga Creek on the river's south side. There they rounded up a small force of rebel pickets and established a beachhead. By the next afternoon Sherman had his whole corps over the river and was preparing for an assault on Tunnel Hill—named for a railroad tunnel that went through it—at the north end of Missionary Ridge. The area was virtually undefended, but when Gen. Braxton Bragg saw Sherman's troops moving up from the river, he sent urgent orders to his best division commander, Gen. Patrick Cleburne, to shift his division to Tunnel Hill and hold it at all hazards.

While this was going on, great events also were under way at the other end of Bragg's line on Lookout Mountain. Under cover of morning fog, three federal divisions were assaulting the imposing heights of the mountain. It looked impregnable, but the rebel forces holding the mountain were heavily outnumbered and bluecoated troops began forcing their way up the precipitous slopes and ravines.[31]

The 78th had been "ordered out at 4 o'clock a.m.," Batchelor wrote. "Got to a pontoon bridge four miles up the river." The pontoon bridge had been thrown across the Tennessee at Caldwell's Farm, and Beatty's brigade crossed shortly after 1:00 p.m., joining the rest of Davis's division on the south bank. "Our division was held in reserve; so we stacked arms and lay upon the grass midway between the river and the foot of Missionary Ridge, and listened to the preliminary music of the guns as the national line was being adjusted for tomorrow's battle," General Beatty wrote.[32]

Sherman, it developed, had seriously misunderstood the topography of the north end of Missionary Ridge. His troops had not been advancing on Tunnel Hill as he thought, but rather on two detached hills that stood in the way. This gave Cleburne's tough men enough time to reach Tunnel Hill and dig in, ready to defend that vital piece of real estate.

The crisp, cold morning of November 25th revealed the stirring sight of the United States flag flying atop Lookout Mountain. The Union assault, which would become known as "the battle above the clouds," had succeeded, and the troops that seized the mountain were now free to advance on what remained of the Confederate's left flank.

Morning also brought early renewal to the fighting at the north end of Missionary Ridge. "Fireing brisk at 7 a.m.," Batchelor recorded. "Rebels falling back from Missionary Ridge. Our lines chargeing frequently."[33] He was correct about the frequent charges but mistaken about the rebels falling back. Sherman's attack had started late and the Confederates took advantage of the delay to feed more reinforcements to Cleburne.

When his assault finally did get under way, Sherman sent his forces in piecemeal instead of all at once, and their separate charges were stopped on the slopes of Tunnel Hill by Cleburne's stubborn troops. Fighting continued until late in the afternoon, when rebel counterattacks finally cleared the last of Sherman's men from hard-won lodgments on the hill. The hill remained in Confederate hands.

With most of the day gone and little progress on the left, Grant finally ordered Thomas to advance with the Army of the Cumberland and seize rebel entrenchments at the base of Missionary Ridge, hoping the move would relieve pressure on Sherman's front. With an overwhelming numerical advantage, Thomas's men quickly evicted the Confederates from their rifle pits, but then found themselves exposed to heavy rifle and artillery fire from the top of Missionary Ridge. The hot fire made it impossible for them to stay where they were, so, without orders, first in squads and companies, then in regiments, brigades, and finally in whole divisions, the federal troops started up the ridge. From his vantage point on Orchard Knob, Grant watched in astonishment as the troops began to scale the slopes. Still smarting from its defeat at Chickamauga, the Army of the Cumberland was not to be denied. In ragged lines, its soldiers scrambled up the slopes and ravines toward the summit and kept going all the way to the top, where Bragg's weakened lines broke and the defenders fled from the ridge.

To those watching from below, it seemed a miracle. Withrow enjoyed a center-stage view of the action. "As nice a fall day as could be invented for a battle which has now been progressing for 50 hours all along the line," he wrote. "A constant roar of cannon & musketry like clock work. We (the guard at the carell) [corral] are enjoying ourselves hugely & finely fixed [with] any ammount of beef which fills the rations out well. 50 or 40 cattle butchered here today. Beautiful nights these.

"Our lights are all over Missionary ridge."[34]

Withrow's comrades in the 78th also had been passive spectators of the battle. From their position on the far left they had a fairly good view of the action on Tunnel Hill and probably could see at least part of the Army of the Cumberland's spectacular assault on Missionary Ridge, but they did no fighting that day.

They would get their chance the next day.

II

"My Men Are Almost Literally Naked"

NOVEMBER 25, 1863–FEBRUARY 29, 1864

WITH THE CONFEDERATE RETREAT FROM MISSIONARY RIDGE, CLEBURNE'S DIVISION was forced to abandon its position on Tunnel Hill. Davis's division was ordered to join the pursuit.

"We reached the brigade bivouac and laid down on the leaves, already covered with frost, and remained until about an hour before dawn, and then led out on the road around the northern end of Missionary ridge," wrote Sergeant Payne of the 34th Illinois. "This was the first time we had been outside of camp with our new brigade, and we naturally felt some degree of strangeness in the association with regiments of which we had scarcely any knowledge.

"The morning was chilly and very dark, and our advance was made slowly and with great caution, not knowing whether the enemy had left a guard for observation, with which we might come in conflict at any moment."

The troops followed the north bank of South Chickamauga Creek until first light revealed a thick fog. The fog became so dense it was impossible for those at the head of the column to see anything, so Davis ordered a halt. His men took advantage of the pause to make coffee and eat breakfast. Eventually the fog began to disperse and the division resumed the march. When the leading elements reached the railroad crossing of Chickamauga Creek they ran into rebel skirmishers, who put up a stiff fight until they were driven off.

That was just the beginning of Confederate opposition. "Going very slow as every foot is contested," Batchelor wrote. "Passing dead Rebels occasionally and leaveing some dead and wounded. Found 2 Rebels in a house [and] took them prisoners. We are scrimishing [skirmishing] all the time."[1]

With Morgan's brigade leading and Beatty's following, the division drove the rebels until the federals came within view of the hamlet of Chickamauga Station on the far side of a field bordered by earthworks. The only approach was by crossing the field, which appeared a hazardous proposition, so Davis ordered up a battery and opened fire. There was no reply from Confederate artillery, so Morgan's brigade was ordered to advance. Rebel skirmishers posted in the earthworks resisted stubbornly but were soon driven out. They fled through Chickamauga Station, leaving huge quantities of stores burning at the depot. "We found the building all on fire and provisions of corn meal and sutch-like lay in piles in the road which we picked up to eat," Batchelor scrawled in his diary.[2]

"General Sherman arrived at the head of the column at this time, and by his direction the troops were allowed a short rest, after which the pursuit was renewed with increased vigor," wrote Henry J. Aten of the 85th Illinois in McCook's brigade. Davis changed the order of march, with Beatty's brigade taking the advance. The 78th Illinois was at the head of the column. It followed the Western & Atlantic Railroad across the Georgia state line toward the little town of Graysville, passing broken-down Confederate wagons and other flotsam of retreat. Late in the day the 78th reached a place called Mrs. Sheppard's Spring Branch, where the narrow, muddy road was bordered on either side by thick woods and swampy ground. Here the regiment suddenly came under fire from a rebel battery.

Van Vleck deployed six companies as skirmishers, keeping three in reserve (with the consolidation of companies I and F, the regiment had only nine companies). The skirmish line ran into "a galling fire of grape and musketry," Van Vleck wrote later, and when he tried to rally them in "a dense thicket of timber" the reserve companies opened fire on their own men. "Considerable confusion was occasioned in my regiment by the inadvertent and unauthorized firing of some of our own regiment upon my line of skirmishers," the lieutenant colonel reported. Apparently, no one was hurt in the incident.

Beatty deployed the rest of the brigade and McCook's brigade came up to join them. The troops fixed bayonets and charged from the woods onto open ground. The enemy, a full brigade, "was soon driven in disorder from his position, and I was sure that nothing but the darkness that covered his retreat saved him from capture or a complete rout," Van Vleck wrote. "The night was too far advanced to follow, and we rested for the night."[3]

The fight lasted an hour and claimed the life of Sgt. Moses McCandless of Company I, a Macomb resident. He was struck in front of his right ear by a shot that exited through his right eye, killing him instantly. Pvt. William Bowman of the same company was wounded in the thigh and taken to a nearby farmhouse. He was later transported back to Chattanooga, but would die of his wounds December 22nd. Two other men were wounded but would survive.

As for McCandless, "we carried him into a cabin and covered him with his blanket," Edward Mott Robbins wrote later. "While we were preparing for the night, the faithful Jack [the man who had taken charge of Robbins's horse and personal effects at Chickamauga] came in with a chicken and we proceeded to cook it and have a supper . . . but I assure you there was no levity, for our dead comrade was lying cold and stiff in our midst.

"Early in the morning we dug a hole as best we could, wrapped our comrade in his blanket and covered him over, found a piece of board and marked it as best we could by carving the letters of his name, with a pocket-knife."[4]

There was scarcely time to finish the hurried burial before the regiment was back on the road. This time McCook's brigade led the division, which marched through Graysville without further opposition and continued until it reached the road to Ringgold, which was crowded with other federal troops. The division continued to the vicinity of Ringgold, where it broke off the pursuit.

Davis's division spent the next day tearing up railroad track, but Van Vleck found time to write home for the first time in nearly a week. He told Patty he had just received orders for the regiment to start on a ten-day expedition. "Now the idea of being compelled to go two weeks longer, is gloomy," he wrote. "I am not only short of shirts but every thing else except what I have on & my rubber blanket & shawl. I succeeded in borrowing two blankets which make me comfortable. I miss my knives & spoons & have lost my pocket knife & there are but a few in the reg't., so we go it with fingers, but as we have but little to eat it don't take long.

"I laid out doors & on the ground last night & it rained all night, but I feel none the worse to day. To night I took a good wash & turned my shirt wrong side out & feel fine. But I am as well off as any of the rest except that my shirt has been on longer than the others, but none of the officers have a change with them."[5]

The 78th was not alone in having little in the way of tents, clothing, or other equipment. In their haste to pursue the Confederates, most of Beatty's regiments had left their baggage behind. Now they were about to join an expedition with Sherman to relieve Burnside's force at Knoxville, and they would have to make the march under harsh winter conditions without proper equipment or rations.

Davis's division began the march the morning of Sunday, November 29th. "March at daylight, go about 27 miles to day over rough roads," Batchelor wrote. Their route led through McDaniel's Gap to Cleveland, Tennessee, where they rendezvoused with two divisions of Sherman's XV Corps and Maj. Gen. Oliver Otis Howard's XI Corps. Next day those divisions took the road from Cleveland through Athens to Loudon, Tennessee. Davis elected to stay off that crowded road and followed a parallel route. "March about 20 miles on very short rations," Batchelor recorded.[6]

"The weather was cold, and a good deal of discomfort was experienced on account of scarcity of clothing," wrote Sergeant Payne of the 34th Illinois. "The men were in pitiable condition. Many were absolutely without any sort of shoes, and tried to make some substitute by cutting up part of a blanket and wrapping the feet. The ground was frozen nearly all the time, and the roads were rough and gravelly. Sometimes we marched on the railroad track, which was no better than the roads. It was a very common thing to see bloodstains on the road and the railroad ties, from the bare and lacerated feet of the men of our regiment, as well as of many others.

"Supplies were scarce and hunger the fixed condition. The nights were bitter cold, and there were none too good facilities for getting fuel. Every expedient was resorted to make wind-breaks and to find such minus degree of discomfort as would allow a little sleep."

Van Vleck's report of the expedition was similar. "At no time since the organization of the regiment have we been so poorly equipped for such a trip," he wrote. "Many of the men were barefooted and a majority of them without shirts and overcoats, but they all understood the importance of their mission and went with alacrity and cheerfulness.

"On two different days we were without rations of any kind, and for many days had nothing but unbolted corn meal, or fresh meat and corn meal without salt. The roads were very muddy, and the weather, a portion of the time, cold and wet. The men necessarily suffered a great deal, but I heard no murmurings or complaints."[7]

While the men of the 78th endured the cold and hunger of the march, Withrow was enjoying a relative life of ease in Chattanooga. "Ev[e]rything passing off smoothly," he wrote December 3rd. "We are now having quite enough to eat. A little rice, some beans, 2/3ds rations, bread, all the choice cuts of beef we wish, plenty of coffee. Also ¼ rations of pork, which serves us finely in cooking our stakes [steaks] &c &c. Once in a while a little hominy, by getting corn of those having horses."

The day after Withrow made that entry in his diary, Payne recorded the following: "Rations were entirely exhausted, and he was a lucky man who could find an ear of corn by hunting through the fields. For four days there was less than one good ear of corn per day to a man, or the equivalent of it in any other supplies. Parched corn as a steady diet became tiresome, and our regiment [the 34th] was in great luck in being sent to a mill to grind for the division. The division teams scoured the country for long distances, and brought in such supplies of grain as could be found, and we, fairly or otherwise, managed to get full toll for our services as millers."[8]

Sunday morning December 6th found Odell in a hospital in Murfreesboro, Tennessee, writing another letter to his wife, Beliscent. He had been sent by boat from Chattanooga to Bridgeport November 26th, then on a train to Murfreesboro. "About a hundred of us were . . . placed on beds in sleeping cars," he wrote. After an overnight journey, "I was taken out and carried to this place by some black soldiers. Great care is taken of the sick and wounded here . . . We are in a large brick building formerly used as a tavern." His wound was better; the danger of amputation had passed.

While Odell was writing his letter, the 78th was "some 20 miles this side of Knoxville [when] we heard with joy the expedition had been highly successful," Van Vleck wrote, "and that Longstreet had been driven into North Carolina, with the loss of his wagon and siege trains and of many men as prisoners and deserters." It was true. Longstreet's attack on Burnside's garrison at Knoxville had been soundly repulsed and Lee's lieutenant had retreated eastward. "We gladly received the order to 'right about' and march toward camp and the supposed depot of rations and clothing," Van Vleck said.

The regiment marched about seventeen miles the next day, passing through Madisonville, "a neat little village of sixty or seventy houses," according to Sgt. F. M. McAdams, who later became historian of the 113th Ohio. They covered another twenty miles December 8th and camped in Polk County, Tennessee. There Davis halted the division for five days while waiting for a pontoon bridge to be thrown across the Hiwassee River.[9] By then his men were exhausted "and many of them lay down in the mud, unable to go any farther, and became drenched by the pouring rain, suffering everything but death itself," wrote Capt. Levi Ross of the 86th Illinois of McCook's brigade.

While waiting for the bridge to be finished, Davis sent his men foraging in the surrounding countryside and put some to work at several local mills, grinding corn and grain brought in by the foragers. Batchelor was with a foraging party December 10th. "Went out with L[ie]utenent of Co. D to find a mule for our reg[i]ment wagon," he wrote, omitting the lieutenant's name. "Found a good one at Warner [word illegible]. A conscripting officer give him [the owner] a voucher for $75.00 for it. Voucher no good."[10] Davis also sent out infantry mounted on horses and mules seized from nearby farms to capture or disperse gangs of "guerillas and murderers" inhabiting the neighborhood.

There was no way for the men of the 78th to know it at the time, but they had lost another comrade December 10th when Pvt. John W. Roberts of Company K died of wounds at Nashville. Roberts had been wounded at Chickamauga and left on the battlefield, where he was captured by Confederates and subsequently paroled.

The division resumed its interrupted march to Chattanooga December 15th, going about twenty-two miles before camping for the night. It covered another twenty miles the next day, arriving at McDonald's Gap in a driving rain, where it made an uncomfortable camp in the dark. The division marched thirteen miles on the 17th, camped on Chickamauga Creek, and spent a miserably cold night.[11]

The march resumed the morning of the 18th. Soldiers in the 78th started "with half a cracker a piece & marched 6 miles to Chattanooga & stood on the river bank till night without fires & it was freezing cold & there we had to stay all night, the pontoon having broken away & started [down river] for New Orleans," Van Vleck wrote Patty. "We got some crackers & coffee at night but Oh, how cold. We could not sleep a wink. It seemed hard to stay in sight of camp all night & not to be able to cross. . . ."

"Awfull cold nearly froze," Batchelor wrote in his diary. Some members of the 34th Illinois, desperate for shelter, broke into a guard house and spent the night where prisoners were ordinarily held.[12]

The 78th was finally able to cross the river on boats the next day and returned to its old camp on Stringer's Ridge. But "at least one-third of the men [were] unfitted for immediate duty on account of being barefooted and footsore," Van Vleck reported.

Withrow was glad to see them. *"Glory!"* he wrote in his diary. "Our brig[ade] has returned & I had the pleasure of a hearty shake of Col. Van's hand, also Capt. R[eynolds]. Boys all look worse than ever I saw them before . . . No chance for any kind of business at 78th today on acc't of a general 'scrub up & fill in.' Weather quite raw. Some of the boys came in without shoes. An awful hard tramp on [the] 78th."[13]

For the next several days, the regiment concentrated on scrubbing away caked-in mud, obtaining rations, and replacing worn-out shoes and clothing from such supplies as were available. Supplies were now flowing regularly into Chattanooga, but the army still was not on full rations and clothing stocks were not yet up to par. The regiment also spent much time gathering wood and tending fires to keep the men as warm as possible in the cold temperatures of late December.

Van Vleck tended to some unfinished business. When he had returned from his furlough, he had found the regiment "somewhat lax in di[s]cipline." Just how lax became evident when the 78th was ordered out of camp November 24th to join Sherman's forces; about fifty men stayed behind without permission. Van Vleck hadn't forgotten, and when the regiment returned to Stringer's Ridge he "court-martialed every one of them & had [them] fined $2 to $13 each."

Withrow wasn't court-martialed because he had been absent on an authorized detail, so he was in the lieutenant colonel's good graces as much as he ever was.

On the 22nd he took advantage of the opportunity to apply for a furlough. "Went up to 78th this beautiful morning & obtained permission of my Col. [Van Vleck] & a certificate of Surgeon Moss which was forwarded much against the will of my Cap't [Reynolds], he declaring 'there were married men more deserving of furlough than I was in his com[man]d.' Know not how it will result, but it was my first application." The certificate presumably was to attest that Withrow suffered from rheumatism.

Van Vleck spent part of the day writing home. "We have not an overly pleasant camp, being stationed on the top of a very high ridge about a mile & a half or two miles north of the town, in full view of all the fighting grounds that were the theatre of the late battles, which were plainly seen by those who were left in camp," he told Patty. "The day I arrived here I could see the rebel camps along the base of Mission Ridge for miles in length but they are all gone now."

A few days of rest apparently benefited the men, for "the general health of the reg't. is the best it ever has been," he wrote. "We now have 500 men here and only 16 are taking medicine . . . We are living in log huts. Head quarters are in an old stable which we have fitted up, but find it rather cool in this cold weather. My health is excellent, but my arm is not any better than when I left you. I cannot dress or undress without help nor get on to my horse except I am up on something, but every body seems anxious to help me so I am never in trouble."

Van Vleck said he had asked a man named T. S. Vail to join the regiment as chaplain. "I hope he will be liked & do good," the lieutenant colonel said. He also reported the death of a mare belonging to Mrs. Broaddus—probably the late major's horse—adding, "we took up a subscription & raised her some $125 in consequence." This would be added to one hundred dollars the major's son, Thomas, had been paid for the sale of Broaddus's other horse, which Van Vleck had ridden on the march to Knoxville. "I have no horse [now] & know of no chance to buy one," he said. "Major Green has none. Dr. Moss lets me use his when I desire."[14]

December 24th dawned calm and bright, but it was just another routine day in the camps. "Christmas Eve and nothing doing until after night when quite a rattling has been commenced with guns of all descriptions," Withrow wrote. "Not much Christmas here. Some foolish soldiers and Niggers are drunk with $25 whiskey. Visited a citizen lady friend tonight."

Christmas Day was equally bleak. "We have no turkeys and pot-pies," wrote Henry J. Aten of the 85th Illinois, "no claret and champagne to cheer us on the occasion. But we must be content with hard bread and fat meat."

It was the same for Van Vleck. "Oh how much I wish I might spend the day with you & partake of your sumptuous fare," he wrote Patty, "but instead of that I must be content to spend the day in my tent alone with only my every-day army fare. There is no chance to buy anything here except from [the] gov't. There is not even a suttler in all this army, that I have heard of."

The lieutenant colonel did receive another visit from Withrow. "Christmas day and very little doing," Withrow wrote. "Saw Col. V. & visited 78th generally . . . Boys all in pretty good spirits . . . Of all the dull holidays ever I saw this has surpassed them. A gun fired occasionally."[15]

Christmas was even less cheerful for Sergeant Butler of Company K, who had long since returned from his furlough. He was in the regimental hospital, where he had been for a week. The attending surgeons did not make note of the nature of his ailment.

The day after Christmas Davis's division left camp, crossed the river to the muddy streets of Chattanooga, and marched to McAfee Church, where the men had waited in suspense on September 20th before being ordered into the inferno of Chickamauga. This time they were going there to build winter quarters.

It was a miserable day. Rain had begun falling about midnight and continued through the day. The march also took them through a desolate landscape—abandoned Confederate camps, legions of graves, discarded clothing, empty redoubts, "and miles of rifle pits," Aten wrote. When the division reached its destination late on the soggy day, the men made camp on the border between Tennessee and Georgia. "My quarters are in the State of Tennessee, those of my troops in Georgia," General Beatty wrote. "The line between the states is about forty yards from where I sit."

Next morning, "as soon as it was light the men began active preparations to construct quarters," Aten recorded. "Axes and hatchets were kept busy in cutting trees and preparing building materials. Though the rain fell in uncomfortable profusion, the work went on uninterrupted."[16]

"It seems as though we always have a bad time to move in," Van Vleck wrote Patty on the 28th. "It began to rain Friday afternoon & rained incessantly, a cold bitter rain, until this morning it stopped. We moved Saturday through the rain & mud, & got here just before 8 & the men went at once to work building cabins & they kept their axes going in the rain all night, & all day yesterday & they have their cabins so far advanced that they will afford comfortable shelter to night.

"We have a very pretty hillside for a camp, except head qtrs. We have got our tents down too far where it is getting very muddy. Our camp is not more than a quarter or half a mile from where we were posted in line Saturday night before the battle [of Chickamauga], & about 4 miles from the old battle field. We shall go out in search of Maj. Broaddus' body as soon as the weather will permit. We are a little east and south of Chattanooga & about seven miles away, on the south slope of Missionary Ridge. We will probably remain here during the winter.

"We are still further from supplies than ever. The poor mules have not had anything to eat since Saturday morning. The men get from ½ to ¾ rations, enough so that [they] can get along & I think do much better than as though they got full rations."

The weather changed for the better on the 29th, and Withrow, back in Chattanooga, called it "one of the lov[e]liest days of the season . . . Gay times these, far better than our boys at the reg't. are having. My little Rebel as gay as a lark and not much larger." This was apparently a reference to the "lady friend" Withrow had visited Christmas Eve.

His assignment to the cattle detail had allowed him to set up a little business on the side, selling tallow from butchered cattle, from which he recorded a profit of twenty-one dollars. On the 29th he decided to take a gamble and buy some beef heads in hopes of selling them at a profit. Next day he proudly reported that he had earned $1.30 on his investment.[17]

On the 29th Pvt. Sylvester Ruddell of Company C, a resident of Blandinsville, McDonough County, died of disease in a Nashville military hospital.

Rain returned to Chattanooga again on the 30th and it was still stormy and wet on the morning of the 31st. "Many fine bands of music playing this morn[ing]," Withrow wrote, but the rain put a damper on most New Year's Eve celebrations. Only a "few guns" were fired that night and a few more the morning of January 1st. By then the rainstorm had passed and cold weather had come in its wake. "The very coldest day of the season by *all* odds," Withrow penned. "Last night the soldiers suffered sever[e]ly from cold."

The temperature moderated a little over the next two days, though it was still too cold for most soldiers. That wasn't their only complaint. "Nothing to eat," Batchelor wrote in his diary January 3rd.

January 4th was a "very nasty, icy, sleety day," in Withrow's words, but at the 78th's camp near McAfee Church most of the soldiers were snug in their newly constructed winter huts. 1st Sgt. William E. Summers of Company K wrote home on the 5th to say that "Sergeant Butler [out of the hospital and back with the regiment] and myself have built a cabin and covered it with boards and are living at home as cozy as you please . . . I wish you could see us in our cabin, all so neat, with a dirt floor. The fireplace could not be done better. The chimney has such a draft that I have to pull my partner out of it for fear the suction will spout him out the top. Uncle Sam furnishes us with flour, so now we have slapjacks for breakfast that don't go up the chimney . . . but down our throats."[18]

Withrow made the last entry in his diary that day. "Worked hard all day," he wrote. "Day fine. Many cattle butchered. *All is well.* News is very good." He offered no explanation why he stopped keeping his diary; perhaps his furlough had been approved.[19]

That same day, under a somber sky, Lieutenant Colonel Van Vleck led a sixty-man detail from the 78th down the La Fayette Road toward the Chickamauga battlefield, the same route the regiment followed on the fateful 20th of September. There were constant reminders of what happened that day: splintered trees, patches of burnt brush and blackened ground, discarded clothing, canteens, other debris, and scattered graves. Their destination was Horseshoe Ridge, where the 78th had received its baptism in battle. Their mission was to try to find Major Broaddus's remains.

They easily found the place where they had fought; its memory was etched in the mind of every man who had been there. They also found many graves, but only one that appeared relatively fresh. The rebels had buried their dead after the battle but left federal corpses unburied; they were finally interred on General Grant's order after the Confederates were driven away from Chattanooga.

The fresh grave was very near the spot where the men who carried Major Broaddus's body from the field remembered leaving it. It was large, and Van Vleck assumed it contained the remains of all the 78th's dead who had been left on the field. "I ordered the whole grave to be opened," he wrote Martha Broaddus next day, "for although I knew that decomposition would have advanced so far that the features of none could be recognized, yet I knew that inasmuch as we had but one officer killed, there could be but one officer buried there, and he would readily be distinguished from the others by his dress.

"I was not disappointed. There was the body of an officer in the center, laid out with much more care than the others. I at once recognized the coat and the vest, and through the col[l]ar of each was the mark of the fatal bullet that pierced his neck. His overcoat, pants and boots and even the buttons from his vest had been purloined by his fiendish enemies, but there remained the striped shirt, the knit drawers, and the bright blue socks with white toes, that I could never forget. The flesh had all moldered from his head and face, but there still lingered as a faithful witness of his identity, a single lock of his light brown hair.

"But you will remember a more distinguishing mark than any I have mentioned: I did not forget it, and although I was satisfied beyond a doubt, yet I could not neglect a single test." The skull's lower jaw was "entirely without teeth & for a long time had been, as the process was entirely absorbed & no sockets remained, and in the upper jaw were the few teeth so peculiar to the Major. I could ask for no stronger proof of his identity." He called Thomas Broaddus, the major's son, and he "at once recognized all the marks that I have mentioned as well as the general shape of the head and the peculiar shape of the feet which were still perfect in form.

"Every person present having fully concurred with Thomas and me as to the identity of the corpse, I ordered it to be carefully removed and folded in a blanket and placed in the ambulance. We returned slowly to camp with our precious charge & reached here just before dark.

"This morning I sent the body to Chattanooga in charge of Major Greene, accompanied by Thomas and several of his company, with instruction to bury it in a common coffin at Chattanooga, there to remain until we can get a metal[l]ic coffin, for which we will have to send to Bridgeport. As soon as that can be obtained, the body will be sent to Macomb by express.

"It having proved impossible to obtain a discharge for Thomas, I have applied for a furlough for him which I am greatly in hopes I shall be able to procure. If so, he will go with his father's remains. . . .

"I am grateful to God for having been permitted to recover the body of your lamented husband and my dear friend, for it will be a very great consolation to me, as well as to you, to know that it no longer molders in the soil of our barbarous foes and that it shall hereafter rest beside his children, his kindred and friends, where a monument may be erected to his memory to perpetuate his glorious deeds of valor. . . ."

It was a final irony: The lack of teeth which had caused Major Broaddus such difficulty in life had led finally to his identification in death.[20]

Van Vleck spared little in his account to Mrs. Broaddus, but perhaps to save her further grief he omitted a few grim details. These, however, he shared with his wife. The grave, he said, "presented a most horrid sight" when opened. "The remains—probably of all the 78th who were left dead upon the field—were here piled together in a common mass. Here a bunch of ribs, there a pile of heads, in another place a quantity of hair, feet or hands. The bodies had remained unburied until decomposition had so far taken place that the parts would not hold together, & they had been piled together with that carelessness which we would be led to expect from a careless lot of soldiers, who had been detailed to perform a very disagreeable task & were anxious to get through with it as soon as possible. Not more than six inches of earth covered the general mass of remains." The major's body was in several pieces.

No one knows what emotions Thomas Broaddus experienced when called to identify his father's decomposed body, but Mrs. Broaddus had been concerned about her son since the major's death. In the same letter describing the recovery of her husband's remains, Van Vleck tried to address those concerns:

"As to the inquiries in relation to Thomas I will say that I have watched him with all the interest I could have done had he been my own child, and I do not believe that he is in the habit of drinking. I have never seen the least indication of it. There is not a boy in the reg't. that does his whole duty with more alacrity and cheerfulness than he does. During all that tedious march to Knoxville and return, he was at all times on hand and in his place; he never straggled and never murmured. No one could have performed his duty more faithfully than he did.

"That a boy of his vivacious temperament and independant spirit should have enemies, is not to be wondered at. Perhaps he is *too* independant, and cares too little for the opinions of others. If I find this to be the case I will from time to time caution him against the evil consequences that naturally flow from such a course. I think that his habits and general conduct are quite as good as you could expect were he at home under your own observation & scrutiny."[21]

The soldiers of the 78th awoke January 8th to find a light dusting of snow on the ground. They also welcomed 169 men from the 34th Illinois into the regiment. Veteran members of the 34th—those who had served two years or more—were being sent home on a recruiting mission. Those who had served less time were not permitted to go, so they were transferred into the 78th while their comrades were away. An unexpected result of the transfer was that it brought the strength of the 78th to more than the 850-man minimum required for the regiment to be commanded by a full colonel, making Van Vleck eligible for promotion.

He shared the news in a letter to his wife, but his mind was on more pressing concerns. "My men are almost literally naked," he wrote. "A large proportion of them, at *least two thirds* of them all, have not the least shred of a shirt or sock or overcoat, & none of them have coats excepting the thin summer blouse unlined & which has been worn almost to tatters, and their pants in very many instances refuse to hide their nakedness, and yet am I obliged to send these men [into] this raw winter weather which I find to be as trying to my well-fed and well-clad body as an Illinois winter, to stand picket, 'In their shirt tails (except the shirt) & with empty bellies.'

"Who is to blame I don't know . . . I have no idea how long this thing is to continue nor how long the soldiers will endure it without discontent, but I suppose they will submit as long as they can be induced to believe that it can't be helped."[22]

Three days later Van Vleck wrote home again, describing more of what he had seen on his visit to Horseshoe Ridge. "No one can know how terrible the conflict was without visiting the ground," he said. "Although I was in the very thickest of the fight, I could not realize how fearfully the battle raged until I calmly examined the field and saw that not a tree, not a bush, no, not a twig was left without the marks of the missels of death. One little bush not more than 2½ feet high and not a stalk of which was larger than your smallest finger & which stood right behind one of my companies, bears the marks of seven rebel bullets. In one little tree just in front of our position, which is not more than five inches in diameter, I counted 26 bullet holes. In another not more than 7 inches through, I counted 56 bullet holes.

"On one part of the field I saw trees so furred by *musket* balls that the marks could not be distinguished one from another & therefore could not be counted. Now how do you suppose that whole bodies of men can live through such a leaden hail? Such a rain of death? He alone who believes in the protecting care of Providence, can answer the questions. While I notice with gratitude, in view of the escape of so many of us, the evidences of the terrible work done by the enemy, I had the melancholy satisfaction of seeing the evidences of our own fearful work. Many, very very many, are the graves of rebels, buried upon the ground commanded by the guns of the 78th. In one place is a large square excavation made by the uprooting of a large oak. Herein I saw the most ghastly sight I ever have seen. It was filled litterally full of the enemies' dead, & only covered with a few sticks [and] a few rotten bits of logs, any or all easily removed, and oh what a sight was then presented, a mouldering mass of human forms, virtually left unburied."

He went on to tell about "being able to trace our line of battle distinctly by the clothing & trappings of the killed & wounded. Along the whole line are strewn straps, canteens, haversacks, knapsacks, cartridge & cap boxes, hats, shoes, socks & clothing, hastily stripped off when wounded, or killed, by the men themselves, or their comrades, or left by the rebels when they had exchanged with our dead. Very many are the hats, shoes, socks, pants & indeed every article of clothing of rebel style & wear which were cast off by the side of our slain, in exchange for like articles which they had on when they died.

"The rebel line of battle in front of the line of my reg't. can also be distinctly marked by the remnants of clothing & accoutrements cast off by the wounded & dying. It seems almost incredible, but it is true, that the distance between those two lines so marked is by actual measurement, only 48 paces. And the distance from our line to the position of their battery is only 300 paces. Do you wonder that there are many rebel graves on that ground? As they charged time after time up that fatal steep, in the vain effort to drive us from our position, they would come so very near to us, but the deadly fire of my faithful men, would then hurl them back to their old positions."

—◆—

The dull routine of winter camp ended January 12th when the regiment marched three miles to a railroad bridge, which it was ordered to guard for the next week.

Van Vleck, however, did not go along; he was again stuck with his least favorite duty, sitting on a court-martial board. He asked General Beatty to relieve him from the duty, but the general refused. Major Greene still had not returned from transporting Broaddus's remains to Chattanooga, so the regiment had to go under temporary command of a captain.

Beatty's refusal to excuse Van Vleck from court-martial duty did not keep the general from adding an endorsement to a letter the lieutenant colonel had written Illinois Governor Yates to advise him the regiment's increase in size had made him eligible for promotion. Beatty wrote: "Lt. Col. Carter Van Vleck is one of the best officers in this Department, and is in *every* respect well qualified for the position of Col. I earnestly recommend his immediate promotion, & certify to the correctness of the statement made herein."

"Such an endorsement, asked for, would be of no value, but when it is volunteered by such a man as Gen'l. Beatty, it is of some value to him for whom it is intended," Van Vleck wrote his wife. He also complained that his chimney was smoking so badly it "most puts my eyes out," but he expected to move to new quarters the next day. His new hut had "a large & fine stone fire place, with [a] mud & stick chimney in it [and] a nice greased paper window some 15 inches square, and a good shirt-tail door . . . The roof is made of clapboards held to their places with weight poles."

While Van Vleck was moving, the rest of the regiment left for picket duty at the railroad bridge. But its horse and mule teams were "so week [weak] [they] can hardly walk," Batchelor wrote. "Been without feed seven days, except bark off trees."[23]

Major Greene returned from Chattanooga on the 15th and Van Vleck sent him to take command of the regiment at the railroad bridge. Van Vleck himself remained occupied with the court martial, which resumed every morning, but he was able to report the regiment "has at last got a supply of shoes, socks, shirts & drawers," though it was "still destitute of coats. We have also begun to draw full rations again for the first time since the Battle of Chickamauga."

The men of the 78th were looking forward to returning to camp after a week guarding the bridge, but the day they expected to return they received new orders to stay put until further notice. Another week passed before more orders came and they called for Beatty's entire brigade, including the 78th, to join a reconnaissance in force toward Ringgold to see if the rebels were still there.

The march got under way early on January 28th. Batchelor had his usual succinct version of events: "Ordered out at daylight with 3 days rations," he wrote. "We go to Ring[g]old hunting some bushw[h]acker. Get supper and lay down five minutes when 5 shots where [were] fired from the top of the mountain. The Rebels run the cavilery [cavalry] in but stop[p]ed on finding us infantry. We returned."[24]

Van Vleck, who went along, had a different account. "We only went a little way beyond Ringgold when we found the rebels in force & the cavalry had quite a sharp skirmish with them, killing four & taking several prisoners," he wrote. "We had none killed & only 4 wounded. We remained the other side of Ringgold all night & started back this morning about nine o'cl'k." Ringgold, he said, was the most heavily damaged town he had seen in the war. "All the business part of the town was burned the 30th Nov. last by Gen'l. Hooker's command."

The regiment finally arrived back at its camp near McAfee Church about 2:00 p.m. on the 29th. Next day it received word of the death from disease of Pvt. James P. Stickney of Company B, a resident of Woodville, Adams County.

Van Vleck wrote Patty on the last day of January complaining he had heard nothing from T. S. Vail, the man he had invited to join the regiment as chaplain, and was wondering why. He also said, "I have got no place for Mr. Magee [Magie] yet," indicating the enterprising former postmaster was at least temporarily at loose ends as far as his position in the regiment was concerned.

—✦—

Back in its winter quarters, the regiment resumed daily drill, with time out to gather wood and keep fires going for cooking and comfort. Their routine was interrupted occasionally by the arrival in camp of rebel deserters, some alone, others in groups.

Early in February, Company G welcomed back its captain, Thomas L. Howden, who had recovered from his Chickamauga wound. "There is no captain in the regiment who is more loved and esteemed by his company than is Captain Howden," wrote an unidentified soldier, who signed himself "High Private," in a letter published in the *Quincy Whig & Republican*. "His men were exceedingly glad to see him once more, and they resolved to present him with some mark of their favor and esteem. Accordingly, they raised a sufficient sum and purchased an elegant sword, belt and scabbard, which were presented to him. . . .

"The captain was taken completely by surprise. When called out to receive the present prepared for him, he saw his company drawn up in line . . . Orderly [Daniel] Long stepped forward with the sword in his hand, and in a neat and appropriate speech, presented it to the captain. The captain thanked his company in the most cordial manner for the magnificent present, but he was inclined to think he had been somewhat slighted or abused in the fact that they had kept him so completely in the dark about the proceedings."[25]

2nd Lt. Vilasco Chandler was still recovering from his wound, and Van Vleck lamented that his absence left the regiment without an adjutant. "I am waiting for [Elisha] Morse to be exchanged or Vilasco to get well," he wrote Patty. "There is no one here that quite suits me, & I have concluded to appoint Vilasco, if he comes back soon. Lt. [William D.] Ruddell of Co. B is acting [adjutant]. Capt. [George] Pollock is improving and has gone home on leave of absence [Pollock, commander of Company E, also had been wounded at Chickamauga]. After so long a time the cars are running to Chattanooga & we get a plenty of everything except coats, which the men need very much yet."

The lieutenant colonel also had received word from Governor Yates's office that the application for T. S. Vail's appointment as chaplain was "informal" and would have to be resubmitted. Finally, he said the brigade had orders "to move camp tomorrow, to Tyner's Station on the Chattanooga & Knoxville Railroad about ten miles from Chattanooga. I hate to give up these good quarters & go again to our poor tents, but such is soldier life."

Batchelor was surprised when he got orders "to take General Davis' division headq'rs ambulance to go to Chattanooga every day for the mail."[26]

The brigade, including the 78th, marched to Tyner's Station February 7th. Tyner's was little more than a speck on the Tennessee map, about twelve miles north of Ringgold as the crow flies. Except for the boxlike little station building, there was hardly anything there, but it would be home to the brigade for the next two weeks.

The brigade also would have a new commander. About noon on Tuesday, February 9th, Van Vleck received orders to take command. General Beatty, who had earlier submitted his resignation, finally received its acceptance. Col. John G. Mitchell, who had commanded the brigade before Beatty, was on leave of absence, which left Van Vleck the senior officer. He left Major Greene in charge of the regiment and assumed brigade command February 10th.

"I have no idea how long this arrangement will continue, but it will last only during Col. Mitchell's absence to Ohio or until a brigadier gen'l. is sent to us," Van Vleck wrote Patty. "We were exceedingly sorry to loose Gen'l. Beatty, he being the only *decent* brigadier we have ever had. I drew up a very flattering address which was cordially & unanimously signed by the regt'l. commanders & which was very flattering to the gen'l. & which made him feel very kindly towards me (for suggesting & carrying out the matter) & for which he seemed unable to thank me enough."

The flattery was mutual. In his farewell address to the brigade, Beatty concluded: "Lieutenant Colonel Carter Van Vleck, 78th Illinois Volunteers, assumes command. My acquaintance with his character as a soldier and a man satisfies me that I shall leave the management of the brigade in competent and faithful hands, and that you will have no cause to regret the change."

Van Vleck soon discovered he liked his new post. "I find the duties of brigade commander very light and pleasant," he wrote Patty, "much less laborious and perplexing than of a regimental commander . . . There is a staff officer for every branch of duty in the brigade & I have nothing to do but to make suggestions or give commands & the work is done. It is really a very pleasant position."

His wounded arm also was slowly getting better, "but the improvement is almost imperceptable. I am just as helpless in dressing and undressing as when I first came back to the reg't. . . . I can use it with ease in washing my face, but it is with great difficulty that I get it into my trousers pocket, & cannot get it into my coat pocket, behind, at all. I hurt it on an average about thirteen times a day, but it is not so painful as it used to be . . . I am in hopes to recover full use of it at the coming of warm weather."[27]

A few days after Beatty's departure, there was also a temporary change of command at the division level. Gen. Jefferson C. Davis turned the division over to Brig. Gen. James D. Morgan, the senior brigade commander, and left for Nashville to testify at an inquiry into the conduct of Generals Alexander McCook and Tom Crittenden at Chickamauga.

About this time the officers of the 78th held another election. With Van Vleck awaiting his colonel's commission, there was a general assumption that Major Greene was in line for promotion to lieutenant colonel, and Van Vleck did not think another election was necessary. But Greene "said that he would prefer to have an expression of the officers; & I made no objection but told him if there was to be another election my claims must again be submitted & they were accordingly," Van Vleck wrote Patty. He was again elected unanimously, but when the vote was held for lieutenant colonel, Capt. Maris R. Vernon of Company K was the surprise winner by a count of nine to five over Greene, which "left the Major to be Major still."

Greene "was very much disappointed, & so was I, for I did not think they would vote against him although they might not be entirely satisfied with his course," Van Vleck wrote. "To elect a capt[ain] over a major, for lt. col. is a pretty strong verdict of disapproval of his administration." Greene had done well at Chickamauga and had held the regiment together while Van Vleck was recovering from his wound—even if there was some laxity of discipline—which left Van Vleck puzzled why Greene was repudiated by his fellow officers. He made inquiries and "found it the same old complaint, that ruins so many good officers, *viz.*, inconsiderate & hasty action, especially in matters of discipline."

That was a polite way of saying Greene was guilty of occasionally going off half-cocked, but there was more to it than that. The major, after all, was only twenty-one years old and probably lacked the maturity to deal with older subordinate officers. Rightly or wrongly, some saw him as something of a tyrant. Van Vleck did not share that view; he agreed Greene had committed some "indiscretions," but attributed them to "a very laudible ambition to do his whole duty & to require others to do the same, without that *caution* which is so necessary to temper all zeal . . . I think him an excellent officer, & he is naturally very kind & still I fear he will always labor under the same disadvantages that lost him promotion at the late election."

As for Captain Vernon, "I think [he] will make a very fine field officer. He is a very fine looking officer, the finest looking of any in the reg't. He is six feet tall, well proportioned & good features. He is of a mild, pleasant disposition & I doubt not will please all. When Vilasco [Chandler] returns to the reg't. & assumes the duties of adj't. to which I have assigned him, & when Mr. Vail arrives [as chaplain], I shall have altogether the finest looking 'field & staff,' in this part of the country."

Vail, however, was still missing. "I cannot understand why he has never written to me," Van Vleck complained. "I have written him three letters in relation to his appointment, but have as yet heard no word from him. In the last letter, I requested an immediate reply, but I have not yet rec'd. any, although it is high time."[28]

On February 22nd, immediately after Davis returned from Nashville and resumed division command, he got orders from General Thomas to make a reconnaissance in force toward Dalton, southeast of Ringgold. He put the division's first and third brigades on the road to Ringgold on the afternoon of the 23rd and they marched to the outskirts of Ringgold, where Davis reported to Maj. Gen. John M. Palmer, commanding the XIV Corps of the Army of the Cumberland. Late that evening word was sent to the second brigade, still at Tyner's Station, to join the others. Van Vleck put the brigade in motion and it arrived at Ringgold sometime during the night.

Since the second brigade had marched most of the night, Davis left it to secure Ringgold Gap while he advanced with the other brigades, under Morgan and McCook, to support an attack by Gen. Richard W. Johnson's division on Tunnel Hill, another promontory named for its railroad tunnel.

Johnson's division encountered stiff resistance, so Davis ordered Morgan's brigade to attack. It drove the rebels from their position and the combined forces of Johnson and Davis continued advancing toward Buzzard's Roost, a gap through Rocky Face Ridge on the road to Dalton. Fighting continued the next day, with the divisions of Baird and Cruft joining Johnson and Davis, but Van Vleck's brigade, including the 78th, was not involved. It spent most of the day demolishing fences and outbuildings in Ringgold for lumber to build temporary quarters. Colonel Mitchell also returned to the brigade that day and resumed command, ending Van Vleck's temporary stint as brigade commander.

With the purpose of the reconnaissance having been accomplished—it revealed the Confederates held a very strong position protecting the gaps through Rocky Race Ridge—Davis on the 27th marched Morgan's and McCook's brigades back to their camp at McAfee Church, but "in compliance with orders, I left the Second

Brigade, now command by Colonel J. G. Mitchell, to report to General Baird," Davis wrote in his report. Baird deployed the brigade along Pea Vine Creek and kept it there until Leap Year's Day—Monday, February 29th—when it was released to return to McAfee Church.[29]

While all this was happening, Thomas Goldsborough Odell, still in the hospital at Murfreesboro, finally received a furlough and started home to Quincy. There, for the first time in eighteen months, he was reunited with his wife, Beliscent, and their children.[30]

"Brave Men Were Falling on Every Hand"

March 1–May 22, 1864

As of March 1, 1864, the men of the 78th Illinois had served exactly half their three-year commitment to the service. "Now each day will shorten the last half, which if it be as short as the first, will not seem long," Van Vleck wrote his wife. That day he also received his pay, collecting $670. But to his consternation, he also got word he had been assigned to yet another court martial.[1]

The regiment cheered the return of 2nd Lt. Vilasco Chandler March 5th, at least partly recovered from his Chickamauga wound. "He looks very slim yet, but I hope he will be able to perform the duties of adj't," Van Vleck wrote. "He will not be able to march for a good while to come, but as adjutants are allowed horses to ride, he will be able I think to keep along with us. He still limps, considerably."

The lieutenant colonel also received a letter from 1st Lt. Elisha Morse, still incarcerated at Libby Prison in Richmond. "He was quite well & resigned to his fate," Van Vleck wrote his wife. The mail also brought photographs of Major Broaddus, sent by his widow, one for each officer who contributed to the $125 they had sent her.

On Sunday, March 6th, the veterans of the 34th Illinois returned from their recruiting mission with 184 recruits. Their arrival at McAfee Church meant the 169 men who had temporarily transferred from the 34th to the 78th would return to their old regiment. This in turn would reduce the 78th to about 735 men, well below the threshold required for a full colonel to command, but it no longer mattered; Van Vleck's promotion to colonel was already in the works.[2]

The paperwork arrived later that week. Van Vleck was promoted to full colonel and Maris Vernon to lieutenant colonel. The two were formally mustered at their new ranks March 15th. Vernon's promotion created a vacancy in command of Company K, so 1st Lt. William B. Akins was promoted captain and took over the company. In anticipation of the change, 1st Sgt. William E. Summers had earlier been promoted to first lieutenant to replace Akins and Sgt. Jonathan Butler was promoted first sergeant to replace Summers.[3]

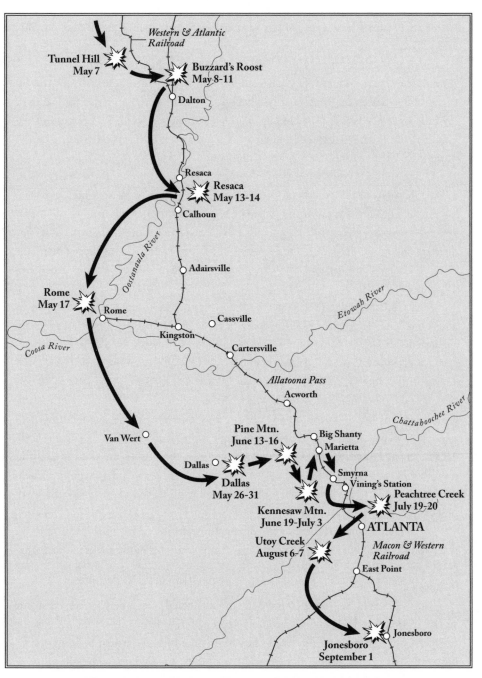

Western & Atlantic Railroad

Tunnel Hill
May 7

Buzzard's Roost
May 8-11

Dalton

Resaca

Resaca
May 13-14

Calhoun

Oostanaula River

Adairsville

Rome
May 17

Rome

Cassville

Etowah River

Kingston

Cartersville

Coosa River

Allatoona Pass

Acworth

Chattahoochee River

Pine Mtn.
June 13-16

Big Shanty

Marietta

Van Wert

Dallas

Dallas
May 26-31

Smyrna

Vining's Station

Peachtree Creek
July 19-20

Kennesaw Mtn.
June 19-July 3

ATLANTA

Utoy Creek
August 6-7

Macon & Western Railroad

East Point

Jonesboro
September 1

Jonesboro

ATLANTA CAMPAIGN - MAY 7 – SEPTEMBER 1, 1864

Ulysses S. Grant, whose string of victories included Forts Henry and Donelson, Shiloh, Vicksburg, and Chattanooga, got his reward when Congress revived the rank of lieutenant general, previously held only by George Washington. Grant received his commission in Washington, D.C., March 9th. On March 18th he named his trusted friend and subordinate, Maj. Gen. William T. Sherman, commander of the Military Division of the Mississippi, including the Departments of Ohio, Tennessee, and the Cumberland. Each department had an army named after it. Davis's division was part of the XIV Corps of the Army of the Cumberland.[4]

Grant would remain with the Union Army of the Potomac in the East, which meant Sherman would command the spring campaign in the West, which everyone knew would be aimed at capturing Atlanta. Preparations for that campaign would soon get under way, but meanwhile the men of Davis's division kept to the routine of winter quarters, including daily drill and picketing duty. They were also visited by members of the Sanitary Commission, who distributed religious materials, writing paper, and other useful articles.

Snow fell the night of March 22nd and by next morning had accumulated to a depth of nine or ten inches. "The snow being in good packing condition probably suggested the idea to some of the men that a snowball battle would be a source of grand fun," wrote F. M. McAdams of the 113th Ohio. "The preliminaries were soon arranged. The 98th O.V.I. [Ohio Volunteer Infantry] and 78th Illinois arrayed on one side, and on the other the 121st O.V.I. and the 113th O.V.I. Positions were taken, the strength of the opposing forces was carefully ascertained by reconnoitering parties, which played their several parts with tactical precision. At length the main body became engaged and the charging and retreating by turns went on at an interesting rate. The war was carried to Germany, for at length the 108th O.V.I. [a regiment made up largely of German stock] finally shared in the contest, and in the end each party proclaimed his side victorious.

"All ended well and the occasion will long be remembered because of the solid fun it furnished. If nations could only settle their difficulties by snowballing battles, or by pounding one another over the head with pillows, war would be stripped of most of its horrors."[5]

Van Vleck told his wife that local inhabitants could not remember a snowstorm so late in the year. In the same letter, he expressed renewed support for Lincoln in the forthcoming election. "I don't hesitate to say that he is the wisest & best man we have ever had in the presidential chair," he wrote, "& it would be the height of madness, at this critical moment, to engage in experimental trials for a better." He also expressed frustration that he still had heard nothing from Mr. Vail. "There is only one chaplain in the brigade & he is an itinerant 'no-account,' & has but little influence for good," he wrote. "I have had a good deal of preaching recently from the other brigades, whose chaplains I have invited over." But he also had good news to impart: "My arm is nearly sound."

Next day, in a letter to an unnamed uncle, Van Vleck lamented the lack of transportation available in Sherman's army. "We have no mules nor horses of account," he wrote. "We have not more than one quarter of a supply of artillery horses, & have not even that proportion of mules for our wagons. This terrible deficiency in our supply of mules & horses is only *one* of the sad consequences of our defeat at Chickamauga, of which our people at the north can never have the remotest conception."

The men of the army, however, were far better off—"never better provisioned & clothed." The government "furnishes a full supply of all the rations ever issued in our army, including light bread, as often as it is prefer[r]ed, to the hard bread. There is no deficiency in the rations drawn, except a supply of vegetables, & that is, to a great extent, made up by the Sanitary Commission . . . Last year at this time, at least two thirds of my command, officers & men, were sick . . . whereas now, not more than two per cent of the reg't. are on the sick list, & there is a buoyancy & sprightliness of spirits in all who are well, to which we were all entire strangers a year ago. I may well say that the soldiers of the Army of the Cumberland, were never in so good fighting trim as now."[6]

Ironically, the same day Van Vleck was writing about the regiment's good health, Pvt. Levi Fry of Company E died of disease in a Nashville hospital. Fry was a resident of Liberty, Adams County.

By March 24th, the snow had melted, leaving a morass of mud in its place.

—⁓—

Since his return to the 78th, Vilasco Chandler had enthusiastically embraced his new duties as adjutant, but it soon became obvious the lingering effects of his Chickamauga wound would prevent him from taking part in the forthcoming campaign. On March 25th he reluctantly submitted a letter of resignation on "account of a severe gunshot wound in the right thigh received at Chickamauga September 20, 1863, which disables me from active duty. I tender the resignation now, that this place may be filled before active operations, for when the coming campaign does open, I would necessarily be compelled to do this." The letter was accompanied by a certificate from Surgeon Samuel Moss, who said Chandler's wound resulted in "contraction of the flexor muscle of the leg . . . which renders it impossible for him [Chandler] to march and is very painful riding horseback." Moss estimated it would be nine to twelve months before Chandler might recover sufficiently to return to active duty.[7]

Chandler's resignation disappointed his commanding officer. "Vilasco is feeling very badly & has sent up his resignation, but don't want it known in Macomb for fear it will not be accepted, but I think it will be," Van Vleck wrote Patty. "He is not really fit for the service & never will be again, but I am very sorry to give him up." Once again he expressed hope that 1st Lt. Elisha Morse, still held at Libby Prison, would be exchanged and assume the duties of adjutant.

"You ask how I like Sherman as a commander," Van Vleck wrote in the same March 27th letter. "I like him first rate. You will remember he had command of our expedition to Knoxville. I think he is one of the finest officers in the army. With him & [George] Thomas & [John] Palmer & [Jefferson C.] Davis for successive commanders I could wish for nothing more, only that Gen'l. Beatty was still in command of the brigade.

"I like the idea of promoting Grant very well. Every thing considered, he is probably the most suitable person that could have been appointed. He is not the most brilliant of our generals, but he is as safe as any & has caution very happily developed for a commander."

He wrote again on the 30th to "tell you of a very pretty present which I received yesterday from Col. Mitchell. He sent me a very pretty haversack, which cost $4.50, and a beautiful pair of Col's. French Bullion shoulder straps, which cost $12." Along with the gifts, Mitchell enclosed this note:

My dear Colonel Van Vleck:

Accompanying this note please find the Col.'s passants [insignia] of which I spoke a few days since. You will accept them from me with the assurances of my highest regard for you as a gentleman and a soldier.

I know you will confer as much honor upon the country in this new position as you did in one inferior.

Believe me always, Dear Col.

Very truly your friend and obedient servant,

John G. Mitchell, Col. Commanding[8]

Not all the news on March 30th was good. Capt. John K. Allen of Company H submitted his resignation that day for reasons of disability. He had not recovered use of his left hand, wounded by a bullet at Chickamauga, and surgeons had advised him to have two fingers amputated. "He was a splendid officer & I hated very much to lose him," Van Vleck wrote. Allen's successor as commander of Company H would be 1st Lt. George T. Beers, who was promoted to captain.

On the final day of March, Davis's division was reviewed by Maj. Gen. George H. Thomas, commander of the Army of the Cumberland, and Maj. Gen. John M. Palmer, commander of the XIV Corps of that army. "Each of the several commanders was accompanied by his respective staff officers, and there was parade and pomp in profusion," wrote McAdams of the 113th Ohio. The second brigade had a new brass band that played festively for the occasion.[9]

"I got rid of a very worthless officer yesterday, a 2nd Lt. of Co. G, from Adams Co.," Van Vleck wrote Patty on April 3rd. "He has not done any duty for the last ten months just from a lack of ambition. I sent up five different resignations for him before I got it accepted, only one of which ever reached department head qtrs. The trouble was that the doctors couldn't find any thing the matter with him & therefore couldn't approve his papers, & for disability an officer has to be examined, not only by the regt'l. surgeon but by the brigade, division and corps surgeons. The last resignation I sent up for him stated the whole case, & begged that Gen'l. Thomas might get a sight of the papers. The result was, they came back accepted in three days & the lt. was not called before the surgeons at all. I am now rid of the most of my poor officers & get along pretty well." [The officer was 2nd Lt. Charles Thompson.][10]

Pvt. John Monahan of Company died of disease that day in a Chattanooga hospital. He was from Blandinsville, McDonough County.

~

It began raining that night and the rain soon became a torrential downpour, making life miserable for those on picket duty. By the next afternoon streets in the camps around McAfee Church had again been churned to mud by the traffic of soldiers. The church itself was full of military stores.

The cool, wet weather persisted, and the men of the 78th huddled around fires to keep warm. The gloomy mood occasioned by the weather did not improve with word that Pvt. James T. Moore of Company F died of disease in Chattanooga April 7th. He was a resident of Columbus, Adams County.

Van Vleck and Mitchell traveled together to Chattanooga on the 9th and Van Vleck told his wife Mitchell had proposed the two join in a law partnership after the war. "He wants that we should come to Nashville & open a lawyers' office & general claim agency, & proposes to furnish any am[oun]t of money necessary for the business to the am[oun]t of $50,000," the colonel wrote. "Which I suppose he could furnish, as his father-in-law is reputed to be the wealthiest man in the city of Columbus, & his father is also a very influential man & was formerly rich but in '57 lost an immense am[oun]t in railroading. He is also highly connected, being a relative of [Ohio] Gov. [William] Dennison, a nephew of the present sec[retary of] state of Ohio & being related to several other public functionaries in Ohio. He is young & has never practiced, having come into the army three years ago & being now only 25, but he is a graduate of college, & got his legal education with Judge Swan, formerly Chief Justice of Ohio. He is the ranking col. in this brig[ade] and is soon, he thinks, to be a brigadier. He is a man of more than ordinary abilities & with the political influence at his command, can do a great many things that we lone stars can't. I am disposed to think quite favorably of his proposition as I have no doubt but there are innumerable fortunes in waiting at Nashville, to be gathered by the early adventurers after the war, but of course it is unwise to make any calculations for the future, while we remain in the army, for it is peculiarly true that we do not know 'what a day will bring forth.'"

That last sentence got Van Vleck to thinking. "Since my return to the reg't.," he wrote, "I have much of the feeling that you speak of, 'an undefinable dread,' a fearful apprehension of some personal ill, or some great calamity, which if I should fall in battle, might perhaps be properly termed a presentiment, yet I can not term it this, for I have always had the fondest and most confident hope that we shall survive the present painful separation & be permitted to spend many years of happiness together. Whether we do or not, this we know, that our destiny is in the keeping of an infinitely wise & merciful God, and we can do no better than to move forward with alacrity, in the discharge of our duty, as it is from day to day disclosed to us, and meet our fate with boldness, whatever it may be, trusting in Jesus for strength according to our day."[11]

The "78th Ills. gets marching orders starts at sunrise," Batchelor wrote in his diary April 10th. The regiment and two companies of cavalry had orders to make a reconnaissance southward to La Fayette, Georgia, then westward to the base of Lookout Mountain.

The regiment left camp soon after daylight Monday, April 11th, with 437 men, and marched down the La Fayette Road, passing through the full length of the Chickamauga battlefield, until it was within a mile of La Fayette. With the exception of four Confederate scouts, there was no evidence of the enemy. "From all I could learn, I am satisfied that there is no considerable force this side of Taylor's Ridge, and the enemy seem to be concentrating all their forces at or near Dalton," Van Vleck wrote in his report. "From La Fayette I passed through Blue Bird Gap [on Pigeon Mountain] (which I found very much obstructed, so as to be entirely impassable for wagons or artillery), and encamped 1 mile this side of Thornton's, in Chattanooga Valley, having crossed Mission Ridge at a point opposite Blue Bird Gap." The regiment was back in camp at McAfee Church by 3:00 p. m. Wednesday, April 13th, after marching between fifty and sixty miles.[12]

After returning from the reconnaissance, Van Vleck and all the other field officers of Mitchell's brigade went to Chattanooga "to serenade Gen'l. Steedman [who had just been promoted] & we were of course invited in & handsomely treated," Van Vleck told his wife. "After a toast had been drunk to the Gen'l. & to Mitchell as brigade commander I was much embarrassed by having to respond to an exceedingly flat[t]ering toast which delated upon my conduct at Chickamauga & upon my unprecedented early return from home after being wounded in time to participate in the Battle of Chattanooga, and upon my satisfactory & popular administration of affairs for the short time I commanded the brigade. I should have thought nothing of the toast under many circumstances, but the occasion and the hearty response of all present, led me to believe that I had been entirely ignorant of the feelings which were entertained for me, & I was confirmed in this belief at the dinner today. I hope I may have grace sufficient to maintain the position I so unexpectedly find myself in."

The dinner, also in honor of Steedman, was held Sunday, April 17th, hosted by Colonel Mitchell. Steedman "was there in all his glory" and "the dinner was a most sumptious affair. The room (a large log house) was decorated with flags & evergreens, & at one end was a transparent with two stars suspended, & 'Chickamauga' emblazoned on the sides.

"The table was very fine, & furnished with written bills of fare, which was comprised, in part of, roast beef, porterhouse steak, soup, potatoes in all styles, tomatoes, coffee with *cream* & sugar, green apple & peach pies, custard pie, rice pudding, pine apples, peaches, sardines, cheese, nuts, light bread, rusk [sweet bread or cake], fresh butter, baked beans, champagne, etc. It was the finest dinner I have seen for a long time. It does not seem right to attend to such matters on Sundays, but it has long been the practice to attend to them on that day & no other, & it seems impossible that such old customs can ever be changed, & it is impracticable to entirely disregard them. The party was very pleasant and quiet."[13]

After nearly two weeks of wet and unseasonably cold weather, the temperature finally moderated, but "time drags heavily," wrote McAdams of the 113th Ohio. "During the past ten days, the monotony of duties has been almost distressing." General Davis, he noted, "has issued an order prohibiting enlisted men from wearing boots in our future movements . . . Many of the men have boots that have cost high prices, and to be compelled to abandon them and wear shoes will be next to an outrage.

"I notice that General Davis wears boots."

Batchelor broke the monotony by paying a visit to the Chickamauga battlefield April 19th. "I saw one mound with a board notice by it saying Line of Battle of 27th Indiana. Burried here 19 Union Solders. Another one with 17 Union Solders, another with 10 Union Solders. This was joining our reg[i]ment on the battle field. I dropped my pocket knife down a well on the Chic[k]amauga battle field while stooping to get a drink."[14]

The regiment lost another man April 23rd when Pvt. Joshua D. Potter of Company K died of disease in a Chattanooga hospital.

As April drew toward its close, there were unmistakable signs the army was getting ready to move. Although the weather remained cool, the men were ordered to pack their overcoats, extra blankets, and clothing and send them home or ship them back to Bridgeport for storage. Officers were told to leave any baggage they could not carry on their persons or on horseback. From the camps around McAfee Church, the men of Davis's division watched other divisions of the Army of the Cumberland march eastward. The long-awaited spring campaign was about to begin.

Pvt. James McRae of Company E, who had been sent home ill, died at his home in Liberty, Adams County, April 27th.

The expected marching orders came May 1st and triggered a frenzy of last-minute preparations in Davis's division. Most of the 78th's officers sent home extra possessions rather than ship them to storage in Bridgeport. Since Lieutenant Colonel Vernon had no family, and no place to call home, he sent his valise to Van Vleck's wife to be stored in the colonel's garret.

The division was ordered to march to Ringgold, with Mitchell's brigade leaving from McAfee Church, Morgan's from Tyner's Station, and McCook's from Lee & Gordon's Mills, south of the Chickamauga battlefield. Once the division was united at Ringgold, everyone expected an advance would be made on Dalton. Sherman had placed the army on three-fifths rations and ordered officers to subsist on the same rations as the men. Davis's division, with a normal complement of 172 supply wagons, would start the march with only thirty-seven. It was obvious Sherman wanted the army to move quickly, without being encumbered by huge trains.[15]

At 8:30 a.m. on Monday, May 2nd, the 78th Illinois, with twenty-three officers and 516 enlisted men, left McAfee Church and began the march to Ringgold, where it arrived about 3:00 p.m.[16] But it proved to be a case of "hurry up and wait," for once it reached Ringgold, the regiment and the rest of Davis's division stayed put another three days while other elements of Sherman's huge army moved into position. Finally, on May 6th, orders came for the regiment to march at daylight next morning. An anonymous member of the 78th, who signed himself "Old Soldier," gave this version of subsequent events:

"Morning came and the army was in motion. The XIV Corps took the road leading to Dalton. We had not proceeded but a few miles until we came on the enemy's pickets, and the sound of muskets told us that the contest for Atlanta had commenced.

"We drove their pickets in and advanced; we found them in force perhaps one mile north of Tunnel Hill. We were placed in position and had a very nice fight with the Johnny Rebs. The entertainment was commenced by paying our respects to them with artillery and musketry, they saluted us in the same way, but our boys were in earnest and it soon got too warm for the Johnnys and they fell back to Tunnel Hill where they had fortifications. They thought we would halt, but we talked to them a while at long range, and then went up and Johnny thought we were going to come [and repeat] Mission[ary] Ridge on him. So he fell back towards his strongholds, and we took possession of the fortifications and camped for the night, after giving him a few hints from one of our batteries now in position in the works so recently occupied by the Johnnys."[17]

"Old Soldier" supplied a similar flowery account of the next day's events:

"Sunday morning, May 8th, the sun made his appearance in all his usual loveliness, and seemed to say to all beholders, 'this is the Sabbath, this is the day of rest,' and it seemed for a while that the armies would rest and not renew the conflict. At 8 o'clock there was preaching in our brigade; the old white-haired minister preached an excellent sermon, and was near the conclusion when the roar of artillery caused all to look up. The old man told us to remain quiet, and he would soon be through. He said that our friends in the front would take care of the rebels, and that if it was necessary for us to go, he would say go, and when we did go in for us to do our duty.

"The fight continued quite brisk and when meeting was over your correspondent went up on the hill to look at Johnny. There he was on Rocky Face Ridge, and on a very steep rugged ridge in front of Buzzard Roost Gap [also known as Mill Creek Gap], and in the valleys. He had a very strong position, and seemed to be determined to give us a hard fight here."

Robbins remembered that while the skirmishers were marching toward Mill Creek Gap, following the route of the Western & Atlantic Railroad, they saw "what we supposed to be a masked battery" which they approached cautiously. As they got closer they found the "battery" was "nothing more than the front wheels of a wagon with a small log mount[e]d on them to represent a piece of artillery, covered with bushes in order to disguise it. We did not experience much difficulty in taking that particular piece of ordinance. But as we advanced a number of the Rebel rear guard threw down their guns and came running towards us with hands up and a white cloth indicating they wanted to surrender, and they were permitted to enter our lines."

About 3:00 p.m. Mitchell's brigade, supported on the left by a brigade of the IV Corps, was ordered to charge the ridge overlooking Buzzard Roost Gap. Mitchell deployed the 78th Illinois and 113th Ohio in front as skirmishers, with the 78th on the right. On their way forward the skirmishers splashed across Mill Creek, holding rifles and cartridge boxes over their heads.

The rest of the brigade followed, and then, as "Old Soldier" resumed his narrative, "the word to advance was given. We started through the brush in line of battle. On we went, and when near the foot of the ridge, which rises very abrupt, the order to charge was given." The charge was made by two companies of the 78th, under command of Major Greene, accompanied by four companies of the 121st Ohio and two companies of the 113th Ohio.

"Old Soldier" again: "A yell was raised, and up the rugged hill the brave men of the Second Brigade went, supported on the left by the brigade of the IV Corps. It was a rugged march up that steep and rocky hill, and the afternoon was very warm; but on they went with determination written on every man's countenance. They knew no such word as fail; for those very men had met charge after charge of the enemy, and returned the same on Chickamauga's bloody fields last September. On they went, right up the hill. The rebels reserved their fire, and we came up on them so suddenly that they became panic struck and ran like so many sneaking curs. They seemed perfectly surprised to think that we would charge such [a] hill.

"Our regiment [the 78th] had the honor of being the first regiment on the to[p] of the hill, and the boys made the old forrest ring with their cheers when we got full possession of the heights. There was a large rebel force on the hill at the commencement of the charge, but on our gaining the summit they were all going down the other side as fast as if Old Nick had been after them. We sent some leaden messengers after them, and they returned the compliment, but did not do us much damage. The fighting continued pretty brisk until after dark; we laid on the ground we occupied that night, the Johnnys having fallen back nearer their strong works on Buzzard Roost."[18]

Pvt. Francis M. Beezley of Company H, who joined the regiment as a recruit on February 12th, 1864, was wounded in the attack, the 78th's only casualty. However, Pvt. Hugh White of Company F, who had been left behind due to illness, died at McAfee Church that day.

~~

While the 78th Illinois and the 113th and 121st Ohio troops were charging up the hill, Mitchell deployed the 34th Illinois and 108th Ohio to their right and ordered them to seize "a round knob, about 250 feet across the base and 25 feet in height, which was occupied by the enemy's pickets," Payne wrote. To get there, they had to ford a flooded part of Mill Creek that was twelve to fifteen feet wide and about four feet deep, with steep banks on either side. The rebels had dammed the creek by blocking a culvert, flooding several acres to obstruct the entrance to Mill Creek Gap.

Confederate pickets fled when they saw Union troops approaching on the run, and the knob was taken. Over the next twenty-four hours, troops from the 34th Illinois and 113th Ohio made two valiant attempts to force their way to the blocked culvert so they could try to open it, but they were repulsed each time.[19]

The rest of the brigade spent the night of May 8th occupying the positions captured that day, but fighting resumed early on the 9th. Two guns belonging to Battery C of the 1st Illinois Artillery were dragged up the hill taken by the 78th and put into position to return fire from rebels posted in redoubts and rifle pits on Rocky Face Ridge. Late in the afternoon the fighting increased in intensity and continued until after dark, with soldiers in the 78th "shooting at the flash of the [rebel] gunns," Batchelor wrote.

"The scene was one of the grandest & most awful I ever witnessed," Van Vleck told Patty. "The position of the rebels is the strongest I ever have seen. It is a gap between two very high & precipitous mountains that cannot be ascended from this side by man or beast . . . Last night after dark, the crest of these mountains, & of the fortifications between them, was one continuous sheet of flame."[20] The 78th had five men wounded during the day's fighting, but other regiments suffered much worse.

That night three more guns were hauled to the top of the hill and put in position, protected by infantry pickets. The rest of the brigade moved back to shelter behind the crest of the hill and dug in, but next morning "scrimishing [skirmishing] commenced at daylight all along the lines," Batchelor recorded. Weather added lightning, thunder, and heavy rain to the noise and flash of artillery, and the troops spent a miserably cold night in their wet uniforms, unable to light fires because they were under the eyes of the enemy.

May 11th passed in similar fashion, with continual skirmishing and artillery firing, but in the evening Mitchell's brigade was pulled back off the hill into the valley below, where it spent a far more comfortable night than the previous one.[21]

━ ━

Sherman's plan had been to send Thomas's Army of the Cumberland against the west side of Rocky Face Ridge while Maj. Gen. John M. Schofield's Army of the Ohio moved against the north end of the ridge to hold the Confederates in position, and Maj. Gen. James McPherson's Army of the Tennessee sliced through lightly defended Snake Creek Gap at the ridge's south end to cut the railroad between the rebels and Atlanta. The plan worked to perfection, up to a point; McPherson chased away rebel pickets, drove through the gap, and approached the railroad, but then took counsel of his fears, pulled his army back to the gap, and dug in. Sherman would later tell McPherson he had missed the opportunity of a lifetime.

Alerted to the danger on their southern flank, the Confederates—now under command of Gen. Joseph E. Johnston (Bragg had resigned after the Missionary Ridge debacle)—realized their position along Rocky Face Ridge was untenable. During the night of May 12th, they withdrew and moved south into previously prepared positions near Resaca.

They soon had company. At sunrise May 12th, the XIV Corps, including Davis's division, headed south toward Snake Creek Gap, "which was reached after a march of 14 miles at dark," wrote Aten of the 85th Illinois. "After a brief halt for supper the march was resumed, and continued until near daylight.

"The night trip, through this famous gap, was one to be remembered. The division was in the rear of the corps, and through the long hours the column toiled on through the narrow, crooked defile. The night march was not a long one when the number of miles traversed is considered, for this wild and picturesque defile is but six miles in length. But the road was only such a track as country wagons had worn in the bed of a stream that meanders through Rocky Face Mountain, or passed over projecting spurs. The artillery and ammunition trains in front delayed the march, yet the men were not allowed to tarry more than a few moments at any point for rest. Many sank down from exhaustion, feeling they could not go another step. At last, near daybreak, the weary column halted, and the soldiers set about preparing coffee and frying meat over quickly kindled bivouac fires."[22]

The division was up and on the road again early the next morning, moving "into comparatively level but heavily wooded country, and were delayed for some time, apparently waiting for orders while held in ranks," Payne recorded. About 3:00 p.m. the brigade was ordered to pile knapsacks, then resume the march toward Resaca. Sounds of heavy firing were audible ahead, but the brigade finally halted for the night without becoming engaged.

The Confederates had dug entrenchments across the northern and western sides of a narrow neck of land between Camp Creek and the Conasauga River. On May 14th, Davis's division took up a position on the western face of the rebel salient. The brigades of Morgan and McCook were only lightly engaged, but Mitchell's brigade was detached to relieve Brig. Gen. John Turchin's brigade of the XIV Corps, which had been repulsed in an assault on the Confederate lines. Mitchell launched his own attack to screen Turchin's withdrawal, and once that was accomplished, Mitchell's brigade held its position under heavy fire. "Colonel Mitchell's conduct was conspicuous on this occasion for personal gallantry," Davis wrote later.[23]

"Old Soldier," the anonymous correspondent of the 78th, weighed in with an account of the day's action: "The battle was raging on our right, left, and in front. Brave men were falling on every hand. This was one of the days that will occupy a conspicuous page in our country's history. At night three of our companies were placed on the skirmish line close to the enemy's works. We were released in the night and moved a short distance to the rear to draw rations."

The rations were eagerly received, but not by Batchelor. "I have a terrable head acke and vomiting at 12 o'Clock at night," he scribbled in his diary.

"Old Soldier" resumed his account next day: "The morning of the 15th found the 78th again in the front line with skirmishers out, and facing Johnny. A heavy fire was kept up all day. We built strong breastworks and were in a fine position that night. At dark the firing nearly ceased, and the skirmishers of the contending armies held a very animated conversation with each other. Johnny Reb asked our boys who they were going to elect for next President; they told them that we were going to re-elect Old Abe, certain. Johnny seemed surprised at the announcement. Our boys asked them if they had anything new; they said they had a new general. On being asked who it was, they said it was 'General Starvation.'

"Our boys invited the Johnnys to come over and have some coffee with us, but they declined, although they said they would like some of the coffee. Johnny told us he was coming over that night to take us in, but we told him we could not see it in that light. About midnight they made a feint, as though they were going to make a night attack, but we proved to them that was dangerous business, and they withdrew. When morning came we found the enemy had evacuated during the night, and the rebel army was in full retreat."[24]

The 34th Illinois and the 108th Ohio had both suffered severely in the fighting, losing many killed and wounded, but the 78th had gotten off relatively easy with only two or three men wounded. However, one of those, Pvt. Samuel H. Fugate of Company A, would die of his wounds May 17th. Pvt. Thomas Broaddus had a narrow escape when a bullet went through his clothing and another shot away the shank of his bayonet.[25]

Sherman, meanwhile, had received a message from Brig. Gen. Kenner Gerrard, which was interpreted to mean that Gerrard's cavalry division had located a bridge across the Oostanaula River on the way to Rome, Georgia. Thinking Gerrard's discovery presented an opportunity to cut the railroad between Rome and Kingston, Sherman ordered Thomas to send "a good division" from the XIV Corps to support Gerrard. Thomas gave the assignment to Davis.

Responding to the order, Davis pulled his division out of line on the 16th and marched it back toward Snake Creek Gap so the men could retrieve their knapsacks and draw rations. Then, at 2:00 p.m., they started for Rome. It was a very warm day and the men quickly became fatigued, but they continued the march. Along the way, the 78th passed an old woman standing at the gate of a "respectable" residence, and Sgt. John E. James of Company C spoke to her and said that all the country behind the 78th was back in the Union now. The old woman burst into tears and said that had it always been so, there would be fewer broken-hearted mothers.

Despite the men's fatigue, the division marched fifteen miles and made camp for the night. During the night, Gerrard's cavalry division passed through their camp, withdrawing eastward. Gerrard told Davis his message to Sherman had been garbled or misunderstood and he had not found a bridge over the Oostanaula, so he had decided to rejoin the main army at Resaca. "This condition of affairs placed me in an embarrassing position as to how to act under the circumstances," Davis wrote later. "Believing, however, that the main object of the expedition could best be obtained by pushing on to Rome with my command, and try to secure the bridge and capture that place, I immediately sent a communication to Major-General Thomas of my determination, and early on the morning of the 17th resumed the march in that direction."[26]

The city of Rome, clustered around the confluence of the Oostanaula and Etowah Rivers, which together form the Coosa River, was a rich target. Several key roads intersected there and the city was accessible by medium-sized steamboats navigating the Coosa River. It was also an industrial center, site of the Noble Brothers Foundry and Machine Works, which manufactured cannons for the Confederacy. Davis's decision to try to capture the city without waiting to see if General Thomas might have other ideas was perfectly in keeping with the division commander's combative personality.

Leaving his wagon train under guard, Davis pushed his troops forward under rain on the 17th, with Mitchell's brigade in front. Six miles from Rome, at a place called Farmer's Bridge over Armuchee Creek, Mitchell's men ran into rebel skirmishers and "drove them rapidly, allowing no time for formation, until, when within one mile of the city, they opened on us with artillery from a fort," Mitchell said. This was Fort Attaway on De Soto Hill, the most prominent topographic feature in the area, which included a network of infantry trenches and dug-in artillery positions.

Mitchell formed his brigade in line and requested support from the 5th Wisconsin Battery, which came forward and unlimbered. "Colonel McCook's brigade was on my left, General Morgan's on the right, massed," Mitchell wrote. "The enemy had advanced from his works and was rapidly coming toward us. The plan adopted was to draw back my skirmish regiment [the 34th Illinois] before the enemy's advance, the entire remaining force concealed, inducing him to think that regiment constituted our entire force. When he had come sufficiently far to receive our fire from the front line he would have been enveloped on either flank."

Things didn't work out that way. McCook received permission "to take a range of hills in his front, and in doing so wheeled to the right, and struck the enemy on the right flank, thus discovering to him some estimate of our force," Mitchell continued. "He fell back at once behind his works."

That evening, a courier reached Davis with an order from Thomas to countermarch his division back over the route Gerrard had taken and rejoin the main army.

But Davis thought Rome was within his grasp and ordered his men to dig in and rest on their arms for the night.

Batchelor summed up the day's action in his usual few words: "The fighting is pretty heavy. We have 15 killed, good many wounded."[27]

⸺⸺

A dense fog obscured the enemy works on the morning of the 18th, finally lifting about 9:00 a.m. At that time Davis "ordered the works to be vigorously attacked in front of each brigade with a strong line of skirmishers," he wrote later. "This was done and the works soon taken possession of, having been abandoned during the night, except by a skirmish line, which fled rapidly across the river." The retreating Confederates tried to set fire to pontoon bridges across the river but were pursued so closely by the federals that they were only partly successful.

"The city was now completely at our mercy," Davis reported. "This fact, considered in connection with the best information I could obtain, convinced me that the enemy intended to evacuate the city, and was only prolonging his resistance in order to remove, as much as possible, his public stores.

"To complete the capture of the city it was necessary to throw troops across the Oostenaula . . . The hazardous enterprise of effecting the first crossing was gallantly accomplished by the 85th Illinois Regiment [of McCook's brigade], commanded by Colonel [Caleb] Dilworth, on rafts built of rails and logs hastily collected on the bank." The 85th crossed quickly and began driving the enemy's pickets back toward the city. "The enemy, finding himself unexpectedly attacked from a direction which soon must result in his capture, retreated in the most precipitate manner over the Etowah River.

"Dilworth advanced his skirmishers down the Oostenaula, driving in those of the enemy, until his line reached the city and extended to the Etowah, thus covering the railroad and all approaches to the city between the forks of the two rivers. This enabled us to reach the crossings over the Oostenaula, and secure what yet remained undestroyed of the bridges. The main bridges were entirely destroyed, but the pontoons were secured and repaired, and a bridge made in a few hours sufficient to cross the whole of McCook's brigade."

Rome proved to be a rich prize. Federal troops captured a trainload of supplies, ten pieces of artillery and large quantities of cotton, tobacco, quartermaster stores, and medical supplies. "The large iron-works and machine-shops of Noble & Co., upon which the enemy relied for a large part of his ordnance supplies and repairs, were captured in good condition," Davis reported. "It was the intention of the enemy to destroy these shops and stores, but so sudden was the attack of Dilworth's skirmishers that he precipitately fled, and they fell into our possession."

McCook's men occupied the city while Mitchell's and Morgan's brigades camped on the west bank of the Oostenaula. "The enemy's pickets continued to hold the south bank of the Coosa for several days, and kept up at intervals a vicious skirmish firing into the city, killing and wounding soldiers and citizens indiscriminately, until the 22nd, when in compliance with instructions, Morgan crossed a part of his brigade in pontoon boats, which had been sent me from the main column by order of Major-General Thomas, and took possession of the opposite bank of the river," Davis wrote. "The pontoon bridge was soon laid, and the whole of Morgan's brigade moved across and occupied the works, driving the enemy from that entire front."[28]

Batchelor liked Rome. "Rome is one of the prettyest little towns I ever saw," he wrote in his diary. "We got a lot of tobacco. Each man drew 1 plug chewing tobacco, 1 pound smokeing [tobacco] and 12 cigars."

Many Union soldiers remarked on the beauty of the roses that seemed to be blooming everywhere in Rome. Van Vleck was among them. He picked one and put it in a letter to Patty, where historians found it, long-dried and well-pressed, nearly 140 years later.[29]

13

"It Appeared Like Certain Death to Remain"

MAY 23–JUNE 30, 1864

THE SOLDIERS OF THE 78TH ILLINOIS HAD THREE DAYS TO SMELL THE ROSES IN Rome, a welcome rest after ten days of nearly nonstop marching and combat. The regiment's camp was near a home with a large garden filled with a variety of flowers. The weather was oppressively warm and the sweet scent of flowers hung heavily in the lazy air. The men spent time bathing in the river, washing clothes, sleeping, or wandering about the town. Batchelor, the ever-vigilant forager, and his comrades got "about 400 pounds of meat from under a house."[1]

Van Vleck visited two law offices in the town and "found the books all scattered over the floor, & everybody helping themselves. I thought I could make as good use of some of the books as the soldiers, & brought away two or three good books to read. The proprietors are in the Rebel army."

The days of rest ended May 24th. Mitchell's brigade led Davis's division out of Rome that morning, on its way to rejoin Sherman's armies. In the week since Davis had cut loose, those armies had driven south from Resaca through Adairsville, Cassville, and Kingston, where they swung right to bypass tough Confederate defenses along the railroad at Allatoona Pass.

Davis's men marched eighteen miles and camped that night in a peach orchard under a steady downpour. Next morning they resumed the march, passed the village of Van Wert, paused for dinner in a cornfield, then continued toward the town of Dallas. About 3:00 p.m. they began to hear heavy firing from that direction, where Gen. Joseph Hooker's troops were fighting the Confederates at New Hope Church. Davis ordered his men to quicken their pace, and the troops pressed forward in gathering darkness and more rain. Finally a halt was called, and the division—wet, hungry, and tired—went into camp about three miles from Dallas.[2]

Next morning, while the men of his division were trying to dry their clothes and tents, Davis reported to General Thomas and received orders to make a reconnaissance toward Dallas "with a view of finding out the enemy's position on that flank." With Morgan's brigade leading, the division started down Burnt Hickory Road, crossed Pumpkin Vine Creek, drove away some enemy pickets, entered the town of Dallas, and formed line of battle on East Marietta Road. "The head of General McPherson's column arrived at this time and went into position, his lines running across the Villa Rica Road," Davis reported. "Skirmishers . . . soon found [Confederate Lt. Gen. William J.] Hardee's Corps intrenched in a strong position."

Davis's men dug temporary breastworks, received mail, and drew rations, then rested on their arms through the night. Next day Davis ordered Mitchell's brigade to "open communication with the right of General Hooker's corps." Mitchell sent the 34th Illinois to make the connection while the 78th waited north of town in the morning, then advanced a half mile eastward in the early afternoon.

Batchelor thought the advance was more like two miles. "So mutch fighting and at 9 o'Clock p.m. was charged by the Rebels," he wrote in his diary. "They took four prisoners. We took 27 prisoners, one a captian [captain]."

On the morning of the 28th, "in order to render the position between my left and General Hooker's right more secure, I selected a strong position about midway between the two points, the distance being three miles, and ordered Mitchell to intrench his brigade there and to cut [build] roads to his rear connecting with the main command," Davis wrote. Mitchell's brigade had to cover the entire distance between Davis and Hooker, variously estimated at two to three miles, so the line necessarily was very thin. The 78th moved a mile to its left that evening to take its place in line and dig temporary fortifications.

"I am 25 years old to day," Batchelor wrote in his diary May 28th. He almost didn't survive the day. "We make an attempt to go to the left," he wrote. "As we make the turn a shell from the rebel fort burst so close that I could not see for a while."[3]

Fighting continued almost incessantly along the line, though the 78th was largely spared except for one man who was severely wounded in the hip. The regiment remained briskly engaged on the skirmish line through most of the night of May 29th. "The shells fly thick and fast," Batchelor wrote. "The Rebels charge us seven times in succession but [were] repulsed every time. They then commenced falling back and our men sang *We Will Rally Round the Flag Boys.*"

May 29th also was the day 1st Lt. Tobias E. Butler of Company G died of his Chickamauga wound. He was at his home in Camp Point, Adams County, when he died.

The morning of the 30th found the men of the 78th exhausted from the night's fighting, but Van Vleck nevertheless put them to work building more fortifications.

Each company had only one ax and four spades, but every man had a tin cup and a bayonet, and it was amazing how much dirt a few hundred men with poor tools could move in a short time when motivated by the expectation that someone would soon be shooting at them. By midafternoon, Van Vleck wrote, they had constructed an earthwork ten feet thick at the base and as high as a man's head, topped with heavy logs, "and half as long again as the reg't. in line . . . The men are *entirely* protected by it, from musketry & artillery, except during the act of firing, & they then only expose their eyes to a crack [in the logs] some four or five inches wide."

The work was scarcely complete when Generals Sherman and Davis and Colonel Mitchell rode up to inspect it. Sherman told the others they were the best temporary works he had ever seen, "which, considering the high authority, flattered the boys & *their Col.* considerably," Van Vleck wrote.

The works afforded some protection, but the stress of the campaign was beginning to take its toll. The constant shelling, night attacks, and steady picket-line firing were bad enough, but the troops also had to contend with sleeplessness, exhaustion, stifling heat, relentless rain, sticky red Georgia mud, filth, poor food and too little of it, bad water, mosquitoes, flies, chiggers, ticks, and an everlasting stink, all with no apparent end in sight. It took a man of extraordinary mental and physical toughness to endure all that, not to mention the ever-present risk that a bullet or shell might instantly snuff out his life or leave him crippled. Not all men were that tough, and some were beginning to suffer what today would be called battle fatigue.

"This *continued* fighting has a great effect on the nervous system of many men, a constant state of dreadful fear & excitement," Van Vleck wrote. "Many men maim themselves to get out of it. I have had two such cases in my reg't. One deliberately shot off his great toe, the other his forefinger, when they knew it would not take them out of the service, but only out of this campaign.

"Such cases seem to be frequent. One man in the 98th O[hio] V[olunteers], who has heretofore borne a good character as a brave & honorable soldier, deliberately shot himself through the head & put an end to his existence. It seems difficult to account for these cases, more especially the last, upon any rational or philosophical principles. The contrary effect is produced upon many of the men. They become careless & indifferent. This is the case with the larger proportion, but there is no denying, but a large part of the human family are constitutional cowards."[4]

This was a harsh judgment on the colonel's part, given that the great majority of men in the 78th had served faithfully in miserable conditions with little complaint. Perhaps the continuing stress of the campaign was also beginning to affect Van Vleck.

The 78th remained behind its earthwork and continued skirmishing May 31st. Van Vleck was writing a letter to his wife when a shell "burst over my head & covered me & my paper with powder & a large piece fell near to me, but no one fortunately was hurt. They are trying our new works, & now I have got the men into them I am not fearful of the result." That night, about ten o'clock, the regiment received orders to prepare to move.

On the first day of June, under a scorching sun, the whole division moved some five miles to the left and relieved a division of the IV Corps. "The enemy's lines being very close here, we had several casualties," Lt. Col. Maris Vernon reported. The heat gave way to a violent thunderstorm and heavy rain, which continued on the 2nd.

The 78th was still on the skirmish line the night of June 3rd and "repelled an advance of the enemy," Vernon continued. "Scirmishing all the time," Batchelor wrote. Payne of the 34th reported firing all day from rebel sharpshooters in and behind trees or concealed in thick weeds and underbrush. "Rain again fell in great quantities," he recorded, and some soldiers had to stand in flooded rifle pits.[5]

It was still raining on the 4th when Mitchell's brigade moved again, passing New Hope Church, and finally rejoined the rest of the XIV Corps. Batchelor reported that "Jim Thomson, orderly at Davis' H'dQ'rs and another orderly went out after food this morning and never returned."

That night the enemy withdrew and "we passed through his works on the following morning, and moved in the direction of Acworth, going into camp some two miles to the southwest of it," Vernon reported. Batchelor recorded the movement as a march of about seven miles. As always, he had his forager's eye peeled. "Get plenty of wheat, oats and rye," he said.

Davis's division made camp near the banks of Proctor's Creek in position to control the road from Acworth to Big Shanty. It remained there three days, the men resting as well as they could under relentless rain. They waited for supplies to be brought up, especially rations, but rain had turned the roads into bottomless mud so it was nearly impossible for wagons to come forward. For the time being at least, however, the men were no longer under constant fire.[6]

While the men rested, Van Vleck wrote Patty that he had finally given up on T. S. Vail as his choice for regimental chaplain and instead selected John L. Jones, a Presbyterian minister from Schuyler County. "I hope he may prove acceptable & profitable," the colonel wrote.[7]

***

The fighting around Dallas and New Hope Church had been extremely bloody and intense, and some regiments in Mitchell's brigade had suffered significant losses, but the 78th had been remarkably lucky; only one man had been seriously wounded and a few others suffered minor wounds. Sherman's force had gained ground steadily, repeatedly flanking the shorter rebel lines. For his part, Confederate General Joseph Johnston had maneuvered skillfully, parrying each federal thrust and holding position stubbornly until flanked again. He was also watchful for any opportunity to employ his smaller army at temporary advantage against Sherman, but the opportunity never seemed to come. With the federal armies now only about twenty-five miles from Atlanta, he was rapidly running out of maneuvering room.

Johnston's situation was causing increasing anxiety in the Confederate capital at Richmond. As far as President Jefferson Davis and his advisors could tell, Johnston had done nothing but retreat and had no plan to take the offensive against Sherman. This view was reinforced by letters from Lt. Gen. John Bell Hood, one of Johnston's corps commanders, who sought the army command for himself.[8]

For the 78th Illinois and the rest of Sherman's armies, the campaign's next phase began with a general push on Friday, June 10th. The movement, toward Marietta, was made along narrow, muddy roads bordered by thick woods that dripped constantly from continuing rain. Rebel skirmishers contested nearly every foot of the advance, but the federal troops kept pressing forward.

Mitchell's brigade took the advance for Davis's division on June 13th and Company B of the 78th, under command of 1st Lt. Freeman Woodruff, "advanced the skirmish line, capturing six prisoners," Lieutenant Colonel Vernon reported. That evening the division came upon the enemy line at Pine Mountain, where the rebels had a signal station and artillery battery on the bald crest. The federals had barely taken position when an entire rebel company, including the captain and two lieutenants, came over the lines to surrender. "They reported that the brigade to which they belonged had made arrangement to desert in case the rebel army fell back any farther," Van Vleck wrote.[9]

About 11:00 a.m. the next day, federal troops spied a cluster of rebel officers near the signal station, apparently observing Union lines through field glasses. General Sherman was among those who saw the rebel officers and ordered two artillery batteries to open fire on them. Several salvos were fired, scattering the officers, and shortly afterward a message from the Confederate signal station was intercepted and decoded as a request for an ambulance to retrieve the body of Lt. Gen. Leonidas Polk.

That was how Union forces learned their cannon fire had killed the general, one of Johnston's corps commanders. A shell, probably fired by the 5th Indiana battery, had struck Polk in the chest and passed through his body, killing him instantly. His death brought tears to Generals Johnston and Hardee, who had been with him moments before. He was also mourned by Confederate President Jefferson Davis, who had been

Polk's friend. Their remorse was undoubtedly genuine, but the loss was more personal than military, for Polk—an Episcopal bishop in civilian life—was probably a better clergyman than general.[10]

"Lay arround till noon, then go about one mile," Batchelor wrote in his diary June 14th. "Drive Rebels and capture a few prisoners." That was his description of a federal attack on the rebels' Pine Mountain defenses. Mitchell's brigade went forward with the 78th along with the 113th and 121st Ohio in the first line. They advanced through a heavy fire of musketry and artillery, ending the day at the edge of a large field, where they dug rifle pits for protection.[11]

Next afternoon Davis's division crossed the field and advanced at the double-quick. Rebel skirmishers saw them coming and many "threw down their arms & started for our lines, every fellow shaking his hat or something white as evidence of his peaceful intention," Van Vleck wrote. "The deserters not only came into our lines but immediately set themselves to work caring for our wounded & digging entrenchments."

The rebels made a furious counterattack on the Union line about nine o'clock that night, but were repulsed. "Cannonading and musketry all night," Batchelor wrote.[12]

Federal batteries poured a heavy fire into the rebel positions during most of June 16th. While that was happening, the soldiers of Mitchell's brigade took time to draw new clothing for the first time since the beginning of the campaign. Many were in dire need of it.

That night the rebels attacked again and once more were driven back, but not without loss in the 78th. Cpl. Jeremiah M. Stuart of Company D was shot through the head and killed on the picket line, and Sgt. William S. Hendricks, the regimental sergeant major, took a bullet through the left heel, a wound that would eventually force his discharge.[13]

Things were relatively quiet in front of Davis's division on the 17th, although rain continued falling almost without interruption. The men could hear brisk fighting off to the left, however, as other federal troops slogged through rain and rebel bullets to gain yet another lodgment on the rebel flank. This compelled Johnston to withdraw yet again, which he did the afternoon of June 18th, and the soggy Confederates filed into entrenchments around the base of Kennesaw Mountain. Davis's men moved forward about five hundred yards across a cornfield and took possession of the rebels' old works.

The new Confederate line stretched about six miles from the railroad on their right across Kennesaw, Little Kennesaw Mountain, and Pigeon Hill to a ridge on their left that would later become known as Cheatham Hill. Rebel soldiers dragged heavy cannon up the slopes to emplacements that dominated the approaches to this formidable line, and cavalry was posted to guard their flanks.[14]

On Sunday, June 19th, the 78th and its sister regiments advanced about two miles under torrential rain through an ocean of mud and came up against the new rebel line. Creeping forward through heavy brush, they moved in close and dug rifle pits under heavy skirmish fire, which continued through the day. In the afternoon artillery joined in, with Confederate batteries opening first and federal gunners responding in kind. Many of the federal shells fell short, however, endangering soldiers on the skirmish line and adding to their misery from rain and oppressive heat.

"Troops are lying at the foot of Kinesaw Mountain," Batchelor scrawled in his diary. "We get a number of prisoners." In fact, more and more Confederates were deserting, and they were beginning to "talk very different[ly] from what they did at the beginning of the campaign," Van Vleck wrote. "They exhibit none of that vindictiveness, & but little of the confidence that characterized them then. Desertions are ten *times* more frequent & extensive.

"Their pickets [also] are much more communicative & friendly with ours, keeping up a constant conversation, & every day small parties from their picket line & from ours may be seen along the disputed ground between the two lines in friendly confab, and busily engaged trading—our boys for tobacco, which the rebels have in abundance, and the rebs for coffee, of which our men are ever supplied in quantities greater than they can use. This is a new mode of warfare, you will think, but is it not another harbinger of an early peace?"[15]

"Heavy fog but heavy cannonading all day," Batchelor wrote on the 20th. Payne of the 34th Illinois thought about thirty federal cannon were engaged, but "without any visible results except damage to the lines of rifle-pits and lunettes on the mountain...."

Van Vleck agreed with Payne's estimate of the number of cannons and lack of damage. "One continuous roar & one continuous screeching of shells filled the air & made the earth to tremble," he wrote Patty. "It was sublime in the highest degree. But you would be surprised as I have been, to see how little damage the shells are capable of doing." Only two men in the 78th had been slightly wounded by the bombardment, he said. "It seems almost miraculous how so many escape."[16]

Their escape may have been aided by the fact they could see the men firing at them, which gave them time to take cover. "We can see the gunner as he rams the charge home," wrote McAdams of the 113th Ohio. "Then comes a puff of smoke, and in two or three seconds the shots come shrieking through the air, sometimes striking in the timber in our rear, sometimes plowing up the dirt in our front, and bounding over our heads and landing a thousand feet behind us."

June 22nd was the first dry day in what seemed like weeks, and although the men of the 78th remained under nearly constant artillery and skirmish fire, they tried to dry things out. "We found everything either mouldy, rusty or sour from the continued dampness or rather *wetness,*" Van Vleck wrote. "To sleep in wet blankets one night is not very dangerous but to do it for weeks has at last made me sick, not seriously but has brought on one of my billious derangements, but I hope I am past the most of it."

The rain continued to hold off on the 23rd, but artillery fire increased as more batteries joined on each side. "This great shelling, as little damage as it does, has a very demoralizing effect," Van Vleck told his wife. "When a shell bursts within a few feet of your head, & tears up the trees & the ground about you, although it does not hurt your bones or muscles, yet it produces a very peculiar feeling that no one is partial to . . . And then these rifled shells have the most outrageous screeching sound that ever pained the human ear. To hear some three or four score of them screeching & bursting at once, in connection with the booming of as many cannon, & to see the smoke rising from the different fortifications, as from so many lime kilns, is really one of the most awfully sublime scenes I have ever witnessed." Despite all the shelling, the 78th suffered only one man slightly wounded.

The rebel artillery fire eased off on the 24th, which had been declared a national day of fasting and prayer in the Confederacy. In Chattanooga on this date, Pvt. Thomas Lindsey of Company C died of disease in an army hospital. He was from Blandinsville, McDonough County.

The Confederate artillery fire resumed the next day in all its fury. Late in the afternoon of that clear, warm day, Davis's division got orders to move.[17]

Sherman had been unfairly critical of the Army of the Cumberland for its habit of entrenching after every advance, which he thought delayed its progress. The general's other armies probably behaved no differently, but perhaps partly because he was irked at the Cumberlanders Sherman decided to abandon his flanking tactics temporarily and use them to make a direct assault on the rebel works at Kennesaw Mountain. On June 24th, he issued Special Field Order 28, which called for an attack to be made at 8:00 a.m. Monday, June 27th.

Shortly after midnight June 26th, the men of the 78th and the other regiments of Mitchell's brigade crawled out of their rifle pits and trenches and filed quietly to the rear. After the entire division was assembled, it marched about four miles through thick woods and deep ravines, a route purposely chosen to mask the movement from the enemy. The line of march was around the west end of Kennesaw Mountain and behind the federal lines at that point, and it was daylight when the division finally halted. "Very hot we[a]ther," Batchelor wrote.[18]

The division camp was in the rear of Maj. Gen. David S. Stanley's IV Corps. "It was Sunday, and for the first time in weeks the men had an opportunity to spend a day in the silence of the shady woods," wrote Aten of the 85th Illinois of McCook's brigade. "There were no bugle calls that day, and after a quiet inspection of arms and an issue of extra ammunition, the time was devoted to undisturbed rest. In the distance an occasional cannon could be heard, but the camp was out of reach of shot and shell, and beyond the sound of the rifles on the skirmish line."[19]

While the men relaxed, General Thomas informed Davis "of the distinguished duty" for which his division had been designated. With General Stanley and other officers, Davis "made a thorough reconnaissance of the enemy's works and selected the point of attack. The point selected was immediately in front of General Whitaker's brigade of Stanley's division of the IV Corps." The rebel works at this point followed rising ground that formed a salient angle. "In the absence of abatis, fallen timber, and other obstructions which generally confront their works, this point seemed the most assailable."

Davis selected McCook's and Mitchell's brigades to make the assault, with Morgan's to be held in reserve. Early the next morning, June 27th, "the brigade commanders accompanied me to the ground and familiarized themselves with it," Davis wrote. At 7:00 a.m. the two brigades "were massed in an open field in rear of our breastworks . . . some 600 yards from the point to be carried," Davis continued. "No place nearer the enemy's line could the troops be massed without receiving the enemy's fire, both of infantry and artillery. The ground to be passed over was exceedingly rocky and rough, and considerable parts of it covered with forest trees, interspersed with undergrowth." The troops were ordered to leave knapsacks, tents, and cooking utensils behind.

The day was already sizzling hot, with the sun a fiery hole in a gunmetal sky, and the men stood in ranks for more than an hour with sweat trickling down their faces while they waited for whatever was coming. They watched as regimental commanders were summoned by Mitchell to receive orders, then returned to pass the orders along to company commanders.[20]

The plan was for three brigades of Brig. Gen. John Newton's IV Corps division to attack the left side of the rebel salient while McCook's and Mitchell's brigades of Davis's division struck the point and right side. McCook would aim for the point with Mitchell on his right, where the Confederate line curved southeast around the hillside. The 34th Illinois was designated to provide skirmishers for Mitchell's attack, with Companies A and B in the first line, without bayonets, followed closely by Companies F and I with fixed bayonets. The rest of the brigade was to follow in column of regiments—the 113th Ohio in front, followed by the 121st Ohio, 98th Ohio, and 78th Illinois.

Col. Henry B. Banning of the 121st Ohio later reported that he received very explicit orders to deploy his men so they would overlap the 113th Ohio on the right by two companies. "The other regiments, I understood, were to form in echelon, guiding and overlapping in like manner," he wrote. "I was also instructed to deploy my regiment to the right when I struck the enemy; that my left would probably strike an angle in the enemy's works, and that I would have to wheel my regiment to the left, and that I would be supported on my right by the regiments in my rear." In other words, according to Banning, each regiment was supposed to deploy so that it slightly overlapped the right of the regiment in front, then wheel to the left when it struck the enemy line where it curved away from the point of the salient. Van Vleck, however, later complained heatedly that he never received such orders. Lt. Col. John S. Pearce, commanding the 98th Ohio, third in line, also said nothing of such orders in his report of the action.[21]

The attack was scheduled for 8:00 a.m., but some units were still getting into position at that hour, so General Thomas delayed the starting signal. Federal artillery opened fire on the rebel salient about 8:00 a.m., however, accomplishing little except to alert the enemy an assault was probably coming.

While Mitchell's troops waited silently in line, still sweating from the rising heat, the 34th Illinois skirmishers heard some of the brigade's officers making bets "that our skirmish line would, or would not, capture the picket line," Payne wrote. Not surprisingly, this "caused a strong feeling of resentment in the minds of the men. It seemed too much like gambling with their lives."

Finally the order came for the brigade to move into position for the attack. "We passed through the lines of the first brigade [Morgan's], which was well protected behind their rifle-pits," Payne wrote, "and taking position outside, deployed our skirmish line steadily and deliberately, sufficiently to the front to allow the other lines to deploy in our rear.

"Having gained position, we had from 20 to 30 minutes to look out the situation in front, before the signal gun should send us on the perilous charge against the most strongly fortified position we had ever seen, either our own or the enemy's. Our skirmish line halted on the brow of a hill which immediately sloped towards the east and the lines of the enemy, through scattering timber on the right and a small wheat field on the left, ending in a shallow ravine and rising to higher ground beyond, upon which were the rifle-pits of the enemy, and in front, varying from 100 to 250 feet, were the pits of the [enemy] picket line.

"The main line of the enemy was about 300 yards from our position, and our skirmish line was in plain view of the enemy and his picket line, but we were not molested.

Not a shot was fired. The silence became painful, and foreboded preparation to meet the attack. The men on the skirmish line were alert and attentive, intense and determined, but very quiet."

It was about 9:00 a.m. before Thomas was satisfied everything was ready (Payne thought it was a little earlier and Van Vleck thought it was later) and gave the order to fire the signal guns and start the attack. "The expected signal came, clear and sharp, from our left rear, and the double skirmish line sprang away like a trained racer, directly for the [rebel] picket line in front," Payne wrote. "In less than 60 seconds every man of the [rebel] picket line was off his post, and all except perhaps a half dozen were in our lines as prisoners."

Mitchell's four regiments went forward like a blue ocean wave breaking against a reef. The reef in this case was two ragged rows of red earth where the rebels had dug trenches and piled up dirt parapets topped with headlogs. The soldiers behind the earthworks were from Brig. George Maney's Tennessee Brigade of Maj. Gen. Benjamin Cheatham's division, the same brigade that Mitchell's men had fought at Graysville.

As the Union troops raced uphill toward the rebel lines, there came a long series of flashes from gaps in the headlogs, accompanied by a giant peal of musketry, followed instantaneously by the ugly sounds of bullets smacking into human flesh and bone and the sudden gasps or strangled yells of wounded men. "The lines halted voluntarily, and the efforts of the officers to urge the men forward were unavailing," Payne wrote. "The trail of the charging column was crimson with the blood of those who fell at every step of the way, and to attempt farther would only double the size of the 'butcher's bill' without results."

Mitchell's lead regiment, the 113th Ohio, "proceeded through thick woods up one hill and down across a small creek," Capt. Toland Jones later reported. "Owing to the rough nature of the ground, the lines were not kept in as perfect order as desirable . . . When crossing the creek we found before us a hill of some size, at the summit of which were the main works of the enemy.

"Our regiment advanced up, exposed to the full fire of the enemy. It was not until we had advanced halfway up the hill that the enemy poured into our ranks his heaviest fire. Our left was then in close proximity to a salient angle in the hostile works, toward which Colonel McCook's brigade was charging with his entire line. The firing then became most terrific, the rebels opening up with two batteries upon either flank and delivering from the left a most galling musketry fire. The men, however, advanced without faltering, the 121st [Ohio] taking position on our right.

"We charged rapidly forward, and our men falling by scores, until the left had nearly reached the works, some of the men falling immediately upon them. At this time Lieutenant Colonel Warner [the regiment's commander] was severely wounded, and the brigade upon our left behind forced to retire, the order was given to fall back."

The ground in front of the rebel line "for two or three hundred feet had been cleared of every bush, but a dangerous sharp-pointed stub was left where every bush and shrub had stood," Payne wrote. "Trees from four to ten inches in diameter had been felled, with the tops outward, the limbs trimmed off so as to leave as many sharp points as possible, and the limbs fixed rigidly in place by stakes driven in the ground. The trunks of trees ten inches in diameter were pierced with two-inch holes at right angles alternately every ten or twelve inches, and stakes six feet long driven through and sharpened at each end. These logs were fastened together at the ends with chains, securely bolted, and set up a few feet outside the rifle-pits. These lines of 'cheval du frise' [chevaux-de-frise] were the most perfect and impassable of any we had ever seen or ever saw afterwards. In addition, there was a complete line of 'headlogs' on the parapet, leaving two and a half inches through which to thrust the muzzles of their guns, and was the only vulnerable point at which we could direct our fire."[22]

The 121st Ohio followed the 113th and, as Colonel Banning said he had been ordered, started a left wheel to close with the angle of the enemy's breastworks. When the regiment "got close up to his ditches" the rebels "opened upon my single line with grape and canister from both flanks and a full line of small arms from my front," Banning reported. Four of his company commanders and most of their sergeants went down almost immediately. "The enemy now opened another battery from an angle to his works on my right. On this flank I was entirely without support." That was a veiled reference to the 98th Ohio and 78th Illinois, which Banning evidently expected would be in echelon on his right.

The flanking fire came from a battery the rebels had concealed behind piles of brush. The branches were suddenly cast off, exposing four cannon that opened fire with canister and cased shot, which clattered across the landscape, striking trees and rocks and men.

"Believing it would be impossible to carry the strong position of the enemy with my now weak and thin line, I closed my regiment to the right and withdrew some 20 paces to the rear, and had my command to lie down, where the formation of the ground offered some protection," Banning wrote. "Having made these dispositions, I sent a written statement of my position to Colonel Mitchell, commanding the brigade, who sent me orders to refuse my right and hold and intrench if I could do it without too great a sacrifice. Leaving one-half of my men on the line to keep up the fire, with the other half I built a line of earthworks in the rear of the line under cover of the woods, refusing my right."[23]

The 98th Ohio, third in line, "advanced amidst a perfect shower of canister and bullets to within a few yards of the enemy's lines," Lt. Col. John S. Pearce reported, "but so strong was their position that their [his regiment's] front lines were compelled to give way and come back hurriedly through the two rear lines, carrying with them Companies G and B of the regiment. These two companies, however, were soon in position and intrenching, along with the balance of the regiment, which held the ground it occupied at the time it was ordered to halt and lie down . . . .

"As soon as the regiment lay down, they commenced with their bayonets to dig, and their hands, spoons, and tin mess-pans to construct earthworks for their protection and defense . . . There, under one of the heaviest fires, both of canister and ball, during this campaign, did they erect a work in one hour which afforded them much protection. Now they could raise their heads from the ground with some safety, where before it was almost sure death to take your face out of the dust."[24]

The 78th Illinois, last in line, moved forward at the double-quick, "my position in line being the right," Van Vleck wrote two days after the assault. "We moved forward to the very foot of the enemies' works, where our two front lines were repulsed with very great loss. The two rear lines however, consisting of the 98th Ohio (Col. Pierce) & my reg't., maintained our position on the ridge we had gained & [advanced] within 50 yards of the enemies' works, & immediately went to work fortifying, & are now fixed to stay."

If Batchelor's account is accurate, the 78th may have gotten even closer to the enemy works than Van Vleck said. "We attact [attacked] with a charge which was desperate so as to throw rocks at each other," he scribbled in his diary. "Picks and spades are used to fight with. Colonel McCook is killed. He commanded 3rd brigade." Batchelor was premature concerning McCook's fate; the colonel was wounded but lingered nearly three weeks before he died. Brig. Gen. Charles Harker, commander of one of Newton's brigades, also was mortally wounded in the attack.[25]

James K. Magie also described the attack in a letter to an unknown recipient. The first page of the letter is missing, and his narrative begins with the second page: "Such wounded as could walk were passing by us to the rear where portions of those regiments in advance of us were fleeing in confusion through our ranks to the rear, [but] as far as I could observe from my position, every man of the 78th was pressing forward with gallant tread, ready to obey every order from our Colonel.

"At length the enemy opened a cross fire upon us of grape, cannister and shell, and then came a grand rush from our front of panic-stricken men saying they had orders to fall back . . . I was upon the left of the regiment in rear of Co. B. There were some two or three in that company that could scarcely resist the tide that was bearing to the rear, but the 78th had as yet received no orders to halt or to retreat, and it became every man as a true soldier to keep his place and obey orders.

Assault by Mitchell's Brigade

Four regiments, the 113th Ohio, 121st Ohio, 98th Ohio and 78th Illinois attack in echelon, each regiment slightly overlapping the one in front.

(1) The 113th Ohio begins the charge of Mitchell's Brigade. It meets intense fire and turns back when its commander is wounded.

(2) The 121st Ohio, next to attack, wheels left and comes under heavy fire. Forced to fall back a short distance, it finally digs in to face the rebel line and follows orders to refuse its right flank.

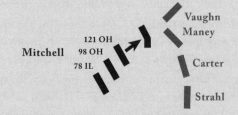

(3) The 98th Ohio rushes in next but encounters an avalanche of fire and breaks apart. Some troops flee to the rear while others dig in and hold on.

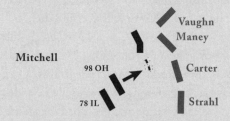

(4) The 78th Illinois, believing friendly forces are hidden by smoke in its front, holds fire as it advances under fire and digs in near the Confederate works. It remains there, fighting off counterattacks, until July 2.

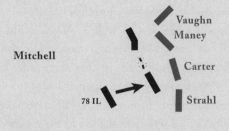

■ Union Units   ■ Confederate Units

KENNESAW MOUNTAIN - MORNING JUNE 27, 1864

"Sergeant Joseph Strickler noticed the few that wavered, and instantly ordered the men to keep their places. It was a trying moment—it appeared like certain death to remain or to advance, but Strickler, knowing that if a break was made disorder and confusion would ensue, seemed to throw his soul into the work. He was determined that no man of Co. B should break to the rear, and by his persuasion, encouragement and example, every man remained at his post of duty.

"We soon had orders to halt and lie down and in that position our danger was not so great. I was not far from Wm. C. Dixon, [Pvt. William C. Dixon of Company B] when he was wounded. I saw him jump up with his right arm dangling by his side and bleeding profusely, but before he would leave for the rear he went and notified Lieut. [Freeman] Woodruff, who was in command of the company, that he was wounded and obtained his permission to go to the rear. Dixon was a good soldier, and I am sorry to learn that it was found necessary to amputate his arm.

"After the firing had pretty much closed, our regiment was ordered to hold the ground and to throw up breastworks. There was then some canvassing in each company to ascertain who was killed, wounded or missing. Co. H was found to have suffered the least of any other company in the regiment, but there was one man missing—[Pvt.] Philo Ogden. No one could tell where he was; he had been seen in the thickest of the fight, but where he had gone no one seemed to know. Lieut. [Samuel] Simmons, who was in command of the company, inquired of me if I had seen Ogden. I had not. Someone then remarked that he must have gone to the rear. I knew Ogden, and I knew that a braver or better soldier could not be found in the Army of the Cumberland. I remarked to the Lieutenant—'if Ogden has gone to the rear, he has been carried there.' A little further investigation developed the fact that Ogden was in the extreme front, only a few yards from the rebel breastworks, loading and firing as fast as he knew how."[26]

The attack had been soundly repulsed at every point, and the survivors of Mitchell's regiments—those who had not fled—now sought shelter behind every rock or tree, or burrowed into every small depression in the earth, or tried to make their own holes using bayonets as digging tools. Some even took shelter behind the bodies of dead comrades—anything to get out of the howling storm of bullets and canister. There they huddled, under the merciless sun and continuing heavy fire, with only canteens full of warm water to relieve their thirst.

Many wounded men lay between the lines where stretcher bearers could not reach them. "The day was very hot"—some estimates placed the temperature at well above 100 degrees—"and nothing could be done to relieve the fearful condition of the wounded," Payne wrote. "Their piteous calls for help had to be disregarded, as the enemy kept up a straggling fire to prevent the making of rifle-pits so close to their lines, and it is quite probably some of the wounded were accidentally killed."

But there were no orders to withdraw; to do so would only expose more men to deadly fire. So the men stayed put while the searing sun continued its slow circle across the smoky sky. "I had four or five men sunstricken yesterday," Van Vleck wrote the next day, "some of which, it is said, will die."[27]

At last evening shadows crept slowly—oh, so slowly!—across the battlefield, and when it was too dark for the enemy to see, parties of men armed with picks and shovels began digging proper earthworks on the hillside where Mitchell's survivors still held their grip. General Davis organized men to fill empty cracker boxes and sacks with dirt, then carry them forward to add to the shelters being built in the darkness.

"A great many of our wounded were left on the ground by the reg'ts. in advance, & could not be brought off until night," Van Vleck wrote. "It was almost heartrending to hear the poor fellows calling for help, & to be unable to get to them or to send them any relief. Major [John] Yager of the 121st, was one of these, & Major [George] Greene thought he could get him off the field, & taking a corp[oral] with him started out, but the corporal was killed instantly before they got half way to the spot, & the Major returned, filled with self-condemnation for the part he had taken in an affair which resulted in the death of a good man."

Parties were sent to gather up the wounded after dark, but "the boys had lain in the hot sun all day, with their wounds open, and they were too sore to be carried except on a stretcher," wrote Lt. J. M. Branum of the 98th Ohio. "We worked until 2 o'clock, bringing them back and giving them water. It was a dark night's work as we groped our way among the bushes, guided by calls of the wounded and occasional flashes of [heat] lightning. By 3 o'clock the wounded were all taken back, under a severe fire from the enemy."[28]

Tuesday, June 28th, dawned as bright and warm as the preceding day. "Our men have works built within 50 yards of the Rebels," Batchelor scrawled in his diary. "The dead begin to smell very badly."

There was "no material change in position," Colonel Mitchell reported. "Continued to advance my lines by system of gradual approaches, keeping up constant firing." But he said his men also "were much annoyed by the enemy's sharpshooters."[29]

Preliminary returns indicated the 78th had ten killed and forty-nine wounded in the assault, but part of the 28th was spent trying to confirm these numbers. The final figures were eleven killed and fifty-one wounded. The dead included Pvt. James Thomas of Company A; Cpl. Julius Rice and Pvt. Elijah McWilliams of Company B; 1st Sgt. John E. James and Pvt. Jacob H. Michaels of Company C; Cpl. William Manlove of Company D; 1st Sgt. William Pierce and Pvt. Charles H. Blake of Company E; and Pvts. Isaac W. Adkins, John W. Mewmaw, and William B. Stahl of Company K. Five of the wounded, including 1st Lt. George A. Brown of Company A, would later die of their wounds. Two other officers—Capt. Thomas L. Howden of Company G and Capt. William B. Akins of Company K—were slightly wounded. Each was struck a glancing blow on the head by shell fragments. In addition to Pvt. William C. Dixon, whose arm was amputated, at least two other soldiers lost limbs. Pvt. Robert L. Laughlin of Company I, nephew of Major Broaddus, lost an arm, and Pvt. Richard C. Terry of Company C lost a leg. Several soldiers also were listed as "deranged by concussion of shell."[30]

"The greater portion of the killed and wounded were by shell," wrote Sgt. Martin L. Stewart of Company G, "as the 78th laid in the second [line] of battle. Many of the wounded are very slight and are now being well taken care of, considering the number of surgeons [we] have to work with, and the boys appear to be in good spirits and hate to leave the field, as many of the wounded have never been in a hospital."

That night the rebels charged the positions occupied by Mitchell's brigade, but were repulsed. Mitchell's regiments doggedly continued to hold the works they had scratched out of the hillside.

June 29th was another hot morning and the stench of corpses in front of the rebel entrenchments was becoming unendurable. "Our men go in with a flag of truce for permission to bury the dead," Batchelor wrote. "Terms are from 10 a.m. to 3 p.m. Officers meet between the lines and stand back to back and talk until time was up."

Van Vleck said it was the rebels who asked for the truce, but it didn't really matter because burying the dead "became a necessity, for the enemy as well as ourselves," Payne wrote. "The bodies were in a terrible condition, and the atmosphere was almost unbearable." When the two sides had agreed to the truce, "a guard line composed of men from both armies was established midway between the lines, and all [the dead] on the farther side were brought to the guard line and delivered to our burial party."

While that was going on, the officers and men who had so recently been trying to kill each other "fraternized on the most friendly terms, and exchanged commodities with each other, principally tobacco and coffee," Payne continued. "The officers and guards of both sides had difficulty in restraining their men from crowding the guard line. Among the Confederate officers who came out to the front lines were Gen'ls [Benjamin] Cheatham, [Thomas] Hindman and [Patrick] Cleburne. The men of both sides who were not engaged otherwise, sat on the head-logs of their respective works as quietly and peacefully as two farmers on a rail fence on opposite sides of a road, discussing crops and prices. . . .

"The grewsome task was completed and the graves mostly marked with pieces of board from cracker boxes, and at 4 o'clock in the afternoon everybody was out of sight and the racket began again."[31]

While the truce was in effect, Van Vleck was writing a blistering letter to his wife. His anger was not directed at her—he rarely if ever had a harsh word for his beloved Patty—but he needed to pour out his feelings about what happened during the June 27th assault.

"As almost always happens, there was a great blunder, for which some body, (& I suppose it is Col. Mitchell) is responsible," he wrote. "It seems now that instead of my reg't. forming the fourth line, I was really for the most part in the front line, of which I was ignorant until to day. Col. Banning of the 121st Ohio had positive orders to deploy the line as soon as he passed the skirmish line, which would place his reg't. on the right of 113th, the 98th on his right & I on the right of the 98th. But nobody but Banning it seems had any such orders, & consequently his was the only reg't. that deployed, & when the 113th was repulsed it would have left the 98th in front had not a large share of the 78th worked their way past them.

"As it was I can safely say that the 98th & 78th laid together *in the front line,* receiving the rebel fire & fearing to return it lest they should kill some of the 113th or 121st which, though we were ignorant of it, were all a long way out of our way. And do you know that such is the most trying position soldiers can possibly be in, to be compelled to remain under a destructive fire of musketry, canister and case shot, and be unable to return the fire? Yet such was our case, & our orders were explicit not to fire, unless the two front lines fell back, and as the fight was in a dense thicket, where we could not see a dozen yards to our front, and as our front was unmasked by the 121st without our having the least intimation of it, and we consequently had no other idea than that they were still before us, neither the 98th nor 78th were able to fire a gun & yet I lost more men than either of the other reg'ts if you deduct the loss of the 113th & 121st inflicted while they were falling back.

"A terrible loss has been suffered by our div[ision] but I suppose as long as the generals feel paid for the loss, by advantage of position, we have no *military* right to complain, but in a humanitarian point of view, I beg leave to say that there was a very unnecessary sacrifice. I am willing to sacrifice my own limbs or my life and those of my gallant men, if I can there by accomplish a corresponding good in helping to crush this wicked rebellion, but to sacrifice near a thousand men, to gain a position which might have been gained by a loss of one tenth the number, appears to me to be worse than folly.

"Still we are not to look for infinite wisdom in man, & our military leaders for the most part are not only men, but men of small caliber, or of small experience. You may think that this remark reflects upon my friend Mitchell. I intend that it shall. Although I entertain the highest regard for him as a man and as a regimental commander, I have reluctantly concluded that in the first place he is too young, & in the next place he is too nervous, for a brigade commander in time of an action. As for Davis, he has neither the native genius [n]or education, to command with success, anything more than a reg't."

What triggered this outburst? Someone, perhaps Banning, apparently told Van Vleck that his regiment was out of position in the attack because it failed to follow orders to deploy as Banning's regiment had done. But if those orders were never communicated to the 78th or the 98th Ohio, Van Vleck and Lieutenant Colonel Pearce of the 98th Ohio could not have known what they were supposed to do. What they did instead was push straight ahead, which explained why Banning complained he had no support on his right. With Banning's regiment out of the way after wheeling to the left, the 78th and 98th Ohio in effect became the front line without knowing it, and they went forward until they struck the enemy works at an oblique angle. At that point they went to ground and held their fire, believing the 113th and 121st Ohio regiments were still somewhere in their front, concealed by woods and the smoke of battle. How long the two regiments waited under heavy fire without shooting back is unrecorded.

In the end, the miscommunication did not affect the outcome of the battle; the attack never had a chance of succeeding. But Van Vleck was obviously angered by what was at least an insinuation that he hadn't followed orders.

He was, however, proud of the 78th. "I have renewed cause of thankfulness for the gallant conduct of my reg't.," he wrote. "Their praise is in the mouth of every body in the brigade. Even during the thickest of the fight an adjutant of one of the other reg'ts. came & took his place by my side, leaving his own reg't., & said to me, 'I want to be with this bully regiment, for I know they will stand their ground.' I heard similar expressions from many other officers. Several of the col[onel]s expressing to me great admiration of my reg't. from the fact, probably, that my reg't. was all present when we halted, which no other col[onel] can say. Another point, the provost guard picked up all the stragglers, but it was remarked by all, that none had a '78' on their hats, although there were many of every other number known to this brigade.

"Am I not justified in being proud of such a reg't.? They have my confidence & give me theirs in return, & this has much to do with their valor & my willingness to brave the greatest dangers with them wherever duty calls."

Van Vleck also reported he had promoted James K. Magie to first sergeant of Company C, replacing 1st Sgt. John E. James, who was killed in the assault. "I greatly deplored the death of James for he was a good man & a consistent Christian, but at the same time it affords me pleasure to be able to promote Magie, who I had expected to promote in some other position," the colonel wrote. "He has served a long time as a private, & is every way competent for any position, & his family need[s] greater support than his pay as a private afforded." Magie, he said, "appears very thankful."

Van Vleck probably didn't know just how much Magie needed money to pay his debts and finance his son's operation, nor was he aware of the irony that Magie, who once thought he might be able to make a thousand dollars selling stamps and papers, was now thankful for an increase from a private's pay of thirteen dollars to a first sergeant's pay of twenty dollars a month, if and when a paymaster ever visited the regiment.[32]

<hr />

During the night of June 29th the rebels attacked again, trying once more to dislodge the federal troops from their hard-won positions. "This morning at 2 o'Clock Rebels charge us but get repulsed," Batchelor wrote. "We continue to extend our works."

Van Vleck thought it was about midnight when the rebels attacked. "We had the advantage of breast works this time, & we repulsed them handsomely," he wrote Patty on the 30th. "They however got near enough so that one left his hat, & two left their guns on the works of the 98th Ohio. I had one man killed & there was one killed in the 98th Ohio, this is the sum total of the loss in our brig[ade] . . . I know nothing of the loss of the enemy, but it must have been very severe.

"I wish you could realize the terrible sublimity of a battle at midnight, especially to the minds of the assaulted. Imagine yourself to be awakened out of a sound & peaceful slumber, into the midst of a most fearful battle, every square inch of space around and above you seemingly filled with deadly missiles, the senses bewildered, by the complicated, terrible & overpowering sounds of roaring musketry, whizzing bullets, booming cannon, & shrieking, and bursting shells, and the scene fitfully lit up by the lurid flames that flash from the artillery, along the line of infantry or from the bursting shells, or that stream along, in the wake of the shells, like a comet's tail, you being ignorant of the enemies' strength or designs, & unable to see anything of his movements, and obliged to remain at your post in the storm of death that rains over you.

"Excepting the day of final judgment, and the scene of the resurrection of the dead, as foretold & partially described in the Bible, I can concieve of nothing so awefully grand, so highly sublime, as a great battle at midnight."[33]

Late that afternoon a brief but heavy rain shower brought an end to the scalding heat of the past few days—and an end to the bloody month of June.[34]

14

"The Northern Sky Is Exceedingly
Dark Just Now"

JULY 1–AUGUST 23, 1864

IN THE EARLY MOMENTS OF FRIDAY, JULY 1ST, THE REBELS MADE ANOTHER ATTACK on the Union regiments clustered on the hillside below the Confederate works. The result was another repulse, "a heavy loss of ammunition and some swearing," wrote McAdams of the 113th Ohio. "A soldier hates to have his rest broken."

The men of the 78th Illinois continued crouching uncomfortably in their improvised earthworks while skirmish firing went on almost without interruption throughout the day. The 98th Ohio, which had ended up alongside the 78th in the June 27th assault, was relieved that day and returned to camp, much to the disgust of the 78th.

Pvt. Byron Grubb of Company E of the 78th died of disease July 1st. He was a resident of Liberty, Adams County.

By July 2nd Van Vleck was growing angry because the 78th had not been relieved. As usual, he vented in a letter to Patty: "Those of us particularly, who are within a stone's throw of the rebel works, as *we* have been, now for nearly a week, keeping up a heavy skirmish fight with the enemy night and day, & having to repel the enemies' charges every night, being thus unable to get any sleep, are completely used up," he wrote. "We have all remonstrated, begged & entreated, hoping to be relieved by fresh troops. Morgan's brigade is lying in our rear, was not engaged at all in the fight, and could just as well as not, come forward and relieve either McCook's brig[ade] or ours, or a part of both, but Davis refuses to have it done, but compells us . . . to remain here day after day, wearing ourselves out as I have described, until we are nearly all sick."

The condition of his regiment wasn't the colonel's only concern. A newspaper correspondent had reported him wounded in the battle of the 27th. "I knew nothing of this until last evening . . . or I should have tried to get a telegram to you one way or another, he wrote."[1]

The colonel's entreaties apparently got through to someone, because that evening the 98th Ohio returned to the lines and relieved the 78th. The worn-out, sunburned, half-sick men filed gratefully out of the works under cover of darkness and headed for the rear for some much-needed rest.

The rest proved brief. About 2:00 a.m. on July 3rd there was a great crash of fire from the rebel skirmish line, continuing about five minutes. Then all fell silent. The federal troops recognized it as a familiar tactic, one usually signaling a rebel retreat. Sure enough, when daylight came the rebel works were empty.

"Rebels vacate, we follow," Batchelor wrote. "Go through rebel works. They are strong." Payne of the 34th Illinois agreed. "It was the unanimous verdict that we had never seen such an absolutely unassailable line of works," he wrote. "The one hundred or more lonely graves between the lines spoke of the heroic effort to accomplish the impossible that is sometimes required of the man in the ranks."[2]

Sherman's latest flanking move had forced the Confederates to abandon their Kennesaw Mountain line and fall back again. Davis's division was ordered in pursuit, which cut short any chance for the 78th to rest from the exertions of the previous week. Instead, the troops joined the army's march through Marietta and bivouacked at Nickajack Creek, within sight of the next line of enemy works.

"Marietta is a beautiful town," Van Vleck wrote Patty on the 4th, "although I could see but little of it, having been compelled yesterday for the first time to go with the reg't. in an ambulance." The colonel had suffered diarrhea for a month before the ordeal at Kennesaw Mountain, which he described as "a whole week of intense excitement & fatigue, & without two consecutive hours of sleep. Under such treatment you need not be surprised to learn that the diarrhea soon gave place to dysentery." The weather was intensely hot and "the doctor constrained me to ride in the ambulance, which I doubt not was greatly to my advantage, for I slept nearly all day." He got another day of rest on the 4th while the regiment remained in bivouac. "I feel a great deal better to day, but am very weak," he told Patty.[3]

From their new position, "we now see the ste[e]ples in Atlanta, Georgia," Batchelor wrote. The regiment spent the day digging rifle pits but had little time to occupy them. Next morning "we were again following up the enemy's retreating columns, skirmishing all day, and capturing several prisoners," wrote Lieutenant Colonel Vernon. "In the evening we went into position, and fortified in sight of, and within musket-range of, his strong defenses on the Chattahoochee [River]."[4]

It was anything but a comfortable day for men in the ranks. Payne complained that "orders from brigade headquarters forbid laying off the blouse, but required them to be worn. The day was hot and sweltering, and the line of march was through the very dense pine underbrush where no breeze could penetrate [and] the road was crooked, requiring a frequent right or left wheel as rapidly as it could be made. As a consequence, the men were boiling externally, and when the word was passed that the command was on the wrong road, the boiling 'struck in,' and manifested itself orally. . . ."

"Scrimising [skirmishing] all the time," Batchelor wrote on the 6th. "We now build breast works. Take about 100 prisoners. The we[a]ther is very hot."

Van Vleck told his wife he was feeling a little better. "We are beginning to get considerable fruit which is a great advantage to us," he wrote. "I have feasted all day on huckleberries, & blackberries are getting ripe, & apples & grapes are matured enough to make a first rate sauce, & is doing much to restore the health of the men."

— ⁓ —

The 78th and its sister regiments were awakened at 3:00 a.m. on the 7th with orders to prepare to march, but it turned out to be a false alarm. Instead, they spent the day digging entrenchments "and put up bowers over our 'pup tents'" to provide a little shade, Payne wrote. That evening "the brigade band, from which we had heard nothing for a long time, in the cool of the evening gave some concerts, which were well attended by an appreciative audience." July 8th was marked by "heavy cannonading all day," according to Batchelor.[5]

"We still occupy the ground where we first took position here," Van Vleck wrote on the 9th. "This rest is of great advantage to us, but we are in a deep ravine, with nothing but artificial shelter, & the weather continues most intensely hot, & is making a good many sick." His health had taken another turn for the worse. "This is the worst day I have had, & have been kept in bed the most of the time. I have not yet missed duty except on the one days' march through Marietta, but should be unable to go with the reg't. if it was to move to day.

"I hope I shall at least hold out until Atlanta is ours. I should then be able to leave the army (if sickness compelled me) without an uneasy conscience . . . I hear of no news along the line. We have simply come to a halt because the enemy have the river bank most thoroughly fortified & we can't cross."

It was true no crossing could be made against the formidable defenses opposing the Army of the Cumberland, but on July 8th Sherman sent Schofield's Army of the Ohio several miles upriver past the Confederate right flank where Schofield's men crossed the Chattahoochee on pontoon boats and established a beachhead south of the river. Next day Kenner Gerrard's cavalry also forced a crossing; Atlanta's last significant natural barrier had fallen to the federals. That evening, the

Confederates withdrew from their works along the Chattahoochee and fell back to Peachtree Creek.[6]

With the rebels no longer in their front, Mitchell's brigade made camp on the north bank of the Chattahoochee. "I have put my reg't. into regular camp, on a beautiful spot of ground beside a splendid spring, have put up my tent, am living on Sanitary stores," Van Vleck wrote Patty. Sanitary stores, he explained, "are furnished through the hospitals, to officers as well as men. They sent me some condensed milk, tea, soft crackers, white sugar, onions, & corn starch, which I relished very much being unable to eat hard tack & bacon without a relapse, whenever I began to get better. They also sent me some good brandy & a bottle of ale, all of which was much to my taste and I think did much good." Without the racket of musketry or artillery to keep him awake, the colonel also was sleeping soundly and feeling better. "If we can be left alone as we hope to be for three or four days longer, I expect to be good as new."

As usual, he was more concerned about his soldiers. "You can have no idea how dirty the men have become, & how alive with vermin," he wrote. "We have had soap but two or three times on the campaign, & many of the men have no change of under clothing, & by being compelled to be together in the trenches night & day, they necessarily communicate their filth from one to another. Thus far I have managed to change & take a thorough bath every week, & still expect to, but a company officer can't carry a change with him very well as we only have one wagon to the reg't. & do not see that for a month at a time, some times."

Since the carnage at Kennesaw Mountain, the 78th had suffered few casualties, but it lost three men from July 12th to 15th, though none were at the front. Pvt. Francis Fryer of Company K died in Chattanooga July 12th of wounds suffered at Kennesaw Mountain. The unlucky Fryer had also been wounded at Chickamauga but recovered and returned to duty. Next day Pvt. Charles S. Neida, of Littleton, Schuyler County, a recruit who had joined Company A in November 1863, died of disease at Nashville. And on the 15th, Pvt. Benjamin Shirl, Company K, a resident of Melrose, Adams County, also died of disease at Nashville.

Van Vleck wrote home again on the 15th: "You need not think this is an old sheet of paper," he told his wife. "It has been exposed but a very short time, but [the many black spots on the page] will give you perhaps a faint idea of the flies. I thought they were bad last year, but they are much worse this year & do nearly eat us up. But they are only one of the pests of life here: Fleas, muskitoes, & chiggers by the million, wood ticks that bury their heads beneath the skin & die, cattle ticks, & worms & insects of ever[y] kind, including scorpions. Lizzards & spiders greatly abound as you might expect they would at this season, in this latitude! And as we have to live in the woods

& sleep on the ground we get the full benefit of them all. We devote all our leizure [leisure] time night & day scratching, even those of us that are able to keep rid of the ordinary vermin of the army. I am broken out like one with the measles in full blast, but I hope for better things soon."

On Saturday, July 16th, the regiment drew rations and received orders to move. At 5:00 a.m. the next morning it was on the march to Pace's Ferry on the Chattahoochee, where it waited until a pontoon bridge was completed, then crossed the river—about 150 yards wide—and turned south toward Peachtree Creek, following the route of Ridgewood Road.[7]

The 78th advanced about a mile when it ran into Confederate cavalry at Nancy's Creek and "had quite an engagement just at sundown," Robbins wrote later. [Pvt.] "Samuel Naylor of Co[mpany] E of my regiment, was wounded. From this wound he suffered all the rest of his life, and still many begrudged him the insignificant pension he got."

When the fight was over, the regiment dug trenches "in a very dense woods with abundant underbrush."[8]

—◦—

As the Army of the Cumberland advanced south of the Chattahoochee, fateful events were taking place on the rebel side. Confederate president Jefferson Davis, having grown exasperated at Johnston's continued retreat, issued a temporary full general's commission to John Bell Hood and sent word to Johnston on the 17th that Hood was relieving him as commander of the rebel Army of Tennessee. Davis earlier had asked Robert E. Lee his opinion of Hood as a potential commander. Lee famously replied that "Hood is a bold fighter [but] I am doubtful as to other qualities necessary." That was about as close as Lee ever came to outright condemnation of a fellow officer, and it must have given Davis pause. But he thought he needed a "bold fighter" to defend Atlanta and there was no other obvious choice, so Hood got the job.

Hood, however, was not the same man he had been at Gaines Mill, Second Manassas, or Antietam. A wound at Gettysburg made his left arm almost useless and a thigh wound at Chickamauga resulted in amputation of his right leg. He needed help mounting a horse and had to be strapped into the saddle once he got aboard, and he suffered nearly constant pain from his wounds. It has been suggested, though never proven, that he took laudanum to ease his pain. In any case, when he took command of the Army of Tennessee, Hood clearly understood his mission was to fight. And fight he did.[9]

—◦—

On July 18th, the XIV Corps of the Army of the Cumberland crossed Nancy's Creek and headed south on the Howell Mill Road toward Peachtree Creek. Mitchell's brigade was on the right, covering the area between Ridgewood Road and the Chattahoochee River. Elements of Davis's division camped that night on the north bank of Peachtree Creek.

Van Vleck wrote his wife that he had received a letter from Martha Broaddus. "She is almost heartbroken about [her son] Thomas of whom she hears nothing but reports of ill conduct," he said. "The foolish woman seems to think if he was only at home he would be a better boy, when he was notoriously the worst boy in the community before he came to the army. But I have concluded to try & get him discharged. He is so quarrelsome that no body in his co[mpany] will either mess or tent with him. His hand is against every body & everybody's against him. He is constantly fighting with somebody and all my nice talk to him & severe punishments go for naught. His capt[ain] told me that he had taken the boys off him until he was tired [of rescuing him]. He now intends to let him take his fill of fighting until he has been soundly thrashed by every man in the co[mpany]. He thinks he will then behave himself. But it is bred in the bone & I think will stay there till he either gets killed in some of his fracases, or meets with God's grace to change his heart."

The colonel said he also was still troubled with diarrhea and doubted he would get better "as long as the hot weather continues. I am getting very poor, but think my general health is rather on the increase. I still keep at the head of the reg't. & hope I may be permitted to continue there, although the surgeon has tried very hard to send me back to the hospital. If however I get no worse, as I hope, I shall not go to the hospital very soon, for I should get worse there faster than here, from anxiety for the reg't."

———

History records the Battle of Peachtree Creek was fought July 20, 1864. That was indeed when the largest forces were engaged, but the fighting actually began on the 19th and quickly developed into a desperate struggle involving Davis's division.

It began when Davis ordered his third brigade, now commanded by Col. Caleb J. Dilworth (successor to McCook, mortally wounded at Kennesaw Mountain), to cross Peachtree Creek. The rebels had destroyed the bridges, so the brigade spent the morning of the 19th searching for a place to cross. At length a "foot log" was found near the mouth of a tributary called Green Bone Creek. The "foot log" allowed men to pass over single-file, and five companies of the 52nd Ohio crossed in that manner, deployed a skirmish line, and charged enemy pickets atop a 50-foot bluff near the stream. The pickets withdrew, but when the men of the 52nd reached the crest they came under heavy fire. Then a rebel brigade emerged from a wooded area and started across an open field toward the small Union contingent on the crest. The 85th Illinois and the remainder of the 52nd Ohio crossed the stream as rapidly as possible and charged into the open field to meet the oncoming rebels.

"On the right of the 85th it was a desperate hand-to-hand conflict, in which muskets were clubbed and the bayonet was freely used," Aten wrote. The Confederates gained the federals' right flank and poured an enfilading fire into the two regiments. Dilworth's other regiments, the 86th Illinois and 22nd Indiana, crossed the stream and tried to join the fight, but the federal line was already starting to disintegrate. Dilworth called urgently for support, and Davis sent Mitchell's brigade.

Mitchell's men crossed the stream "on logs and rafts" under heavy musket fire and Mitchell "threw forward the 34th Illinois to check the enemy attempting to turn the left flank." He then ordered the 78th Illinois to take position on the left of Dilworth's brigade and ordered the 98th Ohio to move in behind them.[10] "We luckily reached them in the very nick of time to save them as the Rebels had closed entirely around their flanks ... and the river, with only a single log to cross on, with a deep swift current, was in their rear," Van Vleck wrote the next day. "One reg't. had been driven pell-mell through the river with considerable loss (the 22nd Ind.). The 85th Ill. was routed, a large portion of them captured, and many killed and wounded ... The 52nd Ohio (Dan McCook's old reg't.) fared no better, and the lt. col. commanding was captured.

"Such was the condition of things when my reg't. as the advance of the brigade crossed the river, there being only the 86th Ill. of [Dilworth's] brigade left intact, and moved into position under a severe fire from the front and both flanks on the crest of a steep ridge. I had been in position but a few moments when I could plainly see that I was entirely surrounded by the enemy except [for] a strip of almost impassible river in my rear, which was separated from me by a broad open field, over which it would be certain destruction to pass, under the concentrated fire which the enemy had. I had scarcely begun to realize my critical situation when the 86th Ill., my only support on the right (there was nothing on my left), had a panic and came near being routed.

"If ever I thought fast of southern dungeons and my acquaintances there, it was then. I could see no salvation for us, but happily the 86th was checked and kept in position; the rest of the brigade succeeded in getting across the river and we held the hordes at bay until the 3rd div[ision] got across and then we drove [the rebels] back to their lines.

"I have in no engagement been in half the danger of capture and in none have I been in more danger of Rebel bullets. But I have renewed cause of thankfulness to

God for his merciful care for me and my reg't., having had up to this time only seven or eight men wounded, three of whom, however, I fear are mortally wounded. One of the wounded men (not dangerously) was my Color Sergt., Thomas Edmonson, of McComb [Sgt. Thomas Edmondson of Macomb]. The 22nd Ind. and 85th Ill. both lost their colors."

The fighting continued until dark, after which the 78th and Mitchell's other regiments "put up fortifications within 200 yards of their [the rebels'] works."

Van Vleck again was critical of federal leadership, blaming both Davis and Dilworth for what he called "ignorance and criminal ambition." He added: "I am heartily disgusted with the whole army management and sometimes feel determined to tender my resignation at once. But when I think of leaving my brave boys in the hands of an untried commander I cannot make up my mind to do it."

Mitchell's and Dilworth's brigades held their positions the next day, listening to heavy cannon and musket fire on their left, where Hood had launched his first big attack in defense of Atlanta, which became known as the Battle of Peachtree Creek. But Mitchell's men remained busy. "We have kept up a most intensely hot fire on the Rebels all day," Van Vleck wrote. "We have also now got artillery into position on the right of my reg't., so that I think our position impregnable now."

The 78th Illinois's fire was indeed "intensely hot." Vernon reported the regiment expended seventeen thousand rounds of ammunition that day. "The result was he [the enemy] abandoned his works before sunset."[11]

The following day Van Vleck told Patty the 78th's new chaplain, John L. Jones, had arrived. "I like his appearance very much," the colonel wrote. "He is a much better appearing man than I anticipated, in fact he is allowed to be the best looking man in the reg't. & I hope he will have grace sufficient for a proper, faithful, & profitable discharge of his ardiuous duties. The only objection I have noticed thus far is that he smokes a pipe."[12]

⌣

The XIV Corps, including Davis's division, advanced again the morning of the 22nd. "The lines in our front were abandoned in the night . . . leaving a few dead and wounded to fall into our hands," wrote Payne of the 34th Illinois. The division halted "on an elevated piece of ground from which we could see the church spires and tall buildings in that much-coveted City of Atlanta, southeasterly and about four miles away . . . Our Corps formed line and fortified at once, along Proctor's creek, in position at the right of the army."

That same day, far to the left, the so-called Battle of Atlanta was fought. Hood had ordered a flanking attack on McPherson's Army of the Tennessee. Like the Peachtree

Creek fight, the result was another costly reverse for the Confederates, but the popular McPherson, a rising star in the Union army, was killed. The fighting was miles away from the position occupied by Mitchell's brigade, but "the uproar was fierce and continuous, and plainly heard by us during the whole of the engagement," Payne wrote.

Also that day, Pvt. John Steen of Company A, who had been wounded in the recent fighting, died from his injuries.

"Move about four miles, then draw five days rations," Batchelor recorded on the 23rd.[13] Satisfied there would probably be no more fighting on their part of the line for a while, Van Vleck—"at the earnest & repeated solicitations of Dr. Moss"—turned over command of the regiment to Vernon "& retired to our div[ision] field hospital." The hospital was about three quarters of a mile in the rear, the colonel told Patty, and "the only advantage over camp is that I am away from the excitement & continual disturbance incident to my position as a reg't. commander, & have a diet somewhat more suitable to my case than it is possible to get in camp.

"The quarters are not so comfortable as my own, being only a hospital tent fly, 12 ft. high at the ridge & five ft. high on the sides, & entirely open all around," he wrote. "Rather airy you will say, but I reply, comfortable during these intensely hot days. The only diet offered me thus far has been rice & corn starch. From the nauseous effects of the medicine I am taking, I have been able thus far to eat nothing to day. The doctor thinks, & I earnestly hope, that a few days rest will bring me out all straight. I hope so the more earnestly since Major Green[e] has been sent back to the hospital at Chattanooga with erysipelas in the face, which will keep him away for several weeks. Col. Vernon is thus left alone."

Batchelor reported "scrimishing [skirmishing] heavy" on Sunday the 24th: Pvt. John A. Edmonson of Company B, another casualty of the recent fighting, died that day of his wounds.

Pvt. Ingram Pace of Company C was preparing breakfast for the 78th's headquarters at sunrise on July 25th when a stray bullet struck him in the right thigh. The bullet passed through his leg without striking bone, but it was enough of a wound to put Pace out of action for several months. It was also a disturbing reminder that even when the 78th wasn't in line close to the enemy, there was always a danger of being hit by a stray shot or artillery round.

Pace's limited culinary skills would not be missed. "We hired Ingram Pace & paid his wages & all he could do for us was to fry a little meat, occasionally make *his kind* of biscuit, & boil a few coffee grounds in water," Van Vleck wrote. "He had no more faculty for cooking than a mule, & so with every body we ever yet have employed."

Pace's loss from the regiment was offset by the return of Pvt. George Hogue of Company I. Hogue had been "injured on the head by concussion of a shell at

Kennesaw & was crasy for a while," the colonel wrote, "but he is now well & with the reg't. again."

Van Vleck's own spirits were buoyed by receipt of "a barrel of fine ale at the hospital last eve, so that I have renewed cause of hope for a speedy recovery. This is the strongest beverage I indulge in now, & I think that will prove highly beneficial to me, or would if I could have a continued use of it. But one barrel will not last long here among so many patients & visitors."

The 78th remained in line parallel to the Turner's Ferry Road for another three days. Skirmishing continued almost without interruption, but those not on picket duty enjoyed "the freedom from close confinement to the trenches and the opportunity to attend to personal matters, writing letters, mending and washing," Payne recorded. "The nights were cool and refreshing, allowing restful sleep."[14]

On the 27th, the men of the 78th and Mitchell's other regiments watched the Army of the Tennessee march past on the Turner's Ferry Road. The army, now under command of Maj. Gen. Oliver O. Howard, McPherson's replacement, was headed to the right in another flanking movement ordered by Sherman. Hood learned of the movement and tried to counter it with another attack, hurling two rebel corps at the federal advance near Ezra Church. The battle, fought the afternoon of July 28th, was another costly repulse for the rebels. Gen. William J. Hardee, sent by Hood to take command of the rebel assault, arrived too late to influence the outcome, but was horrified by the slaughter. "No action of the campaign probably did so much to demoralize and dishearten the troops engaged in it," he said.

Hardee wasn't the only late arrival. Davis's division, temporarily under command of Brig. Gen. James D. Morgan of the first brigade—Davis being ill—"was ordered to march by a circuitous route in the rear, to the right of the Army of the Tennessee," Payne wrote. "We start out on the Turner's Ferry Road, and about noon struck the Skillet-Town [Lickskillet] Road and halted for dinner, moving again at 1 o'clock, soon taking the Green Ferry Road . . . At 3 o'clock, we received orders to leave the road and march straight to the right of Gen. Howard's position, which we were able to do by following the sound of the guns.

"It was the usual misfortune that our division did not get up in time to strike the enemy in flank and capture thousands . . . If we had not made so great a detour we would have been on time, but Gen. Morgan had never been over the roads, nor at the right of Howard's line. Neither he nor anybody else knew just where to go nor when the enemy would strike."

Quarters 78th Regt Ills vols Infy
Tennessee Aug 10th 1863

Nathan Butler of Co K 78th Regt Ills vols
in the last month been unfit for duty
sick in the Regimental Hospital
this place Most Respectfully asks for
Thirty days leave of furlough to visit his home
in Adams County Illinois. Sergt Butler
has had little or no sickness prior to this since
entering the service, he has always been with
the Regiment on the march, and without
regard to weather has ever discharged his
duties in a prompt and Soldierly like manner.
A Furlough would not only benefit him
in health and spirits, but would also afford
him an opportunity to arrange his business
matters at home in a more satisfactory
manner for his absence, Sergt Butler
has never before asked for a Furlough
*   Maris R Vernon*
*   Capt Co K 78th Regt Ills vols*

The letter that triggered the author's search for the history of the 78th Illinois Volunteer Infantry: Capt. Maris Vernon of Company K requests a furlough for Sgt. Jonathan Butler.

Period photograph of the Old Stone Church at Dallas City, Illinois, where the men who would become Company H of the 78th met for the first time on August 2, 1862. (COURTESY WILLIAM AND MARVEL ALLEN)

Capt. John Knox Allen, commander of Company H, who was wounded at Chickamauga. His wound eventually forced his resignation from the service. (COURTESY WILLIAM AND MARVEL ALLEN)

Carte de Visite (calling card) image of Col. Carter Van Vleck, the sad-eyed officer who became the 78th Illinois's second commander and shaped the regiment into a first-rate fighting outfit. (ABRAHAM LINCOLN PRESIDENTIAL LIBRARY AND MUSEUM)

On its maiden voyage the steamer *John H. Groesbeck* carried the 78th Regiment on a cold, unpleasant journey up the Cumberland River to Nashville. (COURTESY OF WILLIAM AND MARVEL ALLEN AND THE MURPHY LIBRARY, UNIVERSITY OF WISCONSIN–LA CROSSE)

Postwar image of James K. Magie, the debt-ridden newspaper editor in civilian life who thought he had discovered a way to get rich when he became an army postmaster. Things didn't turn out as he hoped. (ABRAHAM LINCOLN PRESIDENTIAL LIBRARY AND MUSEUM)

James K. Magie's sketch of the hanging of two Confederate spies at Franklin, Tennessee, published in *Harper's Weekly* July 4, 1863. (REPRODUCED BY PERMISSION OF APPLEWOOD BOOKS AND HARPERSWEEKLY.COM)

Postwar photo of Pvt. Edward Mott Robbins, who narrowly escaped capture while serving as a hospital steward at Chickamauga. His brief 1919 memoir contains some of the best anecdotes about the 78th Illinois. (ABRAHAM LINCOLN PRESIDENTIAL LIBRARY AND MUSEUM)

Postwar image of Pvt. James Edgar Withrow, who suffered from homesickness and hated life in the 78th Illinois. Withrow kept a diary for about three months following the Battle of Chickamauga. (ABRAHAM LINCOLN PRESIDENTIAL LIBRARY AND MUSEUM)

James D. Morgan was a militia captain when the Civil War began. Still recovering from a broken leg, he hobbled off to war on crutches. Morgan rose to the rank of brigadier general and took command of the 2nd Division of the XIV Army Corps after Jefferson C. Davis was promoted to corps command. The 78th Illinois was part of the 2nd Division. (ABRAHAM LINCOLN PRESIDENTIAL LIBRARY AND MUSEUM)

Jefferson C. Davis, the frail but fiery general who shot and killed General "Bull" Nelson, escaped punishment and became commander of the 2nd Division of the XIV Army Corps, including the 78th Illinois. Davis later was promoted to corps commander. (COURTESY OF NATIONAL PARK SERVICE)

Capt. William B. Akins became commander of Company K of the 78th Illinois after its original commander, Maris Vernon, was promoted to lieutenant colonel. (SHELBY COUNTY HISTORICAL SOCIETY COLLECTION, US ARMY MILITARY HISTORY INSTITUTE)

John Grant Mitchell twice commanded the brigade including the 78th Illinois, first as a colonel in the Atlanta campaign, then later as a brigadier general in the Bentonville campaign. (RUTHERFORD B. HAYES PHOTOGRAPH COLLECTION, RUTHERFORD B. HAYES PRESIDENTIAL CENTER, FREMONT, OHIO)

Capt. Robert M. Black, commander of Company D of the 78th Illinois, was killed at Jonesboro. (RICHARD TIBBLES COLLECTION, US ARMY MILITARY HISTORY INSTITUTE)

Carte de Visite (calling card) image of 1st Lt. John B. Worrell, who recovered from an accidental gunshot wound to succeed Robert M. Black in command of Company D. Worrell was later promoted to captain. (COURTESY OF ARCHIVES AND SPECIAL COLLECTIONS, WESTERN ILLINOIS UNIVERSITY LIBRARIES)

Robert S. Blackburn began the war as captain of Company A of the 78th Illinois. His promotion to major became official March 20, 1865, while the regiment was fighting at Bentonville. (ABRAHAM LINCOLN PRESIDENTIAL LIBRARY AND MUSEUM)

This photo, probably the only surviving wartime image of the 78th Illinois, shows a company from McDonough County, Illinois, probably either Company C or Company I. The photo was likely taken late in the war when the company's numbers had been severely reduced, or it may show only part of the company. (COURTESY OF ARCHIVES AND SPECIAL COLLECTIONS, WESTERN ILLINOIS UNIVERSITY LIBRARIES)

The 78th Illinois held numerous reunions after the Civil War. This group photo of the 1897 reunion was taken in front of the Pace Hotel in Macomb, Illinois. First on the left in the second row is Charles Vilasco Chandler, whose Chickamauga wound forced him to resign from the service. Third on the left in the second row is Benjamin Gill, the blacksmith who kept the 78th's horses and mules shod. Fifth from the left in the first row is Morris Chase, who survived eighteen months in rebel prison camps. No others are identified. (COURTESY OF ARCHIVES AND SPECIAL COLLECTIONS, WESTERN ILLINOIS UNIVERSITY LIBRARIES)

Morgan's force also was delayed by continual skirmishing with rebel cavalry. At one point it "routed a large dismounted cavalry force," according to Vernon of the 78th. After a long, frustrating day, and with nothing to eat, the division finally went into camp sometime after midnight near the Ezra Church battlefield.[15]

The men of the 78th had marched twenty miles, the hardest march "they have had since they have been in the service," Van Vleck wrote. "Dr. Moss was here [at the hospital] to see me this morning, & he says that he never saw the reg't. half so near used up as it is now. Six of them have just been brought to the hospital & more of them are coming." Next morning the division, still under Morgan's command, advanced over the Ezra Church battlefield to the White Hall Road and entrenched. "Found the enemy's dead unburied and many of their wounded uncared for," Col. Henry Banning of the 121st Ohio reported.[16]

"The battlefield around Ezra Church presented a sickening sight," Aten wrote. "Almost 700 dead Confederates were scattered over the field in front of the XV Corps. The ground occupied during the battle by that corps was a high ridge and the sloping ground in its front was dotted over with open fields. As the charging columns of the enemy advanced they met a murderous, well-directed fire which no troops could stand." The stench from the rebel corpses was sickening and Batchelor reported that "Negro[e]s have been burning dead Rebels all day."[17]

On the last day of July, Mitchell's brigade was sent several miles on a reconnaissance, trying to pinpoint the location of the Confederate flank. It returned to its camp "in a tremendous rain," wrote McAdams of the 113th Ohio. "We had left our baggage in our line, and as a consequence we got very wet, and we remained wet all night."

The division hospital was moved to a new location that day, "a very much pleasanter camp for a hospital than the other was," Van Vleck wrote. "We had barely got our tents spread yesterday when it began to rain, & it rained very hard until night (from about 1 o'cl'k. p.m.) & the atmosphere is cool and delightful this morning, but it is still cloudy. The rain was needed for the health & comfort of the men."

The colonel had written his wife almost every day that week. His stay in the hospital had left him with plenty of time on his hands, and the result was increasing homesickness, growing contempt for senior officers, especially Davis, and a general feeling of depression. At one point he wrote of seeing his image in a mirror for the first time in months "and I confess that I was in some doubt as to whether the face belonged to me."[18]

***

"I did not write you the usual Sunday letter yesterday because we were moving [the] hospital," William H. Githens, the 78th's assistant surgeon, wrote his wife August 1st.

"There is no firing or very little to'day—and but little fighting for some days . . . We have had but two or three wounded for some days—one of the 16th [probably 16th Illinois] boys was hit yesterday—piece of his nose knocked off. . . .

"We have over a hundred patients all the time none of them very sick and present[ly] none seriously wounded. I do hope that we will not have to go through any more such terrible scenes as we have—of operating and amputating &c—persons may talk of getting accustomed to such things—but it is not my nature—I can operate on them with a steady hand as any body—at the same time I can sympathize with them as deeply as any one—and pray that the day may soon come when the terrible butchery will cease.

"It may cost many a life yet to get full possession of Atlanta—but we are bound to have and hold it at all hazards—sooner or later . . . the Army feeds up [us?] all the corn in the country—and in fact every thing else—leaving the country perfectly desolate. Maybe it will come out new and take a better start next time—it's certainly a hard enough looking country now scarcely anything but old dilapidated log houses—occasionally a frame [house]—but all shabby—the country through here is very rough and hilly—and the soil quite poor—Just about Atlanta I think it is better. . . ."

The division hospital, which had been in two locations, was reunited by the move. Van Vleck had been at one location while three other officers from the 78th—Captain Ruddell of Company B and Captain Black and Lieutenant Puntenny of Company D—had been at the other. Their complaint—dysentery—was the same as Van Vleck's.

Pvt. William C. Dixon of Company B, whose right arm was amputated after he was wounded at Kennesaw Mountain, had been sent back to a hospital in Chattanooga. He died there on the first day of August.

⁓

While the 78th's commander and three other officers were in the division hospital, Major Greene was returning to the regiment from the hospital at Chattanooga, where he had recovered from his bout with erysipelas. He had also managed to collect seven months' back pay, still owed to all the other members of the 78th. "There are very many men of my reg't. whose families are really suffering for want of these just dues," Van Vleck wrote his wife on the 2nd. He was feeling much better that day, although still very weak.[19]

The men whose families were suffering for want of pay were at least given an opportunity to rest in their wet trenches until August 3rd. But on Thursday, August 4th, Mitchell's brigade moved again, trekking a mile southeast to take a position along Utoy Creek. The 78th manned the brigade skirmish line that night. Next day the brigade went another six miles by Batchelor's estimate, driving back rebel pickets and reaching the Sandtown Road.

The 78th made these movements without its new chaplain, John L. Jones. "Our chaplain became terribly scared at the bullets what little time he was here," Van Vleck told Patty. "He could neither eat nor sleep, & after about a week of anguish, he started for home without saying a word to any body. He had not yet been mustered into the service, on account of the absence of blanks [mustering forms], and he thought he wouldn't be, that his duty was with his vacant churches at home, so he wrote me from Marietta. But by the time he got to Nashville he changed his mind & wrote me again asking it *'as a favor,'* that I let him come back after this campaign (the *fighting*) is over. I don't know what to do. He seemed like a good and pleasant man & preached a first-rate sermon, but I fear that this exhibition of insubordination and arrant cowardice, will destroy his influence with the reg't. A preacher whose place is away in the rear, that can't trust the Lord for his personal safety, I am afraid would be a poor hand to preach courage to the boys that go to the front."

Patty Van Vleck had asked her husband to consider resigning from the service, which "made me think about it more than I ever did before," he wrote. "You ask if I should be subject to the draft [if he resigned]. I never have been subject to the draft on account of having no teeth, but after the 1st of next month, in fact after the 16th of this month, I shall have served two years, which will also exempt me from draft. But you know that question has never troubled me. I came to the Army only from a strict sense of duty & I expect to remain as long as it appears to be my duty so to do; but I do not think it to be my duty to remain after I am disabled for duty, nor to sacrifice my life or health in the hospital.

"I know how much my interest & how much yours & Nellie's [interest] demands that I should be at home & that we should again keep house. But what are all our interests compared with those of the gov't. which must ever be first considered? I have pretty much given up all hope of getting strong again while I am compelled to remain in the field. I expect therefore as soon as Atlanta is taken to make an application for a leave of absence, & if successful, & I have but little doubt but the change in climate & diet will restore me to full health & strength, & I shall be able to remain with the reg't. until their time expires, which is only little more than a year. But if I am unsuccessful in my application for leave, I shall not hesitate to tender my resignation on account of physical disability, provided I get no better."[20]

Three federal corps, including the XIV, attacked Confederate positions south of the Sandtown Road August 6th in what became known as the Battle of Utoy Creek.

Mitchell's brigade played only a minor role in the conflict, but came under heavy artillery fire and had several men wounded. Next day, under heavy rain, Mitchell's skirmishers advanced, captured a line of rebel rifle pits and some of their occupants, and constructed a new line of entrenchments. That night the 78th Illinois, supported by a battery of artillery, established a picket line "within 300 yards of the enemy's works," according to Colonel Mitchell.

The day's events inspired one of the longer entries in Batchelor's diary: "Fireing is heavy," he wrote. "We captured a Scrmish [skirmish] line to day. I was stung last night by a scorpian on the left cheek. Took 40 more prisoners. The excitement and bite seem to affect me a little."[21]

Pvt. Marshall C. Cline of Company C, a resident of Blandinsville, McDonough County, was killed in the skirmishing that day.

The division hospital made another move while this was going on. Its new location was "a little more than a mile to the rear of our div[ision], which is nearly west of East Point . . . five miles southwest of Atlanta," Van Vleck wrote. The colonel was feeling well enough to make an attempt to return to the regiment that day and rode as far as the XIV Corps headquarters of General John Palmer, where he "broke down & stopped to rest & remained there until noon & then went back to the hospital. I concluded from this that it was hardly worth while for me to try to do duty for a few days longer.

"I reached Palmer's [headquarters] only in time to bid him good bye. He & Gen'l. Sherman have not had a very good understanding between them for some time past, & when Sherman day before yesterday ordered Palmer to report to & receive orders from [Gen. John M.] Schofield (who is, as Palmer claims, his junior in rank), Palmer refused & asked to be relieved & Sherman relieved him." Brig. Gen. Richard W. Johnson was appointed temporary commander of the XIV Corps.

On Monday, August 8th, Mitchell's brigade advanced about a half mile and faced to the east, parallel to the rebel lines. "Rifle trenches were made in front of a small open field with ground sloping to the rear, and strong defences with embrasures for two pieces of artillery were made on the front line, and guns brought up," wrote Payne of the 34th Illinois. "The front lines of the enemy were about eighty rods distant, across a ravine in which there was a dense underbrush, reaching up close to our lines. Skirmishing was lively in this position, the two pieces of artillery joining in . . . There was rain in the afternoon and at night, making everything nasty and uncomfortable."

Sgt. Adam Walters of Company B died at a hospital in Chattanooga that day. He was from Marcelline, Adams County.

August 9th found Van Vleck still in the hospital. "I thought I knew something of the horrors of war before I came to the hospital," he wrote Patty, "but I was as ignorant as a child, as everybody must be who has not been present at a field hospital in time of battle, where all the wounded of a division are brought, to have their wounds dressed & to have the necessary operations performed, where arms and legs are amputated and flung into a common pile with as little ceremony as the butcher cuts up & prepares the beef for the brine.

"But you cannot imagine how much of the horror has been taken from these horrible places, by the invention of chloroform. It is administered in every case, not only with no bad effect but with the most salutary effect . . . The patients rally from the severest amputations, almost as soon as the influence of the chloroform is gone, & seem less prostrated, if any difference, than before the operation was performed. This is a discovery the value of which is not realized by any of us, but especially by people in civil life. I think it should be a special cause of thankfulness to God, for no human mind can have the remotest conception of the am[oun]t. of suffering and anguish it saves the soldier from.

"But there are many cases where chloroform fails to save the poor sufferer from untold misery, cases where the wounds are mortal but where the poor fellows must live & suffer ten thousand deaths, for many hours or even days. Cases where they are shot through the bowels, or where the back is broken as in a case we had here yesterday, or where a whole limb or a large portion of the body is torn away by a shell. It is indeed a most piteous sight to see such cases where no help can be tendered except to deaden their sensibilities as far as possible. How long must this terrible war continue? Will not God have mercy on us & cause this fearful slaughter & desolation to have a speedy end?"

Major Greene had just been brought to the hospital, sick with dysentery. "I have taken him into the tent with me," Van Vleck wrote. "This makes me all the more anxious to get out to the reg't. I am feeling a great deal better to day & if I continue to get better shall go to the reg't. day after to morrow. How long I shall be able to stay remains to be seen, but I cannot remain here a day longer than it is absolutely necessary, so long as Vernon is alone with the reg't. Capt. Reynolds [Granville Reynolds of Company I] is also here quite sick with bilious fever. The fact is, every body is worn out & unless the army gets rest soon it will all be in the hospital. It is wonderful how much we have already endured, but there is an end of human endurance, and that is not far away in the case of this army."[22]

Van Vleck had many visitors during his hospital stay, including Batchelor. "Go to the hospital to see Colonel Van Vleck sick with flucks [flux]," Batchelor wrote in his diary August 10th. "Also Captian Reynolds and Major Green[e]."

That evening the 78th Illinois was relieved from its position on the front line and ordered back to the second line of works at a place called Willis Mills, about three miles from East Point and a little more than six miles from Atlanta. The rain that had begun August 8th was still falling and the soaked soldiers returned to earthworks and rifle pits that in many cases were filled partly with water.[23]

The rain finally ended and the morning of August 11th dawned warm and clear. "I am feeling considerable better today & have determined to go to the reg't. (unless it rains) this afternoon," Van Vleck wrote Patty that morning. "I think there is no longer any specific disease which I have to contend with. It is only general debility from which I can as well recover at the reg't as here. I am tired of this place & every body connected with it, & am much needed at the reg't . . . .

"The Northern sky is exceedingly dark just now, in fact, I have never come so near the verge of despair as I now am. Hope seems almost gone, but I still have faith in God, but in no other body and in nothing else. Let us pray more earnestly than ever & still cling to Him."

As good as his word, the colonel left the hospital late that morning and made his way to the regiment, where he was warmly received by officers and men. But his welcome took an unhappy turn when Captain Ruddell of Company B, who had also recently returned from the hospital, was struck in the back of the head by a Minie ball and seriously wounded. His injury was another reminder that although the regiment was in the second line of works, men still were not safe from stray shots or long-range sniper fire.

—◆—

Van Vleck's turn came at dusk. The colonel was on his way into his tent when the bullet hit him. It had traveled a long way and was nearly spent when it struck two inches above his left eye, but it still had enough momentum to punch a hole through his skull and enter his brain.

Those who saw it happen rushed to his side and found to their astonishment that Van Vleck was still conscious and able to speak and move normally. It was almost as if nothing had happened—except there was a large, bloody hole in his forehead. The colonel was taken immediately back to the hospital where the second division's chief surgeon, Dr. Edwin Batwell, hurriedly examined him.

"When brought into the hospital he was perfectly sensible, and exhibited the same calm and collected manner that exemplified him on the battle-field as well as in the council of military leaders," Dr. Batwell wrote later. "If it was not for the blood, which, mixed with cerebral matter, oozed from the wound, one never could have imagined, that he had received so fatal an injury. Much difference of opinion prevailed as to whether the ball had entered the [skull] cavity, or not, as the entire absence of any urgent or unfavorable symptom, almost precluded the idea in the minds of some."[24]

The colonel was well enough that at "8 ½ p.m." he was able to write the following:

> *My dearest Patty,*
> *This is probably the last letter I shall be able to write you. I went to the reg't. at noon, & was struck in the head by a stray bullet just at dark, the bullet still being in my head. I thank God that I have been spared to write you a few words.*
> *Through God's grace I am prepared to die as I have long lived, faithful to Him, to you and to my country. I hope I may possibly see you & Nellie before I die, if not I shall meet you both in Heaven. Goodbye. The grace of God bless you infinitely & bring you to me in Heaven when God has finished His will with you here.*
> *Much love to all, & a kiss for Nellie & my whole heart's love for Pattie.*
> *Carter*[25]

News of the colonel's wound sent shock waves through the regiment. "Colonel Van Vleck comes back to the reg[i]ment after dinner and in a very few hours is shot in the partin[g] of his hair [on] top of his forehead," Batchelor wrote in his diary. "Very little hopes of his recovery."

"The worst thing that has happened to the Seventy-eighth Regiment was the wounding of Colonel Van Vleck last eve," Lt. William E. Summers wrote his family. "He was just back from the hospital and had not been in the regiment but a few hours. It was after sundown. A Minie ball struck him over the left eye. The doctors say he will not live but a few hours. The boys are very sad over the loss of their colonel."[26]

"On the 11th a calamity, the most melancholy of the campaign, occurred to the regiment," Lieutenant Colonel Vernon wrote. "Its beloved commander and honored chief, Colonel Carter Van Vleck, received a mortal wound . . . A stray shot from the enemy nearly a mile distant winged its way over two lines of works, selecting for its victim one of the bravest and best of men, the ball striking just above the left eye and penetrating the brain."

Word spread quickly to other regiments in Mitchell's brigade. "Col. Carter Van-Vleck, of the 78th Illinois, was mortally wounded by a musket ball in the head," wrote Payne of the 34th Illinois. "He was an excellent officer, and highly esteemed in the brigade."[27]

It often took weeks during the Civil War for a letter from the front to reach its destination, and the note Van Vleck wrote to tell Patty of his wound could not have reached her quickly. Someone—perhaps Vernon, maybe Van Vleck himself—must have arranged for the news to be sent by telegraph. However it came, the colonel's wife started immediately on a desperate journey to try to reach her husband's side while he yet lived.

The ordeal of Patty Van Vleck's journey to reach her wounded husband is one of the great untold stories of the Civil War. She left no record of the trip, or the obstacles she had to overcome, but they were surely many. She may have had help, but in any case it would have been necessary to argue or plead with officers for permission to pass through areas normally closed to civilians, or gain passage on military trains where she was probably the only woman among hundreds of men. She had to travel through disputed territory where Confederate cavalry was a continuing menace, and finally manage somehow to gain entry into a live combat zone—and all the while she did not know whether she would still find her husband alive when, or if, she arrived at her destination. But she would not be denied.

While she tried desperately to reach her husband's side, the second division surgeons were treating Van Vleck according to the best medical knowledge of the time. "All interference with the wound was omitted," Dr. Batwell wrote. "Cold water was the only local application. He [Van Vleck] lay with his face toward his pillow, both for the exit of any discharge, and in the hope that the [Minie] ball, if within the cavity, might by gravitation, come toward the external opening, and be removed.

"Absolute quiet was of course enjoined. All the [mental and physical] functions were natural, and everything seemed to indicate that a successful termination might possibly result. Thus it continued from day to day, no pain or uneasiness indicating inflammatory action. Rationally and calmly, he spoke of his death as a natural consequence from such a wound."

For five days the colonel's condition remained unchanged. Then, "on the sixth day, a tendency to sleep became more evident, which increased gradually, until coma supervened," Dr. Batwell noted. But Van Vleck was still "capable of being aroused," and while awake his mental and physical functions continued to appear normal.[28]

The men of the 78th were astonished by their leader's continued survival and did what little they could to help. "Try every way to take the colonel to the rear but he is so weak [and] his head so painfull he cannot stand it," Batchelor wrote in his diary on the 19th.[29]

Surgeons had traced the path of the bullet that struck Van Vleck "directly backward [into his brain], but no tendency to paralysis developed itself, nor were any of the natural functions of the body interrupted," Dr. Batwell wrote. As days passed, the colonel slept more and more, though he could still be awakened "even to within a few hours of his death."[30]

The colonel was still alive when Patty Van Vleck arrived and found him in a hospital tent "put up on his account a short distance in rear of the lines." And there, in the hot, still air of the tent, with the Georgia summer sun beating down outside, Van Vleck and his wife spent their last hours together, to the monotonous accompaniment of countless droning flies and the continual stutter of distant gunfire.

On Tuesday, August 23rd, with Patty at his side, Carter Van Vleck went to sleep for the last time. He was thirty-four years old.

15

"This Will Undoubtedly Be a Hard Battle"

AUGUST 23–NOVEMBER 15, 1864

THE SOLDIERS OF THE 78TH ILLINOIS REACTED SORROWFULLY TO NEWS OF VAN Vleck's death, though it was not entirely unexpected. Since the colonel had been in the hospital even before he was wounded, they had been without their commander for a month, which gave them a chance to grow accustomed to Lt. Col. Maris Vernon as their temporary commander. Now he would be in command permanently, although he was not eligible for promotion because the 78th's numerical strength remained well below the minimum for a full colonel to command.

The regiment also had remained active while Van Vleck lingered in his hospital tent. It took its turn on the brigade skirmish line August 15th, where its crisp performance prompted McAdams of the 113th Ohio to write: "They are first-class soldiers. We have known them a long time." It also lost another man when Pvt. Peter S. Camery of Company G died of wounds on the 12th.

On the 19th the regiment was dispatched with other units to try to cut the Macon & Western Railroad, the sole remaining umbilical keeping Atlanta alive. The attempt failed, but another effort was made the next day and this time it succeeded. "This drew the Rebs out then Killpatrick's cavelery [Brig. Gen. Judson Kilpatrick's cavalry division] cut it [the railroad] more," Batchelor wrote.[1]

General Davis had been ill and bedridden for nearly the past month, but on August 22nd Sherman appointed him new commander of the XIV Corps, replacing Richard Johnson, the interim commander. Brig. Gen. James D. Morgan, who had commanded Davis's first brigade, took over for Davis as division commander. Morgan, a Quincy resident, was familiar to the 78th, but most of its men probably knew little about his colorful background. Born in Boston, Massachusetts, the son of a sea captain, Morgan started work as an apprentice cooper at age nine, then went to sea himself at age sixteen. The crew of his ship mutinied and burned the vessel, and Morgan spent weeks adrift in a small boat before making landfall on the South American coast. The experience persuaded him to forsake a career on the high seas, so he returned to Boston and worked in a fish market. At age twenty-four he moved to Quincy, set up a cooperage, and tried his hand at several other occupations until he got into the business of packing pork, which eventually made him prosperous.

Small, tough, and wiry, Morgan took part in the army's campaign against the Mormons and was a captain of volunteers during the Mexican War, where he won brevet promotions for gallantry. He later organized the Quincy militia company known as the Guards, and after hobbling out of town on crutches at the beginning of the Civil War, he served as colonel of the 10th Illinois and was promoted to brigadier. At age fifty-four he was one of the oldest division commanders in the Union army, but he was popular with his men because of his willingness to share their miserable lives in the trenches, eschewing most perquisites of senior officers.

Sherman had concluded it was useless to try to batter his way into Atlanta through the nearly impregnable defenses surrounding the city, so he ordered Maj. Gen. Henry D. Slocum with the XX Corps to protect his railroad lifeline while he sent his remaining forces on another wide sweep around the Confederate left, hoping to make a permanent lodgment on the Macon & Western Railroad and force evacuation of Atlanta.[2]

The position of Mitchell's brigade near the Utoy Creek battlefield remained largely unchanged while preparations were made for the movement. Men on picket still exchanged fire with the rebels, but occasionally an informal truce would be declared, continuing until pickets on one side or the other were relieved by men who were not parties to the understanding, and firing would resume.

The move to the right began August 27th. Mitchell's brigade started at 4:00 a.m. and marched south until it "halted in an orchard near a farmhouse and cotton mill," McAdams recorded. "Several good-looking women and a Negro with six toes attracted our attention."

Early next morning the brigade was on the move again. "For several miles we marched briskly," McAdams wrote. "Halted at 7 a.m., stacked arms and rested. At 9 a.m. we moved southward, passed the IV A.C. [Army Corps] and again halted." The 121st Ohio deployed "and drove the rebels from a woody hill on our left flank. At 2:30 p.m. we reached the railroad leading westerly from Atlanta."[3]

The brigade camped near the railroad that night. Next morning, the 78th Illinois "advanced out two miles due east on a reconnaissance and to protect the operations of destroying the railroad," Lieutenant Colonel Vernon reported. At 4:00 p.m. the regiment returned and rejoined the rest of the brigade, which had been busy tearing up the track. "The rails were torn loose from the cross-ties, which were piled up with rails in layers," wrote Payne of the 34th Illinois. "When the ties were burned, the rails were easily bent around trees and telegraph poles, and so thoroughly damaged that they could only be repaired in a rolling mill." Sherman watched the work with satisfaction.[4]

On August 30th the 78th marched "in a southerly course a distance of 10 miles [Batchelor thought it was six miles], occupying a position at night three miles east of the Macon railroad and some six miles north of Jonesborough," Vernon wrote. The regiment went on the skirmish line at sunset.[5]

"Lay still untill about 3 p.m., then go 3 miles," read Batchelor's diary entry for August 31st. The 78th and the rest of Mitchell's brigade had been detailed to support Brig. Gen. Absalom Baird's division on a reconnaissance feeling for enemy positions along the railroad. The reconnaissance revealed enemy troops and wagon trains moving on a road toward Jonesboro. Baird reported his findings to Davis and put his men to work destroying more of the railroad.

Gen. John Bell Hood had sent most of his cavalry on a raid into Tennessee and had no means to detect the federal movements, so he was slow to realize Sherman had turned his flank and was closing on Jonesboro. It was August 30th before he figured out what was happening and ordered Lt. Gen. William Hardee to take his corps and the corps of Lt. Gen. Stephen D. Lee and rush to Jonesboro. When the rebels arrived late in the afternoon of the 31st, they discovered Maj. Gen. Oliver O. Howard's Army of the Tennessee was already dug in along the Flint River west of the town. Hardee attacked, but was easily repulsed and fell back on the town.

Hood meanwhile received an erroneous report that Union forces were advancing on Atlanta, so he sent orders for Stephen D. Lee's corps to hasten back to the city and assist in its defense, leaving Hardee and his corps to defend Jonesboro. Hardee stretched his line to occupy the works abandoned by Lee's troops, which extended north from Jonesboro, roughly paralleling the west side of the railroad track. About a mile north of town, the line made an abrupt turn to the southeast, crossing the tracks at an acute angle, so that the right flank was sharply refused. The ground fell away from the point of the angle, giving the defenders a commanding view of the approaches. There was no time to throw up abatis or other obstructions, but it was still a strong position, although Hardee's troops were spread very thin. They were good troops, however—Patrick Cleburne's division, the best in Hood's army. The angle itself was held by Brig. Gen. Daniel C. Govan's veteran Arkansas brigade.[6]

The morning of Thursday, September 1st, was cool and breezy, offering pleasant relief from the heat of recent days. The relief was short-lived, however, for the day began warming as the sun climbed higher in the sky.

The day marked two years since the 78th Illinois had been mustered into service, and for all that time the parents of Pvt. Perry Lesure of Company K had been trying to get him discharged from the army. Lesure had enlisted on a whim and his aging parents wanted him home.

Their efforts had finally paid off. Lesure's discharge papers arrived that morning and were presented to him by Capt. William B. Akins of Company K. Lesure could have started for home immediately, but he was reluctant to leave his comrades and decided to stay with the regiment at least long enough to see what the day might bring. Shortly before 10:00 a.m. the regiment was ordered to form in line, and Lesure joined the ranks as he always had. Soon the entire XIV Corps was marching southward, one of three federal corps converging on Jonesboro, where Sherman wanted them to link up with Howard's Army of the Tennessee and attack Hardee's corps.[7]

Davis's corps was first to arrive, reaching the area north of Jonesboro about noon. Morgan's division, approaching from the west, was directed to cross Chamber's Mill Creek and take position on the right of Brig. Gen. William P. Carlin's division. Morgan's right, in turn, was to connect with the left wing of Howard's troops, still in position after their victory the previous day. When Morgan got into position, however, he found he did not have enough room to deploy a full division front, so he advanced farther until his line overlapped in front of Howard's works on the right.

The movement "was impeded by deep ditches, which it was necessary to bridge, during which time we were exposed to a raking fire from the enemy's batteries less than three-quarters of a mile distant," reported Capt. Toland Jones of the 113th Ohio. Mitchell's brigade had to bridge one ditch and cross in single file under heavy artillery fire, but once across the brigade found shelter on the reverse slope of a wooded knoll less than a half mile from the enemy lines. Here the troops rested while they waited to see what would happen next.[8]

While the troops were resting, Edward Mott Robbins remembered, Private Lesure sought out his company commander. "'Captain, what would you do if you were in my place, go into this fight or not?'" he asked.

"'You don't have to go, you have always been a good soldier, and we all know the circumstances under which your discharge was obtained, and it is for your father's and mother's sake,'" Captain Akins replied. "'This will undoubtedly be a hard battle, and were I in your place I would turn in my musket and take no chances.'" By this time other men of Company K had gathered around and urged Lesure not to take the chance. "But his answer was, 'I have been lucky for two years, never had a wound, and I believe I will be [lucky] now, and I am going with you,'" Robbins wrote.

The brigade remained in its sheltered position until about 2:00 p.m., when it formed in line of battle. The 78th Illinois was on the right in the first line with the 113th Ohio on the left. The 34th Illinois was on the left of the second line and the 121st Ohio on the right. Three companies of the 98th Ohio deployed in front as skirmishers. Dilworth's brigade deployed on Mitchell's right while Carlin's and Baird's divisions deployed on his left. "To the left as far as we could see brigades were massed for a charge," wrote Aten of the 85th Illinois in Dilworth's brigade. "With batteries thundering from the intervals between them, flags waving and flashing in the sunlight, staff officers dashing here and there, all made a martial scene grand and inspiring in the highest degree."[9]

The three companies from the 98th Ohio, commanded by a captain, went forward "by a rapid and daring movement [and] captured nearly the entire rebel skirmish line," the 98th's commander, Lt. Col. John S. Pearce, reported. "The enemy, calling to the captain from their main lines, said they would surrender. The captain, supposing them to be in good faith, advanced his skirmishers close to the enemy's works, when he discovered that their object was to entrap and capture him with his entire line." The skirmishers fell back, except for one man who was taken prisoner. "In the meantime, the remaining companies [of the 98th] were brought forward . . . to within 150 yards of the enemy's line and there intrenched," Pearce wrote. There they stayed until the order was given for the whole brigade to charge.

It was late in the afternoon—some sources say 4:00 p.m., others 5—when the order was finally given. "As the men rose up and passed over the crest of the knoll, a terrible fire of shell, grapeshot, and musketry was opened upon the line," wrote Lieutenant Colonel Vernon of the 78th. "Major Green[e] was among the first to receive a wound [in the left arm], which compelled him to leave the field. The men were now falling at every step, yet their brave comrades pressed steadily forward, ready to meet death rather than defeat." Capt. Robert M. Black, commander of Company D, went down with a fatal wound and 1st Lt. John B. Worrell took over the company. First Sgt. Jonathan Butler of Company K also fell gravely wounded.[10]

"The line crossed a corn-field into a deep ravine, where our progress was impeded by deep ditches and a thick canebrake," wrote Jones of the 113th Ohio. "These obstacles being overcome, the line was well dressed up and again ordered forward."

It wasn't as easy as Jones indicated. "When we had charged about half way across the field . . . a halt was ordered, guides thrown out and the charging line ordered to dress on the guides," Edward Mott Robbins wrote after the war. "This movement was executed under a galling fire from the Rebel line. The coolness with which this

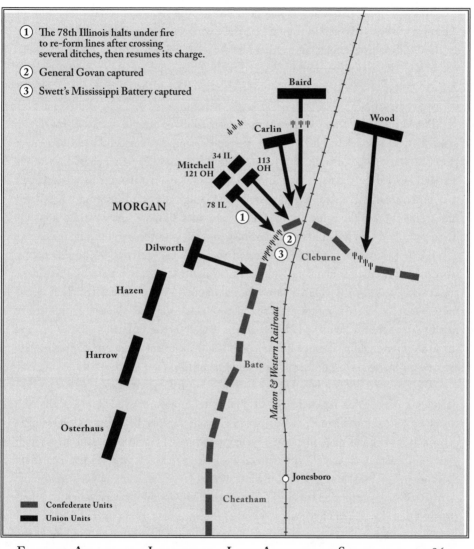

1. The 78th Illinois halts under fire to re-form lines after crossing several ditches, then resumes its charge.

2. General Govan captured

3. Swett's Mississippi Battery captured

Baird

Carlin

Wood

34 IL

113 OH

Mitchell
121 OH

78 IL

MORGAN

1

2

Cleburne

Dilworth

3

Hazen

Macon & Western Railroad

Harrow

Bate

Osterhaus

Jonesboro

Confederate Units

Cheatham

Union Units

FEDERAL ASSAULT ON JONESBORO - LATE AFTERNOON SEPTEMBER 1, 1864 maneuver was executed, I have heard commented on many times since the war. But I think it was the most trying ordeal I ever experienced during my three years of service.

"When the battle line was properly dressed, the command 'Forward!' came and we went forward with a yell."[11]

Through murderous fire, the regiment charged up the slope toward the point of the angle in the rebel line. "In front of the right wing the enemy continued to work his artillery with terrible effect, until, either killed or borne down at the point of the bayonet, he fired his last piece, double-charged with grape, when my two right companies, A and D, were less than ten paces from it," Vernon wrote. The blast nearly decimated the two companies.

Pvt. William H. Thompson was among those in Company D struck down by the giant shotgun blast. A ball hit his lower jaw, splintering the bone, and he lost so much blood he was unable to walk. Sgt. James Abbott and another man helped him to his feet and headed for the rear when Thompson was hit again, this time by a Minie ball that penetrated near his spine and passed out through his side. The wound paralyzed him instantly from the waist down, and his comrades, thinking there was no hope for Thompson, laid him down in the underbrush and left him there.[12]

By then most of the 78th had scaled the parapets and was inside the enemy works. After moments of vicious hand-to-hand fighting with rifle butts and bayonets, the enemy "at last . . . yielded a stubborn resistance," Vernon wrote. The fight lasted only twenty or thirty minutes, but "the victory was complete. We carried his entire line of works from where the left first struck it to the crest of a ridge, where his line made another angle, a distance greater than the front of the regiment, capturing one brigadier-general and a number of field and line officers."

The captured general was Daniel Govan. As usual in such cases, there was disagreement over which regiment got to him first, but according to Robbins, the oft-maligned Pvt. Thomas Broaddus was one of Govan's captors. Broaddus "addressed the general [Govan] and said, 'General, I took a good many chances on your arrest with your staff,'" Robbins wrote. "The general said, 'I don't know, why do you say that?' 'Because my gun was empty. I fired my last shot as I entered your works.'"[13]

The 78th also captured the six guns of Swett's Mississippi Battery, which had fired the shot that decimated Companies A and D. Many prisoners also were taken.

Maj. James A. Connolly of Baird's division, which had been on the left in the charge against the rebel earthworks, offered a stirring account of the battle in a letter to his wife, Mary: "Oh, it was a glorious battle!" he wrote. "There was no chance for flinching there. Generals, colonels, majors, captains and privates, all had to go forward together over that open field, facing and drawing nearer to death with every step we took, our horses crazy, frantic with the howling of shells, the rattling of canister and the whistling of bullets, ourselves delirious with the wild excitement of the moment, and thinking only of getting over those breast works—great volleys of canister shot sweeping through our lines making huge gaps, but the blue-coated boys filled the gaps and still rushed forward right into the jaws of death—we left hundreds of bleeding comrades behind us at every step, but not one instant did that line hesitate—it moved steadily forward to the enemy's works—over the works with a shout—over the cannon—over the rebels, and then commenced stern work with the bayonet, but the despairing cries of surrender soon stopped it, the firing ceased, and 1,000 rebels were hurried to the rear as prisoners of war.

"When the cheer of victory went up I recollect finding myself in a tangled lot of soldiers, on my horse, just against the enemy's log breast-works, my hat off, and tears streaming from my eyes, but as happy as a mortal is ever permitted to be. I could have lain down on that blood-stained grass, amid the dying and the dead, and wept with excess of joy. I have no language to express the rapture one feels in the moment of victory, but I do know that at such a moment one feels as if the joy were worth risking a hundred lives to attain it."[14]

The victory celebration was cut short when the rebels gathered for an effort to retake their works. "A staff officer from Colonel Mitchell brought me orders to hasten to the right to the support of the 78th Illinois," wrote Colonel Banning of the 121st Ohio. "I moved on double-quick, by the flank, to the right about 200 yards through the woods, and found the 78th Illinois had possession of a six-gun battery, from which it had driven all of the enemy that it had not either killed or captured. Simultaneous with my arrival the 34th Illinois came up. Our arrival was in good time; the enemy had rallied and was coming back upon the 78th Illinois (which had already lost largely) in heavy force. But he was turned back from this, and another attempt to retake the guns was most severely punished.

"The guns were captured by the 78th Illinois. The 121st Ohio and the 34th Illinois held the guns and repulsed two desperate charges of the enemy to retake the battery. The second charge was made about 6 o'clock, and from this time until darkness put an end to the conflict the battle raged fiercely."[15]

As darkness approached, the 113th Ohio received orders to relieve the 121st Ohio, which was almost out of ammunition. "We moved to the right across a deep ravine up to the crest of a hill under a sharp fire from the enemy," said Captain Jones of the 113th.

"The firing grew less and less active as the night lengthened," wrote F. M. McAdams, also of the 113th, "and finally only an occasional flash could be seen in our front. Toward midnight a call was made for a man from each company to stand at some distance in front of the line, the object being to watch the movements of the rebels and prevent a surprise. I volunteered and took my position at a large tree nearly a hundred feet in front of our line. A naughty rebel found out my hiding place, and wasted several shots at me. He grew tired, and finally parted without saying good night.

"My attention was attracted by the groans of a wounded man some distance from me. I groped my way toward where he lay, listened, and again moved cautiously forward. In this way I at length found the unfortunate sufferer. His name was Albert Fonnest, of Company C, 78th Illinois. He was wounded through the body below the ribs, and his life blood was fast flowing away. I went back to our line, reported the fact to Captain Shepherd, of the 113th, and he sent a messenger to the 78th to inform the man's comrades of his dying condition. I returned to my post at the tree. Half an hour later, four men of the 78th Illinois came out near me, looking for their wounded comrade. I led them forward to the place where he lay, spoke to him, felt his pulse, and found that he was dead. They carried him off the field, and I returned to my company." [There was no Albert Fonnest in the 78th; the dead soldier was probably Pvt. John S. Forrest of Company C, a resident of Blandinsville, McDonough County.][16]

While the fighting sputtered out in the darkness, surgeons in the second division hospital two miles to the rear were busy treating the most seriously wounded as fast as they were brought in. Jonathan Butler of Company K was among them. He had been hit in the upper right chest by a Minie bullet that shredded his right lung, blew out through his right side, breaking several ribs, and passed through his upper right arm.[17]

Sergeant Payne, the 34th Illinois historian, also was taken to the division hospital. Ever the dutiful reporter, Paine recorded that forty-nine amputations were performed at the hospital that night. One was his own right arm. Henceforth Payne had to rely on diaries kept by other members of the 34th to complete his history of the regiment.[18]

During the night, each company of the 78th took roll to see who was left. Many men did not answer when their names were called. The survivors busied themselves carrying the wounded to hospitals and burying the dead where they fell. Company K had eight men wounded but only one killed. The body of Pvt. Perry Lesure was found on the field with his discharge papers still in his pocket.[19]

As the men dug shallow graves, they saw great flashes on the northern horizon and heard the distant rumble of heavy explosions. Everyone assumed the XX Corps was attacking Atlanta; they did not realize the Confederates were blowing up ammunition and other stores in preparation for evacuating the city.

Captain Jones of the 113th Ohio celebrated the morning of September 2nd by firing "a salute with canister from the guns captured by the 78th Illinois." There was no response; the Confederates had left during the night. "None but the dead and a few wounded were found on the field," Jones wrote.

Sergeant Abbott of Company D of the 78th was eating breakfast with his men when he suddenly remembered the wounded Pvt. William Thompson. "Thompson wasn't dead when I left him," he told the others, "and if some of you boys will go, we'll try and find him." They went to the spot where Thompson had been left in the underbrush and found him still alive. They put him on a blanket and carried him to a hospital.[20]

The final count showed the regiment had fifteen killed and sixty-seven wounded in the brief fight. The dead included two officers, Captain Black of Company D and 1st Lt. Daniel W. Long of Company G. The others were Pvt. Richard H. Scott, Company A; Pvt. William Beatty, Company B; Pvts. John W. James, John S. Forrest, John W. Rush, and Henry Venning, Company C; Sgt. Albert Wallace, Pvt. George W. Crotts, and Pvt. Samuel S. Davis, Company D; Sgt. Robert Wilburn, Company F; Pvt. John S. Beckett, Company G; Sgt. William J. Thomas, Company H; and Private Lesure of Company K. Seven of the wounded would die later from their injuries.[21]

Late in the morning of September 2nd, the 78th Regiment—what was left of it—marched into Jonesboro, a small town with a railroad running down its middle instead of a main street. It was raining and the town looked wet and shabby. "Go into Jonesborough," Batchelor wrote in his diary. "Our Corps took nearly 900 prisoners and they are still comeing in."

General Davis also rode into the town, cheered by each regiment he passed. He made an impromptu speech, congratulating his men on their victory, and was applauded heartily. Then the troops were given news "of the evacuation of Atlanta by the enemy and the glorious termination of the campaign," Vernon wrote.

After four months of nearly incessant fighting, Atlanta had fallen at last.

It rained even harder Saturday, September 3rd, and after a brief rest Morgan's division went back to work tearing up railroad track. Many rebels were still coming into federal lines to surrender. "Sending many prisoners back," Batchelor wrote the next day.[22]

The division remained at Jonesboro until September 6th. At noon that day it began marching north toward Atlanta in another heavy rain, camping that night at the village of Rough and Ready. After another nine-mile march on the 7th, the division made camp on the outskirts of Atlanta, now firmly in Union hands.

Next morning "we had an early breakfast, but did not move until 11 o'clock," wrote McAdams of the 113th Ohio. "Moved out to the road, halted two hours, and then moved in the direction of Atlanta . . . When within three miles of Atlanta, a halt was ordered, and the brigade formed in close column, fronting toward the railroad. General James D. Morgan, our division commander, then mounted a stump in our midst, secured our attention, and read special congratulatory orders from General Grant and President Lincoln . . . As the general concluded reading, he remarked that we should never cheer ourselves, and that he was opposed to noise except when it was made in order. He then proposed three cheers for our *cause,* three for General Sherman, and three for 'the Old Warhorse, General George Thomas.' When General Morgan had finished and left the stump, Colonel John G. Mitchell, commanding the second brigade, proposed three cheers for our old and new division commanders, meaning Generals Davis and Morgan."

After that the division marched another three-quarters of a mile "and went into camp near the Macon & Western Railroad, and near a suburb of the city of Atlanta, called Whitehall."

Batchelor had a much more concise version of the day's events: "Move to the suberbs of Atlanta," he wrote. He also noted that rebels had cut the railroad north of Chattanooga. "Stops everything," he said.[23]

The 78th Illinois remained at Whitehall for three weeks. This allowed the men a well-deserved rest, although there were still the daily tasks of guard mounting, occasional picket duty, and other camp chores. Badly needed new clothing was issued and officers tried to catch up on paperwork and reports neglected during the campaign. Some men went into the city and gawked at the sights, which included wrecked trains and the burnt ruins of a rolling mill destroyed by the Confederates. Those who remained in camp witnessed the passage of many refugees fleeing the city. Sherman had ordered the civilian population evacuated.

On the 14th, while Batchelor complained in his diary about not having enough to eat, the regiment's surviving officers attended to a duty they had not had a chance to perform, meeting to draft a tribute to Carter Van Vleck. The results were conveyed by Lieutenant Colonel Vernon in a letter to Patty Van Vleck:

"My dear Madam," he wrote, *"Enclosed I send you a copy of the proceedings of a meeting held by the officers of the regiment lately commanded by your lamented husband, expressive of their feelings for the loss of a loved commander and their sympathy with you in your grave affliction. I might further add that the feeling of the officers is shared by the men of the regiment. The loss of one highly esteemed by his whole command as was Col. Van Vleck is irreparable. Melancholy for a time was written upon the countenance of each and every one and gloom pervaded the regiment.*

"My own associations with him, for the three months immediately preceding his death, were of the most intimate nature: During the campaign we tented together

and shared the same couch, and I feel in his death the loss of one to me as a brother. I can indeed sympathize with you in your great bereavement.

"Trusting that you may be sustained in this your day of trial and sorrow by the spirit of Him who giveth and taketh away, I remain,

> *With much respect,*
> *M.R. Vernon*
> *Lt. Col. 78th Ill."*

The tribute read, in part: "With sorrowing hearts we bow with reverence before the 'will' of the 'Almighty Ruler of the Universe' who has seen fit in His wisdom to take from among us our late beloved Commander, Col. Carter Van Vleck.

"Thus passed from Earth one whose life had been spent in beautiful contrast to the tumultuous scenes of war among which he died. Alas! We shall never again behold that placid countenance nor hear, as we so often have on drill and on the field, that full melodious voice.

"Professing to be, he lived a Christian in his everyday life, and died with a firm trust in God.

"As a Patriot there was no one more devoted to his country, giving his counsel in peace and his life in war.

"In his death we have lost a valuable friend and the regiment a loved commander. One, who, while he enforced obedience to orders, elicited the universal respect of his command.

"To his bereaved wife and little daughter we offer our heartfelt sympathy as mourners and condole with them the melancholy affliction that has fallen so heavily upon them. With his aged father we share the grief brought to his declining years.

"But while we mourn the loss of him who was so recently our companion in arms, we have the consolation of knowing that the sacrifice was given in a cause which he deemed worthy the offering."

Copies of the tribute were sent to the *Macomb Journal* and *Quincy Whig & Republican* for publication.[24]

The day after the tribute was composed, the regiment learned of the death from disease of Pvt. Reason Van Cecil of Company B. He was from Marcelline, Adams County. Two days after that, Pvt. Thomas H. Wingfield of Company K died of wounds suffered at Jonesboro. He was a resident of Payson, Adams County. And three days after that, on September 20th, Pvt. Henry Vandivier of Company A succumbed to his Jonesboro wounds. He was from Brooklyn, St. Clair County.

On September 26th, Batchelor recorded the return to the regiment of Sgt. Thomas Edmondson of Company I, the color bearer who had been wounded a year before at Chickamauga. "His wound is not quite well," Batchelor wrote, but his company was glad to see him anyway.[25]

After three weeks in camp, the men of the 78th and other regiments of Morgan's division were growing bored and restless, but that ended September 28th when they received orders to prepare to move by rail to Chattanooga, leaving all convalescent men and nonessential baggage in camp. The first brigade left that day while the second and third brigades waited until the following day. At 5:00 p.m. on the 29th, "a train of box cars ran down to our camp from Atlanta," wrote McAdams of the 113th Ohio. "Into and upon this we climbed, and at dusk, with bands playing and colors flying, we ran back to Atlanta. An hour later we were moving northward in the direction of Chattanooga.

"Many of us had not been on a train for nearly two years, and the novelty of riding and sleeping on top of a box car did not wear off immediately. By the time the majority had fallen asleep a brisk rain set in, and comfortable rest was at an end. Our train had a heavy load and moved slowly. Daylight found us halted at Allatoona, 40 miles from Atlanta and 96 miles from Chattanooga."

They reached Chattanooga at 3:30 p.m. September 30th. At 5:30 the next morning they were on their way again, stopping briefly at Stevenson, Alabama, then starting again around 11:00 a.m. About eight o'clock that evening they arrived at Huntsville. "The rebel cavalry had been threatening the place" and had demanded its surrender, wrote Sgt. William Enderton of the 34th Illinois, "but they fled at the aproach of our division."

Late the next afternoon the division left Huntsville bound for Athens, Alabama, but about four miles from town it found the railroad track "badly torn up," in the words of General Morgan. He put the men to work repairing the track and they worked all night in a heavy downpour. By daylight the track was fixed and the train started again, but two miles from Athens they found more track destroyed and a bridge burned. "Marched from this point to Athens," Morgan wrote. "Here I found that the enemy had left the day previous, the gallant little garrison having replied that they were there to fight and not to surrender."[26]

Early the next morning the division took up the march again on the road to Florence, Alabama, going ten miles until a halt was called for dinner in a cornfield. The march resumed in the afternoon and the troops reached the Elk River at Benford's Ferry about 4:00 p.m. "The troops stripped off their clothes, tied them in bundles, and, placing the bundles on the muzzles of their guns, waded the river, which at this ford was about 3½ feet deep," McAdams wrote. "It was rare sport and a grand sight." Since the soldiers were already wet, it didn't matter that it had started raining again, as it had been doing for most of the past few days.

After trudging another four miles, the division went into camp near Rogersville. By then the rain had increased to a deluge "and we slept wet."

They stayed wet the next day as rain continued. "We moved ahead, passing through the dirty little town of Rogersville," McAdams recorded. "The roads are deep with mud, sand and water, and the men are suffering with sore feet." They got even wetter fording First, Second, and Blue Water Creeks, covering nineteen miles until they made a soggy camp near Shoal Creek, about seven miles from Florence.

October 6th dawned bright and pleasant, a welcome respite from the rain. The 78th and the 34th Illinois made a reconnaissance and collected forage three miles out on the Lawrenceburg Road, returning to the brigade in the evening. While they were away, other elements of Morgan's division made contact with Confederate cavalry, apparently the rear guard of Gen. Nathan Bedford Forrest's command, which was driven through the town of Florence. Next day the entire division moved to Florence and camped that night within a mile of the town.

On Saturday, October 8th, "our brigade marched through the principal streets of Florence, with music sounding and banners flying," McAdams wrote. "Of course we attracted the attention of the citizens, consisting of women and Negroes. Some of the women are good-looking, but the greater number are of the razor-blade and elm-peeler pattern, long as rails and sour looking."[27]

That night the troops shivered through the season's first frost. At 10:00 a.m. the next day the 78th went on picket duty, relieving the 34th Illinois. The brigade spent the night in camp outside Florence, then started back toward Athens next morning. This time the road was dry, which made marching easier, and the brigade marched about twenty miles. Starting again the following morning, the troops forded the Elk River and camped about six miles from Athens.

Athens was reached next day and the division went into camp while waiting for repairs to be made to the railroad track and bridge. These were finished and trains arrived the following day. The men boarded and were taken to Huntsville, arriving at dusk. After some delay caused by a car that ran off the track, the trains got under way again after dark. It was a cold night and men riding on top of boxcars were uncomfortable. They reached Stevenson about 1:30 a.m. on the 14th, passed through Bridgeport, crossed the Tennessee River at daylight, and arrived in Chattanooga about 10:00 p.m. Mitchell's brigade camped east of the town that night, then shifted to a site near Fort Wood on the 15th. "Here was obtained clothing, for which the men were suffering," Vernon reported.[28]

Important things had been happening while Morgan's men were off vainly chasing Confederate cavalry. After losing Atlanta and much of his army along with it, Gen. John Bell Hood had been forced to adopt a new strategy. He reasoned that if he could cut Sherman's supply line by breaking the railroad between Chattanooga and Atlanta and keeping it broken, Sherman might be compelled to relinquish his grip on the conquered city and retreat northward. This was not very likely to happen, as Hood himself may have realized, but he had few other options just then. So with his army, he circled west past Sherman's right flank and came down on the railroad at Big Shanty and Acworth, north of Atlanta, capturing the federal garrisons at those places, and began tearing up track. He was between Sherman and Allatoona Pass, where the tracks squeezed through a narrow defile that could be easily blocked. If that happened the railroad might be shut down indefinitely.

Alert to the danger, Sherman started in pursuit of Hood, but had to stop when he ran into the track Hood's men had wrecked. Realizing Hood would reach Allatoona before his troops could get there on foot, Sherman sent an urgent message to Brig. Gen. John M. Corse, whose division was in Rome, to rush to Allatoona and defend the place. Hood, meanwhile, sent Brig. Gen. Samuel G. French with his division to take it.

Corse won the race, barely, with about two thousand men. On October 6th, French attacked with a little more than three thousand men. The result was a fierce battle with remarkably high casualties on both sides. It went on most of the day, but late in the afternoon French's men intercepted wigwag messages from Sherman that help was on the way, so French decided to break off the action. Allatoona Pass was saved, though it had been a near thing.

Hood withdrew westward toward Dallas, then turned north again and fell upon Resaca October 12th, wrecking much of the railroad between Resaca and Dalton. He captured the Union garrison at Dalton October 13th, then moved toward Tunnel Hill, destroying more track as he went. Sherman came after him again, but Hood slipped away through Snake Creek Gap and marched to La Fayette, south of the Chickamauga battlefield, where the 78th Illinois had made its reconnaissance back in April.

At that point Morgan's division joined the chase. The division left Chattanooga about 7:00 a.m. on the 18th and marched twelve miles to Lee & Gordon's Mills, south of the Chickamauga battlefield. Next day it marched another fifteen miles to La Fayette, where it found Hood already had gone, so the division camped there for the night.

"We are ordered to live off the country as mutch as possible," Batchelor wrote in his diary, no doubt with a gleam in his forager's eye. "We get sweet patatoes princaply [principally], some beef, some pork, some chickens, lots of sorg[h]um."

The march resumed at 6:00 a.m. on the 20th and the division covered thirteen miles, camping that night near the Chattooga River. On the 21st it made another sixteen miles and bivouacked at Doherty's Plantation. The division reached Gaylesville, Alabama, October 22nd, where it rendezvoused with the other divisions of the XIV Corps. But Hood's army was still somewhere out in front of them, and Sherman decided further pursuit was useless.

———

In Sherman's mind, the futile experience validated his own preferred strategy: He had his mind set on a march across Georgia to the sea. His idea was to destroy the railroad between Chattanooga and Atlanta so it would be of no use to anyone—it would take a huge force to guard it otherwise—burn what was left of Atlanta, then set out for the coast with his men living off the land. He proposed the scheme to General Grant, whose initial reaction was cool. Grant worried about what Hood might do if Sherman left him and started marching eastward. But Sherman already had sent Maj. Gen. George H. Thomas with two divisions to Nashville, and he assured Grant that they could combine with other forces to create an army strong enough to deal with any trouble Hood might cause. Grant finally gave approval, and Sherman began making preparations for a march to the sea.

———

Morgan's division remained at Gaylesville for five days. It rained on two of those, and the nights were cold, sometimes with heavy frost. The troops found the countryside picked clean, so foraging was difficult. "We have three days' rations to last five days," complained Sergeant Enderton of the 34th Illinois.[29]

The division finally left Gaylesville on the afternoon of the 28th, crossed the Chattooga River, and marched seven miles before camping for the night. It was back on the road at daybreak the next morning and reached the familiar vicinity of Rome, Georgia, by midafternoon, making camp outside the city. The rest of the XIV Corps came up the next day.

Mitchell's brigade rested the last day of October, but reveille came at 3:30 a.m. November 1st and the brigade was on the road to Kingston by 5:30 a.m. By then, however, it was at least temporarily no longer Mitchell's brigade; Colonel Mitchell had gone home on leave of absence and his place had been taken by the brigade's senior lieutenant colonel, John S. Pearce of the 98th Ohio. There were changes at the regimental level, too. Vernon still commanded the 78th Illinois, Lt. Col. Oscar Van Tassell remained in command of the 34th Illinois, and Capt. Toland Jones was still at the head of the 113th Ohio, but the 121st Ohio was now under command of Maj.

Aaron B. Robinson, and the 108th Ohio, also attached, was commanded by Lt. Col. Joseph Good.

The brigade arrived at Kingston about 1:00 p.m. November 1st, made camp, and spent an uncomfortable night under rain. John B. Worrell of Company D was mustered at his new rank of captain, taking the place of Capt. Robert M. Black, killed at Jonesboro.

The brigade remained at Kingston nearly a week. The weather was bad most of the time—cold, rainy, sometimes windy—but at long last a paymaster visited the brigade. "Signed pay rolls in the rain," Sgt. Enderton of the 34th Illinois wrote on the 2nd. Two days later, after finally receiving his pay, he wrote; "Cold weather, no news, plenty of money, and nothing to buy."

The 78th got its money November 4th. "Our reg[i]ment paid off up to August 31st," Batchelor wrote. It was the first time in eight months the regiment had been paid.[30] The regiment also received the news that Pvt. Charles L. Norris of Company C had died of disease in Chattanooga two days earlier.

※

Reveille sounded at 3:00 a.m. Tuesday, November 8th, and three hours later Morgan's division marched out of Kingston. After four hours on the road it passed through Cassville, where "every house has been burned except the churches and the houses of a few poor families," Sergeant Enderton noted. The division halted near Cartersville at 1:00 p.m. and the soldiers cast ballots in the presidential election. They knew the capture of Atlanta had virtually assured Lincoln's re-election, which had seemed highly unlikely less than three months earlier.[31]

They remained at Cartersville four days, two of them under rain. While there they drew "all the provisions we can take as the R.R. [railroad] is being torn up as we go," Batchelor wrote. They also received new clothing, filled wagons with rations, sent all their surplus baggage to the rear, and burned whatever was left. All signs pointed to a new campaign in the offing, and Lieutenant Colonel Van Tassell of the 34th Illinois decided it would be one campaign too many. He resigned November 12th and went home. His place was taken, at least temporarily, by Capt. Peter Ege.[32]

Cartersville was left in flames on the 13th and the division marched a short distance to the railroad where the soldiers stacked arms and began destroying the tracks. They ripped up six miles of track, all the way to Allatoona, then marched another five miles to Acworth, where they camped.

They left Acworth the next morning, which was bright and cold, and marched twenty-one miles before making camp on the north side of the Chattahoochee River. They were up again at 6:00 a.m. on the 15th, crossed the river at 8:00 a.m., and got to Atlanta about noon, where they "found two-thirds of it burned and the embers of hundreds of buildings still smoking," Enderton recorded. "A pall of smoke hangs over the ruined city, and great black clouds of smoke and forked tongues of flame roll up from many a house-hold which have just caught fire." Batchelor noted some buildings contained unexploded shells "which explode when hot enough."

The division camped about two miles east of the city. That evening the men received another issue of clothing. Each private drew two pair of shoes, a new haversack, a canteen, a wool blanket, a rubber blanket, half a tent shelter, a knapsack, and an extra shirt.[33]

Back in the city, more fires were breaking out "and it soon became evident that these fires were but the beginning of a general conflagration which would sweep over the entire city and blot it out of existence," wrote Major Connolly of Baird's division. "So quartermasters and commissaries ceased trying to issue clothing or load rations; [instead] they told the soldiers to go in and take what they wanted before it burned up. The soldiers found many barrels of whisky and of course they drank of it until they were drunk; then new fires began to spring up, all sorts of discordant noises rent the air, drunken soldiers on foot and on horseback raced up and down the streets while the buildings on either side were solid sheets of flame, they gathered in crowds before the finest structures and sang 'Rally around the Flag' while the flames enwrapped these costly edifices, and shouted and danced and sang again while pillar and roof and dome sank into one common ruin.

"The night, for miles around was bright as mid-day; the city of Atlanta was one mass of flame, and the morrow must find it a mass of ruins."[34]

16

"They Are Going Somewhere Toward Freedom"

NOVEMBER 16, 1864–MARCH 8, 1865

FOR THE SOLDIERS IT WAS THE GRANDEST OF ALL ADVENTURES, A 250-MILE MOVABLE feast, a chance to "make Georgia howl," as Sherman put it. His men took him at his word—and Georgia howled. Despite some dark moments along the way, the troops would always remember they had been cut loose to do things they would never again be allowed to do, and they took full advantage of the opportunity.

The rail-thin, red-headed Sherman had reorganized the army that would make the march to the sea, dividing it into two wings. The right wing, under Maj. Gen. Oliver Otis Howard, included the XV Corps with four divisions and the XVII Corps with three. The left wing, commanded by Maj. Gen. Henry W. Slocum, included the XIV and XX Corps, each with three divisions. Brig. Gen. Judson Kilpatrick's cavalry division of two brigades also was attached.

In the XIV Corps, still commanded by Bvt. Maj. Gen. Jefferson C. Davis, the first division was led by Brig. Gen. William Carlin, the second—including the 78th Illinois—by Brig. Gen. James D. Morgan, and the third by Brig. Gen. Absalom Baird.[1]

The great march began the morning of November 16th. The 78th Illinois left its camp east of Atlanta about 11:00 a.m. and filed past the graves left by the July 22nd Battle of Atlanta northeast of the city. The regiment's route paralleled the Georgia Railroad, passing through the town of Decatur before camp was made for the night. Next day the 78th covered seventeen miles, taking time out to destroy a half-mile of railroad and marching through the village of Lithonia, where several buildings were aflame. Their camp that night was near Conyers Station on the railroad.

Batchelor was already pleased with the forage opportunities. "Forrage is plenty," he wrote. "Patatoes and chicken, Mollasses and feed."

On the 18th the regiment crossed the Yellow River, marched through Covington and destroyed about a mile of railroad east of the town. The regiment made camp after marching about seventeen miles.[2]

Next day brought rain and movement was difficult over muddy roads. Late in the morning the 78th passed through Sand Town, which Major Connolly of Baird's staff described as "a little weather-beaten village of about 250 or 300 inhabitants." Batchelor continued gloating over easy pickings along the way. "Lots of forage and pea nutts," he wrote.

Connolly noticed the good foraging, too. "Our men are foraging on the country with the greatest liberality," he wrote. "They go where they please, seize wagons, mules, horses, and harness; make the Negroes of the plantation hitch up, load the wagons with sweet potatoes, flour, meal, hogs, sheep, chickens, turkeys, barrels of molasses, and in fact everything good to eat, and sometimes considerable that's good to drink."

Sherman had issued instructions that every regiment should send out a twenty-man foraging party each day; all other soldiers were forbidden to forage. The twenty-man parties were sent out, but the rest of the order was ignored and there were so many foraging opportunities right along the roadsides that soldiers could not resist. Men broke ranks and joined in the fun until there was "scarcely one that does not forage from morning till night," wrote Sergeant Enderton of the 34th Illinois.

Runaway slaves flocked to fall in behind the blue-clad ranks. "The Negroes stare at us with open eyes and mouths, but generally, before the whole column has passed, they pack up their bundles and march along, going, they know not whither, but apparently satisfied they are going somewhere toward freedom," Connolly observed.[3]

The 78th crossed the swampy Ulcofauhatchee River on the 19th, marched twenty miles, and made camp in a thicket near a place called Shady Dale. Next day the 78th and the 113th Ohio were assigned as wagon train guards. "The trains moved slowly and the men improved the time in appropriating whatever had escaped the vigilance of troops in the advance," wrote McAdams. "One fellow, lacking a jug for the purpose, filled a plug hat with molasses at Whitefield's store and carried it to his company. Everything in this store worth carrying, and some things that were not, was taken." Another man "went into a building to fill his canteen with molasses, and found the floor two inches deep with it."

The regiment marched seventeen miles that day and made camp four miles east of Eatonton. Heavy rain fell that night. "We find mules, horses, Negro[e]s plenty," Batchelor recorded. "Get some candy, nutts, patatoes, pork &cetra." Cooking utensils also were popular items for appropriation.[4]

Word spread quickly among the inhabitants of the country that nearly everything they owned was fair game for the roving foragers, and local citizens began frantically seeking ways to conceal food and valuables, or find some other way to deter foragers. One trick was to hang out a yellow flag, signaling there was smallpox on the premises. This worked until the troops figured out the ruse; after that, any house displaying a yellow flag was first to be searched.

It became something of a game, fun for the soldiers but deadly serious for the inhabitants. The troops learned to look for fresh dirt, usually evidence of buried valuables or provisions. They also learned where to search in or under houses for goods concealed by the occupants. If that didn't work, and the family owned slaves, soldiers would convince the slaves—sometimes by terrorizing them—to reveal where things were hidden. Little escaped their efforts.

When they had found all there was to find, the torches would come out and outbuildings, barns, storage sheds, and warehouses would be set aflame. Most homes were spared, depending on the attitudes of the occupants. The army's route was traceable from afar by pillars of smoke rising high on either side of its line of march, and in its wake it left a forest of "Sherman's sentinels"—gaunt, fire-blackened chimneys, the only things left standing.[5]

Slocum's left wing marched southeast while Howard's right wing headed south toward Macon, but on November 21st Slocum also turned south toward Milledgeville, then Georgia's capital. "Rained all night," Batchelor complained. "Makes four nights in succession and rains all day." The going was slow and heavy on the muddy roads and the long column had an especially difficult time crossing Murder Creek. It managed eleven to thirteen miles that day, depending upon who was asked, and made a wet camp near Cedar Creek.[6]

Morgan's division, including the 78th, remained in camp November 22nd, permitting Baird's third division, which had been trailing behind, to take the advance. The rain had finally stopped and the day was clear and cold. Men searched eagerly for firewood and fence "rails are growing scarcer every hour," McAdams recorded. That evening there were snow flurries.

Reveille was early on the 23rd and the division was on the road by 5:30 a.m. The roads were drying and the command marched fourteen miles, with the 78th's brigade halting for dinner on the plantation of Howell Cobb, who had chaired the secession convention in Montgomery, Alabama, and was a major general in the Confederate Army. The division camped about two miles northwest of Milledgeville.

By this time a great caravan of runaway slaves—men, women, and children—was trailing in the division's wake, "like a sable cloud in the sky before a thunderstorm," as one soldier put it. They had no idea where the army was headed, but they were sure it would be someplace better than where they had been. They came by the thousands, "poor little children 'toting' their little bundles, footsore and weary, sobbing and limping," wrote one Illinois soldier. Many women carried bundles on their heads and babies on their backs. Others were weighted with plunder taken from their former masters' homes.

Some of the runaways joined the soldiers' ranks, trying to ingratiate themselves in various ways—cooking, washing or mending clothes, gathering wood or tending fires, or digging sinks (latrines). Others volunteered as foragers, servants, informants, or teamsters, and some offered entertainment, playing musical instruments, singing, and dancing. Others carried gamecocks and staged cockfights, which were great favorites with the soldiers.[7]

November 23rd marked a year since Pvt. John W. Sapp, of Birmingham, Schuyler County, joined Company A of the 78th as a recruit. It was also the day he died of disease in far away Nashville.

Morgan's division entered Milledgeville on the 24th, eight days after the march from Atlanta began. "Boys go into the State House and get swords, spears and knifes," Batchelor wrote in his diary. "We tear up the R.R." But the 78th had little time to plunder the capitol because the division kept going, camping for the night six miles east of the city. Baird's division remained at Milledgeville, giving Major Connolly time for a good look around the place. Though it was late November, he was impressed by the fragrance of late-blooming flowers and shrubs. He also admired the homes he saw, which, he said, gave evidence of "refinement within." All in all, he thought Milledgeville "an old, aristocratic city."[8]

The 78th and the other regiments of Pearce's brigade were on the road again at 6:00 a.m. November 25th. They "marched very hard until noon and halted for dinner and to put down a pontoon bridge across a creek, where the enemy had burned a bridge," Sgt. Charles S. Gaylord of the 34th Illinois wrote in his diary. They also encountered their first meaningful opposition: "Rebel bushwhackers shot several foragers to-day." The country was swampy and thickly wooded with pine, mostly uninhabited except for an occasional "miserable-looking little cabin," in Connolly's words.[9]

The following day Pearce's brigade ran into more opposition. "We have quite a scrmish [skirmish] with Rebels," Batchelor wrote. "Few wounded, one or two killed." Lieutenant Colonel Pearce reported the incident in more detail: "November 26, marched toward Sandersville, Washington County, Ga., and when within about two miles of that place we met the enemy's cavalry. The brigade having the advance that day, I was ordered by General Morgan, commanding the division, to send forward a regiment to support the skirmish line which had been formed from the several foraging parties . . . The 113th Ohio Volunteer Infantry, commanded by Captain [Toland]

Jones, being on the right of the brigade, I sent it forward, when the skirmishers advanced, driving the enemy through the town, this regiment following and being the first to enter the place. We marched ten miles this day and encamped a short distance east of Sandersville."

The 113th Ohio had one man killed and two wounded in the fight. The 108th Ohio also had a man killed and the 121st Ohio had one wounded. The 78th Illinois suffered no loss. The rebel cavalry belonged to Maj. Gen. Joseph Wheeler.[10]

At Sandersville General Davis decided to divide his column. He ordered Carlin's division and the XIV Corps wagon train to keep going on the road to Davisborough while the divisions of Baird and Morgan took a road slightly to the north where they could screen the trains from further assaults by Wheeler.[11]

On they marched, a sight unlike any seen on the North American continent before or since, a blue river of men flooding across the land, sweeping everything in its path. Their approach was audible from a distance—the rhythmic tread of thousands of marching men, the heavier thud of horses and mules, the squeak and creak of hundreds of wagons, gun carriages, and limbers, the shouts of teamsters, and the continuous rattle and clank of pots, pans, and skillets dangling from men's belts or the sides of wagons. They also had "all kinds of music," according to one farmer—"horns, cow bells, tin pans, everything they could pick up that would make a hideous noise."

"It was the XIV Corps that came through my place," the same man said. "They looked like a blue cloud coming . . . They burned everything but occupied dwellings. They cut the belluses [bellows] at the blacksmith shops. They took every knife and fork and cooking utensil we had." The blue cloud might have been a storm of locusts because it picked clean everything in its path. It left a shocked, barren-looking landscape, and the trailing black cloud of runaway slaves was quick to harvest anything the army might have overlooked.

The soldiers were mostly interested in edible things, but they could not resist gathering souvenirs. They picked up fancy hats, dress shoes, and formal clothing, and some marched off with stolen garments draped around their shoulders. Others took knives or antique weapons, lanterns, photographs, books, looking glasses, or any number of other items. After a while they forgot why they had taken them and tossed them along the roadsides, where they were gathered up by the following horde of escaped slaves. Sometimes, on the horizon, the soldiers could see pillars of smoke marking the progress of their comrades in Howard's army farther south.

"Our march was conducted in a very systematic manner," wrote Edward Mott Robbins of the 78th. "The brigade or regiment that was in the advance today was put in the rear tomorrow. We marched 50 minutes and rested ten." During one such rest period the 78th halted "in front of one of those beautiful southern mansions. It had been raining all day and was still raining. We had only stopped for a few minutes, when an old man came to us from the mansion and asked to see the flag. It was taken from its cover and unfurled. The old man took its folds in his hands and said, 'Beautiful emblem, flag of our country,' and tears came to his eyes, and then he walked away."[12]

From southern newspapers the troops learned that Lincoln had been re-elected by a substantial margin. They also took notice they were entering a more productive country with larger plantations and more cultivated land. "Persimmons grow by the roadside in abundance," Major Connolly wrote. "Our orderlies gather them in their handkerchiefs as they ride along, and bring [them] up to us, so that we just ride along and eat persimmons, until we are almost tired of them."

On Wednesday, November 30th, Pearce's brigade rested in camp two miles north of the town of Louisville. "Some of the forage squads had picked up some race horses, and there was a difference of opinion as to who had the best one, so we took this opportunity to test them," Robbins wrote. "We had to go some little distance from camp in order to find a suitable piece of road that would make a race track, but just as we were in the zenith of our expectations of seeing a horse race, Wheeler's Rebel cavalry showed up and we had to form a skirmish line in order to protect ourselves from being captured. Needless to say, our ardor for a horse race was cooled to the extent that we did not care who had the best horse."

Fortunately for the would-be racers, six companies of the 113th Ohio were in the vicinity, guarding a six-wagon forage train. They joined the skirmish line, which was forced back until the rest of the brigade came up on the double-quick and the rebels broke off the attack. But eight men of a "forage party" led by Capt. William Akins of the 78th's Company K were captured in the affair. At least Lieutenant Colonel Vernon called it a "forage party" in his tactful report of the incident, though its mission might actually have been to see who had the fastest horse. "In justice to Captain Akins," Vernon wrote, "I must say it was through no neglect on his part that the men were captured. The enemy, vastly superior in number, charged upon him in front and on flank, and it was with great difficulty he evaded the capture of his whole party."[13]

The eight men captured were not the regiment's only loss that day. Back in Chattanooga, Pvt. Jesse Cunningham of Company E died from wounds suffered at Jonesboro.

After leaving Louisville, Davis's column veered south toward Millen, entering low, swampy country. The flat country made it easier to see the smoky spires that marked the path of the other federal troops off to the right. Rebel cavalry continued hovering off the XIV Corps' flank and there were also "bushwhackers" about, but the

Confederates did not have enough force to mount any serious opposition. Instead, they burned bridges and felled trees across the roads to slow the march of the XIV Corps.

"Our division is again with the corps train," McAdams wrote December 2nd. "It has been a hard day on man and beast. The road is almost a continuous swamp and the heavy trains require frequent assistance. It is reported that six of our foragers were killed to-day. Some say their throats were cut and a card pinned to each read, 'Death to all foragers.'"

Batchelor's diary entry for Saturday, December 3rd, read: "Cross pontoon. Some scrimishing. All the refugees following not employed are stopped. Heavy cannonading to left." The crossing was over Buckhead Creek, and General Davis had ordered the bridge taken up as soon as the last infantry crossed so the pontoons could be hurried forward to the next crossing. Most of the runaway slaves following the division were left stranded, except those "employed" in some fashion by the troops, who were allowed to cross. Nobody in the army seemed particularly concerned about the refugees left behind.

"Our division is guarding the entire corps train, which is strung out 4½ or 5 miles," wrote Sergeant Gaylord of the 34th Illinois. The corps marched ten or twelve miles that day—again depending on who was asked—and Morgan's and Carlin's divisions spent the night camped at Lumpkin's Station.[14]

Next day they "marched at 6 a.m., rapidly, and soon reached the Waynesboro and Augusta Railroad," Gaylord wrote. "The railroad has been destroyed by our troops. We crossed the road and took an easterly course through a fine pine forest. The plantations are rather distant from each other, but very large. Heard considerable cannonading and musketry off to our left . . . Passed through a small place called Buckhead, in Burke County. Marched about 15 miles and camped in a pine grove."[15]

Because of the swampy country and obstructions in its path, the XIV Corps had fallen a day behind Howard's right wing, and Sherman was pressuring General Davis to speed up his march. As a result, the men were "hurried so but few get to eat breakfast," Batchelor recorded December 5th. As with most things in the army, it turned out to be a matter of hurry up and wait; since Pearce's brigade was in the rear of Morgan's division, it didn't get on the road until after 11:00 a.m. Once it did start moving it made rapid progress, marching about eighteen miles before going into camp near Brier Creek about 8:00 p.m.

Next day was a repeat, except "the sand is deep and loose and often fills our shoes," McAdams reported. "We have reached nearly parallel with the Savannah River and not far from it. Crossed Beaver Dam Creek early this morning on a pontoon which had been built during last night. We have made some 20 miles today, and our camp is in the vicinity of Hudson's Ferry, on the Savannah River."[16]

"Find all kind of obstructions in the road," Batchelor wrote December 7th. "The rebels run one of our foragers almost to our lines. There is a small gun boat in the [Savannah] River. About 26 miles to Savan[n]ah. We pass one end of the Dismal Swamp." Morgan's division had the advance that day and encountered a number of enemy cavalrymen, capturing several. After marching seventeen miles the division camped near Little Ebenezer Creek.

Most of the refugees who had been left behind at Buckhead Creek had somehow found their way across that stream and were again trailing after the XIV Corps, much to General Davis's displeasure. He thought they were a drag on the corps, keeping it from moving as rapidly as it should.

"Heavy scrimishing," Batchelor wrote on the 8th. "The rebels shell us from their gun boat." Surgeon John L. Hostetter of the 34th Illinois had other details: "Two bridges had to be put in to-day, which delayed the march. To add to the vexation, Gen. Morgan advanced four miles farther than he ought, and was ordered to retrace the distance. After we crossed the first bridge, the brigade halted near Ebenezer Church, on a creek of the same name."[17]

The first of the two bridges mentioned by Hostetter was over Little Ebenezer Creek; the second over Ebenezer Creek itself, a larger stream. Col. George P. Buell of the engineers and his men had worked through the night to finish the crossing, which was at the end of a causeway that traversed a swamp. "When the bridge was completed, the work of crossing Ebenezer began, but progressed slowly," McAdams wrote.

Morgan's and Carlin's divisions were first to cross, so they may not have witnessed what happened next, but Major Connolly of Baird's division did. "The crossing of Ebenezer Creek was a very delicate undertaking," he wrote. "The enemy was just in our rear, undoubtedly listening for every sound that would indicate a movement on our part, and to cross the creek we had to pass through at least a mile of the most gloomy, dismal cypress swamp I ever saw, on a narrow causeway, just wide enough for a wagon to drive along."

When Connolly reached the bridge, he found several officers "turning off the road, into the swamp all the fugitive Negroes that came along. When we should cross I knew it was the intention that the bridge should be burned, and I inquired if the Negroes were not to be permitted to cross; I was told that Gen'l. Davis had ordered that they should not. This I knew, and Gen'l. Davis knew, must result in all these Negroes being recaptured or perhaps brutally shot down by the rebel cavalry tomorrow morning. The idea of five or six hundred black women, children and old men being thus returned to slavery . . . was entirely too much." Outraged, Connolly protested vigorously to Davis's officers.

It did no good. As before at Buckhead Creek, a few able-bodied refugees—men who had made themselves useful to the troops—were permitted to cross before the bridge was taken up (not burned). Some left their families behind, and it was reported that a number of frantic family members plunged into the deep creek and drowned trying to cross. The others—estimates range from several hundred to more than a thousand—were left in the swamp, where Connolly supposed they would be shot or forced back into slavery. Some probably did suffer unpleasant fates, but as before many of them eventually found a way across the creek and rejoined the march.

Connolly, however, was unwilling to forget the incident. He wrote a letter to his congressman protesting Davis's action. A copy of the letter was published in the *New York Tribune* and came to the attention of Secretary of War Edwin Stanton, who called Davis to account. Davis and his superiors, including Sherman, defended his actions as a military necessity. Davis "took up his pontoon bridge not because he wanted to leave them [the refugees], but because he wanted his bridge," Sherman said. In the end, nothing came of all this, and Davis, a professional survivor, escaped with nothing more than another blot on his reputation to go along with the shooting of "Bull" Nelson.[18]

On Friday, December 9th, Pearce's brigade had marched about eight miles beyond Ebenezer Creek when it came to a small rebel earthwork blocking the road at Cuyler's Plantation. A pair of cannon in the earthwork opened fire "in a lively manner," McAdams wrote, "and for a time we were at a standstill." The brigade deployed on both sides of the road and brought up a pair of guns from Battery I of the Second Illinois Light Artillery under command of Lt. Alonzo Coe. The guns, posted in the roadway, began dueling with the Confederates, but a rebel shell struck Coe and killed him.

What happened next is unclear. General Davis's report of the incident says he did not order an attack because the rebel position was on the far side of a swamp. The reports of Morgan, the division commander, Pearce, the brigade commander, and Vernon, commander of the 78th, also make no mention of an attack; they say only that the Confederates abandoned their position after dark. Batchelor, however, recorded a sharply different version. "We meet the Rebs," he wrote. "Charge their works. Capture 25 men, two pieces of artillery. The Lutenant of Battery I Second Illinois was shot in two." No explanation exists for the divergent accounts. Exactly what happened at Cuyler's Plantation remains something of a mystery.[19]

The march resumed about eight o'clock the next morning, the men filing past Lieutenant Coe's fresh grave next to the road. The brigade covered about ten miles, overtaking the XX Corps, which they found destroying the Savannah & Charleston Railroad near its crossing of the Savannah River. The brigade camp that night was at a place called Ten Mile House.

The brigade was on the road again at 7:30 the next morning and marched to within five miles of Savannah. There, about 2:00 p.m., the division "took position behind light breastworks within 600 yards of a rebel battery at the junction of the Charleston & Savannah and the Georgia Central Railroads," wrote Surgeon Hostetter of the 34th Illinois. Pearce's brigade relieved troops of the XVII Corps. The rebel battery greeted them by throwing a few shells in their direction, but no damage was done.

"Our protracted picnic is now at an end," wrote McAdams of the 113th Ohio. "We are here to stay, and sooner or later we shall hold dress parade in the streets of this historic old city."[20]

The following day, December 12th, Pearce's brigade moved about two miles to the right and took position "with the right of the regiment near the [Savannah and Ogeechee] canal, and some four miles from the city," Vernon wrote. "Remained in this position [until] the fall of Savannah."

This was Vernon's concluding report of the campaign. He had faithfully recorded distances marched, but was less meticulous naming landmarks or river crossings, and his report is almost totally devoid of details about the regiment's daily activities on the march. But Vernon did have an eye for statistics, and he appended the following to his report:

"There was issued to the regiment by the brigade commissary from and including the 16th of November, the date of leaving Atlanta, up to the 21st of December, the following amount of rations: Six days' rations bread, six days' rations bacon, six days' rations soap, six days' rations salt, 24 days' rations coffee, 11 days' rations sugar, nine days' rations beef. The rest required to subsist upon was foraged off the country. I am unable to give the amount brought into the regiment, but I do know the men did not suffer; in fact, they lived well.

"The regiment destroyed two miles of railroad, brought and turned over 23 head of mules, 11 head horses, and 22 head of cattle. Number of Negroes that followed the regiment into camp, 23. Cotton and cotton gins destroyed, none.

"In conclusion I must say that both officers and men performed the march in fine spirits; none were lost through sickness or fatigue."[21]

Vernon's report skipped the nine days from December 12th until December 21st, when the rebels evacuated Savannah and the city fell to the federals. But those were not easy days for the men. The food and forage they had enjoyed on the march were now missing. "Our men are now living almost entirely on rice," Major Connolly wrote. "We have no meat and no crackers, but little coffee and very little sugar . . . Our horses and mules are living on rice straw, and the Lord only knows how the ten or twelve thousand fugitive Negroes within our lines are living. . . ."

It had also turned cold. "The ice this morning is an inch thick on water-pails, and the ground is frozen hard," wrote Surgeon Hostetter of the 34th Illinois. "Those who have overcoats and blankets are fortunate."

Lack of mail was another complaint. "This is the 26th day out from Atlanta, and it is over a month since we had a mail," Hostetter said. "Even the Southern papers are not easily obtained. They as usual are full of bombast, stating that Sherman's army is scattered and starving."[22]

On December 13th, however, Brig. Gen. William B. Hazen's division captured Fort McAllister on the bank of the Ogeechee River near its confluence with Ossabaw Sound, where a federal fleet was waiting. This allowed Sherman to communicate with the navy, and that in turn meant supplies and mail would soon be forthcoming.

"Orders to write as we get mail out in the morning," Batchelor wrote jovially in his diary on the 14th. The men waited anxiously for incoming mail and rations. "Have to use swamp water for cooking and making coffee," wrote Sergeant Enderton of the 34th. "We put the rice in bags and beat with sticks to get the hull off. It takes about half of our time, and then we cannot get it clean."[23]

The weather had warmed, making things more bearable, but nothing did more for the spirits of the men than the delivery of mail on December 17th. Batchelor received seven letters.

That day orders came to dismount all foragers and turn over to the quartermaster's department all horses and mules seized along the march. The orders also directed that all Negroes were to be sent to Port Royal, except those employed by the government or as servants to officers.[24]

~⁓~

Savannah was garrisoned by about ten thousand Confederate soldiers commanded by the familiar Lt. Gen. William J. Hardee. On the night of December 20th, Hardee and his army evacuated the city via pontoon bridge, and the next morning "the news sped along our line that there was no enemy in our front," McAdams wrote. "In a few minutes some of our men were inspecting the rebel works and scouting far beyond the lines held by them yesterday."

"Bugles sounded reveille at 5 o'clock," wrote Hostetter of the 34th. "The morning is freezing cold. Marched at 7 o'clock. Delayed in the road by the dilatory movements of our first brigade. Moved 1½ miles towards the city and went into regular laid-out camp, on the south bank of the Savannah and Ogeechee canal." Later he ventured into the city. "Savannah is the finest Southern city I have seen," he wrote. "Its streets are wide, shaded with rows of live-oaks . . . Numerous parks, well shaded with the live-oak and China tree, are formed at street crossings . . . Large quantities of rice and cotton were burned in the city." Hostetter wasn't the only visitor. "Go Into town," Batchelor wrote. "Rebels evacuated last night leaving gunns, locomotives, steam boats."[25]

Next couple of days were spent getting camps established and making preparations for building quarters. Then it was Christmas Eve, and the men of the XIV Corps celebrated by firing muskets into the air, raising such a clamor that other troops were called out in alarm. Next day, Sunday, was Christmas Day. "Some of the men are drunk," Batchelor scrawled in his diary.[26]

Two days later the XIV Corps was reviewed by General Sherman. Will Z. Corin of the 121st Ohio penned an account of the proceedings: "In Sherman's rear rode Brig. Gen. 'Jimmy Morgan'—the gallant commander of our division. He is about Sherman's age or perhaps a little older—was mounted on his old 'pacer'—wore an old oil cloth cap—a new dress coat (the first time he was ever known to wear one) and silver spurs—very short whiskers . . . Further off—and on the right of Gen. Sherman rode our brave Corps commander . . . Brevet Maj. Gen. Jeff C. Davis. He rode a fine black stallion—wore a nice uniform with mustache and chin whiskers—is about 35 years old—has sandy hair and whiskers and an eye that can look through a stone wall . . . He has an awful wicked look but is the idol of the Corps—because he is brave and sharp, and, like Hooker, feeds his corps better than any other corps commander can. He wore a slouched hat pulled down over his eyes (he always does) so that he could just cock one eye on us."

Next day Batchelor got some unexpected orders. "General Jeff. C. Davis sends for me to take his H'dQuarters ambulance and take General Foster's wife and daughter to steamboat," he wrote. On December 30th he was sent to get mail for the regiment. On the 31st, he wrote: "Have no feed for horses & mules. Very little rations. Buy some tabacco cheap. Sell it again. Make $5.00."

That night, New Year's Eve, all the regimental commanders in the XIV Corps called their men into line and ordered them to stack arms. Guards were posted over the arms and the men were sent to their quarters. The object was to prevent a repeat of the celebration on Christmas Eve, but it didn't quite work. The enterprising men bored holes in stumps and logs and filled them with powder, and about ten o'clock a terrific series of explosions ensued.[27]

The 78th Illinois and the rest of the XIV Corps remained in Savannah until January 20th. It rained much of the time, which added misery to the monotony of camp life, picket duty, and work on fortifications. Officers wrote reports and saw to it their regiments were brought up to strength in terms of arms, ammunition, and other essentials. Rations improved, thanks to supplies brought in by the fleet, and there were some opportunities for relaxation. Many men attended concerts or plays, took meals at Savannah's restaurants, strolled through the city's streets or along its wharves, and attended services at its churches. Those who had money enough could get a shave and a haircut for seventy-five cents.

The 78th Illinois suffered several losses during its stay at Savannah. Pvt. Lewis Shehawny of Company E, a resident of Liberty, Adams County, died of disease January 13th. Disease also claimed the life of Pvt. Daniel Groves of Company B on the 18th. He was from Marcelline, Adams County. Maj. George Greene, still disabled from an arm wound suffered at Jonesboro, resigned from the service January 15th, and regimental sergeant major William S. Hendricks was discharged on the 17th, also because of wounds. This left the regiment with sixteen officers and 305 enlisted men.[28]

The other regiments in Pearce's brigade had been similarly reduced, and most were now commanded by captains or majors; besides Pearce, Maris Vernon was the only lieutenant colonel in the brigade.

Orders came on January 19th to be ready to move the next morning. The march into South Carolina was about to begin. In the flurry of activity surrounding preparations to break camp, General Davis summoned Batchelor again. "I take General Foster and General Davis to the steam boat on the river," he wrote in his diary. "They boath compliment [me] very highly for good driving and keep[ing] up the team."

The march began about 11:00 a.m. the next day in another heavy rainstorm. The XIV Corps went north about ten miles on the Augusta Road, which was wet and swampy, before making a miserable camp. Orders went out for each regiment to detail a sergeant and one man from each company to serve in a "pioneer corps." The XIV Corps remained in camp on the 21st while the "pioneers" went to work cutting trees and making corduroy roads.[29]

It wasn't until January 25th that Davis deemed the roads passable enough to resume the march. The weather continued wet, but some parts of the column managed to make fifteen miles that day. Next day they marched another eight miles, but "our progress to-day has been exceedingly slow," McAdams wrote. "The second brigade was [wagon] train guard, and we had plenty of work to do in helping the wagons out of the deep holes and quicksand. The country is flat and much water stands on the surface. We built small fires of pine knots in the woods during the day, and while the weary mules dragged their heavy loads along at almost a snail's pace, we stood around our smoking fires until our faces were dusky."

Their camp that night was near Springfield, Georgia, where the 78th had "to put up in a swamp," according to Batchelor. On January 27th they marched seven more difficult miles, fording a creek "swollen by recent rains and difficult to cross," in McAdams' words. "The water was very cold and small sheets of ice adhered to the chunks and logs. Soon as we had crossed our clothes began freezing and were soon stiff and uncomfortable; but building a number of big fires in the woods we danced around them, joking and cheering until we were somewhat comfortable." That night they camped near the home of a "Mr. Dasher." "The grass caught fire near our tent in the night, and our bedding was partially destroyed by the fire."

They marched all day again on the 28th, finally arriving at Sisters Ferry on the Savannah River. There the XIV Corps remained nearly a week, waiting for high water to subside and a pontoon bridge to be thrown across the river. The work went slowly because of "the immense amount of labor to be done in clearing out the old road of drift wood and fallen timber," Davis reported. "The frequent explosion of torpedoes, concealed under the water and drift, [also] subjected the working parties to considerable danger, and several men were killed and wounded by these infernal machines."

While the 78th and its sister regiments waited for the bridge to be completed, Batchelor went foraging on the 29th. "We get 2 pigs and some corn," he wrote. "The Rebs fire on [us] from the boats. One of the boys [was] rideing a mule, the mule was shot."

The bridge was finished February 4th and the crossing began that day and continued the next until part of the pontoon bridge was carried away in the afternoon. Repairs were made and the rest of the XIV Corps completed crossing before dark. Pearce's brigade was last to cross, leaving the 34th Illinois on the west bank to cover removal of the bridge. "Cross the river, then a cordoria [corduroy] road put up," Batchelor recorded.[30]

The corduroy road led to high ground about two miles east of the river, and there the brigade remained in camp until February 7th, when the 34th Illinois rejoined after being ferried across the river. With it came John G. Mitchell, now a brigadier general. After his leave in Ohio, Mitchell had gone to Tennessee to command a provisional brigade in the Battle of Nashville, where federal troops broke and scattered the remains of John Bell Hood's army. Now Mitchell was back to resume command of his old brigade, relieving Lieutenant Colonel Pearce, who would return to the 98th Ohio.

The weather remained wet and dismal, and to the men of the 78th Illinois it began to look as if nearly all of South Carolina was under water. The brigade broke camp February 8th and marched about seven soggy miles over "awfull roads," in Batchelor's words, camping again near Brighton's Cross Roads.[31]

Next day's march was on a better road, which allowed the brigade to cover eighteen or twenty miles. But it was "the coldest day of the season," according to 1st Lt. William C. Robinson of the 34th Illinois.

The brigade covered another seventeen miles on the 10th, with time out for foraging. "Plenty forage," Batchelor recorded. "Pork, patatoes, and mollases." South Carolina was considered the "cradle of secession" by the troops, who were determined to punish the state even more severely than they had punished Georgia. They set fire to nearly every dwelling they passed, despite an order from General Sherman that "burning of property is strictly prohibited, unless accidental; and any soldier caught attempting to fire any incombustible material will be arrested."

That order got four men from the 78th into trouble on February 11th. The regiment reached Barnwell Court House that day and "here General Baird arrested four men and tied them behind wagons," Batchelor wrote. "They was our sold[i]ers. He thought they was destroying property." The four miscreants were not identified, but Baird's action did little to stem the destruction. "This town was mainly in ashes by the time our division entered," McAdams wrote.

February 12th was a Sunday, but the troops did not get the day off. "March at 6 o'clock," Batchelor wrote. "We reach Williston." The weather was mild and the road good. Mitchell's brigade crossed the Augusta & Charleston Railroad at Williston Station and camped on the bank of the South Edisto River.[32]

Mitchell's brigade was in the rear when the division made a difficult crossing of the South Edisto the next day. "Continued our march in the direction of Columbia," McAdams wrote. "A great quantity of supplies was brought in by the foragers, and we have more now than we can care for ... The torch of destruction has been freely applied to-day, and we have at no time been out of sight of fire and smoke from burning buildings. It looks hard, and *is* hard, but then war means death and suffering, and the innocent often suffer with, as well as for, the guilty." The 78th spent the night camped near a place called Dean's Swamp.[33]

The regiment marched nineteen miles in rain and sleet on the 14th and crossed the North Edisto River at Horsey's Bridge. Foragers ran into small parties of Confederate cavalry and the 78th was "looking for a fight," Batchelor wrote, but "[the] rebels left."

Next day the regiment got its wish. "Heavy scrimishing," Batchelor recorded. "Boath sides takeing prisoners." Lieutenant Robinson of the 34th had the details: "Soon after starting this morning, we found a very large [rebel] cavalry force moving on the same road, and about dinner time, while some of them were chasing a few of our foragers, they ran against our column and fired into us, wounding two men." They also captured Pvt. John Vandivier of Company A of the 78th. The rebels wore blue overcoats and were mistaken for friendly troops, which allowed them to get close to the federal column. Despite the skirmish, the regiment marched nineteen miles that day and camped a mile southeast of Lexington Court House.[34]

On the 16th, Mitchell's brigade marched within three miles of Columbia, the capital of South Carolina, and halted for dinner. Lieutenant Robinson of the 34th Illinois rode forward with General Mitchell to a point where they "had a fine view of the city through a glass. The city was afterward occupied by the right wing, and destroyed by them." The brigade resumed marching in the afternoon and the 78th covered sixteen miles, crossed the Saluda River on a pontoon bridge, and camped for the night.[35]

Next day's march took the regiment fourteen miles to a point near Freshly's Mill on the Broad River. "Have to wait for pontoons comeing, then lay them," Batchelor wrote. At 2:00 a.m. on the 18th, the 78th crossed the river in boats to work on the bridge while the regiment's other brigades worked from the other side. After "mutch trouble with pontoons" the bridge was finished about daylight. The river at this point was about two hundred yards wide.

Once the brigade was across it "took a position across the Columbia & Greenville Railroad, stopping further shipments by that line," Lieutenant Robinson wrote. "Our foragers found a rich harvest, bringing in any amount of flour, meal and meat, besides horses and mules. They found the rebel cavalry rather plenty, and brought in some prisoners, though some of our boys were captured . . . The rebels were in the habit of killing foragers, and we are fearful about the fate of these two boys."

On February 19th the regiment marched about five miles and camped near Thompson's Post Office after destroying about half a mile of the Columbia & Greenville tracks. Next day it was Morgan's division's turn to guard the XIV Corps wagon train, an unpopular assignment rotated among the corps' three divisions, usually for four or five days at a time. Camp was made early at Ebenezer Meeting House. "A hundred mules and horses were killed this morning, they having become used up and worthless," McAdams noted.

Next day the regiment marched "12 miles to Winnisburg [Winnsborough]," Batchelor recorded. "Here we meet the XX Corps. They steal everything they can see, even to a silver bugle from the bugler." The regiment camped for the night about five miles from White Oak Station. That day Pvt. William W. Harmon of Company C, who had been left ill in Savannah, succumbed to disease. He was from Blandinsville, McDonough County.

Back on the road at dawn, Mitchell's brigade covered about twelve miles on the 22nd, Washington's Birthday. "About noon we passed an extensive plantation, with the mansion on the left," Sergeant McAdams wrote. "This was on fire as we passed out of sight."

February 23rd was another day of wet, miserable weather. The XV Corps wagon train did not get under way until nearly noon and made slow progress in mud that was quickly churned up by horses, mules, and wagons. "When night came on we had moved but five miles," McAdams wrote. "Hour after hour we plodded on—moving and halting, cursing, sulking, singing, moving and halting. Thus the whole night passed, and as morning dawned we moped into camp, wet, hungry and disheartened." Their camp was on the west bank of the Catawba River near Rocky Mount Ferry.

"Rained all night—raw meat for breakfast," Batchelor wrote in his diary on the 24th. A bridge of thirty-three canvas pontoons had been thrown across the Catawba, which was deep and swift and nearly a thousand feet wide at that point. The current was so strong the pontoon anchors kept dragging and portions of the bridge kept breaking and had to be repaired again and again. Wet weather also had softened the approaches at both ends of the bridge and the going was treacherous for wagons and teams. The division started across the river late in the morning and took all the rest of the day to finish crossing.[36]

The 78th slogged two miles beyond the river and made a muddy camp at Warrenton's Farm. "Raining all day," Batchelor wrote on the 25th. "Nothing to eat cooked." The regiment remained in camp that day. "Weather wet and roads almost impassable," Vernon reported. The regiment stayed put again the next day, but the men were put to work building corduroy roads. "My but I am sick," was Batchelor's diary entry for the day.

He was "very little better" on the 27th. The regiment continued building corduroy roads while engineers struggled to keep the bridge across the Catawba intact. "The river is so swift—the pontoon is washed away," Batchelor wrote. "They go and take many of the fifth chains off the wagons to hold the boats."

It rained all night. "Troops moving all night across river," Batchelor recorded. "Scrimish line falling back as the Rebels are following." The Confederates were pressing so closely that "our artillery fire[d] on them across the river so we can take up [the] pontoon." Once the bridge was removed, the well-soaked men of the 78th trudged about four miles over the just completed corduroy road and stumbled into another muddy camp as the last hours of February ebbed away.[37]

General Davis pushed the XIV Corps harder than ever during the first few days of March. Morgan's division took the lead as the corps extracted itself from the sticky mud near the Catawba and resumed its march on the first day of the month. It was more a struggle than a march. Though the division managed to cover eighteen or twenty miles that day, it did so mostly by felling trees and corduroying roads, and when not doing those things, the men were manhandling wagons stuck deep in the mud. They also had to cross two streams.

It was no time for the faint of heart, the infirm, or the ill. Batchelor was still among the latter. "I am to[o] sick for duty but keep on doing duty," he wrote. His duty, like that of every man, was strenuous and exhausting, and it was late in the day when the 78th and Mitchell's other regiments staggered into camp at Clyburn's Plantation.

Each regiment in Mitchell's brigade was issued a box of new shoes on March 2nd. Those who got them were fortunate; every man's shoes had suffered from repeated immersions in mud and water, and many were falling apart. But those with new shoes barely had time to pull them on before the brigade was on the road again. "We pass the safes and papers of the Camden Bank as they could not get them away," Batchelor wrote. Men from the XX Corps had found the bank president in the woods the day before, attempting to hide the bank's assets. The men relieved him of about eight hundred dollars in gold and silver, plus Confederate bonds with a face value of more than a million dollars, now virtually worthless. The division marched about twelve miles that day, again over miserable roads, and camped on Big Lynch Creek.[38]

"Rebs capture a few of our men to day," Batchelor wrote on the 3rd. "Go 20 miles. Awfull muddy hard marching." General Mitchell recorded the distance marched as twenty-three miles. "Reached Thompson's Creek and found the bridge burned," he reported. "The water was several feet deep and about 40 yards wide. By 9 o'clock the brigade pioneers and two companies of the 113th Ohio . . . had completed a fine bridge across the stream, so that the column was not delayed one hour by the destruction of the old bridge." That wasn't how Lieutenant Robinson of the 34th Illinois remembered it. He said the bridge detail worked nearly all night to finish the job.[39]

With Mitchell's brigade leading, Morgan's division crossed into North Carolina March 4th, but the route it followed, over "an old, worn-out plank road" in Robinson's words, took it back into South Carolina by day's end. They camped near the Pee Dee River, waiting for a pontoon bridge to be built, but "owing to a want of proper management and energy on the part of the officers and the lack of material to lay so long a bridge (920 feet), it was not completed until late in the evening of the 6th," General Davis reported.[40]

On the 5th, while the division waited for the bridge, the men of the 78th were astonished to see a gaunt, almost unrecognizable figure enter their camp. Batchelor celebrated the moment in his diary: "Captian Hawkins of Co. F of 78 Ills captured at Chic[k]amauga has made his escape and returned to the reg[i]ment." Capt. Henry E. Hawkins had been among those captured on picket September 22, 1863. He had been held in several different Confederate prison camps, finally escaping less than three weeks previously from a camp at Winnsborough, South Carolina. Somehow he had made his way back to the 78th, despite suffering malnutrition and chronic rheumatism.[41]

Construction of the bridge across the Pee Dee was taking a long time because there were not enough pontoons to reach across the river, so Davis ordered his troops to unload wagons, cover the empty wagon beds with canvas, and float them in the river to serve as makeshift pontoons. Sometimes it worked and sometimes it didn't. "Great trouble to lay the pontoon[s]," Batchelor wrote. "Use the wagon beds. They sink. Have to build temporary trestle." His carpenter's skills came in handy for that job.

The bridge was finally completed early in the evening of March 6th. Davis started his corps across next morning, but "owing to the frequent interruptions caused by the breaking of the bridge, it [the crossing] was not completed until 9 p.m.," he reported. Each of those "frequent interruptions" required men to turn out in freezing weather to repair the breach. By the time the whole corps was across and the bridge could be taken up, the men had "been up two nights in succession," wrote the chaplain of an Indiana regiment. "The men were falling asleep continually . . . yet the generals were hurrying, hurrying, all the time." Morgan's men had the task of taking up the bridge, and finally went into camp about a mile from the east bank of the river.[42]

The corps moved again at an early hour on the 8th, but Mitchell's brigade, in the rear, did not start until 8:00 a.m. "We marched on the Rockingham Road until noon, entering the State of North Carolina in the forenoon," McAdams recorded. "It rained nearly all day, and the men suffered much from fatigue." At noon they turned northeast on the Fayetteville Road and finally went into camp near Rockingham about 11:30 p.m., having covered twenty-three to thirty miles, depending on who was asked. This time, they were in North Carolina to stay.[43]

17

"God Bless Their Brave Souls"

MARCH 9–JUNE 21, 1865

AFTER A BRIEF NIGHT'S REST, THE BRIGADE MOVED AGAIN THE MORNING OF MARCH 9th. "The column crossed Love's Bridge over the Lumber River about midday," McAdams recorded. "A resin factory was burning on the stream above the bridge, and, as our column passed over, the surface of the water under our feet was ablaze with burning resin and turpentine, presenting a sight not easily forgotten." They marched through mud under a heavy downpour until just before noon, when the column reached a plank road and the marching became easier. They covered twenty-two or twenty-three miles that day.

At 8:00 a.m. on the 10th, Mitchell's brigade "moved five miles to the left . . . to the support of General Kilpatrick, attacked by the enemy's cavalry," Lieutenant Colonel Vernon reported. "The enemy having fallen back, we returned to the main road and camped 14 miles from Fayetteville; distance marched, 21 miles." Batchelor offered more details: "After going eight miles a bridge is burnt so we are stopped," he wrote. "General Kilpatrick was supprised this morning as the Rebs charged his camp. He finely [finally] rallied his men and took 250 Reb prisoners."[1]

Mitchell's brigade remained at the rear of the column on train guard Saturday, March 11th, but still covered about eleven miles and went into camp within a mile of Fayetteville. Baird's division had captured the place earlier that day, driving Confederate general Wade Hampton's cavalry out of the city and across the Cape Fear River. "Put up at Fayitville," Batchelor scrawled in his diary. "There is [a] great ammount of liquor captured here. Many are drunk."

A pontoon bridge was laid across the Cape Fear on Sunday, replacing a bridge burned the day before, and Morgan's division crossed and established a bridgehead on the opposite side of the river. Baird's division remained in Fayetteville, wrecking everything that might be useful to the enemy. "Enginears are at work destroying the arsnall [arsenal] and other public buildings," Batchelor wrote. The same day a federal gunboat, the *J. McB. Davidson,* came up the river from Wilmington, re-establishing communications with the outside world. Mail, supplies, and reinforcements would soon follow.

⁓

On the 13th, Mitchell's brigade moved camp to Lock's Creek, four miles from Fayetteville. There the troops rested two days and tried to wash the mud out of their clothes. They sorely needed new clothing, but none was to be had at Wilmington. However, boats loaded with coffee and sugar did come up the river, and those commodities were very welcome.[2]

The brigade started again about 8:00 a.m. on the 15th, following the XX Corps on the Raleigh Road, and marched about twelve miles under another steady fall of rain. Sounds of skirmishing by the XX Corps could be heard in the distance. Mitchell's men camped that night in the vicinity of Taylor's Hole Creek.

Reveille came early on the 16th and the brigade was on the road at daylight. "The roads are very soft and next to impassable," McAdams wrote. Late in the morning the soldiers heard sounds of a major engagement ahead, where the XX Corps had run into a pair of Confederate divisions blocking the Raleigh Road. The federals drove the rebels back through two lines of works but were stopped by a third line, and Maj. Gen. Henry Slocum asked Davis to send a brigade to assist. Davis sent Mitchell's brigade, but the road was jammed with wagons and pack mules so the troops "were compelled to march through the woods," Davis reported later. "This was very difficult to do, in timber so thick, and ground so swampy." Mitchell pressed forward anyway, and when his brigade finally reached the front it went into line left of the road, next to Ward's division of the XX Corps. Mitchell posted the 78th Illinois in front on the left with the 34th Illinois on the right. The 98th and 108th Ohio made up the second line and the 113th and 121st Ohio the third.

The brigade was ordered forward and the men in front soon came under heavy fire from rebel skirmishers. But they pushed on "and soon developed the enemy in a new line of strong earthworks, with artillery, which they opened upon us," wrote Lieutenant Robinson of the 34th. "Our lines were extended to the right and left, skirmishing briskly, but failed to flank them out of their position. It was soon found their works extended across a neck of land, with flanks resting on the Cape Fear and the Black [Rivers]. Artillery was placed in position and an old-fashioned artillery duel ensued."

The rebels still held their position when the fighting eventually died out in darkness, so preparations were made for the federal troops to storm their works the next morning. "But to our infinite relief," the enemy evacuated during the night, Robinson wrote. The fight would become known as the Battle of Averasborough, sometimes also called the Battle of Taylor's Hole or Black River. It cost the life of Cpl. Jesse E. Cundiff of Company B of the 78th, a resident of Ursa, Adams County.[3]

When they discovered the rebels had left during the night, Mitchell's skirmishers went forward, occupied their empty trenches, and busied themselves tending to the wounded. It was noon before they resumed the march, again under steady rain. They "dragged our slow length along, wading swamps and floundering through mud of unmeasurable depth," wrote McAdams. "Crossed [the] Black River by wading and walking [on] logs. We crossed other streams not deserving a name. I cannot understand what such a country was made for." After marching about ten miles, they went into camp about 9:30 p.m.[4]

❧

The XIV Corps was now on the road to Goldsborough, and the Confederates were preparing to receive them. Gen. Joseph E. Johnston had been restored to command, heading an all-star cast of Confederate generals whose corps and divisions had been nearly obliterated by four years of grinding warfare. Together they had scraped up the dregs of rebel manpower, including a few survivors of John Bell Hood's shattered army.

The federal strategy was obvious to Johnston: Sherman planned to drive through North Carolina into Virginia and link up with Grant and the Army of the Potomac, which had Robert E. Lee's Army of Northern Virginia under siege around Petersburg and Richmond. The Confederacy's only hope was to prevent this from happening. Johnston thought it was already too late; he believed the fledgling nation's military resources were exhausted. But he dutifully took on the task of trying to stop Sherman.

Johnston knew he did not have enough men to defeat Sherman's huge army in a head-to-head fight. His only chance was to catch one of Sherman's advancing wings beyond supporting distance of the other and try to deal it a crippling blow. To that end he contrived to set a trap for Sherman's left wing near the hamlet of Bentonville. His idea was to use a blocking force that would compel the federals to deploy and attack, then launch an all-out counterattack that, with luck, would crush their flank.

While Johnston and his commanders worked to assemble their meager forces, Morgan's division took the lead as the XIV Corps resumed progress toward Goldsborough early March 18th. The troops marched through alternating periods of bright sunshine and occasional rain showers. Mounted foragers in front of the column ran into rebel cavalry, which fell back after a skirmish. The foragers followed and the scenario was repeated over a distance of several miles until the foragers came under fire from a pair of rebel cannon. They halted and waited for Morgan's infantry to come up.

Morgan's first brigade, now under command of Brig. Gen. William Vandever, deployed right of the road and Mitchell's brigade deployed on the left. Skirmishers went forward, but the rebels withdrew rapidly when they saw the size of the federal force. Sherman rode up and watched the action, then told Morgan to halt and give the XX Corps, then at the rear of the column, a chance to close up. It took all afternoon for that to happen, and Morgan's men finally made camp at the junction of the Averasborough-Goldsborough and Smithfield-Clinton Roads, where they made fires of fence rails, and spent the night.[5]

March 19th was the first pleasant day the men of the XIV Corps had seen in a long time. Carlin's division took the advance, starting on the Goldsborough Road about 7:00 a.m. and passing the camp of the 34th Illinois "with colors flying and bands playing the national airs," Robinson wrote. "It was a splendid scene. All felt gay and joyous under the influence of the mild spring weather." Morgan's division started after Carlin about an hour later.

Carlin had mounted foragers in front, as usual, and they had not gone far when they ran into enemy pickets. The pickets yielded ground "with unusual stubbornness for cavalry troops," General Davis later reported. He ordered Carlin to "attack vigorously and push on, which he did until reaching [Willis] Cole's house; here the enemy opened with his artillery from behind works on the left of the road, which completely controlled it." The federals had run into Johnston's trap.

Carlin "deployed his troops and brought forward his artillery, which soon opened fire, and was sharply answered by the enemy's," Davis wrote. Brig. Gen. George P. Buell, commanding Carlin's second brigade, was deployed on the left and Brig. Gen. Harrison C. Hobart's first brigade in the center, both left of the road, which at that point ran almost in an east-west direction. Carlin's third brigade, under Lt. Col. David Miles, was posted on the right, abutting the south side of the road.

Carlin then ordered Buell to make a flanking movement to ascertain the enemy's position and strength. "This movement was in progress when I arrived at the front and gave orders for this reconnaissance to be pushed boldly," Davis said. "This was done and the enemy's works attacked. Prisoners and deserters captured by this movement gave ample information . . . that Johnston's whole force was rapidly being concentrated in our front with intention of giving battle."[6]

Never one to decline an invitation to fight, Davis sent a courier to tell Morgan's division to hurry forward as quickly as possible. The men of Mitchell's brigade, in the advance of Morgan's division, could already hear rising sounds of musketry and cannon fire ahead when the courier rode up and passed the order to each regimental commander: "General Davis instructs that you come forward as rapidly as possible without fatiguing the men."

"The men were soon on a double-quick," wrote McAdams, "and after 20 minutes rapid marching we passed General Davis and staff on the side of the road, on their horses, looking anxious and peering in the direction of the contending forces." Davis was worried about Carlin's right flank, where Miles's brigade was posted, which was "in the air" south of the Goldsborough Road. He told Morgan to deploy his men on Miles's right and extend the flank. Mitchell's men "filed right into the woods," McAdams said, "and, going some distance ahead, fronted in line." An officer in General Buell's brigade saw them go. "Morgan's men were swinging into line with all the precision of a dress parade," he wrote. "Morgan always went into battle that way."

The dress parade didn't last long. Mitchell's troops soon found themselves in a swamp. The men plunged into shallow pools of cold, stagnant water, struggled through patches of deep, clinging mud, and fought their way through thickets of underbrush and vines. They also began to exchange fire with rebel pickets hidden in the underbrush. Finally they came abreast of Miles's troops, who were building log breastworks, and Mitchell ordered "both lines of my command to shelter themselves in like manner." He deployed part of the 78th as skirmishers, keeping the remainder of the regiment in reserve. The 98th, 108th and 113th Ohio regiments were posted from left to right to form the brigade's first line, while the 34th Illinois and 121st Ohio made up the second line.

The 78th's skirmishers pushed forward through the underbrush, trading shots with rebels in their front, while the remainder of the brigade set to work building breastworks. They had only a few axes, hatchets, and spades, but they did what they could, cutting trees and brush and heaping up mounds of smelly black swamp soil. "Logs, stumps, limbs, and everything that could be found, had been piled in our front," McAdams said.[7]

Morgan's first brigade, under Vandever, meanwhile was taking position on Mitchell's right. The third brigade, now commanded by Brig. Gen. Benjamin D. Fearing, was placed in reserve behind the first two.

The 78th skirmishers kept going, pushing back Confederate pickets until they saw enemy troops in large numbers up ahead. Believing the enemy "was preparing to take the offensive," Vernon ordered the companies he had kept in reserve to deploy on his right, and opened a "heavy fire" on the rebels.

The rebels came on in two lines of battle, the 78th's skirmishers "were driven in, and when the enemy approached within easy range, the reserve opened fire which broke his first line," Vernon wrote later. "The second line advanced, and perceiving my position would soon be flanked, I fired a volley, and under the smoke of it fell back to the main line of works."

"All at once our skirmish line came bounding over our works, telling us to be ready, for they [the rebels] were coming close in their rear," McAdams wrote. "Every man of us dropped to our knees in two ranks, and made ready for the contest. The woods in our immediate front were thick with brush, and the advancing foe came within short range of our guns before we could see his line. Then we opened upon him with such a fire as carried destruction and death with it, and before which a man might not hope to advance and live. This was kept up for a long while, the men in the rear rank loading the guns and those in the front rank firing." The rapid firing continued until the rifles became too hot to handle, but it was effective; the rebel charge finally petered out, and the survivors stumbled back into the woods.

By then it was about 2:30 or 3:00 p.m. A brief lull followed the Confederate retreat, but then Mitchell's men heard a sudden great roar of musketry and cannon fire north of the road where Carlin's division was posted. "The enemy burst upon them in one of those terrific charges for which they are famous, carrying everything before them like an avalanche," wrote Robinson of the 34th Illinois. Johnston had launched his counterattack.[8]

Carlin's division crumpled before the massive rebel assault and men began streaming back toward Mitchell's position. General Davis, seeing what was happening, ordered Fearing's brigade to cross the road and establish a new line. It did so and held for perhaps a quarter of an hour before it too was swept away in the flood of Carlin's retreat and the rush of screaming Confederates that followed. Fearing retreated nearly a quarter of a mile, leaving Mitchell's brigade on its own, unsupported except for Vandever's men on the right.

Many of Carlin's men had fled across the Goldsborough Road and "commenced a rapid and disorganized retreat through my lines," Mitchell wrote later. "It was impossible to gather any definite information from them; all that was known was that the troops on their left had given way and the enemy had turned their flank." Mitchell tried to rally some of the fleeing men, ordering the commanders of the 21st Wisconsin and 79th Pennsylvania to form a line covering his left flank. He also ordered the 34th Illinois to change front and face north toward the oncoming rebels. The 98th Ohio was ordered to refuse its left, swinging back at a ninety-degree angle until it also faced north and joined the right of the 34th. "The brigade then was fortified on two sides of [a] square and in each side were posted three regiments," Mitchell wrote.

The 21st Wisconsin, 79th Pennsylvania, and another regiment, the 38th Indiana, were placed left of the 34th Illinois, extending its line, and the 121st Ohio "formed upon the left of these," in the words of its commander, Maj. Aaron B. Robinson. "All this was done in a swamp covered with water and thickly overgrown with underwood and brambles as well as larger trees, and under a continual fire, which was growing hotter every minute."

The movements reduced Mitchell's brigade from two lines to only a single line formed in a right angle, with one side facing east and the other north. The right flank,

① Mitchell's Brigade forms south of the Goldsborough Road. Pickets from the 78th Illinois advance until driven back by a large rebel force. After a heavy firefight, the rebels withdraw.

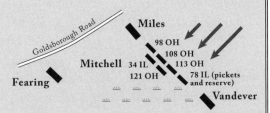

② A massive rebel attack north of the road routs Carlin's Brigade. Mitchell refuses his left flank to meet the rebel charge and rounds up the 38th Indiana, 79th Pennsylvania and 21st Wisconsin of Carlin's Brigade and places them in line with his own regiments.

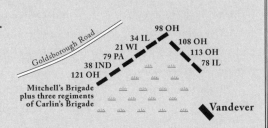

③ The Confederate attack breaks through Carlin's regiments, cutting off the 121st Ohio of Mitchell's Brigade. The 121st withdraws about 400 yards, leaving Mitchell's other regiments isolated in right-angle formation.

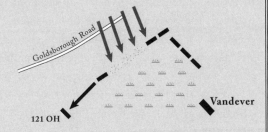

④ Rebels attack Mitchell's line from the east but are driven back again. Others charge through the gap let by Carlin's regiments and attack the 108th and 113th Ohio and 78th Illinois from behind. The defenders jump over their breastworks and fire in the opposite direction.

■ Union Units   ■ Confederate Units

BENTONVILLE – MARCH 19, 1865

facing east, included the 78th Illinois and 108th and 113th Ohio, while the left flank, facing north, consisted of the 98th Ohio, 34th Illinois, and 121st Ohio, plus the regiments that had been flagged down from Carlin's retreat.

Mitchell ordered "every axeman in the brigade" to fell trees for breastworks in front of the north-facing line, but "in less than half an hour . . . our skirmishers were driven in and a strong line of battle opened fire upon both fronts of our works." The main force of the attack hit the angle where Mitchell's line changed directions, and "the enemy's position at this point gave them an enfilading fire down both of my lines. They were driven back, however, with serious loss." The regiments of Carlin's division, however, had "inferior protection" and "were compelled to retire." Their retreat left the 121st Ohio isolated and created an opening for the rebels, who drove through it and swung around into the rear of Mitchell's brigade, which was now effectively surrounded on three sides.

Major Robinson of the 121st saw them coming, but "the similarity in appearance of their uniform to the dusty, threadbare, and faded uniform of our troops" left him in doubt as to who they were, so he "ordered the men to lay down, reserving their fire." He sent a patrol to ascertain the identity of the approaching troops, but then "I saw their colors emerging from the brush, and I ordered the men to fire, which was quickly returned. The fire was now kept up for about 15 minutes with great obstinacy, the enemy slowly advancing and we holding ground." The rebels began to close from the left "and the fire upon our right became a perfect tempest. To remain longer in that position would have been madness, and we fell back about 400 yards."[9]

While the 121st Ohio was fighting for its life, the Confederates in front of Mitchell's original east-facing line, now held by the 78th Illinois and the 108th and 113th Ohio, charged again. "Again we welcomed them by a fire more fatal, if possible, than the first," wrote McAdams of the 113th. As before, the charge was repulsed, but the bloodied rebels had scarcely faded back into the smoking woods when the Confederates who had pushed back the 121st Ohio turned up in the rear of Mitchell's three east-facing regiments. "For a moment we were confused, not knowing whether they were friends or foes, and the enemy seemed equally puzzled at the situation," McAdams reported. "Then, climbing over our works and changing front to rear, we delivered into their ranks a raking fire, which drove them back." Eventually the retreating Confederates blundered into Vandever's brigade on the right, and many were captured.

But the fighting wasn't over. "Recrossing our works, we again met the foe in our original front," McAdams said. In fact, survivors of the battle remembered having to change fronts three times that afternoon. By the last time, their ammunition was nearly exhausted and they had to search among the wounded for extra cartridges.

There was still more to come. Just at sunset the rebels mounted another attack from north of the Goldsborough Road. It was a disjointed affair, with units going astray in the failing light and thick smoke that shrouded the battlefield. One small Confederate brigade lost its way and blundered into the north-facing segment of Mitchell's brigade, where it was quickly repulsed by a heavy volley of musketry.

The day's events prompted one of Batchelor's longest-ever diary entries. "Go three miles," he wrote. "Find Rebels well fortified. Our first and second divisions are badly cut up . . . the Rebels break their lines and the rebels get to the rear of my reg[i]ment and division. Some cut their way to the rear, some jump the works and hand-to-hand fight with the Rebs. Many of the Rebs are dressed in our blue clothes which dec[e]ive us. A great many prisoners are taken. Some seems to want to come in now [that] they are whip[p]ed."[10]

The fighting gradually died out, and after the guns fell silent the survivors could hear the cries of wounded men lying in the swamps or in burning underbrush, gradually weakening and then dying out. "Near midnight, when all seemed hushed and no enemy seemed to threaten our line, we sought out the knolls and high places in the swamp through which our line ran, and, spreading our beds thereon, lay down to rest, keeping our equipments on, and our arms within reach," McAdams wrote. And there the living spent the night among the dead.

Monday came on even warmer than the day before, and the weary men of Mitchell's brigade slowly picked themselves up from the muddy terrain where they had spent the night and made ready for another day of fighting.

They did not have long to wait. General Slocum had ordered Davis to advance his skirmish line without bringing on a general engagement, and the order was passed down the chain of command to Mitchell, who sent his line forward through the swampy underbrush. It was greeted almost immediately by shots from the rebels. Skirmishing continued until about noon, when the rebel fire suddenly slackened. Mitchell's men probed and discovered the Confederates had abandoned their positions. "The lines were immediately advanced and the old rebel works occupied," wrote Lieutenant Robinson of the 34th Illinois, "but the skirmishers soon discovered a new line, full of 'Johnnies,' covering and parallel with the Goldsborough Road . . . Their artillery was so placed as to rake the works they left, which made a pretty warm place." Baird's division came up on the left, and "getting some artillery in position, soon had the rebel battery engaged, while our lines were being advanced, which was immediately done and works erected in front of and parallel with those of the enemy," Robinson reported. Skirmishing continued, but there was no general engagement.

That was just as well, because through some misunderstanding Baird withdrew his division later in the afternoon, again leaving Mitchell's brigade unsupported on its left. General Morgan ordered Lt. Col. James W. Langley, commanding Fearing's brigade—Fearing had been wounded in the previous day's fighting—to post two regiments on Mitchell's left. This was done, but there were still no friendly forces on Langley's left. The rest of the XIV Corps came up and formed to the right, but again without any connection to Mitchell. His men would spend another night in the open.

"Scrmishing all day," Batchelor recorded. "General Davis out with his men all night last night . . . My reg[i]ment lost 57 men killed, wounded and missing. Orderly J.J. Clark one of them."[11]

Although he probably had little or no time to think about it, March 20th was the effective date of promotion for Capt. Robert S. Blackburn of the 78th to the rank of major. For the first time since Maj. George Greene went down at Jonesboro, the 78th again had two field officers.

Tuesday morning Mitchell's brigade again sent skirmishers forward. They crossed the Goldsborough Road, moving north, and passed Willis Cole's farmhouse on their left. Some of Mitchell's men, probably from the 34th Illinois, entered the house and posted sharpshooters in the second-story windows, which gave them a good view of three rebel batteries. The sharpshooters "annoyed the rebels by shooting down in their works, killing many artillery horses," Lieutenant Robinson wrote. "This, it seems, they could not bear, so they advanced a line of battle, driving in our skirmishers, and burnt the house."

The heaviest action of the day took place farther to the right, but Mitchell's men remained under heavy artillery fire from the batteries whose horses they had killed. At least one shot found its mark. "Lutenant Summers, put in command of my company belongs to Co. K was killed by a solid shot," Batchelor wrote. "All my co[mpany] officers are killed, wounded or captured."

Summers, brother of Lucia Summers and the man who had shared a winter hut with Sgt. Jonathan Butler at Rossville, had been first sergeant of Company K before promotion to first lieutenant. Lieutenant Colonel Vernon had just placed him in command of Company H after its commander, Capt. George T. Beers, the last officer remaining in the company, was killed in Sunday's fighting. Summers' death came at the end of the day's fighting. "The Rebels seemed to want to give us a parting shot and fired two cannon shots before retiring, the last one taking the head off of Capt. Summers of Co. K," wrote Edward Mott Robbins. Summers would be the last man of the 78th to die on the battlefield.[12]

Beers and Summers were the only officers the 78th lost in the three days of confused fighting. Six others were killed, including Pvt. Alexander S. Talley, Company B;

Pvt. Thomas Cunningham, Company D; Pvts. James H. Gay and Sulphen Harelson, Company E; Sgt. Edward McKim, Company H, and Pvt. James E. Drury, Company K. Thirty-two men were wounded, including several who would die later of their wounds. Two were listed as missing.[13]

—◆—

The Confederate attacks had failed, and with all of Sherman's army—the XIV, XV, XVII, and XX Corps—now on the field, the rebels were hopelessly outnumbered. They had no option but retreat. "The enemy fell back last night . . . leaving his pickets, his dead and his wounded, and his hospitals in our hands," McAdams wrote. Batchelor was more succinct: "The Rebs have left," he wrote. "We move out towards Goldsborough."

"Everybody has something to say about the battle," wrote Surgeon Hostetter of the 34th Illinois—"hair-breadth escapes, bullet holes through hats and clothes are exhibited, and charges and changes of line discussed. Every soldier looks as though the fact of his being yet alive was a subject for everlasting congratulations. Joy is depicted on every face. In addition to the bright morning, the bloom of the peach trees lends beauty to the day."[14]

Leaving the battlefield, Mitchell's brigade marched about eight miles toward Goldsborough and camped near the Neuse River in a windstorm that blew sand and dirt into the men's eyes. The brigade resumed the march next morning along with the rest of the XIV Corps, crossing the Neuse on a pontoon bridge and arriving in Goldsborough around 2:00 p.m., where there was an impromptu review by Generals Sherman, Slocum, Howard, John M. Schofield, and Alfred H. Terry. On the way into town the brigade passed some of Terry's troops, just up from Wilmington. "He has two divisions of colored troops, the first our boys have seen," said Lieutenant Robinson of the 34th. "They lined the road as we marched by with bands playing and colors flying, and seemed delighted at the sight of Sherman's army, and I don't see but our boys looked upon the colored soldier as they would on any other man—good friends in a fight."

The XIV Corps went into camp two miles beyond town, having marched about twelve miles. The camp was "pleasantly situated," McAdams noted—except there were no fence rails to burn and the wind kept blowing sand in soldiers' eyes and cooking kettles. "The boys are engaged in fitting up tents, drawing clothing, and are ready to receive a few greenbacks," Robinson wrote. "The wounded are comfortably cared for in hospitals, hastily fitted up in the seminary, churches, etc., and are generally doing well. Those slightly wounded have been sent to New Bern."

The XIV Corps remained outside Goldsborough until April 10th. "The camp was staked off, and our tents were arranged in proper order," McAdams wrote. When not engaged in camp duties, the men wrote letters or went sightseeing in town.

Batchelor noted on the 25th that General Sherman had issued "complementary orders to the troops on the success of our campai[g]n and that it has been long and teadious and we will now rest a while with plenty to eat." As if in response to the general's order, Batchelor reported next day that the "carrs arrive with rations and mail. All quiet. Resting up." The cars also brought new clothing and ammunition. Cpl. James M. Beckett of Company G, wounded at Bentonville, died of his injuries on the 27th. He was a resident of Camp Point, Adams County.[15]

<hr />

Even with the long rest, a number of men remained ill, and Morgan's division sent all its sick to a hospital in New Bern. Those still healthy were finding it hard to adjust to the monotonous camp routine after the daily exertions and privations of the past few weeks. But they shared a sense of expectancy—there were rumors Richmond had fallen, that the war was nearly over, and soon they could all go home.

On Thursday, April 6th, Mitchell assembled the brigade and read a dispatch confirming Richmond had indeed fallen, news greeted "with such cheering as seldom vibrates on mortal ears," in McAdams' words. "The men are in a state of excitement bordering on insanity."

Two days later there was more good news. "General Grant is pressing General Lee very hard," Batchelor wrote. "We go to Sherman's Head Q'rs and call him out. He comes out and says a few cheering words then has the latest dispatch read of Grant's success and for us to press General Johnston and close this war."

Company I of the 78th had another reason for celebration next day. "Morris Chase and John Myers come to day," Batchelor wrote. "They was captured at Chic[k] amauga." Chase and Myers were among the twenty men of their company captured September 22, 1863. They survived more than eighteen months in rebel prison camps before making their way back to the 78th.

The 78th and the rest of Morgan's division also got orders that day to be prepared to march. After more than two weeks in camp, the men were restless and ready to move, but they decided to have a little fun first. Surgeon Hostetter of the 34th Illinois reported what happened:

"On the evening before departure, the men of the first [Vandever's] and second [Mitchell's] brigades of our division engaged in a sham battle, in which the second fell back to the vicinity of the brigade sutler's tent, and then, at a given signal, both brigades charged, and declared a dividend on sutler's stock (in trade) in less time than it takes to relate the transaction. The sutler fought bravely, but after having one of his own cheeses bursted over his head and his eyes filled with sand, yielded to the inevitable and consoled himself with such philosophy as he could command."[16]

Next day brought a quick reminder that the war wasn't over yet. Mitchell's brigade, with the 108th Ohio in front, led the XIV Corps out of camp. "Move at 6 a.m. on the Raleigh Road," Batchelor wrote in his diary. "Heavy scrimishing. Five to Seven killed and wounded in our brigade." The 108th drove the enemy for about two miles, losing one officer, until it came under artillery fire, which was quickly answered. A "spirited fire" ensued, and the 113th Ohio lost one man. About noon, four companies of the 113th took the advance and pushed the rebels back another mile until they also came under artillery fire near a place called Holt's Mill. Again the fire was answered and the Confederates eventually fell back. The brigade marched fourteen miles, most of the time under rain, and camped for the night at Moccasin Creek.

Baird's division took the lead April 11th but there was more "heavy scirmishing," Batchelor wrote. "Go to Smithfield then have to build two pontoon bridges accross Nuce [Neuse] River during the night." Baird's men had to drive rebel cavalry out of the town and the rebels burned a bridge over the Neuse, necessitating the construction of two pontoon bridges.

Wednesday, April 12th, brought the news all had been waiting for: "A dispatch comes that General Lee has surrendered to General Grant," Batchelor wrote. "Causes more cheering and rejoicing than I ever saw or heard." "The end certainly approaches," wrote McAdams of the 113th.

Morgan's division remained in Smithfield until noon, then "we march forward with bright prospects," Batchelor wrote with unusual eloquence. "Cross the pontoon and press toward Raleigh, capital of North Carolina. Scirmishing all day."

They were on the road again at 6:00 a.m. of the 13th and marched within fourteen miles of Raleigh when "the Governor comes in and surrenders the City of Raleigh," Batchelor recorded. "Men in good spirits" but there was "still a little scirimishing. We pass the best orchard to day I have seen in the South. As General [Judson] Kilpatrick enters the town a Rebel shoots at him. He orders him hung at once. We find plenty of apple jack [and] a box of liquiorish [licorice]. Many of us visit the State House where the stars and stripes were flying above the dome."

Morgan's and Baird's divisions marched a mile beyond the city and camped near the state insane asylum, while the first division, now under command of Brig. Gen. Charles Walcutt, occupied the city. "The paroled men of Lee's army passed through the lines of our troops by the hundreds, on their way to their homes," Surgeon Hostetter wrote.

The XIV Corps resumed the march on the morning of the 14th, pursuing what remained of Johnston's army. They followed a railroad about eight miles west of Raleigh until about noon when the column turned left at a "new depot" and followed "an obscure road running a snaky course through a woody district," as McAdams described it. They also met more "deserters and some parrolled men from Lee's Army," Batchelor said. After marching seventeen or eighteen miles, they camped in the woods. The troops were again living off the country and foragers returned with "plenty of bacon and meal."

Morning brought a severe thunderstorm and heavy rain, making roads difficult. Several streams also had to be waded. "Halted early," Batchelor wrote. After marching about eighteen miles, Mitchell's brigade set up a wet camp at Avon's Ferry (sometimes called Aiken's Ferry) on the Cape Fear River. Foragers brought in "flour, meal, meat and poultry," but two foragers from the 34th Illinois were shot, one fatally.[17]

Morgan's division was still at Avon's Ferry on the 18th when news came that Sherman and Johnston were scheduled to meet that day to discuss terms of surrender. "With this glorious news we can afford to endure the monotony of camp," McAdams wrote. Shortly afterward, however, the "glorious news" was totally eclipsed by a thunderclap report: "Presedent Lincoln is assas[s]inated in the theater," Batchelor wrote in his diary. The awful news was confirmed in an order from General Sherman. "Thus it seems that our enemy, despairing of meeting us in manly warfare, begin[s] to resort to the assassin's tools," Sherman wrote. "Your general does not wish to infer that this is universal, for he knows that the great mass of the Confederate army would scorn to sanction such acts, but he believes it the legitimate consequences of rebellion against rightful authority."

The announcement "creates a feeling of indescribable gloom in all our hearts, and the feeling is entertained that, if we again move against the enemy, the worst deeds of the past will be humane with what will follow," McAdams wrote. "Every heart is sad, all heads are bowed in mourning, and every mind is filled with thoughts of the awful crime."

April 19th brought hot weather and rumors of peace. It also brought orders for Morgan's division to march for Holly Springs. The division broke camp at 5:00 a.m. on the 21st and marched fifteen miles to its destination, "a small village of two stores and a very few houses," according to McAdams. The division remained at Holly Springs on the 24th, "occupied with normal camp duties." There was no word on peace negotiations. "I take the General Davis ambalance [ambulance] and go to Raleigh for mail," Batchelor jotted that day. "I see General Grant here [in Raleigh] reviewing the XVII Corps."

On Tuesday, April 25th, word came that Sherman and Johnston had concluded a surrender agreement that was disapproved by authorities in Washington. The war was back on and "Sherman will assume the offensive at noon tomorrow."

Sherman's far too generous peace terms had indeed been rejected by the federal government. That was the reason for General Grant's visit to North Carolina—he came to assure Sherman returned to the negotiating table and imposed the same terms Grant had given Lee at Appomattox. The evening of April 26th brought rumors to the troops at Holly Springs that Johnston had surrendered—again.[18]

Next day Pvt. John H. Wood of Company B of the 78th died of wounds suffered at Bentonville. He was from Marcelline, Adams County.

Late that evening "a dispatch was received confirming the rumor that Johnston had surrendered on the terms accorded to General Lee by General Grant," McAdams wrote. "Good enough. Our suspense is at an end and the war is closed." The news may have been anticlimactic to McAdams—his hopes had been raised and dashed so many times—but others were still ready to celebrate. "Last night heavy firing was heard to the northwest, and we were unable to account for it," McAdams wrote next morning, "and therefore felt some uneasiness." But it was merely "a jubilee in one of our camps, the soldiers giving vent to their joy by firing off a few hundred dollars' worth of ammunition." Batchelor heard the celebration because he was "sick all night. The first division fired off some ammunition last night so the third division rush[ed] out to help them thinking it is an attact on them," he wrote.

Morgan's division broke camp at 5:00 a.m. the following day and started for Raleigh. "I am awfull sick," Batchelor wrote. "We go four or five miles beyond town. Reports are we are going to start for home via Richmond and Washington. Each man to carry . . . a sufficient supply of rations so no man will be allowed to forage in any way and to march 15 miles a day so not to tire the men."[19]

It was supposed to be an easy march. "Gen. Sherman issued orders to the corps commanders to march slowly and easily, which would mean from 15 to 18 miles each day, according to the weather and roads," wrote Surgeon Hostetter of the 34th.

The division marched twelve miles on the 29th and camped at Morrisville. It remained in camp next day and Mitchell held brigade drill. "It is a busy day—and Sunday at that," McAdams wrote. That was also the day Sgt. Jerome J. Clark of Company I, wounded at Bentonville, died of his injuries.[20]

Reveille for Morgan's division sounded at 3:00 a.m. Monday, May 1st, and the division was on the march with the rest of the XIV Corps two hours later. It crossed the Neuse River about 2:30 p.m., marched twenty-two miles, and camped on the road. They started early again on the 2nd. "Start at daylight [and] go to Oxford [North Carolina], a nice little town," wrote Batchelor, apparently feeling better. The division tramped more than twenty miles that day and camped at a place called Fishing Creek.

Davis's corps made another 5:00 a.m. start on the 3rd. "Marched 22 miles," wrote Sergeant Enderton of the 34th Illinois. "Camped in the State of Virginia, near [the] Roanoke River . . . The troops are much fatigued. Weather hot." Batchelor thought they covered twenty-six miles that day.

It was turning out not to be an easy march after all. There were rumors Davis and the new XX Corps commander, Maj. Gen. Joseph A. Mower, had a wager over which corps could reach Richmond first, explaining why they were pushing their troops so hard.

Reveille came even earlier—at 2:00 a.m.—on the 4th, and Morgan's division "crossed the Roanoke at sunrise on a pontoon bridge," Enderton recorded. "Marched 25 miles, passing through Boydstown [Boydton]." Late in the day it began to rain.

It continued raining the next day. "Start at Sunrise, go to Lewiston, 28 miles," Batchelor wrote. "Here is a ruff [rough] made gallows to hang Negroes on." Enderton reckoned they marched twenty-six miles. "It is an outrage to march us over 16 miles a day," he wrote, "but it appears that Jeff C. Davis, our corps commander, and [the] commander of the XX Corps are running a race to Richmond. It will kill many men to march us in this manner a few days more."[21]

"Resuming the march at an early hour we reached Nottaway C. H. [Court House] at 8 a.m.," McAdams wrote on the 6th. "Here the sick and disabled were put on board the cars and sent on to Petersburg . . . Pursued our march till late in the evening, and having marched 32 miles, went into camp at Good's Bridge, on the Appomattox. The day has been warm and hundreds of the men, unable to keep up with the column, fell out, and taking their own time came into camp late in the night. Many are cursing the officers, some are cursing their sore feet. . . ."

Enderton heard a report "that six men in one division dropped dead on the road. Many of the men gave out—could not keep up. Many bleed at the nose. I never saw such outrageous marching. Weather very hot." Batchelor heard a rumor that seven men had died of sunstroke.

"Go to Manchester on the bank of the James River," Batchelor wrote on the 7th. "We are in full view of Richmond. We can see the Rebel capital with Old Glory waveing over it."

The day's march was somewhere between twenty-two and twenty-five miles. Again it took a severe toll. "Two of the Zouaves [17th New York] died last night," Enderton wrote. "Poor fellows! After fighting through the war and starting for home, [they] were actually marched to death." McAdams also was indignant. "Nearly half the men are exhausted and lie scattered along the road for miles in the rear," he said. The XIV Corps had won the race to Richmond, but it lost eight men in the process, Enderton reported. The XX Corps lost twenty.

Perhaps as a reward for its efforts, the XIV Corps was allowed to rest in camp for the next three days. Batchelor kept busy, though. "I go to [the] city to take in the mail," he wrote. "I then go see the monument of Washington [on] horse back. Very large and fine." He saw other monuments, then "went and saw Jeff Davis' fine residence, then saw Libby Prison and Castle Thunder," where so many federal troops had been held captive.

On the 11th the XIV Corps was marching through Richmond by 7:00 a.m. The 34th Illinois led the way for Mitchell's brigade. "The boys get bacon or sweet patatoes or anything to stick their bay[o]nets through and carry it on the bay[o]net as they go through the city," Batchelor related. "Many have roosters on their knapsacks, some crowing ones as they march." McAdams reported "large crowds of citizens crowded the sidewalks to witness the movements of our column." Leaving the city behind, the corps crossed the Chickahominy River and camped within three miles of Hanover Court House, having marched twenty-two miles.

The corps rested in camp until noon the next day, then resumed the march, crossed the Pamunkey River on a pontoon bridge and started across country. After marching ten miles the men stopped, leveled the furrows in a farmer's ploughed field, and made camp.[22]

During the next week, as the men of the 78th Illinois and their XIV Corps comrades marched through northern Virginia, they passed places with names now etched in their country's history, including Spotsylvania Court House and the Wilderness, where the Army of the Potomac and Army of Northern Virginia had slugged it out in some of the war's bloodiest fighting. They waded the Rapidan River at Raccoon Ford, still guarded by abandoned Confederate earthworks, and marched through a country wiped clean by the passage of armies. Where once there had been forests, there were now only stumps. Not a fence remained standing, and only a few houses were still occupied; most stood empty with broken windows and doors hanging open.

On the afternoon of May 17th, the corps marched across the fields where the First and Second Battles of Bull Run had been fought, "where many relics and evidences of the bloody contests were visible," wrote Sergeant Gaylord of the 34th Illinois. They crossed Bull Run itself and went into camp. "Washington papers were brought into camp, from which the capture of Jefferson Davis was first learned," Gaylord added.

Next day the corps marched through Fairfax Court House in a storm of rain and hail. "Several of our men who where [were] tired and strag[g]ling behind where [were] robbed of all they had," Batchelor wrote.

On May 19th the XIV Corps moved within two miles of Alexandria and went into camp at Fort Ward. Their long, arduous march was finally ended.[23]

Sherman's whole army camped around Alexandria while Maj. Gen. George Gordon Meade's Army of the Potomac camped near its namesake river across from Georgetown. Plans were afoot for both armies to march through Washington in a grand review, Meade's army first on May 23rd, and Sherman's army the following day. The next few days would be spent in camp preparing for the review. After that, Batchelor wrote, the men of the 78th "expect to be mustard [mustered] out soon." In anticipation, he sent home a box of extra clothing. He also got a pass to visit the city of Washington. "Visit the Patent office," he related. "See models of many inventions."

At the Patent Office Batchelor saw a scale, climbed aboard, and learned that he weighed 148 pounds. He had last weighed himself in Kentucky on November 23, 1862, when his weight had been 154 pounds. In the two and a half years since, he had marched more than a thousand miles, fought in four major and many minor battles, endured poor food or none at all, and suffered several bouts of illness—and lost only six pounds.

Batchelor also took in exhibits featuring George Washington's sword "and some of his private property," plus the coat worn by Andrew Jackson at the Battle of New Orleans, "and many other curiosities." He returned to camp with "a large mail in the general's ambulance."

Back in camp new uniforms were being issued for the men to wear in the Grand Review. Sherman's men wanted no part of them; they decided to march in the same stained, sun-faded, dirty, tattered uniforms they had worn on their long march across the Carolinas and Virginia.

Assistant Surgeon Githens of the 78th visited Washington on the 22nd and wrote his wife about preparations for the review. "Thousands of feet of staging are being built upon the principle streets," he said. "I had formed an opinion of how the public buildings would look but I had not come near the reality. The Capitol is grand . . . the Senate chamber is beautiful and it almost dazzles with gilding . . . The President's House is very fine also—in fact it is a much larger and more beautiful city than I had supposed."[24]

Sherman's men spent most of May 23rd in camp while the Army of the Potomac marched through the streets of Washington. Batchelor bought an album and purchased photographs of Lincoln, President Andrew Johnson, and Sherman to put in it. Late in the day the XV, XVII, and XX Corps crossed Long Bridge over the Potomac and bivouacked near the city in preparation for the next day's march, while Davis's XIV Corps closed up to the bridge in position to cross.

Next day it was their turn. It was a beautiful day and the XIV Corps crossed the Long Bridge about noon and marched into the city. It formed in platoons and, "with the long, swinging, steady step of the veteran, acquired from practice by thousands of miles of marching, over mountain and vale of a dozen states, moved through the vast throngs that lined the streets of the Capital City," wrote Gaylord of the 34th.

But it was McAdams of the 113th Ohio who had perhaps the best of many descriptions of the review: "For miles there was a surging, admiring multitude filling the sidewalks, windows, balconies, and every conceivable spot from which a view of our column could be had. There was waving of handkerchiefs by fair hands and cheers from husky voices, together with flags, mottoes, emblems and decorations, which no one can describe with tongue or pen.

"Garlands, wreaths, festoons and evergreens added beauty and brilliancy to the scene. There was little or no effort on our part to make a display. Commanding officers seemed to take pride in having the men appear in their every-day attitude of marching or fighting. The forager was on hand, with his pack mule loaded down with bacon, forage and poultry; the pioneers carried spades, hatchets and shovels, and the artillery men trundled their heavy guns . . . The tattered banners told of conflicts on distant battle fields, and the decimated ranks of the infantry companies told how nobly some had fought and how bravely they had fallen."

Robbins of the 78th added his version: "One feature . . . that seemed to please the onlookers was our pack mules that carried the officers' equipage, camp equipage, such as tent flies, headquarters clerical supplies, medical supplies, etc. These mules were led by Negroes and during the march these Negroes had picked up a good many fighting cocks, in order to have something to amuse themselves; while in camp they would have cockfights and many a Negro and soldier for that matter, would stake their money on the result of these fights, and when on the march, these cocks were fastened on top of these pack mules, and they were on this Grand Review, just as on march."[25]

When it was over they crossed back over the Potomac and returned to their camp at Fort Ward, after a day that none would ever forget.

—◦—

On May 25th the XIV Corps again crossed the Potomac, marched through Washington, and made camp north of the city. Mitchell's brigade was assigned a spot that required considerable cleaning up before a reasonably comfortable camp could be established, but once camp was ready the brigade would remain there until, one by one, its regiments were mustered out of the service and started for home.

It would be two weeks before that happened to the 78th Illinois. Meanwhile, the men had little to do but wait, and many whiled away the hours wandering about the city and taking in its sights.

Batchelor kept busy "driving General Davis' team of grays and ambulance," ferrying officers back and forth from camp to Willard's Hotel and other locations in the city, sometimes not returning until the early hours of the morning. On May 28th he celebrated his 26th birthday. Three days later he noted that the paperwork necessary for the regiment to muster out had been completed and its headquarters teams were being turned over to army quartermasters.

The weather June 2nd was "very hot," he wrote. "Being out so mutch nights I have a terrable head acke [ache]. The boys are shooting away their ammunition." That probably didn't help his headache.

That day fifty men from the 78th were transferred to the 34th Illinois. These were men recruited into the regiment after its original date of muster who had not yet served their full enlistments. The 34th had many men in the same category. All, however, would be mustered out in about another six weeks.

June 2nd also was the day the 98th Ohio became the first of Mitchell's regiments to muster out and start for home. "We have been brigaded with them for so long that they seemed like brothers to us," wrote McAdams of the 113th Ohio. What remained of the XIV Corps was reviewed the next day by its old commander, Maj. Gen. George H. Thomas, the "Rock of Chickamauga," whom the soldiers affectionately called "Old Pap."

Finally, on June 7th, the 78th was mustered out. By then many men who had been ill or wounded had recovered and returned to the regiment, as had those who survived rebel prison camps, so the number receiving discharges was 492, many more than had begun the last campaign. That was still far less than the reported 934 men who had set out from Quincy on September 20, 1862, and it included thirty-two recruits who had joined the regiment sometime later. Deaths from disease and combat, plus attrition from discharges and desertions, had erased something like 474 names from the original muster rolls.

Company H, the Dallas City contingent originally commanded by Capt. John K. Allen, was typical. Of eighty-eight men and three officers on its original muster roll, forty-seven came home, including four recruits, and one officer. Company F suffered the greatest loss. Of three officers and ninety-one men on its original muster roll, only one officer and twenty-five men returned—and one of the men was a recruit. Company D fared best, returning two officers and fifty-nine men from its original compliment of three officers and ninety men, although seven of the returning veterans were recruits.

John Batchelor had one piece of unfinished business to attend to before starting for home. "Being discharged and expecting to start home in a few days, I go and see General Jeff C. Davis to bid him good bye," he wrote. "He then asked me if I would stay with him. He said if I would he would make it worth my while." Batchelor's expertise as an ambulance driver and his all-around reliability apparently had made a deep impression on the general. But if Batchelor ever gave serious consideration to the general's offer, he made no mention of it in his diary.[26]

The veterans of the 78th Illinois boarded a train for Illinois on Thursday, June 8th. Unlike their departure for the war, when they had to ride in open cars full of coal dust, this time they would travel in reasonable comfort.

Sergeant McAdams of the 113th Ohio watched them go. "The old reliable 78th Illinois left for their homes to-day," he wrote. "God bless their brave souls; they have done honor to their state on many well-fought fields."[27]

The train pulled into Chicago on Sunday, June 11th, but if the men expected a welcome they were disappointed. "Arrive at Chicago [and] have to lay in rail road yards all day as the officer in charge of the barricks and locating of returning troops has left town on a pleasure trip," Batchelor wrote. "So we don't get into camp untill about 5 o'clock p.m." More waiting was ahead. The regiment remained at the Chicago barracks for another ten days before a paymaster finally appeared to settle their accounts and pay them off. Only then did the men board another train for the last leg of their trip home.

It was around 2:00 p.m. on June 21st when the train carrying the 78th slid to a noisy stop at the Quincy depot of the Chicago, Burlington & Quincy Railroad. "News of their coming had been received in time to prepare a reception and grand dinner," the *Quincy Daily Whig* reported. "The citizens assembled at the depot sometime before the arrival of the train, with banners flying, and a martial band, which was gotten up for the occasion, discoursing excellent music.

"On the arrival of the train, the members of the 78th were marched around on the east side of the depot and formed in line—two ranks. A general rush was made by the acquaintances and friends of the heroes, to grasp their sun burnt hands, and greet them with welcome.

"In the centre of the line of soldiers was a flag which had been presented to the regiment by the ladies of this place. As the breeze occasionally caused it to spread its proportions, it exhibited marks of hard service, as rents, slits and torn places, plainly showed the accuracy with which the traitorous hands had aimed their guns at the noble boys. The old flag was blackened with the powder of many hard fought battles, and floated yesterday as if proud of the achievements which had been performed by its owners."

Among those waiting at the station was William H. Benneson, the regiment's first colonel—the *Daily Whig* misspelled his name "Bennison"—who gave a brief speech of welcome. He was not very fondly remembered by the men, but they still gave him three cheers—though, just then, they probably would have cheered for anything. The crowd responded with three cheers for the 78th.

Then the order "right face" was given and the regiment marched in step to a fife and drum to military "Hospital No. 2." There the soldiers passed through a long receiving line while a local "glee club" sang "Tramp, Tramp, Tramp, the Boys Are Marching" with "much spirit and feeling," according to the *Whig*. The soldiers were then seated at long tables where they listened to more speeches and joined in more rounds of cheering—for Sherman, Grant, and the regiment itself—and heard a prayer from a local preacher. Only after all that were the men, who by then must have been ravenous, allowed to dig into a feast prepared by "the ladies of the Needle Pickets Society."

The *Whig* reporter described the meal as "sumptuous," and it was undoubtedly better than any hospital fare the men had known previously. There was a choice of roast beef, turkey, or chicken, along with pies, cakes, "and innumerable other delicacies," all consumed to the accompaniment of "beautiful pieces" sung "in splendid style" by the glee club.

"Great credit is due the ladies who so generously donated the viands and prepared them for the boys," the *Whig* reporter wrote. But then he added something very peculiar in the last line of his report: "The citizens did not receive the boys as we thought and hoped they would, the reception was a *little* too cool." If that was so, it probably went unnoticed by the "boys." Their bellies were full and they wanted nothing more now than to go home.[28]

And yet . . . and yet . . . they were reluctant to leave the tables where they had shared their last meal together, for they knew it was time for final parting. But when he could put it off no longer, each man stood to say farewell, with many a firm handclasp and warm embrace, to the brothers with whom he had shared so many mortal dangers and desperate privations. Then these young men who were now old soldiers left the hall alone, in pairs, or in small groups, and started for the cities, settlements, or lonely farms from which they had answered the call of duty, and the 78th Illinois Volunteer Infantry Regiment passed into history.

ACKNOWLEDGMENTS

CONSTRUCTING A HISTORY SUCH AS THIS IS A TASK BEYOND THE CAPABILITIES OF ONE person, and I have been exceedingly fortunate to have a regiment of volunteers who helped in many ways. Most I have never met in person; they are voices on the phone, e-mail correspondents, or letter writers. But one thing is certain: Without their invaluable assistance this work could never have been completed, and I owe them all a great debt.

Chief among them are Teresa Lehr, Patty Carter Cunningham, her brother, Stephen E. Cunningham, and the late William and Marvel Allen.

I first came upon Terry Lehr's name in an obscure Internet reference listing her as recipient of a small grant for a project involving the Civil War letters of Carter Van Vleck. It was the first clue I had that such letters might exist, so I tracked down Terry's e-mail address at the State University of New York at Brockport, where she was a faculty member, and sent her a query. She responded immediately and told me there was indeed a very large collection of letters written by the late colonel of the 78th. She and Prof. Philip Gerber, also then at SUNY/Brockport, had been jointly involved in a project to publish the letters in book form, but they were too lengthy to publish in entirety and the two came to an impasse over how they should be edited. Dr. Gerber, author of books on Theodore Dreiser, Willa Cather, and Robert Frost, wanted to use only letters covering the period from the Battle of Chickamauga through the siege of Atlanta, emphasizing military aspects. Terry, who admitted she had by then "fallen in love with Van Vleck," believed that "cutting the letters in half would cut out the heart of their writer." She wanted to publish letters that revealed Van Vleck as a person, especially his religious convictions, moral values, and his very close relationship with his wife, Patty. When she and Dr. Gerber were unable to resolve their differences, Terry withdrew from the project. Dr. Gerber later passed away, the letters went unpublished, and although Terry retained a copy of the transcripts, she had done nothing more with them because she felt she did not have permission from the owners of the letters—Patty Carter Cunningham and Stephen E. Cunningham, Van Vleck's descendants—to proceed on her own.

My query revived her interest in the letters, however, and eventually the two of us decided to approach the Cunninghams for permission to publish them. We drafted an agreement that would give Terry permission to publish an edited version of the letters along the lines she had originally proposed, allow me to publish excerpts bearing on the history of the 78th Illinois, and simultaneously define and protect the ownership rights and interests of the Cunninghams. Patty and Stephen reviewed the draft agreement and very graciously agreed to the terms we proposed, the agreement was signed by all parties, and the rest, as they say, is history. Terry's work, *Emerging Leader: The Civil War Letters of Carter Van Vleck to His Wife, Patty, 1862-1864*, will be an admirable companion volume to this one.

Bill Allen was the adopted great-grandson of Capt. John Knox Allen, original commander of Company H of the 78th. Bill and his wife, Marvel, edited and published the diary of Sgt. James M. McNeill of Company H as a small spiral-bound book titled *Call Them Men Then.* When I became aware of the book, I tracked down the Allens at their home in Wisconsin to ask how I might obtain a copy. Their incredibly generous response was to publish a new edition and waive the copyright so that I might use their work in a history of the 78th Illinois.

That, however, was only the beginning of Bill Allen's interest in this project. He voluntarily spent many hours searching the Internet for information or sources I might have missed, and was especially diligent in searching for period photographs. Many of the photos in this volume are the result of his efforts. Late in 2010, as his health declined (he was on his third pacemaker by then), he arranged for his wife, Marvel, to send me all the files he had compiled on the 78th, which provided more useful information. He passed away December 17, 2010, and his wife followed ten months later. I deeply regret they did not live to see publication of this history to which they contributed so much.

Many others helped in significant ways. I am especially grateful to Charles R. Lemons of the Rolling Fork Historical Preservation Society, New Haven, Kentucky, for pinpointing locations of the stockades built by various companies of the 78th. Lemons's fine text, *A Very Good Camping Place: New Haven and the Civil War, 1861–1865,* based in part on the McNeill diaries, is accessible on the Internet at www.rfhpa .or/history.pdf and is very much worth reading.

Others who helped: Ray Oakes of Jonesboro, Georgia, took time away from his business to show me around the area, especially where the 78th made its attack; Jeff Hancks of Western Illinois University, Macomb, Illinois, assisted with the McNeill diary and provided copies of the Benjamin Gill letters; my son, Randy Raymond of Orting, Washington, tracked down a copy of Edward Mott Robbins's memoir, *Civil War Experiences;* my friend Marian Alexander, recently retired head of special collections at the Wilson Library at Western Washington University, Bellingham, Washington, first called my attention to the book by Bill and Marvel Allen and made helpful suggestions for research.

Alyson Barrett-Ryan and Peiling Andrea Li of the Gilder Lehrman Institute of American History, New York, answered my request for copies of the James K. Magie letters; Rita W. Harlan of the Putnam County Public Library, Greencastle, Indiana, provided a copy of Charles Vilasco Chandler's diary; Cheryl Schnirring of the Abraham Lincoln Presidential Library, Springfield, Illinois, copied the John Batchelor diary for me; and John Hoffman of the University of Illinois Library, Champaign-Urbana, provided a copy of the James Withrow diary.

Rod Clare of Durham, North Carolina, assisted with the Broaddus letters at Duke University; Trevor K. Plante of the Textual Archives Services Division, National Archives and Records Administration, Washington, D.C., checked court-martial records; Kathy Nichols of Archives and Special Collections, Malpass Library, Western Illinois University, assisted generously and patiently with photo research and permissions; and Edward C. Fields, supervisor, Information Services, Department of Special Collections, Davidson Library, University of California at Santa Barbara, provided copies of the William Githens letters.

Jason Amico, volunteer researcher, US Army Military History Institute, Carlisle, Pennsylvania, helped with photo research, as did Mary Michals and Roberta Fairburn of the Abraham Lincoln Presidential Library, Springfield, Illinois. Gilbert Gonzalez and Nan Card of the Rutherford B. Hayes Presidential Center, Fremont, Ohio, provided the image of Gen. John Grant Mitchell.

Composing a narrative of events that took place 150 years ago is difficult enough, but it becomes doubly difficult when you live more than 2,500 miles away from the scene of the action, as I do. Without the marvelous resources now available on the Internet, it would simply not have been possible to complete this work.

The most useful Internet source was the Newspaper Archive of the Quincy, Illinois, Public Library, www.quincylibrary.org/library, which has text-searchable online copies of newspapers dating back to the 1850s. These provided letters, casualty lists, and a great deal more important and useful information. Quincy's citizens should be extremely proud of this remarkable and valuable historic resource.

The Illinois Civil War Muster and Descriptive Rolls database, www.cyberdrive illinois.com/departments/, part of the Illinois State Archives, has rosters of all Illinois Civil War units, searchable by regiment, company, or by individual name. The Illinois GenWeb Project also provides rosters, although its roster of the 78th Regiment varies somewhat from the version in the state archives. I have used both sources as references along with contemporary printed copies of the roster, but the version that appears here has been edited extensively to include information uncovered in my research.

I have a CD-ROM copy of the *Official Records of the War of the Rebellion*, but I much preferred to use the online version available from the eHistory website of Ohio State University because of its more powerful and versatile search engine. The easiest way to access this website is to use Google or another search engine and enter the words "Official Records of the War of the Rebellion."

Many other Civil War websites provide useful content, but as with all Internet sites, it is always advisable to independently verify the accuracy of their information.

—◆—

My very dear wife Joan has often said that when I am working on a book it's almost as if I had gone away, and I suppose it must seem that way. This is the tenth time I have made such a literary journey, and the longest yet, but now I am home again—and Joan, as always, was waiting. She has been my faithful companion, biggest fan, and the guiding influence of my life for nearly fifty years, and although my business is words, I can think of none that sufficiently express the depths of my appreciation or affection for her. Neither this book nor any of my others ever would have made it into print without her.

And finally: To Jonathan Butler, first sergeant of Company K, 78th Illinois Volunteer Infantry Regiment, and his wife, Clara Jane West Butler, I literally owe everything, including my very existence. They were my great-grandparents.

Notes

Abbreviations

B&G—*Blue & Gray Magazine*

HG—*Hallowed Ground Magazine*

JDIB— "Jefferson Davis in Blue," Louisiana State University Press, Baton Rouge, 2002

O.R.—The War of the Rebellion: A Compilation of the Official Records of the Union and Confederate Armies. Washington, DC, US Government Printing Office, 128 volumes, 1880–1901

QDH—*Quincy Daily Herald*

QDJ—*Quincy Daily Journal*

QDW—*Quincy Daily Whig*

QWR—*Quincy Whig & Republican*

Chapter 1

1. McNeill, James M. (William J. Allen and Marvel A. Allen, editors): "Call Them Men, Then, 78th Illinois Volunteer Company 'H'." River Falls, WI, third printing, 2009, p. 3. McNeill's service record identifies his occupation as "lawyer," but according to William and Marvel Allen, editors of his diary, he was "a skilled sawyer, a person who saws down trees or operates a saw in a lumber mill." Since Civil War records were kept in handwriting, it's easy to see how a handwritten capital letter "S" might have been mistaken for an "L."

2. Robbins, Dr. Edward M.: "Civil War Experiences, 1862–1865." Carthage, IL, November 1919, p. 1. McNeill's diary says the voyage aboard the *Jennie Whipple* was on August 10th while Robbins says it was June 15th. Independent evidence supports McNeill, and Robbins's memoir, written more than fifty years after the war, shows other evidence of confusion over dates.

3. QWR, October 20, 1860, p. 3.

4. Collins, William H., and Perry, Cicero F.: "Past and Present of the City of Quincy and Adams County, Illinois." Chicago, S. J. Clarke Publishing Co., 1905, p. 291.

5. QDJ, November 10, 1917, p. 11. Lucia Summers was eighty-one years old when her written reminiscences of the Civil War were published in the *Daily Journal*. They included excerpts from letters written by her brother, William E. Summers, originally first sergeant and later first lieutenant of Company K, 78th Illinois Volunteers.

6. Collins, pp. 291, 293.

7. Ibid., p. 294.

8. QDJ, November 10, 1917, p. 11.

9. QDW, July 17, 1862, p. 3.

10. McNeill, p. 2; QDW, July 21, 1862, p. 3, August 11, 1862, p. 3, September 10, 1862, p. 1, September 20, 1862, p. 3; QDH, August 12, 1862, p. 3.

11. Butler's service record says he was twenty-five years old at the time of his enlistment, but census reports show he was born in May 1828, which would have made him twenty-four years old in August 1862.

12. QWR, August 16, 1862, p. 3. Benneson's name appears as Bennison in the Illinois State Archives as well as in the Report of the Adjutant General of the State of Illinois, Victor Hicken's Illinois in the Civil War, the diaries and letters of some soldiers, and in other publications. It is spelled Benneson in the Official Records, in The Past and Present of the City of Quincy and Adams County, Illinois, and other publications. The discrepancies may be another example of confusion in handwritten records, where the letters "e" and "i" could easily be confused. Which spelling is correct? Those who knew him nearly always spelled his name Benneson, including the soldiers in his regiment once they had known him for a while. More significantly, Benneson himself used that spelling in advertisements for his legal practice. It seems safe to assume the man knew how to spell his own name, so Benneson is the spelling used throughout this volume.

13. Collins, p. 273; QWR, August 23, 1862, p. 3.

14. "Army Record of John Batchelor, Co. I, 78th Ills. Vol. Infantry, 2nd Brig., 2nd Div., 14th Corps, Beginning August 1862, Rewritten 1910." Abraham Lincoln Presidential Library and Museum, Springfield, IL, p. 1. Batchelor's diary is the only one known to span the full length of service of the 78th Illinois Volunteer Infantry. The original diary suffered water damage, so Batchelor made a handwritten copy in 1910. That copy now resides at the Lincoln Presidential Library.

15. McNeill, pp. 3–4.

16. Robbins, p. 12.

17. McNeill, p. 3.

18. Virdin, Donald Odell, "The Civil War Correspondence of Judge Thomas Goldsborough Odell." Heritage Books, Inc., 1992, p. 2.

19. With parental consent, boys under eighteen years of age were allowed to enlist in infantry regiments as musicians, usually as drummers. The records of Company I list another fourteen-year-old, Charles W. Bennett, whose hometown was Plymouth, Hancock County. Could this have been the same individual as the Charles N. Bennett listed on the muster roll of Company D? It seems unlikely there would have been two fourteen-year-old Charles Bennetts from the same county in the same regiment; not only that, but a handwritten middle initial "N" could easily have been mistaken for a "W," or vice versa. So it seems possible, given the casual nature of Civil War record-keeping, that the same young man was listed on the muster rolls of two different companies.

20. Landon's reminiscences were published in the QDJ, February 7, 1889, p. 3.

21. William L. Broaddus to wife, August 29, 1862. Letters of Major William L. Broaddus, 78th Illinois Volunteers. David M. Rubenstein Rare Book & Manuscript Library, Duke University, Durham, NC.

22. QDH, November 24, 1867, p. 4. After the war, Dills sued Benneson for compensation or return of the horse. The case was dismissed on the eve of trial and Benneson apparently retained ownership of the horse.

23. Virdin (Odell), pp 4–5.

24. Virdin(Odell), pp. 2–5; McNeill, p. 4.

25. Letter of Carter Van Vleck to wife, September 9, 1862. Letters of Carter Van Vleck, edited by Philip Gerber and Teresa Lehr, 2001; Almond, NY.

26. Virdin(Odell), p. 5; QDJ, November 10, 1917, p. 11.

27. McNeill, p. 4; Batchelor, p. 2; excerpts from the letters of Pvt. Cornelius Pierce published in QDW, December 19, 1909, p. 16; Landon, QDJ, February 7, 1889, p. 3. McNeill's diary, Odell's correspondence, and a letter written by Pvt. Lemuel B. Roseberry of Company G all say the regiment was issued "rifled muskets." Batchelor may have thought the weapons were relics from the Mexican War, hence his reference to them as "Mexican guns." He may have been right; the standard infantry weapon for US soldiers in the Mexican War was the .69-caliber 1842 smoothbore musket. During the early years of the American Civil War, many regiments were issued these weapons, which usually fired "buck and ball"—a large ball and three pieces of buckshot. However, the barrels of some of these old weapons were re-bored and rifled so they were able to fire a .69-caliber Minie bullet, which greatly increased their effective range and accuracy, and the 78th Illinois apparently received some of these rifled muskets. After the skirmish at New Haven, Kentucky, members of the regiment discovered their bullets had penetrated trees and fence rails at distances of as much as 800 yards, and only rifled muskets could shoot that far; the range of smoothbores was much shorter. However, except for the vague reference by McNeill, Odell, and Roseberry to "rifles," there is nothing in any of the 78th's known diaries and letters that describes them any further, so the exact type and origin of the weapons may never be known.
28. Van Vleck to wife, September 18, 1862; QDH, September 20, 1862, page 2.

Chapter 2

1. Batchelor, p. 3.
2. Landon, QDJ, February 7, 1889, p. 3.
3. QWR, October 11, 1862, p. 2.
4. McNeill, p. 5; Batchelor, p. 4.
5. Virdin (Odell), p. 6; Batchelor, p. 4; Broaddus to wife, November 6, 1862.
6. McNeill, pp. 5–7; Landon, QDJ, February 7, 1889, p. 3.
7. Van Vleck to wife, September 23, 1862.
8. McNeill, p. 6; Van Vleck to wife, September 28, 1862.
9. McNeill, pp. 7–8.
10. Robbins, p. 12.
11. Broaddus to wife, September 28, 1862.
12. By coincidence, Lt. Col. Van Vleck, Broaddus's superior officer, also had no teeth. But his letters make no mention of difficulty with food, and he chewed tobacco, so he evidently had a working set of dentures.
13. JDIB, pp. 102–103, 105–109, 111–115, 119–120; Broaddus to wife, September 30, 1862.
14. QDJ, February 7, 1889, p. 3; Van Vleck to wife, October 1, 1862.
15. Broaddus to wife, October 2, 1862; McNeill, p. 9; QDW, December 19, 1909, p. 16.
16. McNeill, pp. 9–10.
17. QDW, December 19, 1909, p. 16.
18. Virdin (Odell), p. 7; Van Vleck to wife, October 7, 1862.
19. Van Vleck to wife, October 19, 1862.
20. McNeill, pp. 12–13.
21. Broaddus to wife, October 8, 12, 1862.
22. McNeill, pp. 13–15; Batchelor, p. 7.
23. McNeill, pp. 15–17; Broaddus to wife, October 17, 1862.
24. McNeill, pp 15–17; Broaddus to wife, October 21, 1862.

25. JDIB, pp. 120–121.
26. Broaddus to wife, October 25, 1862; Lemons, Charles R.: "A Very Good Camping Place: New Haven and the Civil War, 1861–1865," pp. 20–21.
27. McNeill, pp. 17–19; O.R., Series I, Vol. 16, Part 2, pp. 659–661.
28. Van Vleck to wife, October 24, 27, 1862.

Chapter 3

1. McNeill, p. 19; Broaddus to wife, October 29, 1862.
2. Virdin (Odell), p. 13.
3. McNeill, pp. 20–22; Broaddus to wife, November 4, 1862.
4. Van Vleck to wife, November 4, 5, 1862.
5. McNeill, pp. 21–23; Van Vleck to wife, November 5, 1862.
6. Broaddus to wife, November 6, 1862; McNeill, p. 22.
7. Van Vleck to wife, November 8, 1862; QDW, December 19, 1909, p. 16.
8. Van Vleck to wife, November 9, 1862; QWR, December 17, 1862.
9. Van Vleck to wife, November 10, 1862.
10. Van Vleck to wife, November 14, 16, 1862.
11. McNeill, pp. 24–25; Batchelor, p. 10; Virdin (Odell), pp. 10–13.
12. McNeill, pp. 25, 27; Batchelor, p. 10.
13. Van Vleck to wife, November 23, 1862; McNeill, p. 27.
14. Van Vleck to wife, November 25, 1862; Broaddus to wife, misdated November 20, 1862, possibly written about November 30.
15. Broaddus to wife, November 27, 1862.
16. Pvt. Benjamin Gill to wife, November 1862. Letters of Benjamin Gill, Company I, 78th Illinois Volunteers, Civil War Collection, Western Illinois University Libraries, Macomb, IL.
17. QDW, December 19, 1909; Van Vleck to wife, November 28, 1862.
18. Van Vleck to wife, November 30, 1862; McNeill, p. 28.
19. Van Vleck to wife, December 7, 9, 1862.
20. Virdin (Odell), p. 17; Van Vleck to wife, December 9, 1862.
21. Broaddus to wife, December 11, 1862; Van Vleck to wife, December 14, 1862. The use of terms such as "nigger" and "darkey" are quite properly now considered objectionable, and it is only with great reluctance that the author has included them in this text. But such terms were common in the vernacular of those who fought the Civil War—even those, such as Carter Van Vleck, who were sympathetic to the plight of slaves—and a historian's responsibility is to report their words accurately, even at the risk of offending some readers.
22. QWR, December 17, 1862; Van Vleck to wife, December 18, 1862.
23. Broaddus to wife, December 18, 1862.
24. Van Vleck to wife, December 21, 1862.
25. QDW, December 19, 1909, p. 16; QWR, January 17, 1863, p. 4.
26. Van Vleck to wife, December 25, 1862; "The Diaries of Charles Vilasco Chandler, 1861–1863," Transcribed by Ann Robinson Chandler, 1989. Putnam County Public Library, Greencastle, Indiana, p. 32.
27. Catton, Bruce: "Never Call Retreat," pp. 2–3; Virdin (Odell), p. 26.
28. O.R., Series 1, Vol. 20, Part 1, p. 153.
29. For much of the Civil War, the Union and the Confederacy followed a practice of exchanging prisoners based on a system the United States and Britain had used in the

War of 1812. Under the system, a captured soldier could give his parole and would then be allowed safe passage back to his own lines, but would be disqualified from further military service until he was officially exchanged for a prisoner held by the other side. Enlisted men and lower-ranking officers were exchanged on a one-for-one basis with men of equal rank. Senior officers were exchanged for greater numbers if no senior officer of equivalent rank was available. For example, a colonel was judged to be worth fifteen privates if no colonels were held by the other side.

30. O.R., Series 1, Vol. 20, Part 1, p. 153.
31. Chandler, p. 32.

Chapter 4

1. Letter of Pvt. James K. Magie to wife, January 1, 1863. The Gilder Lehrman Collection (accession number GLC05421), courtesy of the Gilder Lehrman Institute of American History, New York, NY.
2. McNeill, pp. 31–36; Virdin (Odell), p. 28; Lemons, pp. 26–30; O.R., Series 1, Vol. 20, Part 1, p. 151.
3. QDW, December 19, 1909, p. 16; Virdin (Odell), pp. 28–29.
4. McNeill, pp. 35–36.
5. Ibid., p. 36; Magie to wife, January 4, 1863.
6. Virdin (Odell), p. 31.
7. Magie to wife, January 8, 1863.
8. Broaddus to wife, January 10, 14, 15, 1863.
9. Robbins, pp. 1–2.
10. Odell, p. 35; McNeill, p. 40.
11. Broaddus to wife, January 16, 1863; QWR, January 17, 1863, p. 3.
12. Batchelor, p. 17; Virdin (Odell), p. 37; Broaddus to wife, January 20, 1863.
13. O.R., Series 1, Vol. 20, Part 2, pp. 342–343; Tucker, Glenn: "Chickamauga: Bloody Battle in the West," Morningside Bookshop, Dayton, OH, 1961, p. 341; Cozzens, Peter: "This Terrible Sound: The Battle of Chickamauga," University of Illinois Press, Urbana and Chicago, 1992, p. 440.
14. Magie to wife, January 21, 1863; Broaddus to wife, January 22, 1863.
15. QWR, February 7, 1863, p. 2.
16. McNeill, p. 40; Virdin (Odell), p. 40; Broaddus to wife, January 24, 1863.
17. Chandler, p. 33; McNeill, p. 41; Magie to wife, January 27, 1863; Virdin (Odell), p. 40.
18. Chandler, p. 33; Magie to wife, January 27, 1863; McNeill, p. 42; Batchelor, p. 17.
19. Chandler, p. 34; Van Vleck to wife, January 31, 1863; Magie to wife, February 2, 1863.
20. Military arrest did not necessarily mean confinement of the arrested officer, but it did mean that he was suspended from duty pending resolution of the charges against him.
21. Van Vleck to wife, January 31, 1863.
22. Broaddus to wife, February 1, 1863; Chandler, pp. 34–35; McNeill, pp. 42–43.
23. McNeill, pp. 43–45. The 83rd Illinois captain killed at Dover was actually Philo C. Reed, commander of Company A, a resident of Monmouth, Warren County, Illinois.
24. Broaddus to wife, February 6, 1863; Magie to wife, February 5, 1863; Virdin (Odell), p. 43; Chandler, p. 35.
25. McNeill, p. 45; Van Vleck to wife, undated but probably written February 5 or 6, 1863; Chandler, p. 36.

Chapter 5

1. McNeill, p. 46; Chandler, p. 36.
2. McNeill, p. 46; Chandler, p. 36; Van Vleck to wife, February 11, 1863.
3. Broaddus to wife, February 10, 1863; McNeill, pp. 46–47.
4. "Archaeological Investigations on Roper's Knob: A Fortified Civil War Site in Williamson County, Tennessee," by Benjamin C. Nance. Tennessee Archaeology, Vol. 2, Fall 2006, No. 2.
5. Van Vleck to wife, February 13, 1865; Magie to wife, February 17, 1863.
6. Van Vleck to wife, February 19, 1863.
7. Chandler, p. 37; Magie to wife, February 20, 22, 1863.
8. Broaddus to wife, February 25, 1863; Magie to wife, February 25, 1863.
9. Van Vleck to wife, February 27, 1863; McNeill, p. 50; Magie to wife, March 1, 1863; Virdin (Odell), p. 45.
10. Batchelor, p. 20; McNeill, p. 51; Magie to wife, March 2, 1863.
11. Officers were able to resign their commissions, but non-commissioned officers and privates were obligated for their full three-year term of service unless discharged.
12. Batchelor, p. 20; Broaddus to wife, March 4, 1863; Van Vleck to wife, March 4, 1863.
13. O.R., Series 1, Vol. 23, Part 1, pp. 85–89.
14. McNeill, pp. 51–52.
15. Broaddus to wife, March 6, 1863.
16. McNeill, p. 52; Virdin (Odell), p. 47; Van Vleck to wife, March 8, 1863; Broaddus to wife, March 9, 1863.
17. McNeill, pp. 52–53.
18. Van Vleck to wife, March 15, 1863; Batchelor, p. 22; McNeill, p. 54.
19. Van Vleck to wife, March 20, 1863.
20. McNeill, pp. 54–55.
21. Batchelor, p. 22; Broaddus to wife, March 20, 1863; Magie to wife, March 20, 1863.
22. Broaddus to Reuben Broaddus, March 22, 1863; Van Vleck to wife, March 22, 1863; Magie to wife, March 22, 1863; Virdin (Odell), pp. 50–51.
23. Magie to wife, March 24, 1863.
24. Van Vleck to wife, March 28, 1863; Magie to wife, March 30, 1863.

Chapter 6

1. Van Vleck to wife, April 1, 3, 1863.
2. Broaddus to wife, April 1, 1863.
3. Virdin (Odell) pp. 52–53; Broaddus to wife, April 3, 1863.
4. Van Vleck to wife, April 4, 1863; Gill to wife, April 5, 1863.
5. Broaddus to wife, April 6, 1863. The Carter family described by Broaddus was almost certainly the one whose home and outbuildings were prominent landmarks in the Battle of Franklin on November 30, 1864.
6. Magie to wife, April 7, 1863.
7. Magie to wife, April 11, 1863.
8. Van Vleck to wife, April 10, 1863.
9. Magie to wife, April 13, 14, 1863; Broaddus to wife, April 15, 1863.
10. Batchelor, p. 24.
11. Broaddus to wife, April 17, 18, 1863; Robbins, p. 12; Odell, pp. 56–57.

12. Van Vleck to wife, April 18, 1863; Broaddus to wife, April 19, 1863; Magie to wife, April 19, 1863.
13. Batchelor, p. 24; Van Vleck to wife, April 22, 1863.
14. Magie to wife, April 23, 1863; Broaddus to wife, April 23, 1863.
15. Magie to wife, April 25, 1863; Van Vleck to wife, April 26, 1863.
16. Broaddus to wife, April 28, 1863; Virdin (Odell), p. 59.
17. Gill to wife, April 1863. This was the last of his letters to be preserved.
18. Magie to wife, April 28, 1863; QWD, December 19, 1909, p. 16. The Magie letter of April 28 is the last in the collection at the Gilder Lehrman Institute of American History except for one from his wife, Mary, dated July 1, 1863, and part of another letter from Magie to an unknown recipient. The first page and date of the latter are missing but it was written sometime in late June or early July 1864 (the Gilder Lehrman Institute has it misdated as having been written in 1863). The two obviously continued their correspondence after April 18, 1863, but what became of their other letters after that date is unknown.
19. Batchelor, pp. 25–26; Broaddus to wife, May 1, 3, 1863.
20. Virdin (Odell), p. 61.
21. Broaddus to wife, May 9, 1863; Van Vleck to wife, May 10, 1863.
22. Broaddus to wife, May 12, 1863; Van Vleck to wife, May 13, 1863.
23. Batchelor, p. 26; Broaddus to wife, May 14, 1863, postscript May 15, 1863.
24. Chandler, p. 48; Broaddus to wife, May 17, 1863.
25. Van Vleck to wife, May 17, 1863; Chandler, p. 39.
26. Chandler, p. 40; Van Vleck to wife, May 24, 1863.
27. Chandler, p. 40; Virdin (Odell), pp. 66–67.
28. Chandler, p. 41; Broaddus to wife, May 28, 31, 1863.
29. Van Vleck to wife, May 31, 1863.

Chapter 7
1. Chandler, p. 41; Broaddus to wife, June 3, 1863.
2. Van Vleck to wife, June 4, 1863. In 2006 archaeologists excavated Roper's Knob and uncovered evidence of many of the features described by Van Vleck. The results of the archaeological investigation are reported in detail by Benjamin C. Nance in Tennessee Archaeology, Vol. 2, Fall 2006, No. 2, pp. 83–106.
3. O.R., Series 1, Vol. 23, Part 2, pp. 388–389.
4. Chandler, p. 42.
5. O.R., Series 1, Vol. 23, Part 2, p. 388; Chandler, p. 42. In a letter dated June 2, Van Vleck told his wife the move back to the fort occurred June 2, but Batchelor and Chandler both recorded the movement as taking place on the 7th. This and other evidence indicates that Van Vleck's letters dated June 1 and 2 were almost certainly written instead on June 7 and 8, respectively.
6. Chandler, p. 42; Van Vleck to wife, June 10, 1863. It was said that Orton had proposed to General Lee's daughter Agnes, but Lee did not approve of the match because Orton had a reputation for recklessness.
7. Broaddus to wife, June 9, 12, 1863; James K. Magie: "The Execution of Williams and Peters," Harper's Weekly, Vol. 7, No. 340, July 4, 1863.
8. Chandler, p. 43; Van Vleck to wife, June 10, 1863.
9. Chandler, p. 43.
10. Chandler, p. 43; Broaddus to wife, June 15, 1863.

11. Van Vleck to wife, June 16, 1863; Haas, John E., and Longacre, Glenn, editors: "To Battle for God and the Right, The Civil War Letterbooks of Emerson Opdycke." University of Illinois Press, Urbana and Chicago, 2008, p. 78.
12. Chandler, p. 43; Virdin (Odell), pp. 72–73.
13. Broaddus to wife, June 18, 1863.
14. O.R., Series I, Vol. XVI, Part I, pp. 1066–1068.
15. Van Vleck to wife, June 19, 1863.
16. Chandler, p. 44; Broaddus to wife, June 20, 21, 1863. Private James S. Carroll of Industry, McDonough County, a member of Company I, would be discharged July 7, 1864, for reasons of disability.
17. Van Vleck to wife, June 21, 1863; Broaddus to wife, June 22, 1863. Fort Granger in Franklin may be the only place where enduring marks left by the 78th Illinois can still be seen. The sprawling twelve-acre earthwork was purchased by the city of Franklin in the 1970s and visitors may inspect the eroding ramparts of the fort, which were in no small part constructed by shovel-wielding members of the 78th. The regiment also contributed to the works on nearby Roper's Knob, which are not as well preserved, but it is still possible to climb to the top of the knob where Major Broaddus once gazed out at the surrounding countryside and pronounced it the best he had ever seen.
18. Broaddus to wife, June 23, 1863; Van Vleck to wife, June 23, 1863.
19. Van Vleck to wife, June 26, 27, 1863; Batchelor, p. 30.
20. Ibid., p. 30; Chandler, p. 45; Virdin (Odell), pp. 77–78.
21. Broaddus to wife, June 28, 29, 1863; Chandler, p. 45.
22. Ibid., p. 45. General Granger had issued a strict order against foraging or pilfering from private citizens.

Chapter 8

1. Batchelor, p. 31; Chandler, p. 46.
2. Mary Magie to James K. Magie, July 1, 1863. Mary spelled their son's name Eddie, while Magie spelled it Eddy.
3. Broaddus to wife, July 3, 1863; Van Vleck to wife, July 4, 6, 1863; Chandler, p. 46.
4. Ibid., p. 46; Batchelor, p. 32; Broaddus to wife, July 6, 1863.
5. Virdin (Odell), p. 79; Van Vleck to wife, July 6, 1863. The stolen horse may have been the one given to Benneson in Quincy by Mr. Dills, the man who hoped to become the 78th's sutler but later changed his mind.
6. Batchelor, p. 32; Broaddus to son, Reuben, July 7, 1863.
7. Batchelor, p. 32; Chandler, pp. 46–47; Broaddus to wife, July 10, 1863.
8. Van Vleck to wife, July 10, 1863.
9. Chandler, p. 47; Broaddus to wife, July 12, 1863.
10. Broaddus to wife, postscript to letter of July 12, 1863; Batchelor, p. 32.
11. Virdin (Odell), pp. 80–81; Broaddus to wife, July 16, 1863.
12. Van Vleck to wife, July 16, 19, 1863.
13. Broaddus to wife, July 20, 1863; QDW, December 19, 1909, p. 16.
14. Van Vleck to wife, July 25, 1863; Chandler, p. 48; Broaddus to wife, July 22, 1863. "Copperheads" was a derisive term used by Unionists to describe opponents of the war. It was derived from the name of the poisonous snake.
15. Van Vleck to wife, July 26, 1863; Virdin (Odell), pp. 82, 84–85.

16. Van Vleck to wife, July 30, 1863; Chandler, p. 50.
17. Ibid., p. 50; Broaddus to wife, August 2, 1863.
18. QDW, December 19, 1909, p. 16; Van Vleck to wife, August 3, 1863.
19. Virdin (Odell), pp. 86–87; Chandler, p. 50.
20. Broaddus to wife, August 5, 1863; Van Vleck to wife, August 5, 1863.
21. Chandler, p. 51; Broaddus to wife, postscript to letter of August 5, 1863.
22. Chandler, p. 51.
23. Van Vleck to wife, August 8, 1863; Chandler, p. 51; Broaddus to wife, postscript to letter of August 7, 1863.
24. Broaddus to wife, August 9, 11, 1863; Virdin (Odell), p. 89; Van Vleck to wife, August 10, 1863.
25. QDW, December 19, 1909, p. 16; Van Vleck to wife, August 12, 1863.
26. Broaddus to wife, August 13, 1863; Van Vleck to wife, August 13, 1863.
27. Van Vleck to wife, August 14, 15, 1863; Virdin (Odell), p. 89.
28. Cozzens, "Terrible Sound," p. 440; Tucker, pp. 341–342.
29. Van Vleck to wife, August 16, 1863; Broaddus to wife, August 16, 1863.
30. Broaddus to wife, August 18, 1863; Van Vleck to wife, August 19, 1863.

Chapter 9
1. Van Vleck to wife, August 21, 1863.
2. Broaddus to wife, August 23, 1863; Pvt. John B. Curl's service record erroneously recorded his death as having occurred August 31, 1863.
3. Chandler, p. 51; Van Vleck to wife, August 30, 1863.
4. Broaddus to wife, August 30, 1863; to son Reuben, August 30, 1863.
5. Van Vleck to wife, August 30, 1863; Virdin (Odell), p. 92.
6. Broaddus to wife, August 31, 1863, September 2, 1863.
7. Van Vleck to wife, September 4, 1863; Chandler, p. 52; Broaddus to wife, September 5, 1863.
8. Van Vleck to wife, September 6, 1863; Broaddus to wife, September 6, 1863.
9. Chandler, p. 52.
10. Van Vleck to wife, September 9, 1863.
11. Chandler, p. 52; Batchelor, p. 33; Virdin (Odell), p. 93.
12. Van Vleck to wife, September 10, 11, 1863.
13. Chandler, p. 52; Broaddus to wife, September 11, 1863.
14. Chandler, pp. 52–53.
15. Aten, Henry J.: "History of the Eighty-Fifth Regiment Illinois Volunteer Infantry," Hiawatha, KS, 1901, p. 101; Tucker, pp. 106–108; Cozzens, "Terrible Sound," pp. 93–94.
16. Van Vleck to wife, September 15, 1863.
17. Broaddus to wife, September 15, 16, 1863.
18. Broaddus to wife, September 17, 1863; B&G Vol. XXIV, No. 3, p. 42; Chandler, p. 53; Robbins, p. 3; O.R., Series 1, Vol. 30, Part 1, p. 859; Virdin (Odell), p. 94.
19. Broaddus to wife, September 18, 1863; Batchelor, pp. 33–34; Chandler, p. 53.
20. O.R., Series 1, Vol. 30, Part 1, pp. 922–923.
21. B&G, Vol. XXIV, No. 3, p. 48; Vol. XXIV, No. 6, p. 7; Cozzens, "Terrible Sound," pp. 121–124; O.R., Series 1, Vol. 30, Part 1, p. 866.
22. Batchelor, p. 34; Chandler, p. 53; O.R., Series 1, Vol. 30, Part 1, p. 870.

23. Aten, pp. 104–105; McAdams, F.M.: "Every-Day Soldier Life, or a History of the Hundred and Thirteenth Reg't, Ohio Volunteer Infantry," Chas. M. Cott & Co., Book Printers, Columbus, OH, 1884, p. 41; Virdin (Odell), p. 94.

24. Batchelor, pp. 34–35; Aten, p. 105; Cozzens, "Terrible Sound," pp. 440–441.

25. O.R., Series 1, Vol. 30, Part 1, p. 860; Tucker, pp. 343–346.

26. Cozzens, "Terrible Sound," pp. 440–441; Chandler, p. 54; O.R., Series 1, Vol. 30, Part 1, p. 868.

27. Cozzens, "Terrible Sound," p. 443; Robbins, p. 3.

28. Tucker, p. 347; O.R., Series 1, Vol. 30, Part 1, pp. 867–869; Robbins, p. 4.

29. Van Vleck to wife, September 21, 1863; Batchelor, pp. 34–35; Hicken, Victor: "Illinois in the Civil War." Second Edition, University of Illinois Press, Urbana and Chicago, 1991, p. 209. When Batchelor copied his water-damaged diary in 1910, he inserted the following note: "I forgot to say [in his original diary] that on Sep 20th on the afternoon of the Battle of Chic[k]amauga on Sunday that we still had those very large bore muskets issued to us at Quincy Illinois so mutch larger than the Springfield rifle that for about 2 hours we was nearly out of ammunition [and] had to hold the line with the bay[o]net." It was true the 78th ran low on ammunition, as did most or all of Steedman's division, but after nearly fifty years Batchelor's memory was hazy about the regiment's weapons. The .69-caliber rifles had been exchanged for .58-caliber Springfield rifles before the regiment left Portland, Kentucky, for Nashville.

30. O.R., Series 1, Vol. 30, Part 1, pp. 860, 867, 869; QDW, September 10, 1870, p. 1. Butler survived and appeared to be recovering, but finally died of his wounds in May 1864.

31. Van Vleck to wife, September 21, 1863; O.R., Series 1, Vol. 30, Part 1, p. 869; Virdin (Odell), pp. 96, 99.

32. Virdin (Odell), p. 96; O.R. Series 1, Vol. 30, Part 1, p. 867. The ammunition shortage was due partly to the fact that Steedman's division had earlier given its extra supply, ninety-five thousand cartridges, to Gen. John M. Brannan's division.

33. Horseshoe Ridge has been preserved as part of Chickamauga National Battlefield Park and is easily accessible today. There are no earthworks; the ridge itself served as a natural earthwork, and there was no time for soldiers on either side to dig in. A small monument marks the area defended by the 78th.

Chapter 10

1. Van Vleck to wife, September 21, 1863; Robbins, p. 4.

2. It would be several weeks before a reasonably complete list of the 78th's casualties at Chickamauga could be tabulated; even then there were questions about its accuracy. Analysis of various lists suggests a total of ninety-eight casualties, including seventeen killed, four mortally wounded, sixty-six wounded, four listed as wounded and missing, and seven listed as wounded, captured, and paroled. The latter were left on the field after the battle and captured by Confederates. A full listing of the wounded: *Officers:* Lt. Col. Carter Van Vleck, Capt. George Pollock, 2nd Lt. Phillip Mercer, Capt. T. L. Howden, 1st Lt. Tobias Butler, Capt. John K. Allen, 2nd Lt. Samuel Simmons, 2nd Lt. C. V. Chandler. *Company A:* Mortally wounded (died after battle): John T. Miller. Wounded: Benager Davis, Jasper Wilson, O. L. Pitney, Sam N. Fugate, Martin V. Fugate, James M. Groves. Wounded and listed as missing: James E. Belote, Jasper Wilson, William H. Lansden. *Company D:* Wounded: Egbert Newman, Francis McMahon, Jacob Lairley, Samuel Crum, Edward Limpus, Henry C. Thompson, Charles Johnson, Robert Hamilton,

John W. Howard, Charles Swygleson, James Abbott. Wounded, captured, and paroled: James Mayfield, John L. Miller. *Company E:* Mortally wounded (died after battle): John Nations. Wounded: William Glenn, Thomas Wyatt, Russell L. Gallaher, Samuel McLean, Joseph Matthews, William F. McRae, John H. Steele, Ephraim Winner, Julius Younghein. Wounded, captured, and paroled: Thomas W. Fordyce, John B. Nations (note: John Nations and John B. Nations were different individuals). Wounded and missing: Charles Kuntz. *Company G:* Mortally wounded (died after battle): James R. Wisehart. Wounded: William T. Becket, Harlow E. Selby, Thomas Goldsborough Odell, Presley Riley, William Long, George Iler. *Company H:* Wounded: Thomas M. Scott, James Ward, Joseph Beerman, George Gasaway, Edmund Arnold, Martin Kinman, John Cosgrove, John W. Robinson, Jeremiah Ward. *Company I:* Wounded: Perminion Hamilton, James C. Buchanan, George H. David, Thomas J. Downen, Jacob Faber, James P. Shannon, Douglas M. Chapman, Joseph Mayfield, Thomas Edmondson. *Company K:* Mortally wounded (died after battle): Peter L. Felt. Wounded: Samuel Mills, John H. Dool, Artemus Curtis, Isaac W. Adkins, Charles Preshuer, Francis M. Fryer, Thomas J. Tramill, George Buskirk. Wounded, captured, and paroled: John Reed, James Kinkade, John W. Roberts.

3. O.R., Series 1, Volume 30, Part 1, p. 970; Robbins, p. 4; Chandler, p. 54.

4. The enlisted prisoners from Company F were William Henderson, Anthony Howell, Henry Sammons*, Clarkson Akers*, Milton Johnson, Thomas McLaughlin, William Manard, John Robinson, David Trout*, Charles Akers, Hardin Asher, Henry Brewer*, John Beal*, Charles Cummins*, David Coovert*, Benjamin Demoss*, John Frost, Henry Felsman, John A. Guymon*, John Garig*, James W. Howell*, John Hogan*, Samuel Jacobs, John S. Kelly, Thomas Lawless, John A. McNeal*, John Odear*, Thomas Odear, Charles Plowman, Samuel Trout, and James Taylor*. Those from Company I were John R. Carroll*, Richard C. Allen*, Libeus Allshouse*, Theodore Austine, Christopher Brown*, James M. Chase, Simeon Craig*, Hugh Doran*, Nathaniel Decker, Samuel T. Gibson*, George P. Hall, John V. Myers, Harvey Ricketts, John Sims, William R. Reed, Francis M. Stewart, Joseph A. Smith, William F. Smith, David A. Vincent, and William A. Wilhelm. Asterisks identify those who died in rebel prison camps. The capture of these men, combined with battle losses, raised the 78th's Chickamauga casualty total to the highest of any regiment in Mitchell's brigade.

5. QDW, September 22, 1863, p. 3; Aten, p. 109; Chandler, p. 54.

6. Batchelor, p. 36; Chandler, p. 54; Virdin (Odell), p. 96.

7. Van Vleck to wife, October 2, 1862; "Diary of James Edgar Withrow," University of Illinois at Urbana-Champaign, p. 2.

8. Aten, pp 109–110; Withrow, p. 3.

9. Chandler, p. 54.

10. Withrow, pp. 3-4; Van Vleck to Martha Broaddus, September 27, 1863; Chandler, p. 54.

11. Chandler, pp. 54–55; Van Vleck to wife, September 29, 1863.

12. Withrow, pp. 4–5; Batchelor, p. 37.

13. Van Vleck to wife, October 2, 5, 1863; Withrow, p. 6.

14. Batchelor, p. 37; Withrow, p. 6.

15. Ibid., p. 7; Van Vleck to wife, October 7, 1863.

16. Withrow, p. 7; Batchelor, p. 38.

17. QDJ, November 12, 1917, p. 9; JDIB, pp. 195–197; Robbins, p. 4.

18. QDH, November 5, 1863, p. 2.

19. Withrow, p. 8; William H. Githens Civil War Correspondence, Wyles Collection, Department of Special Collections, Davidson Library, University of California, Santa Barbara, letter to wife, October 12, 1863.

20. Batchelor, p. 38; Withrow, pp. 8–11; Cozzens, Peter: "The Shipwreck of Their Hopes: The Battles for Chattanooga." University of Illinois Press, Urbana and Chicago, 1994, pp. 4, 7.

21. Withrow, pp. 11–13; Batchelor, p. 38.

22. Withrow, p. 14.

23. Batchelor, p. 40; Withrow, pp. 15–16; Cozzens, "Shipwreck," pp. 102–104.

24. QDJ, November 12, 1917, p. 9; National Archives court-martial records.

25. Batchelor, p. 41; Withrow, pp. 17–18; Beatty, John: "The Citizen Soldier." Wilstach, Baldwin & Co., Cincinnati, OH, 1879, pp. 352–353.

26. Withrow, pp. 18–19; Batchelor, p. 41; Virdin (Odell), p. 107.

27. Payne, Edwin W.: "History of the Thirty-Fourth Regiment of Illinois Volunteer Infantry, September 7, 1861–July 12, 1865." Allen Printing Company, Clinton IA, 1902, p. 78.

28. Withrow, pp. 20–21; Virdin (Odell), p. 108.

29. Withrow, p. 21; Cozzens, "Shipwreck," pp. 122–123; JDIB, p. 202.

30. Withrow, p. 21; Van Vleck to wife, November 23, 1863.

31. Withrow, p. 22; Cozzens, "Shipwreck," pp. 130, 160–175.

32. Batchelor, p. 42; Beatty, pp. 357–358.

33. Withrow, p. 22; Batchelor, p. 42.

34. Cozzens, "Shipwreck," p. 282; Withrow, p. 22.

Chapter 11

1. Payne, pp. 90–91; Batchelor, pp. 42–43.

2. Aten, p. 137; Batchelor, p. 43.

3. Aten, pp. 137–138; O.R., Series 1, Vol. 31, Part 2, pp. 501–502.

4. Van Vleck to wife, November 28, 1863; Robbins, p. 5. Robbins's memory again did not serve him well, for he mistakenly identified his dead comrade as "Lieutenant" McCandless. The only Lieutenant McCandless in Company I was James H. McCandless, who resigned May 29, 1863. The man killed at Graysville was Moses McCandless, who enlisted as a private and was later promoted to sergeant, although his service record was never updated to reflect the promotion. Three days after the informal burial near Graysville, McCandless's remains were recovered and taken to Chattanooga.

5. Aten, p. 138; Van Vleck to wife, November 28, 1863.

6. Batchelor, pp. 44–45; JDIB, pp. 211–212.

7. Payne, pp. 93, 95; O.R., Series 1, Volume 31, Part 2, p. 502.

8. Withrow, pp. 24–25; Payne, p. 93.

9. Virdin (Odell), p. 112; O.R., Series 1, Volume 31, Part 2, p. 502; McAdams, p. 55.

10. JDIB, p. 214; Batchelor, p. 45.

11. Aten, p. 139; McAdams, p. 55.

12. Van Vleck to wife, December 19, 1863; Batchelor, p. 45; Payne, p. 95.

13. O.R., Series 1, Volume 31, Part 2, p. 502; Withrow, pp. 28–29.

14. Ibid., p. 29; Van Vleck to wife, December 22, 1863, January 31, 1864.

15. Withrow, p. 30; Aten, p. 56; Van Vleck to wife, December 25, 1863.

16. Aten, pp. 56–57; Beatty, p. 362.

17. Van Vleck to wife, December 28, 1863; Withrow, pp. 31–32.

18. Batchelor, p. 46; Withrow, p. 32; QDJ, November 12, 1917, p. 9.

19. Withrow, p. 32.
20. Van Vleck to Martha Broaddus, January 6, 1864.
21. Ibid.; Van Vleck to wife, January 6, 1864.
22. Payne, p. 97; Van Vleck to wife, January 8, 1864.
23. Van Vleck to wife, January 11, 12, 1864; Batchelor, p. 46.
24. Van Vleck to wife, January 17, 27, 29, 1864; Batchelor, pp. 46–47.
25. Van Vleck to wife, January 31, 1864; QWR, May 7, 1864, p. 2.
26. Van Vleck to wife, February 6, 1864; Batchelor, p. 47.
27. Van Vleck to wife, February 10, 1864.
28. Van Vleck to wife, February 21, 1864.
29. O.R., Series 1, Vol. 32, Part 1, pp. 455–458.
30. Virdin (Odell), p. 124. Odell was discharged January 23, 1865, after sixteen months in military hospitals. After the war he held several positions in Adams County government, served as postmaster of his hometown of Camp Point, then moved to Rush County, Kansas, and took up farming. He was later elected county probate judge. His wounded foot bothered him the rest of his life. He died in 1899. His younger brother, Risdon, survived the war and was mustered out in June 1865.

Chapter 12
1. Van Vleck to wife, March 2, 3, 1864.
2. Van Vleck to wife, March 6, 1864; Payne, p. 101.
3. Van Vleck to wife, March 14, 1864.
4. Payne, 102; McDonough, James Lee, and Jones, James Pickett: "War So Terrible: Sherman and Atlanta." W.W. Norton, New York and London, 1987, pp. 14–15.
5. McAdams, pp. 70–71.
6. Van Vleck to wife, March 22, 1864; Van Vleck to unnamed uncle, March 23, 1864.
7. Chandler, pp. 55–56. Chandler had recovered sufficiently a year later to become captain of Macomb's Excelsior Baseball Club. He later became the city's leading citizen, building an empire in banking, real estate, and manufacturing. During the 1890s he bought an entire city block, razed the buildings on it, and converted it to a public park that bears his name and remains in use today. He married and fathered six children, but economic and political circumstances eventually forced him into bankruptcy. He died in 1934 at age ninety-one and was buried in Macomb's Oakwood Cemetery, not far from his old commander, Carter Van Vleck.
8. Van Vleck to wife, March 27, 30, 1864.
9. Van Vleck to wife, April 3, 1864; McAdams, p. 71.
10. Van Vleck to wife, April 3, 1864.
11. Van Vleck to wife, April 10, 1864.
12. Batchelor, p. 48; O.R., Series 1, Volume 32, Part 1, p. 661.
13. Van Vleck to wife, April 17, 1864.
14. McAdams, p. 75; Batchelor, pp. 48–49.
15. Van Vleck to wife, April 24, 1864, May 1, 1864.
16. McAdams, p. 76; O.R., Series 1, Volume 38, Part 1, p. 687.
17. QWR, June 25, 1864, p. 2.
18. Ibid.; Robbins, p. 5; O.R., Series 1, Volume 38, Part 1, pp. 696, 701; JDIB, pp. 238–239.
19. Payne, pp. 106–107, 356–358.
20. Ibid., p. 107; Batchelor, p. 50; Van Vleck to wife, May 10, 1864.

21. McAdams, p. 78; Batchelor, p. 51.
22. Scaife, William R.: "The Campaign for Atlanta." Third Edition, Atlanta, GA, 1990, pp. 12–15; Aten, p. 164.
23. Payne, p. 108; JDIB, p. 204; O.R., Series 1, Vol. 38, Part 1, p. 627.
24. QWR, June 25, 1864, p. 2; Batchelor, p. 51.
25. Van Vleck to wife, May 16, 1864.
26. Castel, Albert: "Decision in the West: The Atlanta Campaign of 1864." University Press of Kansas, Lawrence, 1992, p. 191; JDIB, p. 242; Van Vleck to wife, May 18, 1864; O.R., Series 1, Vol. 38, Part 1, p. 628.
27. Ibid., pp. 628, 679; JDIB, p. 244; Batchelor, p. 52. Batchelor was apparently referring to the number of men killed in the entire brigade; there is no record of any member of the 78th being killed in the fighting at Rome.
28. O.R., Series 1, Vol. 38, Part 1, p. 630.
29. Batchelor, p. 52; Van Vleck to wife, May 20, 1864.

Chapter 13
1. O.R., Series 1, Vol. 38, Part 1, p. 630; Aten, pp. 171–172; Batchelor, pp. 52–53.
2. Van Vleck to wife, May 20, 1864; McAdams, p. 81.
3. Ibid., p. 81; Batchelor, pp. 53–54; O.R., Series 1, Vol. 38, Part 1, pp. 630–631, 688.
4. Batchelor, p. 54; Van Vleck to wife, May 31, 1864. The men in the 78th who shot themselves were not identified.
5. Van Vleck to wife, May 31, 1864; Batchelor, p. 54; Payne, p. 118; O.R., Series 1, Vol. 38, Part 1, p. 688.
6. Ibid., p. 688; Batchelor, p. 55; JDIB, p. 255.
7. Van Vleck to wife, June 7, 1864. Jones never was formally mustered into the regiment.
8. Castel, pp. 76–77, 211, 356.
9. Aten, p. 175; O.R., Series 1, Vol. 38, Part 1, p. 688; Van Vleck to wife, June 14, 1864.
10. Aten, p. 175; B&G, Vol. VI, No. 5, pp. 13–14.
11. Batchelor, p. 55; Payne, p. 120; McAdams, p. 84.
12. Van Vleck to wife, June 17, 1864; Payne, p. 120; Batchelor, p. 56.
13. Payne, p. 121; Van Vleck to wife, June 17, 1864.
14. McAdams, p. 85; Van Vleck to wife, June 19, 1864; Scaife, p. 39.
15. Payne, p. 122; Batchelor, p. 56; Van Vleck to wife, June 19, 1864.
16. Batchelor, p. 57; Payne, p. 122; Van Vleck to wife, June 22, 1864.
17. McAdams, pp. 86–87; Van Vleck to wife, June 22, 24, 1864.
18. HG, Fall 2007, p. 30; Payne, p. 124; JDIB, p. 256; Batchelor, p. 57.
19. Aten, pp. 179–180.
20. O.R., Series 1, Volume 38, Part 1, p. 632; Payne, p. 126. Abatis consisted of felled trees with sharpened limbs facing toward the enemy.
21. Payne, p. 126; O.R., Series 1, Volume 38, Part 1, pp. 703–704.
22. Payne, pp. 127–129; O.R., Series 1, Volume 38, Part 1, p. 698.
23. O.R., Series 1, Volume 38, Part 1, pp. 703–704.
24. O.R., Series 1, Volume 38, Part 1, pp. 692–693.
25. Van Vleck to wife, June 28, 1964; Batchelor, pp. 57–58.
26. The first page of Magie's letter, including the date it was written and the name of the intended recipient, is missing. The remaining four pages, identified as document GLC05241.45 in the collection of the Gilder-Lehrman Institute of American History,

is misdated as having been written "circa July 1863." The 78th Illinois did not take part in any major action such as that described in the letter during June or July 1863. Furthermore, the descriptions in the letter fit closely with events at Kennesaw Mountain on June 27, 1864. Finally, Magie's account of the wounding of Pvt. William C. Dixon of Company B removes all doubt that Magie was describing the Kennesaw Mountain attack; that is where Dixon suffered the severe arm wound that required amputation and later resulted in his death. So it is clear that Magie wrote the letter shortly after the battle. Why there is a gap between this letter and the last previous one in the Magie collection—dated July 1, 1863—remains unknown.

27. Payne, p. 130; Van Vleck to wife, June 28, 1864.
28. JDIB, p. 261. Van Vleck to wife, June 28, 1864. The corporal killed in the rescue attempt was not identified. Lieutenant Branum of the 98th Ohio was later killed in the battle of Bentonville; his account of retrieving the wounded at Kennesaw Mountain was published posthumously in the National Tribune in 1900.
29. Batchelor, p. 58; O.R., Series 1, Volume 38, Part 1, p. 680.
30. A full listing of the wounded: *Officers:* 1st Lt. George A. Brown of Company A (died of his wounds June 30, 1864), Capt. Thomas L. Howden of Company G, Capt. William B. Akins of Company K. *Company A:* Sgt. Oliver Brooks (died of his wounds July 3, 1864); Cpl. Joseph Curtis; Pvt. James Curtis; Pvt. William Hellyer; Pvt. John Johnson; Pvt. John W. Mullen; Pvt. Theodore C. Noell; Pvt. Nelson Vandivier; Pvt. Edward N. Wheeler. *Company B:* Sgt. John S. Grimes; Pvt. Walter S. Baldwin; Pvt. William C. Dixon (died of his wounds August 1, 1864); Pvt. John H. Parsons. *Company C:* Pvt. James R. Huddleston; Pvt. Richard L. Terry. *Company D:* 1st Sgt. William H. Crotts (died of his wounds August 11, 1864); Cpl. William Frost; Pvt. William Cecile; Pvt. Joseph M. Parish. *Company E:* Pvt. Francis N. Barnard; Pvt. John Kuntz; Pvt. John A. Pottorf; Pvt. Fielding R. Smith. *Company F:* Pvt. Henry E. Barnett. *Company G:* Cpl. Jesse Haley; Pvt. James A. Becket; Pvt. Isaac A. Bottorf; Pvt. Thomas F. Bottorf; Pvt. Madison Henley; Pvt. Benjamin O. Hildreth; Pvt. Joseph D. Pickler; Pvt. Alexander Simons; Pvt. John H. Wisehart. *Company H:* Sgt. Edward McKim. *Company I:* Sgt. Jesse B. Scudder; Pvt. George P. Hogue; Pvt. Robert F. Laughlin; Pvt. John C. Pembroke; Pvt. John E. Pritchard. *Company K:* Sgt. John Bucklew; Cpl. John A. Hymen; Pvt. Norman R. Butler; Pvt. Francis Fryer (died of his wounds July 12, 1864); Pvt. Oscar L. Harkness; Pvt. Paschal Hickerson; Pvt. John Zimmer.
31. QDW, July 13, 1864, p. 3; Batchelor, p. 58; Payne, p. 133.
32. Van Vleck to wife, June 28, 29, 1864. Magie survived the war and became postmaster of Macomb in August 1865. By January 1866 he had saved enough money to realize his dream of purchasing sole proprietorship of the *Macomb Journal.* He later sold the paper and bought the *Canton Register,* taking over as its editor.
33. Batchelor, p. 58; Van Vleck to wife, June 30, 1864.
34. The area where Davis's division made its charge against the rebel lines has been preserved in Kennesaw Mountain National Battlefield Park. The earthworks assaulted by Mitchell's brigade remain mostly intact.

Chapter 14

1. McAdams, p. 93; Van Vleck to wife, July 2, 1864.
2. Batchelor, p. 59; Payne, pp. 135–136.
3. O.R., Series 1, Volume 38, Part 1, p. 634; Van Vleck to wife, July 4, 1864.
4. Batchelor, p. 59; O.R., Series 1, Volume 38, Part 1, p. 688.

5. Van Vleck to wife, July 6, 1864; Payne, pp. 136–137; Batchelor, p. 59.

6. Van Vleck to wife, July 8, 1864; Scaife, p. 43.

7. Van Vleck to wife, July 12, 15, 1864; Scaife, p. 45.

8. Robbins, p. 6; Payne, p. 138.

9. Van Vleck to wife, July 18, 1864; Castel, pp. 353–359, 360–361.

10. Aten, pp. 197–198; O.R., Series 1, Volume 38, Part 1, pp. 681, 689, 694.

11. Van Vleck to wife, July 20, 1864; O.R., Series 1, Volume 38, Part 1, p, 689.

12. Van Vleck to wife, July 22, 1864.

13. Payne, pp. 139–140; Batchelor, p. 60.

14. Van Vleck to wife, July 24, 27, 1864; Payne, pp. 139–140.

15. Scaife, pp. 62–63; Payne, p. 140; O.R., Series 1, Volume 38, Part 1, p. 689.

16. Van Vleck to wife, July 30, 1864; O.R., Series 1, Volume 38, Part 1, p. 705.

17. Aten, p. 215; Batchelor, p. 61.

18. McAdams, p. 95; Van Vleck to wife, July 29, 1864, August 1, 1864.

19. William H. Githens to wife, August 1, 1864; Van Vleck to wife, August 2, 1864.

20. O.R., Series 1, Volume 38, Part 1, p. 689; Batchelor, p. 61; Van Vleck to wife, August 5, 1864.

21. O.R., Series 1, Volume 38, Part 1, p. 681; Batchelor, p. 62.

22. Payne, p. 143; Van Vleck to wife, August 7, 9, 1864.

23. Batchelor, p. 62; O.R., Series 1, Volume 38, Part 1, p. 689.

24. Harold Havelock Kynett, Samuel Worcester Butler, and D. G. Brinton, editors; Medical & Surgical Reporter, Vol. XIII, July 1865–January 1866, Philadelphia, Alfred Martien, printer. Report of Edward Batwell, MD, chief surgeon, 2nd Division XIV Army Corps, p. 291.

25. Van Vleck to wife, August 11, 1864.

26. Batchelor, p. 62; QDJ, November 12, 1917, p. 9.

27. O.R., Series 1, Volume 38, Part 1, p. 689; Payne, p. 144.

28. Kynett, et al., p. 291.

29. Batchelor, p. 63.

30. Kynett, et al., p. 291.

Chapter 15

1. McAdams, p. 97; Batchelor, p. 63.

2. Hughes, Nathaniel Cheairs, Jr.: "Bentonville: The Final Battle of Sherman and Johnston." University of North Carolina Press, Chapel Hill, 1996, pp. 95–96; Scaife, p. 91.

3. O.R., Series 1, Volume 38, Part 1, p. 681; McAdams, p. 98.

4. O.R., Series 1, Volume 38, Part 1, p. 690; Payne, p. 145.

5. "Jonesborough" was the spelling used during the Civil War. The modern spelling is Jonesboro.

6. JDIB, pp. 276–277; Scaife, pp. 91–93.

7. Robbins, p. 7; O.R., Series 1, Volume 38, Part 1, p. 690.

8. O.R., Series 2, Volume 38, Part 1, p. 699; JDIB, p. 277.

9. Robbins, p. 7; Aten, p. 224.

10. O.R., Series 1, Volume 38, Part 1, pp. 690, 695.

11. O.R., Series 1, Volume 38, Part 1, p. 695; Robbins, p. 7.

12. QDJ, July 29, 1914, p. 12.

13. Robbins, p. 7.

14. Connolly, James A.: "Three Years in the Army of the Cumberland," edited by Paul M. Angle. Indiana University Press, Bloomington, 1959, pp. 257–258.
15. O.R., Series 1, Volume 38, Part 1, pp. 690, 707.
16. O.R., Series 1, Volume 38, Part 1, p. 699; McAdams, p. 102.
17. There is a tradition in Butler's family that when he was hit he fell into a ditch full of water and lay there until litter bearers found him the next morning. This is a dramatic story, but at least some of it is almost certainly not true. It is possible Butler fell into a ditch full of water—there were a number of ditches and intermittent streams in the path of the 78th— but it is virtually certain he did not lie there all night. Records of the 78th regimental hospital show Butler was admitted September 1, the same day he was wounded. He was later transferred to the 2nd Division hospital, where records show he was also admitted September 1. It's possible one hospital orderly might have been mistaken about the date, but extremely unlikely two different orderlies would have made the same mistake. Moreover, sunset at Jonesboro was at 7:02 p.m. local time September 1, 1864, so there would have been at least an hour and a half of good light after the attack for orderlies to find and collect the wounded.

     Butler spent months in military hospitals until his discharge in February 1865. With only one lung and a paralyzed right arm, he was rated 75 percent disabled by surgeons and was unable to return to his pre-war occupation of blacksmith. He was awarded a pension of eight dollars a month starting in June 1866. Though plagued by frequent pain and occasional hemorrhages, he raised a large family and lived into his seventieth year.
18. Payne, p. 150.
19. O.R., Series 1, Volume 38, Part 1, p. 699. The slope where Private Lesure fell and the 78th Illinois charged through a hail of canister to capture General Govan and Swett's battery is now a residential subdivision. Nothing remains of the battlefield.
20. QDJ, July 29, 1914, p. 12. Thompson miraculously survived his injuries. He spent more than six months in army hospitals before he was discharged March 11, 1865. By then he had learned to walk with the aid of crutches. After several years he was granted a pension of six dollars a month, later increased to as much as thirty dollars a month. He served fifteen years as postmaster of Coatsburg, Adams County, and lived well into the twentieth century.
21. The following list of wounded at Jonesboro was prepared by 1st Lt. Harmon Veatch, acting adjutant of the 78th Illinois, and published in the *Quincy Whig Republican* September 24, 1864: *Officers:* Maj. George Greene. *Company A:* Sgt. John D. Corria (left arm); Pvt. William H. Curtis (neck, severe); Pvt. Alex Shamell (neck, severe); Pvt. Charles L. Willson (left shoulder); Pvt. Harvey F. Hendrick (right hand); Pvt. Henry Vandivier (head); Pvt. Thomas R. Alway (head); Pvt. William K. Ruggles (finger); Pvt. Henry C. Bodenhammer (thigh). *Company B:* Sgt. James A. Miller (left arm); Pvt. Crist Mangle (burned, severe); Pvt. William T. Patterson (wrist and hand); Pvt. Daniel Newcomer (bowels, severe); Pvt. Leonidas Thompson (right leg). *Company C:* Sgt. Michael Mealey (neck, severe); Cpl. Luther Meek (right arm, slight); Pvt. William C. Freeland (thumb shot off left hand); Pvt. Marion D. Bond (right leg amputated); Pvt. John F. Green (left side contusion); Pvt. Joseph A. James (right shoulder, slight); Pvt. George Martin (left shoulder, slight); Pvt. Cyrell Tyft (right thumb, severe). *Company D:* Pvt. Mitchell E. Wallace (right arm); Pvt. William H. Thompson (jaw broken, flesh wound in left hip); Pvt. Jacob J. Fry (left foot amputated); Pvt. John C. Cormack (contusion right side); Pvt. Jacob Gerst (left shoulder, severe); Pvt. William S. Davis (right thigh, severe); Pvt. James W. Craig (left hand, slight).

Company E: Cpl. Francis M. Barnard (thigh, slight); Cpl. Edward Williams (thigh, slight); Pvt. Samuel Deighton (thigh); Pvt. Jesse Cunningham (thigh); Pvt. John W. Hendricks (head, slight); Pvt. Peter Hoffmaster (right shoulder, slight). *Company F:* Pvt. Theodore Chandler (left shoulder). *Company G:* Sgt. John C. Malthener (left breast); Cpl. George W. Wiseheart (right shoulder); Pvt. William T. Beckett (left thigh and left arm); Pvt. Daniel Hompsher (foot contusion); Pvt. John M. Farlow (face, slight); Pvt. Richard Flack (leg); Pvt. Samuel G. Reed (contusion, right side); Pvt. Alfred Pollock (head); Pvt. Clayton W. McGill (leg, slight). *Company H:* Sgt. John Gibbs (right heel); Pvt. Jeremiah Ward (side, severe); Pvt. Joseph W. Walker (left side, slight); Pvt. Henry Gilbreath (both hands); Pvt. Thomas Robinson (left side, severe); Pvt. William H. Stanley (left side and arm, severe); Pvt. Philo Ogden (head, slight); Pvt. Thomas S. Rice (left side, slight); Pvt. John Beerman (right shoulder). *Company I:* Cpl. Sophroneous Carnahan (neck, slight); Pvt. John C. Pembroke (right arm); Pvt. Henry Parker (right arm, slight); Pvt. William Weaver (head, severe). *Company K:* 1st Sgt. Jonathan Butler (breast and right arm, severe); Cpl. John H. Riley (left thigh, severe); Cpl. John P. Beers (wrist, severe); Pvt. William Cray (neck and shoulder, severe); Pvt. David M. Coulter (right leg and left foot); Pvt. Charles Gurn (left leg contusion); Pvt. Thomas H. Nichols (both legs); Pvt. Thomas H. Wingfield (both legs).

22. Batchelor, pp. 64–65.
23. McAdams, pp. 104–105; Batchelor, p. 65.
24. Lt. Col. Maris Vernon to Patty Van Vleck, September 16, 1864.
25. Batchelor, p. 66. Batchelor's diary for the period September 26 to October 18 contains some puzzling entries. At various times during this period Batchelor says he was in Kingston, Rome, Resaca, and Dalton, all in Georgia, but every other documented source, including Lieutenant Colonel Vernon's reports, says the 78th Illinois started by rail for Chattanooga on September 29, then moved into Alabama where it remained until late October 14, then returned to Chattanooga where it stayed until October 18. No explanation for the discrepancies in Batchelor's diary has been found.
26. O.R., Series 1, Volume 39, Part 1, pp. 620–621; Payne (Enderton), p. 159. As noted in the text, Payne was wounded at Jonesboro and was thereafter forced to rely on the diaries of other soldiers in the 34th Illinois. The entry on page 159 was from the diary of Sgt. William H. Enderton of Company A. Subsequent entries from Enderton's diary are identified as Payne (Enderton). Names of other soldiers whose diaries are quoted are identified in similar fashion.
27. McAdams, pp. 110–111; O.R., Series 1, Volume 39, Part 1, p. 642; Payne (Enderton), p. 160.
28. Payne (Enderton), p. 160; McAdams, pp. 111–112; O.R., Series 1, Volume 39, Part 1, p. 642.
29. O.R., Series 1, Volume 39, Part 1, p. 622; Payne (Enderton), pp. 161–162.
30. Payne (Enderton), p. 162; Batchelor, p. 68.
31. Payne (Enderton), p. 162; McAdams, p. 114.
32. Batchelor, p. 69; JDIB, p. 295; Payne (Enderton), p. 162.
33. Ibid., pp. 162–163; McAdams, p. 115; Batchelor, p. 69; JDIB, p. 295.
34. Connolly, p. 301.

Chapter 16
1. Jefferson C. Davis actually held a brevet, or temporary, major general's rank.
2. O.R., Series 1, Volume 44, Part 1, p. 194; Batchelor, p. 70.

3. McAdams, p. 117; Batchelor, p. 70; Payne (Enderton), p. 166; Connolly, pp. 311–312.
4. McAdams, p. 117; Batchelor, p. 70; O.R., Series 1, Volume 44, Part 1, p. 194.
5. Hicken, pp. 281–283.
6. JDIB, p. 301; Batchelor, p. 70; O.R., Series 1, Volume 44, Part 1, p. 194.
7. McAdams, p. 118; JDIB, pp. 305–306; Hicken, p. 284.
8. Batchelor, p. 70; Connolly, p. 307.
9. Payne (Sgt. Charles S. Gaylord), p. 165; Connolly, p. 322.
10. Batchelor, p. 71; O.R., Series 1, Volume 44, Part 1, p. 190; McAdams, p. 118.
11. JDIB, p. 302.
12. Hicken, p. 282; Robbins, p. 9.
13. Connolly, pp. 325–326; Robbins, p. 9; McAdams, pp. 119–120; O.R., Series 1, Volume 44, Part 1, p. 190.
14. McAdams, p. 120; Batchelor, p. 72; Payne (Gaylord), pp. 168–169.
15. JDIB, p. 304; Payne (Gaylord), p. 169.
16. Batchelor, p. 72; Payne (Gaylord), p. 169; McAdams, p. 122.
17. Batchelor, p. 72; Payne (Surgeon John L. Hostetter), p. 170.
18. McAdams, p. 123; Connolly, pp. 353–354; JDIB, pp. 308–314.
19. McAdams, p. 123; Batchelor, p 73.
20. McAdams, p. 124; Payne (Hostetter), p. 171.
21. O.R., Series 1, Volume 44, Part 1, p. 195.
22. Connolly, p. 362; Payne (Hostetter), p. 172.
23. Batchelor, p. 73; Payne (Enderton), p. 174.
24. Batchelor, p. 73; McAdams, p. 126; Payne (Hostetter), p. 175.
25. McAdams, p. 127; Payne (Hostetter), p. 177; Batchelor, p. 73.
26. Payne (Hostetter), p. 182; Batchelor, p. 73.
27. JDIB, p. 317; Batchelor, p. 74; Payne (Hostetter), p. 182.
28. Payne, p. 178; O.R., Series 1, Volume 47, Part 1, p. 515.
29. Batchelor, p. 75; Payne, p. 185.
30. McAdams, p. 132; Batchelor, p. 76; O.R., Series 1, Volume 47, Part 1, pp. 429, 509, 513, 515.
31. O.R., Series 1, Volume 47, Part 1, p. 509; Batchelor, p. 76.
32. Payne (1st Lt. William C. Robinson, later promoted to captain), p. 190; Batchelor, pp. 76–77; McAdams, p. 135.
33. Ibid., p. 136; O.R., Series 1, Volume 47, Part 1, p. 514.
34. Batchelor, p. 77; Payne (Robinson), p. 192; O.R., Series 1, Volume 47, Part 1, pp. 509, 514.
35. Payne (Robinson), p. 192; O.R., Series 1, Volume 47, Part 1, p. 514. The location of the Saluda River crossing is in dispute; Mitchell said it took place at Leaphart's Ferry, Vernon said it was at Youngling's Ferry, and McAdams said it was Hart's Ferry.
36. McAdams, pp. 137–139; Batchelor, pp. 78–79; Payne (Robinson), pp. 193–194.
37. Batchelor, pp. 79–80; O.R., Series 1, Volume 47, Part 1, p. 516.
38. O.R., Series 1, Volume 47, Part 1, p. 432; Batchelor, p. 80; Payne (Robinson), pp. 194–195.
39. Batchelor, p. 80; O.R., Series 1, Volume 47, Part 1, p. 510; Payne (Robinson), p. 195.
40. O.R., Series 1, Volume 47, Part 1, p. 432.
41. Batchelor, p. 81; Virdin (Odell), pp. 28–29.
42. JDIB, pp. 326–327; Batchelor, p. 81; O.R., Series 1, Volume 47, Part 1, p. 432.
43. McAdams, p. 141.

Chapter 17

1. O.R., Series 1, Volume 47, Part 1, p. 516; Batchelor, p. 82.
2. JDIB, pp. 327–328; Batchelor, p. 82; McAdams, p. 142.
3. Ibid., p. 143; O.R., Series 1, Volume 47, Part 1, p. 433; Payne (Robinson), pp. 198–199.
4. JDIB, p. 331; McAdams, p. 143.
5. Hughes, "Bentonville," pp. 17–18, 22, 47; Payne (Robinson), p. 199; McAdams, p. 144.
6. Hughes, "Bentonville," p. 64; Payne (Robinson), p. 199; O.R., Series 1, Volume 47, Part 1, p. 434.
7. Hughes, "Bentonville," p. 96; McAdams, p. 144; O.R., Series 1, Volume 47, Part 1, pp. 510, 516–517.
8. Ibid.; McAdams, pp. 144–145; Payne (Robinson), p. 200.
9. O.R., Series 1, Volume 47, Part 1, pp. 510–511, 526–527.
10. McAdams, pp. 145–146; Hughes, "Bentonville," pp. 146–147; Batchelor, pp. 84–85.
11. Hughes, "Bentonville," pp. 159–160; Payne (Robinson), p. 204; Batchelor, p. 85. 1st Sgt. Jerome J. Clark of Company I, a Macomb resident, was shot in the groin. He died of his wound on April 30, 1865. The final total of casualties was not as high as Batchelor indicated (see note 13).
12. Payne (Robinson), pp. 204–205; Batchelor, pp. 85–86; O.R., Series 1, Volume 47, Part 1, p. 517; Robbins, p. 20. Large portions of the Bentonville battlefield have been preserved, including much of the ground where Mitchell's brigade was virtually surrounded during the first day's fighting. Breastworks constructed by the defenders have been located and mapped in this area, sometimes called the "Bull Pen," but are difficult to visit because of thick brush, downed trees, and swampy ground.
13. The following list of wounded from the period including the Battles of Averasboro and Bentonville was published in the Quincy Whig Republican April 8, 1865: Company A: Sgt. Amos Scott, left hand, severe; Cpl. David M. Sapp, right side and hip, slight; Pvt. Peter Burmond, left hand, slight; Pvt. Abraham Hite, both feet, severe; Pvt. John R. Gott, right thigh, slight; Pvt. Edward Morgan, thigh and privates. Missing: Pvt. Theodore G. Noell (it was later determined that Noell had been captured; after repatriation, he mustered out with the regiment at war's end). Company B: Sgt. Joshua Colvin, left arm, severe; Sgt. William E. Miller, right hand, slight; Pvt. John W. Breneman, left hand, slight; Pvt. Walter S. Baldwin, abdomen; Pvt. Francis M. McNamara, head, slight; Pvt. Crist Mangle, hip, slight; Pvt. John H. Wood, face, severe. Company C: Sgt. Alfred J. Stafford, left thigh, severe; Pvt. John Gorham, arm, slight; Pvt. Philip Chaffin, side, slight. Company D: Cpl. Adolphus W. Drager, left hand, slight; Cpl. Robert M. Hamilton, left leg, slight; Pvt. Thomas Newland, head, slight; Pvt. Martin V. Wares, left hand, slight. Company E: 1st Sgt. William Lawson, head, slight; Cpl. James H. Pettit, back, slight; Pvt. James Galagher, left thigh, severe. Company G: Sgt. Jesse Haley, right arm, severe; Cpl. James M. Beckett, right leg, severe; Cpl. Anson Castle, arm, slight; Pvt. George Loukor, arm, slight. Company H: Sgt. Samuel L. L'Homidieu, body; Pvt. Joseph Bartlett, left breast; Pvt. Gideon Z. McElhiny, left breast. Missing: Sgt. William Hetrick (it was later determined that Hetrick had been captured; after repatriation, he mustered out with the regiment at war's end). Company I: 1st Sgt. Jerome J. Clark, right groin. Company K: Sgt. Thomas Jolly, face, severe.
14. McAdams, p. 147; Batchelor, p. 86; Payne (Hostetter), p. 209.
15. McAdams, pp. 147–148; Payne (Robinson), p. 205; Batchelor, pp. 87–88.
16. McAdams, p. 149; Batchelor, p. 89; Payne (Hostetter), p. 210. The unfortunate sutler's name was Nick White.
17. Batchelor, pp. 89–92; McAdams, pp. 149–151; Payne (Hostetter), pp. 210–211.

18. McAdams, pp. 151–153; Batchelor, p. 93.
19. Batchelor, pp. 95–96. Perhaps it was because Batchelor was feverish from his illness, but his diary contains two separate entries for April 28, 1865. As a result, subsequent entries are misdated—the second entry for April 28 actually describing events that occurred on April 29, and so on—until he got back on track May 7. It is also possible he made the error when he copied his diary from the original in 1910, although that seems less likely.
20. Ibid., pp. 95–96; Payne (Hostetter), pp. 211–212; McAdams, p. 154.
21. McAdams, p. 154; Batchelor, pp. 97–98; Payne (Enderton), p. 212.
22. McAdams, pp. 154–155; Payne (Enderton), pp. 212–213; Batchelor, pp. 99–101.
23. Batchelor, pp. 101–104; Payne (Gaylord), p. 214; McAdams, pp. 156–157.
24. Batchelor, pp. 104–105; JDIB, p. 355; Githens to wife, May 23, 1865.
25. Payne (Gaylord), p. 214; McAdams, p. 158; Robbins, pp. 10–11.
26. Batchelor returned home to his wife and son, now more than three years old. After just five days at home he returned to work as a carpenter. "There was plenty of work and good wages for several years," he wrote later in his last diary entry. As for Davis, his postwar career included three years as military governor of the Territory of Alaska, recently acquired by the United States from Russia. He also commanded US forces in the Modoc Indian War on the Oregon-California border. Continually plagued by ill health, he died of pneumonia in 1879.
27. Batchelor, pp. 106–110; Payne, p. 216; McAdams, pp. 160–161.
28. Batchelor, p. 111; QDW, June 22, 1865, p. 3.

Roster

78th Illinois Volunteer Infantry Regiment

Civil War record-keeping was done mostly by hand and often without much regard for accuracy. Handwritten records offered ample opportunity for different interpretations, sometimes resulting in different spellings of names. Many such errors persist to this day. The following roster was compiled from the Report of the Adjutant General of Illinois, the Illinois State Archives, the Illinois US GenWeb Project, individual service records, and other sources. Wherever it has been possible to reconcile differences in the spelling of names from these various sources, or to correct other errors, those changes have been made. However, no claim is made for absolute accuracy; at this distance in time, 100 percent accuracy is probably not possible.

The 78th Illinois Volunteer Infantry Regiment was mustered into federal service at Quincy, Illinois, September 1, 1862. Soldiers listed as "recruits" in the following roster usually joined the regiment later.

Abbreviations:
> Des.—Deserter
> Disab.—Disabled
> Disch.—Discharged
> KIA—Killed in Action
> M.O.—Mustered Out
> POW—Prisoner of War
> Ptd.—Promoted
> Res.—Resigned
> Trans.—Transferred
> VRC—Veteran Reserve Corps
> Wds.—Wounds

Headquarters and Staff
> **Colonels**
> BENNESON, William H. Res. Sept. 2, 1963.
> VAN VLECK, Carter. Died of wds. Aug. 23, 1864.
> **Lieutenant Colonels**
> VAN VLECK, Carter. Ptd. colonel.
> VERNON, Maris R. M.O. June 7, 1865.

Majors
BLACKBURN, Robert S. M.O. June 7, 1865.
BROADDUS, William L. KIA at Chickamauga, Sept. 20, 1863.
GREENE, George. Res. Jan. 15, 1865, due to wds.
Adjutants
ANDERSON, John D. M.O. June 7, 1865.
CHANDLER, Charles V. Res. Apr. 3, 1864, due to wds.
GREENE, George. Ptd. major.
Surgeons
GITHENS, William H. 2nd asst. surgeon. Ptd. 1st asst. surgeon. M.O. June 7, 1865.
JORDAN, Thomas M. Res. Apr. 5, 1863; disab.
McINTIRE, Elihu S. 1st asst. surgeon. Res. March 25, 1863.
MOSS, Samuel C. 2nd asst. surgeon. Ptd. 1st asst. surgeon, ptd. surgeon. M.O. June 7, 1865.
Quartermaster
HUMPHREY, Abner V. M.O. June 7, 1865.
Chaplains
TAYLOR, Robert F. Res. Jul. 8, 1863.
Non-commissioned staff
BURNS, Edward P. Quartermaster sgt. M.O. June 7, 1865.
CARROLL, Daniel M. Principal musician. M.O. June 7, 1865.
CHANDLER, Charles V. Sgt. major, ptd. 2nd lt.
CREEL Durham. Hospital steward. M.O. June 7, 1865.
GRAMMER, Seth W. Sgt. M.O. June 7, 1865.
HENDRICKS, William S. Sgt. major. Disch. Jan. 17, 1865, wds.
MAYNARD, Reuben L. Principal musician. M.O. June 22, 1865.
STRICKLER, Joseph R. Sgt. major. M.O. June 7, 1865.
VEATCH, Harmon. Sgt. major, ptd. 2nd lt.

Company A
Recruited from St. Clair, Schuyler, McDonough, and Hancock Counties.

Captains
BLACKBURN, Robert S. Ptd. major.
HITE, Christian W. M.O. June 7, 1865.
First Lieutenants
BROWN, George A. Died of wds. June 30, 1864.
CHIPMAN, Philip. Res. Feb. 1, 1863.
GRAHAM, Archibald H. Res. Apr. 5, 1863.
HITE, Christian W. Ptd. captain.
SCOTT, Amos. M.O. May 19, 1865.
Second Lieutenants
BROWN, George A. Ptd. 1st lt.
GRAHAM, Archibald. Ptd. 1st lt.
HITE, Christian W. Ptd. 1st lt.
WOODS, Nathan P. Res. Apr. 21, 1864.
First Sergeants
HITE, Christian. Ptd. 2nd lt.

Sergeants

BROOKS, Oliver. Died Jul. 3, 1864, at Chattanooga.

CORRIA, John D. M.O. June 7, 1865; was POW.

CURTIS, Jesse. M.O. June 7, 1865.

FRISBY, Abraham. M.O. June 7, 1865.

SCOTT, Amos. Ptd. 1st lt.

WALKER, John N. M.O. June 7, 1865.

Privates

AVERY, Stephen. Disch. March 31, 1863; disab.

BAIN, Alexander. M.O. June 7, 1865; was POW.

BALL, Albin. M.O. June 7, 1865.

BELOTE, Darwin. Died at Franklin March 5, 1863.

BELOTE, James E. KIA at Chickamauga, Sept. 20, 1863.

BESSELL, Augustus C. M.O. June 7, 1865; was POW.

BODENHAMER, Henry C. M.O. June 7, 1865.

BOX, John. M.O. June 17, 1865; was POW.

BROWN, George A. Ptd. 2nd lt.

BRUNDAGE, George W. Disch. Aug. 24, 1863; disab.

BRUNDAGE, James. Ptd. cpl. M.O. June 7, 1865.

BURNETT, William. M.O. June 7, 1865.

CORRIA, John D. Ptd. sgt.

COX, William. Disch. May 5, 1865; disab.

CURTIS, James. M.O. Jul. 17, 1865.

CURTIS, Jesse. Ptd. sgt.

CURTIS, John. M.O. June 7, 1865.

CURTIS, Joseph. Ptd. cpl. M.O. June 7, 1865.

CURTIS, William H. Disch. March 11, 1865, wds.

DAVIS, Benager. Died of wds. Oct. 7, 1863.

DAVIS, John. Died at Nashville, March 18, 1863.

DAVIS, Philip. Disch. Aug. 31, 1863; disab.

DAVIS, Robert H. Disch. Dec. 8, 1864; disab.

DRIVER, Samuel R. Died at Franklin, Feb. 19, 1863.

EWING, Samuel M. Died at Nashville, Aug. 2, 1863.

FRAKES, Joseph. Disch. May 8, 1863.

FRISBY, Abraham. Ptd. sgt.

FUGATE, Martin V. KIA at Chickamauga, Sept. 20, 1863.

FUGATE, Samuel H. Died of wds. May 17, 1864.

GILLELAND, Benjamin C. Trans. Engineer Corps.

GOTT, John R. M.O. June 7, 1865.

GRAHAM, Shepard. Died at Franklin March 28, 1863.

GROVES, James M. M.O. June 7, 1865.

HARRISON, George. M.O. June 7, 1865.

HELLYER, George. M.O. June 7, 1865; was POW.

HELLYER, William. M.O. June 7, 1865.

HITE, Abraham. Absent wounded at M.O. of regiment.

HITE, Abraham L. Disch. Dec. 31, 1862; disab.

HITE, Christian. Ptd. 1st sgt.

HOW, Samuel W. M.O. June 7, 1865.

HOWELL, John. M.O. June 7, 1865.
HUSTED, Talmon. Trans. VRC March 24, 1864.
JOHNSON, John. M.O. June 7, 1865.
LANSDEN, William H. Died as POW at Andersonville Oct. 6, 1864.
McCLAIN, William H. M.O. June 7, 1865.
McKEE, William. M.O. June 7, 1865.
MILLER, John T. Died of wds. Sept. 27, 1863.
MINER, Samuel J. Des. Feb. 3, 1863.
MINTS, Lorenzo. M.O. June 7, 1865.
MORGAN, Edward T. M.O. June 7, 1865.
MULLIN, Martin. M.O. June 7, 1865.
NOELL, Theodore C. M.O. June 17, 1865; was POW.
PELSOR, Tracey. Died at Quincy Apr. 27, 1863.
PETERSON, Francis M. Ptd. cpl. M.O. June 7, 1865.
PITNEY, Orville L. Ptd. cpl. M.O. June 7, 1865.
RECORD, Josiah S. Des. Jan. 30, 1863.
REED, John E. Died at Nashville March 28, 1863.
RIGSBY, George W. Died at Quincy Oct. 11, 1862.
ROBINSON, Israel. Disch. Apr. 17, 1863; disab.
ROBINSON, Nimrod. M.O. June 7, 1865.
ROBINSON, Richard. M.O. June 7, 1865.
SAPP, David M. Ptd. Cpl. M.O. June 7, 1865.
SCOTT, Amos. Ptd. sgt.
SCOTT, Hiram. Died at Nashville March 27, 1863.
SOWARD, Charles W. M.O. June 7, 1865.
STEEN, John. Died of wds. Jul. 22, 1864.
TANKERSLEY, Andrew J. Disch. Sept. 30, 1863; disab.
TOLAND, Solomon. KIA at Chickamauga Sept. 20, 1863.
TOLAND, William. Disch. Feb. 14, 1863; disab.
VANDIVIER, John. M.O. June 17, 1865; was POW.
VANDIVIER, Nelson. Ptd. cpl. M.O. June 7, 1865.
WALKER, John N. Ptd. sgt. M.O. June 7, 1865.
WALKER, William T. Died at Nashville Feb. 28, 1865.
WHEELER, Joel B. M.O. June 7, 1865.
WHEELER, John H. M.O. June 7, 1865.
WHITE, Benjamin F. Disch. Sept. 12, 1863; disab.
WIER, William. Ptd. corporal. M.O. June 7, 1865.
WILSON, Jasper. KIA at Chickamauga Sept. 20, 1863.
WOODS, William S. Trans. Engineer Corps.
WYKOFF, William H. H. M.O. June 7, 1865.
WYLES, Henry H. Trans. VRC, Oct. 22, 1864.
WYLES, Samuel S. M.O. June 7, 1865.

Recruits
ALWAY, Thomas R. Trans. Co. H, 34th Ill. Inf.
BODENHAMER, Christopher G. Taken prisoner Nov. 27, 1864.
BODENHAMER, Isaac H. Trans. Co. H, 34th Ill. Inf.
BROOKS, Oliver. Ptd. sgt.
BURMOND, Peter. M.O. June 7, 1865.

BURTON, James E. Trans. Co. H, 34th Ill. Inf.
BURTON, William C. Trans. Co. H, 34th Ill. Inf.
CLARK, James T. Trans. Co. H, 34th Ill. Inf.
COX, Christopher C. Trans. Co. H, 34th Ill. Inf.
CURTIS, Joseph. Ptd. cpl. M.O. June 7, 1865.
DAVIS, John W. Trans. Co. H, 34th Ill. Inf.
DAVIS, William H. KIA at Chickamauga Sept. 20, 1863.
EWING, George W. M.O. June 7, 1865.
FRAKES, Robert. Des. Jan. 20, 1865.
GRANGER, Robert. M.O. June 7, 1865.
HENDRICK, Harvey F. Trans. Co. H, 34th Ill. Inf.
HOW, Isaac C. Trans. Co. H, 34th Ill. Inf.
HOW, James. Trans. Co. H, 34th Ill. Inf.
JAMES, Samuel J. Trans. Co. H, 34th Ill. Inf.
JOHNSON, David. Trans. Co. H, 34th Ill. Inf.
LACY, John S. Trans. Co. H, 34th Ill. Inf.
MULLEN, John W. Trans. Co. H, 34th Ill. Inf.
NEIDA, Charles S. Died at Nashville Jul. 13, 1864.
NOAH, Alexander. African undercook. M.O. June 7, 1865.
RUGGLES, William K. Trans. VRC May 4, 1865.
SAPP, John W. Died at Nashville Nov. 23, 1864.
SCOTT, Richard W. Died of wds. Sept. 2, 1864.
SHAMELL, Alexander. Trans. Co. H. 34th Ill. Inf.
STEVENS, Alexander. African undercook.
STEWART, James. No further information.
THOMAS, James. KIA at Kennesaw Mountain June 27, 1864
THORP, Lorenzo D. Trans. Co. H, 34th Ill. Inf.
VANDIVIER, Henry. Died of wds. Sept. 20, 1864.
WHEELER, Edward N. M.O. May 22, 1865.
WIER, William H. Trans. Co. H, 34th Ill. Inf.
WILDS, Howard. Trans. Co. H, 34th Ill. Inf.
WILLSON, Charles L. Disch. March 15, 1865, wds.
WOODS, Nathan P. Ptd. 2nd lt.

Company B
Recruited from Adams County

Captains
ANDERSON, John C. Res. March 15, 1864.
RUDDELL, William D. M.O. June 7, 1865.
First Lieutenants
RUDDELL, William D. Ptd. captain.
WOODRUFF, Freeman. M.O. June 7, 1865.
Second Lieutenants
ANDERSON, John D. Ptd. regimental adjutant.
TAYLOR, David M. Res. Apr. 20, 1863.
WOODRUFF, Freeman. Ptd. 1st lt.

First Sergeants
MILLER, William E. M.O. June 7, 1865.
WOODRUFF, Freeman. Ptd. 2nd lt.
Sergeants
ANDERSON, John D. Ptd. 2nd lt.
COLVIN, Joshua. Absent sick at M.O. of regiment.
GRIMES, John S. M.O. June 7, 1865.
MILLER, James A. M.O. June 7, 1865.
MILLER, William E. Ptd. 1st sgt.
NICHOLS, Joseph W. M.O. June 7, 1865.
RUDDELL, George H. M.O. June 7, 1865.
WALTERS, Adam. Died at Chattanooga Aug. 8, 1864.
Privates
ADARE, Richard. Absent sick at M.O. of regiment.
ADARE, William T. Absent sick at M.O. of regiment.
ARTERBURN, Samuel. M.O. June 7, 1865.
BALDWIN, Michael. Ptd. cpl. M.O. June 7, 1865.
BALDWIN, Walter S. M.O. June 7, 1865.
BEATTY, William. KIA at Jonesboro Sept. 1, 1864.
BISELL, Levi P. Disch. Jul. 16, 1863.
BRENEMAN, John W. M.O. June 7, 1865.
BRENEMAN, William H. M.O. June 15, 1865.
BRUGMAN, Samuel N. Des. Dec. 1862.
BRYANT, David. Trans. VRC, Feb. 11, 1864.
BRYANT, George W. Des. Jan., 1863.
BURKE, John A. Died at Boston, Ky., Nov. 2, 1862.
BURKE, Leander. M.O. June 7, 1865.
CARMACK, Samuel B. Ptd. cpl. M.O. June 7, 1865.
CARTER, William E. Trans. VRC.
CAWLEY, James G. Disch. Feb. 23, 1864, disab.
CAWLEY, William. Des. Dec. 1862.
CECIL, Reason Van. Died at Atlanta Sept. 15, 1864.
COLVIN, Joshua. Ptd. sgt.
CRAWFORD, Orville. M.O. June 7, 1865.
CUNDIFF, Jesse E. Ptd.cpl. KIA at Averasborough March 16, 1865.
CUNDIFF, John B. M.O. June 7, 1865.
DILLON, Thomas L. M.O. June 7, 1865.
DIXON, William C. Died of wds. Aug. 1, 1864.
DOBBS, Elias M. Des. Jan. 1863.
DUNCAN, James W. Disch. Oct. 25, 1862; disab.
EDMONSON, John A. Died of wds. Jul. 24, 1864.
ELSTON, William L. Disch. Nov. 17, 1863; disab.
FRAZIER, Theophilus L. M.O. June 7, 1865.
GROVES, Daniel. Died at Savannah Jan. 18, 1865.
GUESSMAN, William A. Disch. Nov. 3, 1863; disab.
HEARN, Jasper A. Ptd. cpl. M.O. June 7, 1865.
HEATH, John R. M.O. June 7, 1865.
HEDGES, Thadeus S. Ptd. cpl. M.O. June 7, 1865.

JOHNSON, William A. M.O. June 7, 1865.
JORDAN, Curtis W. M.O. June 7, 1865.
KINKADE, David. M.O. June 7, 1865.
KINKADE, Thomas. M.O. June 7, 1865.
LAPP, William D. Des. Jan. 1863.
LEACHMAN, John F. M.O. June 7, 1865.
LEE, Charles H. M.O. June 7, 1865.
MANGLE, Crist. M.O. June 7, 1865.
MAYFIELD, Henry C. M.O. June 7, 1865.
MAYFIELD, James W. Disch. Oct. 1863; disab.
McKENZIE, William A. Musician. M.O. June 7, 1865.
McMULLEN, John. M.O. June 7, 1865.
McNAMARA, Francis M. M.O. June 7, 1865.
MILLER, James A. Ptd. sgt.
MILLER, John L. Died of wds. Oct. 26, 1863.
MILLER, Uriah K. Disch. Jan. 12, 1863, wds.
NEWCOMER, Daniel. Disch. May 3, 1865; disab.
PAINTER, Joseph. M.O. June 7, 1865.
PARSONS, James D. M.O. Jul. 22, 1865.
PARSONS, John H. M.O. June 7, 1865.
PARSONS, Lafayette. Absent sick at M.O. of regiment.
PATTERSON, Clifton. M.O. June 7, 1865.
PATTERSON, William T. Disch. Feb. 25, 1865, wds.
PITT, Charles W. Absent sick at M.O. of regiment.
RALPH, Joseph. M.O. June 7, 1865.
RICE, Julius. Ptd. cpl. KIA at Kennesaw Mountain June 27, 1864.
SIMONS, Benjamin. M.O. June 7, 1865.
SOWELL, William C. M.O. June 7, 1865.
SPICER, Charles R. Disch. June 5, 1865.
SPICER, James A. Disch. June 21, 1865.
ST. CLAIRE, David. M.O. June 7, 1865.
STICKNEY, James. Died Jan. 30, 1864.
STRICKLER, Joseph R. Ptd. regimental sgt. major.
TALLEY, Alexander S. KIA at Bentonville March 19, 1865.
TAYLOR, John T. Des. Jan. 1863.
THEITON, Henry. M.O. June 7, 1865.
THOMPSON, John. M.O. June 7, 1865.
THOMPSON, Leonidas. Absent wounded at M.O. of regiment.
THORNTON, Louis L. Absent sick at M.O. of regiment.
TUTTLE, Enos B. M.O. June 7, 1865.
WADE, James A. Disch. Oct. 25, 1863; disab.
WEISTER, Jacob W. M.O. June 7, 1865.
WILLSON, William H. M.O. June 7, 1865.
WOOD, John H. Died of wds. Apr. 27, 1865
Recruits
ADAIR, Daniel W. Trans. Co. G, 34th Ill. Inf.
AUSTIN, Timothy W. Trans. Co. G 34th Ill. Inf.
BARNETT, Commodore. Disch. June 1863.

BRENEMAN, David J. M.O. June 7, 1865.
GERARD, Benjamin F. M.O. June 7, 1865.
GLASS, George. Trans. Co. G, 34th Ill. Inf.
McWILLIAMS, Elijah. KIA at Kennesaw Mountain June 30, 1864.
McWILLIAMS, Joseph. M.O. June 7, 1865.
McWILLIAMS, William. M.O. June 7, 1865.
PEW, Nelson G. Trans. Co. G 34th Ill. Inf.
SELLICK, Edward J. Trans. Co.G 34th Ill.

Company C
Recruited from McDonough County

Captains
BLANDIN, George W. M.O. June 7, 1865.
HUME, Charles R. Res. Dec. 18, 1864.
First Lieutenants
BLANDIN, George W. Ptd. captain.
CARTWRIGHT, Oliver P. Res. Oct. 6, 1863.
O'NEIL, Andrew J. M.O. June 7, 1865.
Second Lieutenants
BLANDIN, George W. Ptd. 1st lt.
First Sergeants
JAMES, John E. KIA at Kennesaw Mountain June 27, 1864.
MAGIE, James K. M.O. June 7, 1865.
Sergeants
KIRKPATRICK, Francis A. M.O. June 7, 1865.
MEALY, Michael. Died of wds. Sept. 4, 1864.
MEEK, Luther. M.O. June 7, 1865.
SPELLMAN, Charles L. M.O. June 7, 1865.
STAFFORD, Albert J. M.O. Jul. 12, 1865.
Privates
BENTLEY, Joseph H. Disch. Apr. 8, 1863; disab.
BOND, Marion D. Disch. May 5, 1865, wds.
BOYLAN, Thomas C. M.O. June 7, 1865.
BRIDGES, Thomas B. Trans. Co. I.
CARNES, Henry. M.O. June 7, 1865.
CARTER, Isaac G. M.O. June 7, 1865.
CHAFFIN, Philip. M.O. June 7, 1865.
CLARK, Edward. Disch., Oct. 3, 1862, disab.
CLINE, Marshall C. KIA near Atlanta Aug. 7, 1864.
COLE, Eleazer. Des. Jan. 3, 1863.
CURTIS, Joseph P. M.O. June 7, 1865.
CURTIS, Mark M. Ptd. cpl. Des. Jan. 3, 1863.
DAVIS, Thomas J. Disch. Feb. 1, 1865, disab.
DECKER, Nathaniel. Trans. Co. I.
DIXON, William. Des. Jan. 3, 1863.
DOWELL, George W. Died at Nashville Oct. 29, 1863.

DOWNEN, Thomas J. Trans. Co. I.
DUFFIELD, William H. M.O. June 17, 1865; was POW.
DUNCAN, James M. Ptd. cpl. M.O. June 7, 1865.
DUNCAN, John. Musician. Disch. March 13, 1863; disab.
FORREST, John S. KIA at Jonesboro Sept. 1, 1864.
FRANK, John. M.O. June 7, 1865.
FREELAND, William C. M.O. June 22, 1865.
GALBREATH, John T. M.O. June 7, 1865.
GIBSON, Samuel. Trans. Co. I, Oct. 1, 1862.
GORHAM, John. M.O. June 7, 1865.
GREEN, John F. M.O. June 7, 1865.
HAINLINE, John R. M.O. June 7, 1865.
HAMILTON, Elisha. M.O. June 11, 1865.
HARMON, John. M.O. June 7, 1865.
HARMON, William W. Died at Savannah Feb. 21, 1865.
HENDRICKS, Lewis. Ptd. cpl. M.O. June 7, 1865.
HUDDLESTON, James R. M.O. June 7, 1865.
JAMES, John E. Ptd. 1st sgt.
JAMES, John W. KIA at Jonesboro Sept. 1, 1864.
JAMES, Joseph A. Ptd. cpl. M.O. June 7, 1865.
JAMES, William E. M.O. June 7, 1865.
JENKS, Joel H. Musician. M.O. June 7, 1865.
KEITHLEY, Joseph H. M.O. June 7, 1865.
KEITHLEY, Perry. M.O. June 7, 1865.
KIRKPATRICK, Francis A. Ptd. sgt.
LAWSON, Joseph D. Des. Sept. 30, 1862.
LINDSEY, Thomas. Died at Chattanooga June 24, 1864.
MAGIE, James K. Ptd. 1st sgt.
MAGIE, Charles H. Died at Nashville Aug. 19, 1863.
MARSHALL, Josephus. Des. Jan. 9, 1863.
MARTIN, George. M.O. June 7, 1865.
MAYHUGH, Francis T. Des., May 21, 1863.
MAYHUGH, John T. M.O. June 7, 1865.
MAYHUGH, Laban D. Des. May 21, 1863.
McFALL, Sylvester. Ptd. cpl. Disch. Dec. 10, 1864, wds.
McGEE, William F. M.O. June 7, 1865.
MEALY, Michael. Ptd. sgt.
MEEK, Luther. Ptd. sgt.
MESSACHER, Silas. M.O. June 7, 1865.
MESSACHER, William D. Ptd. cpl. M.O. June 7, 1865.
MICHAELS, Jacob H. KIA at Kennesaw Mountain, June 27, 1864.
MIDCAP, Nathaniel. M.O. June 7, 1865.
MONAHAN, John. Died at Chattanooga Apr. 3, 1864.
MORGAN, Clinton. Drummed out of service, Nov. 4, 1862.
NORRIS, Charles L. Died at Chattanooga Nov. 3, 1864.
O'CAIN, James. Disch. Sept. 13, 1863; disab.
O'NEIL, Andrew J. Ptd. 1st lt.
PACE, Ingram. Trans. Co. I. Oct. 1, 1862.

ROBERTS, Peter B. M.O. June 7, 1865.
RUDDELL, Sylvester. Died at Nashville Dec. 30, 1863.
RUSH, John W. KIA at Jonesboro Sept. 1, 1864.
SHERRY, Marion. M.O. June 7, 1865.
SIMS, John. Trans. Co. I. Oct. 1, 1862.
SMITH, William. Disch. March 7, 1863; disab.
SPELLMAN, Charles L. Ptd. sgt.
STAFFORD, Albert J. Ptd. sgt.
TERRY, Richard L. Wounded at Kennesaw Mountain, June 27, 1864; leg amputated.
TIPTON, James. Disch. Nov. 11, 1862; disab.
TYFT, Cyrell. Died of wds. Sept. 3, 1864.
VENNING, Henry. KIA at Jonesboro Sept. 1, 1864.
WARNER, William H. M.O. June 7, 1865.
WELSH, James L. M.O. June 7, 1865.
WILHELMS, William A. Trans. Co. I. Oct. 1, 1862.
WILSON, Andrew. M.O. June 7, 1865.
WILSON, Elias H. M.O. June 3, 1865; was POW.
WOODSIDE, John W. Disch. March 7, 1863.
WORLEY, John L. M.O. June 7, 1865.
WORLEY, William H. H. M.O. June 17, 1865.
Recruits
BAYLES, Joseph W. M.O. June 7, 1865.
BROWN, Fredrick P. Des. Jan. 3, 1863.
CHAFFIN, Michael. M.O. June 7, 1865.
CHARTER, Smith W. Trans. Co. E, 34th Ill. Inf.
GRIFFITH, William. Trans. Co. E, 34th Ill. Inf.
KIRK, John W. M.O. June 22, 1865.
WARNER, Jesse. M.O. June 7, 1865.

Company D
Recruited from Hancock and Adams Counties

Captains
BLACK, Robert M. KIA at Jonesboro Sept. 1, 1864.
WORRELL, John B. M.O. June 7, 1865.
First Lieutenants
CUBBAGE, Wilford. M.O. June 7, 1865.
WORRELL, John B. Ptd. captain.
Second Lieutenants
KINCHELOE, Issac N. Res. Jul. 16, 1863.
PUNTENNY, Samuel W. Res. Nov. 29, 1864.
First Sergeants
ABBOTT, James. M.O. June 7, 1865.
CROTTS, William H. Died of wds. Aug. 11, 1864.
Sergeants
BRYAN, Rice B. Trans. Invalid Corps 1864.
DRUM, James T. Died at Franklin Apr. 12, 1863.

FROST, William. M.O. May 20, 1865.
NEWLAND, Isaac. Disch. Jan. 17, 1864; disab.
TALBERT, William. M.O. June 7, 1865.
WALLACE, Albert. KIA at Jonesboro Sept. 1, 1864.
WALLACE, John. M.O. June 7, 1865.
WELLS, William. M.O. June 17, 1865; was POW.
Privates
ABBOTT, James. Ptd. 1st sgt.
ALLISON, David. Died at Atlanta Sept. 8, 1864.
ASHBAUGH, Lewis. M.O. June 7, 1865.
BARGER, Philip. M.O. June 7, 1865.
BELL, John L. Died at Louisville Feb. 3, 1863.
BENNETT, Charles N. M.O. June 7, 1865.
BOTTS, Joseph O. Disch. June 10, 1863; disab.
BOTTS, Sidney. Ptd. cpl. M.O. June 17, 1865; was POW.
BOYLES, Archibald. M.O. June 7, 1865.
BURTON, Luther C. Died of wds. June 26, 1864.
CARROLL, John. KIA at Chickamauga Sept. 20, 1863.
CARY, Freeman. Ptd. cpl. M.O. June 17 1865; was POW.
CECIL, William. M.O. June 7, 1865.
COON, James W. M.O. June 7, 1865.
CORMACK, John C. M.O. June 7, 1865.
CRAIG, David B. M.O. June 7, 1865.
CRAIG, James. M.O. June 7, 1865.
CROTTS, George W. KIA at Jonesboro Sept. 1, 1864.
CROTTS, William H. Ptd. sgt.
CRUM, Theodore P. Trans. Invalid Corps 1864.
CUBBAGE, John H. M.O. June 7, 1865.
CUBBAGE, Wilford. Ptd. 1st lt. Sept. 1, 1864.
CUNNINGHAM, Thomas. KIA at Bentonville March 19, 1865.
DAVIS, Samuel S. KIA at Jonesboro Sept. 1, 1864.
DAVIS, William S. Died of wds. Sept. 17, 1864.
DRAGER, Adolphus W. Ptd. cpl. M.O. June 7, 1865.
DRUM, James T. Ptd. sgt.
EARL, William. Disch. Sept. 12, 1863; disab.
FAUGHT, Virious. M.O. June 7, 1865.
FROST, William. Ptd. cpl, then ptd. sgt.
FRY, James M. M.O. June 7, 1865.
FRY, Solomon. M.O. June 7, 1865.
FUTHY, Henry. Ptd. cpl. M.O. June 7, 1865.
GERST, Jacob. M.O. June 7, 1865.
GILLILAND, Leander. M.O. June 7, 1865.
HAGAR, Rufus I. Disch. Apr. 1863; was POW.
HAMILTON, Robert M. Ptd. cpl. M.O. June 7, 1865.
HAMILTON, William J. M.O. June 7, 1865.
HAWKINS, Daniel G. Died at Louisville May 12, 1863.
HOWARD, John W. Ptd. cpl. M.O. May 22, 1865.

HUCKINS, Jacob O. Disch. May 24, 1863; disab.
JOHNSON, Charles. M.O. June 7, 1865.
KIMMEL, George. Died at Beech Fork, Ky. Oct. 29, 1862.
KIMMEL, Henry. M.O. June 7, 1865.
LAIRLEY, Jacob. Died of wds. Oct. 2, 1863.
LANEY, Charles. Des. Feb. 1, 1863.
LANEY, Peter. Des. Feb. 1, 1863.
LIMPUS, Edward F. M.O. June 7, 1865.
LONG, William R. M.O. June 7, 1865.
MAHILL, Daniel H. Des. Sept. 26, 1862.
MANLOVE, Wilford W. M.O. May 18, 1865.
MANLOVE, William. Ptd. cpl. KIA at Kennesaw Mountain June 27, 1864.
MARSHALL, Mordecai. M.O. June 7, 1865.
MATHEWS, Eli. M.O. June 11, 1865.
MATHEWS, Samuel. M.O. June 7, 1865.
McCANDLESS, Alexander. M.O. June 7, 1865.
McMAHON, Francis M. Disch. June 10, 1864.
MILTON, William E. Ptd. cpl. M.O. June 7, 1865.
NEWLAND, Isaac. Ptd. sgt.
NEWLAND, Thomas. M.O. June 7, 1865.
NEWMAN, Egbert. M.O. June 7, 1865.
ORMSBEE, Ephraim. M.O. June 7, 1865.
PARISH, Joseph M. M.O. June 7, 1865.
PUNTENNY, Samuel W. Ptd. 2nd lt.
RAMPLEY, John. M.O. June 7, 1865.
RAMPLEY, Riley. M.O. June 7, 1865.
SHORT, Eli E. M.O. June 7, 1865.
SMITH, Thomas B. Trans. VRC Jul. 25, 1864.
STOUT, William G. M.O. June 7, 1865.
STUART, Andrew H. Des. Nov. 1, 1862.
STUART, Jeremiah M. KIA near Big Shanty, Ga., June 16, 1864.
SWYGLESON, Charles. M.O. June 7, 1865.
SWYGLESON, Robert. M.O. June 7, 1865.
TALBERT, William. Ptd. sgt.
THOMPSON, Henry C. Died of wds. Sept. 25, 1863.
THOMPSON, Mason M. M.O. June 7, 1865.
THOMPSON, William H. Disch. March 11, 1865, wds.
WAGGONER, Josiah. M.O. June 7, 1865.
WALLACE, Albert. Ptd. sgt.
WALLACE, John. Ptd. sgt.
WALLACE, Mitchell E. M.O. June 7, 1865.
WARES, Martin V.B. M.O. June 7, 1865.
WELLS, William. Ptd. sgt.
WHITAKER, Benjamin F. M.O. June 7, 1865.
WRIGHT, Samuel H. M.O. June 7, 1865.
YARNALL, Joseph. Trans. Engineer Corps Jul. 25, 1864.
YARNALL, William. M.O. June 7, 1865.

Recruits
ALLISON, Justice M. Disch. Feb. 16, 1865; disab.
BATES, William. M.O. June 7, 1865.
BROWN, Warren P. Trans. Co. E, 34th Ill. Inf.
CECIL, Thomas J. Trans. Co. E 34th Ill. Inf.
CRUM, Samuel. M.O. May 11, 1865.
DICKINSON, Jonathan H. Des. Oct. 1, 1863.
DICKINSON, Rufus B. Des. Oct. 1, 1863.
DORMAN, James M. Trans. Co. E, 34th Ill. Inf.
DRAGER, Augustus J. Trans. Co. E, 34th Ill. Inf.
FRY, Jacob J. M.O. Jul. 11, 1865.
GREEN, Julius. Trans. Co. E, 34th Ill. Inf.
GREWELL, Christopher H. Trans. Co. E, 34th Ill.Inf.
KING, Joel B. M.O. May 23, 1865.
KING, William A. Trans. Co. E, 34th Ill. Inf.
LAW, Robert. M.O. May 23, 1865.
MAHIL, William. Des. Sept. 26, 1862.
MOORE, Enos P. Trans. Co. E, 34th Ill. Inf.
PAXTON, John C. M.O. June 7, 1865.
STUMP, Edward T. Died at Camp Butler, Il., March 17, 1864.
THOMPSON, John M. No further information.
WAGGONER, Ephraim. Trans. Co. E, 34th Ill. Inf.
WILLIAMS, Joseph. N. Trans. Co. E, 34th Ill. Inf.
WILSON, John H. Trans. Co. E, 34th Ill. Inf.
WINSTON, James M. Trans. Co. C, 61st Ill. Inf.
WRIGHT, Samuel M. M.O. May 23, 1865.

Company E
Recruited from Adams County

Captains
MERCER, John J. M.O. June 7, 1865.
POLLOCK, George. Res. June 27, 1864.
First Lieutenants
HENRY, Mathew. Res. March 2, 1863.
MERCER, John J. Ptd. captain.
MERCER, Philip H. Disch. May 4, 1865.
Second Lieutenants
MERCER, John J. Ptd. 1st lt.
MERCER, Philip H. Ptd. 1st lt.
First Sergeants
LAWSON, William. M.O. June 7, 1865.
PIERCE, William. KIA at Kennesaw Mountain June 27, 1864.
Sergeants
BARTLETT, James. M.O. June 7, 1865.
GLENN, William. Died of wds. Oct. 16, 1863.
ROBERTSON, Nathaniel B. Disch. June 16, 1864.

TOMLIN, William. M.O. June 22, 1865.

Privates

AKERS, Charles. M.O. June 7, 1865.

ALLEN, David. Disch. Sept. 14, 1863.

ALLEN, Wilson. Disch. June 8, 1863.

ASKEW, George W. Died at Nashville June 3, 1863.

ASKEW, William P. M.O. June 9, 1865.

BARNARD, Francis N. Ptd. cpl. M.O. June 7, 1865.

BARTLETT, James. Ptd. sgt.

BEARD, David. M.O. June 7, 1865.

BENFIELD, Samuel. M.O. June 7, 1865.

BERGETT, Albert G. Ptd. cpl. M.O. June 7, 1865.

BIRDSALL, Isaac. Trans. Engineer Corps Jul. 29, 1864.

BLIVEN, William. KIA at Chickamauga Sept. 20, 1863.

BUFFINGTON, Peter B. Disch. June 13, 1863.

CAMPBELL, George W. KIA at Chickamauga Sept. 20, 1863.

CASTERLINE, George F. Trans. Invalid Corps Feb. 15, 1864.

CASTERLINE, John F. M.O. June 7, 1865.

CHANDLER, John B. M.O. June 7, 1865.

CHANDLER, William R. Trans. Invalid Corps Apr. 10, 1864.

COLE, Charles W. Ptd. cpl. M.O. June 7, 1865.

CORBIN, Parker. Disch. Oct. 29, 1863.

COVERT, William. Disch. May 7, 1863.

CRAIG, Milton. M.O. June 7, 1865.

CUNNINGHAM, Jesse. Died at Chattanooga Nov. 30, 1864.

DEAL, Henry. M.O. June 7, 1865.

DEIGHTON, Samuel. M.O. Jul. 14, 1865.

DEISER, Alexander. M.O. June 7, 1865.

DEISER, Samuel. Died at Franklin May 17, 1863.

FESSENDEN, Charles B. M.O. June 7, 1865.

FLORA, John. Disch. Sept. 14, 1863.

FORDYCE, Thomas W. Disch. May 27, 1864.

FRAZELLE, Azariah. Died at Louisville March. 4, 1863.

FRY, Levi. Died at Nashville March 23, 1864.

FRY, Tillman K. Disch. March 14, 1863.

FULMER, Bernard. M.O. June 7, 1865.

FULMER, Valentine. KIA at Chickamauga Sept. 20, 1863.

GALLAHER, Russell. M.O. June 7, 1865.

GARDINER, Robert. Died at Louisville Apr. 22, 1863.

GATES, William N. M.O. June 7, 1865.

GOTT, Thomas. M.O. June 7, 1865.

GRAMMER, Seth W. Ptd. regimental commissary sgt.

GRUBB, Byron. Died at Chattanooga Jul. 1, 1864.

GRUBB, Perry D. M.O. June 17, 1865; was POW.

HARELSON, Sulphen. KIA at Bentonville March 19, 1865.

HASTINGS, John K. KIA at Chickamauga Sept. 20, 1863.

HEDRICK, George W. Died at Franklin Apr. 7, 1863.

HENDRICK, William F. M.O. June 7, 1863.

HENDRICKS, David C. Disch. Jul. 24, 1863.
HENDRICKS, Israel. KIA at Chickamauga Sept. 20, 1863.
HENDRICKS, John W. M.O. June 7, 1865.
HERALDSON, Jacob V. M.O. June 7, 1865.
HILL, Philip. Des. Oct. 4, 1862.
HOFFMASTER, Julius. M.O. June 22, 1865.
HOFFMASTER, Peter. M.O. June 7, 1865.
HUFF, Aaron. M.O. June 7, 1863.
KELLEY, John L. M.O. June 7, 1863.
KUNTZ, Charles. Reported missing at Chickamauga Sept. 20, 1863.
KUNTZ, Henry. M.O. June 7, 1865.
KUNTZ, John. M.O. June 7, 1865.
LAWSON, William. Ptd. 1st sgt.
MATTHEWS, Joseph. Died of wds. Oct. 17, 1863.
McLANE, Samuel. M.O. June 7, 1865.
McRAE, James. Died at Liberty, Il., Apr. 27, 1864.
McRAE, William F. Absent sick at M.O. of regiment.
MERCER, Philip H. Ptd. 2d lt.
NATIONS, John. KIA at Chickamauga Sept. 20, 1863.
NATIONS, John B. Disch. May 28, 1864.
NAYLOR, Samuel. Disch. May 2, 1865.
PATE, Noah. Disch. Feb. 3, 1864.
PETTIT, James H. Ptd. cpl. M.O. June 7, 1865.
POTTORF, John A. Ptd. cpl. M.O. June 7, 1865.
PRICHARD, William H. M.O. June 7, 1865.
ROBERTSON, Nathaniel B. Ptd. sgt.
ROSS, Alexander R. Absent sick at M.O. of regiment.
SCOTT, Gordon. Trans. from Co. F. Died at Nashville June 14, 1863.
SHEHAWNY, Lewis C. Died at Savannah Jan. 13, 1865.
SIMPSON, Robert B. M.O. June 7, 1865.
SLACK, Benjamin F. M.O. June 7, 1865.
SLIPPER, Joseph. Trans. Engineer Corps Jul. 29, 1864.
SMITH, Fielding R. M.O. June 7, 1865.
STARKS, Andrew. Absent sick at M.O. of regiment.
STARNES, Josiah. KIA at Chickamauga Sept. 20, 1863.
STAUFFER, Jacob. M.O. June 7, 1865.
STEELE, John H. M.O. June 7, 1865.
THOMAS, William. M.O. June 7, 1865.
TOMLIN, William. Ptd. sgt.
VANCIL, Tichnor. Ptd. cpl. M.O. June 7, 1865.
WHITTAKER, Nicholas. M.O. June 7, 1865.
WILLIAMS, Edward. Ptd. cpl. M.O. June 7, 1865.
WINNER, Ephraim. M.O. June 7, 1865.
WINNER, Joseph N. M.O. June 7, 1865.
WYATT, Thomas. Trans. VRC Jan. 15, 1865.
YOUNGHEIN, Julius. M.O. June 22, 1865.
Recruits
BLAKE, Charles H. KIA at Kennesaw Mountain June 27, 1864.

GALAGHER, James. Trans. from Co. F. Absent sick at M.O. of regiment.
GALAGHER, Samuel. Trans. from Co. F. Disch. May 17, 1863.
GAY, James H. Trans. from Co. F. KIA at Bentonville March 19, 1865.
GLENN, William. Trans. from Co. F. Ptd. sgt.
SCOTT, Gordon. Trans. from Co. F. Died at Nashville June 14, 1863.

Company F
Recruited from Adams County

Captains
HAWKINS, Henry E. Disch. May 15, 1865.
First Lieutenants
CANNON, Clinton B. Res. May 28, 1863.
MORSE, Elisha. Ptd. captain June 6, 1865, but M.O. as 1st lieutenant. Was POW.
Second Lieutenants
EARL, Seldon G. Res. Dec. 23 1862.
IRWIN, Leander. Disch. May 15, 1865.
Sergeants
HENDERSON, William. M.O. June 17, 1865.
HOWELL, Anthony. M.O. June 7, 1865; was POW.
JONES, Ellis D. Disch. Feb. 24, 1863; disab.
WILBURN, Robert. KIA at Jonesboro Sept. 1, 1864.
Privates
AKERS, Charles W. Died as POW at Richmond Feb. 17, 1864.
AKERS, Clarkson. Died as POW at Andersonville Aug. 16, 1864.
AKERS, John W. M.O. June 7, 1865.
AKERS, Stephen. Claimed as deserter by 3rd Missouri Cavalry Sept. 9, 1862.
ARTERBURN, Brannum. M.O. June 7, 1865.
ASHER, Hardin. M.O. June 17, 1865; was POW.
BARRY, Thomas. M.O. June 7, 1865.
BEAL, John. Died as POW at Andersonville June 12, 1864.
BEARD, William J. Died at Nashville May 20, 1863.
BIRD, George H. Trans. Engineer Corps Jul. 29, 1864.
BUCKNER, John W. Des. Aug. 1862.
BURN, William. Des. Feb. 1, 1863.
BUTTS, Lindorft. Died at Nashville Feb. 22, 1863.
CAMERY, Peter. Trans. Co. G.
CARSON, Archibald. Disch. Aug. 27, 1863; disab.
CARSON, James. Des. May 1, 1863.
CHANDLER, Charles. M.O. June 7, 1865.
CHANDLER, Theodore. M.O. Jul. 11, 1865.
COOVERT, David. Died as POW at Andersonville Jul. 5, 1864.
CUMMINS, Charles. Died as POW at Richmond Feb. 17, 1864.
CUMMINS, Joseph. Disch. Apr. 21, 1863, disab.
DAVIS, James S. Died at Atlanta Sept. 7, 1864.
DEMOSS, Benjamin F. Died as POW at Andersonville Aug. 29, 1864.
EBBEN, Henry. Des. Feb. 14, 1863.

EYMAN, George. Died at Nashville May 17, 1863.

FELT, Peter F. Disch. March 22, 1863; disab.

FRENCH, Joseph. M.O. June 7, 1865.

FROST, John. M.O. June 7, 1865; was POW.

GALLAGHER, James. Trans. Co. E.

GALLAGHER, Samuel. Trans. Co. E.

GAY, James. Trans. Co. E.

GILKEY, Edwin. M.O. June 7, 1865.

GLENN, William. Trans. Co. E.

GUYMON, John A. Died as POW at Andersonville Oct. 25, 1864.

HAYES, John A. Disch. March 11, 1863; disab.

HENDERSON, Benjamin C. Des. Jan. 23, 1864.

HENDERSON, William. Ptd. sgt.

HENDRIX, Joseph. Disch. Apr. 21, 1863; disab.

HOGAN, John. Died as POW at Savannah Oct. 1, 1864.

HOWELL, Anthony. Ptd. sgt.

HOWELL, James W. Died as POW at Andersonville Jul. 12, 1864.

ILER, George W. Trans. Co. G.

IRWIN, Leander. Ptd. 2nd lt.

JACOBS, Samuel. M.O. June 7, 1865; was POW.

JAMISON, Thomas. Trans. VRC Apr. 1865.

JOHNSON, Milton. Ptd. cpl. M.O. June 7, 1865; was POW.

JONES, Ellis D. Ptd. sgt.

KELLY, John S. M.O. Jul. 25, 1865; was POW.

KING, David G. Trans. Co. G.

KINSALA, Patrick. Disch. Jul. 6, 1864; disab.

KISHNER, John. Des. Oct. 1, 1862.

KITCHEN, John. Disch. Feb. 9, 1864; disab.

LAWLESS, Thomas. M.O. June 7, 1865; was POW.

LEISTER, Emmerson. Trans. Co. G.

LONG, William. Trans. Co. G.

LOUKOR, George. Trans. Co. G.

MANARD, William G. Ptd. cpl. M.O. Jul. 11, 1865; was POW.

McCAFFREY, Edward B. M.O. June 7, 1865.

McLAUGHLIN, Thomas. Ptd. cpl. M.O. June 7, 1865; was POW.

McNEAL, John A. Died as POW at Andersonville Sept. 26, 1864.

MILLER, Joseph S. Trans. Co. G.

MOORE, James P. Disch. Apr. 18, 1864; disab.

MOORE, James T. Died at Chattanooga Apr. 7, 1864.

MOORE, William. Des. Feb. 1, 1863.

MORSE, Samuel S. Trans. Engineer Corps Jul. 29, 1864.

MYERS, William. Absent sick at M.O. of regiment.

ODEAR, John. M.O. June 7, 1865; was POW.

ODEAR, Thomas. Died as POW at Andersonville June 14, 1864.

PLOWMAN, Charles. M.O. June 7, 1865; was POW.

REED, Samuel. Trans. Co. G.

RICHARDSON, John A. Des. Jan. 2, 1863.

ROBINSON, John. Ptd. cpl. M.O. June 7, 1865; was POW.
SAMMONS, Henry. Died as POW at Florence S.C. Oct. 18, 1864.
SCOTT, Gordon. Trans. Co. E.
SKIRVEN, William. Trans. Engineer Corps Jul. 29, 1864.
SMITH, Andrew. Absent sick at M.O. of regiment.
SMITH, George. M.O. June 7, 1865.
SMITH, William. M.O. June 7, 1865.
SWETT, William. Disch. May 29, 1863; disab.
TATMAN, Ezra. Died at Franklin May 25, 1863.
TAYLOR, James. Died as POW at Richmond Jan. 9, 1864.
THOMAS, James H. Disch. Aug. 27, 1863, disab.
TROUT, David. Died as POW at Florence S.C. Oct. 29, 1864.
TROUT, Samuel J. M.O. June 17, 1865; was POW.
VIARS, Thomas J. Des. Jan. 26, 1865.
WHITE, Hugh. Died at Rossville, Ga. May 7, 1864.
WHITE, Thomas C. Disch. March 22, 1863.
WILBURN, Robert. Ptd. sgt.
WILLIAMS, Stephen A. Des. Jan. 26, 1863.
Recruits
BARNETT, Henry T. Trans. Co. G, 34th Ill. Inf.
BREWER, Henry. Died as POW at Andersonville Aug. 22, 1864.
CAMPBELL, John. Absent sick at M.O. of regiment.
FELSMAN, Henry. M.O. June 17, 1865; was POW.
GARIG, John. Died as POW at Andersonville Aug. 18, 1864.
GORDON, Green. African undercook. Des. Dec. 17, 1864.
MALONE, Francis. Des. May 24, 1864.
PHILLIPS, Berry. African undercook. Trans. Co. G, 34th Ill. Inf.
PIERCE, Cornelius. Died at Quincy Aug. 11, 1863.
VIARS, Charles. Died at Nashville Jul. 11, 1863.

Company G
Recruited from Adams County

Captains
HOWDEN, Thomas L. M.O. June 7, 1865.
JOSEPH, Jacob F. Res. Apr. 2, 1863.
First Lieutenants
BUTLER, Tobias E. Died of wds. May 29, 1864.
DEHAVEN, James T. M.O. June 7, 1865.
HOWDEN, Thomas L. Ptd. capt.
LONG, Daniel W. KIA at Jonesboro Sept. 1, 1864.
Second Lieutenants
HERNDON, Pleasant M. Res. Apr. 2, 1863.
THOMPSON, Charles. Res. March 30, 1864.
First Sergeants
MILLER, Joseph. M.O. June 7, 1865.
THOMPSON, Charles. Ptd. 2nd lt.

Sergeants

BECKETT, William. Trans. VRC Apr. 10, 1864.

HALEY, Jesse. Absent sick at M.O. of regiment.

LONG, Daniel W. Ptd. 1st lt.

MALTHENER, John C. M.O. June 7, 1865.

SEATON, James A. Disch. as private.

SELBY, Harlow E. M.O. June 7, 1865.

STEWART, Martin L. M.O. June 7, 1865.

Privates

ALBERT, John W. Trans. VRC Jan. 15, 1864.

ALBERT, Louis C. Disch. Aug. 7, 1863; disab.

ASHER, Jasper. Disch. Apr. 27, 1863, wds.

BARRY, William B.Y. Disch. Feb. 12, 1863; disab.

BECKETT, James A. Ptd. cpl. M.O. June 7, 1865.

BECKETT, James M. Ptd. cpl. Died of wds. March 27, 1865.

BECKETT, John S. KIA at Jonesboro Sept. 1, 1864.

BECKETT, William T. M.O. June 7, 1865.

BLICKSON, George. Des. Feb. 5, 1863.

BOOKER, Samuel J. Disch. Apr. 18, 1863; disab.

BOTTORF, Isaac A. Trans. VRC March 15, 1865.

BOTTORF, Thomas F. Ptd. cpl. M.O. June 7, 1865.

BRIDGES, Ca. African undercook. Trans. Co. K 34th Ill. Inf.

BUTLER, Tobias E. Ptd. 1st lt.

CAMERY, Peter S. Trans. from Co. F as cpl. Died of wds. near Atlanta Aug. 12, 1864.

CANNON, William E. Absent sick at M.O. of regiment.

CASTLE, Anson. Ptd. cpl. M.O. June 7, 1865.

CURL, John B. Died at Shelbyville Aug. 22, 1863.

DEHAVEN, James T. Ptd. cpl., then 1st lt.

DEMOSS, Jonathan. M.O. June 7, 1865.

DEWITT, Delancy. M.O. June 7, 1865.

DICKINSON, Thomas. Trans. VRC June 27, 1864.

DILLEY, Valentine. KIA at Chickamauga Sept. 20, 1863.

DOWNING, William M. M.O. June 7, 1865.

EDWARDS, Asa T. M.O. June 7, 1865.

ERDMAN, Sebastian A. Musician. Disch. Feb. 22, 1863; disab.

ESNSMINGER, Franklin. M.O. June 7, 1865.

FARLOW, John M. M.O. June 7, 1865.

FLACK, Richard. M.O. June 7, 1865.

FLACK, Samuel. Trans. VRC 1865.

FRY, John. Trans. VRC March 15, 1864.

FURGUSON, Henry. M.O. June 7, 1865.

GIBSON, James. Trans. VRC Jan. 15, 1864.

HALEY, Jesse. Ptd. sgt.

HALEY, William. M.O. June 7, 1865.

HAMRICK, William W. Disch. May 16, 1863; disab.

HAND, Thompson. Trans. VRC Nov. 13, 1863.

HEDRICK, James. Trans. Co. A 34th Ill. Inf.

HENLEY, Madison. M.O. June 7, 1865.

HOMPSHER, Daniel. M.O. June 13, 1865.
ILER, George W. Trans. from Co. F. Ptd. cpl. M.O. June 7, 1865.
KING, David J. Trans. from Co. F. M.O. June 7, 1865.
LESTER, Emmerson. Trans. from Co. F. M.O. June 7, 1865.
LONG, William. Trans. from Co. F. M.O. June 7, 1865.
LOUKOR, George. Trans. from Co. F. M.O. June 22, 1865.
MAJORS, Archibald C. No further information.
MALTHENER, John C. Ptd. cpl., then sgt.
McCLELLAND, Hugh M. Disch. Mar 22, 1865; disab.
McFARLAND, Henry M. Ptd. cpl. M.O. June 7, 1865.
McGILL, Clayton W. M.O. June 7, 1865.
METHINGHAM, John. Disch. Mar 26, 1863; disab.
METHINGHAM, William. M.O. June 7, 1865.
MILLER, Daniel S. Disch. Nov. 14, 1863; disab.
MILLER, Franklin. Disch. Oct. 15, 1862; disab.
MILLER, Joseph. Ptd. 1st sgt.
MILLER, Joseph S. Trans. from Co. F. Disch. May 30, 1863; disab.
NEWLAND, Daniel R. Absent sick at M.O. of regiment.
ODELL, Risdon M. M.O. June 7, 1865.
ODELL, Thomas G. Ptd. cpl. Disch. Jan. 23, 1865; wds.
OLSSON, John. Absent sick at M.O. of regiment.
OUREY, Abner. Des. March 17, 1863.
PAYNE, Bennett A. M.O. June 7, 1865.
PICKLER, Joseph D. M.O. June 7, 1865.
PILCHER, William. Trans. VRC Apr. 6, 1864.
POLLOCK, Alfred. Disch. May 18, 1865.
PRETTYMAN, David. Musician. Disch. May 1, 1863; disab.
REED, Ralph C. KIA at Chickamauga Sept. 20, 1863.
REED, Samuel G. Trans. from Co. F. M.O. June 7, 1865.
RILEY, Presley. Ptd. cpl. M.O. June 7, 1865 as private.
ROE, Bernard F. Died at Shelbyville Sept. 3, 1863.
ROSEBERRY, Lemuel B. M.O. June 7, 1865.
ROSS, Benjamin F. Died at Quincy Oct. 29, 1862.
SANBURN, Alonzo. M.O. Jul. 31, 1865.
SIMONS, Alexander. Disch. Apr. 7, 1865; wds.
SMITH, William M. M.O. June 7, 1865.
STEWART, Martin L. Ptd. cpl., then sgt.
TAYLOR, Christopher. M.O. June 7, 1865.
TAYLOR, David P. M.O. Jul. 22, 1865.
TAYLOR, Thomas S. Trans. Engineer Corps Jul. 27, 1864.
THOMPSON, George W. Ptd. cpl. Trans. VRC Apr. 30, 1864.
WELCH, George W. On detached duty at M.O. of regiment.
WHITE, William J. Ptd. cpl. M.O. June 7, 1865.
WHITFORD, James T. M.O. June 7, 1865.
WILSON, Clark. Trans. Engineer Corps Jul. 21, 1864.
WISEHART, George. Ptd. cpl. M.O. June 7, 1865.
WISEHART, James R. Died of wds. at Chattanooga, Oct. 8, 1863.
WISEHART, John H. M.O. June 7, 1865.

WISEHART, Philip C. M.O. June 7, 1865.
Recruits
DICKINSON, Charles. Trans. Co. K, 34th Ill. Inf.
HILDRETH, Benjamin O. Disch. March 17, 1864, wds.
LONG, Harvey. Trans. Co. K, 34th Ill. Inf.
MARSH, Elijah M. M.O. June 7, 1865.
McCLURE, Hugh. Disch. March 22, 1865; disab.

Company H
Recruited from Hancock and Henderson Counties

Captains
ALLEN, John K. Res. March 30, 1864; disab.
BEERS, George T. KIA at Bentonville March 19, 1865.
First Lieutenants
BEERS, George T. Ptd. captain.
GIBBS, John. In hospital at M.O. of regiment.
Second Lieutenants
SIMMONS, Samuel. Disch. March 11, 1865.
First Sergeants
SCOTT, Thomas M. Ptd. captain March 30, 1864, but declined commission; was POW.
Sergeants
GIBBS, John. Ptd. 1st lt.
HETRICK, William. M.O. June 17, 1865; was POW.
L'HOMIDIEU, Samuel L. Died of wds. March 30, 1865.
McKIM, Edward. KIA at Bentonville March 19, 1865.
McNEILL, James M. Disch. June 16, 1863.
RICE, Jonathan. Disch. May 8, 1863.
RICHART, Cyrus C. M.O. June 7, 1865.
ROSE, Henderson. M.O. June 7, 1865.
THOMAS, William J. KIA at Jonesboro Sept. 1, 1864.
Privates
ARNOLD, Edmund. Captured near Atlanta Aug. 4, 1864.
BARTLETT, Joseph. M.O. June 7, 1865.
BECKWITH, Samuel. M.O. June 7, 1865.
BEERMAN, John. M.O. June 7, 1865.
BEERMAN, Joseph. Died of wds.
BEESLEY, Henry F. M.O. June 7, 1865.
BLAN, William H. M.O. June 7, 1865.
BROWN, Martin M. M.O. June 7, 1865.
CALEY, Wilson S. M.O. June 7, 1865.
COKE, Joseph. Died at Nashville March 7, 1863.
COSGROVE, John D. M.O. June 7, 1865.
DEIBERT, Charles H. KIA at Chickamauga Sept. 20, 1863.
DUNHAM, George. M.O. June 7, 1865.
ECKLES, Stephen. Disch. June 19, 1863.
ELLIS, Martin. Died near Nashville Feb. 7, 1863.

ETTEN, Isaac. M.O. June 7, 1865.
FLORY, Jonah. M.O. June 7, 1865.
GABHART, John. Des. Feb. 2, 1863.
GILBREATH, Henry. M.O. June 7, 1865.
GREEN, William. Trans. Invalid Corps.
HANCOCK, Alvin. M.O. June 7, 1865.
HETRICK, William. Ptd. sgt.
HIGGINS, David J. M.O. June 7, 1865.
HILB, Morritz. Ptd. cpl. Disch. Apr. 18, 1863.
HILLIARD, Daniel. Trans. Invalid Corps.
HOUK, Harmon. M.O. June 7, 1865.
HOUSEWART, Robert. Absent sick at M.O. of regiment.
HUCKINS, Jacob. Trans. Invalid Corps.
HUFF, Solomon. Died at Franklin May 9, 1863.
HUGHES, Thomas J. Disch. May 27, 1863.
JONES, Thomas J. Disch. June 1, 1863.
KEIL, William. Trans. VRC June 7, 1864.
KINMAN, Martin V. M.O. June 7, 1865.
KRAIG, George. Disch. at Quincy; date not recorded.
L'HOMIDIEU, Samuel L. Ptd. sgt.
LINCOLN, Albert. Died at Franklin March 9, 1863.
LUDINGTON, Allen B. M.O. June 7, 1865.
LUDINGTON, John M. Ptd. cpl. M.O. June 7, 1865.
MARISE, Frederick. Engineer Corps, Jul. 13, 1864.
McELHANEY, Andrew J. M.O. June 7, 1865.
McINTIRE, Elihu S. Ptd. regimental 1st assistant surgeon.
MENDENHALL, Benoni. Ptd. cpl. Disch. Oct. 12, 1864; disab.
MILLS, John H. M.O. June 7, 1865.
MISNER, Peter. Disch. March 31, 1865.
MOTLEY, Francis. Captured at Louisville, Ga. Nov. 30, 1864.
MUDGE, Daniel W. Ptd. cpl. M.O. June 7, 1865.
NICHOLS, John. Disch. March 24, 1863.
OGDEN, Philo. Ptd. cpl. M.O. June 7, 1865.
PATE, John W. Died at Nashville Feb. 7, 1863.
PECK, Elera P. Disch. May 11, 1863.
PERKINS, Thomas B. M.O. June 7, 1865.
PORTER, Lewis. Trans. Engineer Corps, Jul. 13, 1864.
RAY, John. M.O. June 7, 1865.
REED, Elisha D. M.O. June 7, 1865.
RICE, Thomas S. M.O. June 7, 1865.
RICHARDS, James. M.O. June 7, 1865.
RICHART, Cyrus C. Ptd. sgt.
RICHTER, Henry William. Des. Sept. 19, 1862.
RIEMAN, David R.P. M.O. June 7, 1865.
ROBBINS, Edward M. M.O. June 7, 1865.
ROBINSON, John W. Absent sick at M.O. of regiment.
ROBINSON, Thomas. Died of wds. Sept. 2, 1864.
ROSE, Henderson. Ptd. cpl., then ptd. sgt.

RYNEARSON, Joel H. Disch. 1864.
SANFORD, Elijah M. M.O. June 7, 1865.
SCOTT, David. M.O. June 19, 1865.
SEWARD, Oren P. M.O. June 17, 1865; was POW.
SHAIN, Elijah A. Ptd. cpl. Disch. Jul. 18, 1863.
SHAW, Isaac M. Died at Savannah Jan. 15, 1865.
SPENCER, Austin W. M.O. June 7, 1865.
STANLEY, William H. Died of wds. Sept. 10, 1864.
STRICKLER, Burris W. M.O. June 7, 1865.
TAYLOR, Joseph. M.O. June 7, 1865.
THOMAS, William J. Ptd. sgt.
THOMPSON, Sails. M.O. June 7, 1865.
UHLER, Francis. M.O. June 7, 1865.
VANHORN, John W. Ptd. cpl. M.O. June 7, 1965 as private.
WALKER, Joseph W. Ptd. cpl. M.O. June 7, 1865.
WARD, Jeremiah. M.O. June 7, 1865.
WARD, William J. I. Ptd. cpl. Died at Nashville Feb. 28, 1863.
WIBBELL, John. Disch. Sept. 14, 1864.
WILLIAMS, Isaac. Disch.; no date recorded.
WOOD, Waterman S. Ptd. cpl. M.O. Aug. 9, 1865 as private.
YOCUM, Elijah L. M.O. June 7, 1865.
Recruits
ATHERTON, John R. M.O. June 7, 1865.
BEEZLEY, Francis M. Trans. Co. G, 34th Ill. Inf.
DEUSENBERRY, William. M.O. June 7, 1865.
GASAWAY, George. M.O. June 7, 1865.
McELHINEY, Gideon Z. M.O. June 7, 1865.
McLELLAN, Nash. African undercook. Died at Chattanooga June 1, 1864.
MILES, Cannon. African undercook. Trans. Co. H, 34th Ill. Inf.
RANDALLS, Hiram. M.O. June 7, 1865.
TULL, John B. Trans. Co. G, 34th Ill. Inf.

Company I
Recruited mostly from McDonough County

Captains
REYNOLDS, Granville H. Res. Dec. 19, 1864.
VEATCH, Harmon. M.O. June 7, 1865.
First Lieutenants
HOVEY, Hardin. Disch. May 15, 1865.
Second Lieutenants
CHANDLER, Charles V. Ptd. regimental adjutant.
McCANDLESS, James H. Res. May 29, 1863.
VEATCH, Harmon. Ptd. captain.
First Sergeants
CLARK, Jerome J. Died of wds. Apr. 30, 1865.
SHANNON, John F. M.O. June 7, 1865.

Sergeants

BUCHANAN, James C. M.O. June 7, 1865.

EDMONDSON, Thomas. M.O. June 7, 1865.

GARRISON, Zachariah M. M.O. June 7, 1865.

HAMILTON, Perminion. Died of wds. Oct. 15, 1863.

McCANDLESS, Moses A. KIA near Graysville, Ga. Nov. 26, 1863.

McCLELLAN, James C. Disch. Aug. 4, 1864, for promotion in US Colored Troops.

SCUDDER, Jesse B. M.O. June 7, 1865.

SMITH, James H. M.O. June 7, 1865.

Privates

ALLEN, Richard C. Died as POW at Andersonville May 28, 1864.

ALLSHOUSE, Libeus. Died as POW at Richmond, Feb. 14, 1864.

AUSTINE, Theodore P. M.O. June 17, 1865; was POW.

ARNOLD, Ira. M.O. June 13, 1865.

BATCHELOR, John. M.O. June 7, 1865.

BATIE, Simon R. Ptd. cpl. M.O. June 7, 1865.

BAYMILLER, Michael. M.O. June 7, 1865.

BEAR, John O. Ptd. cpl. M.O. June 7, 1865.

BENNETT, Albert C. Died at Boston, Ky. Nov. 12, 1862.

BOWMAN, William H. Died of wds. Dec. 22, 1863.

BRIDGES, Thomas B. Trans. from Co. C. Disch. Aug. 24, 1863; disab.

BROADDUS, Thomas H. M.O. June 7, 1865.

BROWN, Christopher. Died as POW at Richmond Jan. 23, 1864.

BROWN, Daniel. M.O. June 7, 1865.

BUCHANAN, James C. Ptd. sgt.

CARNAHAN, Sophroneus. Ptd. cpl. M.O. June 7, 1865.

CARROLL, Daniel M. Ptd. regimental principal musician.

CARROLL, James S. Disch. Jul. 7, 1863; disab.

CHANDLER, Charles V. Ptd. 2nd lieutenant.

CHAPMAN, Douglas M. Absent at M.O. of regiment.

CHASE, James Morris. M.O. June 7, 1865; was POW.

CLARK, Jerome J. Ptd. 1st sgt.

COWGILL, John F. Disch. Jan. 30, 1864; disab.

CRAIG, Simeon. Died as POW at Andersonville Sept. 22, 1864.

CREEL, Durham M. Ptd. regimental hospital steward.

DALLAM, Samuel W. M.O. June 7, 1865.

DAVID, George H. Died of wds. Oct. 2, 1863.

DECAMP, Goin S. M.O. June 7, 1865.

DISERRON, Daniel. M.O. June 7, 1865.

DORAN, Hugh H. Died as POW at Andersonville May 28, 1864.

DOWNEN, Thomas J. Disch. Apr. 20, 1864; wds.

EDMONDSON, Thomas. Ptd. sgt.

FOLLETT, Robert. Trans. Engineer Corps.

GARRISON, Zachariah M. Ptd. sgt.

GIBSON, John. Disch. Apr. 6, 1863; disab.

GILL, Benjamin F. M.O. June 7, 1865.

HALL, George P. M.O. June 7, 1865; was POW.

HOGUE, George P. Ptd. cpl. M.O. June 7, 1865.

HOWE, John B. M.O. June 7, 1865.
HUMMER, John. Ptd. cpl. M.O. June 7, 1865.
LANE, Frank. KIA at Chickamauga Sept. 20, 1863.
LAUGHLN, Robert F. M.O. May 24, 1865.
MAXWELL, John C. Ptd. cpl. Disch. Aug. 9, 1863; disab.
MAYFIELD, Joseph. M.O. June 17, 1865; was POW.
MAYNARD, Reuben L. Ptd. regimental principal musician.
McCANDLESS, Moses A. Ptd. sgt.
McCANDLESS, Wilson. Ptd. cpl. M.O. June 7, 1865.
McCLELLAN, James C. Ptd. sgt.
McCLELLAN, John. Disch. Apr. 30, 1863; disab.
McCLELLAN, William G. Disch. Dec. 12, 1864, for promotion in US Colored Troops.
MONFORT, Lawrence M. Disch. Jul. 24, 1863; disab.
MORSE, Elisha. Ptd. 1st lt. Co. F.
MYERS, John V. Ptd. cpl. M.O. June 7, 1865.
PAINTER, George. Trans. VRC Sept. 1, 1863.
PARKER, Henry. M.O. June 7, 1865.
PEMBROKE, John C. M.O. June 7, 1865.
PENNINGTON, Joseph L. Disch. Jan. 19, 1863; disab.
PITTMAN, Burress E. Disch. Aug. 18, 1863; disab.
PITTMAN, George. Disch. Aug. 24, 1863; disab.
PLOTTS, Thomas M. M.O. June 7, 1865.
REED, Henry G. M.O. June 7, 1865.
REED, William R. M.O. June 17, 1865; was POW.
RHEA, Elias B. M.O. June 7, 1865.
RICKETTS, Harvey. M.O. June 3, 1865; was POW.
SCUDDER, Jesse B. Ptd. sgt.
SCUDDER, Martin V. Disch. June 30, 1863; disab.
SHANNON, James P. M.O. June 7, 1865.
SHANNON, John F. Ptd. 1st sgt.
SMITH, James H. Ptd. sgt.
SMITH, Joseph A. M.O. June 17, 1865; was POW.
SMITH, William F. M.O. June 7, 1865; was POW.
SOWARD, John W. Died Oct. 22, 1863.
STEWART, Francis M. Disch. Aug. 20, 1865; was POW.
STEWART, John F. Trans. VRC, Apr. 28, 1864.
STEWART, Thomas B. Trans. VRC Apr. 28, 1864.
TUNIS, Isaac. M.O. June 7, 1865.
TUNIS, Joseph. Disch. May 1, 1863; disab.
VAIL, Thomas J. Died at Nashville Jul. 3, 1863.
VEATCH, Harmon. Ptd. 2nd lt.
VINCENT, David A. M.O. June 11, 1865; was POW.
WEAVER, John. M.O. June 7, 1865.
WEAVER, William. Died of wds. Sept. 6, 1864.
WILSON, Louis R. M.O. June 7, 1865.
WILSON, Rufus R. M.O. June 7, 1865.
WITHROW, James E. M.O. June 7, 1865.

Recruits

BENNETT, Charles M. Musician (drummer). Disch. date not recorded.
BRIDGES, Thomas B. Disch. Aug. 24, 1863; disab.
CARROLL, John R. Died as POW at Andersonville Aug. 27, 1865.
CUPP, Jonas P. Disch. May 5, 1865.
CUPP, William C. Trans. Co. F, 34th Ill. Inf.
DECKER, Nathaniel. M.O. June 6, 1865; was POW.
ELLIS, James C. Apr. 5, 1864. Trans. Co. F, 34th Ill. Inf.
FABER, Jacob. M.O. June 7, 1865.
GIBSON, Samuel T. Died as POW at Andersonville Jul. 29, 1865.
McCLURE, Hugh. Trans. Co. F, 34th Ill. Inf.
McKLINTOCK, Karr. M.O. June 7, 1865.
PACE, Ingram A. Disch. Dec. 13, 1864; disab.
PRITCHARD, John E. Disch. Sept. 29, 1864.
SIMS, John. M.O. June 17, 1865; was POW.
THORN, Samuel. Trans. Co. F, 34th Ill. Inf.
WATSON, Polk. African undercook. Des. Oct. 4, 1864.
WATSON, Robert. African undercook. Trans. 34th Ill. Inf.
WILHELM, Samuel P. Disch. Oct. 1, 1864; disab.
WILHELM, William A. M.O. June 9, 1865; was POW.

Company K
Recruited from Adams County

Captains
AKINS, William B. M.O. June 7, 1865.
VERNON, Maris R. Ptd. lt. col.
First Lieutenants
AKINS, William B. Ptd. captain.
HYMAN, John. M.O. June 7, 1865.
PARSONS, Jeremiah. Res. June 17, 1863.
SUMMERS, William E. KIA at Bentonville March 21, 1865.
Second Lieutenants
AKINS, William B. Ptd. 1st lt.
First Sergeants
BUTLER, Jonathan. Disch. Feb. 10, 1865, due to wds.
SUMMERS, William E. Ptd. 1st lt.
Sergeants
ADKINS, Thomas S. M.O. June 7, 1865.
BUCKLEW, John. M.O. May, 1865.
BUTLER, Jonathan. Ptd. 1st sgt.
FRYER, Andrew J. M.O. June 7, 1865.
HOWLAND, Nathaniel. Disch. May 30, 1863; disab.
JOLLY, Thomas L. M.O. June 7, 1865.
PHIPPS, Elijah G. M.O. June 7, 1865.
REED, John. M.O. Jul. 25, 1865 as private.
ROBERTS, Christopher C. M.O. June 7, 1865.

SMITH, Charles A. Died at Nashville March 30, 1863.
Privates
ADKINS, Isaac W. KIA at Kennesaw Mountain June 27, 1864.
ADKINS, Thomas S. Ptd. sgt.
ALPS, John F. M.O. June 7, 1865.
BAILEY, Alfred K. Ptd. 2nd lt. in 109th US Colored Troops Feb. 20, 1864.
BARGER, Christian. M.O. June 7, 1865.
BARROW, Henry H. Died at Nashville May 4, 1863.
BEERS, John P. Disch. Feb. 24, 1865; wds.
BROWN, Brigham D. Died at New Haven, Ky. Nov. 7, 1862.
BUCKLEW, John. Ptd. sgt.
BURNS, Edward P. Ptd. regimental quartermaster sgt.
BUSKIRK, George W. M.O. Jul. 5, 1865.
BUSKIRK, John P. M.O. June 7, 1865.
BUTLER, Norman R. M.O. June 7, 1865.
CHEDELL, George C. M.O. June 17, 1865; was POW.
CHISM, Caleb A. Disch. Dec. 9, 1862; disab.
COOKSON, Andrew J. M.O. June 7, 1865
COULTER, David M. M.O. May 13, 1865.
CRAY, William. M.O. June 22, 1865.
CURTIS, Artemus. Disch. for promotion in US Colored Troops Nov. 28, 1863.
DAVIS, William. Trans. Invalid Corps.
DONOVAN, Thomas. M.O. June 22, 1865.
DOOL, John H. Absent sick at M.O. of regiment.
DRURY, James Elias. KIA at Bentonville March 19, 1865.
DYER, Jacob E. Disch. Feb. 12, 1865.
FELT, Peter L. Died at Chattanooga Oct. 9, 1863.
FISK, Parsons C. Ptd. cpl. M.O. June 7, 1865.
FLANDERS, Orrin J. Disch. March 7, 1863.
FRENCH, Stillman A. Died at New Haven, Ky. Dec. 26, 1862.
FRYER, Andrew J. Ptd. sgt.
FRYER, Francis. Died of wds. Jul. 12, 1864.
GARD, Jeremiah. Ptd. cpl. M.O. June 7, 1865.
GUNN, Henry H. Died at Quincy Sept. 25, 1862.
GURN, Charles. Ptd. cpl. M.O. June 7, 1865.
HAINES, Thomas B. M.O. June 17, 1865; was POW.
HARTWELL, John D. Died at Franklin May 17, 1863.
HICKERSON, Paschal. M.O. June 7, 1865.
HOWARD, Alfred. M.O. June 7, 1865.
HUBBELL, Mortimer B. Ptd. cpl. M.O. June 7, 1865.
HYMAN, John A. Ptd. cpl., then 1st lt.
JOHNSON, George B. M.O. June 7, 1865.
JOLLY, Daniel T. M.O. June 7, 1865.
JOLLY, Thomas L. Ptd. sgt.
KINKADE, James. Died of wds. Oct. 22, 1863.
KNIGHT, Zelotus. Disch. May 7, 1863; disab.
LAMBERT, Jesse. Musician. M.O. June 7, 1865.
LANDON, Isaac W. M.O. June 7, 1865.

LAWBER, Uriah. M.O. June 7, 1865.

LESURE, Perry. KIA at Jonesboro Sept. 1, 1864.

McKEE, John. Died at Louisville Jan. 31, 1863.

MEWMAW, John W. KIA at Kennesaw Mountain June 27, 1864.

MILLS, Samuel. Ptd. cpl. M.O. June 7, 1865.

MOORE, Albert G. Trans. Pioneer Corps Jul. 29, 1864.

MOORE, Francis M. KIA at Chickamauga Sept. 20, 1863.

MOORE, Preston. Disch. May 2, 1863; disab.

NICHOLS, Thomas H. M.O. June 7, 1865.

PHIPPS, David E. Disch. Dec. 15, 1862.

PHIPPS, Elijah G. Ptd. sgt.

PHIPPS, Joseph M. KIA at Chickamauga Sept. 20, 1863.

PRESHUER, Charles. Absent sick at M.O. of regiment.

REED, John. Died at Franklin Feb. 24, 1863.

RILEY, John H. Disch. Feb. 8, 1865; wds.

ROBBINS, Jacob B. M.O. June 7, 1865.

ROBERTS, Christopher. C. Ptd. sgt.

ROBERTS, John W. Died of wds. Dec. 10, 1863.

SHANNON, Joseph P. M.O. June 7, 1865.

SHANNON, William W. M.O. June 7, 1865.

SHIRL, Benjamin. Died at Nashville Jul. 15, 1864.

SMITH, Charles A. Ptd. sgt.

SMITH, George W. Ptd. cpl. Disch. Nov. 4, 1862; disab.

STAHL, William B. KIA at Kennesaw Mountain June 27, 1864.

SWAN, George W. Died at Nashville March 20, 1863.

TATMAN, Hiram. M.O. June 7, 1865.

THOMPSON, William H. M.O. June 22, 1865.

TILTON, David A. M.O. June 7, 1865.

TRAMILL, Thomas J. M.O. June 7, 1865.

UNDERWOOD, William O. M.O. May 13, 1865.

WEBSTER, Noah. M.O. June 7, 1865.

WELDON, Samuel M. M.O. June 7, 1865.

WINGFIELD, Thomas H. Died of wds. Sept. 17, 1864.

WOOD, Leonard. Died at Rolling Fork Bridge, Ky. Jan. 27, 1863.

ZIMMER, John. M.O. June 7, 1865.

Recruits

ELLINGTON, William T. Trans. Co. E, 34th Ill. Inf.

HARKNESS, Oscar L. M.O. June 7, 1865.

HICKERSON, John P. Trans. Co. E, 34th Ill. Inf.

JOLLY, Henry H. Trans. Co. E, 34th Ill. Inf.

JOLLY, Joseph. Trans. Co. E, 34th Ill. Inf.

NEWSOM, John R. Trans. Co. E, 34th Ill. Inf.

POTTER, Joshua D. 1863. Died at Chattanooga Apr. 23, 1864.

Bibliography

Newspapers and Other Periodicals

Blue & Gray Magazine, Vol. VI, No. 5, June 1989: "The Battle of Kennesaw Mountain and Related Actions," by Dennis Kelly.

Blue & Gray Magazine, Vol. VI, No. 6, Fall 1989: "Atlanta Campaign," by Stephen Davis.

Blue & Gray Magazine, Vol. XXIII, No. 4, Fall 2006: "The Chickamauga Campaign: The Fall of Chattanooga," by William Glenn Robertson.

Blue & Gray Magazine, Vol. XXIV, No. 3, Fall 2007: "The Chickamauga Campaign: The Armies Collide," by William Glenn Robertson.

Blue & Gray Magazine, Vol. XXIV, No. 5, Winter 2008. "Wiley Sword's War Letters Series," Letter from Pvt. J. P. Graves of Swett's Mississippi Battery.

Blue & Gray Magazine, Vol. XXV, No. 2, Summer 2008: "The Battle of Chickamauga, Day 2, September 20, 1863," by William Glenn Robertson.

Civil War Times Illustrated, Vol. XXVIII, No. 4, Summer 1989: "The Atlanta Campaign," by David Evans.

Hallowed Ground, Vol. 8, No. 3, Fall 2007: "Kennesaw Mountain," by Willie Ray Johnson.

Harper's Weekly, Vol. VII, No. 340, July 4, 1863: "The Execution of Williams and Peters," by James K. Magie.

Macomb Eagle, February 12, 1858–August 16, 1862.

Macomb Journal, October 4, 1861–August 15, 1862.

Medical & Surgical Reporter, Vol. XIII, July 1865–January 1866, Philadelphia, Alfred Martien, printer, 1865; Harold Havelock Kynett, Samuel Worcester Butler, and D. G. Brinton, editors.

Quincy Daily Herald, 1858–present.

Quincy Daily Journal, 1858–present.

Quincy Daily Whig, 1858–present.

Quincy Daily Whig & Republican, 1858–present.

Tennessee Archaeology, Vol. 2, Fall 2006, No. 2: "Archaeological Investigations on Roper's Knob: A Fortified Civil War Site in Williamson County, Tennessee," by Benjamin C. Nance.

Books

Aten, Henry J.: "History of the Eighty-Fifth Regiment Illinois Volunteer Infantry." Hiawatha, KS, 1901.

Beatty, John: "The Citizen Soldier." Wilstach, Baldwin & Co., Cincinnati, OH, 1879.

Bonner, Robert E.: "The Soldier's Pen: Firsthand Impressions of the Civil War." Hill & Wang, New York, 2006.

Carter, Howard Williston: "A Genealogy of the Descendants of Thomas Carter." Norfolk, CT, 1909.

Castel, Albert: "Decision in the West: The Atlanta Campaign of 1864." University Press of Kansas, Lawrence, 1992.

Catton, Bruce: "Never Call Retreat." Doubleday & Co., Garden City, NY, 1965.

Collins, William H., and Perry, Cicero F.: "Past and Present of the City of Quincy and Adams County, Illinois." S. J. Clarke Publishing Co., Chicago, 1905.

Connolly, James A.: "Three Years in the Army of the Cumberland," edited by Paul M. Angle. Indiana University Press, Bloomington, 1959.

Cozzens, Peter: "The Shipwreck of Their Hopes: The Battles for Chattanooga." University of Illinois Press, Urbana and Chicago, 1994.

Cozzens, Peter: "This Terrible Sound: The Battle of Chickamauga." University of Illinois Press, Urbana and Chicago, 1992.

Daniel, Larry J.: "Days of Glory: The Army of the Cumberland, 1861–1865." Louisiana State University Press, Baton Rouge, 2004.

Dyer, Frederick H.: "A Compendium of the War of the Rebellion." The Dyer Publishing Company, Des Moines, IA, 1908.

Haas, John E., and Longacre, Glenn, editors: "To Battle for God and the Right, The Civil War Letterbooks of Emerson Opdycke." University of Illinois Press, Urbana and Chicago, 2008.

Hicken, Victor: "Illinois in the Civil War." Second Edition, University of Illinois Press, Urbana and Chicago, 1991.

Hughes, Nathaniel Cheairs, Jr.: "Bentonville: The Final Battle of Sherman and Johnston." University of North Carolina Press, Chapel Hill, 1996.

Hughes, Nathaniel Cheairs, Jr., and Whitney, Gordon D.: "Jefferson Davis in Blue: The Life of Sherman's Relentless Warrior." Louisiana State University Press, Baton Rouge, 2002.

Kautz, August V.: "Customs of Service for Non-Commissioned Officers and Soldiers." Stackpole Books, Harrisburg, PA, 2001 (reproduction of 1865 original).

Kelly, Dennis: "Kennesaw Mountain and the Atlanta Campaign: A Tour Guide." Kennesaw Mountain Historical Association, Inc., Marietta, GA, 1990.

Luvaas, Jay, and Nelson, Harold W. (editors): "US Army War College Guide to the Atlanta Campaign: Rocky Face Ridge to Kennesaw Mountain." University Press of Kansas, Lawrence, 2008.

McAdams, F. M.: "Every-Day Soldier Life, or a History of the Hundred and Thirteenth Reg't, Ohio Volunteer Infantry." Chas. M. Cott & Co., Book Printers, Columbus, OH, 1884.

McDonough, James Lee, and Jones, James Pickett: "War So Terrible: Sherman and Atlanta." W. W. Norton, New York and London, 1987.

McNeill, James M. (William J. Allen and Marvel A. Allen, editors): "Call Them Men, Then, 78th Illinois Volunteer Company 'H'." River Falls, WI, third printing, 2009.

Noe, Kenneth W. "Perryville: This Grand Havoc of Battle." University Press of Kentucky, Lexington, 2001.

Payne, Edwin W.: "History of the Thirty-Fourth Regiment of Illinois Volunteer Infantry, September 7, 1861–July 12, 1865." Allen Printing Company, Clinton IA, 1902.

Robbins, Dr. Edward M.: "Civil War Experiences 1862–1865." Carthage, IL, November 1919.

Scaife, William R.: "The Campaign for Atlanta." Third Edition, Atlanta, GA, 1990.

Secrist, Philip L.: "Sherman's 1864 Trail of Battle to Atlanta." Mercer University Press, Macon, GA, 2006.

Sherman, William Tecumseh: "Memoirs of General William T. Sherman." Second Edition, revised and corrected, two volumes. D. Appleton & Co., New York, 1889.

Simpson, Brooks D., and Berlin, Jean V., editors: "Sherman's Civil War: Collected Correspondence of William T. Sherman, 1860–1865." University of North Carolina Press, Chapel Hill, 1999.

Smith, Charles H.: "The History of Fuller's Ohio Brigade, 1861–1865." Press of A. J. Wyatt, Cleveland, OH, 1909.

Tucker, Glenn: "Chickamauga: Bloody Battle in the West." Morningside Bookshop, Dayton, OH, 1961.

Virdin, Donald Odell: "The Civil War Correspondence of Judge Thomas Goldsborough Odell." Heritage Books, Inc., Bowie, MD, 1992.

Wagner, Margaret E.; Gallagher, Gary W., and Finkelman, Paul, editors: "The Library of Congress Civil War Desk Reference." Simon & Schuster, New York, 2002.

Warren, Ezra: "Generals in Blue: Lives of the Union Commanders." Louisiana State University Press, Baton Rouge, 1988.

Watkins, Sam R. "Company Aytch, A Side Show of the Big Show." Broadfoot Publishing Co., Wilmington, NC, 1990. (Original edition Nashville, 1881.)

Woodworth, Steven E. "Nothing but Victory: The Army of the Tennessee, 1861–1865. Alfred A. Knopf, New York, 2005.

Official Documents

Report of the Adjutant General of the State of Illinois. Revised by Brigadier General J. N. Reece, Adjutant General. Springfield, IL, Phillips Bros. State Printers, 1901.

The War of the Rebellion: A Compilation of the Official Records of the Union and Confederate Armies. Washington, D.C., US Government Printing Office, 128 volumes, 1880–1901.

Public Records

Census Records of Farmer Township, Rice County, KS, 1880.

Census Records of Franklin Township, Edwards County, KS, 1890.

National Archives: Pension Records of Jonathan Butler, First Sergeant, Company K, 78th Illinois Volunteer Infantry Regiment.

National Archives: Service Records of Jonathan Butler, First Sergeant, Company K, 78th Illinois Volunteer Infantry Regiment.

Veterans Records of Jonathan Butler, General Reference Branch, National Archives and Records Administration, Washington, DC.

Diaries and Letters

"Army Record of John Batchelor, Co. I, 78th Ills. Vol. Infantry, 2nd Brig., 2nd Div., 14th Corps, Beginning August 1862, Rewritten 1910." Abraham Lincoln Presidential Library and Museum, Springfield, IL.

"The Diaries of Charles Vilasco Chandler, 1861–1863," Transcribed by Ann Robinson Chandler, 1989. Putnam County Public Library, Greencastle, IN.

"Diary of James Edgar Withrow," University of Illinois at Urbana-Champaign, IL.

Letters of Benjamin Gill, Co. I, 78th Illinois Volunteers. Civil War Collection, Western Illinois University Libraries, Macomb, IL.

Letters of Carter Van Vleck, edited by Philip Gerber and Teresa Lehr, 2001 (unpublished); Almond, NY.

Letters of James K. Magie, the Gilder Lehrman Collection (accession number GLC05421), courtesy of the Gilder Lehrman Institute of American History, New York.

Letters of Major William L. Broaddus, 78th Illinois Volunteers. David M. Rubenstein Rare Book & Manuscript Library, Duke University, Durham, NC.

William H. Githens Civil War Correspondence, Wyles Collection, Department of Special Collections, Davidson Library, University of California, Santa Barbara, CA.

Internet Sources

Civil War Vignettes: A Civil War Genealogy Research Service. www.civilwarvignettes.com. Information on Pvt. Samuel S. Davis, Co. D, 78th Illinois Volunteer Infantry, killed at Jonesboro, Georgia.

Illinois Civil War Muster and Descriptive Rolls Database, Illinois State Archives, Springfield, IL. www.cyberdrive.ill. Illinois regimental rosters.

Illinois US GenWeb project. www.ilgenweb.net. Rosters, photos, other information.

Lemons, Charles R.: "A Very Good Camping Place: New Haven and the Civil War, 1861–1865." www.rfhpa.or/history.pdf (Rolling Fork Historic Preservation Association).

INDEX

ABOUT THE AUTHOR

Steve Raymond, a retired newspaper editor, is author of nine previous books. A member of the Civil War Trust and Puget Sound Civil War Roundtable, he also reviews books on history for the *Seattle Times* and is a member of the National Book Critics Circle. He and his wife, Joan, live on Whidbey Island in Puget Sound.